AFRICA

A HANDBOOK

Volume 2

HANDBOOKS TO THE MODERN WORLD
General Editor: Andrew C. Kimmens

WESTERN EUROPE
THE SOVIET UNION AND EASTERN EUROPE
THE MIDDLE EAST
AFRICA
ASIA AND THE PACIFIC
CANADA
THE UNITED STATES
LATIN AMERICA AND THE CARIBBEAN

AFRICA

Volume 2

Edited by

SEAN MORONEY

New York • Oxford

Library of Congress Cataloging-in-Publication Data

Handbooks to the modern world. Africa / edited by Sean Moroney.—
  Rev. and updated ed.
     p. cm.—(Handbooks to the modern world)
  Includes index.
  ISBN 0-8160-1623-2 [set]
  1. Africa. I. Moroney, Sean. II. Series: Handbooks to the
modern world (Facts On File, Inc.)
  DT3.H36   1989
  960—dc19   88-28649
  ISBN 0-8160-2200-3 (Vol. I)
  ISBN 0-8160-2201-1 (Vol. II)
  ISBN 0-8160-1632-2 (set)
Printed in the United States of America

10 9 8 7 6 5 4 3 2 1

CONTRIBUTORS

PITA ADAMS was an editor of the *Africa Research Bulletin* for several years. She is now a free-lance editor, continuing to specialize in African affairs. Recently she has become an annual contributor to the *Africa Contemporary Record*.

TAFFY ADLER received B.A. and P.Phil. (African studies) degrees from the University of the Witwatersrand. Between 1976 and 1986 he was a full-time trade-union official, serving as Transvaal regional secretary and national education secretary for the Federation of South African Trade Unions and the National Automobile and Allied Workers Union. He is now a researcher for the Labour and Economic Research Centre in Johannesburg, which serves the needs of the nonracial trade-union movement. Adler has contributed articles on labor history and industrial sociology to various journals, and has lectured on these subjects at the universities of Cape Town and the Witwatersrand.

ABDULA RAHMAN MOHAMED BABU was born in Zanzibar in 1924. He studied philosophy and literature there and in England. Babu took a leading role in the struggle for independence as secretary-general of the Zanzibar Nationalist party, and later as chairman of the Umma party. He was the first foreign minister of the Republic of Zanzibar and for eight years, from the time of the formation of Tanzania in 1964, served in various ministries of the government of President Julius K. Nyerere. Detained as a prisoner of conscience in 1972, he was finally released in 1978, and the following year went to the United States as visiting professor of international relations at the University of California, Berkeley, and San Francisco State University. From 1981 to 1984 he taught African affairs at Amherst College in Massachusetts, then went to London to do research and write. Besides lecturing in Africa, Asia, England and the Americas, he is now a contributing editor to *African Concord* and *Africa Events*. He is the author of *African Socialism or Socialist Africa;* his books on the political history of East Africa and on U.S. involvement in East African politics are to be published in 1989.

LALAGE BOWN, O.B.E., who holds an M.A. from Oxford University, is head of the department of adult and continuing education at the University of Glasgow, and in 1987 was Silver Jubilee lecturer at the University of Ibadan faculty of education. Previously, for 31 years, she was a professor of adult education at the African universities of Zambia, Ahmadu Bello, Zaria and Lagos. A member of the research committee of the International African Institute, she is author or editor of books and articles on African studies, development studies and adult education, as well as a number of reports for UNESCO and the Ford Foundation.

DERRICK CHITALA, a public policy analyst who holds B.A. and M.A. degrees in politics and public administration from the University of Zambia, is now a development consultant with MRPD, Ltd. In 1985 he founded this network of consultants for promoting, organizing and coordinating research in eastern and southern Africa. He was also a founder of the *Journal of African Marxists,* of which he is now secretary. Chitala coedited *SADCC: Prospects for Disengagement and Development in Southern Africa* and has written numerous articles on the problem of African development.

JOHN I. CLARKE is pro-vice-chancellor and sub-warden of the University of Durham, England, and chairman of the International Geographical Union Commission on Population Geography. His main academic interests lie in population geography and urbanization, especially in Africa, the Middle East and Britain. Clarke received a Ph.D. from the University of Aberdeen in 1956; his dissertation topic was on nomadic migrations in Tunisia and in the course of his research he spent 18 months in that country. Following two years' service in the Royal Air Force (1952–54) he taught at Aberdeen and Durham. From 1963 to 1965 he was professor of geography at Fourah Bay College, University of Sierra Leone, after which he returned to teach at Durham. He has held visiting professorships at several universities worldwide. Among Clarke's many publications is *Population Geography and the Developing Countries* (1971); he was editor of and contributor to *An Advanced Geography of Africa* (1975) and *Geography and Population: Approaches and Applications* (1984).

BASIL DAVIDSON, born in Bristol, England, in 1914, is a writer on and historian of Africa. He worked extensively as a journalist on such publications as the *Economist, Times, New Statesman* and *Daily Mirror.* He has been visiting professor at the universities of Ghana, California at Los Angeles, Edinburgh, Manchester and Birmingham, and holds honorary degrees from the universities of Ibadan, Dar es Salaam and Edinburgh. He was the author and presenter of the eight-part documentary television series *Africa* (1984). Davidson has published dozens of books on African subjects, and is especially known as the chronicler of various national liberation struggles. Among his most recent books are *Africa in History: Themes and Outlines* (rev. ed., 1974), *In the Eye of the Storm: Angola's People* (1975), *Let Freedom Come: Africa in Modern History* (1978), *The African Slave Trade* (rev. ed., 1980), *The People's Cause: A History of Guerrillas in Africa* (1981), *Modern Africa* (1983), *Africa: History and Achievement* (1984), *Southern Africa: Progress or Disaster?* (1984) and *The Story of Africa* (1984).

WENDY DAVIES taught in Ghana and in London before working for several years as education officer at the Africa Centre in London, where she took a particular interest in increasing the availability of educational programs for women. Since 1984 she has been working as a free-lance writer, specializing in educational and cultural affairs. She has produced educational material for the International Broadcasting Trust, Save the Children, the Commonwealth Secretariat, the Commonwealth Institute and various educational publishers; and has contributed articles to *West Africa, New African, Africa Now,* the *Zimbabwe Herald, Spare Rib* and *Women in Education.*

COLE P. DODGE, who holds advanced degrees in anthropology and public health, is UNICEF representative in Sudan. Previously, he held the same post in Uganda (1981–86), and he has worked in India, Bangladesh, Nigeria, Somalia and Ethiopia. He is coeditor of *Crisis in Uganda: The Breakdown of Health Services* (1985), *Beyond Crisis: Development Issues in Uganda* (1987) and *War, Violence and Children in Uganda* (1987).

EFUA GRAHAM holds bachelor's and master's degrees in the human sciences and is also a trained nurse, with special experience and interest in the fields of health, human development and the promotion of human rights. She is the research and development director of the Foundation for Women's Health in London, which promotes projects to improve the physical well-being of African women.

PETER GUTHRIE is a civil engineer with experience doing road projects in Africa and the Far East. He spent a year in northern Nigeria connected with Voluntary Service Overseas and two years in Lesotho on a labor-based construction and maintenance program; he has also served in Iran, Malaysia, Sudan, Botswana and the Philippines. He is an associate with the consulting engineering firm of Scott Wilson Kirkpatrick & Partners, Basingstoke, England, and lectures on appropriate technology in civil construction.

JOSEPH HANLON is a journalist and writer on southern Africa. He is the author of *Mozambique: The Revolution under Fire* (1984), *SADCC: Progress, Projects, and Prospects* (1985), *Apartheid's Second Front* (1986) and *Beggar Your Neighbours* (1986); and is coauthor of *The Sanctions Handbook* (1987).

BARBARA E. HARRELL-BOND holds a diploma in social anthropology and a D.Phil. from Oxford University. Since 1982 she has been coordinator of the Refugee Studies Programme, Queen Elizabeth House, Oxford. Previously, she was associate for Africa, Universities Field Staff International (1979–81) and visiting professor of anthropology at the University of Illinois, Urbana (1970). She has participated in international conferences on the problems of refugees in various parts of the world, held at Oxford between 1984 and 1986; served on the editorial advisory committee of *Third World Affairs* (1986); and was consultant on Sudan for the Office of the U.N. High Commissioner for Refugees (1982–83) and a member of the board of directors of the International Third World Legal Studies Association (1983–86). A correspondent for *West Africa,* she is also the author of several books—including *Modern Marriage in Sierra Leone: A Study of the Professional Group* (1975) and *Imposing Aid: Emergency Assistance to Refugees* (1986)— and coauthor of *Family Law in Sierra Leone* (1975).

ARTHUR HAZLEWOOD was research professor in Commonwealth studies at Oxford University, warden of Queen Elizabeth House and director of the Oxford University Institute of Commonwealth Studies. He is a professorial fellow of Pembroke College, Oxford. He has been concerned with African affairs since 1950 and was director of the Common Market Secretariat in Kenya during the negotiation of the Treaty for East African Cooperation. His books include *The Economy of Africa* (1961), *Economic Integration: The East African Experience* (1975) and *The Economy of Kenya:*

The Kenyatta Era (1979). He was coauthor of *Nyasaland: The Economics of Federation* (1960), *Aid and Inequality in Kenya* (1976) and *Irrigation Economics in Poor Countries* (1982); and he edited *African Integration and Disintegration* (1967).

ADRIAN HEWITT is deputy director of the London-based Overseas Development Institute and research adviser to the All-Party Parliamentary Group on Overseas Development, which produced the report *U.K. Aid to African Agriculture* (1985). He has also worked as a consultant for the World Bank, the U.N. Food and Agriculture Organization and the U.N. Conference on Trade and Development, and was economic adviser to Malawi for two years. He is the author of *Business Guide to World Aid Funds and Projects* (1983) and contributed to *Does Aid Work?* (1986).

MICHAEL HODD teaches at the School of Oriental and African Studies of London University, specializing in the economies of East Africa. He is the author of *African Economic Handbook* (1986) and editor of *Tanzania after Nyerere* (1988).

EBOE HUTCHFUL, born in Ghana in 1946, received a B.A. from the University of Ghana and a Ph.D. from the University of Toronto in 1973. He has taught at the universities of Ghana, Port Harcourt (Nigeria) and Toronto, and is now associate professor of political science at Trent University, Ontario. His fields include militarism, debt rescheduling, the policies of the International Monetary Fund and the World Bank, and environmental protection. He is the author of *The IMF and Ghana* (1987) and a forthcoming book on oil, ecology and public policy in Nigeria.

DEREK INGRAM, a London-based journalist, has specialized in Commonwealth affairs for 30 years. He was a governor of the Commonwealth Institute for many years, and is now president of the Commonwealth Journalists Association and deputy chairman of the Royal Commonwealth Society. In 1980 he was media adviser to the Commonwealth Observer Group in Zimbabwe. The founder and editor of Gemini News Service, he is also the author of several books in his field.

GEORGE JOFFE is a writer and broadcaster on the Middle East and North Africa. He is also consultant editor for the Middle East and North Africa for *The Economist* publications, and he is a member of the editorial board of *Arab Affairs,* the English-language journal of the Arab League. He has also specialized in consultancy on the historical development of maritime and land boundaries and on issues relating to the oil industry in the Middle East and North Africa.

TONY KILLICK holds a B.A. from Oxford University. Formerly director of the Overseas Development Institute (1982–87), he now serves there as senior research fellow. He was lecturer at the University of Ghana (1961–65) and tutor in economics at Ruskin College, Oxford (1965–67). Subsequently, he served as economic adviser in the British Ministry of Overseas Development (1967–69) and the Ministry of Finance and Planning, Ghana (1969–72), as well as with the World Bank and the governments of Kenya and Zimbabwe. From 1972 to 1979 Killick was a research fellow at Harvard University and Ford Foundation visiting professor at the University of Nairobi; in 1987–88 he was a visiting fellow at Wolfson College, Cambridge. He has contributed articles to *Problems of International Money 1972–85* (1986) and *The African Debt Problem* (1986); and he directed an Overseas Development Institute research project on the International Monetary Fund and economic management in developing countries, published in two volumes: *The Quest for Economic Stabilisation: The IMF and the Third World* and *The IMF and Stabilisation: Developing Country Experiences* (1984).

NEIL LAZARUS is assistant professor of English and of modern culture and media at Brown University, Providence, Rhode Island. He writes on contemporary cultural theory and on African and other postcolonial literatures. He has just completed a book about Ayi Kwei Armah and the discourse on postcolonialism in African literature.

COLIN LEGUM was born in South Africa, where he worked as a journalist for many years. He is the editor of the *Africa Contemporary Record* and former editor of the *Middle East Contemporary Survey* and of the two earlier editions of the present Handbook. Until 1981 he was associate editor of *The Observer*. Now engaged in freelance journalism, he writes an internationally syndicated column, "Third World Report." He is the author of *Pan-Africanism* (1962) and coauthor of *South Africa: Crisis for the West* (1964).

TOM LODGE is senior lecturer on African political studies at the University of the Witwatersrand. He was educated in Britain and received a doctorate in southern African studies from the University of York. He is the author of *Black Politics in South Africa since 1945* as well as articles on black South African resistance movements, both historical and contemporary. He is at present writing a book on the African National Congress.

MICHAEL F. LOFCHIE is professor of political science and director of the African Studies Center at the University of California, Los Angeles. He is a coeditor of *Agricultural Development in Africa* (1980) and *Africa's Agrarian Crisis: The Roots of Famine* (1986). Lofchie is currently completing a book on agricultural performance in Kenya and Tanzania, *Policy Makes a Difference*.

JOHN LOXLEY is professor and head of the department of economics of the University of Manitoba, Canada. He was in 1987–88 visiting professor in the School of Economic Studies, Leeds University, England. Loxley has served as an economic adviser on structural adjustment policies to the governments of Tanzania and Uganda and the Central Bank of Madagascar. He has recently been involved in a study of the structural adjustment experiences of Ghana and Zambia for the North-South Institute, Ottawa, and for the Canadian International Development Agency. He is the author of *Debt and Disorder—External Financing for Development* (1986).

ANDREW LYCETT is a free-lance journalist and consultant specializing in international politics and economics. He writes regularly for *The Times* and other British newspapers, and is the coauthor of *Qaddafi and the Libyan Revolution* (1987).

JANET MACGAFFEY, an anthropologist, has taught at Haverford, Bryn Mawr and other colleges in the United States. She has worked in Zaire as a researcher and consultant. Her publications include *Entrepreneurs and Parasites: The Struggle for Indigenous Capitalism in Zaire* (1987), as well as contributions to other books and journals.

PATRICK MATLOU is on leave as lecturer in politics from the University of Liberia. He is now attached to the Refugee Studies Programme, Oxford University and the University of Essex.

ALI A. MAZRUI holds a B.A. from Manchester University, an M.A. from Columbia, and a D.Phil. from Oxford. He is currently professor of political science at the University of Michigan and the Andrew D. White professor-at-large at Cornell. From 1963 to 1973 he was successively lecturer, professor of political science and head of the department, and dean of the faculty of social sciences at Makerere University in Kampala, Uganda. From 1981 to 1986 he was research professor at the University of Jos, Nigeria. Mazrui has been visiting professor at many universities: London, Chicago, Manchester, Harvard, Nairobi, California at Los Angeles, Northwestern, Singapore, Australia, Stanford, Cairo, Sussex, Colgate, Ohio State and Leeds. He was the BBC Reith lecturer in 1979 and presenter of the six-part television documentary *The Africans* (1986). He is the author of numerous books on African affairs, among the most recent of which are *The Political Sociology of the English Language: An African Perpective* (1975), *A World Federation of Cultures: An African Perspective* (1976), *Africa's International Relations: The Diplomacy of Dependency and Change* (1977), *Political Values and the Educated Class in Africa* (1978), *The African Condition: A Political Diagnosis* (the Reith Lectures, 1980), *The Africans: A Reader* and *The Africans: A Triple Heritage* (both 1986).

SEAN MORONEY, an African journalist and consultant, is the publisher of Africa File Ltd. and its constituent publications, *EASA: Trade and Investment in Eastern and Southern Africa* and *Computers in Africa*. He has also been editor of *African Business*, coeditor of *Africa Currents* and executive editor of *Africa Contemporary Record*. Previously he was lecturer in African government at the University of the Witwatersrand, researcher with the South African Institute of Race Relations and research assistant at the London School of Economics and Political Science.

JIMOH OMO-FADAKA, born in Benin City, Nigeria, in 1938, received a Ph.D. in economics from the London School of Economics and Political Science in 1965. His career began as assistant secretary in the Nigerian government Ministry of Economic Planning and Development. Subsequently, he was government adviser on environment and ecological development in Papua-New Guinea, Fiji, Zaire and Nigeria; and from 1980 to 1983 was Regents professor of environment studies at the University of California, Santa Cruz. A member of the IUCN commissions on environmental planning and ecology, he is also a counselor of the World Resources Institute, Washington, D.C. and executive chairman of the African Non-Governmental Organizations Environment Network. He is the author of *The State of the Environment in Africa* (1988).

BADE ONIMODE is an economist specializing in Africa's debt crisis and the policies of the International Monetary Fund and the World Bank. He is professor of economics at Ibadan University and chairman of the council of the Institute for African Alternatives, London. Onimode served as consultant for the U.N. Council on Trade and Development, the World Health Organization and the Nigerian federal government. He is the author of the books *Economic Development of Nigeria: The Socialist Alterantive* (with Ola. Oni, 1975), *Imperialism and Underdevelopment in Nigeria: The Dialectics of Mass Poverty* (1982), *Mathematics for Economics and Business* (1984) and *An Introduction to Marxist Political Economy* (1986). His book on the political economy of Africa's debt crisis was scheduled for publication in 1989.

RUSSELL J. PARKES holds an M.A. and a diploma in economics from Oxford University, as well as a Ph.D. from Ahmadu Bello University. Now a free-lance lecturer, editor and consultant, he was until recently reader and head of the department of political science at the University of Nigeria. His special field is the politics of West Africa, particularly Nigeria.

ALAN RAKE, a journalist and broadcaster, is the managing editor of the magazines *New African* and *African Business*. He edited the *New African Yearbooks*, 1978–82, and since 1983 has edited the *Travellers' Guides to Africa*. He started his career in Africa as correspondent for and then editor of *Drum* magazine (1957–62), before returning to Britain to edit *Africa Confidential*, a newsletter. He joined Gemini News Service, becoming editor of its magazine *African Development* in 1970. Besides broadcasting regularly for the BBC African and Arabic services, he was for a long period a reporter on Africa for the business section of the *Economist*. His books include *Tom Mboya* (1963) and *Africa* (1971).

PETER ROBSON has held the chair of economics at St. Andrews University since 1968. He was previously professor of economics at the University of Nairobi. International economic integration is one of his major interests. He is the author of *Economic Integration in Africa* (1968) and *The Economics of International Integration* (1980). He was coauthor of *The Economies of Africa* (1969) and edited *International Economic Integration* (1971).

ANN WILLCOX SEIDMAN is currently adjunct professor of international development and director of the Southern Africa program at Clark University. She has been professor of economics and head of department at the universities of Zimbabwe and Zambia, and a U.N. consultant for the Special Committee Against Apartheid and the Transnational Corporate Center. She is a graduate of Smith College and Columbia University, and holds a doctorate from the University of Wisconsin. Seidman is the author of *An Economics Textbook for Africa* (3rd ed., 1980), *Southern African Impact Audit* (1985) and *Money, Banking and Public Finance* (1987); and coeditor of *Aid and Development in Southern Africa* (1987) and *Rethinking Agricultural Transformations in Southern Africa* (1988).

KEITH SOMERVILLE is a writer and broadcast journalist covering African affairs. Formerly a special correspondent on southern African affairs for *Africa* magazine, and a regular contributor to *Africa Now* and *African Business,* he now writes for *New African* and *Modern Africa.* His articles on Soviet and Chinese involvement in Africa have been published in the *Journal of Modern African Studies* and *Millennium.* The author of *Angola: Politics, Economics and Society* (1986), Somerville is currently cowriting and coediting a book on Benin, Congo and Burkina Faso, and is preparing a study of contemporary political developments in Malawi.

BEN TUROK, who holds degrees in engineering, philosophy and political science, is director of the Institute for African Alternatives, London. He was formerly senior lecturer at the Open University of Great Britain and at the University of Zambia. He has also worked in Tanzania and Zimbabwe, and in South Africa, from which he is in exile. Turok is the author or editor of the books *Strategic Problems in South Africa's Liberation Struggle* (1974), *Development in Zambia: A Reader* (1979), *Revolutionary Thought in the 20th Century* (1980) and *Africa: What Can Be Done?* (1987).

LINDA VAN BUREN, editor of the pan-African economics monthly *African Business,* has contributed articles on business and tourism to numerous publications. She is editor of the *Travellers' Guide to North Africa,* and has herself traveled extensively in all parts of the continent.

NICHOLAS VAN HEAR holds a Ph.D. in labor and agricultural development in Ghana from the University of Birmingham, 1982. Now based in London, he does research and writes on African agriculture and rural development, industrialization, labor, the debt problem, migration and refugees. He is the coauthor of *Refugees: Dynamics of Displacement* (1986).

CONTENTS

Contributors   v
Maps   xvi
Preface   xix

Volume 1

Basic Information *compiled by Pita Adams, Russell Parkes, Keith
    Somerville and Nicholas Van Hear*   1
Algeria   3
Angola   13
Benin   25
Botswana   35
Burkina Faso   45
Burundi   59
Cameroon   67
Cape Verde   81
Central African Republic   89
Chad   99
Comoros   113
Congo   121
Djibouti   133
Egypt   141
Equatorial Guinea   159
Ethiopia   169
Gabon   181
Gambia   191
Ghana   201
Guinea   217
Guinea-Bissau   227

Ivory Coast   235
Kenya   247
Lesotho   267
Liberia   279
Libya   289
Madagascar   303
Malawi   313
Mali   327
Mauritania   337
Mauritius   347
Morocco   355
Mozambique   365
Namibia   375
Niger   393
Nigeria   401
Rwanda   415
São Tomé and Príncipe   423
Senegal   431
Seychelles   443
Sierra Leone   451
Somalia   463
South Africa   473
Sudan   505
Swaziland   517
Tanzania   525
Togo   543
Tunisia   551
Uganda   561
Zaire   579
Zambia   597
Zimbabwe   607

Comparative Statistics *compiled by Alan Rake*   623

Volume 2

PART ONE: POLITICAL AFFAIRS

Two Decades of Decline: A Burden for the Future   *Basil Davison*   669
The Organization of African Unity   *Colin Legum*   686
Africa's War Zones   *Andrew Lycett*   693
The Superpowers and Africa   *A. M. Babu*   706
Militarization and Economic Development in Africa   *Eboe Hutchful*   716
South African Politics   *Tom Lodge*   730
South Africa's War on Its Neighbors   *Joseph Hanlon*   748
Africa and the Commonwealth   *Derek Ingram*   762
The European Community and Africa   *Adrian Hewitt*   770

CONTENTS

PART TWO: ECONOMIC AFFAIRS

A Survey of the African Economies   *Michael Hodd*   787
Africa, the International Monetary Fund and the World Bank:
   Adjustment and Finance   *Tony Killick*   811
Africa's Response to International Monetary Fund-World Bank
   Programs   *Bade Onimode*   823
The African Debt Crisis   *John Loxley*   841
Banking Institutions in Africa   *Ann Seidman*   858
The African Underground Economy   *Janet MacGaffey*   871
State-Sector Policies in Africa   *Ben Turok*   882
African Regionalism   *Arthur Hazlewood and Peter Robson*   890
African Industrial Development   *Derrick Chitala*   912
Africa's Agrarian Malaise   *Michael F. Lofchie*   926
Africa's Environmental Crisis   *Jimoh Omo-Fadaka*   944
Road Transportation in Africa   *Peter Guthrie*   953

PART THREE: SOCIAL AFFAIRS

Africa's Population   *John I. Clarke*   969
Refugees in Africa   *Barbara Harrell-Bond et al.*   988
African Health and Medical Services   *Cole P. Dodge*   1002
Labor Issues and Trade Unionism in Africa   *Nicholas Van Hear
   and Taffy Adler*   1014
Women in Africa   *Efua Graham and Wendy Davies*   1041
Religion and Social Forces in Africa   *Ali A. Mazrui*   1053
Islam in Africa   *George Joffe*   1067
Education in Africa   *Lalage Bown*   1087
Literature and Politics in Africa   *Neil Lazarus*   1101
African Tourism and Business Travel   *Linda Van Buren*   1113
The Media in Africa   *Sean Moroney*   1123

INDEX   1133

MAPS

Algeria	2
Angola	14
Benin	26
Botswana	34
Burkina Faso	46
Burundi	58
Cameroon	68
Cape Verde	82
Central African Republic	88
Chad	100
Comoros	114
Congo	122
Djibouti	134
Egypt	140
Equatorial Guinea	160
Ethiopia	168
Gabon	180
Gambia	190
Ghana	200
Guinea	218
Guinea-Bissau	228
Ivory Coast	236
Kenya	246
Lesotho	268
Liberia	278
Libya	290
Madagascar	302
Malawi	312
Mali	326
Mauritania	338
Mauritius	346
Morocco (including Western Sahara)	354
Mozambique	364

Namibia	376
Niger	392
Nigeria	402
Rwanda	416
São Tomé & Príncipe	424
Senegal	432
Seychelles	444
Sierra Leone	450
Somalia	464
South Africa	474
Sudan	506
Swaziland	518
Tanzania	526
Togo	542
Tunisia	552
Uganda	562
Zaire	580
Zambia	596
Zimbabwe	608
Mean Annual Precipitation	932
Vegetation	933
Average Annual Population Growth, 1985–86	971
Birth Rate per Thousand, 1985	973
Death Rate, 1985	979
Life Expectancy at Birth (Years), 1985	980
Urban Population, 1985	983

PART ONE

POLITICAL AFFAIRS

TWO DECADES OF DECLINE: A BURDEN FOR THE FUTURE

BASIL DAVIDSON

INTRODUCTION

WHAT future can Africa now expect? By the late 1980s this question had begun to be asked with growing pessimism. Planners were already at work on what was labeled Africa's "agenda for the 21st century," but the indications were not reassuring. Crisis looms on every side, and it seems likely that the 1990s will be no different. More Africans are hungry than memory can recall and declining standards of subsistence seem bound to continue. A grim period of cyclical drought eased about 1987, and food production is now showing some improvement after years of disaster. The population rate, however, is still rising rapidly, at a probable average of three percent a year in most regions—promising to double the number of Africans, perhaps to some 800 million, by early in the 21st century.

Food imports in ever-increasing quantities had become indispensable in the 1970s, and in some cases long before that. Few of Africa's now chronically fragile economies could pay for these essential imports. Each year most African countries continued to lose buying power. During 1986—a somewhat unusually adverse year in this respect, but by no means atypical—the continent lost as much as U.S. $19 billion through collapsed export prices. Africa's overseas debts climbed correspondingly. This inexorable rise of indebtedness to foreign lenders was an unbearable burden, with refusal to meet debt-service obligations beginning (not surprisingly) in the mid-1980s. In 1974, for example, the continent's debt-service ratio (the percentage of export earnings mandatorily allocated to foreign debt-service before exports are used to pay for imports) had stood at a manageable 4.6 percent. Thirteen years later it was close to 25 percent, and was expected to be higher still by the early 1990s. Even running hard in order to stand still is now an impossibility; in these circumstances, misery must deepen.

The political condition of most of Africa often seems no better than its economic plight. Nigeria's military rulers may have promised, with every good intention, to restore civilian government early in the 1990s, but with what hopes of achieving stable institutions? Uganda's new reforming rulers seemed at last to have resolved the murderous confusions of the 1970s and early 1980s, but with what assurance of peace and reconciliation? The brutal reign of Jean Bedel Bokassa in the Central African Republic may be no more than a sordid memory, and the dictator himself long powerless, but can the wounds be felt as healed—any more than in Guinea, which had suffered from Sékou Touré, or in several other countries under similar conditions? Throughout the southern part of the continent, hopes of postcolonial progress have been long deferred, undermined or even wrecked by the apartheid regime in South Africa and its agents of violence and aggression, whether white or black. As to the attitudes of the so-called first and second worlds of "development and industry," the portents there are of growing indifference to the plight of the Third World in general, and of Africa in particular.

Thus it is no wonder that pessimism about the future has become a common mood, quite submerging the euphoria of the years that signaled independence. If it is not a dominant mood, this may be because of the belief of the poverty-stricken (in itself a sort of optimism) that things have become so bad that they can only get better. Yet it is also true that this is an optimism that draws strength and resilience from all the springs of human effort and ingenuity set free in the earlier days of independence. It often seemed then that everything was possible, that all good roads were open, that the years ahead must allow an ascent toward a life that would be far more than mere difficult survival. Some of this resilience is still alive, even in the dim years toward the end of the 1980s, and understandably so. There have been many educational, medical and general social achievements. Measured against those of the industrially advanced world, these achievements are small, erratic and often insecure; measured against the colonial condition, however, which many people can still remember or easily imagine, they are solid and even remarkable. And this optimism is also the optimism of the young. Half or more than half of the total African population is under the age of 15; and the future, for the young, is a promised land to be enjoyed eventually.

The adult population, moreover, is far better prepared than were its recent ancestors to understand its situation and realistic prospects. There again the comparison with advanced countries can still be painful. Levels of spending on African secondary and higher education, as on all forms of graduate research, are much greater than 30 years earlier but still deplorably small. In 1987, for example, UNESCO calculated that Africa was spending only 0.3 percent of the world's $207 billion allocated to scientific research and development, and was continuing to fall further behind in the race for technological development and application. It remains, though, that the number of Africans (although there are far more men than women in this total) who are capable of understanding the rest of the world as well as, or better than, the rest of the world understands Africa, has grown enormously since the 1960s.

All this being so, questions about Africa's future insistently raise questions about Africa's past, above all about the 30 years or so of political independence. How and why has crisis occurred? Individual chapters in this volume look at specific areas of experience; here, a summation is attempted.

Current questions concern large and controversial issues: the nature of the colonial experience, which began, broadly speaking, in the 1880s; the real content of the transfer of power from European colonial governments to African ones; and then the many relevant aspects of Africa's precolonial history. In respect to this last, the achievements made since independence are of crucial importance, for among them is a lively record of learning and inquiring, sometimes at the elementary level, about Africa's own history. New Africa-centered textbooks in the humanities became available in the early or mid-1960s; new programs of teaching and of teacher training likewise emerged and were progressively enlarged and often improved. It could be said by the mid-1970s—save in the territories then released from Portuguese rule, where all forms of reconstruction had still to begin—that the larger part of once-colonial Africa had acquired a syllabus for viable self-enlightenment. Here is another reason why questions about the future imply questions about the past.

Three aspects of Africa's more or less recent history provide reasons for a crisis that is clearly of a profound and structural nature.

Most obvious are the historical reasons, which have been endlessly discussed, and with much self-accusation, by Africans impressed with the consequences of human frailty. Yet no amount of self-laceration can hide the fact that the failures of the past 30 or more years—aside from the triumphs and achievements—remain inexplicable unless seen in their relation to the colonial systems and the legacy of inhibitions and constraints those systems imposed. Whether or not as manifestations of neo-colonialism (a term coined in 1961 to describe the extremely partial nature of the transfer of power), the particular structures of politics and economics inherited from colonial systems have stood at the center of the stage of public and often of private life. Why falling food production? Why soaring urban populations? Why coups or political rogues and bandits? Only colonial history has offered firm ground for answers.

The weight of blame attached to colonial legacies is made heavier still, in this turn-of-the-century mood and atmosphere of debate, by various kinds of analysis. Among these, a second order of reasons for crisis lies in a very general perception (whether in Africa or elsewhere) of the coercive influence of what became known, at least by the 1970s, as the "north-south divide." Although glibly set forth in a good deal of specious "dependency" theory, this perception has been accepted as possessing unassailably strong foundations. Direct political imperialism may have come to an end with the hauling down of colonial flags and the disbandment of colonial armies, but economic imperialism continues to exist; it appears even to be strengthening its hold and purpose. Africa, relatively, grows poorer year by year; the developed nations—above all, the former imperialist powers—grow relatively richer.

The inescapable legacy of colonial times is that Africa continues to export cash crops, minerals or other raw materials in return for the manufactures of the industrialized world. There may be talk of developing industry

671

in Africa, but even if modern forms of manufacture could be promoted with success, rising levels of technology in the industrialized world ensure that the essential relationship, the inherited division of labor, will be little changed. Within this inherited dispensation, the poor in Africa are bound to become poorer, even absolutely poorer, when measured against the living standards of the industrialized countries of Europe, North America or Asia; and the poor in Africa, by the 1990s, will be the vast majority of all Africans everywhere. Economic imperialism, like the improvident loan bankers of the 1980s, is the parent of postcolonial bankruptcy.

Such were the general conclusions arrived at in the late 1980s. They are proving hard to shake, even by the emollient prescriptions of international financial organs such as the International Monetary Fund. Yet this second kind of explanation of Africa's crisis, however persuasive, is beginning to seem inadequate on the threshold of the last decade of the 20th century. Blaming other people may have been a natural and probably unavoidable reaction in the immediate wake of the colonial period; by the 1980s it is decreasingly acceptable. A third kind of reason for crisis, deriving from African history as well as from colonial history—a reason that is a product of Africa's own evolution outside of or alongside colonial misery—ought also to be expected, and therefore defined and discussed.

THE LONG ARM OF THE PAST

There was little debate, 30 years ago or so, into the nature of the colonial inheritance, and not much more awareness of its enormous relevance. Was not Africa at last set free? The arrival of independence (rather easily in West Africa but with huge difficulty in all of "white-settler Africa") seemed for a while like a complete and irreversible change of status. Having sought "the political kingdom," as Kwame Nkrumah emotively urged, the nationalists had found and seized it; with that, by most expectations, they needed only to turn the "transferred power"—however much or little this really was—into an instrument for the public good. A few left-wingers saw things otherwise, but they were quickly thrust aside in the scramble for benefits. Realistic discussion was in any case sorely hampered, and even for a long time rendered impossible, by an acute lack of reliable information.

This sparsity of facts applied both to available statistics and to other administrative sources of knowledge. The new rulerships had everything to learn about the facts of government. Unavoidably, they had to learn within the situations they had taken over; and they governed, more and more, by prolonging those situations. A few tried for originality, but the odds were always strongly against their success in breaking from their inheritance.

It was true, of course, that the circumstances of decolonization (another term of subsequent invention) were various; they differed, often acutely, from one former imperial outpost to another. But however diverse in the details, decolonization was in substance exactly comparable everywhere. It concerned the handing over of strongly centralized and dictatorial administrative machines from which any form of democratic control was absent— and necessarily absent, since any democratic control would have been a dereliction of colonial power and sovereignty. This was the case everywhere. Even in the four British West African colonies, where there was some development of consultative or "advisory" councils in which Africans could participate, colonial dictatorship had remained intact. In the British East and Central African colonies the settler minorities had acquired a share in this dictatorship, but the effect was merely to increase antiblack discrimination. Nothing in the colonial dispensation, here or anywhere else, provided for the access of Africans to any experience of the responsibilities of self-rule.

Hastily put together at the last moment, imperial plans for handing over power generally insisted on the installation of the parliamentary institutions of democracy; even the Facist-style dictatorship of Portugal claimed to have that in mind. Was it not, after all, to be seen as a proof of Europe's "civilizing mission?" Thus the British provided for parliamentary institutions on the Westminster model and the French on that of the Palais Bourbon. And with this there appeared a first major contradiction in the legacy: that between the sovereignty of parliaments created by universal suffrage on the one hand and, on the other, the rigid administrative dictatorships that actually ruled these African countries. Similar contradictions appeared in the colonies of other empires. Whereas in practice the Belgians merely abandoned power over their African colonies, the Portuguese had power taken from them; the contradictions nonetheless remained.

A second of these contradictions emerged in the "parliamentary colonies," if they may be so labeled. The winning nationalist movements had carried the day by mass acclaim and support, as though contrasts of class, region or personal ambition were of little importance to what was going to happen. Some of the nationalist leaders were well aware of the unreality of this stance and tried to compensate for it by programs of radical innovation. Among such leaders were Kwame Nkrumah in Ghana and Sékou Touré in Guinea, with several others elsewhere, of whom Nasser in Egypt was probably the most important. In general, though, little time passed before it became clear that the winning nationalists, the "petty bourgeoisie" of the colonial condition, were going to be loyal chiefly to their own sectional and personal interests. The few, in short, would rule the many, no matter what parliaments might exist or survive.

The few with power would combine politics with business, and business with as useful a collaboration as might be possible with overseas entrepreneurs. To that end they would use the instruments that were to hand; and by far the handiest of these instruments were the habits and capacities of the inherited state, the dictatorial state of colonial imposition. Consequently, as could be widely seen (perhaps most instructively in Kenya), the mass-elected parliaments of the years of independence became the property and arena of rival groups and factions, each with its minority interests in view; and out of this situation, as in Kenya, there evolved a one-party, in effect a "no-party," authoritarianism that was often indistinguishable from the colonial dictatorship that had preceded it.

A third contradiction duly flowed from the first and second: a contradiction between town and country. Here again the problems of independence were found to be inseparable from those of the closing years of colonial rule. Rural Africans continued to flock into towns. These towns became enlarged into sprawling slums and *bidonvilles* ("tin-can towns," so named from the beaten-out gasoline cans and sheets of corrugated iron with which the better buildings were constructed; the rest made do with mud and thatch). There had been towns in precolonial Africa as sophisticated and comfortable as old Kumase or Benin, as prosperous as Djenne or as handsome as Kilwa, and as universally admired as the Cairo of the Middle Ages. There had been towns in colonial Africa. Sometimes they were rich and memorable like the great city of Cape Town, more often they were centers of small white settlements, like Salisbury (the Harare of today), or mere administrative *bomas* furnished with police lines on the British pattern evolved in India and populated by civil servants, specialist technicians, a handful of business settlers but little else in the way of civilization.

Yet all these old towns, with some exceptions such as Cairo, had been relative pinpoints of habitation, tiny urban islands in a vast rural continent. After the 1930s recession, prolonged in Africa almost until World War II, the towns and cities ceased to be pinpoints of habitation. They became monsters of uncontrollable expansion.

THE URBAN EXPLOSION

The "flight from the villages" begun in the 1930s increased enormously during World War II and its aftermath, and continued into the 1980s despite every effort to bring it to a halt. It has been one of the most far-reaching changes of the entire time since the onset of colonial invasion. Rapidly doubled and quadrupled in size, new conurbations (although the word suggests some planning where actually there was none) absorbed people from villages that no longer, as it seemed, held any hope of a life promising more than hunger and oppression. Powerless to stem the tide, baffled colonial administrators simply stood by and let it happen.

A social and moral quagmire, comparable to that of the towns of early industrial England, spread out and soon began to engulf tradition and its codes of behavior or restraint. Many years passed before new forms of urban self-organization became feasible. In 1948, with the tide still rising high, the sociologist Kofia Busia (later to be a prime minister of Ghana) embarked on a survey of conditions in the port of Sekondi-Takoradi, and found that the old cultural norms and customs were giving way, "most prominently and most obviously of all in increased crime, prostitution, juvenile delinquency, unbridled acquisitiveness, bribery and corruption . . . the symptoms of a maladjusted society." In 1955 a British royal commission, commenting on urbanization under Kenyan colonial decrees that prevented husbands from bringing their wives into the towns where the men lived and worked, observed that "the evils associated with the absence of family life—drunkenness, prostitution, and venereal disease—are rife in the towns with large African populations."

There was much other evidence to the same effect, which spoke volumes for the real crisis of society within which and against which the nationalism

674

of the postwar years had to emerge and grow. A grim burden of confusion accompanied the campaigns for independence. As soon as the new governments had taken over they were faced with imperative demands for urban spending of one kind or other. Aside from this, the sheer size of urban populations meant that the politics of nationalism became more and more the politics of the towns rather than of the villages. The towns were where the new rulers worked and increasingly resided, and were where the votes for politicians were most easily accessible. They were also where the new business interests of the nationalists in power could find ready support from foreign capital. The heart of Africa might still be in "the bush," but by the 1970s it was a heart that was scarcely beating.

Other consequences flowed from this. The terms of trade between town and village, city and countryside, turned ever more markedly in favor of the urbanized populations or, at least, in favor of the political-cum-business groups that had dominant influence in the new states. This too was to have a painful sequel.

MILKING THE RURAL AREAS

Late 20th-century problems that grew out of all these earlier and sometimes contradictory trends had their roots in every field of life, but none more significant than the patterns of land and labor usage. Forced labor by rural Africans, whether for administrative or white-settler purposes, was widespread until 1946 or even until the early 1970s in the case of the Portuguese colonies, but it was more common in the white-settler colonies than in West Africa. In the colonies of West Africa, with little or no white farming settlement, coercion of rural labor took the form of an insistence upon the production of cash crops for export—for example, cocoa in the Gold Coast and groundnuts in Senegal—grown by Africans but delivered to the international market through the highly profitable channel of large European trading companies.

The result was much the same. Whether as forced or migrant workers on European farms, plantations and mines, or as more or less eager cash crop producers "in their own right" (save for having no control over prices, in practice a heavy handicap), the peoples of rural Africa turned away from growing food for home consumption to growing crops for sale abroad. Some development of this kind must in any case have been desirable. But the price for its wholesale and unbridled development was disastrous. Several communities certainly continued to gain. One example is the coffee-growing Chagga of northern Tanganyika (since 1964, with Zanzibar, the United Republic of Tanzania). More generally, the decline in the use of rural land and labor for the growing of food for home consumption led to ever-increasing importation of food.

Warnings of food shortage began to be sounded, especially in West Africa, as early as the 1930s; and they continued to be heard. But nothing was done to reverse the process, and in the circumstances perhaps nothing could have been done. Every colonial government was convinced that national interest and economic wisdom combined to argue that Africa's agrarian exports must be maximized. The economies handed on to the nationalists, when independence came, were very largely dependent on agrarian exports in return for fuel and manufactures and, increasingly, for food. And the nationalists, although making countless gestures in the direction of rural rehabilitation, were held back by the situations in which they had to function. There were persuasive urban demands they had to meet or face electoral uproar. Their business ambitions counseled them to take what share they could in the export-import trade. Foreign creditors anxious for interest payments pushed ceaselessly for more exports—necessarily, in large measure, more agrarian exports—as a means of rescuing the solvency of the new states. In any real sense, rural rehabilitation stayed a dead letter.

While the happy few with access to profits in burgeoning towns became comfortable and even rich, the many in the rural zones found life increasingly harder. Nigeria achieved a population of some 60 million by the early 1970s but in 1978, a year of high prices for Nigerian oil and therefore high profits in the towns, about 82 percent of this population, and 55 percent of the whole labor force, was still rural. Yet the index of real rural wages had fallen from 157.1 nairas in 1954–57 (at constant 1962 prices) to 78.5 in 1970–73, rising only a little after that, whereas the index of real urban wages had almost exactly doubled. It needed no great wisdom to perceive that this imbalance must be fatal to good government.

Discontent came inevitably. Some further statistical evidence may be useful. In 1977, for example, the official Nigerian index of all prices (based on 1962) stood at 423, with food prices somewhat higher at 592. But the index of the minimum wage—urban and rural combined, so that the very low rural figure is obscured—stood at no more than 366. Urban populations had to run ever harder to stay in the same place, but the rural multitudes (still far more than half of all Nigerians) turned to more drastic measures. This became a general rural trend in Africa. Rebelling against the prices offered by the towns and the official authorities—above all, the marketing boards—the rural multitudes in a growing number of farmer colonies turned to the remedies of tradition. Many turned their backs on the towns. They began to resort to their old patterns of economy: subsistence enlarged by local trade. Those who still produced a surplus for sale preferred to get better prices by smuggling their produce across the nearest frontier rather than delivering it to a national market that appeared unrelievedly hostile to their interests.

By the early 1980s, at least, there was no single frontier of the many national frontiers of West Africa across which persons and their goods were not being massively smuggled by stealth or with the connivance of corrupt local officials. Pledged to build nations, the nationalists found themselves in confrontation with rural peoples for whom their nationalism had become a burden and a curse. Meanwhile, with ever more mouths to feed, the towns called incessantly for more food; and often now this food reflected changing tastes and habits. An example is wheat, a cereal ill adapted to or even impossible to grow in tropical Africa. In 1983 the executive secretary of the U.N. Economic Commission for Africa, Dr. Adebayo Adedeji, declared that "a large number of [African] countries are spending up to a third of their foreign exchange earnings on importing food. We reckon that by the turn of the decade Africa will be spending as much on the importation of wheat as it is now spending on the importation of oil." A still largely agrarian continent, always able to feed itself relatively well in the past, could no longer do so. Adedeji's belief was that without drastic reform, above all putting "the priorities where they should have been put 20 years ago, in the agricultural and rural sector (and by agriculture I mean food production and not just production for export), the crisis will get worse."

The forecast has been realized. It is merely reinforced by the few exceptions where genuine rejection or reform of colonial and postcolonial continuities in agricultural policy have occurred. Zimbabwe under its independent government, for example, has scored a startling success in agricultural production, more than trebling maize production since 1979, by giving strong priority to the needs of smallholding black farmers.

WARLORDS OR GUARDIANS?

Against a background of steady misery, the political upheavals of the last decades cannot be surprising. No comprehensive review is possible here, but a glance at the dominant factors, followed by a few brief case studies, may be enough to give the general picture without much distortion of its many complexities.

Given the rivalry for always scarce resources in cash and capital, the ruling nationalists were rapidly forced, as much by the inherited situation as by self-interest, into the politics of factionalism. These had to take the form of regional rivalries, translated as unavoidably into the rivalries of what has been described, often quite misleadingly, as "tribalism."

What then divided the contending nationalist groupings was no kind of ideological or principled program of government—socialist policies, for example, against capitalist policies even though party labels might often claim as much—but an untrammeled contest for bureaucratic jobs, business opportunities or, more generally, a personal slice of the cake. Money being king, corruption naturally followed.

Those who had looked for social progress and reconstruction after the colonial period deplored the rise of greed and careerism among their leaders and the cliques around these leaders. Those who gained from greed and careerism replied that each was inseparable from the building of a proper system of free enterprise; while the few with more education could point out that such had been the case in early capitalist England and France.

In this developing turn-of-the-century crisis, the contest of these opposing views has yet to be resolved. Meanwhile, the politics of nationalism suffers grievously. With the political arena increasingly a dogfight of contending ambitions, ploys and conspiracies, the new nations became correspondingly hard to govern by civilian means. There were exceptions. Tanzania was in most ways one exception, Zambia was another, and for a long while Kenya seemed likely to remain a third. But with uproars ever louder, more and more often the military took over. Sometimes the armed forces took over as anxious and honest guardians of the state, more frequently as ruthless warlords. In one case after another it was seen that the military alone possessed the necessary executive power.

This is another way of saying that the attempt to graft multiparty parliamentary systems (reflecting a long European history of multiclass society) on to stiffly authoritarian colonial institutions had failed. In West Africa the bell was tolled for the Westminster model by a 1966 military coup in Nigeria and another in Ghana, with others soon to follow elsewhere. In the Francophone territories the same knell was heard, sometimes with even worse consequences. In Morocco the parliamentary state gave way to a monarchical state, while in Egypt and later in Libya the military took command. In southern Africa the outcome was rather different, and, as elsewhere, the various military rulers differed greatly from each other in their quality and aims.

It remains that military rule, in whatever form, achieved no popularity. Sometimes, with active support by responsible military rulers, notably in Nigeria, there came a complex search for new forms of democratic stability; this continues. Ghana, for example, reverted to civilian rule in 1969, only to collapse once more into a series of military regimes until finally, in the early 1980s, there came what seemed to promise an effective prelude to new forms of democracy. There were comparable strivings in Burkina Faso, in Benin and latterly in Uganda. Nigeria reverted to civilian rule in the late 1970s after a long and painful civil war between 1967 and 1970, but the newly relaunched parties revealed the same fragility as the old ones. Early in the 1990s Nigeria will presumably still be under a military government that has undertaken, however, to hand over power once again to the civilians.

By now it is widely accepted that no mere transfer of foreign institutions can be the answer. Africa will have to draw upon its own traditions and originality.

A DIFFICULT ROUTE

The same lesson is being learned from an intense and often sharply instructive experience of dealing with the outside world.

Colonial powers, so long as they persisted, had drawn a thick veil between rhetoric and reality, incessantly preaching the exclusive virtues of their own dispensations. Very sure that escape from colonial rule was possible only along the route of nationalism, transforming colonial states into nation-states, the nationalists had generally gone along with that. They had accepted the Western models. Those who demurred—and there were quite a few—proclaimed the saving alternative of other models, including those of the USSR and China. Yet no real understanding of either set of models was available along the way to independence, or soon after it had been achieved. When independent judgments could at last be formed, those of any weight generally concluded that early hopes had been ill founded. Africans were going to have to find their own solutions.

This conclusion has been reinforced by the impact of great-power rivalries and by the developed world's failure to relieve any of the basic causes of Africa's indebtedness to foreign lenders.

A measure of cynicism followed early beliefs that rich and powerful economies would be sufficiently disinterested to promote programs and contracts sincerely aimed at putting African needs first. Soon enough, but perhaps above all through experience with foreign experts or advisers of one kind or another and with those who financed these persons or agencies (whether in the Eastern or the Western bloc), skepticism grew apace. It began to be said, though privately more often than in public, that the project of "winning Africa for the West" or "for the East," was another way of hampering or preventing an independent choice derived from an independent estimate of the continent's capacity for self-help. As this thought evolved, the advocates of nonalignment gained ground. They were again strengthened by great-power attitudes and actions in two important regions. One of these was in southern Africa, the other in the north-easterly region of the Horn. Each situation provided much food for thought even if, by the 1980s, the fragility of most African states made any appropriate counter-action very difficult.

In southern Africa the United States continued, and ever more openly, to succor the apartheid state of South Africa and to assist the latter's violent effort to wreck the newly established republics of Angola and Mozambique. With another but comparable rhetoric, this time of revolution rather than of freedom, the USSR gave massive military support to an Ethiopian regime that was pledged, in fact if not in propaganda, to achieve a dominant influence over the whole region of the Horn. From neither intervention did any constructive peace seem possible.

The foreign-debt crisis came to a head after 1985, and again it was evident that no outside agency was prepared to relieve it. Two years later, a seventh meeting of the U.N. Commission for Trade and Development addressed itself once more to solving the central economic problem that six previous such conferences had entirely failed to solve: the reaching of international agreements that might shield primary-produce countries, African among them, from the consequences of adverse terms of trade. This would involve, by one means or another, the improvement or at least stabilization of primary-produce export prices, and some mechanism for restraining the rise of the prices of imports. Though efforts toward these objectives had been made through the EC aid program, the Lomé Convention, the basic adversity remained. Relatively, the postcolonial world continued to grow poorer.

The conviction grew that the "world conflict" involving Africa had little or nothing of substance to do with any "east-west divide" but a great deal to do with the north-south divide in which the postcolonial countries, notably in Africa, were expected to remain as primary producers for the benefit of a development of resources and technology that would continue to occur elsewhere. At this point, moreover, the debt-service position became untenable. Following South American lead in the mid-1980s, Zambia, Zaire and the Ivory Coast broke with all precedent and orthodoxy by suspending their debt payments, and other countries seemed likely to follow.

THE EXPERIENCE OF SOUTHERN AFRICA

It now appears that any real progress, or even any halting of regression, must depend on a more or less far-reaching reorganization of the legacy bequeathed by colonial rule. In southern Africa, for example, the interests of imperial Britain had for long exercised a virtual hegemony throughout the whole vast area south of the Congo basin. Decolonization in the 1960s raised the prospect of a different, and African, hegemony. Malawi became independent in 1964, as did Zambia, followed rapidly by the three High Commission Territories of Basutoland (Lesotho), Bechuanaland (Botswana) and Swaziland—with the likelihood that other colonies in the region would eventually follow them into independence.

Another claimant to hegemony, however, was also on the scene. South Africa's dependence on Britain began to be broken by the coming to power, in 1948, of the Afrikaner white minority. Potent changes in the South African economy had meanwhile promoted industry and manufacture over farming, a process much advanced by increasing inflows of capital from the United States and other industrialized countries competitive with Britain. Britain's hegemony was over, but which other should succeed it? Was the successor power going to be the apartheid state fueled by its overseas partners? Or were the emergent republics of southern Africa themselves going to take over? The bloodstained history of the years since 1975 shows that everything has turned on the answer.

At least to the end of the 1960s, if not later, the Western expectation or wish was that Britain's supremacy would pass to a white-ruled South Africa, and that this South Africa would become the direct or indirect controller of economic and political life in all the lands south of the Congo. As its spokesmen plausibly claimed, the apartheid state had both the capacity and the opportunity to exert that control. A "southern African common market" under South African hegemony would assure South Africa of limitless supplies of essential raw materials, while South African industry would find protected markets in the countries north of its borders. Assured of this, the South African government hastened to come to terms with the rise of African nationalism, the better to absorb its challenge. It found willing partners in several countries, notably Malawi and Madagascar, and sufficiently consenting partners elsewhere.

The future seemed assured, and the apartheid state, riding high, proceeded to match its growing prosperity with harsher discrimination against its own black peoples, whether African, Indian or Coloured. Those liberal-minded observers who had prophesied that booming prosperity in South Africa would ease and eventually eradicate the racist discrimination of its Afrikaner rulers were shown to have misunderstood the mentality of apartheid. By late in the 1960s every possibility of black advance through black pressure or protest appeared to have been crushed.

But this perspective proved false, and the proof came from a least-expected quarter. It had been taken for granted that the Portuguese colonies of Angola and Mozambique would remain as convenient adjuncts of a South African subcontinental power; and this seemed to be confirmed in 1965 when a hard-pressed Portuguese dictatorship was obliged by financial stress to open the doors of these large territories to non-Portuguese investment. South African corporations at once began to move in. Strong anticolonial nationalist movements might be fighting in Angola and Mozambique, but it was similarly taken for granted that they too would be crushed.

It failed to happen. By the end of 1973 the Portuguese regime had been forced to commit the bulk of all its land and air forces to warfare against the movements in Angola, Mozambique and Portuguese Guinea (now Guinea-Bissau) in West Africa. Yet these nationalist movements—Frelimo in Mozambique, MPLA in Angola and PAIGC in Portuguese Guinea—still held the political and military initiative. With no end in sight to more than a decade of costly warfare, the Portuguese armed forces declared against their regime and its generals; on April 25, 1974 the dictatorship was overthrown and the way soon cleared for the independence of the colonies. Unconditional independence was conceded to Portuguese Guinea in September 1974. Still more reluctantly the same concession was made to Mozambique a year later and—although in complex circumstances—to Angola in November 1975. Cape Verde had achieved the same goal in July of that year, while São Tomé and Príncipe became independent at the same time as Angola.

These events took the South African government by surprise. The independence of Mozambique came with such overwhelming suddenness that nothing was undertaken to prevent it. But the independence of Angola, again under a radical government quite certain to oppose any spread of South African influence, was at once challenged and even anticipated by South African military invasion. This failed in its objective and was called off in March 1976, only to be resumed a little later.

From 1978 on, the apartheid regime embarked on a long series of invasions of Angola and then of Mozambique, partly by South African forces and partly by surrogate agencies of various kinds, such as the UNITA organization in the case of Angola and that of Renamo in Mozambique. In these violent efforts to achieve South African hegemony, Pretoria found a strong ally in the administration of President Ronald Reagan; and this ensured that the aggressions would continue. Aggression went far to wreck all hope of constructive change in these territories, but it still failed to overturn their independent governments.

In 1980, moreover, the project of South African subcontinental hegemony was further assailed by the success of nationalist fighting movements in Rhodesia, principally the Zimbabwe African National Union. White-ruled Rhodesia became black-ruled Zimbabwe, and again with a government, headed by Robert Mugabe, that seemed certain to be a stubborn adversary of the apartheid system. What remained to that system, outside its borders, was the former German colony and subsequently U.N. trusteeship territory of Namibia. But there, too, Pretoria had to face the rising protest and guerrilla warfare of the South-West Africa People's Organization, as well as the formal condemnation of the Western powers.

Within South Africa itself, meanwhile, renewed black protest led principally by the banned African National Congress, by new and militant trade unions, and by young people in the huge black townships outside such cities as Johannesburg, now called into question the very survival of the apartheid regime. By late in the 1980s, South Africa faced an almost worldwide isolation that threatened to become effective by way of some form or another of economic sanctions. Apartheid South Africa may remain extremely powerful, yet its condition now seems much like that of the dinosaurs: destined to die out from "too much armour and too little brain."

CONFLICTS IN THE HORN

Sorely afflicted by drought-induced famine since early in the 1970s, the diverse peoples of the wide region of the Horn have suffered from a combination of troubles, some of their own making, others derived from the colonial legacy. The colonial partition here was not only the result of European imperialism—that of Italy and Britain, and in a small degree that of France—but also of the building of a purely African empire: that of the Abyssinian or Ethiopian ruler Menelik II and his people, chiefly the Amhara. When Italy established its colonial rule over most of the country of the Somalis and the Eritreans, and Britain did the same in northern Somali country (with France seizing the enclave of Djibouti), Menelik was able to enclose the Somali region of the Ogaden and other non-Ethiopian territory to the south. And when the European powers duly withdrew (mainly in 1960), Menelik's successor, Haile Selassie, not only maintained this Amhara-ruled empire but, in 1962, added to it by engulfing the former Italian colony of Eritrea. Much trouble was bound to follow.

The Eritreans disliked being swallowed. They replied with the guerrilla warfare of a newly matured nationalism, and fighting continued. But Amharic domination, typified by the emperor and his henchmen, now faced a challenge from within. A land-hungry peasant revolt in the southern provinces set off an army revolt that declared, however confusedly, for revolution. The quasi-feudal hierarchies of the old empire were thrust aside. Power passed to an army committee (Dergue) of mostly young officers. Briefly, there was a prospect of far-reaching change within the empire, and of a democratization that could transform this empire into a federation of peoples. It never happened.

What did happen was that a new Dergue under Col. Mengistu Haile Mariam dismissed every proposal for any such reorganization and, in effect, set itself to maintain an Amhara-ruled central power. In 1976 Mengistu turned for military aid to the USSR, which at once hastened to displace the United States as the principal upholder of the empire. With extensive Soviet military supplies and advice, and some from Cuba, the Dergue armies were able to defeat a Somali rising (backed by Somalia) aimed at removing Ethiopian control of the Ogaden seized by Menelik in the 1890s. The Dergue then renewed its attempt to crush Eritrean resistance. But the Eritreans more than held out. New Soviet-backed offensives followed. These were bitterly destructive, but without success.

The upshot was that by the mid-1980s the whole region was in conflict. Inside Ethiopia new guerrilla movements erupted: those of the Tigre, the

Oromo and the southern Bantu-speaking peoples, each demanding that Amhara domination should give way to some form of democratic reorganization. Meanwhile, with persistent Soviet support, Mengistu continued to build and fortify a highly centralized and personal power. The conclusion, here as in southern Africa, once again appeared to be that great-power intervention, whether from the East or the West, could only inflame old problems and worsen new ones.

SAHARAN TROUBLES

Having decided to accept the colonial pattern of frontiers—although with the exception, confirmed in 1964, of the disputed Ogaden—the new nations of Africa were unavoidably involved in various frontier troubles. The early independence years saw a number of such troubles settled peacefully, as for example between Morocco and Algeria where the Organization of African Unity (OAU), formed in 1963 (see pp. 686 ff.), proved its value as a mediator. Other troubles proved resistant to solution. Two may be mentioned here.

In ancient times, occasionally with neighbors, the Sanhaja people of the far western plains of the Sahara (Berber in origin but Arab in language and religion) had made a home in the near-coastal Saquia al-Hamra region. During the colonial partition these Sanhaja lands were enclosed by Spain as the "protectorate" of Río de Oro, often against local armed resistance that continued into the 1930s. As elsewhere, foreign invasion and dispossession gave rise to a nationalism that began to mature during the 1950s.

Spain withdrew from Río de Oro in 1975, ignored the claims of the Sanhaja (now the Sahrawi, the people of the Western Sahara), and agreed to divide the territory between Morocco and Mauritania. At this the Sahrawi renewed their armed resistance, led by a political movement formed in 1973, called the Polisario Front, and followed this up by the declaration in November 1975, of the Democratic Republic of the Sahrawi. With Algerian support, Polisario's fighters induced Mauritania to withdraw its claim to the southern part of the territory. But the Moroccan king, Hassan, with an eye to the mineral deposits of the northern part as well as to his royal prestige, refused to withdraw. With the OAU sharply split in its support of one side or the other, the war continued.

Another largely Saharan dispute found the Republic of Chad (dating from 1960) involved in crippling conflict between (broadly) its Muslim people of the northern oases or mountains and its non-Muslim peoples of the southern grasslands. Other factors in the conflict included the continued presence and influence of French military garrisons, and, in the north, Libyan expansion under Muammar al-Qadhafi. Various efforts at peacemaking, including an attempt by the government of Nigeria, failed to calm the strife. Meanwhile, serious drought in the 1970s and later added famine to the sufferings of a people who had yet to enjoy the advantages of independence. Once again it was seen that the long arm of the past, whether colonial or African in nature, could be too strong in its destructive power for any statesmanship available.

NEW WAYS AHEAD?

Any brief overview of a subject as complex as this must leave so much unsaid that it may easily mislead. Nevertheless, it can be summarily stated that if disasters were many in these 30 years or so, there was nonetheless no lack of positive achievements. The quality of life improved, often in ways that can scarcely be formally recorded in statistics. Once the constraints of foreign rule were removed—constraints that were relatively mild in the British West African colonies, but ruthlessly severe in most of the white-settler colonies (whether British or otherwise)—an often dazzling profusion of talents and initiatives rapidly evolved in the sciences as well as in the arts. Fiction, poetry and drama; music, both traditional and modern; popular sports, such as football; oratory and debate—all these flourished as never before. The African voice was heard worldwide in assemblies of opinion or research, while at home the study of the humanities, not least the study of history, gave weight and substance to a confidence that African peoples were indeed an integral and equal part of the human family. All this was profoundly healing after the traumas of dispossession.

The end of the 20th century may have to preside over many-sided crises, but it sees as well the onset of a new realism, of a better grasp of the challenges of independence and of the emergence, however tentative as yet, of original approaches, of indigenous solutions, of new ways ahead. An agenda for the 21st century, it has begun to seem, need not be condemned to repeat the past. On this agenda, as it further appears, two areas of constructive change may come to occupy the scene. One of these concerns the structures of power within the nation-states; the other has to do with intraregional cooperation.

The chronic fragility of nation-states where strongly centrialized power is so often usurped by the soldiers, is likely to persist until far-reaching devolutions of authority can be implemented. The dissidence of rural populations will continue until ways can be found of persuading them back into the arena of national unity. In either case the solution would seem to lie partly in improving the terms of trade to the advantage of the countryside as against the town, even if earlier goals of rapid industrialization by a process of milking the countryside have to be modified.

But the solution would also seem to lie, as many now say, in raising effective forms of local self-government as a counterforce and corrective to the power of central government. Time after time it has been shown—as for example in Zimbabwe—that African farmers can produce abundant crops for sale in towns if they are once assured of their rights and opportunities. Time after time it has been evident—as in Ugandan political developments after 1985—that a government capable of devolutions of power can restore peace to zones of embittered conflict. There has been much useful experiment already in several countries in the promotion of new types of local-government control and self-rule.

A second area of constructive change according to this agenda likewise takes shape in renewed efforts to move toward regional cooperation and instrumental unification. Here, almost everything remains to be done or even attempted. Nation-state "me-firstism" had long dismissed the old visions of African unity that led the debates of the 1950s. And yet it would seem that the tasks set before the 16-state Economic Community of West African States, formed in 1975, are still urgent: downgrading the inherited frontiers, ensuring mobility of persons and their wealth, creating a vast region of production and exchange so that the impoverishment of recent years may be reversed. At least the outline of a comparable reorganization of southern Africa, anticipating the day when the skills and capital of a democratized South Africa may become freely available on cooperative terms, has emerged among the countries bordering on South Africa. The obstacles may be great; the potential gains are greater still.

Africa's problem in the second half of the 20th century has been to acquire the powers of independence in the modern world. Against whatever failures or setbacks, this has been substantially achieved. The challenge that remains is to complete the command of these powers and use them to win the material benefits, as well as the political and moral freedoms, of a new internationalism within this continent of many peoples and many cultures.

FURTHER READING

Carlsson, Jerker, ed. *Recession in Africa*. Uppsala: Scandinavian Institute of African Studies, 1982.

Davidson, Basil. *The Fortunate Isles: A Study in African Transformation*. Trenton, New Jersey, Africa World Press, 1988.

————. *Let Freedom Come: Africa in Modern History*. Boston: Little, Brown; London: Allen Lane, 1978.

Egerö, Bertil. *Mozambique: A Dream Undone*. Uppsala: Scandinavian Institute of African Studies, 1987.

Hanlon, Joseph. *Beggar Your Neighbours: Apartheid Power in Southern Africa*. London: Catholic Institute for International Relations; Bloomington: Indiana University Press, 1986.

Lewis, I. M., ed. *Nationalism & Self-Determination in the Horn of Africa*. London: Ithaca Press, 1983.

Markakis, J. *National and Class Conflict in the Horn of Africa*. Cambridge: Cambridge University Press, 1987.

Martin, David, and Phyllis Johnson. *The Struggle for Zimbabwe: The Chimurenga War*. London and Boston: Faber & Faber, 1981.

Pallister, D., et al. *South Africa, Inc.: The Oppenheimer Empire*. London, 1987.

THE ORGANIZATION OF AFRICAN UNITY

COLIN LEGUM

THE Organization of African Unity (OAU) celebrated its 25th anniversary on May 25, 1988. It has grown from 32 member-states at its formation to 50, embracing all the independent countries on the continent, with the exceptions of Morocco and South Africa, the latter of which is excluded from membership because of the racist nature of its political system. Morocco had initially refused to sign the charter of the OAU because at the time it still laid claims to Mauritania, whose independence was recognized by the OAU and so qualified for membership. Morocco later changed its position on Mauritania and joined the OAU, only to withdraw in 1984 because of a decision to admit the Sahara Arab Democratic Republic (SADR, or Western Sahara) to membership despite the fact that it was ruled by a government in exile. Morocco, which had been granted sovereignty over the territory when Spain ended its colonial occupation, insisted that Western Sahara was part of its precolonial kingdom—just as it had once insisted on reestablishing its historic sovereignty over Mauritania.

The OAU's achievement as an organization covering virtually an entire continent makes it the first successful unification movement in history. Over the centuries a number of efforts have been made to achieve some form of political unity over continents, regions or ethnic groupings: Pan-Slavism, Pan-Americanism, Pan-Arabism, for example. However, the fulfillment of this goal was finally achieved first in Africa. Four main reasons account for this historic breakthrough: the seeding of the ideas of Pan-Africanism since the beginning of the 20th century; the emergence to independence of the great majority of African countries at roughly the same time, between the late 1950s and the mid-1960s; the common colonial experience of African peoples, which gave them a broadly shared interest in establishing their rights and status in the world community; and a commitment to ending the "remnants of colonialism" in the continent, especially in the white-ruled region of southern Africa.

THE ORIGINS OF PAN-AFRICANISM

Pan-Africanism had its earliest roots not in the African homeland but in the diaspora of black peoples in the New World. It developed through

686

what has been described as "a complicated triangle of influences" between the New World, Europe and Africa. In the nascent period of Pan-Africanism—from the middle of the 19th century until the beginning of the 20th century—the future leaders of the African independence struggle imbibed these new ideas as students in the United States and Britain.

Pan-Africanism is essentially a movement of ideas and emotions; at times these have remained at the level of thesis and antithesis, while at other times they have achieved a synthesis. On a functional level, Pan-Africanism can be likened to international socialism; in another sense it can be likened to a world federation, Atlantic union or federal union—each allowing for considerable scope of interpretation in its practical application. In its deepest sense, however, it differs from these concepts because of its original idea of exclusivity, the embracing of black consciousness in a world dominated by white powers. Its closest parallel, perhaps, is to Zionism, the dream of a dispersed people to gain their own homeland and restore a sense of Jewish dignity. As the outstanding intellectual apostle of Pan-Africanism, Dr. W. E. B. Du Bois, a black American, wrote in 1919: "The African movement means to us what the Zionist movement must mean to the Jews, the centralization of race effort and the recognition of a racial fount."

The emotional impetus for Pan-Africanism flowed out of the experience of a widely dispersed people—those of African stock—who felt themselves physically discriminated against, either dispossessed of their lands by colonialists or sold into slavery. This historic experience involved a loss of independence and freedom and was felt to have robbed black people of their dignity. *Dignity* is the key word in the vocabulary of Pan-Africanists; to regain dignity in the eyes of the world is the mainspring of all their actions.

In 1897 Du Bois declared that "if the Negro were to be a factor in the world's history, it would be through a Pan-Negro movement." At the first Pan-African congress, held in London in 1900 at the initiative of a Trinidadian barrister, H. Sylvester Williams, Du Bois spoke his famous prophetic lines: "The problem of the 20th century is the problem of the colour line—the relation of the darker to the lighter races of men in Asia and Africa, in America and the islands of the Sea."

Five subsequent Pan-African conferences were held in the United States, England and France between 1901 and 1945. At these conferences young intellectuals and politicians from Africa imbibed the ideas and spirit of the growing movement. This experience was deepened by contact between the proponents of Pan-Africanism and African students at American and British universities. Among the score or so of black South African students in the United States at the turn of the century were P. K. Isaka Seme, Sol T. Plaatje, J. L. Dube, D. D. T. Jabavu and A. B. Xuma, all of whom became associated with the birth and development of the African National Congress. They were later followed by students from East and West Africa like Dr. Nnamdi Azikiwe of Nigeria, Dr. Hastings Kamuzu Banda of Malawi, Peter Mbiyu Koinange and Jomo Kenyatta of Kenya, and Kwame Nkrumah of Ghana.

A parallel movement developed among French-speaking colonial peoples who met as students in Paris. They developed the idea of negritude, described by them as "anti-racist racism," using *racism* in a purely ethnic, nonpejorative sense. Negritude was inspired by two poets from Martinique, Etienne Léro and Aimé Césaire, who found disciples in men like Rabemananjara from Madagascar, and Léopold Senghor and David Diop from Senegal.

Pan-Africanism, seeded in the diaspora, was planted in the African continent when the new class of politically active young anti-colonial students returned to their homes to lead nationalist movements. Since Ghana was the first sub-Saharan country to achieve its independence, it fell to Kwame Nkrumah to take the initiative in launching a Pan-African organization in Africa itself. The first conference of Independent African States was held in Accra in 1958 and was attended by leaders of all the then independent states (excluding South Africa)—Ghana, Egypt, Ethiopia, Liberia, Morocco, Tunisia, Libya and Sudan.

In the subsequent 15 years the movement had a checkered career for a number of reasons. Nkrumah's ambition to make Accra the headquarters of the liberation movement and his active support of dissident movements in neighboring countries provoked suspicion and hostility, especially in Francophone African countries and in Nigeria. Gamal Abdel Nasser, then at the peak of his career, vied with Nkrumah to make Cairo the headquarters of the continent's liberation movements. There were also national and personal rivalries among political leaders. But the major rift was between those regarded as "the radicals" and "the conservatives." Men like President William Tubman of Liberia, Emperor Haile Selassie of Ethiopia, President Félix Houphouët-Boigny of the Ivory Coast and Abubakar Tafawa Balewa, prime minister of Nigeria, were antagonistic to the radical camp led by Nkrumah, President Sékou Touré of Guinea and President Modibo Kéita of Mali.

These divisions led to the formation of two rival groupings: the Casablanca group and the Monrovia group. (Although King Hassan of Morocco himself belonged to the conservatives, he chose to identify himself initially with the radicals for pragmatic reasons.) In the various attempts to heal the breach between the two rival groups, a fundamental difference emerged that cut across the lines of radicals vs. conservatives. This was over the issue of whether the emerging OAU should seek to begin by building institutions for the political unification of all African states (as demanded by Nkrumah, Touré and Keita), or should proceed along more pragmatic lines to achieve the highest level of political and economic cooperation possible, while keeping alive the final objective of a "United States of Africa." The pragmatists (who included radicals like Julius Nyerere of Tanganyika, as it was then still known) won decisively at the inaugural conference that launched the OAU in Addis Ababa in 1963, where Nkrumah found himself virtually alone on the issue of political unification. Haile Selassie, in deference to his status, was elected as the first chairman of the OAU. He was also successful in getting his capital accepted as the headquarters of the new organization.

THE CHARTER OF THE OAU

The preamble to the OAU Charter, setting the general aims and objectives of the organization as follows:

Convinced that it is the inalienable right of all people to control their own destiny;

Conscious of the fact that freedom, equality, justice and dignity are essential objectives for the achievement of the legitimate aspirations of the African peoples;

Conscious of our responsibility to harness the natural and human resources of our continent for the total advancement of our peoples in spheres of human endeavour;

Inspired by a common determination to promote understanding and collaboration among our States in response to the aspirations of our peoples for brotherhood and solidarity, in a larger unity transcending ethnic and national differences;

Convinced that, in order to translate this determination into a dynamic force in the cause of human progress, conditions for peace and security must be established and maintained;

Determined to safeguard and consolidate the hard-won independence as well as the sovereignty and territorial integrity of our States, and to resist neo-colonialism in all its forms;

Dedicated to the general progress of Africa;

Persuaded that the charter of the United Nations and the Universal Declaration of Human Rights, to the principles of which we reaffirm our adherence, provide a solid foundation for peaceful and positive co-operation among States;

Desirous that all African and Malagasy States should henceforth unite so that the welfare and well-being of their peoples can be assured;

Resolved to reinforce the links between our States by establishing and strengthening common institutions.

The OAU established three institutions: the Assembly of Heads of State and Government, which was to meet annually at summit meetings; the Council of Ministers, composed of foreign ministers or such other ministers as might be designated, and which was to meet at least twice a year; and the General Secretariat, headed by an administrative secretary-general.

A Commission of Mediation, Conciliation and Arbitration was set up to implement the pledge of member-states to settle all disputes among themselves by peaceful means. Five specialized commissions were also established: economic and social; educational and cultural; health, sanitation and nutrition; defense; scientific, technical and research.

Nothing was said in the charter itself about respect for the boundaries of member-states, but a subsequent decision laid down that the borders inherited at independence should be respected and that no changes should be brought about except through peaceful means, as a result of mediation and agreement.

The Defense Commission, whose responsibility was to create a Pan-African Military command, has continued in existence but has failed, to date, to make much progress.

A major weakness of the OAU has been the failure of its member-states to pay their dues, so that by 1987 about U.S. $40 million was in arrears, forcing the reduction of the budget to slightly over $23 million. A similar failure to honor commitments to the Africa Liberation Committee has weakened its role. Nevertheless, the committee, which has the role of supporting the anticolonial liberation movements and particularly those in South Africa, has played a major role in promoting their struggle.

SUCCESSES AND FAILURES OF THE OAU

Like all multinational organizations, such as the United Nations, the Commonwealth of Nations and the European Community, the OAU lacks the power to enforce its decisions except in cases of general consensus or when a sufficient number of major member-governments are in substantial agreement. The charter's prohibition against interfering in the internal affairs of member-states prevented it from playing any effective role in the bloody civil war in Nigeria in the late 1960s or in doing anything to restrain the tyrannical regimes of Idi Amin in Uganda, "Emperor" Bokassa in the Central African Republic and Macias Nguema in Equatorial Guinea. These blots on the OAU's reputation have led to the decision to establish a Charter of People's and Human Rights, which provides for a court composed of eminent Africans to accept petitions and give ruling on abuses in member-countries. The necessary majority of OAU members was reached in 1987 when active steps were taken to begin to implement the charter.

The Commission of Mediation, Conciliation and Arbitration later fell into desuetude following its failure to resolve the conflicts between Ethiopia and Somalia in the Horn of Africa, between Morocco and the SADR, or between Chad and Libya. However, the OAU has succeeded in a number of cases through ad hoc interventions to stifle at birth military conflicts between Algeria and Morocco, and between Mali and Upper Volta (now Burkina Faso). Its only attempt at a peacekeeping role in Chad ended disastrously. Through its chairman, it succeeded, however, in bringing an end to the civil war in Sudan in 1973.

Although the OAU cannot lay down policies for its members, it has made three notable contributions toward establishing continental cooperation. These have been developing a collective policy toward Rhodesia (now Zimbabwe), the former Portuguese colonies, South Africa and Namibia; declaring a diplomatic boycott of Israel; and, most importantly, establishing an African Economic Recovery Program (AERP).

African governments were strongly divided in the 1960s over their relations with South Africa. A number of them—led by the Ivory Coast and Malawi—favored a policy of engaging in dialogue with the Pretoria regime rather than maintaining a total economic and diplomatic boycott of the country. When this issue was forced to a vote at an OAU summit, the great majority of members rejected dialogue and halted the move started by the Ivorians to engage in talks with the apartheid regime. Although not all the members abided by the majority decision, the OAU's intervention was effective in restricting, or inhibiting, all except a very few African governments from engaging in negotiations with Pretoria. The attempt to stop trading was less successful.

On the issue of Israel, a call by the OAU for African governments to break their diplomatic links after the 1973 war with the Arabs met with instantaneous success; only three member-states refused to end their ties, although many more maintained covert diplomatic and economic links. This policy of isolating Israel remained largely effective for a decade, until six countries followed Egypt's example in renewing their diplomatic ties in the mid-1980s.

The biggest success of the OAU has undoubtedly been in facing up to the continent's disastrous economic situation in the 1980s. The first step toward collective action was taken at the OAU economic summit in April 1980, with the unanimous endorsement of the Lagos Plan of Action, which endorsed a regional food plan for Africa drawn up by African agricultural ministers in 1978. The significance of this plan was that it gave priority to the importance of producing more food for the continent. Having pointed this way forward, the OAU agreed in 1984 to prepare a program to confront the continent's alarming economic crisis. The AERP was unanimously endorsed in 1985, and African leaders moved in concert to get a special session of the U.N. General Assembly summoned to discuss the plan and gain pledges of support from the world community to enable its targets to be met and to sustain structural reforms. There is no precedent for virtually an entire continent closing ranks in this way to support a collective economic plan and confront the nations of the developed world.

Prophesying the impending demise of the OAU has been a popular sport of the media ever since African governments surprised the skeptics who had argued that the widely different leaders of the continent would never agree to unite. Despite some shaky moments—especially in 1980–81 after the failure to get a quorum for its annual summit in Libya because of the antipathy felt by a majority to the policies of Colonel Qadhafi—the OAU appears to have grown strong roots throughout the continent. Its technical cooperation programs, though seldom written about, have been of special importance, both in coordinating development programs and in pioneering new ones. These include basic work in promoting regional economic cooperation; building new roads such as the Trans-Sahara Highway, and linking the capitals of the continent to each other by direct telephone connections instead of, as used to be the case, having to go through European capitals; cooperation in preventive health schemes; and joint industrial, technical and scientific studies.

While the major concentration of the OAU has been current political issues and, increasingly, on economic questions, the earlier idealism of Pan-Africanism continues to evoke a passionate response despite the hard realities of the difficulties in systematizing the relations among 50 states, few of them as yet 30 years old. The ambition to move gradually toward a meaningful United States of Africa remains alive, as testified to by the Lagos Plan, which proposed the creation of a single African Economic Community by the year 2000.

FURTHER READING

Andemicael, Berhanykun. *The OAU and the UN: Relations between the Organization of African Unity and the United Nations.* New York: Africana, 1976.

———. *Pan-Africanism Reconsidered.* Berkeley: University of California Press, 1962.

Cervanka, Zdenek. *The Organisation of African Unity and Its Charter.* London: Hurst; New York: Praeger, 1969.

Geiss, Imanuel. *The Pan-African Movement: A History of Pan-Africanism in America, Europe and Africa.* London: Metheun; New York: Africana, 1974.

Legum, Colin. *Pan-Africanism: A Short Political Guide.* Rev. ed. London: Pall Mall; New York: Praeger, 1965.

——— et al. *Africa in the 1980s: A Continent in Crisis.* New York: McGraw-Hill, 1979.

Padmore, George. *Pan-Africanism or Communism? The Coming Struggle for Africa.* London: Dobson; New York: Roy, 1956.

Thompson, Vincent Bakpetu. *Africa and Unity: The Evolution of Pan-Africanism.* London: Longmans, 1969; New York: Humanities Press, 1970.

AFRICA'S WAR ZONES

ANDREW LYCETT

INTRODUCTION

AFRICA, a vast continent consisting of over 50 separate states, appears, through the coverage it receives in Western media, to be continually beset by war. But if its war zones are analyzed, it is clear that the majority of the continent—geographically and demographically—lives in comparative peace.

The serious civil and regional wars in progress are primarily the result of the creation of colonial states, followed by rapid decolonialization without consideration of the ethnic and nationalist conflicts that would follow. Chad, Sudan, Uganda, Western Sahara, Ethiopia and Angola offer the prime examples. Angola, for example, is linked to the regional southern African crisis, and conditions there are complicated by the racial and economic tensions within South Africa itself. (See Joseph Hanlon's chapter "South Africa's War on its Neighbors," in this Handbook, for more details.)

Once these conflicts are taken into account, however, there is little other actual armed confrontation to report in the rest of the continent. West Africa is currently strife-free. The same is true for most countries of the Sahel region and the heartland of the continent, though they have had their conflagrations, certainly. The Nigerian civil war (1967–70) was a classic postcolonial struggle, with the Christianized, oil-rich Ibos seeking to stake out their independence from the Islamized rump of Nigeria, and with most observers, including the former occupying power, Britain, supporting the federal government. The other major conflict on the continent in the last 30 years was the Zairian civil war—another classic attempted hijack of the existing postcolonial order. But today both Nigeria and Zaire are peaceful.

One of the cardinal tenets of African diplomacy is that colonial boundaries, however haphazardly drawn, are sacrosanct. The Organization of African Unity (OAU) adopted this as an important principle in 1963, and retains it. This inflexible approach to internal conflict, however understandable, has rendered the OAU totally ineffective in mediating Africa's protracted civil wars.

Although the six main wars noted above—in Angola, Chad, Sudan, Uganda, Ethiopia and Western Sahara—are partly the legacies of colonialism, they involve more than that. The conflict between Chad and Libya in

693

the Sahara can indeed be largely attributed to French neglect of northern Chad, coupled with a disputed boundary drawn by French and Italian colonialists. But it would not have escalated as it did without one other vital factor—the posturing and ambition of Libyan leader Col. Muammar al-Qadhafi.

In Western Sahara, the Qadhafi figure is King Hassan of Morocco, an Arab potentate seeking to take advantage of the departure of the Spanish colonialists in 1977 to extend his territory. He is largely supported by Western powers, who have little to gain by backing the indigenous Sahrawis who are fighting for their independence.

In Sudan, the conflict between north and south can again be described as classically postcolonial. The British clearly neglected the south, while trying to quarantine it against Islamic influences from the north. Nevertheless, Sudan gained its independence in 1956 as one country; there was no inevitability that northerners would antagonize southerners to such an extent as to spark, first, the 17-year-long civil war that ran from 1955 to 1972 and, secondly, the conflict that has continued for much of the 1980s.

Western connivance allowed Ethiopia to claim control of the former Italian colony Eritrea after it had been administered by the British on behalf of the United Nations from the end of World War II to 1952. But it was Ethiopia's territorial ambition that led to this annexation—its desire to create an area of influence in the Horn of Africa in imitation not just of Western imperialism, but of all the empires that have sought political hegemony throughout history.

Southern Africa presents a slightly different case, because the two main conflicts there are caused by the major power, South Africa, which wishes to maintain divisiveness between its neighbors. The war in Mozambique is probably the most unnecessary one on the continent: the rump of a guerrilla group, Renamo (also known as the Mozambique National Resistance, or MNR), being maintained by Pretoria to make life difficult for the Frelimo government in Mozambique and remind it who is boss in the region. To the west, South Africa wishes to keep Namibia within its sphere of influence and postpone the arrival of yet another independent, black, possibly Marxist government on its borders. The situation is complicated by the presence of Cuban troops in Angola, helping to preserve the MPLA government in power against the rival claims of Joseph Savimbi's UNITA movement, in turn supported by South Africa. No other conflict in Africa has so much outside involvement as the complicated struggle for ascendancy in Namibia/Angola. The U.S. assistant secretary of state for African affairs, Chester A. Crocker, has been laboring throughout the two-term Reagan administration to bring about a settlement that would achieve the removal of the Cubans from Angola. The Angolans and Cubans, in turn, wanted a settlement that would secure the South Africans' withdrawal from Namibia (leading to Namibian independence, probably under South-West Africa People Organization (SWAPO) rule.) In late 1987 and during 1988 there were reports of headway in reaching a compromise along these lines. But a settlement seems as far away as ever; and the same is true of Africa's other major conflicts. To understand these better, it is necessary to look at them in greater detail.

The 102,703-sq. mile/266,000-sq. km. country known as Western Sahara was originally inhabited by Islamized Berbers. The Portuguese used it as a staging post on their African explorations in the 14th century. But no Western power made a territorial claim there until 1884. This was done by Spain, which was more interested in developments in the offshore Canary Islands than anything inland. Indeed it was not until 30 years later that Spain began to establish administrative control. Western Sahara has significant phosphate deposits; its 621-mile/1000-km. shoreline gives rights over extensive reserves of fish.

By the mid-1930s Moroccan-backed resistance to Spanish rule had started. In 1958 Morocco invaded. Spain joined forces with France to drive the North African kingdom back, but not before part of the north of the country was ceded to Morocco—under the terms of the Treaty of Sintra in April 1958.

At that time Western Sahara was divided into two regions: Saquia al-Hamra in the sub-Saharan steppe in the north, and Río de Oro (the old Portuguese name) in the desert south. In 1958 the two regions were united by the Spanish as one province; Spanish Sahara (as it was then called) was given a provincial council, with three representatives in the Spanish Cortes.

Within a short time the constitution had been suspended. Both Morocco and Mauritania submitted claims to the United Nations for parts of the country. Spain granted partial autonomy to its colony in May 1967, when a general assembly (Yema'a) was established.

The following year, the first guerrilla organization, the Movement for the Liberation of the Sahara, was formed by exiled Sahrawis. In May 1973 this became the Frente Popular para la Liberación de Saquia al-Hamra y Río de Oro, or Polisario. In 1975, following continued unrest, a U.N. mission visited Spanish Sahara and found that there was considerable support for Polisario, which at that stage had Mauritanian and Algerian backing.

In October 1975 Morocco and Mauritiania signed a secret treaty—backed by historical claims—to divide the territory between them. The matter was before the International Court of Justice when, in November 1975, Morocco assembled an army of 350,000 unarmed men and marched them across the frontier. Within a week of this "Green March" Spain hurriedly decided to leave the Sahara. It agreed with Morocco and Mauritania that it would depart in February 1976, and that the two African countries would take joint control.

Algeria objected to this and threw greater resources and political weight behind Polisario. The Sahrawi Arab Democratic Republic was formed in exile in Algeria by Polisario the day the Spanish left.

Polisario attacks on Moroccan and Mauritanian positions inside Western

Sahara over the next few years caused Mauritania to withdraw, exhausted, from the war in 1979. Morocco responded by annexing the whole territory.

Morocco has subsequently ruled Western Sahara for the best part of a decade, with a mixture of military might and diplomatic maneuvering. Since the early 1980s Morocco has made major arms purchases from the United States, France and Spain. In 1985 it announced a further U.S. $1 billion arms program, which would include the acquisition of sophisticated American and French fighters, as well as fast patrol boats and heavy armor. Although this latter program has not been initiated, owing to financing problems, it was enough to keep Western powers interested in Moroccan ascendancy over the territory.

King Hassan of Morocco is, of course, an important diplomatic figure in his own right—an Arab moderate who has long been close to both Paris and Washington. He has skillfully impressed upon Western powers the advantages of staying close to him. He has held out to the European Community the prospect of a valuable fishing agreement, for example. He has tended to adopt pro-Western positions in African conflicts—for example, in Chad—and this has made him a valued conservative power broker in Africa. Morocco also has the political and, very importantly, the financial support of conservative Arab states, particularly Saudi Arabia. All this has militated against Polisario getting much recognition or backing from the West.

At the same time, Morocco has used its superior military might in Western Sahara to keep out Polisario guerrilla attacks. The most obvious instrument of this policy is the wall that now virtually encloses the territory from southern Morocco to Mauritania. The wall—built largely of sand—is protected by electronic equipment, which gives the Moroccans early warning of impending Sahrawi attack.

Polisario had success in the early 1980s, mounting lightning attacks in Land Rover columns—like the one that temporarily put the important Bou-Craa phosphate mines out of action in 1981. The guerrilla movement has an estimated 25,000 men under arms. It is financed largely by Algeria and Libya, and armed by Yugoslavia and North Korea. Its armory contains tanks, artillery and armored cars captured from Morocco.

This force, however, backed as it is by 150,000 refugees in camps in Algeria, is no real match for the Moroccan conscript army (though technically all the Moroccan soldiers in Western Sahara have volunteered for duty). Polisario is reduced to classic guerrilla hit-and-run tactics. After a period of unilateral ceasefire designed to encourage momentum toward peace talks, Polisario resumed military activity in December 1987, when, according to its own figures, it launched 122 operations against Moroccan positions, killing 110 soldiers, wounding 175 and taking 11 prisoner.

Polisario had been hoping for mediation under U.N. auspices, but this was held back by Morocco's refusal to treat directly with it. After a period of considerable tension between their two countries, progress on the issue seemed to be signaled by the summit between King Hassan and Algerian President Chadli Benjedid in April 1987. However, Morocco, following its ill-fated union with Libya from 1984 to 1986, remains unconvinced by (and probably uninterested in) Algeria's plans for Maghrebi unity (including an independent Sahrawi state). Despite the goodwill it has engendered throughout the world, Polisario looks doomed to further diplomatic isolation, with little real progress toward a solution of its claims in Western Sahara.

CHAD

After a history of competing Islamic kingdoms, most of central Chad was absorbed in the sultanate of the Sudanese ruler, Robah Zobeir, at the end of the 19th century. He was defeated in 1900 by the French, who eight years later began to include Chad in French Equatorial Africa. In 1920 Chad became a colony, and in World War II was an important military staging post.

The French were quite clear about Chad. It was a useful political pawn in their West African empire. But economically it was of little importance. They were interested enough in the commercial potential of the lush south to plant cotton there. But the infertile desert north was not important. Chad became divided between what the French called *Tchad utile* and *Tchad inutile*. The black Sarans of the south had to be educated to run the cotton and other industries. They became a partially Christianized elite, while the northern Muslims were kept out of positions of power and influence.

Political parties first surfaced among the black workers of the south. François Tombalbaye, a school teacher and trade unionist, became the country's first president when it achieved independence from France in 1960. He was leader of the Parti Progressiste Tchadien, a local branch of the Rassemblement Démocratique Africain, the grouping of Francophone West African states led by Houphouët-Boigny, president of the Ivory Coast from the same year (1960).

Almost inevitably the pro-southern bias that had surfaced under the French continued under a government composed largely of southerners. In 1965 a Muslim revolt began in the northern Tibesti region. In 1966 a party representing northern Muslim interests, the Front de Libération Nationale du Tchad (Frolinat), was formed under Dr. Abba Siddick.

Over the next couple of years Frolinat launched a guerrilla war against the government in Chad. In September 1969, following President Tombalbaye's request, France sent 2,500 troops to Chad to help quell the rebellion. They were withdrawn in August 1971 when Chad's president initiated an exercise in national reconciliation. This did not last long, however. In 1972 Frolinat attacked the Chad capital, Ndjamena. Over 1,000 people were arrested, and Libya and Egypt were implicated as supporters of the rebels.

Thenceforth, Libya under Qadhafi, rather than Egypt under Sadat, became the main supporter of Frolinat. In 1973 Libya seized the so-called Aozou Strip in northern Chad—reputedly rich in uranium and other minerals—quoting a 1935 treaty between the Italian Fascists, then ruling Libya, and the neighboring French colonialists.

In April 1975 President Tombalbaye was killed in a coup. The former army chief of staff, Gen. Félix Malloum, was released from prison to lead the country. At this stage Frolinat was a coalition of different tribal potentates. Libyan financial and political support build up Goukouni Oueddei, son of the hereditary leader of the Tibesti, into the dominant force. An earlier leader, Hissène Habré, broke away from the main body of Frolinat in 1977, claiming Libyan influence was too strong and that Tripoli was racist in its attitudes to blacks.

Habré set up a small group, the Forces Armées du Nord (FAN), which in 1978 agreed to establish a government sharing power between south and north in Ndjamena. But this was never an easy relationship. Malloum still controlled the army, and the French helped Habré build up his own firepower. Fighting between Habré's FAN and Malloum's Forces Armées Tchadiennes (FAT), the basic Chad army, broke out in Ndjamena in February 1979.

This was followed by an all-out civil war between northerners and southerners, i.e., between Muslims and Christians. The OAU stepped in to arrange a ceasefire. After a series of conferences—sponsored mainly by Nigeria—it was agreed to set up a broader based coalition, including not only Habré's FAN and Malloum's FAT, but also Goukouni Oueddei's Frolinat. The latter had grown tired of its dependency on Libya, which, in turn, had found another faction to back—Acyl Ahmet's more revolutionary Front d'Action Commune Provisoire (FACP).

In November 1979 a government of national unity, comprising these elements, was set up with Goukouni as president. But again peace was short-lived. In March, resentment between Goukouni and Habré boiled over into fierce fighting. Goukouni called in Libya to help "keep the peace." In January 1981 Qadhafi made the mistake of announcing the de facto union of Chad and Libya. This alienated Chad opinion. By December 1981 Habré had been defeated by a combination of 2,000 Libyan troops and Goukouni's army. Goukouni nominally ruled the country, now in coalition with Ahmet's FACP, and with the strong support of Libya. The OAU then urged Qadhafi to withdraw, which he did in November 1981. An OAU force attempted to keep the peace for a short period from December 1981. But Habré was massing his men once again in Sudan. Before the OAU could withdraw its forces as planned at the end of June 1982, Habré had swept back into the Chad capital on June 7 and routed Goukouni.

Goukouni returned shamefacedly to Libya, from where he started another round in the Chad civil war. In June 1983 he captured the important northern administrative town of Faya-Largeau. Habré immediately recaptured it, but within a few days, backed by 2,000 Libyan troops, Goukouni was back in control.

This was at the height of Western paranoia about Qadhafi. President Reagan promised Habré $10 million in aid and dispatched AWACS planes to Sudan to support him. He encouraged France to return to its former colony to prevent yet another takeover by Qadhafi. (There was no longer any pretense that Goukouni was an independent leader.) In Operation Manta, France sent 3,000 troops to Chad. They positioned themselves on the 15th (and later 16th) parallel as a physical barrier to further Libyan penetration.

France was soon lobbying Libya to negotiate a mutual withdrawal. This was finalized in September 1984; but whereas French troops pulled out, Libyans remained in the northern oases.

Habré spent the next couple of years consolidating his power in Ndjamena. He has been mopping up small centers of resistance to his rule in the south, while managing to establish a fair measure of consensus in the capital.

In March 1987 he chose to strike again against Libyan positions in the north. In a lightning strike his forces routed the Libyans at their last main base at Wadi Doum. Without this, Libya was no longer able to supply its garrison at Faya-Largeau. Habré's men pursued the Libyans into the Aozou and in a celebrated putsch, attacked and damaged an important Libyan base inside the Jamahariya at Mattan as Sarra.

Qadhafi vowed revenge. But the war in Chad is unpopular, and he needs to build up his support again. Meanwhile there are signs of new anti-Habré factions appearing. For the time being, however, the American-backed Chadian strong man holds the ring.

SUDAN

The conflict between north and south in Sudan has had as long a gestation as any in Africa. The seeds were sown during the Anglo-Egyptian condominium when, somewhat similarly to northern Chad under the French, southern Sudan was considered "Soudan inutile." The British were, however, concerned to prevent the incursion of northern Islamic concepts into the unformed south. Therefore, from around 1930 they evolved a southern policy that meant effectively cordoning off the south from northern influence. The south was open to Christian missions but not to Arab traders. As the then civil secretary, Sir Harold MacMichael, put it: "To encourage the spread of Arabic in the South would be to sprinkle gunpowder in the neighbourhood of a powder magazine, or to sow weeds because they grow more quickly than corn."

When Sudan became independent from Britain in 1956, it was already virtually divided into two. But the British were determined that the country should remain a single political entity. In the years up to the British departure, southerners had begun to fear northern intentions in the south. In August 1955, even before the British officially left, a southern garrison mutinied in Torit in Equatoria. This was followed by widespread massacres of northerners throughout the south.

The Torit mutiny is considered the start of the 17-year-long civil war between south and north. Although not all the country was engulfed by conflict—some southerners worked in Khartoum trying to change an uncaring northern policy toward the three provinces of the south (Equatoria, Bahr-el-Ghazal and Upper Nile)—many southerners took to the bush waging guerrilla war against the north.

The southern bush army, known as the Anyanya, operated out of bases in Uganda and Ethiopia. It was led by Col. Joseph Lagu. The opinion of southern political exiles was expressed by the Sudan African National Union, headed by William Deng and Joseph Oduho. (The Southern Front, led by Clement Mboro and Abel Alier, tended to work inside Sudan.)

When the radical young officer Col. Jaafar al-Nimeiry took power in a military coup in May 1969, he was determined to bring an end to the civil war that had held back Sudan's development. In 1972 he negotiated the Addis Ababa agreement, which established the south as an autonomous political region with its own High Executive Council. The initial success of the peace brought Nimeiry considerable international recognition as a statesman.

Problems soon reoccurred. The High Executive Council formula neglected the fact that the Dinka were the dominant tribe in the south. Under the Dinka vice-president, Abel Alier, the Dinka quickly adopted positions of power and influence in the south. Other tribesmen objected, and there was considerable support when in May 1983 President Nimeiry reintroduced the three districts, or provinces, which had existed in the south under the British—each with its own assembly and ministers.

It soon became clear that Nimeiry's motives were not limited to good government. He was determined to weaken southern resolve, which had already begun to show itself following the discovery of oil in the south in the late 1970s. The oil was discovered and due to be exploited by Chevron, an American company; but many southerners believed its proceeds should be used for their own economic development. Nimeiry was adamant on the point that it was the whole country's resource.

Southern opinion was not mollified by a series of central government maneuvers. Khartoum started to excavate the Jonglei Canal, an ambitious works project that would have cut out much of the meandering of the Nile. But southerners feared the north wanted to send down Egyptians—who were partly financing the scheme because of their need for increased flow of Nile waters—to farm the irrigated land around the Canal and Arabize the people.

When in late 1983 Nimeiry introduced *Sharia,* or Islamic law, and announced it would apply to the whole country, including the animistic and partially Christianized South, southern opinion erupted. As in 1955, there were mutinies of southern soldiers in garrisons like Bor. A new party, the Sudan People's Liberation Movement (SPLM), took to the bush under Col. John Garang, its military leader, and Joseph Oduho, its political guru. Garang's Sudan People's Liberation Army (SPLA) made it clear it intended business when it raided Chevron's camp at Bentiu in Upper Nile and kidnapped foreign workers. By the end of 1983 Chevron had pulled out of the south.

Since then the war has been complicated and protracted. The SPLA has gained considerable logistical support from neighboring Ethiopia. Early on it was joined in its attacks against dispirited northern troops by forces calling themselves Anyanya II. But this effective army soon bridled at alleged Dinka dominance of the SPLA; it broke away, and in recent months has been armed by the Khartoum government against the SPLA.

The SPLM put itself forward as a pan-Sudanese movement. It has northerners among its top personnel, including Dr. Mansour Khalid, Nimeiry's former foreign minister. In 1987 Prime Minister Sadiq al-Mahdi's shaky coalition government in Khartoum initiated peace negotiations with the SPLM, but was not inclined to make many concessions. During the year, it extended its control over the south, particularly Upper Nile province, extending even into Blue Nile province in what is officially Northern Sudan, not far from Kosti.

The politics of the conflict are complicated. Al-Mahdi is backed by Arab states, including, increasingly, Libya. The SPLA could not operate without Ethiopia's support. But what other countries are behind the SPLA is not clear.

A solution of the conflict will have to await either Khartoum's total weariness with the war or a regional peace, tackling southern Sudanese complaints along with Eritrean dissatisfaction. If Sudan were to desist from supporting the Eritreans, Ethiopia would withdraw backing from the SPLM.

ETHIOPIA

Ethiopia is somewhat unusual in Africa: a Marxist state attempting to preserve the empire stitched together by its deposed rulers in a fit of European-style colonialism.

The story of modern Ethiopia is one of the domination of the country by Amharic-speaking Shoans who eventually made their capital (in the 19th century) in Addis Ababa. Shoan control over Eritrea, scene of the present-day Ethiopian rulers' worst civil unrest, was never put into practice. Rather, it was an outpost of the Ottoman Empire for three centuries until, following the opening of the Suez Canal in 1869, the British—so as to keep their rivals, the French, out—encouraged Egypt to take a proprietary interest in the province.

But it was another European power, Italy, that showed the most interest in Eritrea. The colonization of the coastal region began at Massawa (now Mits'iwa) in 1885. By 1890 the Italians had occupied most of what is now known as Eritrea. Seeking to advance into the rest of Ethiopia, they were badly defeated by Emperor Menelik II at the Battle of Adwa in 1896—an important affirmation of the fact that a disciplined African army could defeat a better-armed European one.

Italy retreated to its Eritrean colony, to which it gave an administrative and industrial infrastructure, and even a sense of nationality. In 1935 the Fascist government in Rome wanted to extend its African empire; it pushed again into Ethiopia, occupying it until defeated by the British in 1941.

Britain was clear, however, that it did not want to rule Eritrea for long. In 1950 the United Nations determined that the province should become a federated state within Ethiopia. This was carried out in September 1952. But 10 years later, in November 1962, Ethiopia absorbed Eritrea directly under its rule, doing away with any idea of federation. Nominally, the Eritrean assembly voted this through, but Eritrean nationalists argue that its members were subject to undue pressure from the Ethiopians.

Eritrean resistance began in 1961 with the formation of the Eritrean Liberation Front (ELF). Within a short while ELF commanded considerable

701

support. It tended to be dominated by conservative Muslims, and in 1969 more radical elements, many of them Christian, broke away to set up the Eritrean Peoples' Liberation Front (EPLF). Between 1972 and 1974 the two movements were fighting each other rather than Haile Selassie's government.

When that government was deposed in 1974, the Eritrean resistance movements combined and again enjoyed military success. In January 1975 they came close to capturing the main Eritrean town of Asmera. Members of the new military regime, the Dergue, who were suspected of being sympathetic to the Eritrean cause were harshly dealt with. The Ethiopian head of state Lt. Gen. Aman Andom was deposed and killed for this reason.

Eritrea was one of the main thorns in the Dergue's flesh between 1975 and 1977. In 1977 the EPLF captured important towns on the coastal plains and plateaus of the Sahel, such as Nacfa and Keren, while ELF had success further south in the lowlands of the Barca, taking citadels like Agordat and Tessenai.

By now Ethiopia's fissiparous tendencies were beginning to assert themselves in other ways. The EPLF spawned a breakaway group, ELF-PLF, funded by Saudi Arabia and headed by the veteran nationalist leader Osman Saleh Sabbe. An anti-Dergue group, the Tigre Peoples' Liberation Front, raised the banner of revolt in Tigre, and there were similar movements, such as the Western Somali Liberation Front (WSLF) in the Ogaden and the Oromo Liberation Front further south.

In 1977 the Somali government intervened to support the claims of the WSLF. It pushed successfully into the Ogaden, before coming bogged down and having to retreat. During this Ethiopian-Somali war, Addis Ababa bought large amounts of Soviet weapons, which have subsequently been turned on the Eritreans and Tigreans, the two most dogged of the "nationalities" fighting for their independence.

There have been frequent attempts to bring the three Eritrean parties together. In 1986 ELF and ELF-PLF were working together, but largely because their individual influence was diminished. The dominant EPLF refused to sit down with the others—officially because it suspected them of wishing to make a deal with the Ethiopians. Nevertheless, there were well-attested reports that the EPLF itself was talking with Addis Ababa.

After a lull in fighting the EPLF tried in the summer of 1987 to retake the offensive. It launched an assault on four Ethiopian garrisons in Knafina, and claimed to have killed 219 government troops. Meanwhile the Dergue had launched its own "hearts and minds" counteroffensive, seeking to win support through concessions on the nationalities issue in Ethiopia's new constitution, finally adopted in September 1987.

Backed by Soviet hardware, in early 1988 the Ethiopian government enjoyed military superiority over the various secessionist groups in the country. But potential conflicts never seem far below the surface, and some of them have a more serious, international flavor. In February 1987 the Somali government accused Ethiopian ground forces of supporting dissidents in attacks on northern Somali towns in which over 300 people were killed. In July there were clashes between Ethiopian and Sudanese troops along their mutual border around Nazah, some 50 miles/80 km. from Kashm el Girba.

SOUTHERN AFRICA

The conflict in southern Africa is the most complicated on the continent. It revolves around the need of South Africa to ensure that its neighbors remain weak and incapable of giving significant military support to the black majority within its borders.

The conflict is also arguably the oldest. As far back as 1920 South Africa was granted a mandate by the League of Nations to administer the former German colony of Namibia. By 1922 the Bodelswart peoples were already in revolt; in 1925 the Rehoboth rose up. Both uprisings were ruthlessly put down.

In 1946 the United Nations nominally took over control of the League of Nations' trusteeships, but South Africa refused to submit to U.N. authority. Despite repeated rulings by the International Court of Justice at The Hague that the South African position was illegal, the Pretoria government, which had started to apply apartheid in Namibia, refused to budge. In 1966 the U.N. General Assembly passed Resolution 2145 ending South Africa's mandate in the territory. A U.N. Council for Namibia was set up as the de jure government.

Beginning in the late 1950s black political movements had been taking root inside Namibia. The largest of these was the South-West Africa People's Organization (SWAPO), formed in 1964 out of the Ovamboland People's Organization.

By the mid-1970s SWAPO forces were constantly attacking South African positions inside Namibia, while continuing a political battle for independence outside. Moved by international opinion (the United Nations had put a target date of the end of 1978 for independence) and by the breakdown of Portuguese rule in Angola and Mozambique (which both became independent in 1975), South Africa sought a political solution. A draft constitution, leading to a measure of autonomy, was proposed at the Turnhalle in Windhoek in January 1977. But SWAPO was excluded from the political process.

The South Africans engineered a hastily conceived election in December 1978, which returned a Constituent Assembly dominated by the Democratic Turnhalle Alliance. From then on, developments in Namibia became closely linked with those in neighboring countries, particularly Angola. A Marxist party, the MPLA, had emerged as the victor in the independence war against Portugal; it had had to fight not just the colonialists, but also two additional liberation movements: the veteran Holden Roberto's FNLA, which operated in the north, and Joseph Savimbi's UNITA in the south.

Following independence in 1975, the MPLA, based in the Angolan capital of Luanda, continued to be pressed by UNITA, which had long been supported by Zambia. By 1977 the MPLA was alleging that UNITA was also backed militarily and politically by South Africa. This gave Angola cause to call in Cuban troops to defend its revolution against UNITA and the South Africans.

The MPLA alleges that Pretoria assists UNITA, based at Jamba in southern Angola, from its own bases in Namibia. South Africa has indeed conducted raids deep into Angola—reportedly in hot pursuit of SWAPO guerrillas operating in Namibia. In 1987 it committed an estimated 6,000 troops to help UNITA's 60,000 forces push back the Angolan government's 53,000 regulars and 50,000 militia, together with its 30,000 or so Cuban advisers.

Since taking on his job in 1981, Chester Crocker has sought to find a solution to this conflict, based on the principle that if the Cubans quit Angola, the South Africans will follow suit in Namibia, leaving behind a truly democratic government (including representatives of SWAPO) in their place.

Toward the end of 1987 Angola seemed to be on the point of adopting this timetable. But despite its strong trade links with Washington (in 1986, oil exports—largely from fields in the north pumped by Chevron and Texaco—gave it a trade surplus with the United States of $642 million), Luanda remains suspicious of American intentions. Washington does not recognize the MPLA government, citing the presence of the Cuban troops in the country as reason, and gives $15 million a year in arms, including missiles, to UNITA.

Talks therefore broke down in January 1988, as UNITA, backed by South African soldiers, launched its biggest-ever offensive against the Angolan government stronghold at Cuito Cuanavale in the south. Whether this was to force Luanda's hand and encourage it to the negotiating table, or simply to scuttle any idea of negotiations was not clear.

While UNITA has some claim to be described as a legitimate political movement fighting against an unrepresentative and foreign-backed Marxist government in Luanda, the same cannot be said for Renamo in Mozambique. Renamo was originally formed by Rhodesian intelligence in the late 1970s to make life difficult for the new Frelimo government, headed by President Samora Machel, in Mozambique. Following Zimbabwean independence in 1980, South Africa took up the support of Renamo, which operated at that time from bases inside Malawi. In 1986 the Mozambique government reached an agreement with Malawi, which promised to curb the activities of Renamo. Malawian and Tanzanian troops now assist the Mozambicans patrol against Renamo, while up to 15,000 Zimbabwean soldiers protect the Beira corridor through which runs Harare's crucial rail and road links to the sea.

In October 1986 Mozambique's beleaguered President Machel was killed in an air crash, which was widely suspected as being caused by South Africa. Under his successor, Joaquim Chissano, the country's problems have continued, compounded by drought and continued acts of brutality by Renamo forces in the countryside.

Mozambique is weak and unable to offer much lead to Angola or Namibia. As chronicled by Joseph Hanlon in his article in this Handbook, South Africa also keeps up an assault on other neighboring countries, including Zambia, Lesotho and Swaziland. Zimbabwe has suffered sporadic but debilitating civil disturbance in Matabeleland, though by early 1988 this appeared to have ended.

Prognostications for peace in southern Africa are not good, for the South African government clearly sees its policy of military (and economic) pressure on its neighbors as the best way of winning time for itself—and for possible political reform within its own borders.

FURTHER READING

Blundy, David, and Lycett, Andrew. *Qaddafi and the Libyan Revolution.* London: Weidenfeld & Nicolson, 1987.

Halliday, Fred, and Molyneux, Maxine. *The Ethopian Revolution.* London: Verso, 1981.

Hanlon, Joseph. *Apartheid's Second Front: South Africa's War Against Its Neighbours.* Harmondsworth and New York: Penguin, 1986.

Jansen, Godfrey H. *Militant Islam.* London: Pan Books, 1979.

Khalid, Mansour, ed. *John Garang Speaks.* London and Boston: Kegan Paul International, 1985.

Knapp, Wilfred, ed. *North West Africa.* 3rd ed. Oxford and New York: Oxford University Press, 1977.

Malwal, Bona. *People and Power in Sudan: The Struggle for National Stability.* London: Ithaca Press, 1981.

Wolfers, Michael, and Bergerol, Jane. *Angola in the Front Line.* London: Zed Press, 1983.

THE SUPERPOWERS
AND AFRICA

A. M. BABU

As most African countries are celebrating their quarter century of independence from colonialism, many African scholars, intellectuals and out-of-power politicians are beginning to examine seriously whether this independence is real or practical in an age dominated by the two superpowers. The question being asked constantly is: If the former great powers of the period before World War I cannot act independently of the superpowers, how can the young countries of the post-World War II period fare any better under the present conditions? And more specifically, how can Africa, which contains the least developed parts of the world, act independently of either of the two superpowers?

However, these questions are really academic, since the presence of the superpowers in Africa must be acknowledged as a reality to be lived with. The real question is how to accommodate this presence in the interest of stability and prosperity in the region. Is the presence of the superpowers necessarily negative or can it be harnessed to positive ends? To answer these questions it is necessary to trace the historical evolution that brought about their presence in Africa.

BACKGROUND

The end of European colonialism in Africa coincided with the division of the world into two power blocs of opposite ideological persuasion, plunging the world into a bitter cold war in which the respective leaders of the blocs, the United States and the Soviet Union, were engaged in an intense rivalry. Africa inevitably became a fertile ground for these two powers' intervention in the race to fill the perceived vacuum left by the departing colonial powers. Moreover, the manner in which independence was achieved by each African country also determined the extent of the superpowers' respective involvement. Where independence was achieved by means of armed struggle, the superpower that was willing to supply arms gained the upper hand; invariably this has been the Soviet Union. Where independence was achieved peacefully, Western influence initially remained dominant.

To be precise, the end of 1956, which saw the Suez crisis arising out of

706

the Anglo-French invasion of Egypt, will probably be referred to in history as the actual beginning of the end of direct European colonialism in Africa. This also marked the beginning of the superpowers' direct involvement in African affairs. Until then Britain and France were the dominant powers in both the Middle East and Africa. The disastrous failure of their Suez venture, however, made it clear to them that the age of the pre-World War I great powers was over and that the world was on the threshold of a new epoch—the epoch of the two superpowers.

Early in 1957 the famous Eisenhower Doctrine was declared, which asserted the right of the United States to intervene in Middle Eastern and African affairs in order to "defend the area against Communism." This was intended to counter Soviet presence in the area after the signing of a treaty of economic cooperation between the Soviet Union and President Nasser of Egypt in 1956.

Nasser was pushed toward the Soviet Union by the clumsy attempt of the British and French to resort to gunboat diplomacy when they had neither the necessary guns, the boats nor a relevant diplomacy to effectively carry it out. The declared reason and justification for the Anglo-French invasion of Egypt was that it was a response to Nasser's decision to nationalize the Suez Canal Company, which was owned jointly by Anglo-French interests. Egypt needed the revenue from the Canal to pay for the construction of the Aswan High Dam, funding for which had earlier been rejected by the World Bank following U.S. pressure. In retaliation for the nationalization, Britain and France ordered the withdrawal of all their technicians working for the company, in order to weaken Egypt's economy. Egypt responded by inviting the Soviet Union and its allies to replace them. This bold action brought the USSR for the first time into the heart of Middle Eastern and African affairs, with far-reaching consequences.

Inevitably, Nasser's move created an upheaval in the Western world. The new Soviet presence was seen to constitute an encroachment on the West's vital strategic interests in the area. For, in addition to the region's oil reserves, Western military strategic interest in this region at the time was based on the Baghdad Pact—a military alliance comprising Pakistan, Iran, Iraq and Turkey, the objective of which was to encircle the Soviet Union from its southern flank. Soviet presence in Egypt was therefore seen as a serious blow to the objectives of the Baghdad Pact. And to make matters worse, this presence also meant that the Soviet Union was now firmly established on the continent of Africa.

It was indeed a turning point in Africa's history. The Soviet Union undertook not only to embark on the massive Aswan Dam construction project, which was then the biggest such project outside the Soviet Union and the United States, but it also undertook to equip the Egyptian army with a fairly sophisticated war machine. This commitment brought to the area thousands of Soviet technicians and military personnel, which inevitably boosted Soviet influence in the rest of the Middle East and Africa, and correspondingly weakened that of the West. Nonalignment began to have the practical meaning of balancing the involvement of the two power blocs in the area.

Henceforth, the anticolonial struggle took a different form. Cairo immediately became the headquarters of African liberation movements. On the initiative of the Soviet Union and China, an Afro-Asian People's Solidarity Organization was founded and headquartered in Cairo; this brought many future African leaders into direct contact with the representatives from the Soviet bloc, leading to the evolution of a mutual working relationship that was to have a far-reaching influence in the continent.

In response, the United States stepped up activities to strengthen its influence in the continent, not via Cairo but through Ethiopia and Liberia, and through the trade union movement. In Ethiopia it established a military presence, and in Liberia it set up a powerful radio booster for the Voice of America. Working through the newly formed International Confederation of Free Trade Unions (ICFTU)—the American trade union movement under the arch anti-Moscow George Meany and his representative in Europe, Irving Brown, referred to in Phillip Agee's book as a "principal Central Intelligence Agency agent for control of the ICFTU"—the United States virtually controlled the entire trade union movement in Africa, with regional bases in Tunisia and Kenya.

Throughout the 1960s, as African countries were gaining independence one after another, the superpowers were getting further involved in the affairs of the continent. The year 1960 started with the dramatic explosion of the so-called Congo Affair, when the Belgians were forced out of their colony by mass uprisings. Patrice Lumumba, who had emerged out of the ensuing chaos as the prime minister of the new country, immediately telegraphed Moscow requesting Soviet military support. This precipitate move convinced the United States that the new leader was a Communist and had to be dealt with accordingly. The Congo Affair will probably go down in African history as the beginning of extensive Central Intelligence Agency (CIA) involvement in African affairs. The diplomatic and covert skirmishes between the two superpowers that followed this event are now history, but their impact continues to be one of the serious problems afflicting Africa.

AFRICA'S CHANGING FORTUNES

In the last two decades the fortunes of Africa have continued to change in response to the rapidly changing world situation. The 1967 war between Arab states and Israel diminished the importance of the Suez Canal in oil transportation when the oil companies resorted to the use of supertankers after the blockage of the Canal. Henceforth, most of the oil from the Arab/Persian Gulf now went via the Cape of Good Hope, on the continent's southern tip, en route to Europe and the United States. The Cape route immediately became of greater strategic importance for the Western bloc and a potential target for the Eastern bloc.

Various events of the 1970s—President Nixon's withdrawal of the dollar from a fixed rate, which plunged the world into monetary and financial crisis; the emergence of Europe as an economically independent power bloc; the Middle East war, which was followed by an oil price explosion—helped to disrupt the postwar economic status quo, exposed the West's dependence on foreign oil and inevitably shifted the cold war from Europe to the Middle East. It now became clear that any serious upheaval in the Middle East would not only have a direct impact on the Western economics but would also threaten their defense capability. Saudi Arabia, which contains most of the oil reserves needed by the West, immediately became the most strategically important country in the Third World. The Horn of Africa, which is only a few miles away from Saudi Arabia, also became an area of greatly intensified superpower contest. That is to say, Africa now contained two of the three "storm centers" of the world (the third being Southeast Asia), which could spark off superpower confrontation with serious consequences.

It is not surprising, therefore, that the current areas of conflict between the two superpowers in Africa are southern Africa and the Horn. But that is not all. Africa as a whole plays a crucial role in the global skirmishes of the superpowers. For instance, when the Iranian revolution overthrew the shah, and the new Iranian leaders pulled out of the Central Treaty Organization alliance that had replaced the Baghdad Pact, the whole alliance had to be dismantled since Iran was the key link between Pakistan and Turkey in that whole system of defense. In response, the Carter administration immediately set up in 1979 the so-called Rapid Deployment Force to enable the United States to transport troops and equipment directly across the Atlantic to the Middle East. And all the countries (except Oman) that are linked to this operation are on the African continent—namely, Morocco, Egypt, Somalia and Kenya. In addition, Carter decided to flood the Indian Ocean with nuclear-powered warships and submarines, which so alarmed the Soviet Union that it promptly invaded Afghanistan under a pretext of helping what looked like a contrived "socialist revolution." Actually, faced with this massive U.S. presence in the Indian Ocean, it is obvious that the Soviet Union's move was to enable it to have a foothold where its missiles could reach targets in the ocean. This evolution, naturally, has put Africa on the nuclear firing line of superpower confrontation.

SUPERPOWER BLUNDERS

The superpowers' rivalry is motivated by their desire to advance regional political influence or to establish a military presence in order to tip the balance of power in their respective favor. The more strategic the area is, the more intense the rivalry. As Europe ceased to be the primary area of superpower rivalry—having not only recovered from the devastations of World War II, but also having developed into an independent and dominant economic force in the world—the focus of the cold war in effect moved from that area to the Middle East; by extension, Africa has had to suffer the consequences of this shift. Because they are new in the region, ignorant of the myriad postcolonial intricacies and preoccupied largely with global calculations, the superpowers perpetually find themselves getting out of one blunder only to be trapped into another.

For example, a perfectly justified struggle of the Eritrean people against Ethiopian colonial domination has never enjoyed lasting or principled support from either of the superpowers, although during Emperor Haile Selassie's rule the Soviet Union did for a while support the Eritreans morally and diplomatically, if not materially. On the contrary, it is Ethiopia, the colonialist, that has been supported by each one of the superpowers at one time or another. The reason is simply that Ethiopia is of great strategic importance to both of them, owing to its proximity to Saudi Arabia's oil reserves. Consequently, neither of them dares to seem to be too unfriendly to Addis Ababa. The result is catastrophic, not only to the Ethiopians and Eritreans, but to the whole continent of Africa. For as long as the Eritrean colonial question remains unsolved, there will be no peace in the Horn; and as long as the Horn is in turmoil, the whole of Africa is threatened.

Again, Namibia has a right to independence like any other African country, but because of the global strategic needs of the United States the Reagan administration did all it could to hamper it. During the Carter administration there were at least two contending views within the U.S. government, those of the so-called globalists and regionalists, and there was, therefore, more than an even chance for the United States to support Namibia's demand for self-determination.

In Reagan's administration, however, the globalists seem to have an upper hand. Their position is a straightforward one of not yielding an inch to the Communists. According to this globalist view, southern Africa is of strategic importance to the United States and the West because of the Cape route and also because the region contains strategic minerals. If this area were to fall under the Soviet's sphere of influence, then, according to this view, there would be a decisive shift in the global balance of power in favor of the Soviet Union. First, if the USSR dominated the Cape of Good Hope, it would be in a position to interfere with the oil supply en route to the West. Secondly, it would be in a position to control minerals such as chromium, that are vital to the U.S. war machine but are obtainable only in the Soviet Union and southern Africa.

Consequently, to prevent this possibility, the Reagan administration devised the policy of constructive engagement with South Africa. Since its inception seven years ago, the policy has been regarded by many observers as nothing but a smoke screen for perpetuating cold war diplomacy on the continent. Until Reagan came to power, the issue of Cuban presence in Angola was not part of Pretoria's argument against independence for Namibia. The constructive engagement policy, which included making that independence conditional upon withdrawal of Cuban troops and minimizing Soviet influence in Angola, provided South Africa with a convenient excuse to delay Namibian independence.

Reagan has sought to dignify the South African apartheid regime by describing it as the most democratic in Africa, a reliable friend of the West and a force against Communism in the region. He has also made himself thoroughly unpopular in the Third World by consistently vetoing U.N. resolutions hostile to South Africa. For example, despite massive and growing internal pressure, the United States still resists supporting the move for a resolution calling for mandatory economic sanctions against the country. And the Reagan administration killed a U.N.-sponsored five Western powers' mediation initiative designed to seek solutions to the Namibian question. Since Reagan felt that these powers did not regard the Cuban presence in Angola as a hindrance to Namibia's independence, the initiative therefore had to be abandoned. By so delaying the resolution of these southern African problems, his administration has sacrificed peace and stability in the area by perpetuating the myth of Soviet threat.

SOVIET ADVANTAGE IN AFRICA

In this context, unlike what happened in the Horn, in southern Africa the Soviet Union is enjoying a strategic and diplomatic advantage over the United States. The USSR is seen as less "global" and more "regional," in the sense that it sides with the underdog, with the oppressed against the oppressor. Whereas the United States is supporting and arming UNITA, which is opposed throughout Africa and regarded in the region as an extension of the South African army, the Soviet Union is on the side of the legitimate government of Angola, a popular government in the region, which came to power after a protracted revolutionary war against Portuguese colonialism. In supporting the government of Angola, neither the Soviet Union nor Cuba is seen as interfering in that country's internal affairs; their presence is regarded as perfectly justified, morally and legally, since they were invited there by the host government in its struggle against an aggressive foreign power, i.e., South Africa, with UNITA as its "advance contingent."

Even prior to the Reagan administration, the United States had plans for Angola in its global strategy. When Nixon and Kissinger were toying with the idea of establishing a South Atlantic Treaty Organization, comprised principally of Argentina, Brazil and South Africa, they also had Angola in mind, whether under Portuguese leadership or under a reliable African leader like Holden Roberto of the defunct FNLA. But when MPLA came to power instead, the United States not only refused to recognize the new government, but also embarked on organizing a destabilization campaign—including the hiring of mercenaries, through the CIA—intended to topple the government. (A fascinating account of these CIA activities is given in a book by Stockwell who was CIA head of station in Zaire at the time.)

When President Carter came to power, however, there was a slight change of policy in the area. His "regionalist" secretary of state, Cyrus Vance, decided to minimize pressure on Angola and stepped up U.N. pressure on South Africa to free Namibia. In the regionalist view, as long as there was an injustice in the region there would always be an East/West struggle in which the Soviet Union would be invited to support the injured party. In such circumstances the United States would be isolated in the region and its global image would be tarnished, diminishing its credibility among its allies. This regionalist view has to a certain extent proved prophetic, especially in view of the many Reagan policy blunders in the region and the disastrous failure of the constructive engagement fantasy.

711

THE STRUGGLE FOR THE HORN OF AFRICA

While the Soviet Union may benefit from Reagan's blunders in southern Africa, it also is losing credibility in the Horn of Africa. Its military support for the Ethiopian leader Mengistu in his predatory war against Eritrean freedom fighters—when his country is suffering from untold misery and famine—does not present the Soviet Union in a flattering light to the poverty-stricken people of Africa. Whereas Africans support the USSR for coming to the assistance of Angola in the face of foreign aggression, they condemn it for interfering in what the Organization of African Unity (OAU) officially regards as internal affairs of Ethiopia—as opposed to Angola where the threat is from outside. This is a civil war in which the injured party is fighting for its legitimate right to self-determination. The Soviet Union is supposed to be guided by the Leninist principle of the "right of nations to self-determination"; but the Kremlin is seen to be going against all principles laid down by the great revolutionary leaders. Here the people of Eritrea, colonized by Ethiopia in 1962, against their wishes and those of the United Nations as the trustee power, were initially supported by the Soviet Union in their anticolonial struggle. Suddenly they were abandoned by erstwhile comrades in favor of new, unknown comrades now in power in Addis Ababa. This about-turn policy of the Soviet Union is seen as unprincipled, unjust and anything but socialist.

Hopeful signs are the advent of Mikhail Gorbachev as leader of the Soviet Union and new leadership in Washington from 1989. These developments may inaugurate a new era in U.S.-Soviet global relations, to the great relief of Africa.

Gorbachev is quoted in the *Soviet Weekly* of January 16, 1988 as saying: "The present time dictates another morality and other laws. It shows convincingly that today one cannot build one's long-term policy at another's expense but that it is necessary to look for a balance of interests. Not against someone but together with everyone. . . . This is a hard but the only correct path leading toward universal security and equitable cooperation." Building one's policy "at another's expense" has always been the essence of the superpower rivalry in Africa, and the main casualty has always been the well-being of the people of the continent.

Throughout the cold war era both the United States and the Soviet Union have been (mis)guided by their adherence to calculations based on the so-called numbers game theory, according to which if a coup in country X brought into power an anti-American leader, the policy makers in the U.S. State Department, and presumably those in the Kremlin, would, respectively, chalk up a minus sign for the United States and a plus sign for the Soviet Union. Conversely, if the next coup, in country Y, brought an anti-Soviet leader to power, then there would be a plus sign for the United States and a minus sign for the Soviet Union. By the end of the year a "balance sheet" would be drawn up to see which superpower had made gains at the expense of the other. On the basis of such calculations, important policies are seriously formulated and implemented, again with far-reaching consequences.

Although African populations are among the poorest in the world, their governments burden their people with some of the most sophisticated and expensive weaponry available, made either in the United States or in the Soviet Union. Ethiopia, for example has demonstrably the poorest population in the world, but its 350,000-strong regular army is one of the best Soviet-equipped military units in Africa. Forty-five percent of the nation's budget goes for military spending, although a large percentage of its population is faced with almost permanent famine conditions. Ethiopia, incidentally, has never been threatened by any foreign invasion since the days of the Fascist regimes of Mussolini and Hitler that led to World War II, some 50 years ago. Most of this military might is directed against the Eritrean people, who are struggling for their legitimate right to self-determination.

Sudan is another example of a very poor country that is nevertheless heavily committed to massive military spending. Its U.S.-supplied army is confronted by a Soviet-supplied (via Ethiopia) dissident movement in the south. No political solution is in sight because the superpowers are not sure yet which side a strong and peaceful Sudan would lean toward, and what role Sudan would play in Africa's geopolitics.

These are only two examples to illustrate the destructive effects on Africa arising from superpower rivalry. For much of the rest of Africa the story is almost the same. While, of course, no one is suggesting that all of Africa's internal conflicts were caused by either the United States or the Soviet Union, both countries exacerbate these conflicts by their role as arms suppliers, not just for profit but principally to tip the balance of power in their respective favor.

At no time in the history of independent Africa have the superpowers either collaborated for a peaceful settlement in any of the internal conflicts, or embarked on a joint project aimed at economic or social development of any country. Where superpower aid coincides, as in food supply to famine-stricken Ethiopia, the coincidence is purely a result of their rivalry in trying to win over the country concerned.

The experience of these cold war rivalries has taught African leaders the art of exploiting them by constantly threatening to move to the side of the rival superpower. However, while these leaders may think this is an intelligent thing to do in pursuit of a perceived "national interest," experience over the years has shown that their exposure to this kind of game only helps to push them deeper into the superpowers' clutches. Despite the camp they are dependent on, the end result is the same: economic domination and political dependence, much worse than the old colonial experience.

IS SUPERPOWER COLLABORATION POSSIBLE?

In the new epoch of superpower summits and rapprochement (a stage higher than Brezhnev's détente), it may not be wide of the mark to hope for a superpower collaboration in Africa to save the continent from utter devastation and ruin. The superpowers should realize that in the climate of the cold war and global ambitions, neither has made any decisive advance against

713

the other in Africa—despite the billions of dollars wasted in the effort. Commonsense would urge them to think more constructively on how to eliminate poverty and devastation, which ultimately are the cause of world tension. They should now apply their minds to answer the following two questions, political and economic:

- What are the causes of the tensions, insecurity and conflicts in Africa, and what can be done about them?
- What can be done internationally to stop Africa from succumbing to utter misery and degradation?

As to the first question, it is instructive to recognize that all societies have within them some ingredients of instability and conflict, but more experienced and mature societies manage these factors better. The newly independent states are unstable not only because they have no "institutional memory," which transforms past experiences into future guides, but also because their economies are intolerably weak. Superpower rivalry in these unstable countries, needless to say, always tends to aggravate the situation and sharpen internal conflicts. The most glaring examples in Africa are countries that have identified themselves with one or the other superpower; all happen to be countries with intense internal conflicts: Angola, Chad, Ethiopia, Mozambique, Somalia, Sudan, Zaire.

Political instability is also partly a result of the frustration and impatience of the emerging younger generation, which sees the older generation as having messed up their lives and left them with nothing but a bleak future of unbearable external debt burden and mangled economies. In a continent dominated by one-party states or military dictatorships, there is neither public outlet to express this anger nor opportunity for organized peaceful resistance. This makes a fertile ground for internal subversion and underground movements, essential ingredients for instability.

If the superpowers are genuine in their attempt to diffuse world tension, then as far as Africa is concerned they can at least agree not to meddle in internal and local conflicts, however sympathetic they may be to one side or the other.

On the economic front the situation is even more serious. If millions are now dying from starvation or malnutrition when the continent has 400 million people to feed, what will happen by the turn of the century when there will be a population of 800 million to feed? This is the most urgent question, one that must be faced immediately and squarely. The greatest immediate need in Africa today is water to ensure lasting development. Water, scarce in many parts of Africa, is abundant in other parts in the form of rivers and lakes. Can anything be done to harness the resources that do exist? The Soviet Union and the United States have both performed near-miracles in the field of water control and distribution. The former, in fact, has just embarked on yet another gigantic scheme that would redirect rivers and transfer water in a 1,243-mile/2,000-km. canal to some arid parts of Soviet Asia at a cost of only U.S. $10 billion, or 5 percent of Africa's total external debt. Such a project could be undertaken under the

714

auspices of the United Nations or the World Bank, working in consultation with the OAU—rather like the U.N. project of the 1950s to divert Asian rivers in order to satisfy both India and Pakistan in the water disputes that arose because of partition.

This is one practical way to keep Africa from the cold war and superpower rivalry. It is the best form of constructive engagement, a most humanely beneficial venture that will create conditions for genuine superpower cooperation. Such ventures would keep them out of diplomatic mischief in Africa and possibly put them, for once, on the road to world peace.

FURTHER READING

Bertram, Christopher, ed. *Third-World Conflict and International Security*. London: Macmillan; Haddam, Connecticut: Anchor Books, 1982.

Clark, Robert P. *Power and Policy in the Third World*. New York: Wiley, 1978.

Selassie, Bereket H. *Conflict and Intervention in the Horn of Africa*. New York: Monthly Review Press, 1980.

Third World Affairs. London: Third World Foundation for Social and Economic Studies, 1987.

MILITARIZATION AND ECONOMIC DEVELOPMENT IN AFRICA

EBOE HUTCHFUL

MILITARY expenditures in Africa in the decade from the mid-1970s to the mid-1980s took two distinctly opposite directions. From 1976 to 1980 military spending rose steadily for the continent as a whole, peaking in 1980.[1] From 1981 to 1985, however, it declined gradually but steadily, with the biggest drop in 1984 and 1985. On the basis of 1986 U.S. Arms Control and Disarmaments Agency (ACDA) figures, total military expenditures for the continent rose from U.S. $9.4 billion (in 1983 constant dollars) to $16.7 billion in 1979, declining to $15.7 billion in 1984. This represented a rise, on the average, from 2.6 percent of GNP in 1974 to 3.8 percent in 1984, and from 11.8 percent of total governmental expenditures to 13.8 percent; on a per capita basis, military spending rose from $25 to $31 within the 10-year period. Arms imports constituted 8.0 percent of all African imports in 1984 (a decline from 10 percent in 1978), compared with 4.7 percent in Latin America, 15.4 percent in the Middle East and 6.3 percent in South Asia. Between 1975 and 1979 the rate of arms acquisitions by African countries increased by a real growth rate of almost 30 percent annually; between 1979 and 1984, however, the rate of arms deliveries declined by −5.4 percent per year. Arms deliveries to Africa peaked at $8.53 billion in 1978 (1983 dollars), falling progressively to $3.57 billion in 1985.

These trends are roughly representative of general trends among underdeveloped countries (UDCs). The rate of UDCs' military expenditures grew by 4.8 percent per year from 1974 to 1979, but slowed to 2.8 percent between 1980 and 1984, with a real drop of about 0.2 percent between 1982 and 1984. Arms deliveries, however, declined more sharply, with the largest single drop in 1985 and 1986. Deliveries in 1985 were equivalent

---

[1]Or 1979, if SIPRI figures are used. Except where indicated, U.S. Arms Control and Disarmament Agency data is used in the text.

716

in real terms to those of 1976, and represented a drop of 40 percent over 1982 and 37 percent over 1981, with the sharpest contraction occurring in the Middle East.

Different patterns and sequences emerge, however, when these figures are broken down to reflect regional and economic trends and disparities. As noted in the past (by Robin Luckham in 1985 and by Hutchful in 1984), military spending and arms deliveries have been highly concentrated in Africa, with the largest military budgets and arms purchases occurring among oil producers (mainly North African) and in conflict zones in southern Africa and the Horn. Of the total arms deliveries of $27.6 billion in 1981– 85, six countries—Libya, Algeria, Angola, Ethiopia, Morocco and Nigeria—accounted for almost $22 billion, with Libya alone responsible for 37 percent of the continental total. Between 1981 and 1985, however, the oil-exporting countries, traditionally the strongest source of military expenditures and demand, reduced military spending by an average of 9 percent annually, primarily because of reduced oil revenues. Various trends emerge on a regional basis.

In North Africa (including Algeria, Libya, Morocco and Tunisia, but excluding Egypt), military expenditures rose almost uninterruptedly until 1982, after which they dropped sharply, reflecting the effects of drastically reduced oil prices (see graph below). This region accounts for about 60 percent of total arms imports in Africa, with Libya as the single largest importer. In East Africa (Ethiopia, Sudan, Somalia, Uganda, Kenya and Malawi), with the exception of a brief cutback in 1982, military spending again rose consistently from 1976 but fell in 1985, although in relative terms much less sharply than in North Africa. Increases in military spending in this region have been related to some of Africa's longest wars, in Eritrea and the Ogaden, as well as civil wars in the Sudan and guerrilla activity inside Ethiopia. The scale of military spending has been maintained in spite of widespread famine (to which the wars have contributed) in Ethiopia and southern Sudan. A similar trend is visible in southern Africa (including South Africa and the front-line states: Angola, Mozambique, Tanzania, Zambia and Zimbabwe) where a number of guerrilla wars are in progress, involving the African National Congress (ANC) in South Africa, the South-West Africa People's Organization (SWAPO) in Namibia, UNITA in Angola and Renamo in Mozambique, as well as sporadic raids by South African forces into neighboring states, and conventional battles between South African and Angolan forces. South Africa is by far the largest military spender in this area, with approximately two and one-half times the military budgets of the other six states—accounting for about $3.5 billion of the total regional budget of approximately $4.5 billion in 1984. In this area also military expenditure dropped significantly in 1985.

In West and Central Africa, however, military expenditures have shown a more or less consistent decline since 1976, with the exception of small increases in 1977 and 1980. The only active war in this zone (which includes all countries from Mauritania in the northwest to Zaire in the south) is in Chad. Total military spending declined from about $7.5 billion in 1977 to just over $4.5 billion in 1985. The sharpest drop occurred in

AFRICAN MILITARY EXPENDITURES 1976–85 (constant 1980 $ U.S.)

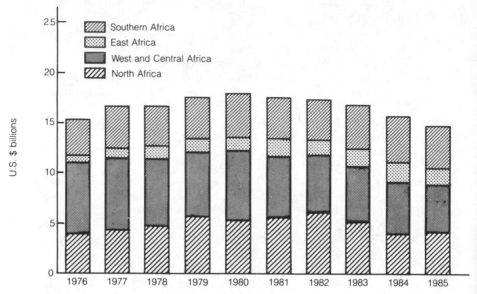

Source: *World Armaments and Disarmaments: SIPRI Yearbook 1987* (London and New York: Oxford University Press, 1987), 146.

Nigeria, the largest spender in the region, where the military budget dropped from a peak of $4.02 billion in 1975 to an estimated $1.17 billion (1983 dollars) in 1984 (ACDA figures) because of the precipitous decline in oil revenues.

Various factors (such as the end of the war in the Ogaden) are involved in the significant contraction in defense spending, but undoubtedly the crucial factor is economic. The drastic fall in oil prices has abruptly slowed the recycling of oil surpluses that had financed the bulk of arms imports and acquisition of other sophisticated military goods. Most of Africa, including oil-exporting countries, has been caught in a severe economic crisis involving inflation, drought and famine, balance-of payments problems, and large, unserviceable foreign debts. Many countries in Africa have thus been placed under rigorous adjustment programs, usually supervised by the International Monetary Fund (IMF), that demand substantial retrenchment and cutbacks in public expenditure. Against this background it has been impossible to sustain the rate of military expansion characteristic of the later 1970s. However, although there have been substantial reductions in absolute levels of military expenditures, the military burden may have remained the same or even increased.

ECONOMIC IMPACT OF MILITARY SPENDING

The present economic climate may tend to suggest the commonsensical view that the economic utility of military expenditures in Africa will be strongly negative. In fact the issue is not so simple. Some studies of the impact of military spending on economic performance claim a positive correlation between high military expenditures and high economic growth, while others argue a negative correlation. On the one hand, military spending has been seen as a form of institutionalized "waste," which is both structurally necessary and beneficial to advanced capitalist economies. On the other hand, military spending has been linked to the declining international competitiveness of the large military spenders (the United States, Britain and, presumably, the Soviet Union) owing to diversion of R & D funding and technical and scientific skills to specialized military sectors; the limited spin-off from military research to the civilian technological sectors; and the inability, in relation to capitalist countries with low defense spending (Japan, Germany), to apply innovations to the mass consumer market. A similar debate has raged on whether military spending stimulates or retards economic growth in Third World countries. Domestic military production is claimed to produce positive spin-offs for economic development through foreign-exchange savings, employment generation and stimulation of domestic industry through imports of sophisticated technology. From a study of 44 UDCs, E. Benoit claimed to have discovered a strong positive relationship between high defense spending and high growth, and between low defense spending and low growth. Benoit stresses both the direct and indirect economic effects of military spending. According to him, military spending leads to inflation; as long as inflation is not excessive it will stimulate growth by creating the additional demand required to bring spare or idle industrial capacity into production. In the area of indirect effects Benoit cites such factors as the role of military training in imparting attitudes and skills beneficial to modernization and nation-building, as well as the impact of public works and civic action programs carried out by the military.[2]

Other studies have uncovered much more negative effects. Increased military spending has been related to lower investment, greater tax burdens, reduced social welfare spending and overall consumption, as well as inflation. Military expenditures have exacted direct costs in terms of health and literacy programs, as well as in agricultural investment; agriculture has been one of the first casualties of expanded defense spending. Arms and other military imports have exacerbated the external indebtedness of UDCs; various studies have placed the additional debt burden resulting from weapons imports in the late 1970s at 20 percent to 30 percent of the total debt burden of UDCs, higher in the case of the heaviest weapons importers.

Several of these studies have been directly critical of those by Benoit and others, mainly on methodological grounds, emphasizing in particular the ambiguity of the relationship between military expenditure and economic development in individual UDCs. Military spending has been found to be positively or negatively correlated with economic growth, depending on the financial circumstances of individual countries, with negative effects

[2] E. Benoit, "Growth and Defense in Developing Countries," *Economic Development and Cultural Change* 26 (January 1978): 279.

realized disproportionately in the poorest countries and in those with serious financial difficulties. Saadet Deger found (in 1986) few of the industrial spin-offs attributed by Benoit and others to local arms production—the reason for this being that military technology was highly specialized, secretive in nature and sheltered from market forces. In a previous (1983) statistical study of 50 UDCs Deger had found the impact of military spending on savings and growth to be negative overall, essentially the same result as had been found for the Organization for Economic Cooperation and Development countries. In a recalculation of Benoit's data, D. Lim discovered an overall negative correlation between defense spending and growth, but also marked regional differences in the nature of the relationship. Economic growth seemed to be most adversely affected in the poorest countries located in Africa and the Western Hemisphere. Lim's conclusion was that in such countries there was "insufficient foreign capital inflow" to offset the negative economic effects of the diversion of domestic investment funds to military spending.[3]

In light of these contradictory findings S. Chan has suggested the need of studies of this kind to: (a) distinguish between correlation and causation (is military spending the cause of rapid growth or merely its product?); (b) take into account divergent national conditions—in particular, generalizations for categories like "developed" and "underdeveloped" countries are considered too broad to be analytically useful; (c) consider the impact on specific economic sectors as well as on the macroeconomy; and finally (d) trace the impact of military spending over specific time periods for the same country, since the nature of the impact and of the trade-offs between military and nonmilitary spending may tend to fluctuate over time.[4]

The domestic economic impact of military spending will obviously depend on a complex of factors, which include the following:

1. The mode of financing of military expenditures, e.g., oil surpluses or other windfall gains from external commodity markets, foreign grants/loans, direct taxation or deficit financing, etc.
2. Actual procurement policies, in other words what proportion of military goods is procured domestically or imported. This will determine what proportion of military spending is retained within the domestic economy.[5] An additional consideration would involve the economic climate in which domestic procurement takes place. Obviously, the effects of the additional demand will differ substantially

[3] D. Lim, "Another Look at Growth and Defense in Less Developed Countries," *Economic Development and Cultural Change* 31 (January 1983): 379.

[4] S. Chan, "Military Expenditure and Economic Performance," in *World Military Expenditures and Arms Transfers* (Washington, D.C.: U.S. Arms Control and Disarmament Agency, 1987).

[5] Chan argues that the proportion of defense spending that stays in the national economy "varies substantially between countries. . . . smaller countries are less able to recapture some of the costs of their military spending through military exports, and are more likely to face the problem of foreign debts and trade deficits." Chan, "Military Expenditure and Economic Performance," p. 33. Although the reference is to NATO countries, this argument is even more applicable to defense spending in most undeveloped countries.

depending on whether there is spare industrial capacity (and if so in what sectors) or full production
3. The sector distribution of military spending—how much is spent on salaries and "consumption" goods like housing for officers as opposed to "capital" goods like armaments
4. The relationship between military industries and research, and the civilian industrial and technology sector. The extent to which military industry and R & D constitute a "baroque" sector, sheltered from the civil sector by security considerations, or on the other hand "meshed" with civilian industry, will obviously constitute a crucial factor

These factors may exist in specific combinations, variable over time, in any particular country and may vary substantially between countries even in the same region and with roughly similar levels of military expenditure.

A number of other difficulties deserve mention. First is the difficulty of determining with reasonable certainty what the components of military expenditure are, since many items of military spending may have both military and civilian effects or function. In many African countries military budgets have over time become less and less explicit and informative.[6] Secondly, the exact level of military expenditure is usually not easy to determine; significant military-related expenditure may be hidden in the appropriations of civilian ministries. Large variations also exist in reportings of military expenditure levels for individual countries, and these can have significant effects on the outcome of calculations of the relationship between military spending and economic growth. In his 1983 study, Deger reached divergent results for Africa using SIPRI and ACDA data. While in both cases the correlation between military expenditure and growth is found to be negative, in absolute value the ACDA coefficient of -0.39 is found to be more than four times the SIPRI coefficient of -0.09. Similarly for Latin America, the effect of military burden on growth is negative using ACDA data but positive for SIPRI data.

Fortunately, with a few exceptions, African economies and military procurement policies are sufficiently similar to permit a number of cautious generalizations. First, African countries are primarily consumers and importers of military goods rather than producers or exporters.

Only one African country, South Africa, has substantial military production facilities. (Egypt, another major manufacturer, is excluded from this study.) Secondly, African countries tend to have a limited industrial base and low level of industrial diversification. Their level of domestic military demand is generally also low. These factors limit their ability to initiate domestic military manufacture. This means that African economies will tend to demonstrate few of the multiplier effects, including R & D, asso-

---

[6] An example of this is Ghana, where military budgets in the first years after independence contained significant details available for public consumption. In subsequent years, however, as the political importance of the military (and controversies surrounding defense spending) grew, defense allocations were sometimes omitted from the budget statement altogether.

ciated with domestic military production where much of the "growth effects" will presumably be located—and possibly the least ability to retain the proceeds of military spending within the national economy. Again, this may depend very much on the sector distribution, and probably procurement practices, associated with each nation's military expenditure. African military forces may differ significantly on how much they spend on (imported) military hardware on the one hand, and on manpower and "consumption" goods on the other. Finally, African countries are severely deficit in investment capital and foreign exchange, suggesting that investment in military goods will tend to have high opportunity costs in terms of capital formation and foreign-exchange utilization. They also do not benefit from high foreign capital inflow, a condition specified by Lim[7] as necessary to overcome the negative impact of military spending on domestic capital formation. Beyond these initial observations, caution is required in generalizing about the actual relationship between military spending and economic growth in Africa because of certain perverse patterns on the continent. In Africa high military spending is positively correlated with strong economic performance, particularly in the form of export surpluses. However, it is also positively correlated with weak economic performance. Some of the highest military spenders in Africa (in terms of military burden)—and this includes Mozambique, Ethiopia, Chad and Angola—are among the most distressed economies on the continent. The intervening factor in the latter case is war.

As far as Africa is concerned, the essentially Keynesian position (advanced by Benoit and others) that military spending will exert a demand-stimulation effect on domestic industrial production rests on a basic misconception. Although considerable industrial spare capacity does exist in most African economies, this is not related to the absence of domestic demand (on the contrary, African economies are plagued by shortages and unfulfilled basic demand) but most frequently to the shortage of imported inputs caused by balance-of-payments constraints. Both industrial spare capacity and balance-of-payments pressures are chronic conditions in African economies, with their fundamental basis in the lack of linkage ("disarticulation") between domestic demand and production structures. Thus the import-intensive character of military demand is only one aspect of a more generalized structural problem in African economies. Military imports do not only compete with imports for civilian and critical economic sectors; in a balance-of-payments squeeze, military spending will create additional demand, but one that in all probability can only be satisfied through further imports. The inflation generated will not, because of the situation of disarticulation referred to above, stimulate domestic production. Rather, its major effect will be to raise domestic costs substantially, leading to currency overvaluation (African exchange rates are administratively determined), declining export competitiveness and other forms of economic distortion.

Domestic military production, particularly of armaments, may not really be the answer; in purely economic terms domestic production has often

[7] Lim, "Another Look at Growth and Defense in Less Developed Countries."

been found to involve higher costs than direct imports and is no guarantee of self-reliance. What domestic production may do in this case is essentially shift the problem of import dependence in the military sector further upstream; by diverting scarce import capacity toward the military manufacturing sector, the problem of spare capacity in nonmilitary industries may actually be exacerbated. Additionally, the large capital outlays, machinery and materials, and skilled technical and scientific manpower that would be required to start and sustain domestic military production can be expected to divert further resources from the civilian economic sector. This is not to disregard the possibilities for production of basic military goods in joint civil-military industries. Such possibilities exist in Africa's import-substituting industrial structure for military items like uniforms, boots, certain types of electronic goods, vehicle assembly and tire manufacture. The Steyr factory in Bauchi, Nigeria, which produces Austrian Steyr trucks for the civilian market and Pinzgaeur transport vehicles for the army, is an example of such ventures. This type of military production may help deepen the market for backward linkages into more complex forms of industrial production.

A different type of analysis must be attempted for South Africa. Here domestic arms production has apparently generated considerable spin-offs for private nonmilitary industry in the form of defense contracts. In 1982, Armscor, the South African state armaments corporation, allocated 70 percent of its budget for domestic arms procurement to private companies and only 30 percent to its own subsidiaries. Military contracting has been critical in the development of microelectronic manufacture (communications equipment, missile guidance systems, radar, minicomputers) in particular, and also significant in the vehicle and other industrial sectors. But according to Leonard this has primarily benefited the transnational corporate sector.

Nevertheless, these are very general observations. A proper and more scientific assessment will have to look much more closely at the concrete circumstances of each African country, not only at the level and origin of defense expenditures, but also at such factors as the actual sector distribution of defense spending, the nature of procurement policies, and so on. As Benoit correctly argued, "the economic effects of a defense program might depend as much on its composition as on its size." From his study of 44 countries he concluded that "substantial variations existed among the various programs in the share of the total allocated to manpower training, imported equipment, domestically produced equipment, etc."[8] The "mix" of defense allocations may also alter significantly over time, making it even more difficult to compare the economic impact of defense programs cross-nationally or to assess the impact accurately even within the same country. As before indicated, there is also the need to calculate more finely the impact of military spending on particular economic sectors rather than for macroeconomics. The information required to do these calculations with any certainty is simply not available for most African countries, so any analysis must necessarily be extremely tentative.

[8] Benoit, "Growth and Defense in Developing Countries."

While the conclusion is likely to be that military expenditures in Africa have, overall, negative effects on economic development in the sense in which that may conventionally be understood, the actual conclusions regarding both costs and benefits may be subject to varying degrees of qualification because of differences posed by specific national conditions, economic sectors or historical periods. Hence, although there is much agreement that military spending relates negatively to capital formation in UDCs, the actual situation is not nearly so straightforward for some of the African countries with the largest military budgets. In countries like Libya, Algeria, Nigeria and South Africa the size of military spending and arms procurement has been tied closely to the performance of specific commodity markets: gold in the case of South Africa, oil in the case of the others. In the case of Organization of Petroleum Exporting Countries' economies, such as those of Nigeria and Libya, capital-absorption limits have to be considered; this makes it doubtful that military spending detracted substantially from the rate of capital formation in the civil sector. On the contrary, high military spending was consistent with high rates of capital formation—as long, of course, as oil prices remained high. Except in countries involved in some form of war it is not the "capital-deficit" countries that have been the big military spenders; and among the big spenders, military expenditures have been scaled down to reflect changing financial and trading conditions.

Similarly, the argument that the military draws specialized manpower away from civil sectors must be taken with caution. In many countries the military was not, at least until relatively recently, directly competitive with the civil sector for trained manpower, but rather benefited from its "surplus."[9] In fact there is evidence that in several countries the military acted as a potential safety valve by absorbing unemployed educated manpower, and in the process did not have access to the best graduates. On the other hand, the military may train its own specialists, particularly since the institution, for reasons of socialization, prefers to recruit the young and may thus be cut off from older civilian professionals. Given the high attrition rate in the officer corps of some African countries, it would not be altogether surprising if the net flow of specialists were in fact from the military to the civil sector.

Since African military forces are primarily labor intensive, emphasis has been placed on the employment-generating effects of military spending. Indeed, Benoit[10] placed considerable emphasis on the labor-intensive rather than capital-intensive character of African armies in arguing their developmental impact. Such armies are said to make their greatest contribution to growth through the dispersion of "modernizing" attitudes and civic action programs that deliberately utilize military forces and equipment for secondary uses on behalf of civilian economic objectives. The response to this kind

---

[9] This has been examined for Ghana by the author in "The Development of the Army Officer Corps in Ghana 1956–66," *Journal of African Studies* 12, no. 3 (December 1985).

[10] Benoit, "Growth and Defense in Developing Countries," pp. 277, 280.

of argument is that such civic action programs tend to be sporadic, unpopular with military officers and hence short-lived. In addition, the so-called modernizing soldier thesis has received little empirical support in Africa; in most of Africa the military is far more often identified with indisicpline, waste and other negative attributes. Although military spending does contribute to employment in the formal sense (particularly in the early days of the expansion of postcolonial African armies) by supporting large military and associated civilian bureaucracies detached from direct production, it in fact places further stress on the fragile productive base of African economies and enhances the possibility of stagnation. Within the military itself labor intensity may well compromise military efficiency, since the cost (in salaries and benefits) of maintaining large standing armies may presumably detract from arms procurement and raising of technical fighting capacity. This means that the "labor-intensive army" may make neither good military nor good economic sense.

The most damaging potential effect of military spending has been argued for an economic sector with which the military has a much less direct relationship—agriculture. Military spending is seen as involving either a direct trade-off with agricultural investment or as exercising negative effects on agriculture through the disruption initiated by militarization and war. The most militarized countries in Africa, such as Ethiopia and Mozambique, are among those with serious problems of hunger. Although the causation is mutual (and also involves intervening factors such as drought), the primary line of determination appears to run from militarization to agricultural collapse. Military spending may not necessarily cause hunger but certainly limits the ability to deal with it effectively. Military imports compete directly with, and may far exceed, food imports. In 1984, in the midst of famine conditions in both countries, arms imports accounted for an estimated 62 percent of total imports into Ethiopia and 48 percent in Mozambique. Even so, the actual relationship between militarization (or even war) and agricultural decline may be more complex and less direct than often portrayed in the literature. There are heavily militarized countries with flourishing agricultural economies (e.g., South Africa, Zimbabwe, Israel), or with fragile agricultures but no famine (Libya), or where agriculture has survived largely intact in spite of civil war and rampant militarism (Uganda). Low military expenditures have not prevented acute agricultural stagnation in other African countries. Obviously, other intervening factors (such as the intrinsic strength or weakness of national agriculture, capital availability, balance-of-payments situation, etc.) are involved. The relationship between the military and agriculture should also be seen in political rather than directly economic terms. In Africa the military and agriculture occupy opposite ends of the spectrum of political influence, with the military representing a powerful and agriculture a weak political interest; the more "closed" the political regime the more this is likely to be the case. Consequently agriculture, the most productive sector, trends to attract low per capita investment while the military, the least economically productive, can lay claim to a higher share of national revenues.

CRITIQUE OF THE "ECONOMIC GROWTH" THESIS

The basic problem with the military expenditure/economic growth equation is that it tends to pose questions not germane to the military function. The military is not an economic institution and does not represent an economic expenditure; consequently, it cannot be assessed or defended in terms of its economic effects. High military expenditures do not always represent deliberate choices, least of all in countries with shattered economies like Mozambique. The implicit insistence on a rational economic calculus in military spending leads to an avoidance of questions relevant to the military function itself, specifically the adequacy of the national defense capability of African states. Events have demonstrated again and again the stark military vulnerability of African states. Africa has been humiliated militarily in the north (Egypt and Libya), and in the south by South Africa, as well as having been the target of intervention by a succession of foreign military forces. It is clear that present spending levels, regardless of the burden on the national economy, have not guaranteed effective defense capability for African states. It is at this point that the economic critique of defense spending (which asserts that too much is being lavished on military resources) comes into conflict with the military critique (which may hold that not nearly enough is being spent—or spent in the right way—to guarantee external security). In the contemporary world, military weakness can be a source of danger; indeed it can probably be argued that certain forms of military conflict in Africa—the repeated South African incursions into neighboring states, foreign interventions executed with impunity, as well as sneak attacks by African states on each other—have been made likely by the military weakness of target countries. The major military conflicts on the African continent, such as those in southern Africa and in the Horn, have also been stalemated and prolonged by the fact that none of the combatants possesses a decisive military advantage.

In several regions of Africa (southern Africa in particular) it has become clear that no economic development is possible without realization of an effective national defense capability. From the standpoint of realpolitik, effective military force may be necessary where other mechanisms for national integration are so weak, particularly if one accepts existing colonial boundaries; the borders of quite a few African countries would have been drastically redrawn if it had not been for an effective military deterrent. (On the other hand, the danger has always been that military solutions will displace political solutions to such "national" questions.) Once the need for an adequate national defense capability is accepted as a legitimate objective, it can then be argued that the real problem in Africa is that defense expenditures have peaked without realizing this objective. Apart from questions regarding the nature of equipment and training levels, crucial gaps still exist in most African force structures—particularly in the areas of logistics and air and sea defense—that rule out their role as instruments of serious offense or defense. As the Organization of African Unity operation in Chad in 1981 demonstrated, no African country (with the exceptions of South

Africa and Libya) has independent capability for long-range military action outside its own borders; for that matter, few have shown themselves capable of sustaining high levels of action within their national borders without foreign assistance. The present economic crisis greatly constraints the possibility of servicing even the existing elementary force structures, thus posing the threat of further military deterioration. The difficult economic conditions also mean that military expenditure may go preponderantly toward maintaining manpower (military salaries and so on) rather than toward renovating the capital stock (new weapons, etc.) This military aspect should be seen as part of a more comprehensive problem of loss of viability, initiative and self-direction on the part of African states in national as well as international arenas.

On the other hand, while the external defense capability of the military in Africa is further weakened by the current economic crisis, its internal security function (for which its depreciated capital stock remains more than adequate) has become a crucial element in the process of economic adjustment. It is in its enhanced internal security role, as well as in its crisis-conditioned assumption of direct politico-economic managerial roles, that the military's contribution to the process of economic developments (or underdevelopment) should be seen. The depth of the economic crisis in many African countries—inflation and critical shortages, famine conditions, serious balance-of-payments problems and debt—combined with institutional collapse and state delegitimation, is posing serious problems of political order and viability. But so are the economic adjustment mechanisms associated with the structural adjustment programs introduced by the IMF and the World Bank and adopted by many African countries. The monetarist orthodoxy associated with these programs lacks political sensitivity essentially because it operates on the basis of economic models that abstract economic processes from political and social relations and determinants. Secondly, these programs' policy instruments are typically brutal, and consciously so, since their primary objectives are to "shock" the economy, over the very short term, into a realignment of domestic price structures with ruling international prices, and into generating forced surpluses in order to resume external debt servicing. They involve sharp currency depreciation, with severe inflationary impact; large-scale labor retrenchment; rigid wage controls; abolition of public subsidies; and large reductions in social welfare, health and educational spending. These measures generate political unrest (the food riots in Zambia and price protests in Khartoum, for instance), the more so since they fall disproportionately on the shoulders of the poor, and thus acquire a repressive context. The fact that they are administered by the state rather than the private sector and concentrate mostly on the public sectors tends to directly politicize the process of economic reform. In this situation the political loyalties of the military—if it is not already in power—and its ability to deploy effective repression become crucial, and a decisive factor in the ability of the reform programs to stay on course. This may appear ironical, since cutbacks in military spending are (at least in theory) one of the targets of economic retrenchment. Whether these reforms, in which the military is directly or indirectly implicated, are consistent with economic growth or may end in crippling African economies altogether (as some argue), remains to be seen.

CONCLUSION

Evidence of the economic impact of military expenditures in Africa remains fragmentary. While the proportion of the increasingly scarce resources in Africa consumed by the military appears substantial and more or less measurable, little evidence exists of the downstream impact of military spending on the economy, particularly in the area of positive spin-offs. This in itself may create a priori support, on political as well as economic grounds, for reduced military spending. Several dimensions to this position should be appreciated, however. First, the position is often based on premises that do not adequately recognize the social utility of force, particularly in fragmented social formations like those of Africa, or its linkage with structural contradictions. Secondly, there is no guarantee that resources released by cutbacks in military spending will find their way into productive investment rather than into forms of wasteful consumption,[11] not to mention the fact that military manpower released by such retrenchment will still need to be reemployed and fed in economies already characterized by chronically high unemployment. Finally, reduced military spending may accentuate the already weakened external defense capability of African states and perpetuate their dependence as military client states, a situation that, by drawing them into cold war calculations, has actually helped to prolong continental wars. The probable response to this is that no amount of funding available to individual African states will ensure adequate conventional defense against South Africa or against technologically superior external forces, and that in the final analysis a contented and well-fed citizenry trained in methods of effective resistance may constitute a more effective national defense tool than any standing army separated from the population. Nevertheless, the urgent question is whether African states should invest more in defense, as in the 1970s (an obviously unaffordable option); should spend little or nothing (an obviously utopian idea); or should fundamentally rethink their defense policies, possibly in the direction of small, well-armed and highly mobile militia forces backed by citizen reserves at the national level, and a coordinated defense force at the continental level along the lines of an African high command.

FURTHER READING

Baran, P. A., and Sweezy, P. M. *Monopoly Capital.* New York: Monthly Review Press, 1966.
Barrow, W. L. "Changing Military Capabilities in Black Africa." In *Arms and the African:*

[11] This is an important caveat that has been ignored in E. Benoit's much criticized thesis. See his "Growth and Development in Developing Countries," p. 276, where he proposes that military expenditures be compared with their "objectively probable substitutes, not with their optimum substitutes."

Military Influences on Africa's International Relations, edited by William J. Foltz and Henry S. Bienen. New Haven, Connecticut: Yale University Press, 1985.

Brzoska, Nichael, and Ohlson, Thomas. *Arms Production in the Third World*. London and Philadelphia: Taylor & Francis, 1986.

Deger, Saadet. "Military Expenditure and Growth in Less Developed Countries," *Journal of Conflict Resolution* 27 (June 1983): 335–53.

——. *Military Expenditure in Third World Countries: The Economic Effects*. London and Boston: Routledge & Kegan Paul, 1986.

Grimmett, R. F. Trends in Conventional Arms Transfers to the Third World by Major Supplier, 1978–1985. Congressional Research Service, Report no. 86–99F. Washington, D.C., 1986.

Hutchful, E. "Disarmament and Development: An African View." *IDS Bulletin* 16 (October 1985): 61–67.

——. "Trends in Africa," *Alternatives* (Special issue on Militarization and Society) 10 (Summer 1984): 115–37.

Kaldor, Mary, and Eide, Asbjorn, eds. *The World Military Order: The Impact of Military Technology on the Third World*. London: Macmillan, 1979.

Kaplinsky, R. "Guns and/or Butter: The Relationship Between the Economy and the Military." *IDS Bulletin* 16 (October 1985): 73–82.

Kennedy, Gavin. *The Military in the Third World*. New York: Scribner, 1975.

Leonard, Richard. *South Africa at War: White Power and the Crisis in Southern Africa*. Westport, Connecticut: Lawrence Hill, 1983.

Luckham, Robin. "Militarisation in Africa." In *World Armaments and Disarmament: SIPRI Yearbook 1985*. London: Taylor & Francis 1985.

Price, R. "A Theoretical Approach to Military Rule in New States: Reference-Group Theory and the Ghanaian Case." *World Politics* 23 (April 1971).

Shiindo, E. "Hunger and Weapons: the Entropy of Militarisation." *Review of African Political Economy* 33 (1985).

Thorsson, I. "Disarmament and Development: An Idea Whose Time Should have Come." *IDS Bulletin* 16 (October 1985): 19–22.

World Armaments and Disarmament: SIPRI Yearbook 1987. London and New York: Oxford University Press, 1987.

SOUTH AFRICAN POLITICS

TOM LODGE

INTRODUCTION

IN May 1987 the white South African electorate went to the polls to vote in, for the 10th time in succession, an overwhelmingly victorious National party administration. Despite the winner being as predictable as in any of the nine preceding contests, the elections attracted considerable speculation in the foreign media, and nearly 70 percent of those eligible to vote did so. White South Africans have long understood the main point of interest in their elections to be the contest for second place; what was unusual about 1987 was the extent their excitement was shared by outsiders. For the first time since 1976, white politicians were cast in the central roles of the South African drama, which had been played out for a decade on the world's headlines and television screens.

For by mid-1987 two states of emergency had seemingly driven back the tide of black opposition that had appeared so inexorable one year before. In their wake the most hopeful prospects of imminent change for the more optimistic observers lay in a realignment of white politics; black protest no longer appeared to contain the dynamic for a victorious confrontation.[1] Whatever the merits of such arguments (and these will be returned to below), there was certainly more movement in white politics than had been the case for a long time, and not all of it was inconsequential. For within white politics there was unprecedented conflict. There was among white South Africans much less ideological consensus than had been the case for decades. The social cleavages that divided whites politically had themselves changed dramatically. Class had become effectively substituted for ethnic identity as a factor determining political loyalties. Because of this, despite the emasculation of parliamentary democracy, with the increasing prominence of intraparty political conflict, white interest in formal electoral contests remained pronounced.

---

[1] For a sophisticated version of this argument see Mark Swilling, "The Politics of Negotiation," *Work in Progress* no. 50 (October 1987): 17–22.

WHITE POLITICAL ALIGNMENTS

The May elections appeared to confound whatever hopes for change survived the emergency. Yet they supplied valuable insights into the character of the political processes and forces at work within the white community. It first needs to be said that white political organizations are chiefly geared to electioneering. The main white parties, permanent bureaucracies that remain between elections, are very skeletal. Consequently, the white political parties are very different in ethos and in their functions from the political organizations and movements that operate in black South Africa. They mostly campaign at a considerable distance from the supporters or constituents. This is reflected by the extent of their dependence on television (particularly in the case of the National party), the declining importance of large public meetings and the heavy reliance on the press to get their message across. Both the National and the Progressive Federal parties in the 1987 election did very little individual canvassing of potential voters. This was not the case with their more working-class opponents; the Conservative party in conjunction with the fascist Afrikaner Weerstandsbeweging held numerous house meetings in blue-collar suburban areas.[2]

Ethnic identity is much less important today than historically in influencing white political behavior. In the election the National party is thought to have drawn nearly half its support from English speakers. Of course, for a long time class affiliations have helped to structure white party politics, though not as obviously as now. The Progressive Federal party (PFP) has customarily been associated with advanced and sophisticated business.[3] The National party was carried to power on the basis of white working-class electoral support and financial contributions from an emergent Afrikaner bourgeoisie.[4] The Conservative party breakaway in 1981 reflected small-farmer, blue-collar, and lower-echelon civil servant dissatisfaction with economic recession, and fears for their own social security generated by government reforms.[5] The movement of government strategies to ground previously occupied by an earlier generation of liberal opposition signaled the interpenetration of state and big business—the gentrification of Afrikaner nationalism and the distancing of its leadership from its original social roots.[6]

The elections left the National party with a still overwhelming parliamentary majority, 123 out of 166 elected seats, but only with a narrow majority of white voters' support (52 percent of the poll). Left-wing oppo-

---

[2] Andrew Kenny, "White Revolution," *Frontline* (June 1987): 33–35.

[3] Brian Hackland, "Incorporationist Ideology as a Response to Political Struggle: The Progressive Party of South Africa, 1960–1980," in *The Politics of Race, Class and Nationalism in Twentieth Century South Africa*, ed. Shula Marks and Stanley Trapido (London: Longman, 1987), 366–88.

[4] Dan O'Meara, *Volkskapitalisme* (Johannesburg: Ravan Press, 1983).

[5] Craig Charney, "Class Conflict and the National Party Split," *Journal of Southern African Studies* 10, no. 2 (1984).

[6] For an overall analysis of this see Heribert Adam and Herman Giliomee, *The Rise and Crisis of Afrikaner Power* (Cape Town: David Philip, 1979).

sition to the government (17 percent) retained for the PFP 19 seats. Two more went to a surviving representative of the New Republican party and a defector from the Nationalists, one of two leaders of an emerging "Independent" movement, Wynand Malan. The other Independent, the former ambassador to London Dennis Worrall, very nearly captured Helderberg from Chris Heunis, minister of constitutional affairs. The really ascendant force in the election was the Conservative party, which by winning 22 seats and over one quarter of the vote became the official opposition.

Notwithstanding their comfortable majority of seats, the elections were very alarming for National party leaders. Their share of the vote had declined from 65 percent in 1977 and 58 percent in 1981. Though Conservative support was regionally concentrated in the Transvaal, in which they won all their victories, Conservative candidates had come respectably second in several Eastern Cape constituencies—in the province hitherto least affected by the right's resurgence. And following the May election, Conservative elation has been enhanced by a string of by-election triumphs. Nevertheless, by April 1988 the Conservatives had yet to win a victory in a large town or capture a constituency outside the Transvaal. Their following still appeared to be limited to the smaller industrial centers and less prosperous agricultural constituencies. Small farmers, industrial and service workers, and junior bureaucrats can supply the support for a formidably obstructive white opposition, but by themselves they are unlikely to vote a party into government.[7] The Conservatives, in contrast to the emerging Nationalists of the 1940s (to whom they are sometimes compared), have a weak intellectual base constituted mainly by an aging and eccentric group of minor academics. In general their middle-class appeal still seems slight.

Poor strategy and lackluster campaigning helped to explain the PFP's failure to gain seats. In Natal an electoral alliance with nearly moribund New Republicans prompted English-speaking conservatives to vote Nationalist and liberal radicals to stay away. The PFP's decreased appeal to young leftish whites contributed to its declining support in Johannesburg. Probably more fundamental to its failure was its inability to outbid the government on the security issue. It could draw comfort from evidence of a continuing trend among affluent professional Afrikaners to switch their allegiance to it (the party did well in the lusher Pretoria suburbs). The Independent candidates were the major beneficiaries of such support, and since the election Wynand Malan has been joined by two Progressives and another refugee from the National party.

Rise of the right

What are the implications of all this? For the government, the threat posed to its continued authority by the Conservatives now seems to be the major consideration in influencing its decisions and policy. The rise of the right in combination with the growing importance of soldiers in maintaining civil order in the black townships have both weakened reformists within

---

[7] For an elaboration of this argument see Karin Brynard, "CP's Recipe for Victory," *The Star* (Johannesburg) 5 March 1988.

the upper layers of the National party and administration. Since the declaration of the 1986 emergency, an effective embargo has been placed upon any talks or negotiations with popular black organizations. The emphasis in government reform rhetoric has shifted from constitutional to economic issues, reflecting the dominant conviction that any constitutional incorporation of blacks should be preceded by law and order, economic recovery and urban social "upliftment." Accordingly, officially conceded outlets for black political expression are likely to remain limited to an advisory National Statutory Council, regional services councils and local municipalities, as well as homeland governments. A freeze on the constitutional front has been accompanied by the announcement of repressive labor legislation, the virtual prohibition of the United Democratic Front (UDF) and some of its major affiliates, the curtailment of the "alternative press," attacks on university autonomy, blustering diplomacy at the United Nations, and a heightened military commitment in Angola. Effectively, the tricameral exercise in racial power sharing is over, the government's unwillingness to repeal the Group Areas Act ending its alliance with the Coloured Labour party. With military expenditure representing at least one-quarter of the government's budget, with a cavalier dismissal of the probability of further foreign economic sanctions, and with the abandonment of any but the most crudely materialistic devices for winning black support (e.g., privatized state housing, tarred roads, water-borne sewage systems), state strategy seems to have diminished the preservation of National party rule and white survival in a state of siege.

Bluster abroad and bullying at home are unlikely to win back significant support from the Conservatives. For underlying the right's advocacy of a Verwoerdian restoration of apartheid are the economic grievances of traditionally subsidized farmers, wage-frozen clerical workers and an increasingly marginalized class of white factory supervisors. Economic conditions for these groups in a state of siege are likely to become even bleaker. The cost of containing black opposition through emergency rule makes a deterioration in white services inevitable. Poor white resentment of de facto integration of inner-city housing, of multiracial regional service councils, and of black patronage of inner-city commercial districts and formerly whites-only beaches, seemed likely to be forcefully expressed in the October 1988 municipal elections.

Role of the National party
Ideology, sentiment and militarism have all had a part in restraining the National party since the election from exploiting its middle-class "reformist" constituency and taking full advantage of the disarray among its left-wing opponents. A succession of opinion polls reveal substantial majorities of white South Africans favoring the orderly abandonment of "social" segregation in such areas as schooling, housing and public services, while retaining a fear of black majority rule and "communism."[8] The election itself

[8] For survey evidence see: "HSRC poll says most people back sharing of power," *The Star*, 17 May 1986; "Poll finds urban whites split on release of Mandela," *The Star*, 9 May 1986,

demonstrated the Nationalist reformist dimension's appeal in traditional Progressive strongholds. Commonsense political sociology indicates the limited nature of the Conservative constituency. In any case, as is beginning to be openly suggested in South African newspapers, should the government lose an election it will have no hesitation in employing the support of the military to keep it in power.[9] Yet Nationalist leaders persist in attempting to win back former adherents rather than consolidating the support of fresh (and possibly opportunist) converts. For example, despite substantial "English" support, President Botha has appointed an entirely Afrikaner cabinet.

In essence, the National party's weakness is an intellectual one; it is incapable of devising a new and coherent ideological identity and long-term strategy. It is a weakness the party shares with the upper echelons of the bureaucracy. Even the army, the most privileged and favored department of state, has no political vision other than a few well-worn maxims of counterinsurgency strategy borrowed from foreign, and long since defeated, colonial generals. The sources of this intellectual vulnerability are complex. They include: political conventions of hierarchy and conformity; an intolerance of academic dissidence that has sterilized Afrikaner scholarship; the prevalence among all whites of a transatlantic suburban culture of consumerism; the effects of international isolation; and a genteelly vulgar religiosity that stimulates a predisposition for sentiment rather than analysis. Paradoxically, though, it is the intellectual debasement of Afrikaner nationalism—its growing incapacity to maintain a hegemonic position even with an exclusively white constituency—that makes contemporary white politics interesting. For to the left of the National party a new middle ground in South African politics has opened up, a terrain the ruling group resolutely refuses to occupy.

Opposition movements
The fluidity of white politics is most perceptible in the area customarily occupied by the liberal parliamentary opposition of the Progressives. In its program and discourse the PFP has traditionally combined hardheaded business objections to apartheid interference with the market, with an older strain of humanitarian concern with human rights. The combination has not always been an easy one to maintain; on the one hand the party has been led in the direction of free enterprise philosophy and conservative notions of federal power sharing; on the other hand liberal compassion and hostility to racialism incline younger members particularly toward social democracy and identification with extraparliamentary protest. In 1986, for example, the party was deeply split at its annual congress over the issue of conscription. The appearance of a substantial Afrikaner "Left opposition"

Jill Nattrass, "Management on the Political Economy of Change," *Indicator SA* 4, no. 1 (Winter 1986); "600,000 votes for true democracy. . . . The problem is how to harness them," *Weekly Mail* (Durban), 25 March 1988.
[9] David Breier, "Nats Would Stage a Coup to Prevent a CP Takeover," *The Star*, 28 February 1988.

to the government and the proliferation of white extraparliamentary groups has helped to widen the gulfs within the party. Demoralization after the disappointment of the 1987 election, in which the PFP had hoped to win 37 seats, served to accelerate the process of disintegration. The PFP's chances of controlling the Johannesburg municipality were ended with the belated announcement of the emigration to Australia of one of its councillors. This helped to set off a fratricidal conflict within the party's Johannesburg membership, leading to the defection of two of its more conservative councillors and the assumption of local leadership by one of the young radicals, former University of the Witwatersrand Sciences Student Representative Council president Tony Leon. Meanwhile, at the national level, two PFP parliamentarians, Peter Gastrow and Jan Van Eck, both admirers of former party leader Frederick Van Zyl Slabbert, announced their conversion to the left end of the Independent spectrum.

The Independent movement has little that is distinctive about its program. While claiming to represent "a new spirit which cuts across political, cultural and racial lines," its emphasis on "constitutional dialogue" and "process politics" is hardly illuminating or original. It is significant more for who it represents than what it says. The movement's origins lay in the ground swell of discontent in Afrikaner intellectual circles, prompted at least partly by the tendency in recent years for authoritarian executive government to deny "insider access" [10] to Afrikaner notables. Both the Afrikaans press and universities have produced a succession of prominent defectors from the National party, including newspaper editor Wiempie de Klerk and economist Sampie Terreblanche. The political restlessness among Afrikaner intellectual elders finds its reflection in Afrikaans student politics in which Nationalist-Conservative conflict led to the dissolution of the Afrikaanse Studentebond and its replacement with the avowedly nonracial Youth for South Africa, an organization of "moderates" with a manifesto very similar to that of the Independents. Significantly, in 1986, the government-funded Human Sciences Research Council found that 42 percent of its respondents in a survey taken at Stellenbosch University would accept a predominantly black government, and that 40 percent thought such a government was in any case inevitable. [11]

Since the election, there have been efforts to transform this loose movement of disaffection into a party, but these efforts have foundered on the problems caused by very disparate personalities, and deeper ideological divisions within the movement. Worrall leads those Independents who seek a credible parliamentary alternative to the National party, not actually very different from it, capable of recruiting mutinous "New Nats" and the less progressive Progressives. Worrall, it should be remembered, was the original architect of the tricameral constitution. Left-wing former Progressives

[10] Andrie du Toit cited by Allister Sparks, "The Independents—just a fuzzy fantasy?" *The Star*, 11 March 1987; see also Tos Wentzel, "Nat academics are disillusioned," *The Star*, 27 February 1987.

[11] "Maties split on black rule," *The Star*, 16 October 1986.

joining the movement at the other end pull it toward the extraparliamentary arena and a mystical religious doctrine of reconciliation.

Significantly, much of the activity of Van Zyl Slabbert's Institute for a Democratic Alternative in South Africa (IDASA) has been focused on Afrikaans students. IDASA's Northern Transvaal director is a Pretoria professor and brother of a leading defense force general. IDASA's goals include the promotion of "a climate for genuine negotiation towards a non-racial and democratic South Africa." It enjoys the qualified approval of black opposition groups (a UDF activist, Eric Mntonga, was until his assassination an IDASA director), but its representatives are also well received within reformist white business. Indeed, the liberal business community itself is now sharply divided over the extent to which it should find common cause with the more moderate voices of black protest. Though one should not overestimate the importance of the relatively radical positions taken by such figures as the South African Permanent Building Society's Bob Tucker, or Premier Milling's Tony Bloom (who in early 1988 announced that he was leaving South Africa), the fact that IDASA or the Five Freedoms Forum can attract corporate funding and business spokesmen to their platforms distinguishes the new white left from the white radical tradition represented by the Communist party in the 1940s, the Congress of Democrats and the Liberal party in the 1950s, and the "End Conscription" campaign and the white UDF affiliates today. This radical constituency is also considerably more significant than it has ever been historically, largely because of the increasing alienation from white society of the English-speaking university campuses. In conscription, with an annual draft evasion rate of 5,000 a year, the radical white left has found an issue in which, for young whites, immediate self-interest and opposition to minority rule coincide.

In summary, white South African politics are complex and volatile. Economic recession has eroded the customary bedrock of the government's support among farmers, workers, and clerks, while the scale and force of black protest has destroyed the credibility of its ideologues within the Afrikaner intelligentsia. Inflation, political uncertainty, and social insecurity have had a polarizing effect on the PFP's constituency, driving sections of it rightward into an almost apolitical support for the National party ("It's fash'nal to be National" was the slogan favored by Nationalists in Johannesburg's northern suburbs in 1987)—leaving the traditional "English" liberal community subject to a variety of different impulses. These include: free marketeering (with its own eccentric brand of right-wing anarchy; religious fundamentalism; the white student left; African nationalism and nonracialism; Afrikaner disaffection; social democracy; and local municipal politics.

INDIAN AND COLOURED POLITICS

On the fringes of white parliamentary politics are the parallel proceedings for the Indian and Coloured communities. Within the (Coloured) House of Representatives, the ruling Labour party controls 75 seats. Its opponents have recently consolidated in a nine-member United Democratic party, the latest of a kaleidoscope of small political groupings in Coloured politics, likely to be as short-lived as its predecessors. In the Indian House of Delegates, the most interesting recent development is the incorporation of the Progressive Reform party, the smaller of two opposition parties, by the white PFP.

It is tempting and commonplace to discount completely the possibility that anything of long-term significance can arise from black tricameral politics. Participation in the parliamentary system has yet to yield for Coloureds and Indians legislative reforms substantially affecting their rights and status. In particular, the government's refusal to consider more than selective adjustments to the Group Areas Act appears to underscore the unwillingness among National party strategists to make the essential commitments required for an effective politics of co-option. Frustration and demoralization help to explain the proliferation of small parties, the frequency of bitter personal disputes between parliamentarians, and the lethargic attendance records of certain members.

On the other hand the junior houses do have a certain obstructive capacity, as is evident at the moment in the Reverend Hendrickse's refusal to support the government's effort to postpone the tricameral elections until 1992. His resignation from Botha's cabinet in August 1987 over Group Areas obduracy seems to have enhanced his standing within his own party. Its recent performance in by-elections has improved, though this may be the effect of these occurring in rural constituencies where Labour party support has always been strongest. Both Labour party politicians and even more obviously those of the (Indian) National People's party do command substantial material resources. Indian education has witnessed significant improvements in recent years, and there has also been an expanded provision of private- and public-sector housing. [12] Judiciously directed public expenditure may create a limited popular base for "collaboration" politics, particularly in those communities where radical opposition has subsided. There has been very little evidence of substantial grassroots organization by UDF affiliates in Indian areas since the 1984 election boycott. In late 1987 a debate within the UDF's Indian affiliates over the merits of participation in elections on a "boycott" ticket began to excite press comment. What it signified for some activists at least was a recognition of the potential attractions within sections of the Indian community of a conservative system of political patronage and the need to displace it. [13]

INKATHA AND INDABA

The dangers to Indian radical resistance movements such a system might represent would be all the more obvious in Natal, where the major repre-

---

[12] State housing expenditure in 1985–86 for Coloureds (R97 million) and Indians (R53 million) was well in excess of money spent on black African housing in the same period (R42 million). For improvements in the course of the 1980s in Indian education, see Elmon Mathonsi, *Black Matriculation Results* (Johannesburg: Skotaville, 1988).

[13] For debate on participation see "Cabal rules Indian politics, claims ex-President," *Weekly Mail*, 29 January 1988, p. 3; Yunus Carrim, "The NIC and the three plagues," *Weekly*

sentative of black African participatory politics, Inkatha, commands a formidable mass following. Inkatha is unusual among those movements that have grown out of the black political culture of involvement with government institutions, for its power does not derive merely from the control of state institutions and resources; it has an authority that is moral, legitimized through an effective ideology.

Inkatha claims the disciplined support of 1.5 million members, though such claims have often been contested.[14] Certainly, Inkatha is capable at chosen moments of orchestrating large crowds of enthusiasts at ceremonial rallies and meetings. More than ever, though, Inkatha is a regional, predominantly Zulu, movement and from its inception has been intertwined with KwaZulu government structures; Chief Buthelezi's presidency of the organization is a corollary of his chief ministership. Inkatha holds all the seats in the KwaZulu legislature and dominates Natal's urban community councils. This does not adequately explain its power, though; the same can be said for other much less apparently effective homeland-based political parties. To a greater extent than parallel movements elsewhere, Inkatha enjoys a degree of public acceptance. On the one hand, it draws upon traditional values—patriarchal discipline, ethnic honor and other facets of Zulu culture that retain considerable attraction for older people especially. But Inkatha combines "traditionalism" with a growing identification with the ideology of reformist capitalism. "Free enterprise," asserts Buthelezi, "goes hand in hand with democratic government."[15] "There is no socialist magic for Africa."[16] Logically accompanying its faith in the progressive character of the private sector is Inkatha's antipathy to disinvestment. Commitment to capitalism reflects the organization's social characteristics. Low-level urban Inkatha leadership is heavily concentrated in the hands of traders, who through their control of community councils are able to manipulate a broad field of patronage. Inkatha's advocacy of capitalism also reflects the presence within its echelons of a growing black managerial middle class. Lending vigor to its economic convictions is the increasingly obvious alliance between Inkatha and big business. In the early 1980s the expansion of radical popular resistance prompted a generalized search among businessmen for the "middle ground"[17] of black politics. Buthelezi and Inkatha were the obvious choices, with their unique combination of social conservatism with apparently authentic African Nationalist appeal.

Inkatha's attraction for businessmen is buttressed by its willingness to embrace federal "power sharing" constitutional blueprints. These take their most recent form in the KwaNatal Indaba, a plan produced through the deliberations of a conference organized by the administrations of Natal and

---

Mail, 12 February 1988; "Who's responsible for NIC row?" Weekly Mail, 19 February 1988, p. 12.
[14] Gerhard Mare and Georgina Hamilton, An Appetite for Power (Johannesburg: Ravan Press, 1987), 70–73.
[15] Clarion Call no. 4 (1985).
[16] Ibid., no. 1 (1985).
[17] Financial Mail, 6 December 1985, pp. 36–39.

KwaZulu. The Indaba recommended two legislative chambers, the first elected proportionately and itself choosing the prime minister, and the second composed of 10 representatives of every ethnic racial group (including a voluntary nonracial "South African" category). The second-chamber representatives would have the power to veto legislation affecting the rights of specific groups. The Indaba proposals continue to find favor with many liberals. They are opposed by black trade unions and the UDF on the grounds that the plan would serve to promote an authoritarian extension of Inkatha's power.[18] Government reaction has alternated; Indaba thinking is very close to some of the wilder projections of cabinet reformists, but the National party explicitly disassociated itself from the Indaba in the 1987 election. Later that year, though, a joint executive authority was established for KwaNatal with Buthelezi as joint chairman.

Inkatha's frequently professed commitment to peaceful "strategic interaction with the state"[19] has been rather eclipsed by a particularly bloody recent phase of its development. Between September 1987 and April 1988, over 400 people died in fighting between UDF and Inkatha partisans in Pietermaritzburg. The origins of the conflict are obviously complex and as yet underresearched. Tensions originally flared up in the course of a consumer boycott organized in 1985 in support of striking workers. Around the boycott there was a proliferation of radical youth organization and activity. High-handed behavior by some of the boycott organizers alienated groups of township residents. In the wake of the boycott, rivalry between a newly established UWUSA (Inkatha trade union) branch and Council of South African Trade (COSATU) affiliates accentuated antagonism between Inkatha supporters clustered around city councillors and civic/youth activists. Pietermaritzburg's African townships were relatively loosely organized until 1987. In August 1987, Inkatha's Youth Brigade began an aggressive recruitment campaign backed with considerable compulsion by armed intimidators led by local chiefs and councillors. Youth organization activists had also stepped up recruitment as part of a often coercive drive against crime, drunkenness, prostitution and smoking on buses. To date, no breakdown is available to indicate the extent to which victims of the conflict had either Inkatha or UDF affiliations. There is court evidence, though, that links local-level Inkatha leadership to violent attacks. UDF leaders did not appear to have a tight control over their youthful constituency. Over a thousand UDF activists were detained under emergency regulations that left Inkatha people unaffected. UDF organizations, already crippled by emergency measures, were in no position to organize an anti-Inkatha offensive. Local Inkatha leaders were noticeably more reluctant to participate in negotiations. Grassroots activists on either side were blameless, but the balance of available evidence suggests that to the extent to which the car-

---

[18] For a discussion of Indaba proposals, mainly favorable, see *Indaba: A Leadership Publication 1987* (Cape Town: Churchill Murray Publications, 1987). For a critical perspective see Gerhard Mare, "Regional Rule for Inkatha," *Work in Progress* no. 46 (February 1987): 7–12.

[19] Lawrence Schlemmer, in the *Financial Mail*, 6 December 1985, p. 37.

nage was caused by the incitement of leadership, Inkatha bears a major responsibility for it. In the short term, in any case, it is the main beneficiary. Its predominance in Natal's second urban center is now likely. But it is a local victory that has been won through coercion (not to mention police partiality) rather than ideology or the dispensation of patronage. It may have detracted very considerably from Inkatha's overall political standing, especially as the representative of "moderation" and the "middle ground."

THE UNITED DEMOCRATIC FRONT

Buthelezi often claims that Inkatha's membership makes it the largest black organization historically. In fact, the numbers game played out between different black political leaders is a fairly tendentious one. There is no question, though, that in its heyday the massive federation of civic, communal and youth organizations, the UDF, represented nationally the largest political movement ever to have emerged in black South Africa. Its strength depended not so much on sophisticated leadership and coordinated organizational structures, but rather on the vitality of its township-based affiliates. Many of these had been built up in preceding years on the basis of effective campaigns about such matters as housing, rents, bus fares and services. Trade unions had sometimes supplied organizational models.[20] Classroom rebellion and swiftly expanding youth unemployment were both creating a disaffected generation of highly politicized teenagers. The UDF's vigorous early growth also reflected the state's willingness to tolerate mass-based structured opposition as one of the corollaries of its efforts to create institutions of legitimization. Between 1977 and 1983 there blossomed a national culture of political resistance informed by a rediscovery of historical traditions and inspired by the revolutionary theater of Umkhonto we Sizwe's (the armed wing of the African National Congress/ANC) "Armed Propaganda."

When the soldiers moved into the townships in the wake of the Vaal Uprising, the UDF became a movement galvanized by local initiatives—with civic and youth congresses organizing a remarkable series of consumer boycotts to compel municipal administrations and businessmen to negotiate the withdrawal of troops, the release of detained leaders and the redressing of local grievances. A state of emergency between July 1985 and February 1986 did little to check the movement, and in fact helped to promote the spread of street-based committees loyal to civic leadership. The government's failure to contain resistance, the increasing level of violent conflict between the occupation forces in the townships and militarized "comrades," and the succession of local victories won through the consumer boycotts all served to stimulate a euphoric belief in the state's vulnerability and the imminence of national liberation. Motivated mainly by the pragmatic need to restore some form of order to fill the vacuum left by the

[20] Jeremy Seekings and Matthew Chaskalson, "Politics in Tumahole," Association of Sociologists of Southern Africa Conference, Durban, 30 June 1986, paper no. 59, p. 22. See also structure of Alexandra Action Committee, as reported in *Financial Mail*, 16 May 1986.

collapse of township administrations, but inspired also by an almost millennial expectancy, civic and youth movements began to construct an alternative institutional framework of "People's Power."

A second, still continuing state of emergency has brought this phase to a shuddering halt. Much fiercer press restrictions, an unprecedented deployment of soldiers and 25,000 detentions affected even the lowest echelons of leadership, driving the movement off the streets and into semiclandestine status. Support for the revolt continued to be evident in a widespread rent boycott, which persisted in some of the main centers even in early 1988. Whistle-blowing teams of comrades and youth organization activists are still capable in Soweto of marshaling demonstrations of mass support for evicted rent boycotters.[21]

At a local level it is likely that activists continue to function in many centers. The Soweto Youth Congress, for example, possesses a shadow leadership structure of people who do not hold elected office and hence are less vulnerable to state harassment. Many of the shadow leaders are ex-Robben Island prisoners, some of them with experience in clandestine organization.[22] Despite, therefore, the embargo on public meetings, house-to-house searches, extensive patroling by police and soldiers, the removal of key local activists, and the presence of a secret military bureaucracy (the joint-management committees), political organization survives in Soweto. But it is discreet and by necessity conspiratorial. It is no longer possible to openly engage the participation of large numbers of people. In contrast with the movement at its peak, politics has receded to being the activity of committed enthusiasts.

Even before its effective prohibition in 1988, the UDF as a national body had for over a year undertaken very little effective campaigning. In the course of 1987 several efforts had been made to restructure the movement in a more conventional, centralized way. A series of national committees was formed or projected to bring together under a tighter coordinating structure the local networks of youth congresses, civic organizations and women's groups. The UDF adopted as its own program the Freedom Charter, formally giving the movement a tighter ideological coherence. An effort was made to initiate a series of centrally directed campaigns: "United Action Against Apartheid" and the "Unban the ANC" drive, the latter launched through an expensive series of press advertisements, funded by a loan from Barclays Bank. Neither campaign progressed beyond its opening salvo, for since June 1986 it has been virtually impossible to mobilize large numbers of people legally.

But why should the UDF confine itself to what is legally permissible? Historically, strong organizations have led huge programs of civil disobedience against ruthless administrations. The UDF's strength, though, was of a different order. It expressed a popular mood and reflected a political

---

[21] For containing rent boycott activity in Soweto see "Panic in White City," *Weekly Mail*, 19 February 1988.
[22] Khehla Shubane (unpublished honors essay, Department of Political Studies, University of the Witwatersrand, 1987).

culture. Much of its driving force came from below and was semispontaneous in character. The UDF's structure was decentralized—it was ill-suited to the task of coordination. It was also more externally dependent than its leaders cared to admit. When the government cut off the flow of foreign funds in October 1986, it deprived central UDF structures of resources that had maintained professional activists, paid for press publicity, supplied equipment and vehicles, helped the organization produce its own printed propaganda, and so forth. The restrictions on the press reportage of UDF and township politics meant that local centers were deprived of a vital channel of communication. As a national organization the UDF was a thin skein of committees holding together a conglomeration of local political cultures of varying character and effectiveness. It proved much easier to immobilize than its ideologues anticipated.

In retreat, in the course of 1987, the activities of surviving UDF leaders began to emphasize the construction of social alliances in efforts to attract business support in a "Friends of the UDF." Classical united-front ideology began to replace the egalitarian anticapitalism that had welled up from local activist culture in the movement's earlier phase. An obliquely expressed (and never publicly acknowledged) debate began within UDF circles over the merits of the boycott tactic. The possibility that UDF affiliates might have sponsored a Sinn Fein style of participation in the parliamentary or municipal elections may have been one of the considerations influencing the restrictions placed on the organization in March 1988.[23] By then, though, despite the proliferation of formal structures in the course of the previous year, the UDF had lost much of its vitality. In the coerced tranquil space it has vacated, the soldiers and civil servants aspire to deflect popular political aspirations with provision of roads, housing, sewerage and patronage.[24] In communities that have been demoralized and demobilized,[25] the prospects of such a strategy securing a measure of public acquiescence should not be underestimated.

LABOR ORGANIZATIONS

The impact of the emergency has been much less telling on trade unions, with their greater strategic leverage and scope of legal protection, and more systematic organization. In the course of 1987 the focus of popular militancy seemed to shift from township- to work place-based organizations. The year was to witness a record level of industrial action, with 5.5 million days lost to employers in strikes. A growing number of these strikes affected several plants simultaneously, reflecting the increasing coordinating capacity of union organization confronted with large and complex corporate

---

[23] Mark Swilling, "The big what if," *Weekly Mail*, 26 February 1988, p. 4.

[24] Houses in Durban's African townships are being sold off for as little as R1,000 and subsequently being resold on the private market for prices exceeding R20,000.

[25] Two perceptive articles on this are: Nomavenda Mathiane, "The Empire Strikes Back," *Frontline* (February 1988): 18–19; Nomavenda Mathiane, "Quiet Collapse," *Frontline* (January 1988): 19–23.

enterprises. The upswing in labor militancy was partly the effect of the conscious intention of unions; COSATU embarked on a "Campaign for a Living Wage." But this itself was prompted by deteriorating economic conditions. Real wages had recently been sharply eroded by inflation, and this had an especially serious effect on migrant workers whose families had been subjected to the most savage drought in postwar rural history. Migrant workers supplied the cutting edge to the year's strike action.

COSATU survived an intensification of employer hostility, vigilante violence and terrorist attacks on its offices to consolidate its position as the leading labor federation. With its membership increasing at a rate of 500 a day, its affiliates in the course of the year completed (not without contention) the process of mergers that concentrated them to build a national organization for farm workers. Accompanying the organizational rationalization of the movement was an at times clumsy effort to induce ideological conformity—with the adoption by COSATU of the Freedom Charter formulated by the ANC and its allies in the Congress Movement in the 1950s and still the ANC's constitutional model for a liberated South Africa. Public manifestations of the conflict between "workerists" and "populists" appeared to subside apart from the continuing breach between two factions each claiming to represent the shopworkers union. COSATU's leadership is today strongly committed to building a united front with "youth, women, and community organizations," which would formally institutionalize the already close relationship it has with the UDF.[26] The dominant group within COSATU's leadership believes that "the interests of the working class can only be advanced by us locating ourselves in the hub of the struggle for democratisation of society, by building a working class as the foundation of the organs of people's power." A commitment to a united front and the Freedom Charter guarantees, in the view of COSATU leaders, a strong position for workers in a postrevolutionary South Africa. Their opponents' contention that links with non-working-class organizations presage the subordination of the labor movement to a postrevolutionary state bureaucracy seems to have less salience in a period in which the labor movement has become the major player in opposition politics. (See pp. 1031ff.).

In 1988 the government appears determined to curb the power of labor. A proposed industrial relations bill will severely curtail normal collective bargaining procedures, outlaw consumer boycotts, extend the scope of unfair labor practices restrictions, and encourage shop floor rivalry between competing unions. The bill enjoys limited employer support and is part of a package of government measures, including the privatization of services and a public-sector wage freeze that would combine to undercut the bargaining capacity of labor. When its passage through parliament is completed, the main concern of COSATU as well as of the black-conscious aligned Azanian Congress of Trade Unions will be a struggle for their very existence. The 1979 labor legislation, opened the era of state reformist efforts at legislation, which helped to unleash the energies of popular political mobilization. The 1988 bill proposed modifications to that legisla-

[26] Frank Meintjies, interviewed in the *Weekly Mail*, 5 February 1988, p. 11.

tion, which more than any other measure threaten the extent to which black political antipathy represents an organized force.[27] Organized labor, though, representing approximately 40 percent of the industrial labor force, may well represent a much more formidable opponent for the government than the comparatively friable structures assembled in the townships and the schools during the early 1980s.

ROLE OF THE ANC

State suppression of its legal radical opponents will certainly bring to the clandestine structures and exiled bureaucracy of the ANC an enhanced strategic importance. Even today, despite its illegality, the ANC occupies a central position in black South African politics, with a recent opinion poll according to it 35 percent of black urban support—twice that of any other organization or leader, and a slight increase over comparable 1985 polls.[28] The ANC's popularity appears to have endured the transition from the excited expectations of impending freedom, which were at a peak in early 1986, to the widening public perception that the struggle is likely to last a long time yet.

Nevertheless, 1987 was a tough year for the ANC. Militarily, the ANC maintained its level of effectiveness, but only just. Two hundred forty-seven insurgent attacks meant that the ANC only barely exceeded the previous annual total of 229. As in 1986, the major proportion of incidents were limpet mine explosions and grenade attacks followed by exchanges of fire with security forces. On the whole, operations were simple, perhaps indicating a dependence on locally trained insurgents. This, too, may explain the incidence of attacks putting civilian life at risk. Land mine attacks were down from the previous year; in 1986 there was concern within the ANC's political military council over civilian casualties caused by land mines.[29] Two car-bomb explosions, one directed at police emerging from Johannesburg's magistrate's court and the other occurring behind the Witwatersrand and South African Defence Forces (SADF) headquarters (both probably radio detonated), were exceptions to the general pattern of simple actions requiring only the minimum of training and preparation.[30] Bearing in mind the logistical and operational difficulties presented by South African conditions for any form of guerrilla warfare, Umkhonto's effectiveness

[27] On labor generally, see contributions by Alan Fine and Rob Lambert to *South African Review* 4 (1987); Greg Ruiters and David Niddrie, "Curbing Union Power," *Work in Progress* no. 52 (March 1988): 16–19; Alan Fine, "COSATU ends year of maturity," *Business Day*, 27 November 1986; Ernest Sideris, "The arena of strife moves from the township streets to the factory floor," *Weekly Mail*, 24 December 1987, p. 7.
[28] *Weekly Mail*, 16 October 1987, pp. 1–2.
[29] "1987: What is to be done?," document prepared by African National Congress Politico-Military Council and circulated to various regional command centers during October 1986. Copy subsequently released to journalists by State President's Office. Reference to land mine attacks on p. 5.
[30] Statistics: *Weekly Mail*, 4 December 1987, p. 4 and *Indicator SA*, 5, no. 2 (Summer 1988): 21.

is impressive, but it does not represent a threat requiring a major redeployment of South Africa's security forces. Counterinsurgency in South Africa remains primarily a police operation. The guerrillas are supplied and reinforced through ANC machinery in Swaziland and Botswana. The current trial of a senior ANC official, Ismail Ebrahim, kidnapped from Swaziland in December 1986, suggests that the police have had reliable inside intelligence on the Swazi regional command structures since early 1986. Agents were able to assassinate Cassius Make, number four in Umkhonto's hierarchy, and Paul Dikeledi, head of the "Implementation Machinery" for the Transvaal, while both were traveling by car across Swaziland. A succession of arrests of incoming cadres at well-timed roadblocks manned by security police seems to confirm that the police are reasonably well informed about the ANC's regional lines of communication. It was claimed that information from such an arrest prompted the SADF raid on Gaborone, in which security officials asserted that Solomon Molefi, a resident Umkhonto commander, was killed. The claim was contested by the Botswana authorities, but in any case the raid is likely to make it even more difficult for the ANC to maintain even a skeletal organizational presence in Botswana. Within South Africa police boast a 90 percent success rate in capturing the men and women they believe are directly responsible for military operations. The 1987 casualty figures (132 guerrillas arrested and 32 killed[31]) suggest that such claims, though inflated, are based all the same on very serious ANC losses. That the ANC was recently able to respond to the murder of its Paris representative and the attempt on the life of Albie Sachs in Maputo with a succession of limpet mine blasts in the four main towns, indicates that despite losses and difficulties it has managed to create durable command structures inside the country. Trials indicate that the 1984–86 period was one of very considerable advance for the ANC in the construction of township-based military and nonmilitary organization.[32] The ANC's January 1988 National Executive statement maintained that much of this organization had remained intact despite heavy military presence in the townships.

Diplomatically, the successes of 1986 and early 1987 in winning public recognition in Western countries seem overshadowed by recent developments. South Africa is only intermittently on American TV screens, and partial sanctions have failed to deliver significant change. (The ANC has said all along such sanctions would fail to accomplish this; their advocacy of sanctions is based on a perception that they weaken the government, not induce it toward reform.) ANC anger at British unwillingness to apply sanctions led to a clash between their representative at the Vancouver Commonwealth Conference and Prime Minister Thatcher. It was an uncharacteristic lapse in the quality of ANC diplomacy. In general, the extent to which South Africa has been perceived to be in a situation of crisis has receded, and this has helped to diminish the ANC's diplomatic leverage.

[31] *Ibid.*
[32] This is especially evident from the evidence in a trial currently proceeding: *State* v. *Sithembiso Ngobese and Thembinkosi Ngobese*, in Durban Magistrate's Court.

ANC strategists are divided between those who favor a classical protracted guerrilla insurgency culminating in an insurrectionary seizure of power, and advocates of a negotiated transfer of authority in which substantial concessions to white apprehensions may be necessary. Partisans of negotiation view guerrilla warfare as an essential source of pressure, whereas insurrectionists view "all-out war" as the means toward an unconditional seizure of power.[33] At the moment, the former view appears to predominate within the leadership. In 1987 the ANC stated that it would include a bill of individual rights in a postapartheid constitution, which would also provide for multiparty democracy.[34] Both ANC and South African Communist party theorists argue that the transition to socialism from national liberation may well be gradual and gentle.[35] This view is shared by Soviet Africanists, who worry that accentuated violence in the region could generate costly superpower tension. They suggest that the quest for a negotiated settlement might in future include a common approach between the Soviet Union and the United States.[36] ANC leaders have simplified their stance on negotiations in a document issued in October 1987, and they also consented to a meeting with an Inkatha representative in New York. At an international conference hosted by the ANC in Arusha, Tanzania, however, Johnny Makatini reiterated traditional ANC bellicosity toward the Pan-Africanist Congress (PAC), their main rival on the left. The Arusha proceedings, according to journalists who attended, did not indicate any exciting new directions in ANC thinking. Clearly, there are disagreements within the ANC over its future strategic direction. The 1988 NEC statement announced that the year would be one of "United Action for People's Power," but was unusually imprecise as to what this would require tactically. Notwithstanding a resolution at its 1985 consultative conference, the ANC has yet to produce an authoritative revision of its strategic and tactical principles. The conditions favoring popular insurrection, which influenced the ANC's strategic thinking between 1984 and 1987, have certainly altered significantly, yet there has been no public recognition of this.

THE PAC

The ANC's competitor, the PAC, claims that in the course of 1986 and 1987 it succeeded in ending the ANC's effective monopolization of armed struggle,[37] but to date the courts have produced no corroboration of such

[33] For an expression of this latter view see Cassius Mandla, "Let Us Move to All Out War," *Sechaba* (November 1986): 24–28.
[34] *Statement of the National Executive Committee of the African National Congress on the Question of Negotiations*, Lusaka, 9 October 1987.
[35] "A conversation with Oliver Tambo," *The Cape Times*, 4 November 1985; "Communist blue print for South Africa," *Guardian Weekly*, 17 August 1986.
[36] Useful summaries on the thinking of Victor Goncharov and Gleb Starushenko appear in *Frontfile: Southern African Brief*, 3 July 1987, July 1987 and August 1987.
[37] For claims see *The Sowetan*, 29 September 1986; *The Star*, 28 February 1987; *The Star*, 18 August 1987.

claims. Several PAC trials, though, are in progress, and it does appear that there has been a revival within the country of active affiliation with the PAC's cause. This is especially the case in the Western Cape, historically a center of PAC strength. Police believe that a link exists between an Islamic fundamentalist organization, Qibla, and the PAC. An Islamic community was established in Cape Town's African townships in the early 1960s, with a few PAC veterans making up the initial group of converts.[38] Abroad, the PAC keeps its most seasoned foreign representative, Gora Ebrahim, in an office in Teheran. More generally the PAC exiles have been experiencing a modest revival in their fortunes, with an unprecedented invitation to send a delegation to Moscow. The visitors will be led by Philip Kgosana, who was reabsorbed into the PAC's Central Committee after a 25-year-long expulsion. Kgosana's return to the PAC is impressive testimony to the current determination within its hierarchy to heal old breaches. Despite possessing an Ethiopian military diploma,[39] Kgosana has no relevant experience of insurgent warfare or clandestine organization. This itself suggests that as a military contender the PAC is likely to remain on the sidelines. For the time being its main priority will be to oppose any international move to grant to the ANC "sole representative" status.

CONCLUSION

The prospects for democratization of South African politics in the near future remain bleak. The government is preoccupied with the requirements of retaining the support of its own electoral constituency. The shift to the Right in white politics and the enhanced influence of the army, resulting from its role in suppressing the township revolt of 1984–86, combine to produce a government preference for majority rule through coercion rather than legitimization. Since 1986 there has been a steady erosion of the legal space previously kept open for the mobilization of black opposition. With the exception of trade unions, legal popular movements have only barely survived the repression of the present state of emergency. Insurgent warfare, while important in sustaining the ANC's domestic following and international stature, has a long distance to go before it can constitute a major threat to the security of the white minority and its rulers. South Africa is low on the list of foreign policy priorities of both superpowers. The chances of a decisive increase in external pressure on Pretoria remain faint. Apartheid, in one form or another, may well last into the 21st century.

[38] The community was built up through the efforts of Imam Abdullah Haroun who died in detention in 1970. For the PAC/Qibla trial see *Work in Progress* no. 47 (April 1987): 15–18.

[39] For biographical details on Kgosana see Joseph Leyleveld, *Move Your Shadow* (London: Abacus, 1987), 317–47; Tom Lodge, *Black Politics in South Africa since 1945* (London: Longman, 1983), chap. 9. See also Philip Ata Kgosana, *Lest We Forget*, Johannesburg: Skotaville, 1988.

SOUTH AFRICA'S WAR
ON ITS NEIGHBORS

JOSEPH HANLON

SOUTH Africa's regime, based on the apartheid system, is waging a full-scale war against its black-majority ruled neighbors. In the eight years from 1980 to 1987, that war has cost at least 940,000 lives and nearly U.S. $35 billion—vastly more than the cost of the growing war inside South Africa itself.[1] This is not accidental. It is part of Pretoria's long-term strategy to use the neighboring states as a buffer against the southward tide of majority rule.[2]

In the 1960s Tanzania, Malawi, Zambia, Botswana, Swaziland and Lesotho became independent. But this did not create serious problems for Pretoria, because continued white rule in Angola, Rhodesia and Mozambique ensured a cordon sanitaire. The defeat of fascism in Portugal in 1974, followed by independence in Angola and Mozambique the following year, created the first crisis for South Africa.

Angola had three liberation movements: the Marxist MPLA, which controlled the largest part of the country; UNITA, which had already signed a secret deal with Portugal; and the FNLA. A joint government was to take office on November 11, 1975, but with U.S. support and encouragement South Africa invaded Angola to install a UNITA-FNLA government. By the end of October South African artillery was 12 miles/20 km. from the capital, Luanda. On November 7, Cuban troops arrived and pushed the South Africans back. Two more South African armored columns invaded in November. In the early part of 1976 the U.S. Congress passed the Clark amendment, banning further U.S. military involvement in Angola. Without U.S. help the South Aricans were forced to withdraw, and in their retreat destroyed as much as they could, causing $6.7 billion worth of damage. In the next three years much of the damage was repaired, however, and the MPLA and FNLA were largely defeated.

---

[1] See appendixes 1 and 2.

[2] Substantial documentation and more detail on the issues raised in the first half of this article are contained in Joseph Hanlon, *Beggar Your Neighbours* (London: CIIR; Bloomington: Indiana University Press, 1986).

Mozambique was left largely in peace, allowed to become independent. Without Angola's oil it was less a prize, and with only one liberation movement (Frelimo) there was no chance of installing an alternative government.

The defeat in Angola combined with internal scandals to bring down the South African government of Prime Minister B. J. Vorster. White South Africa turned to the military. The defense minister and architect of the Angola invasion, P. W. Botha, became prime minister in 1978 (and in 1983, state president).

Botha and the military argued that South Africa faced a "total onslaught"—a Communist plot orchestrated in Moscow and aimed at overthrowing white rule. Botha argued that the total onslaught "includes instigating social and labor unrest, civilian resistance, terrorist attacks against the infrastructure of South Africa, and the intimidation of black leaders and members of the security forces. This onslaught is supported by a worldwide propaganda campaign and the involvement of various front organizations, such as trade unions and even certain church organizations and leaders." It was even alleged that the KGB was behind the disinvestment campaign.

The response to the "total onslaught" was the "total strategy." All aspects of society, including the private sector, diplomacy, commerce, industry and research were to be coordinated by the military under a new "national security management system." The onslaught was seen as being routed through the neighboring states, particularly Mozambique and Angola; control of them became a high priority.

Pretoria's last white-ruled ally was Rhodesia, and it soon became clear that majority rule was inevitable there, too. South Africa had substantial leverage, both because of the international sanctions imposed against Rhodesia and because of its military support of the minority regime of Ian Smith. Surprisingly, South Africa turned against its white allies, however, and pushed Smith to accept majority rule in an effort to defend continued minority rule in South Africa itself.

Rhodesia was geographically central, and also the most industrialized country outside South Africa. Pretoria concluded that it could co-opt a majority-ruled Rhodesia. It proposed a Constellation of Southern African States (Consas), dominated by itself but including at least some of its majority-ruled neighbors. And although it gave financial and political backing to Bishop Abel Muzorewa's campaign for prime minister, in the 1980 elections Muzorewa was overwhelmingly defeated by ZANU and Robert Mugabe.

Rhodesia came to independence as Zimbabwe, and immediately helped to form a new organization, the Southern African Development Coordination Conference (SADCC). All nine majority-ruled states joined SADCC. These included the six frontline states, which had already expressed clear political opposition to apartheid: Angola, Botswana, Mozambique, Tanzania, Zambia and Zimbabwe. But it also included Lesotho, Malawi and Swaziland, which were not part of the frontline states and which South Africa had thought were its allies. Consas was stillborn.

DEVELOPMENT COOPERATION

SADCC is a unique organization, both in outlook and in structure. Its goals are "to liberate our economies from their dependence on the Republic of South Africa, to overcome the imposed economic fragmentation, and to coordinate our efforts toward regional and national economic development."[3]

SADCC recognized that

> southern Africa is dependent on the Republic of South Africa as a focus of transport and communications, an exporter of goods and services, and as an importer of goods and cheap labor. This dependence is not a natural phenomenon nor is it simply the result of a free market economy. The nine states . . . were, in varying degrees, deliberately incorporated—by metropolitan powers, colonial rulers, and large corporations—into the colonial and sub-colonial structures centering on the Republic of South Africa. The development of national economies as balanced units, let alone the welfare of the people of southern Africa, played no part in the economic integration strategy. Not surprisingly, therefore, southern Africa is fragmented, grossly exploited, and subject to economic manipulation by outsiders.

Recognizing the failure of the highly centralized East African Community and the difficulties of the European Community (EC),[4] SADCC opted for a decentralized structure. Its headquarters in Gaborone, Botswana, has a staff of only 12, and it hands down no rulings or policy statements. Instead, each member is responsible for a particular development area: Mozambique for transport, Angola for energy, Swaziland for manpower, Zimbabwe for agriculture, Tanzania for industry, etc. Decisions are made on the basis of mutual self-interest, and members are encouraged to organize two-way and three-way negotiations of specific developments—for example, about a rail link, a river basin, an industrial development. Thus, instead of trying to negotiate a region-wide electricity grid, SADCC stresses the interlinking of existing grids by small cross-border connections; in practice this has led to more rapid progress than trying to negotiate an entire network.

SADCC put forward a program of $6 billion in projects, and by 1987 had raised about 40 percent of this money. Members agreed to negotiate as a bloc with international donors, such as the EC, for regional projects. This would prevent donors from playing one member off against another.

Transport and communications were seen as key. In part because of the sanctions imposed on Rhodesia, and in part because of military action and long-term deterioration of infrastructure, much of the cargo from the inland states passed through South Africa. Yet the SADCC ports of Lobito (Angola), Dar es Salaam (Tanzania), Maputo, Beira and Nacala (all Moz-

---

[3] Southern Africa: Toward Economic Liberation. A Declaration by the Governments of Independent States of Southern Africa Made at Lusaka on the 1st April 1980.

[4] Another important difference is that SADCC is specifically not a "common market" or "free-trade area." In general this leads to industry concentrating in the most developed country—Kenya in the case of the East African Community. In order to prevent this SADCC is based on a policy of balanced trade. This involves some degree of planning and cooperation, and it is hoped that it will lead to a more balanced regional development.

ambique) were closer and cheaper. So SADCC set rehabilitation of existing ports and railways as its top priority. Its effort was successful. By 1982 the six inland states were sending half their cargo through SADCC ports and only half through South Africa.

South Africa saw SADCC as a direct economic threat. Although South African mineral exports go to the developed world, the SADCC states are the main market for South African manufactured exports. These are not competitive on world markets, but can be sold in the SADCC states because of special trading arrangements (such as the customs union with Botswana, Lesotho and Swaziland) and because trade routes pass through South Africa. In 1982 South Africa made a net profit of $1.5 billion on trade with SADCC states—after taking account of customs union payments and wages of migrant miners. Thus the success of SADCC would have profound economic effects.

The real danger, however, was that South Africa would lose the leverage that it gained though economic dominance over its neighbors. At one time or another during the early 1980s it imposed temporary economic sanctions on seven of the nine SADCC states (Angola and Tanzania do not trade with South Africa). These sanctions mainly involved border closures and disruption of rail transport, particularly of fuel, and were usually linked to political demands. If the SADCC states succeeded in reducing dependence on South Africa then Pretoria would lose this power.

ON THE OFFENSIVE

The independence of Zimbabwe, together with the founding of SADCC and the collapse of P. W. Botha's plans for Consas were undoubtedly the biggest regional changes of the period. But the new prime minister faced three other events that changed the regional equation.

First, the fall of the shah of Iran meant that South Africa nearly ran out of oil in early 1980. For the first time, sanctions were seen to be dangerously effective. Second, after being relatively quiet for more than a decade, the African National Congress (ANC) suddenly came alive in the late 1970s. And on June 1, 1980, in an audacious four-part raid, the ANC hit several of South Africa's most tightly guarded oil installations—two Sasol oil-from-coal plants and a refinery.

White rule truly seemed under threat just as the white cordon sanitaire had collapsed. P. W. Botha concluded that if he could not maintain economic and political dominance in the region, then military dominance was essential, and he moved onto the offensive. The third and final change to the regional equation was the election of Ronald Reagan as president of the United States in 1980, which gave Pretoria license to attack.

Earlier attacks had been mounted in 1979, soon after Botha took power. These included a major air raid into southern Angola and a series of bombings in Maseru, the capital of Lesotho. It was not until late 1980, however, that South Africa really began to wage war on its neighbors. During 1981 it attacked seven of the SADCC states. There was a full-scale invasion of southern Angola, and South African troops have not left since. On November 30, 1981 commandos attacked the oil refinery in the capital, Luanda. South African commandos also made several raids into Zimbabwe. An army ammunitions dump was blown up and on December 18, 1981 South African saboteurs blew up the central Harare headquarters of ZANU-PF, just when a meeting of the central committee was scheduled. It was a clear attempt to assassinate Robert Mugabe and the ZANU leadership. In fact, the meeting had been delayed and Mugabe and the central committee escaped, but seven customers in a neighboring bakery were killed and 124 Christmas shoppers on the street below were injured. In Mozambique South African commandos came over the border and hit the capital, Maputo, killing 13 ANC members in raids on three houses; near Beira, commandos blew up two key bridges on the road and railway linking the port to Zimbabwe. In Lesotho there were more bombings in the capital and elsewhere. One government minister was assassinated, and a sophisticated car bomb nearly killed the prime minister, Chief Leabua Jonathan. In Zambia South African troops occupied the southwestern corner of the country. In Swaziland the South African security services kidnapped and killed several South African refugees. In Botswana there was a series of border incidents and incursions. And on November 25, 1981 South Africa failed in an attempt to overthrow the government of the Seychelles (not a member of SADCC and not otherwise a subject of this article).

In the years that followed South Africa kept up the pressure with an almost permanent occupation of southern Angola and frequent raids into neighboring capitals. For example, 42 people were killed in Maseru on December 9, 1982, and 12 were killed in Gaborone on June 14, 1985. The South African Air Force strafed Maputo on May 23, 1983 in what was officially called "Operation Skerwe"—the Afrikaans word for shrapnel. Six people were killed by special fragmentation rockets.

There were also raids on industrial targets, especially railways and ports, oil facilities and major factories. Mozambique, Angola, Lesotho and, to a lesser extent, Zimbabwe and Zambia were hit. Malawi, Zimbabwe, Zambia and Swaziland were also affected by the raids on fuel and transport installations in Angola and Mozambique.

Attacks on neighboring heads of state continued. In January 1986 South Africa provoked the overthrow of Prime Minister Jonathan of Lesotho. There is widespread belief that the South Africans also had a hand in the death of the Mozambican president, Samora Machel. They are alleged to have used a decoy navigation beacon to draw the presidential aircraft off course so that it crashed into a mountain in South Africa. There was strong evidence of such a beacon being deployed, but the subsequent inquiry by South Africa concentrated on the errors committed by the aircraft's crew.

ECONOMIC PRESSURE

While stepping up military pressure South Africa also imposed various types of economic sanctions. The most dramatic was the total closure of the border with Lesotho in January 1986; since Lesotho is completely surrounded by South Africa, this had a traumatic effect. The blockade was lifted only when the Lesotho army—always more sympathetic to South Africa—overthrew the staunchly anti-apartheid Prime Minister Jonathan.

Another major action was an embargo on rail traffic to and from Zimbabwe in mid-1981, which cost Zimbabwe more than $100 million in lost exports and agricultural production.

Mozambique was the only state in the region to have a balance-of-payments surplus with South Africa. Maputo was a major port for South African goods, and at one point Mozambique had over 100,000 miners working in South Africa. Both factors earned Mozambique significant income, while the country bought little from South Africa because it was not part of Pretoria's captive market. After independence, however, and especially after 1980, South Africa imposed sanctions on Mozambique. It forced the mines to cut back on the number of Mozambicans employed (despite objections by the mine owners) and prevented shippers from using Maputo, forcing them to send their goods through more expensive South African ports. By 1987 these sanctions were costing Mozambique more than $100 million per year.

Shorter blockades and border closures were sporadically imposed against Swaziland, Botswana and Zambia, as well as Mozambique, Zimbabwe and Lesotho. Sometimes these were linked to military actions. For example, South African commandos blew up the oil storage facilities in Beira on December 9, 1982. This fuel was largely for Zimbabwe and Malawi, and the raid also cut the oil pipeline from Beira to Zimbabwe. At the same time South Africa attacked the railway from Maputo to Zimbabwe, making it difficult to import fuel that way. And it imposed an embargo on Zimbabwe, banning any fuel imports via South Africa. Inevitably, all sectors in Zimbabwe virtually ground to a halt for two weeks, until the pipeline was reconnected at Beira.

PUPPET ARMIES

Pretoria's most important and successful tactic, however, has been the creation and support of surrogate armies. The model is UNITA, where South Africa was able—with U.S. support—to take over a former liberation movement.

In 1976 Rhodesian security had created the Mozambique National Resistance (MNR, or Renamo) as a fifth column inside Mozambique. It was initially composed of people who had fought with the Portuguese against Frelimo, some of who had committed such serious atrocities that they were afraid to return to Mozambique after independence. With independence in Zimbabwe, the MNR was supposed to be disbanded, and it was defeated inside Mozambique. But South African military intelligence (MI) moved the remnants of the MNR to South Africa, set up new training camps in the northern Transvaal and created an effective fighting force.

Starting from scratch, MI created the Lesotho Liberation Army, which made repeated raids into Lesotho—although almost always within sight of the South African border. Dissident groups were also trained and sent into Zambia and Zimbabwe. There were reports that opposition groups were

753

also being created for Tanzania and Botswana, although by 1987 there was still no evidence of their having been used.

In general, training, command and control of these groups is in South African hands. Thousands of people have been trained inside South Africa, closely linked to the South African Reconnaissance (Recce) Commandos, the group that makes raids into the neighboring states. South African commandos and MI agents also go into neighboring states to provide further support and training. Pretoria also provides arms and other supplies, often making air and sea drops.

The actual foot soldiers are mainly peasants from the countries being attacked. Some had already fought against the government, such as members of the Muzorewa "auxiliaries" in Rhodesia, and of UNITA and FNLA in Angola. Others are criminals released in raids on prisons. Many are illegal migrants who went to South Africa looking for work; their "jobs" often turned out to be serving in the puppet armies. Some soldiers are recruited by South African spies, often with promises of high salaries. Many are simply shanghaied. In Mozambique, for example, the MNR sometimes raids rural schools and kidnaps the entire student body; some escape, some are shot trying to escape and some stay with the MNR. The result is ragtag puppet armies; enough men like the power and excitement, however, to provide a regular supply of local commanders. A few genuine dissidents also join in.

Normally, guerrillas serve only in their own countries. But several better-trained men have been captured who admitted they moved about between puppet armies, and also served with MI and the Recce Commandos.

In the mid-1980s Pretoria began to apply the same tactics at home. They created vigilante groups in the townships, squatter camps and homelands to oppose and attack anti-apartheid activists.[5]

SPREADING CHAOS

It is the puppet armies that have caused the bulk of the destruction in the region. They follow a scorched earth policy, destroying villages and factories, maiming and killing innocent people. Roads and railways are particular targets, because South Africa wants to disrupt both internal and international trade. Attacks on roads, disrupting local traffic, make people afraid to travel; this in turn disrupts agricultural marketing and other commerce, blocking the flow of food for the cities and agricultural exports, as well as cutting off consumer goods and fertilizers destined for the peasants. In both Angola and Mozambique this has had a catastrophic effect on the economy in significant parts of the area.

Activities in each country have been slightly different. In no country but Angola, however, have the puppet armies ever tried to create "liberated zones" with alternative governments, schools, health facilities and so on, as bona fide nationalist guerrilla movements do.

[5]Nicholas Haysom, *Apartheid's Private Armies*, Centre for Applied Legal Studies, University of the Witwatersrand, Occasional Paper no. 10 (Johannesburg, 1986).

In Mozambique the goal seems to have been pure terror and disruption. Economic targets such as factories and shops were destroyed, as well as the social infrastructure like schools and hospitals. By the end of 1985, 196 outlying health posts and health centers had been destroyed, and 288 had been looted and forced to close. This represented one-quarter of the primary health network. More than 1,000 rural shops were burned, blown up or otherwise destroyed. The goal was to bring Mozambique to its knees, but not to install the MNR as an alternative government; Frelimo remained too popular, while the public anger against the MNR for its brutal massacres ensured it could never govern.

In Lesotho, Zimbabwe and Zambia the much smaller puppet groups planted isolated bombs and carried out less extensive raids. The main goal seemed to be to show that the government was not in control, and to try (unsuccessfully) to be a focus for local discontent. In Zambia, South African activity was also linked to support for UNITA in border areas of Angola. In Zimbabwe attacks against government officials and white farmers also seemed designed to cause divisions between white and black, and between the governing ZANU and minority ZAPU parties.

Angola, however, has been different. UNITA had covert support from the U.S. Central Intelligence Agency, and this support became official after the repeal of the Clark amendment in 1985. Some foreign nongovernment organizations also provided medical and economic support. South Africa and the United States appeared to believe it possible to install UNITA as an alternative government. Thus, some attempts were made to create so-called liberated zones.

Throughout the region the puppet guerrilla armies are used as part of South Africa's regional economic strategy—particularly to cut SADCC rail and energy links. Thus, the MNR in Mozambique had by 1985 closed three of the international rail links and sporadically attacked the other three. In Angola, UNITA kept the Benguela Railway closed after 1980; this ensured that the inland countries, particularly Zaire, Zambia, Zimbabwe and Malawi, were forced to send imports and exports via South Africa. This changed somewhat in 1985 when Zimbabwe agreed to take an active military role in Mozambique, particularly defending the railway, road and oil pipeline linking Zimbabwe to the port of Beira. This protection allowed a major SADCC rehabilitation of the port and railway to go ahead. By 1987 Zimbabwe, Zambia and Malawi were all sending significant quantities of goods through Beira, goods which had previously been sent through South Africa.

But the open railways remained under threat, in part because of the way South African commandos use the cover of the puppet guerrilla armies. In Angola, for example, on May 21, 1985, South African Capt. Wynand Petrus du Toit of the Fourth Reconnaissance Commando was captured when he failed to blow up oil storage tanks in Angola. His team carried UNITA propaganda plus a small tin of paint. This, he told a press conference, was so that he could paint "Viva UNITA" in the road. "On most of the operations we usually do," he added, "UNITA claims the responsibility."

STATE TERRORISM

Much of the action of the puppet guerrilla groups may seem mindless and excessive violence: villagers massacred, cars ambushed, people hacked to death. In Mozambique the MNR cuts off ears, noses, and breasts. In fact, however, such actions are not mindless or random at all, but carefully thought out by South Africa. They have three clear purposes: to turn people against the government, to disrupt the economy and to create an international image of black savagery.

In a seminal paper written in 1982,[6] the eminent Afrikaner scholar Deon Geldenhuys suggested that the destabilizers should manipulate food supplies in order to "cause serious hardship to the population, who would in turn direct their frustration and fury at the target's regime."

Pretoria concluded that if it starved Mozambicans they would turn against the Felimo government. In 1983, with South African air support, the MNR invaded a drought-stricken area of southern Mozambique. They burned food stocks and attacked relief vans. More than 100,000 people died—as much victims of destabilization as if they had been shot. In 1986 South Africa tried the same tactic in central Mozambique, but a combined Mozambique-Zimbabwe-Tanzania military effort repelled the invaders. An international relief effort prevented a man-made famine on the level of 1983.

Massacres are also intended to turn people against the government, on the presumption that peasants are unlikely to support a government that cannot protect them.

Some of the terror is quite specific. In rural areas people see health and education as the main gains of independence. When the MNR attacks a village the first thing it does is attack the hospital or health post and burn the school. Health workers are killed or maimed. In one incident in Mozambique the MNR hit an ambulance with a bazooka shell. The ambulance was clearly marked with a red cross and was carrying medicines to a rural area. The accompanying pharmacist was killed instantly but the driver was then bayoneted to death. By killing or mutilating health workers and teachers the South Africans hope to make other teachers and nurses afraid to work in rural areas. The peasants then lose the benefits of a Frelimo government and, Pretoria hopes, see no reason to support Frelimo.

South Africa also wants to disrupt travel. A railroad engineer whose train had been attacked reported that the MNR had kidnapped him but allowed others to flee. His captors said they were instructed by South Africa to kill or capture engineers in order to make other drivers afraid and thus refuse to take trains to Zimbabwe.

Similarly, in road ambushes, some people are killed, often brutally, while others are maimed or even allowed to go free—in order that there be people left to tell the tale. The hope is that people will be so afraid of a painful death or of losing an ear or nose that they will refuse to travel, especially to travel to rural areas, thus disrupting the internal economy.

[6] Deon Geldenhuys, "Destabilisation Controversy in Southern Africa," *Southern African Forum Position Papers* (Johannesburg, 1982) 5, no. 18.

SOUTH AFRICAN OBJECTIVES

In its attacks on neighboring states Pretoria has a variety of overlapping goals. Perhaps the most important is the central international political objective of justifying the necessity of apartheid. This is done by building on racism inside South Africa and in the West, and convincing whites that majority rule means chaos. South Africa thus creates famine in Mozambique, which then is portrayed in the media as the result of black, Marxist misrule. This image is abetted by international charities that want to remain "non-political," and thus portray the famine as a natural, rather than a South African-created, disaster. Similarly, puppet guerrilla armies are pictured as legitimate movements and their actions are simply "black-on-black violence."

Second, South Africa really wants its neighbors to tone down criticism of apartheid. Pretoria apparently feels that if the SADCC states were not leading the international anti-apartheid campaign the West would put less pressure on South Africa.

The third international political goal is to create a buffer against sanctions. This is done in two ways. First, South Africa applies pressure to try to force the neighboring states to make public statements against sanctions; by 1987 only Swaziland, however, had done so. Since Pretoria cannot force its neighbors to oppose sanctions the alternative tactic is indirect. It uses destabilization to ensure that the neighboring states remain economically dependent, particularly on South African ports and railways. Then South Africa and its allies say that sanctions will hurt the neighboring states and thus should not be imposed. Of course the SADCC states vociferously deny this, but South Africa's friends (like Britain) still maintain that such denial is only for public consumption and that "in reality" the SADCC states do not want sanctions.

In fact, in public and in private, the six frontline states strongly support international sanctions against South Africa. But they stress that sanctions must be imposed first by the main trading partners—the United States, Japan and Europe—and only then by SADCC. The lesson of Rhodesian sanctions in the 1970s is that there is little point in the neighbors imposing sanctions, at a significant cost to themselves, if countries like Britain freely break those sanctions.

South Africa also wants to maintain economic dependence for practical reasons. Although SADCC is less important than Europe, it remains a significant market and an important source of foreign exchange. As international sanctions tighten this will become increasingly important. Furthermore, Pretoria hopes to use the neighboring states for sanctions busting. SADCC's goal of breaking away from South Africa is thus a real threat.

Also, economic dependence allows South Africa to impose sanctions on SADCC. The most effective example is Lesotho, where a border closure brought down the government. The greater the economic dependence the more leverage Pretoria retains. Indeed, it might be argued that South Africa has concentrated its military activity in Mozambique and Angola precisely because it has so little economic power in those two states.

Destabilization also has linked political and military goals. There is the obvious need to expel the ANC from the neighboring states and to ensure that the neighbors do not support the uprising inside South Africa. This does not mean simply military assistance but includes moral and political support.

Closely connected with this, however, is the need to convince whites inside South Africa as well as in Europe that the threat comes from outside South Africa, not inside; that the problem is not apartheid and repression inside, but a Communist conspiracy orchestrated in Moscow and Maputo. This means vastly exaggerating the ANC and Red menace in the neighboring states. Thus, South Africa raids targets that have no ANC connection, but says it has hit a terrorist base. For example, on May 23, 1983 the South African Air Force bombed part of Maputo. The author was a journalist there at the time, and arrived on the scene within two hours—while the bodies were still on the ground. The main target was known to be a jam factory, none of the targets were ANC bases, and six people were killed, including a child and a pregnant worker at the factory. Yet South Africa claimed it had hit ANC bases and killed 41 "ANC terrorists." Although this eyewitness account of the story was given prominence at the time, in later years the world media (including the BBC) accepted the South African version. Pretoria therefore need not actually hit the ANC in order to spread a picture of a vast ANC presence in the neighboring states.

Finally, South Africa is simply trying to bring the neighbors to their knees, to ensure that they are more worried about their own problems than about apartheid.

NEGOTIATE OR FIGHT?

During the period 1982–84 there was pressure both internally and internationally, particularly from the United States, for the SADCC states to negotiate with South Africa. In 1982 Swaziland signed a secret nonaggression pact with South Africa. In 1984 Angola signed a limited troop withdrawal agreement, while Mozambique signed the Nkomati nonaggression pact. South Africa violated them all.

The Nkomati accord was always unequal, with Maputo promising to end its limited help for the ANC while Pretoria pledged to end its massive aid for the MNR. In fact, Mozambique halted any help to the ANC, while South Africa *stepped up* its support of the MNR. Previously, supplies for the MNR had been dropped by parachute or were landed on the beach; in 1984, after the Nkomati accord, South Africa actually built a landing strip at the Gorongosa base in central Mozambique. Not only did this allow planeloads of supplies, but the then deputy foreign minister, Louis Nel, actually flew to the base three times during 1984.

It was clear that P. W. Botha could not be trusted, and this ended any attempts to talk with South Africa. Destabilization would only end with the fall of apartheid. Clearly, the SADCC states are no military match for South Africa, and SADCC leaders concluded that the only answer was for the West to put pressure on South Africa. The best form of pressure was comprehensive, mandatory sanctions.

SADCC will undoubtedly pay a price, particularly in the form of stepped-up South African destabilization. But that destabilization had already cost $35 billion by the end of 1987. The cost of sanctions would be relatively small and would be a small investment to bring about the end of the much higher cost of destabilization.

In August 1985 the then president of Tanzania, Julius Nyerere, spoke for all the region's leaders when he said: "Africa also calls for economic sanctions, and we are not stupid either. We know that South Africa's retaliation may well be directed against neighbouring African states. But we also know that our freedom and our economic development will remain under constant threat until apartheid is defeated."

APPENDIX 1: ECONOMIC COST OF DESTABILIZATION

In 1985 SADCC estimated that "South African aggression and destabilisation has cost its neighbours in excess of $10 billion" in the five years 1980–84 (inclusive).[7] This is broken down into categories (in $ million) as follows:

Direct war damage	1,610
Extra defense expenditure	3,060
Higher transport and energy costs	970
Lost exports and tourism	230
Smuggling	190
Refugees	660
Reduced production	800
Lost economic growth	2,000
Boycotts and embargoes	260
Trading arrangements	340
TOTAL	10,120

The only independent estimate is by Reginald Green and Carol Thompson,[8] who concluded that the total cost was $12.9 billion. The main differences are their estimates of lost economic growth as $4 billion and lost exports as $550 million.

Using the same methods as SADCC, UNICEF estimated the costs as $7 billion in 1985 and $8 billion in 1986.[9] A rough extrapolation gives $9.5 billion for 1987. (Note that the compound effects of lost growth become increasingly important as time goes on. This is because factories destroyed or not built in the early 1980s could reasonably be expected to have been generating jobs and profits in the late 1980s, creating wealth that would

[7] Memorandum presented by SADCC to the 1985 summit of the Organization of African Unity, published as Appendix 1 of Hanlon, *Beggar Your Neighbours*.
[8] Reginald Green and Carol Thompson, "Political Economics in Conflict," in *Destructive Engagement*, by P. Johnson and D. Martin (Harare: Zimbabwe Publishing House, 1986).
[9] A. R. Noormahomed and J. Cliff, *The Impact on Health in Mozambique of South African Destabilization* (Maputo: Ministry of Health, 1987).

in turn be invested in more factories.) Thus the best estimate (in $ billion) of the material cost of destabilization is:

Year	$ billion	Source
1980	0.7	SADCC
1981	1.4	SADCC
1982	1.9	SADCC
1983	2.8	SADCC
1984	3.3	SADCC
1985	7.0	UNICEF
1986	8.0	UNICEF
1987	9.5	estimate
TOTAL	34.6	

It is exceedingly hard to establish accurate figures, but these seem to be roughly correct. Indeed, whether the cost is "only" $25 billion or is really more than $50 billion, either figure is certainly very much more than the total development aid to the region during the period—roughly $10 billion.

As SADCC itself admitted in its memo to the Organization of African Unity:

> SADCC's figures can only be estimates at best—the organisation does not keep a score card of destruction. But in making its estimates, SADCC has erred on the side of caution, listing only those things which can be sensibly quantified. . . . And SADCC has only costed bricks and mortar, steel and machinery. There is no price for blood, no cost that can be assigned to the thousands who have died as a result of actions instigated and supported by apartheid.

APPENDIX 2: THE HUMAN COST OF DESTABILIZATION

Since South Africa's war against its neighbors is a hidden war, it is hard to quantify loss of life. In part this is because starvation and infant mortality are the main causes of death that result from the war.

It is widely accepted that at least 100,000 people died in a famine in Mozambique in 1983–84, which, as argued above, was directly caused— as a matter of policy and strategy—by the actions of South Africa and the MNR. More thousands died in a similar war-created famine in 1986–87. The Mozambique government[10] estimates that at least 100,000 people have actually been killed by military actions up to 1986, meaning that at least 120,000 were killed by the end of 1987. In Angola perhaps 75,000 have been killed by UNITA and South African raids, and by war-induced famine.

The 1987 UNICEF study[11] looked at the impact of the destruction of health services, which have become a priority target for South Africa. In

[10] Reginald Green et al., "Children in Southern Africa," in Children on the Front Line (New York: UNICEF, 1987).
[11] Ibid.

both Angola and Mozambique rapid improvements in health services after independence brought a steady decline in child (under the age of five) mortality during 1975–80. But the destruction of health services, and especially the attacks on vaccination teams, reversed this. For the period 1981–86 UNICEF produced estimates for unnecessary child death caused by the war. This seems to have stabilized (in part because health facilities are now being rebuilt about as rapidly as they are destroyed), so it can be assumed that the 1987 figure is probably the same as the 1986 UNICEF figure. This gives a total (in thousands) of:

	Angola	Mozambique
1981	10	15
1982	20	30
1983	31	46
1984	42	63
1985	55	82
1986	56	84
1987 (est.)	56	84
TOTAL	270	404

Although not killed by bullets or machetes, these 674,000 children are still war victims.

The total war toll is at least (in thousands):

Mozambique war	120
Mozambique famine	125
Angola war and famine	75
Mozambican children	404
Angolan children	215
TOTAL	939

FURTHER READING

Commonwealth Eminent Persons Group on Southern Africa. *Mission to South Africa*. Harmondsworth: Penguin, 1986.

Hanlon Joseph. *Apartheid's Second Front: South Africa's War Against its Neighbours*. Harmondsworth and New York: Penguin, 1986.

———. *Beggar Your Neighbours: Apartheid Power in Southern Africa*. London: Catholic Institute for International Relations; Bloomington: Indiana University Press.

Johnson, Phyllis, and Martin David, eds. *Destructive Engagement: Southern Africa at War*. Harare: Zimbabwe Publishing House, 1986.

South African Review. Johannesburg: Ravan Press. Annual.

AFRICA AND THE COMMONWEALTH

DEREK INGRAM

THE involvement of the Commonwealth in Africa in recent years has shown it to be an increasingly important international forum for concerted action with potential to achieve really important results, particularly in the problems of southern Africa.

Fourteen, or nearly one-third, of the Commonwealth's 48 countries are African—including the largest, Nigeria—and some of them are the most politically influential on the continent. In recent years the Commonwealth has, despite differences over Britain's stubborn resistence to a comprehensive sanctions program, proved to be the one international body that has practical, coherent policies aimed at the emergence of a nonracial democratic government in South Africa.

The commitment has been clearly spelled out in Commonwealth summit communiqués—most explicitly after the 1983 meeting in New Delhi. It was unequivocal: "Heads of Government were of the view that only the eradication of apartheid and the establishment of majority rule on the basis of free and fair exercise of universal adult suffrage by all the people in a united and non-fragmented South Africa can lead to a just and lasting solution of the explosive situation prevailing in Southern Africa."

It was crucial that Britain, as the developed country most deeply implicated economically and historically, should be firmly tied in to that commitment. However, at the Heads of Government Meeting in Nassau, Bahamas, 1985 (October 16–22) Britain came into head-on collision with the rest of the Commonwealth over the issue of sanctions against South Africa.

EMINENT PERSONS GROUP—INITIATIVE ON SOUTH AFRICA

As a compromise, the leaders agreed to send an Eminent Persons Group (EPG)—that is, a number of leading figures from Commonwealth countries—to South Africa to find out whether a dialogue could be brought about between the parties there: the South African government, the African nationalist movements, and the white and Coloured communities. Seven people were chosen, led by former Australian Prime Minister Malcolm Fraser and former Nigerian head of state Gen. Olusegun Obasanjo. Their Mission to South Africa (as it became known from the title of their report) was an historic event and made a greater international impact than anyone had thought possible when it was set up. The EPG made extensive tours of South Africa, obtained access to all the leading political figures in the country—including three calls on the long-imprisoned African National Congress (ANC) leader Nelson Mandela—and seemed at one stage to be moving toward a formula for the start of a dialogue between blacks and whites.

Skepticism among the African nationalists within South Africa about the Commonwealth role dissipated as the EPG went about its work. Reluctance at the outset to cooperate was quickly dropped, and leading members of the ANC and the United Democratic Front were impressed by the team's evenhandedness.

On May 19, 1986 the group's apparent progress was sabotaged when South African forces raided Zimbabwe, Zambia and Botswana even as it was still in South Africa and talking to ministers in the government of President P. W. Botha. The EPG immediately left the country and called off its mission.

Its report a few weeks later, however, received a warm reception and may yet prove to be an important document in the long history of the fight for majority rule in South Africa. It sets down a framework within which a beginning might be made to resolve the situation; when the search for a political formula resumes, the EPG proposals could well be picked up.

In essence, the report provides for the release of political prisoners; the unbanning of political parties, such as the ANC; the resumption of normal free political activity; and the suspension (though not, in the first instance, the cessation) of violence.

The group came to the conclusion that the South African government had no genuine intention to dismantle apartheid and that it was not really seriously interested in bringing about a successful dialogue between all the parties. It commented: "Is the Commonwealth to stand by and allow a cycle of violence to spiral? Or will it take concerted action of an effective kind? Such action may offer the last opportunity to avert what could be the worst bloodbath since the Second World War."

The call for tougher action did not find much favor with the British government, and a few months later a Commonwealth summit of seven leaders in London ended without a consensus—an event unprecedented in Commonwealth summit history. The British prime minister, Margaret Thatcher, stood firmly against substantial further sanctions, preferring still to try for dialogue; and it was made clear that the other Commonwealth countries would take tougher measures, regardless of what Britain might do.

A year later, at the full Commonwealth summit in Vancouver, the British position remained unchanged, but now the Commonwealth went a step further by creating a standing committee of eight foreign ministers who would meet at frequent intervals and keep up the Commonwealth momentum. Britain refused to join the committee, which was chaired by Canada and consisted of Australia, Guyana, India, Nigeria, Tanzania, Zambia and Zimbabwe.

At their first meeting in Lusaka, (Zambia, February 1–2, 1988), the eight ministers set about devising ways in which fiscal pressures could be put on South Africa, on the basis that the republic was most vulnerable in the area of foreign-exchange shortage, debt repayment and loans. The committee also decided to do everything possible to counter the increasingly effective censorship that was preventing the facts of the South African situation from reaching the outside world.

It set about preparing studies of South Africa's relationship with the international financial system, and called on banks to press for early payment of debts and not to take part in rescheduling exercises. It aimed, too, to expose and press for closure of breaches in the mandatory arms embargo.

In Vancouver, Britain's prime minister had irritated African countries by taking her case against sanctions a stage further than she had done in Nassau. She now argued that South Africa could be forced to change its ways not by harming the economy but by building it up. A prosperous South Africa was more likely to demolish apartheid than a besieged one. As a balance to this policy, which no other member of the Commonwealth accepted, Britain strongly supported Commonwealth programs to bolster the economies of the front-line states and to make these countries secure against South African efforts to destabilize them.

Britain also continued to support the EPG proposals for a negotiation between the parties in South Africa, and the Commonwealth emerged from Vancouver as the only international organization with an active program for pressure and political dialogue aimed at breaking the deadlock. To African countries, the Commonwealth seemed to hold out the best chance of achieving an eventual breakthrough.

FROM RHODESIA TO ZIMBABWE

As an example of the political importance of the Commonwealth to African countries, they pointed to what it had achieved in Zimbabwe. When in 1965 Ian Smith made his Unilateral Declaration of Independence in what was then Southern Rhodesia, Britain was pressed to take over the country by force. Instead, it agreed to limited and then full sanctions. There followed years of stress within the Commonwealth, with frequent threats by member countries, most notably Ghana, Tanzania and Zambia, to withdraw.

As the 1960s ended, Britain, by its weak stance on Rhodesia, had dissipated much of the goodwill generated in Africa as a result of the comparative ease with which it had acceded to nationalist demands for independence and handed over power. African countries began to see the Commonwealth as a valuable forum in which to put pressure on Britain to secure majority rule in Rhodesia. For several years the Commonwealth, and in particular the African membership, prevented Britain from selling out to the white minority there.

In the end, the Commonwealth was the political instrument that brought about the independent state of Zimbabwe after a 15-year struggle. The 1979 Heads of Government Meeting in Lusaka produced the formula for the Lancaster House talks, which in turn produced a program for a cease-fire, elections and independence.

The Commonwealth provided the monitoring force that supervised the end of hostilities, and a Commonwealth Observer Group drawn from 11 countries pronounced on the fairness of the elections. It was the Commonwealth's greatest political triumph, and it created a fund of goodwill toward the Commonwealth in Africa that remains to this day and will help to underpin it for the solution of the much larger problem of South Africa.

THE LOST MEMBER

South Africa withdrew from membership in the Commonwealth on May 31, 1961. Its departure rendered the Commonwealth an acceptable international institution in African nationalist eyes and established a framework for today's Commonwealth. If South Africa had remained a member it is unlikely that Ghana, then ruled by Dr. Kwame Nkrumah, would have stayed or that any of the other 12 African countries would have continued as members as they became independent in the decade that followed. Nor were other major Third World countries, most notably India, likely to have stayed in the Commonwealth. In this sense Africa can be said to have made the modern Commonwealth.

Looking well ahead into the future, the reality is that the South African problem is bound to be a dominant focus of attention in the Commonwealth for many years to come. The historic connection, the deep economic and political involvement of Britain and South Africa's Commonwealth neighbors, and the traditional commitments to racial equality that countries like India see as a main plank of their foreign policy, make that inevitable—not just in a negative sense but also in terms of the potential usefulness of the Commonwealth in international attempts to reach a South African solution or, in a worst-case scenario, rescuing the inhabitants from large-scale violence.

As with Rhodesia, the British connection with South Africa is a source of grave embarrassment to the Commonwealth; and in some ways the strains put on the association represent, on a larger scale, a repetition of what has gone before. In Nassau in 1985 Thatcher found herself in a situation not dissimilar from the one that confronted her Labour predecessor Harold Wilson in 1966 and later. Thatcher showed a harder face than Wilson in resisting substantive sanctions.

In the meantime the Commonwealth has been in the forefront in trying to combat apartheid and in helping South African refugees, particularly in the field of education. In 1984, for example, the Commonwealth set up the South African Extension Unit in Dar es Salaam to start correspondence courses in English, mathematics and agriculture for exiled South African students. At first the course was offered to 1,000 students in refugee settlements in Tanzania, but now the scheme is being extended to exiles in other African countries.

One of the most effective measures to be taken against South Africa has been the reduction of sports contacts. In 1977, Commonwealth leaders drew up the Gleneagles Agreement, under which governments undertook to do all they could to dissuade athletes from engaging in sports with South Africa. Although there have been substantial breaches, usually by players acting as individuals, the boycott has had a broad impact, perhaps as much by the way it has kept the South African problem and the apartheid system in international focus as by its forcing some changes toward multiracialism in sports in South Africa itself.

The South African situation and the Gleneagles Agreement have, however, greatly strained the Commonwealth's most successful activities, the Commonwealth Games. Boycotts by one or more countries have been a feature of several games, but in 1986 a wholesale boycott led by Nigeria, in protest against Thatcher's resistance to sanctions, decimated the games in Edinburgh and also seriously affected the Commonwealth Arts Festival being held simultaneously.

NAMIBIA STALEMATE

South Africa has now been outside the Commonwealth for a quarter of a century; but Oliver Tambo, president of the ANC, has pointed out that the majority of the population of South Africa were never asked whether they wanted their country to leave the Commonwealth, and so far as the blacks are concerned they still consider themselves members. It is most likely that when at last apartheid disappears and South Africa becomes a fully democratic state it will return to membership.

Furthermore, Namibia, which remains illegally occupied by South Africa, will also have the option of Commonwealth membership when it secures its independence. The offer was put on the table by Commonwealth leaders at their summit in Jamaica in 1973, and the main nationalist party, the South West Africa People's Organization, has indicated that it would want Namibia to join. This would set something of a precedent, since Namibia was never part of the British Empire.

As a result of the 1975 summit, the Commonwealth set up a special program to help Namibian refugees continue their education in Commonwealth countries. The object was to provide a pool of trained manpower for Namibia's development after independence. The work has been funded by the Commonwealth Fund for Technical Cooperation (CFTC) jointly with the United Nations and the Swedish International Development Authority.

Namibian refugees drawn from Zambia and Angola have also benefited from a Commonwealth program of correspondence courses, and the Commonwealth Secretariat has embarked on an English language program for Namibians, since it is anticipated that English will be the official language of an independent Namibia.

Similar help in a wide range of fields was successfully given to Zimbabwean refugees before independence; large numbers of men and women in senior government and other posts in Zimbabwe today are the products of training that took place in many Commonwealth countries, including Australia, Britain, Canada, India, Jamaica, Malta, New Zealand and Nigeria. On the political front, the Commonwealth has taken no independent initiative on Namibia, but instead supports the U.N. plan for independence as set out in Resolution 435, which involves a large U.N. military presence. It has always rejected the linking of Namibia's freedom to the withdrawal of Cuban troops from Angola.

In the light of the Commonwealth performance in the last stages leading to Zimbabwe's independence—which involved a remarkably small number of troops—it has been said that a Commonwealth contribution to a Namibia solution could prove more practical and acceptable than the substantial and costly U.N. intervention proposed.

The stalemate over Namibia increasingly led to its becoming part of the greater South African problem, and the Commonwealth as a result focused on South Africa itself in the mid-1980s, especially when violence in the townships escalated in 1985–86.

Thus the experience in training and preparing Zimbabweans for the day of independence has been used in the case of Namibia and is now underway on a larger scale to prepare the thousands of South Africans presently in exile for the day majority rule is established.

As well as benefiting from Commonwealth cooperation administered multilaterally, African members have gained considerable help bilaterally as a result of the personal contacts regularly maintained through Commonwealth membership.

In 1986, 76 percent of all British aid went to Commonwealth countries—a large proportion of it to Africa. Canadian assistance for Commonwealth Africa is carefully balanced with help to the Francophone countries, but Commonwealth members, most notably Tanzania, receive substantial Canadian help. Australia has become more involved with Commonwealth Africa since Malcolm Fraser struck up personal relationships with African leaders during his prime ministership; and New Zealand chose in 1985 to set up its first mission in Africa in a Commonwealth country—Zimbabwe. Indian technical assistance to Commonwealth Africa has grown in recent years, at least in part as a result of friendships formed between Indian and African leaders at Commonwealth meetings.

MEDIATING RELATIONS WITH EUROPE

Over the years since independence in Africa, economic necessities have dictated changes of attitude by many states. An early example of a major shift in policy came with the birth of the Lomé Convention, under which former colonies of the member states of the European Community (EC) in Africa, the Caribbean and the Pacific (the ACP) became eligible for technical help, preferential trade and other development aid from the EC.

Although the Francophone countries had little difficulty in becoming associated with the EC aid programs under the earlier Yaoundé Convention, the newly independent Commonwealth countries raised strong objections to a similar association for themselves when Britain joined the EC in 1973 and they became eligible.

In the years-long negotiations that preceded the Lomé signing they resisted the idea of becoming what seemed to them apendages of a rich white man's club. In due course they relented. Agreement was finally reached in February 1975, and Lomé has been renegotiated several times since. Today membership in the ACP is not questioned by the African members, although the terms are often bitterly fought over.

Commonwealth countries have found that they are able to secure better terms by working together as a group, with the help of the Commonwealth Secretariat in London and by using the many channels of Commonwealth cooperation available to them.

Many of the benefits of Commonwealth membership for Africa derive from programs of technical help, often in highly specialized areas that are greatly appreciated by governments but are relatively unknown because they are not widely publicizable.

The Commonwealth provides a forum where information and advice can be exchanged with countries on other continents. For example, when a workshop on food supply information systems was held in New Delhi, senior statisticians from 11 African countries were able to study the systems developed by India. A senior Nigerian was able to study storage and mechanization in India; and within Africa itself Malawian researchers were able to study crop protection measures in Zimbabwe.

Soil conservation officers and land use planners from East, central and southern Africa were able to take part in an exercise designed to diagnose land use problems faced by a group of small-scale farmers in Zomba district, Malawi.

The CFTC provides a unique service of technical aid by quickly and economically matching up experts from one Commonwealth country to fulfill a request for help from another. Tax experts, water-supply engineers, conservationists and the like are made available for special assignments.

The CFTC also provides advice to governments on matters of economic complexity and has saved African countries tens of millions of pounds by advising on negotiations with transnational companies. Such help was given to Tanzania in its negotiations for rescheduling its debts with the Paris Club. Five countries—Botswana, Gambia, Ghana, Seychelles and Tanzania—have turned to the CFTC's Technical Assistance Group for advice on petroleum projects. Swaziland was given help in evaluating proposals made by foreign firms to develop its gold resources. Similar help has been given to Mozambique, a non-Commonwealth country that the Commonwealth has agreed to assist because of its importance as a front-line state.

Several African members have asked for help in drafting legislation arising from the U.N. Convention on the Law of the Sea.

Many Africans attend universities in other Commonwealth countries under the Commonwealth Scholarship and Fellowship Plan, which now handles 1,700 scholars at any one time. But in the field of education the most exciting prospect for African students will come from a new plan to create a University of the Commonwealth for cooperation in correspondence education. The aim is to make it possible for learners anywhere in the Commonwealth to study via correspondence courses available from any bona fide college or university in the Commonwealth. Canada promoted the idea at the Vancouver summit and offered a headquarters in Vancouver. Many countries have offered funding, most notably Brunei, with £3 million. Africans living on a continent of huge distances and often in isolated circumstances could benefit greatly from the scheme.

For African member-countries, the Commonwealth works on many levels and holds out the hope of increasing benefits in the years to come. It explains why, despite the political turmoil in the three stormy decades since Ghana became the first British colony to achieve independence in Africa, all 14 member-countries have remained within the Commonwealth. And it explains why a free Namibia and South Africa may in due course increase the number to 16.

FURTHER READING

Accord on Southern Africa, 1985. London: Commonwealth Secretariat, 1985.

A Commonwealth of Learning. Report of a study group on distance education. London: Commonwealth Secretariat, 1987.

Mission to South Africa. Commonwealth Eminent Persons Group on Southern Africa. Harmondsworth: Penguin, 1986.

Okanagan Statement and Programme of Action on Southern Africa, 1987. London: Commonwealth Secretariat, 1987.

Report of the Secretary-General, 1987. London: Commonwealth Secretariat, 1987.

Southern Rhodesia Elections, February 1980. Report of the Commonwealth Observer Group. London: Commonwealth Secretariat, 1980.

Statement on Apartheid in Sport, 1977. London: Commonwealth Secretariat, 1977.

Wright, Stephen, and Brownfoot, Janice N., eds. *Africa in World Politics.* London: Macmillan, 1987.

THE EUROPEAN COMMUNITY AND AFRICA

ADRIAN HEWITT

INTRODUCTION

THE European Community (EC) as a regional grouping has links with Africa which are almost as old as the EC's own internal bonds. As part of the bargain struck in 1957 in establishing the Treaty of Rome, France insisted that a special relationship be established, under part four of the Treaty, with selected African states and Madagascar, almost all of which were then still French dependencies, though shortly afterward destined for independence.

Over the next 30 years, the relationship has been both expanded and diluted. With the increase in EC membership from six to nine (1973) and eventually to 12 (1986), sub-Saharan Africa has remained the firm focus of the EC's development assistance policies, though hardly an important item in its global trading and economic relationships. By the time of the Lomé Conventions, starting in 1975, the EC had drawn into this special cooperative relationship all the independent states in sub-Saharan Africa. Even Mozambique and Angola eventually joined, while neither Ethiopia nor Uganda, during their worst disputes with the governments of EC member states, ever withdrew their memberships. Except for Namibia and South Africa, neither of which enjoys a representative government, the EC's African jigsaw puzzle was complete by the 1980s. The North African countries have had separatae agreements with Brussels outside the Lomé Convention arrangements.

EFFECTS OF EC ENLARGEMENT

New EC members have signaled a dilution in the single-minded concentration on the invented concept of "Eurafrica," so dear to the French policy makers who numbered themselves among the founding fathers of the EC. With the accession of Britain (plus Denmark and Ireland) in 1973, the EC's Yaoundé agreements, which had until then been limited to Africa and been almost the exclusive preserve of Francophone states, were transformed into a more liberal Lomé Convention embracing both Francophone and Anglophone Africa and also extending to the Commonwealth and a few other countries in the Caribbean and Pacific. By 1988 there were 66 signatories to the third Lomé Convention, members of the Africa, Caribbean and Pacific (ACP) Group. Only about 40 of them are in Africa, but because almost all the Caribbean and Pacific members are small islands, Africa remains preponderant in the ACP Group in terms of its share of population, output and in the amount of EC funds it absorbs. (Membership of the ACP Group was not allowed to be extended to the big Commonwealth countries of Asia like India, Bangladesh, Sri Lanka and Malaysia.) The later accession to the EC of Greece, Spain and Portugal has yet to alter this balance. Sub-Saharan Africa remains at the apex of the "pyramid of privileges" which the EC has erected for its relationships with Third World countries. While some see it as a relationship which has failed to mature over the last 30 years—some African countries are now poorer than when the relationship began, in contrast to the excluded Asian countries—others see a partnership to be built on for the future, and an alternative for African governments to superpower blandishments. Still others see the EC, a community of 320 million people not dissimilar in population size to Africa, as itself a future superpower.

COLONIAL ROOTS OF THE "EURAFRICA" CONCEPT

Even if we date the most concerted European involvement in the depths of the African continent from the Congress of Berlin in 1885, this means that European (as opposed to EC) links with Africa are well over a century old. While the EC as a community has no colonial past and no relationship with Africa dating back before 1957, many of the countries which are its member states certainly do. The colonial connections are most important for Britain and France because these were the most durable, but should not be overlooked in the cases of Belgium, Italy and Portugal (historically cast as particularly negative experiences for the Africans involved) or even in the minor African colonial forays of Germany and Spain. Thus seven countries, over half of the EC's 12 member states, had colonies in Africa. In fact, only the smallest EC members—Denmark, Luxembourg, Ireland, Greece and the Netherlands—did not. The contrast with the superpowers is striking: the United States, the Soviet Union, Japan and China never had any colonial possessions in Africa; indeed, until the mid-20th century, none of these countries had any significant economic, cultural or political activity in Africa at all, with the exception of some U.S. business interests. Once Africa ceased being the preserve of the Africans, it was encroached upon only by Europeans, Arabs and Levantines, not by the other major world economic powers. Although this is now rapidly changing, and precisely when the EC itself has come into being, it is in this historical context that Eurafrica and the EC's own nostalgic Third World policies have to be understood.

THREE PILLARS OF EC AFRICAN POLICY

An objective assessment of the EC's relationship with Africa finds it resting on three main supports:

1. The legacy of colonialism, at least some of it fostering understanding and mutual respect
2. The belief in the blocs' complementarity: one temperate, the other mainly tropical; one rich in natural resources, the other rich in skills; one densely urban, the other rural; etc.
3. The assertion that Europe has more to offer Africa in terms of culture, benevolent promotion of development, disinterested assistance, and political cooperation than do the newer superpowers

None of these supports is solid, and scrutiny will show definite flaws in their argument. Yet each bears closer examination as an explanation of the present EC-African relationship and its future dynamics. Each figures prominently as an underlying theme of the Lomé Convention relationship. Selectivity, and hence exclusion from the ACP Group at the EC's behest, relates to colonial history; the exchange of raw materials for manufactures underlies the trade and commodity arrangements; while a cultural chapter has recently been added to the Convention, which has always been a political treaty. The final question to be addressed, however, is whether each of these suports is not unduly backward-leaning and thus incapable of supporting either the changing dynamics of the EC itself or the responses which Africa needs and expects in a global context.

ROLE OF THE LOMÉ CONVENTION

The roots of the Lomé Convention lie in the special trading arrangements negotiated in the postcolonial period. France wished to maintain a close relationship with its former colonies in order to keep open a lucrative export market. Germany, politically weakened, was prepared to do a deal. For their part, the newly independent African nations hoped in the 1960s to benefit from aid and trading concessions. The Yaoundé Convention of 1963 formalized preferential trading arrangements between the original six members of the EC and most of the former French colonies. The accession of Britain in 1973 led to the replacement of the Yaoundé Convention by a new treaty incorporating the former British colonies of Africa, the Caribbean and the Pacific, plus some others. Thus the Lomé Convention was born: it originally had 46 ACP members, with Africa always dominant.

The establishment of the first Lomé Convention in 1975 was heralded by ACP and European governments as a landmark in the evolution of north-south relations. Even the United States later launched a Caribbean Basin Initiative (CBI), which borrowed some elements from the Lomé Conventions.

Lomé I was, perhaps fortuitously, negotiated at a time of brief Third World commodity power, just after the quadrupling of OPEC oil prices and the emergence of world shortages in certain raw materials such as sugar, phosphates and food grains. Throughout the United Nations system, the call was for a new international economic order in which Third World nations, and particularly their governments, would seize a stronger position in negotiating and determining both global economic relationships and their own development patterns.

The EC responded to this new climate with considerable alacrity and at least a measure of presentational aplomb. The Lomé Convention was put forward as a path-breaking "partnership of equals," unknown hitherto in rich-poor global relations. It was claimed to represent a new way of organizing economic and trade relations, negotiated by two groups of countries on the basis of equal partnership. For the first time ever, interlinkages between aid and trade were formally recognized. The interest shown by developing countries in Lomé—in sharp contrast to the criticism repeatedly leveled at the Yaoundé Convention—was doubtless due to the fact that many governments regarded the new framework as a precedent and model for future relations between industrialized and developing countries. The provisions of Lomé offered some major innovations, the most important being the stabilization of export earnings (the Stabex system) and the removal of reciprocity in the EC's granting of trade preferences. ACP states could in theory develop manufacturing export lines and gain free access to the EC's vast market, better access than that accorded to their Third World competitors in Asia and Latin America and to industrialized countries. And they would not have to accord the EC countries similar tariff concessions in return.

Above all, Lomé I offered 3 billion ECUs worth of aid (then the equivalent of about U.S. $3 billion), most of it allocated to Africa. Lomé, like its predecessor agreements, uniquely enjoyed its own special fund, the European Development Fund (EDF), replenished every five years for this purpose and consisting mainly of grants. Other countries outside the ACP Group had no access to it; moreover, its allocations to each individual country were made in advance but programed only loosely, or "indicatively". The EDF is funded directly by the EC member states (Britain, for instance, contributes a fixed 16.6 percent of the current EDF) and does not form a part of the general EC budget. That is why African governments hold Lomé in such high esteem. They regard EC aid as additional to the aid they receive from France, Britain, Germany and other member states. In fact this cannot be the case, although the illusion is powerful. They are, however, correct in judging EC aid as generally "softer," both in financial terms and in general conditions, than that of other donors or of the international financial institutions. That is a phenomenon ripe for modification as the Lomé IV negotiations began. Lastly, African governments are also partially correct in setting great store by the predictability of EDF aid. They know at the beginning of each five-year period the amount earmarked for them, and the sectors or operations in which the aid is to be used. Much chastened since 1975, however, they no longer believe that the aid will be handed over to them to use responsibly (or irresponsibly), nor that the aid will even be committed within the five-year period to which it applies by treaty, let alone disbursed and spent. EDF spending is, in fact, still notoriously slow compared with that of most other donors, and the benefits of indicative programing are arguable at best against the three-year rolling programs used by other aid donors with their main African partner countries.

Appearance, however, is often as important as reality; the apparently generous inducements offered by the Lomé Convention, particularly in the deteriorating general economic climate, tilted the whole balance of the EC-African partnership back into a donor-client aid-dependence relationship. Despite the brave promises of equal political partnership and generous trade-development provisions, the sad fact is that for Africa, the Lomé Conventions have come to represent little more than quinquennial aid-replenishment talks. The whole relationship is ripe for reform.

Perhaps Lomé I raised unrealistic expectations: the scale of resources available and the implementation mechanisms established were not sufficient to bring about significant economic and social development of ACP countries. Neither Lomé I nor its successors reduced poverty levels or improved living conditions for the mass of urban and rural families in ACP countries. Indeed, Africa is facing crisis, and African per capita income and per capita food production are lower now than before the start of Lomé I.

ACP states have not greatly diversified their production or exports. African exports are still highly concentrated in a few products. Primary products still constitute over 95 percent of the EC's imports from ACP countries, with oil from Nigeria and Gabon the major single item. The ambitious industrialization targets of the Lomé Conventions have not been met. The reality of Lomé has been that both aid and trade provisions have acted to confine ACP countries to the export of certain primary commodities. Manufactured and semimanufactured goods have a very small share of EC imports from ACP countries, barely 3 to 4 percent, and this share is not rising. Only Mauritius is a significant exception to this rule.

In absolute terms, aid has increased with each succeeding Lomé Convention. But when inflation and population growth are taken into account, it can be seen that in 1976–85 (Lomé I to Lomé III), EC real per capita transfers to ACP states fell by 40 percent. This was at a time when ACP states' needs for resource transfers were increasing. The African ACP grouping comprises the bulk of the UN's list of 41 least-developed countries (LLDCs), those least viable in commercial terms and least able to secure commercial bank credit. Lomé III provides for a total allocation of 8.5 billion ECUs over 1985–90. This barely covers the rise in prices and, with the number of ACP states now at 66, represents a further decline in real per capita transfers. According to calculations made by the UN Economic Commission for Africa (see Table 1), while Lomé II was already a worse deal than Lomé I for the ACP countries, the aid allocation under Lomé III increased only 10 percent in real terms (EDF only) or 6.6 percent overall at a time when population increases and expansion of the ACP Group to 66 more than offset this in per capita terms. The reality under Lomé III was that Africa's negotiating power was so weakened by the rude economic shocks of 1979–81 and the recession which followed that they were unable

Table 1

RESOURCES UNDER LOMÉ I (1979–84) AND
LOMÉ II (1985–90) CONVENTIONS

	Value of resources allocated (in millions of ECUs)			
	Lomé II	Lomé III current prices	Lomé III at constant (1980) prices[a]	Change in real expenditure of Lomé III over Lomé II (percent)
EDF				
Grants	2,998	4,860	3,371	11.24
Soft loans	524	600	416	−20.61
Risk				
Capital	284	600	416	46.48
Stabex	557	925	641	15.08
Sysmin	282	415	288	2.13
Total	4,645	7,400	5,132	10.48
EIB[b]				
Subsidized loans	685	1,100	763	11.39
Ordinary loans	200	—	—	—
Total resources	5,530	8,500	5,895	6.60

[a]Deflated to allow for inflation over 1980–87.
[b]European Investment Bank
Source: U.N. Economic Commission for Africa; Statistical Office of the EC.

to negotiate hard and coherently with the EC. Africa was already on its knees.

LOMÉ III

Lomé III was signed on December 8, 1984, and came into force belatedly after ratification on May 1, 1986. The trade benefits offered by the EC were substantially the same: strict rules of origin and other nontariff barriers still apply. A change in the distribution of aid has occurred, the amount allocated to soft loans declining by 20.6 percent in real terms and the Stabex (soft commodities) fund being boosted considerably more than the mining-loan facilitiy, Sysmin. Considering the world economy's low level of activity and the austerity policies being pursued in most of the member states of the EC, perhaps the mere fact of maintaining an overall status quo in Lomé III could be considered an achievement. Lomé III contained a number of minor innovations: the principle of self-reliant agricultural development involving full participation of the rural population and the general assertion of priority for agricultural and rural development; a cultural chapter; and for the first time, a general undertaking by all signatories to work towards the eradication of apartheid in southern Africa.

Many negotiators, including many of those in the European Commission, felt this last element—and indeed the cultural chapter too—sat uneasily in an agreement which had been at base an arrangement for economic cooperation. Others argued that apartheid was so pernicious that its continued existence—and, worse, the tacit countenancing of it—negated the constructive work of the economic and social sectors of the Lomé Conventions. In a sense, Lomé III reflected the sense of scant economic progress achieved by the African countries from the relationship over the previous decade; it thus both permitted and justified harder bargaining on the political and cultural fronts.

Lomé III, the longest convention to date, contains five parts. Part 1 provides a guide to the general objectives and expectations of the contracting parties. Part 2 outlines the areas of cooperation: agriculture, industry, transport, and so on. Part 3 describes the operating mechanisms of cooperation, detailing the arrangements regarding trade, Stabex and Sysmin, aid programing and investment. Part 4 describes the functioning of the institutions of Lomé. Part 5 contains a number of minor provisions concerning accession, and is followed by the special protocols, making specific arrangements for protected markets with such uncompetitive ACP imports as cane sugar, bananas, beef and rum, which are generally of minor interest to Africa, though they are important to a few countries. These five parts are followed by the Final Act of Lomé III, which contains a number of annexes of particular interest, such as provisions on migrant workers.

Significantly, special provision is made under Lomé III to channel aid and Stabex benefits disproportionately toward the least-developed member countries of the ACP Group, which are mainly in Africa. The EC uses its own classification of "least developed," and its own list, though limited only to the ACP Group, already exceeds the United Nation list of 41 LLDCs. Under Lomé III, the EC's own list of ACP least-developed countries has risen to 43, accounting for 40 percent of the total ACP population and accorded twice the amount of programed aid given to the other ACP states. This is a "bias towards the poor" which could serve the EC well in its future relations with Africa, were it not for the fact that programed aid has not in practice always resulted in commensurate disbursements when political controversies intervened, allowing the EC to suspend aid at the insistence of its hard-line member states.

Despite these occasional lapses, and the disappointing economic performance of sub-Saharan Africa, there is much to appreciate in the list of general principles which Lorenzo Natali, EC Commissioner for Development, set out as guidelines for the start of Lomé IV negotiations in 1988:

1. The unique, innovatory character of the ACP/EC relationship, steadily built up over more than a decade of joint experience, comes first and foremost from its approach and general principles
2. The ACP-EC Lomé Convention is not only the main pillar of the

776

EC's development policy but also, in the broader context of overall north-south relations, the most comprehensive contractual instrument linking a regional grouping of industrialized nations and developing countries. The number of contracting parties, the scale and diversity of areas of cooperation covered, the volume of financial resources involved, and the innovatory nature of some of its mechanisms—such as policy dialogue, Stabex, or the regional cooperation instruments—make the Lomé Convention today a model for and witness to north-south relations which play a large role in promoting the EC's image in the world. Its main characteristics are:

a. Respect for the sovereignty of states and their economic and political options
b. Institutionalized group-to-group cooperation, preventing political discrimination between recipients
c. Security and foreseeability of aid and trade advantages, based on binding international commitments covering the duration of the convention: this is the often-cited advantage of the contractual nature of Lomé.
d. Comprehensive cooperation arrangements covering a wide range of areas and instruments
e. Permanent dialogue both at technical level (aid programing and policy dialogue) and at political level, in the joint institutions (ACP-EC Council of Ministers, Committee of Ambassadors, Joint Assembly)

This is, at the very least, a package whose potential would be highly appreciated as a basis for relations with Africa by other superpowers, such as the United States or Japan, who do not enjoy such an elaborate network of arrangements and who cannot draw on a history of European colonial links at its base. It is potential which, however, has yet to be realized given the changed circumstances of Africa today. That is why substantial reforms are in order for Lomé IV.

CHANGES FOR THE 1990S: LOMÉ IV

Battle lines for the renewal of Lomé III were drawn as of 1988 and areas of mutual interest identified. A common European position was needed before serious negotiations with the ACP Group could start, and the converse was also true. For Africa, deals are struck among senior government representatives at ministerial and ambassadorial rank, with the Brussels-based ACP Group Secretariat as clearing-house, intelligence headquarters and think tank. For the EC member states, the position is almost infinitely varied according to national parliamentary and executive procedure. In the past, however, on development issues, the EC has tended to travel at the speed of its slowest major member, or else France has asserted its primacy over EDF and development matters in its own peculiar way.

This has meant that the EC's relations with Africa, although apparently dynamic and innovatory during the mid-1970s and early 1980s (before Lomé I was put to the test), had by the late 1980s become something of an anachronism. The operation had become frozen into a past of paternalistic project aid and few useable trade stimuli or concessions, and a cooperation program that, under Lomé III and Lomé II, had failed to address the leading issues of concern to Africa:

1. The impossibility of servicing debt, including for many African countries government-to-government debt
2. Facing up to the demands of the Washington-based financial institutions to submit to tough changes in the economic and social policies of African governments
3. Resolving the problems of turmoil, destabilization and apartheid in southern Africa

On the debt issues, the EC, at least in the Lomé Convention, was almost totally silent until 1988. This was because the EC Commission had chosen to believe that debt problems were separate from the project-based approach to aid and development the EDF had espoused from the beginning almost without change. Stabex was supposed to tide over dependent commodity exporters during the bad years (although it has proved to be repeatedly underfunded, especially in 1981 and 1988), but otherwise Brussels chose to regard the inadequacy of export earnings to service even debt interest (let alone repayments) as a problem for the International Monetary Fund (IMF) and the World Bank. This proved increasingly untenable, as successive governments of the EC's member states produced the Lawson plan, the Balladur plan, and the Mitterrand plan, all purporting to address the African debt problem. Thus in 1987–88, the EC agreed to provide— mainly from recycled funds and unused Lomé-EDF contingency reserves— balance-of-payments support to ACP states to help toward debt relief, initially at the level of 100 million ECUs of import finance, then increased to a pledged 500 million ECUs. There is now a firm agreement that a quick-disbursing sectoral support fund should be offered under Lomé IV in addition to the traditional EDF project aid.

This brings the EC, which under previous Lomé Conventions always prided itself on not exercising political discrimination in Africa, up against the question of policy conditions. The EC's hard liners now insist that strings must be attached to such balance-of-payments support programs. In the interests of policy effectiveness and of Western coordination and solidarity, those conditions must be those of the IMF and the World Bank. The receiving governments must also show evidence of a commitment to undertake significant efforts to carry out economic adjustment in the form of sustainable macroeconomic programs. African governments are concerned that they are about to lose their traditionally "soft" European aid and that the donors of that aid now appear to be "ganging up" on them; in Europe, too, dissenting voices have been heard. This prescription for future EC-African relations on development issues would eliminate much of what has been distinctive about the European contribution in the past, and on which a better future of cooperative relations was to be built. In particular, it casts the American-dominated IMF, an organization firmly devoted to short-term world monetary and payments management with no vocation for promoting longer-term development, in the driver's seat, with its own short-run conditions overwhelming those of all the other partners. While the EC is thus prepared to help constructively with Africa's debt problems, the final design and implementation of that contribution has yet to be resolved politically. Initially, the EC is expected to help African countries with the World Bank's Social Dimensions of Adjustment project, to mitigate the ill effects of enforced public spending cuts.

The other major political issue facing Lomé IV negotiators, and involving all future EC relations with Africa, is the problem of South Africa and the move toward generalized sanctions against Pretoria. Until mid-1988, the EC had been held back mainly by the British and German governments, which were staunchly opposed to sanctions and supported President Ronald Reagan's policy of constructive engagement instead. As Reagan's star waned, and Michael Dukakis came out in favor of both sanctions and naming South Africa a "terrorist state," Britain's position in particular became quite isolated. With the condemnation of apartheid already written into the text of Lomé III, a small aid allocation already made for the victims of apartheid within South Africa from EC funds, and the ACP Group's assent to a proposal to welcome an independent Namibia into the Lomé arrangements, it seemed that the EC had considerable scope for movement on its South African policies for the 1990s.

Five other elements can be identified as significant pressures influencing future EC policies towards Africa. First, the trade provisions offered under previous conventions have almost completely failed to stimulate trade and investment in Africa. Not all the blame can be laid at the EC's door, or at Africa's, but given that the leading declared aim of the Lomé Conventions has been to promote and diversify trade between the EC and the ACP Group, the performance of this instrument has left much to be desired. Africa was also affected at least as badly as the rest of the Third World by the collapse in commercial bank lending during the 1980s. Neither has it yet provided many attractions for direct investment, including investment by multinational corporations, except in the undiversified plantation sector. This is partly because of high labor costs and small national markets, but also because of the lack of political and economic stability. As a result, the conventions' trade and investment provisions have performed poorly. The EC is now expected to offer that trade provisions of Lomé IV can be of indeterminate duration (i.e., permanent), instead of being tied to a five-year renegotiating cycle. The idea behind this proposal, which African governments will treat gingerly, is that longer-term guarantees of trade access will attract more solid investment and investors to benefit economic stability and export expansion. While the EC market access arrangements would not then end after five years, this would not apply to the financial arrangements. The EDF will still be replenished only for a five-year period, and the size of the next EDF will be a closely kept secret, ostensibly not for negotiation with the ACP Group, and to be unveiled at the end of the negotating period as an incentive for ACP governments to sign the new political treaty. Indeed, the actual amounts of EC aid earmarked for each country will not be known formally until *after* the Convention is signed, though obviously such amounts are eagerly discussed in private and bilaterally between government ministers and EC authorities during the negotiating stage.

Second, a new element is introduced by the EC's internal politics. The year 1992, when intra-EC barriers to trade in goods and services are expected to be finally eliminated, will occur midway through Lomé IV; provision must be made for its effects now. The most salient of these effects are expected to be these:

1. For cane sugar exporters, who currently enjoy special access for 1.3 million tons annually of sugar exports: national quotas within the EC on the production of beet sugar should fall away as economic frontiers are removed
2. For banana producers, including African and Caribbean states now heavily dependent on such exports: the present marketing arrangements—whereby Somalia supplies Italy, Cameroon and the *départements* and *territoires d'outre-mer* supply France, and the Windward Islands supply the United Kingdom—will collapse, letting in the cheaper and higher-quality "dollar bananas" from Central and South America which are expected to dominate the wider and unrestricted EC market
3. If 1992 also involves monetary unity, with full membership of the European Monetary System, the European Central Banks will effectively be jointly adopting the monetary burden of the Franc Zone, the African currency arrangements based on the CFA franc which are at present shouldered only by France

Third, Africa can see some major changes in store regarding its own position within the EC's constellation of relationships with the Third World. While the EC has always made clear in the past, mainly on French insistance, that Africa is at the heart of its development assistance efforts, two phenomena are now occurring that are to Africa's short-term disadvantage. On the one hand, there now exists an emerging EC aid program for the so-called nonassociates, shared equally between Asia and Latin America. Though nothing like the size of the EDF, this program is growing fast and has none of the awkward 1960s baggage which has made EDF aid so disappointing in practice. On the other hand, there are pressures on the EC to admit new members outside Africa to the Lomé Convention, and hence effectively to the ACP Group. While Namibia has already been mentioned as a future prospect once political obstacles are overcome, the candidacies of Haiti and the Dominican Republic are already a reality. The EC might find some grounds to refuse Haiti entry, most likely for its democratic record, but on paper Haiti would be a prime candidate as a very poor

Caribbean state which was once a European colony. The Dominican Republic might be easier to reject, but not if Haiti's membership were granted: they share the same island and face fundamentally similar development problems. The Dominican entry without conditions would open the floodgates to generalized Central American and even Latin American membership. This would greatly dilute Africa's strength in the special relationship. This question also reflects the shifting center of gravity of the EC itself. While the Franco-German axis was dominant, France was in full control of Third World policies and Africa was unquestionably put at the apex. British entry failed to disrupt this completely: Asian entries to the special relationship were prevented, and only small far-flung islands were admitted to dilute African dominance. The delayed effects of Iberian entry have yet to be felt, but even Portugal's interests are effectively now more with Brazil than with its former African provinces, and Spain is firmly committed to Latin America. Though the French resist this, neither Germany nor Italy (nor even Britain) would be averse to a shift of aid and concessional resources towards Latin America over the medium term, although all are concerned that Africa should not suffer.

Fourth, Iberian enlargement, plus the earlier membership of Greece, has meant that the EC in the 1980s has already developed a southern tilt. This has been to the benefit of the Mediterranean, hence also to the benefit of the old concept of Eurafrica, although it is mitigated by the Latin American connection just outlined. But how will the next EC enlargement affect Africa? Turkey is not certain to be the 13th member state of the EC; this could be Cyprus or Malta in the Mediterranean, or Norway following another referendum, or almost any of the remaining European Free Trade Association states such as Austria or Sweden. It is possible that after the last southern tilt, the next enlargement could produce a northern shift, with complex implications for Africa.

Fifth, Africa during the 1990s will confront an EC of member-state governments, however cohesive the EC and its dismantled economic barriers is by then. For much of the 1980s, the key EC governments—of Britain, Germany and France under Prime Minister Jacques Chirac were conservative administrations closely attuned to the Reagan line on economic liberalism, monetarism, and international affairs. Although this affected direct EC-Africa policies less than it might have—proof of the institutional strength of parts of the Lomé Conventions—it did severely affect the world economic climate in which African economies had to be managed. No one can describe what an alternative 1980s world economy might have been (it had to recover from the energy crises of the 1970s and the recession starting in 1979), but it is clear that actual 1980s policies have not been kind to Africa. Certain combinations of U.S. and European governments during the 1990s might therefore offer Africa a better deal. Popular support for African concerns in the late 1980s suggests that democratic governments listening to their constituents may do better for Africa in the 1990s. The EC as a budding superpower is thus well placed to update its policies, instruments and institutions.

781

CONCLUSION

EC policies towards Africa have rested on three supports: the legacy of colonialism, the mercantilist idea of exchanging raw materials for manufactures, and the belief that European culture and civilization can be bestowed as part of development. All three supports have been shown here not only to be wanting, but excessively backward-looking. The colonial legacy is the legacy of the member states which did the colonization. This awareness might still be the basis for doing better in future, since knowledge and understanding need never be lost. Even if the idea that raw materials should be exchanged for manufactures for mutual benefit were persuasive, it would no longer be relevant for the future: Africa needs desperately to diversify out of commodity dependence, and Europe is already shifting out of commodity-using manufacturing into services. Although culture has a part to play in relations with Africa, it is not at all obvious that a sterile administrative body such as the European Commission should be empowered to be its vector or to negotiate on behalf of the population of Europe a deal with Africa covering this noneconomic area. And African responses regarding culture are best channeled otherwise than through the arid texts of the Lomé Conventions. These iconoclastic remarks simply mean that if the EC sees itself as a world power on a par with the United States, the Soviet Union and Japan, it needs to begin now to establish a global program of foreign relations and a balanced agenda for the Third World in which its traditional links with Africa will form merely a part. For this, the Lomé Conventions will provide some good building blocks.

FURTHER READING

Afolabi, Peter. *The New ACP-EEC Convention*. Lagos: Nigerian Institute of International Affairs, 1981.

Analysis of Trade between the European Community and the ACP States. Luxembourg: Eurostat, 1979.

Boardman, Robert, Shaw, Timothy M., and Soldatos, Panayotis, eds. *Europe, Africa and Lomé III*. Lanham: University Press of America; Halifax, Nova Scotia: Centre for African Studies, Dalhousie University, 1985.

Cornell, Margaret, ed. *Europe and Africa: Issues in Post-Colonial Relations*. London: Overseas Development Institute, 1981.

Cosgrove, C., and McLeod, J., eds. *Trade from Aid: A Guide to Opportunities from EEC Funding in Africa, the Caribbean and the Pacific*. Reading, Berkshire: CTA Economics and Export Analysts Ltd., 1987.

Djamson, Eric C. *The Dynamics of Euro-African Co-operation*. The Hague: M. Nijhoff, 1976.

Faber, Gerrit. *The European Community and Development Cooperation*. The Hague: Van Gorcum, Assen, 1982.

Frey-Wouters, Adele Ellen. *The European Community and the Third World: The Lomé Convention and its Impact*. New York: Praeger, 1980.

Goubet, Catherine. *The Second Convention of Lomé: EEC aid to the ACP Countries, 1981–1985*. Brussels: Bureau d'Informations Européennes S.P.R.L., 1982.

Hewitt, Adrian. "The Lomé Conventions: Entering a Second Decade." *Journal of Common Market Studies*. Oxford: Blackwell, 1984.

How the European Community Is Helping the Developing Countries: The European Community and the Associated African States and Madagascar. Brussels: Commission of the European Communities, 1975.

Matthews, Jacqueline D. *Association System of the European Community.* New York: Praeger, 1977.

Morino, Lina. *La Comunità europea e l'Africa.* Milano: ISPI; Bari: Dedalo libri, 1975.

Moss, Joanna. *The Lomé Conventions and Their Implications for the United States.* Boulder, Colorado: Westview, 1982.

Ravenhill, John. *Collective Clientelism: The Lomé Conventions and North-South Relations.* New York: Columbia University Press, 1985.

Stevens, Christopher, ed. *The EEC and the Third World: A Survey.* London: Hodder & Stoughton, 1984.

PART TWO

ECONOMIC AFFAIRS

A SURVEY OF THE AFRICAN ECONOMIES

MICHAEL HODD

INTRODUCTION

The African economies, 46 in all located south of the Sahara, are here considered in comparison with other world groupings as classified by the World Bank.[1] In economic terms, South Africa has a considerable influence on averages computed for Africa, and where possible, calculations are made both with and without South Africa; Africa, except where otherwise indicated, is taken to include South Africa. Namibia, Spanish Morocco and Réunion are not included.

This survey begins by considering the structure of the African economies and their recent economic performance, making comparisons mainly with other developing countries (that is, the World Bank's developing country group excluding Africa) and the industrial countries. Data for the high-income oil group and the Eastern European bloc are given where it is available. The oil group is of limited usefulness for comparative purposes, as oil resources make this group very much a special case.

There is considerable variation among the African economies, and features of these differences in terms of geographical location, size, economic type and currency zone are summarized in the third section of this article. The section goes on to examine specific economic problems in Africa, and summarizes economic performance, stability, policies and future prospects.

Averages are computed using the same weighting systems as employed by the World Bank.[2] Although reservations have to be made regarding the reliability of information, particularly for Africa, the view is taken that imperfect figures give a better indication of economic conditions and general orders of magnitude for Africa than no data at all.

ECONOMIC STRUCTURE

Population and land
Table 1 gives the size and growth of population in sub-Saharan Africa in comparison with the other main groupings of countries in the world. Africa

[1] World Bank, *World Development Report* (New York: Oxford University Press, 1987).
[2] *Ibid.*

Table 1
POPULATION 1987

	Population (millions)	Population (% of world total)	Population growth rate (% per year)
Sub-Saharan Africa	489	9.8	3.2
(Sub-Saharan Africa excluding South Africa)	455	9.2	3.3
Other developing countries	3,375	68.2	1.7
High-income oil countries	19	0.4	3.7
Industrial countries	743	15.0	0.4
Eastern European bloc	325	6.6	0.7
World	4,951	100.0	1.6

Source: World Bank, *World Development Report* (New York: Oxford University Press, 1987).

contains roughly 10% of the world's people. Other developing countries make up another 70%, and the high-income oil exporters, industrial market economies and the Eastern European bloc comprise the remaining 20%. The World Bank subdivides the developing countries into low, lower middle income and upper middle income groups. Africa's population makes up 10% of the total population of the low-income group, this group being dominated by India and China which together comprise 75%. Of the lower middle income group, African countries comprise 21%. Of the upper middle income group, Africa makes up 6.4%. South Africa is the dominant African middle-income country in this group, with a population of 33.8 million in 1987, the only others being Gabon (1 million) and Seychelles (65,000).

Population growth rates in Africa are substantially higher than elsewhere, with the exception of the high-income oil group, where some of the population increase is the result of in-migration. What is striking is to compare Africa's rates of population growth, at 3.2% a year, with other developing countries, at 1.7% a year. Africa has a crude birth rate of 48 per 1,000, whereas for other developing countries the rate is 27 per 1,000. Crude death rates in Africa are 17 per 1,000, and they are nine per 1,000 for other developing countries. These figures imply large family sizes, with Africa showing a fertility rate of 6.7, while for other developing countries, the rate is 3.7. High birth rates in Africa, which are only partly offset by higher death rates, imply a population that will grow by 35% in the 15 years up to the year 2000. By contrast, the population of other developing countries will rise by 18% in this period.

Table 2 gives land areas and population densities. Despite fast rates of population growth, Africa has a low overall population density, 20 persons per square kilometer, with only the Eastern European bloc countries sig-

Table 2
LAND, POPULATION DENSITY, URBANIZATION

	Area (1,000 sq. km.)	Population density (persons per sq. km.)	Urbaniza- tion (%)	Urban popula- tion growth (annual % 1980–85)
Sub-Saharan Africa	24,342	20.1	26	5.4
(Sub-Saharan Africa excluding South Africa)	23,121	19.8	25	5.7
Other developing countries	49,342	68.4	32	3.6
High-income oil countries	4,012	76.0	73	6.0
Industrial countries	30,935	24.0	75	1.5
Eastern European bloc	22,778	14.3	66	1.5
World	131,409	37.7	40	2.9

Source: As for Table 1.

nificantly lower. African density is under one-third of that recorded for other developing countries, at 68 persons per square kilometer. However, the nature of the economic structure in Africa, which is highly dependent on agriculture, and the percentage of the land area that is fertile, need to be taken into account when considering the impact of fast population growth on development prospects.

Half of Africa's population fall in the working age-group of 15–64 years. This is 10% lower than in other developing countries, and 17% lower than in industrial countries. These figures imply higher dependency ratios in Africa. Of course, members of the population enter the labor force some-what earlier than the age of 15 in Africa, particularly in rural areas where children begin to help with cultivation, cattle herding and household chores from the age of six or seven. However, this early working age, which reduces the African dependency ratio, is to a great extent at the expense of basic education, and this has an effect on the overall pace of development. The African population structure, with greater proportions in the under-15 age-group, is a result of the faster rate of population growth.

Overall, the picture emerges of Africa containing a small proportion of the population of the world's poorer countries, with significantly lower population density but higher rates of population growth and dependency ratios.

Output and income
Table 3 shows levels of output in 1985 for the main country groupings. It is not possible to make sensible comparisons with the Eastern European bloc. Thus, Africa produces 2% of world output, with the other developing countries recording almost 17%, the high-income oil countries 1.6% and the industrial countries almost 80%.

Table 3
GDP INCOME PER CAPITA, 1985

	GDP (U.S. $ millions)	GDP (% of world total)	GNP per capita (U.S. $)	GNP per capita ICP-adjusted (U.S. $)
Sub-Saharan Africa	228	2.1	515	1,236
(Sub-Saharan Africa excluding South Africa)	160	1.5	400	960
Other developing countries	1,799	16.7	637	1,720
High-income oil countries	170	1.6	9,800	—
Industrial countries	8,568	79.6	11,810	15,353
World (excluding Eastern European bloc)	10,765	100.0	2,456	3,876

Source: As for Table 1.

When level of income per capita is calculated by standard World Bank methods, the Africa level, excluding South Africa, is two-thirds that of the other developing countries. It is almost one-thirtieth of the level in industrial countries.

Cross-national comparisons of output and income are beset by problems. First, consumers in different countries spend their incomes on different goods. Secondly, similar goods have different prices in different countries. Thirdly, the the conversion to U.S. dollars, done in the main by the World Bank at three-year averages of official exchange rates, overestimates GDP when exchange rates overvalue domestic currencies.

The World Bank's International Comparison Project (ICP) makes efforts to allow for these factors. Adjusted incomes per capita are computed for 13 African countries among the 60 countries covered. Unweighted averages of ICP estimates make African incomes per capita 140% higher, and those of other developing countries 170% higher, in comparison with incomes per capita in the United States. Industrial country incomes per capita, excluding the United States, would be 60% higher.

Rough adjustments on the ICP basis would make African incomes per capita one-twelfth of those in industrial countries and two-thirds of those in other developing countries.

Such patchy evidence as exists[3] would suggest that the distribution of income in Africa allocates a smaller proportion of total income to the poorest 40% of the population than in the industrial countries.

Overall, and taking into account the considerable problems involved in making comparisons, sub-Saharan Africa has extremely low average living standards compared with industrial countries, with the poorest groups even further disadvantaged by the more unequal distribution of income.

[3] See *World Development Report,* p. 252.

Table 4
PRODUCTION STRUCTURE, 1985
(% of GNP)

	Agriculture	Industry	Services
Sub-Saharan Africa	25	32	42
(Sub-Saharan Africa			
excluding South Africa)	34	27	40
Other developing countries	19	34	47
High-income oil countries	2	58	39
Industrial countries	3	36	61
World (excluding	6	36	58
Eastern European bloc)			

Source: As for Table 1.

Production structure

Table 4 compares the contributions of the main producing sectors across the main country groupings. One-quarter of the total value of goods and services in Africa is provided by agriculture, and this is over one-third if South Africa is excluded. This is greater than for other developing countries at one-fifth, and the 3% provided by the agricultural sectors of industrial countries. There is greater similarity over the share of industrial sectors, although it must be borne in mind that this sector includes both oil and mineral production, which are prominent features of the African countries with large economies. African economies, with the exception of South Africa, tend to have small manufacturing sectors. The service sectors in Africa contribute two-fifths of output, against almost half in other developing countries and three-fifths in industrial countries.

Over 70% of the African labor force is in agriculture, vastly higher than the industrial group where only 7% of workers are in agriculture. One-tenth of African workers are in industry, compared with 35% in the industrial group. Under one-fifth of the African labor force is in service-sector employment, but three-fifths of industrial country workers are in services.

Rates of growth of the labor force reflect population growth rates of the past 15 years. In Africa and the other developing countries the labor force is growing at 2.4% a year, but it is expanding at under 1% a year in industrial countries. This creates problems in absorbing more of the work force in the industrial and service sectors in Africa.

Despite the heavy concentration of production and manpower in agriculture, Africa imported more than 55 pounds/25 kg. of cereals per capita in 1985. This was roughly in line with the food imports per capita in other developing countries, but the high-income oil and industrial countries imported 353 and 187 pounds/160 and 85 kg. per capita, respectively. There is no reason why food imports should indicate an inadequate ability on the part of the economies in providing for domestic needs. Indeed, it is argued that for many African countries the best use of agricultural resources is in

producing valuable tropical crops for export and using the revenue to purchase inexpensive cereals produced in temperate-zone industrial countries.
However, African governments tend to give considerable emphasis to being
self-sufficient in food, and are prepared to pay a not inconsiderable price
for the independence and self-reliance this represents.

Most agriculture in Africa is rain fed, and compared with other parts of
the developing world, particularly Asia, there is very little irrigation. This
makes agriculture particularly vulnerable to the weather, and drought periods can produce heavy falls in output. Recent droughts in Africa have
caused famines; in 1985, food aid was at a level of almost 22 pounds/10
kg. per capita, whereas in the other developing countries it was just over
4 pounds/2 kg. per capita.

Overall, Africa has a production structure with heavy emphasis on agriculture in terms of both output and manpower committed, and this is
mainly at the expense of services. Nonetheless, there is significant importing of food, and reliance on food aid.

Demand structure

Expenditure for 1985 is compared across the main country groups in Table
5. The main factors are the commitment of almost 70% of GDP to private
consumption, which rises to 76% if South Africa is excluded. Investment
in Africa, excluding South Africa, is 13% of GDP, just over half the allocation in other developing countries. Government consumption is 13% of
GDP and is comparable in other developing countries, but in industrial
countries is about half as great again in percentage terms.

Table 5
STRUCTURE OF EXPENDITURE, 1985

	Private consumption (% of GDP)	Gross investment (% of GDP)	Government consumption	Exports (% of GDP)	Imports (% of GDP)
Sub-Saharan Africa	69	15	13	25	22
(Sub-Saharan Africa excluding South Africa)	76	13	12	21	21
Other developing countries	64	24	12	21	21
High-income oil countries	40	29	31	47	47
Industrial countries	62	21	17	18	18
World (excluding Eastern European bloc)	62	22	16	19	19

Source: As for Table 1.

About one-fifth of all production in Africa, excluding South Africa, is sold overseas and similarly, one-fifth of all spending is on imports of goods and services. This is very similar to other developing countries and the industrial group. The high-income oil group has a very much higher trade dependence.

Africa has low usage of energy, with 243 kilos of oil consumed per capita; if South Africa is excluded, only 100 kilos per head. This compares with 540 kilos per capita in other developing countries, and almost 5,000 kilos per capita in the industrial countries. This is in part a reflection of lower need for heating in the tropics, but also of the lower levels of urbanization and industrialization. Fuel imports take up 7% of export earnings in Africa, although this is 10% if South Africa is excluded. Other developing countries and the industrial group spend 20% of export earnings on fuel.

Overall, Africa's expenditure emphasizes current consumption at the expense of investment. Africa is not noticeably more dependent on overseas trade than other country groupings, with the exception of the high-income oil countries. Africa has relatively low levels of energy usage and energy importation.

International trade
Africa was responsible for 3% of world exports in 1985, and this drops to 2% if South Africa is excluded (see Table 6). Other developing countries are responsible for one-fifth of world exports; high-income oil countries, 4%; industrial countries, 63%; and the Eastern European bloc, 8%. These proportions are closely matched by expenditure on imports.

Table 6
MERCHANDISE EXPORTS AND MERCHANDISE
IMPORTS, 1985

	Exports (U.S. $ billions)	Exports (% of world total)	Imports (U.S. $ billions)	Imports (% of world total)
Sub-Saharan Africa	50.5	2.9	40.4	2.2
(Sub-Saharan Africa excluding South Africa)	34.0	1.9	28.9	1.6
Other developing countries	375.2	21.7	404.0	21.8
High-income oil countries	63.8	3.7	44.1	2.4
Industrial countries	1,089.8	63.2	1,227.0	66.1
Eastern European bloc	143.8	8.3	139.0	7.5
World	1,723.1	100.0	1,854.5	100.0

Source: As for Table 1.

Half of Africa's exports are fuels, minerals and metals, and about one-quarter are other primary products, comprising agricultural, forestry and fishery products. South Africa is the only substantial exporter of manufactures, and when included in the African average, raises the proportion of manufacturing exports from 5% to 16%. This primary-product dependence is in marked contrast to the other developing countries where 45% of exports are manufactures, and to the industrial countries, where the proportion is 75%.

In 1985, food, fuels and other primary products combined made up 35% of Africa's imports, the other 65% being machinery and manufactures. This structure of imports is not too dissimilar to that of other developing countries or the industrial countries. The high-income oil group spends a markedly lower proportion on fuel, but 85% on machinery and manufactures.

In 1985 Africa sold over 8% of its exports to industrial countries and 16% to developing countries, including other African countries. Africa's dependence on industrial markets is greater than other developing countries, who sold 60% of their exports to industrial countries and over 30% to developing countries, including Africa.

Overall, Africa is responsible for a small fraction of world exports and imports, with heavy emphasis on primary products for export revenue, and importing mainly machinery and manufactures. Most exports are sold to industrial countries and very little to other developing countries.

Debt and financial flows
Africa's external-debt position in 1986, in the worldwide context, is shown in Table 7. Africa is responsible for only 10% of the world's outstanding external debt, at U.S. $102 billion. Brazil alone is responsible for $107 billion and Mexico for $97 billion.

However, Africa's outstanding debt is almost 60% of one year's GNP, whereas for other developing countries debt is 35% of GNP. Overall, the burden of debt service (interest payments and repayments of principal) was about the same in Africa and the rest of the developing world, at about 4% of GNP and 20% of export earnings.

Table 7
EXTERNAL DEBT, 1986

	Total debt (U.S. $ billions)	Debt as % of GNP	Debt service (% of GNP)	Debt service (% of exports)
Sub-Saharan Africa	102	57.5	4.3	19.1
Other developing countries	919	35.1	4.5	21.5
World	1,021	36.6	4.5	21.3

Source: World Bank, *World Development Report* (New York: Oxford University Press, 1988).

Table 8
NET AID, 1985

	Net aid, 1985 (U.S. $ millions)	Net aid per capita, 1985 (U.S. $)	Net aid (% of GNP, 1985)
(Sub-Saharan Africa excluding South Africa)	8,260	19.3	3.5
Other developing countries	17,361	5.5	1.1
High-income oil countries	42	2.3	—
All developing countries	25,713	7.2	1.3

Source: As for Table 1.

The lower debt-servicing demands in relation to GNP compared with debt-outstanding is a result of the softer terms on which Africa has borrowed. Interest rates are lower for Africa and maturity periods are longer. This is partly because lending governments have extended more generous terms to Africa, but also because Africa has generally found it less easy to raise commercial loans in the 1970s when the balance-of-payments surpluses of oil exporters were being re-lent by banks.

Table 8 gives new concessionary flows less repayments of principal and interest payments (net aid) in 1985. About one-third of net aid went to Africa. This disproportionate emphasis on Africa, considering that Africa comprises only 12% of the population of the developing world, implies greater receipts of aid per capita. These were over three times as great in 1985, at $19 per capita for Africa and $6 per capita for other developing countries. Africa's net aid receipts were 3.5% of GNP, as compared with 1.1% for other developing countries.

Annual debt-servicing requirements, 1984–86, amounted to $10 billion—more than half the value of new lending to Africa each year. Debt servicing increased to $15 billion annually in the period 1987–89. The International Monetary Fund (IMF) moved, after 1984, to receive net transfers of funds from Africa, although it must be borne in mind that these negative transfers are more than offset by net lending from other multilateral and bilateral donors.

Overall, Africa is a minor debtor in world terms. Although outstanding debts are greater in relation to economy size, debt-servicing demands are comparable to those elsewhere in the developing world as a result of softer terms. Africa receives substantially greater net aid per capita, and as percentage of GNP, as compared with other developing countries.

Government sector
Table 9 shows government budgets in 1985. The governments of Africa, excluding South Africa, and of other developing countries are responsible

Table 9
CENTRAL GOVERNMENT BUDGETS, 1985
(% of GNP)

	Expenditure	Revenue	Budget surplus (+)/ deficit (−)
(Sub-Saharan Africa excluding South Africa)	23.7	19.3	−3.3
Other developing countries	22.2	21.3	−4.2
High-income oil countries	29.1	—	7.0
Industrial countries	29.1	24.5	−5.4
World	27.9	23.9	−5.0

Source: As for Table 1.

for similar expenditures as properties of GNP, at under 25%. Governments do a greater share of spending in industrial countries, at close to 30%. Budget deficits are lower in Africa, excluding South Africa, than elsewhere in developing countries, and certainly lower than the industrial country average.

Central government spending is a poor reflection of total public-sector spending in comparisons made across country groupings, as local government is responsible for a greater degree of educational and housing expenditure in industrial countries than in the developing world. Certain comparisons are perhaps instructive, however, with the African countries devoting almost 40% of central government spending to general administration, whereas this is under 25% in other developing and industrial countries. One-quarter of Africa's spending is on economic services. This is higher, at 36%, in other developing countries, but is under 10% in industrial countries.

On the revenue side, Africa (excluding South Africa) raises almost one-quarter of total revenue from taxes or international trade. This is only 1% in industrial countries. Africa, excluding South Africa, raises only 1.5% of total revenue from social security contributions, other developing countries raise 10% and industrial countries 30%. To a great extent these differences reflect the constraints placed on revenue raising in Africa where most of the population is engaged in subsistence agriculture.

Overall, Africa has relatively modest levels of government spending and budget deficits, with heavy emphasis on general administrative spending by central governments and on revenue raised from taxes on international trade.

Education and health
Literacy rates and enrollments in various levels of education are given in Table 10. The low emphasis that was given to education in colonial Africa is reflected in the low overall literacy rate, where almost two-thirds of

Table 10
EDUCATION

	Literacy 1980 (%)	Primary school enrollment 1984 (%)	Secondary school enrollment 1984 (%)	Higher education enrollment 1984 (%)
(Sub-Saharan Africa excluding South Africa)	38	78	21	2
Other developing countries	59	102	40	8
High-income oil countries	32	75	45	10
Industrial countries	99	102	90	38
Eastern European bloc	99	105	93	21
World	66	100	49	13

Source: As for Table 1, and M. Hodd, *African Economic Handbook* (London: Euromonitor, 1986).

adults were unable to read or write in 1980. Literacy rates are 50% higher in other developing countries. Primary-school enrollments were only four-fifths of Africa's primary-school age population in 1984, whereas they were 100% in other developing countries. Secondary-school enrollments and higher education enrollments were one-half and one-quarter, respectively, of the other developing country rates.

Table 11 gives life expectancy, and infant and child mortalities in 1985. Life expectancy is 20% lower in Africa as compared with other developing countries; infant mortality is 30% greater and child mortality twice the other developing countries' rate. The effect of economic development on quality of life is nowhere more apparent then in these life expectancy and mortality figures. Life expectancy is one-third lower in Africa as compared with industrial countries. Infant mortality is 10 times greater, and whereas 17 children per 1,000 die between the ages of one and four years of age in Africa, there are negligible deaths in this age-group in industrial countries.

There are 10 times the number of doctors per capita in other developing countries than there are in Africa, excluding South Africa. There are 25% more nurses per capita. Daily calorie supply is 25% higher in other developing countries. These comparisons are even starker when Africa (excluding South Africa) is compared with the industrial countries, where the number of doctors per capita is 50 times greater, nurses per capita 10 times greater and average daily calorie supply 70% higher.

Overall, Africa, excluding South Africa, has lower literacy and educational enrollment rates than elsewhere in the world, with the exception of the literacy and primary-school enrollment rates in high-income oil countries. Life expectancy is markedly lower and infant and child mortality higher in Africa and physician, nurse and nutritional provision are markedly inferior.

Table 11
LIFE EXPECTANCY; INFANT AND CHILD
MORTALITY, 1985

	Life expectancy	Infant (under 1 year) mortality (per 1,000)	Child (1–4) mortality (per 1,000)
Sub-Saharan Africa	50	103	17
(Sub-Saharan Africa			
excluding South Africa)	50	105	18
Other developing countries	63	66	8
High-income oil countries	63	61	5
Industrial countries	76	9	—
Eastern European bloc	69	27	—
World	64	59	7

Source: As for Table 1.

ECONOMIC PERFORMANCE

Table 12 shows GDP growth in the 1980s. Africa has had falling GDP over the period 1980–85; and the GDP has been falling faster, at −0.7% a year, when South Africa is excluded. Other developing countries have expanded GDP at almost 4.0% a year in the same period, and the industrial countries have had economies growing at 2.3%.

When population growth rates are taken into account, to give GDP per capita growth rates, Africa (excluding South Africa) has had average output per capita falling at almost −4.0% a year. This implies a fall of almost −20% in the first five years of the 1980s. Other developing countries and the industrial countries have increased GDP per capita at around 2.0% annually, a 10% rise in output per capita in the first half of the 1980s. The oil group of countries have had falling GDP and GDP per capita in the 1980s, but they are very much of a special case, and this contraction follows expansion of GDP per capita at 6.3% a year, the highest of any country group, over the period 1960–79.

Growth performance in the 1980s for Africa, excluding South Africa, contrasts with the period 1960–79, when GNP per capita rose at 1.6% a year. Reasons for this deterioration in economic performance are discussed below.

Table 13 gives the growth performances in the main producing sectors. Although agricultural output in Africa (excluding South Africa) has expanded at 0.9%, this is slower than the population growth of 3.3% a year. The industrial sector has contracted, at −2.4% a year, and the services sector by −0.4% a year. Performances across the sectors is markedly inferior to that of the other developing countries, where both agriculture and industry sectors have expanded output at over 4.0% annually.

Table 12
GDP GROWTH, GDP PER CAPITA GROWTH, INFLATION, 1980–85
(% per year)

	GDP	GDP per capita	Inflation
Sub-Saharan Africa	−0.3	−3.4	15.6
(Sub-Saharan Africa			
excluding South Africa)	−0.7	−3.9	16.7
Other developing countries	3.9	2.2	48.7
High-income oil countries	−2.2	−6.3	−2.5
Industrial countries	2.3	1.9	5.8
World (excluding	2.4	1.5	12.6
Eastern European bloc)			

Source: As for Table 1.

Table 14 shows recent growth of expenditure categories. Africa, excluding South Africa, has expanded private and government consumption by 0.3% and 0.7%, respectively—both rates being lower than the 3.3% rate of population increase. It is the level of gross domestic investment that has borne the brunt of the poor economic performance in Africa. Gross investment has contracted by −11.4% a year. Investment levels in 1985 were 56% of their levels in 1980.

Trade performance is shown in Table 15, with Africa's export volumes falling by over −4.0% a year (and faster, at −5.0%, if South Africa is excluded). This contrasts with other developing countries where export volumes have expanded by 5.0% annually.

Africa's terms of trade have declined since 1980 by almost 10%, implying that a 10% volume of exports has been required to purchase the same volume of imports in 1985. There have been significant changes in the terms of trade for non-oil exporting African countries from 1976, since

Table 13
GROWTH OF PRODUCTION, 1980–85
(% per year)

	Agriculture	Industry	Services	GDP
(Sub-Saharan Africa				
excluding South Africa)	0.9	−2.4	−0.4	−0.7
Other developing countries	4.3	4.1	3.3	3.9
High-income oil countries	7.8	−8.3	5.1	−2.2
Industrial countries	1.5	2.5	2.0	2.3
World	2.9	2.3	2.2	2.4

Source: As for Table 1.

Table 14
EXPENDITURE GROWTH, 1980–85
(% per year)

	Private consumption	Gross domestic investment	Government consumption	GDP
(Sub-Saharan Africa excluding South Africa)	0.3	−11.4	0.7	−0.7
Other developing countries	3.1	1.6	4.6	3.9
Industrial countries	2.2	2.7	2.7	2.3
World	2.3	2.4	2.9	2.4

Source: As for Table 1.

which time they have almost halved. It must be borne in mind, however, that individual African countries have had differing experiences over the terms of trade, depending on the nature of their exports. Adverse terms-of-trade movements and declining export production have combined to reduce imports. Imports in Africa have fallen by −9.0% annually, and in 1985 were at 60% of their 1980 levels. The implications of these factors for economic development are discussed below.

Inflation rates in the 1980s are given in Table 12, above. Africa's record, with an average annual rate of inflation of around 15%, compares well with the record of other developing countries, which have averaged almost 50% annual inflation. The industrial countries have had 6% inflation, while the oil countries have had price levels declining at −2.5% a year.

Table 15
TRADE GROWTH, TERMS OF TRADE

	Exports growth 1980–85 (% per year)	Imports growth 1980–85 (% per year)	Terms of trade (1980 = 100) (% per year)
Sub-Saharan Africa	−4.3	−9.2	91
(Sub-Saharan Africa excluding South Africa)	−5.0	−9.4	94
Other developing countries	5.1	1.3	94
High-income oil countries	−17.1	−1.1	107
Industrial countries	3.7	3.7	100
World (excluding Eastern European bloc)	2.9	2.7	99

Source: As for Table 1.

Overall, Africa has had poor economic performance in the 1980s, in relation to non-oil groups, with falling production (particularly in industry) and declining living standards, investment levels and export performance. Only with respect to inflation has Africa's performance been better than in other developing countries.

THE AFRICAN ECONOMIES

Table 16 summarizes information on the 46 sub-Saharan African countries with respect to geographical region, size as indicated by population level, economy type as classified by the World Bank, and currency zone.

Table 17 summarizes information on recent economic performance, stability, economic reform policies and immediate prospects.

Economic performance is judged on what has happened to average living standards in the period 1980–85. If GDP per capita has fallen, the performance is considered poor; if it has remained more or less unchanged, performance is moderate; rising GDP per capita reflects good performance.

Twenty-two African countries have had poor economic performance, and it is likely that most of the 12 countries for which not enough data is available to prepare complete statistics for the period have also had poor performance. Four countries have managed to hold their own in expanding output, at roughly the same pace as population growth. Eight countries have had good performance in the early 1980s. Overall, only one-quarter of African nations have maintained average living standards or better, and this contrasts with the two decades 1960–79, when this was achieved by over 80% of African countries.

Stability is judged on the record over the past decade, and is a weighted average of factors that adversely effect economic performance. Thus, non-constitutional changes of government, threats of such changes, internal and cross-border armed conflicts, riots and disruptions, and sudden changes in economic policy are all seen as having adverse effects.[4] It is invariably difficult to improve material well-being if there is not internal security, stable government and continuity in economic policy; and the attainment of stability is a prerequisite for economic progress. The 15 countries with very bad stability records have all had poor economic performance or have not collected adequate data for an assessment to be made. Among eight countries with poor stability, the Seychelles has had moderate economic progress; Somalia and Zimbabwe, good performances. But it could be argued that these results would have been even better with improved stability. Of the countries with moderate to good stability, 11 of the 23 have had poor performance, which indicates that stability is in general a necessary but not a sufficient condition for progress.

---

[4]For more detail on stability factors, see Hodd, *African Economies: Stability, Structure, Trends, Performance and Forecasts* (Aldershot: Gower, 1988).

Table 16
REGION, SIZE, ECONOMY TYPE, CURRENCY ZONE

Country	Region				Size			Economy type				Currency zone		
	E	W	C	S	S	M	L	L	M	O	U	F	A	O
Angola				S		M				O				O
Benin		W				M		L				F		
Botswana				S		M			M				A	
Burkina Faso		W				M		L				F		
Burundi	E					M		L						O
Cameroon			C			M				O		F		
Cape Verde Islands		W			S			L						O
Central African Republic			C			M		L				F		
Chad			C			M		L				F		
Comoros	E				S			L				F		
Congo			C			M				O		F		
Djibouti	E				S				M					O
Equatorial Guinea			C		S			L				F		
Ethiopia	E						L	L						O
Gabon			C		S					O		F		
Gambia		W			S			L					A	
Ghana		W					L	L					A	
Guinea		W				M		L						O
Guinea-Bissau		W			S			L						O
Ivory Coast		W				M			M			F		
Kenya	E						L	L					A	
Lesotho				S		M			M				A	
Liberia		W				M			M					O
Madagascar	E					M		L						O
Malawi				S		M		L					A	
Mali		W				M		L				F		
Mauritania		W				M			M					O
Mauritius	E					M			M				A	
Mozambique				S			L	L						O
Niger		W				M		L				F		
Nigeria		W					L			O			A	
Rwanda	E					M		L						O
São Tomé and Príncipe			C	S				L						O
Senegal		W				M		L				F		
Seychelles	E				S						U		A	
Sierra Leone		W				M		L					A	

Country	Region				Size			Economy type				Currency zone		
	E	W	C	S	S	M	L	L	M	O	U	F	A	O
Somalia	E					M		L						O
South Africa				S			L				U		A	
Sudan	E						L	L					A	
Swaziland				S	S				M				A	
Tanzania	E						L	L					A	
Togo		W				M		L				F		
Uganda	E						L	L					A	
Zaire			C				L	L						O
Zambia				S		M			M				A	
Zimbabwe				S		M			M				A	
Total Numbers	13	16	8	10	9	26	10	29	10	5	2	14	17	15

Legend:

E = East	S = Under 1	L = Low income	F = Franc
W = West	million	M = Lower middle	zone
C = Central	M = 1 million–	income	A = Anglo-
S = Southern	10 million	O = Oil exporter	phone
	L = Over 10	U = Upper middle	O = Other
	million	income	

Analysis of economic performance

Explanations of the deterioration in African economic performance in recent years have centered around assessments of the relative impact of external events as against the domestic policies pursued.

The first set of explanations emphasizes the poor educational preparation of the labor force during the colonial period, the impact of the two major oil price rises in the 1970s, droughts and declining terms of trade. Some instability has external origins, particularly in southern African states as the result of South Africa's activities. There has also been the recession in the industrial countries in the early 1980s, which has affected the volume of Africa's exports as well as their prices. High interest rates have increased the burden of servicing external debts, especially for those middle-income oil and mineral exporters that have borrowed from commercial sources.

The other view, while acknowledging the adverse impact of some of the external factors, emphasizes poor domestic economic policies in Africa.

In the 1950s and 1960s, the period in which most African countries were approaching and attaining political independence, the consensus among economists was that the market mechanism was not adequate to meet the development needs of poor countries. There were a number of theoretical reasons to support this, in particular the argument that restricted competition and monopolies in markets, imperfect knowledge and poorly established private property rights led to impaired economic efficiency. Further, markets were thought to result in distributions of income that did not meet with the social values of society; and it was feared that in the early stages

803

Table 17
ECONOMIC PERFORMANCE, STABILITY, REFORMS, PROSPECTS

	Economic performance			Stability					Economic reforms			Prospects		
	P	M	G	B	P	M	G	V	N	S	Y	P	M	G
Angola	P			B						S		P		
Benin	P					M					Y			G
Botswana			G					V			Y			G
Burkina Faso		?		B					N				M	
Burundi		M		B							Y		M	
Cameroon			G					V			Y			G
Cape Verde Islands		?					G			S			M	
Central African Republic	P			B							Y	P		
Chad		?		B						S		P		
Comoros		?		B					N			P		
Congo			G			M					Y			G
Djibouti		?						V		S			M	
Equatorial Guinea		?		B							Y		M	
Ethiopia		?		B					N			P		
Gabon		?						V			Y		M	
Gambia	P						G				Y		M	
Ghana	P			B							Y		M	
Guinea		?			P						Y		M	
Guinea-Bissau		?		B							Y		M	
Ivory Coast	P							V			Y		M	
Kenya	P							V			Y			G
Lesotho			G			M				S				G
Liberia	P				P				N			P		
Madagascar	P				P						Y		M	
Malawi		M						V			Y		M	
Mali	P				P					S			M	
Mauritania	P			B							Y		M	
Mauritius			G					V			Y			G
Mozambique	P			B							Y	P		
Niger	P					M					Y			G
Nigeria	P			B							Y		M	
Rwanda	P						G		N				M	
São Tomé and Príncipe	P						G				Y		M	
Senegal			G					V			Y		M	
Seychelles		M			P					S				G

804

	Economic performance			Stability					Economic reforms			Prospects		
	P	M	G	B	P	M	G	V	N	S	Y	P	M	G
Sierra Leone		?			P						Y		M	
Somalia			G		P						Y		M	
South Africa		M					G		N			P		
Sudan	P			B					N			P		
Swaziland		?					G			S			M	
Tanzania	P							V			Y		M	
Togo	P						G				Y		M	
Uganda	P			B							Y		M	
Zaire	P						G				Y	P		
Zambia	P						G		N			P		
Zimbabwe			G		P				N				M	

Legend:

P = Poor	B = Very poor	N = No reform
M = Moderate	P = Poor	S = Some
G = Good	M = Moderate	reforms
? = No data	G = Good	Y = Substantial
	V = Very good	reforms

P = Poor
M = Moderate
G = Good

Source: M. Hodd, *African Economies: Stability, Structure, Trends, Performance and Forecasts* (Aldershot, Hampshire: Gower, 1988).

of a development strategy reliant on markets there would be a movement toward a more unequal distribution of income.

These views were reinforced by an impression that planning had performed well in the Soviet Union in the interwar period when the market economies of the West had experienced a debilitating depression. During World War II, Western economies were subject to greater government control, overall planning and rationing regulations, which distributed goods according to perceived need rather than via the price mechanism. This experience encouraged the view that government intervention was necessary if urgent national objectives were to be achieved.

The colonial period had established regulations, controls and institutionalized monopolies to protect settler and colonial interests in Africa. The creation of export-crop marketing boards, and restricting the growing of the more valuable cash crops to settlers, were notable examples. The performance of China after 1949 in successfully collectivizing agriculture and introducing socialist planning provided a model that several African countries admired. In the colonial period the ownership of most capitalist enterprises was in the hands of the colonial rulers. The new African leaders at that time, with little vested interest in supporting large-scale capitalist enterprises, pursued a set of policies that emphasized the role of the state rather than corporate business.

The 1960s saw independent African countries increasing their role in their economies. Marketing boards with monopolies over cash-crop purchasing were retained, and were seen as mechanisms whereby governments could effectively tax agriculture by passing on less than the eventual sale price of the crops to domestic producers. Industrialization rather than primary-product production was seen as essential for fast development. Consequently, African countries began setting up manufacturing plants to produce goods previously imported, invariably with monopolies in domestic markets, tariff protection and state ownership. Foreign investment was discouraged and subjected to controls, and in many instances existing foreign-owned enterprises were nationalized. Prices of goods in domestic markets were often regulated. Official exchange rates were kept fixed, and when balance-of-payments problems arose, governments reduced imports by imposing licenses and introducing restrictions on foreign-exchange movements. Concern to be self-sufficient in food led to pricing policies that favored foodstuffs rather than cash-crop production in agriculture. Governments undertook substantial public-sector programs in health, education and the provision of the infrastructure necessary for industrialization.

A change in view among economists began to emerge in the 1970s. However, it was almost a decade before international institutions began to press for changes in policy by African countries, and African governments began to receive similar advice from their own advisers.

It gradually became clear that developing countries that had relied on international markets had experienced good economic performance in the postwar period. The best use of their resources was judged to be in producing goods in which they either had a natural advantage (such as tropical agricultural products or minerals) or in which they had built up experience and expertise, and in trading these for goods more efficiently manufactured by other countries.

At independence there were few university graduates in Africa, and these had degrees mostly in medicine or arts subjects; they lacked the ability to implement comprehensive economic plans. Planning failure began to be seen as more serious than market failures. A new generation of economic advisers began to head government ministries, and many of these advisers had received postgraduate training in economics in the West where there is heavy emphasis on the efficiency of competitive markets.

Shortcomings of the interventionist policies in Africa also became apparent. The export-crop marketing boards often passed on very low percentages of the realized world price to domestic producers. And instead of the margin between the world price and the producer price being used to augment government revenues for productive investment, it was often defrayed in paying salaries in overstaffed institutions. Many export-crop marketing boards, far from adding to government revenue succeeded only in incurring losses that were funded from other government receipts or increased budget deficits. The marketing boards responsible for domestic foods paid high prices to encourage self-sufficiency, but sold goods at subsidized prices to urban consumers. These marketing boards also suffered losses as a result of the negative trading margins, to which were added their operating costs. These policies conspired to reduce export-crop output as farmers moved out of export crops into domestic food production.

The exchange-rate policies pursued exacerbated the adverse effect of marketing boards on exports. Heavy levels of domestic public-sector spending led to acceleration in domestic inflation. With fixed exchange rates, this led to overvalued domestic currencies. The official rates could only be maintained by controls on foreign-exchange dealings and restrictions on imports by licensing. Black markets in foreign exchange emerged in most countries. In the 1970s, Africa's black market exchange rates were on the average 60% higher than official rates.[5] Overvalued currencies further reduce receipts by producers of export crops in domestic currencies, and encourage smuggling. Allied to this is the effect of cheaper imports in discouraging domestic producers of manufactures. These production effects, added to the pressure on the balance of payments, and in the absence of corrective means, led to even greater domestic currency overvaluation.

Those import-substituting industrial projects with tariff protection or domestic monopolies used their market position to produce high-cost goods from inefficient, overmanned enterprises. Lack of experience and expertise in manufacturing, particularly the shortage of managerial skills, added to poor production performance in these sectors. Control over prices of domestic goods led to shortages and the emergence of black markets in basic commodities.

With the rises in oil prices in 1974 and 1979, and the increased burden of debt servicing resulting from higher interest rates, African countries found that the shortage of foreign exchange caused by poor export performance was intensified. Import licenses restricted the availability of fuel, industrial and agricultural inputs, and machinery spare parts. Manufacturing began to operate at low levels of capacity, agriculture grew slowly and the transport system began to fall into disrepair.

Although the effects of government intervention were apparent, it was argued[6] that the predominantly one-party states in Africa, acting as self-perpetuating oligarchies, had no incentive to improve efficiency. Political power required the support of the urban population, a minority that comprised 20% of the total. Ruling groups discriminated through the exchange-rate policy and marketing-board operation to favor urban communities. Thus, low prices to rural export producers, subsidized food prices for urban consumers and cheap imports of manufactures all served to distribute income toward town dwellers. Inflated staff of marketing boards and state-owned enterprises comprised urban residents. In addition, those lucky enough to receive import licenses were in a position to resell the goods at black market prices.[7]

Reform programs of the 1980s

In the face of political factors that have favored intervention in African economies it requires some explanation as to why the 1980s have witnessed

[5] See Hodd, *African Economic Handbook* (London: Euromonitor, 1986).

[6] See R. L. Bates, *Markets and States in Tropical Africa* (San Francisco: University of California Press, 1981).

[7] See A. O. Kreuger, "The Political Economy of the Rent-Seeking Society," *American Economic Review* (1974).

a series of reforms in African economies that have seen the beginnings of returns to market-orientated policies. Table 17 lists the economies that have introduced some reforms, eight in all, and the 29 that have instituted fairly comprehensive changes to their economic policies. Only eight countries have resisted making changes.

The reforms involve devaluation to close to market valuation of currencies, and in some cases, exchange rates set by weekly auctions. Marketing boards have had their monopolies ended and in some cases have been wound up or had their operations severely curtailed. Private trading has reemerged in these markets. Subsidies have been reduced or abolished on foodstuffs, and controls have been lifted on domestic prices. Foreign investment has been encouraged and state-owned enterprises are in the process of being closed down or sold off.

The changes have been more comprehensive and have been introduced more rapidly than observers of the entrenched political positions in the 1960s and 1970s considered possible. Several influences appear to have been important.

In the first place, the interventions in the economy produced redistributions in favor of ruling elites and urban populations at the expense of long-run development of the economy. After two decades of intervention, the new ruling elites of Africa have now accumulated substantial assets and have more to gain by making these assets more productive by more efficient economic policies than by continuing redistribution in their favor.

Secondly, there has been a change in the pressure from the IMF and the World Bank. Up to 1979 the IMF lent on the condition that borrowing countries undertook policies to correct the balance of payments, usually by reducing government spending. From 1979 on it has demanded more wide-ranging reforms to improve efficiency of resources use. In this it has worked in cooperation with the World Bank.

More important than the financial sanctions that the IMF and World Bank have been able to impose via their own lending has been their influence on bilateral donors and policy advisers in African countries.[8] They have succeeded in persuading these groups to support their market-oriented policies by arguing that markets work more efficiently than planned economies, and that as a result, all sections of the community can be better off.

Experience of the reform program has been mixed. Hurried implementation in Zambia and Sudan caused urban unrest at the ending of food subsidies, and the programs were aborted. Elsewhere, results have been encouraging, with return to positive growth rates and improved living standards, most notably in Ghana, Mauritius, Malawi and Tanzania. However, most of these reform programs are in their early stages. Reforming South American countries have experienced deteriorating performance after initial improvements. There is thus reason to be cautious about the overall impact of reforms in Africa.

Future prospects

Table 18 presents forecasts based on World Bank projections up to 1995. The World Bank gives high and low estimates, depending on world con-

[8] See Hodd, "Africa, the IMF and the World Bank," *African Affairs* (1987).

Table 18
FORECASTS, 1986–95
(% per year increase)

	GDP	GDP per capita	Export of goods	Import of goods	Inflation
(Sub-Saharan Africa excluding South Africa)	3.6	0.3	3.0	4.0	8.6
Other developing countries	5.1	3.4	8.1	6.1	—
Industrial countries	3.4	3.0	—	—	3.0
World	3.7	3.0	—	—	—

Source: As for Table 1, and M. Hodd, *African Economies: Stability, Structure, Trends, Performance and Forecasts* (Aldershot, Hampshire: Gower, 1988).

ditions and the nature of policy responses. The estimates presented here are averages of the high and low forecasts.

GDP in Africa, excluding South Africa, is forecast to grow by 3.6% annually up to 1995—about the same rate as the industrial countries—but slower than other developing countries, where GDP is expected to expand at 5.1% a year. Taking population growth into account, Africa (excluding South Africa) is forecast to expand GDP per capita at 0.3% annually. This will produce an increase in GDP per capita of 3% over the decade, and there is thus little scope for optimism concerning improvement in Africa's living standards. Other developing countries and industrial countries are expected to increase their GDP per capita at 3.4% and 3.0%, respectively.

Africa (excluding South Africa) is forecast to expand export volumes by 3.0% annually, and import volumes by 4.0% annually. Both these rates are slower than for the rest of the developing world, for which the forecasts are 8.1% and 6.1%, respectively.

Inflation is projected to be in single figures, at 8.6% a year for Africa (excluding South Africa).[9]

All these forecasts are considerable improvements on the record for 1980–85, when GDP and GDP per capita fell in Africa, as did export and import volumes, while inflation was above 15% annually.

Table 18 lists immediate prospects for 46 African countries, derived from a model[10] that obtains individual country forecasts based on World Bank aggregate projections. Poor prospects indicate falling GDP per capita; moderate prospects, GDP increasing roughly in line with population; and good prospects, GDP per capita rising.

Ten countries have poor prospects, and they are in all cases countries with poor stability or showing unwillingness to introduce reforms, or both. Twenty-six countries have moderate prospects, and for 10 the prospects are good. The countries with good prospects are invariably stable, with economic reform programs in place.

[9] See Hodd, *African Economies*.
[10] *Ibid.*

Overall, Africa is forecast to experience static living standards in the immediate future, although some 10 countries will be in a position to improve the material well-being of their citizens.

FURTHER READING

Bates, R. L. *Markets and States in Tropical Africa*. Berkeley: University of California Press, 1981.
Hodd, Michael. *African Economic Handbook*. London: Euromonitor, 1986.
————. *African Economies: Stability, Structure, Trends, Performance and Forecasts*. Aldershot, Hampshire: Gower, 1988.
World Bank. *Accelerated Development in Sub-Saharan Africa*. Washington, D.C.: World Bank, 1981.
————. *World Debt Tables*. Washington, D.C.: World Bank, 1988.

AFRICA, THE INTERNATIONAL MONETARY FUND AND THE WORLD BANK: ADJUSTMENT AND FINANCE

TONY KILLICK

BY common consent, the economic situation in most African countries is parlous—far worse than in any other Third World region. Similarly, there is little dispute that shortages of foreign exchange are a central obstacle to achieving a turnabout in this situation, the so-called balance-of-payments constraint. The International Monetary Fund (IMF) and the World Bank have sought to respond to the crisis by providing more payments support for African member-states—but on conditions. Their credits are available only in support of "adjustment programs," involving changes in a wide range of policies. This article is about Africa's balance-of-payments (BoP) position, its financing needs, and the great proliferation of adjustment policy conditionality it has experienced in its desperate search for financial support.

BACKGROUND

Although the African continent is indeed in a uniquely poor economic situation, it is imperative to warn against overgeneralizations. The economies of Africa vary enormously in size, structure and vulnerability, and in the living standards they can offer their peoples. While many have acute BoP difficulties and large debts, some run payments surpluses and have no difficulties in servicing modest debt levels. And though in the majority of countries living standards are falling—and in some have been falling for a long time—there is a sizable minority in which average incomes are rising despite rapid population growth.

It is necessary to generalize somewhat, however, and the overall picture

811

is one of acute difficulty. Thus, sub-Saharan Africa as a whole showed a current BoP deficit in 1986 of well over U.S. $8 billion, and similar deficits in 1987 and 1988 were forecast. This understates the problem, however, because these deficits were incurred despite stringent cuts in imports by many countries. This had severely damaging effects on the output of manufacturing, and to a lesser extent in agriculture and other branches of production. It also held back investment and prevented the adequate maintenance of the basic infrastructure. Finally, it held back living standards and, because imported goods act as "incentive goods," reduced the rewards for increasing productivity.

Much of the difficulty, of course, was attributable to the decline in the world prices of most of the primary products on which African countries remain heavily dependent. In consequence there was a drastic deterioration in their terms of trade—the price of exports relative to the price of imports—which are estimated to have fallen, on the average, by no less than 26 percent in the period between 1980 and 1987. For countries already in difficulties in the late 1970s this fall in the purchasing power of their exports was catastrophic. It was also aggravated by a generally stagnant output of export commodities.

Another major factor was the burgeoning cost of interest and amortization payments on external debts. Since debt is the subject of the chapter "The African Debt Crisis," p. 841, suffice it to say here that a high proportion of the BoP deficits already mentioned was represented by the cost of interest payments alone, to say nothing of amortization.

The BoP deficits on current account would not, in fact, be a large problem—nor would the "import strangulation" have occurred—were adequate inflows of capital on soft terms available from the rest of the world. The truth is, however, that net financial inflows have declined drastically during the 1980s. Thus, for sub-Saharan Africa as a whole the net transfer of resources fell from $16.8 billion in 1982 to only $4.4 billion in 1985 (latest figures available). The countries worst affected by this trend were those like Nigeria and the Ivory Coast, which had been borrowing from the commercial banks up to 1982. From these countries there has actually been a net outflow in recent years. But even the poorer African countries, largely dependent on official sources of capital, were not exempt—with net flows declining from around $6 billion in 1980–82 to under $4 billion in 1984–85.

For much of Africa, therefore, the BoP has emerged as the key source of economic weakness. That it has done so is a result of domestic shocks like the drought of the earlier 1980s; domestic policy mistakes; and a world economic environment turned severely, and perhaps irreversibly, more hostile. It is to this changed set of circumstances that African governments have been struggling to adjust, urged on by the IMF, the World Bank and the industrial countries that control these institutions.

ADJUSTMENT AND THE CONDITIONALITY EXPLOSION

Adjustment, then, is the imperative, but there is a question about what this should actually entail. In the broadest terms, adjustment involves shifts in the structures of production and demand to move resources into the production of exports and import-substitutes relative to those (nontradable) activities that do not enter into the BoP. But what does that mean in specific policy terms?

The creditor countries, as well as the IMF and the World Bank, have been rather confident in supplying answers, and their influence has become pervasive throughout the continent. Conditionality—the policy strings that are attached to the provision of BoP credits—is the means by which this influence has been exerted, and today only a few African countries are still going it alone and do not have an adjustment program associated with the fund and/or the bank.

Various forces have conspired to produce this explosion of conditionality. The BoP and debt crises themselves have been the principal culprits, in many cases leaving governments with little choice but to seek the credits available from the IMF and the World Bank and to accept, therefore, the policy conditions with which they are associated. The force of this necessity has been all the stronger because of the insistence of the creditor clubs—official and private alike—that a program must be agreed on with the fund before a debt rescheduling can be set up. Other factors, however, have intensified the spread of conditionality.

One factor is the erosion within the IMF of the value of resources that can be made available by it without rigorous conditionality. To an historically exceptional extent fund resources are now tied to compliance with strict policy conditions. Related to this is a restriction of the fund's facility for compensating countries for unexpected shortfalls in export earnings—access to which compensation used to be automatic but which is now increasingly linked to full conditionality. Yet another factor is the higher level of conditionality attached to the fund's new structural adjustment facility (SAF) than was true of the old trust fund from which the SAF is being financed. Even with the fund's traditional fare, its standby credits, there is today a wider range of policy conditionality than was true some years ago, with more supply-side measures being grafted onto its traditional demand-control policies.

The movement of the World Bank into the business of "policy-related" BoP financing at the beginning of the 1980s was another factor, not the least because of the wide-ranging policy content of its SAF and related loans. Mention should be made too of the increased tendency for bilateral aid donors to link their own program aid to conformity with the conditions of the IMF and the bank, or—particularly in the case of the U.S. Agency for International Development—to develop their own policy conditionality.

Taken together, these developments have resulted in a veritable explosion of conditionality in the 1980s—and have been intended to do so. It would, of course, be a mistake to think that all the policy content set out in stabilization and adjustment programs has been imposed upon reluctant governments. No doubt they would have chosen to introduce some of these actions themselves; and no doubt, too, it has been convenient to use the IMF and the World Bank as scapegoats, to be blamed for unpopular measures that are, in truth, inescapable. It would equally be a mistake to think that all the policy promises made are faithfully executed. There is often a large implementation shortfall and hence a tendency to exaggerate the power of the external agencies over African governments.

Nevertheless, the governments of Africa are today subject to international pressures—the intensity and range of which are without precedent in modern economic history—to adopt often highly specific and sensitive policy measures.

Of what does this conditionality consist? From the creditors and the international agencies a new orthodoxy has been developed about the measures that the debtor countries of Africa—and elsewhere—should undertake in order to achieve adjustment. The chief components of this orthodoxy are as follows:

- Greater and more efficient use of price incentives—in contrast to more planned or regulated approaches—in order to improve the efficiency of resource use. Currency devaluations and the subsequent maintenance of realistic exchange rates are a particularly important example of this approach. Improved producer prices, removal of price controls and subsidies, and interest-rate reforms provide other illustrations.
- Greater reliance on private enterprise and the encouragement of entrepreneurship, with a correspondingly reduced role for the public sector. The privatization of ailing public enterprises—of which the United States is a particularly fervent advocate—is among the nostrums urged under this heading.
- The liberalization of trade and payments, the encouragement of foreign private investment and the promotion of exports.
- The reduction of budgetary deficits, largely through reduced government expenditures, and associated reductions in domestic credit and money supply, along the lines commonly associated with the IMF.

UNSETTLED QUESTIONS

While there is a good deal of agreement both with the general proposition that substantial policy reforms were needed in many African countries and with the broad thrust of the new orthodoxy, there remain a large number of unresolved questions.

One group of questions concerns the consistency of present-day approaches to adjustment with the long-range development of the economies of Africa. Faced, as so many of these economies are, with a critical BoP constraint, adjustment can be seen as a necessary step toward a resumption of longer-term development. At the same time, however, current preoccupations with adjustment represent a shortening of time horizons, a shift from the 10-year time spans of a development strategy to the search for a quick—or at most medium-term—BoP fix.

There are real dangers in this. In the end, the speed of development will be crucially affected by the pace at which productivities can be raised. This requires long-term investments, most particularly in people and skills, but also in the physical infrastructure. There are already too many examples of governments that have had to cut back their spending on education, health and major infrastructural projects in order to produce desired reductions in budget deficits. Although the World Bank—and perhaps even the IMF— show increased sensitivity to this, there is also a danger that distributional concerns, particularly poverty alleviation, will be lost sight of in the preoccupation with the BoP. Since adjustment is far from costless it cannot fail to affect the distribution of income, and there is a real danger that it will worsen the lot of the poorest parts of the population, particularly the urban poor. Much the same could be said for environmental considerations, although here again the bank is responding to criticisms about this matter. In an atmosphere of crisis management and shortened planning horizons there is a rather obvious danger that the longer-term benefits from protecting renewable and nonrenewable assets will be set aside.

Another controversy concerns the role of export promotion in adjustment. The depressed and vulnerable state of world primary-product markets has added to fears that the export orientation of many World Bank and IMF country programs will have the aggregate effect of creating an oversupply on these markets, thus further depressing prices and undermining the purpose of adjustment itself. With manufactured exports—and Africa has few of these—the concern is rather with market access: the willingness of the industrial countries to tolerate further "import penetration," and their increased protectionism. Lest it be thought that African countries are immune to such actions because of the small volume of their manufactured exports, the experience of Mauritius stands as a warning. It came up sharply against market barriers as soon as it began to achieve success, albeit on a tiny scale, with its textile and other processed exports.

So adverse has been the world economic environment to Africa in the last decade or more, and so large are the continuing uncertainties that many see merit in policies that place some premium on risk reduction and self-sufficiency, particularly in food. But risk reduction has yet to be fully incorporated in the new orthodoxy on adjustment design. Indeed, in stressing the value of full integration into world trade and capital movements it seems to have little room for an approach that would have the effect of limiting that integration.

A closely related topic concerns the role of industrialization in African adjustment. The sectoral emphasis in the new orthodoxy is strongly upon the need to improve the performance of agriculture. There are good reasons for this, not the least being the past poor record of agriculture in either adequately feeding Africa's expanding populations or in even maintaining Africa's share in world agricultural-product markets. Nevertheless, beyond the medium term a strategy based upon agriculture has strictly limited potential. Indeed, the depressed state of primary-product markets is already pointing to the need to diversify out of such products—and therefore into industry. The new orthodoxy, however, has little to say about African industrialization, except to (correctly) decry the inefficiency of past attempts and emphasize the need to reduce competitive barriers.

A more general—and politically sensitive—question concerns the respective roles of the public and private sectors. While there is substantial agreement within Africa that postcolonial governments overexpanded the role and scope of the state in the economy, there remain real differences about the extent to which the balance needs to be redressed and the precise forms this should take. There is, for example, considerable skepticism about the

815

appropriateness of, and scope for, the privatization of public enterprises so strongly urged by the Reagan administration. There is skepticism within Africa, too, about the assumption outside agencies sometimes appear to make that private enterprise can be relied upon to do better than the state and to move in to fill any lacunae left by a withdrawal of the public sector.

Another aspect of this disagreement, with its strong ideological over-tones, concerns the efficacy of policies to "get prices right." Here again there is substantial agreement that in the past governments paid too little heed to the power of the market as a mechanism for the efficient allocation of resources, that many distortions exist, and that there is much scope for improved price incentives. The basic change that has occurred through much of the continent in attitudes toward exchange-rate policy is a clear example of the acceptance of the need for improved price relativities. The agreement sometimes breaks down, however, over the extent to which non-price in-terventions by government are also necessary in order to increase the effec-tiveness of improved price incentives.

Disagreements of a rather different kind occur in attempts to reconcile the demand-management approach of the IMF with the structural adjust-ment approach of the World Bank. The fund designs its programs around the resources it expects to be available, whatever their adequacy, and views government spending, domestic bank credit and imports negatively as all weakening the BoP in the short run. The bank instead asks the question, what program and resources will be necessary in order to achieve given BoP *and growth* targets? It is more likely to recognize the positive contribution to adjustment of government programs of capital expenditure, of credit as facilitating improved capacity utilization and structural change, and of im-ports as necessary inputs into the adjustment process. The demand-control policies of the fund have long been criticized by developing countries as excessively deflationary; U.S. Treasury Secretary James Baker is a more re-cent—and surprising—convert to this view, calling for fund programs to become more growth oriented. To be able to do so adequately, however, the fund would need more resources to on-lend to deficit countries, and neither the American treasury secretary nor his European counterparts seem willing to provide them.

Other questions that are asked about the new orthodoxy on adjustment are concerned less with its policy content than with its sustainability.

• Are the modalities of conditionality—the ways in which they are negotiated and the extent to which they are dictated by Washington—such as to ensure the greatest possible meeting of minds between the government and the agencies? Experience teaches that imposed programs are the first to break down and the least likely to be imple-mented.

• How well, in any case, do economists and others engaged in the design of adjustment understand the problem and the connections between their policy recommendations and the program objectives? There is a strong suspicion that the problems and their solutions are not well understood, and therefore that there is a strong case for greater experimentation in program design than occurs at present, especially in IMF programs but in the World Bank's as well.

• How much, in any case, is it reasonable to expect of adjustment programs in the face of limited supporting finance and a generally unfavorable world environment? There is a major danger that unrealistic expectations are being placed on the efficacy of such programs and that there will be a backlash of disillusionment when many of them appear to fail.

• Given the same combination of an adverse world economy and inadequate supporting finance, and adding to it the inevitable economic and social costs of adjustment, will the new adjustment orthodoxy prove to be politically sustainable? Are the political fabric and the perceived legitimacy of governments sufficient to sustain programs involving austerity and greater personal insecurity, or will the programs become politically intolerable as soon as it is realized that the benefits they offer are at best medium-term ones? The example of Zambia is widely cited in this connection.

There thus remains much uncertainty, much controversy. To the long-standing dispute about the policies of the IMF in Africa has now been added a wider range of questions about the policies of the World Bank and of the creditor countries that stand behind these institutions. As has already been hinted, these controversies are closely bound up with the adequacy of the finance the West is willing to make available in support of the efforts of African governments to improve policies and adjust to the shocks that have so affected their economies over the last 15 years. This financial aspect will now be examined in more detail.

THE CASE FOR EXTERNAL SUPPORT

It is sometimes taken as axiomatic that adjustment programs require external support, but this may be a mistake for it is not immediately obvious why a devaluation, an improvement in the budgetary balance or measures to raise the efficiency of public enterprises should require external finance. In this spirit, a U.S. representative to the United Nations was reported recently as arguing that "improved productivity of existing resources, especially if combined with increased domestic savings, is very likely to be more important than additional external resources in the foreseeable future. This is particularly true in the current tight budgetary situation throughout the world." It is therefore worth spelling out the case for external support with some care. A number of overlapping and reinforcing arguments in support of external aid can be marshaled along the following lines.

First, and most important, if the donor community takes its arguments for some resumption of economic growth seriously, then external support is necessary to supplement domestic saving in order to raise investment to high enough levels so that resumed growth can become a realistic aspiration. Domestic saving has, in fact, fallen to extremely low levels in Africa, with inevitably adverse effects on investment. In the context of deteriorating economies and adverse world economic conditions, the prospects for substantial and quick results from policies to raise saving are small. If "adjustment with growth" is to be converted from a slogan into a reality there must be enlarged capital inflows.

Second, there is no serious disagreement that in an overwhelming majority of sub-Saharan African countries it is structural adjustment that is required, as distinct from the classic IMF-type stabilization. But such adjustment is necessarily a lengthy process, involving the implementation of measures to change the productive system. Such measures inevitably take time to achieve results, as people respond to changed price relativities and new opportunities. In the meantime, however, BoP deficits have to be financed until the supply-side measures take effect—and that requires outside support.

Third, there is similarly little dispute that many African countries are suffering from acute shortages of imported goods and services, and that import-purchasing power constitutes the binding constraint upon their economic performance. Thus, adjustment itself requires additional imported inputs—fertilizers, seeds, fuel, spare parts, raw materials—to allow a greater utilization of existing capacity to produce tradable goods, as well as an often crucial refurbishment of the infrastructure. In addition, imports of consumer goods will also sometimes be necessary as incentive goods, to persuade farmers and others that they will be able to convert higher money incomes from their output into higher real living standards. There is thus a need to augment the adjusting countries' import-purchasing power by outside aid.

Fourth, given both the background of economic decline in many African countries and the often heavy social costs of adjustment, assistance is needed to ease the burden on the poor and other vulnerable groups during the transition. However, even carefully targeted programs to raise standards of health, nutrition and education and to provide employment are not cheap.

Fifth, and linked to all the preceding points, assistance is needed in order to ensure the sustainability of the adjustment process. For this to be done in the absence of severe political repression or turmoil people have to believe that the sacrifices they are making will lead to improved living conditions, and this has to be signaled by at least some short-term economic gains. In fact, prospects for living standards in Africa are bleak. Reference has been made above to the importance of breaking the import strangulation, and to the requirements for the resumption of at least some economic growth. If adjustment programs are to hold out sufficiently plausible prospects of economic betterment for them to be politically sustainable, they will need additional external support.

The thrust of these arguments can be underlined by consideration of the speed and success with which it is reasonable to expect countries in the region to achieve adjustment. The point here is that a number of the characteristic features of African economies tell against quick and extensive results, by comparison with Latin America and Asia. One of these features is heavy reliance on the production and export of primary products, with a correspondingly small industrial base. Another is the low average level of income, providing a small base for taxation and saving. Continued low levels of literacy and shortages of skills provide another drag, aggravated by the brain drain many countries have experienced. The still fragile and underdeveloped nature of the institutional infrastructure, and inefficient information flows provide yet further reasons why these countries find it hard to effectively implement an extensive package of adjustment measures. These considerations underscore the earlier point that there will be an inevitable and possibly lengthy time lag between policy actions and their results, which needs to be financed; such considerations also suggest that the needs of Africa are greater in this respect than in many other developing countries.

Finally, the case for assistance is further strengthened by pointing out the frequency with which past programs have failed as a result of inadequate support, turning not only the World Bank but the IMF into strong advocates of larger aid programs. Thus the fund has argued that, in the past, standby programs have broken down as a result of delays or shortfalls of development assistance in such countries as Mauritania, Kenya, Sierra Leone, Tanzania and Ghana. The bank has argued along similar lines, and suggested that for Madagascar, Niger, Senegal, Tanzania, Zaire and Zambia aid inflows would have to increase by 28 percent over expected levels simply in order to avert another fall in per capita consumption, and by 88 percent in order to achieve the bank's own target of restoring real per capita imports to 1980–82 levels.

ESTIMATES OF FINANCIAL NEEDS

If the case for external assistance is accepted, how much will be needed? The best-known attempt to estimate this is presented in the World Bank's 1986 Africa report, although its coverage was confined to the low-income countries of the region. This started from the objective of halting the decline in per capita consumption by 1990, and achieving some growth thereafter. The bank judged that to achieve this it was necessary, *"at a minimum"* to restore per capita imports to average 1980–82 levels. Allowing for debt-service obligations and certain assumptions regarding the value of export earnings, the bank estimated that the total capital inflow requirements of this group of African countries would be $15.3 billion a year, from 1986 to 1990. Of this sum, it expected $12.8 billion annually to be received by way of concessional and nonconcessional flows, including the value of debt-rescheduling arrangements. This left an unfilled financing gap of $2.5 billion a year, of which the bank hoped that $1.0 billion could be forthcoming from increased lending by itself and other multilateral sources. If filled by additional bilateral aid and debt rescheduling, this would imply a 30 percent increase over the 1984 level and a 20 percent rise over then-expected levels.

Estimates of this kind necessarily depend upon a variety of judgments, one of which is about the tactical pros and cons of arriving at a large or small financing gap. It appears that the World Bank formed the view that it would be better to end up with a figure that, being conservative, could not be criticized by the donor community as having been inflated; as a result, there is a systematic downward bias in the bank's estimates.

First, its objective was kept very modest: merely to halt the decline in average living standards by 1990 and permit some improvement thereafter.

Second, the estimate of need rested upon extremely optimistic assumptions about the terms of trade, envisaging improvements in export prices relative to imports that few expect to occur. It therefore assumes a sharp reversal of Africa's export performance by the end of the 1980s. Third, the World Bank's calculations of the import levels necessary to achieve the objective appear low. Finally, the bank makes optimistic assumptions about the value of debt relief, which would require major improvements over the settlements arrived at hitherto.

All in all, then, the World Bank's estimates of Africa's requirements seem a clear underestimate, and when the actual prospects are considered it becomes easier to see why it might have wanted to err on the conservative side.

PROSPECTS FOR CAPITAL FLOWS

The essential background to this discussion is the very sharp fall in net capital inflows into Africa mentioned earlier. It is not surprising, in the face of this, that there are a number of countries where adjustment programs have either broken down or are at risk because of inadequate external support.

Turning now to look forward to prospects for the region, one overriding principle that must be borne in mind is that the overwhelming need of African countries is for finance on *concessional* terms. Even if there were the prospect of large amounts of new commercial money becoming available, it would, with few exceptions, be highly undesirable for the countries of the region to borrow it. Their export and debt-service prospects simply do not justify borrowing, so that the end result would likely be merely to aggravate an already grave debt-service problem. On the other hand, there could be no realistic prospect of any revival of domestic investment and growth if there were any significant net outflow of capital from the region. Thus, for the credits of the commercial banks and the IMF—on commercial or near-commercial terms—what is desirable is a rolling over of the existing stock of debt. It has, in addition, long been the case that only a small proportion of direct investment by multinational companies has gone to Africa, and there is little prospect of any quick, major change in this situation. Thus, the question about the adequacy of likely future flows to most of the region boils down to the future of official concessional flows. On this it is a good news/bad news story.

Beginning with a consideration of multilateral sources of assistance, the World Bank family can be discussed first. The bank can claim to have demonstrated responsiveness and flexibility in the face of the African economic crisis. The share of its lending to the continent has increased greatly, as has the proportion of its assistance in quick-disbursing forms. It set up a special facility for Africa, and a rising proportion of its soft-terms International Development Association money has been allocated to low-income African countries. The decision to set up the low-interest SAF in the IMF, which will mainly be used by African countries, was another positive development, although credits from the SAF are small.

A more negative aspect relates to net flows with respect to upper-tranche credits from the IMF. The fund's major shareholders have, in fact, enforced a deliberate policy of reducing its exposure to African and other uncreditworthy debtor countries. During 1986–87 there was a net return flow from Africa to the fund, although the SAF will help to reverse this situation and Managing Director Michel Camdessus's call for a tripling of the SAF has won some important support. This leads the discussion to the position regarding bilateral aid.

Here as well there is a mixed picture. In some ways the bilateral donors can also be said to have been responsive to Africa's special needs, for they too have substantially increased the share of their total assistance going to the region. Thus, Organization for Economic Cooperation and Development (OECD) data show that the share of total aid going to Africa has risen from 20 percent in 1973 to 32 percent in 1985, with all the increase in share concentrated on low-income countries. The main source of difficulty is that the total size of these countries' aid programs has generally not been growing in real terms and in some cases has declined. This has reduced donors' ability to respond on the necessary scale. The limited willingness or ability of donors to switch their African aid to quick-disbursing, non-project forms has been another deficiency. As a result, one senior OECD official has commented that African governments "are getting ahead of the donor community in formulating the kind of economic programs called for but to which the donors are not able to respond with the kinds of aid and the degree of flexibility that are essential to the whole idea."

The willingness of the French, German, Italian and Japanese governments to allocate money to Africa has been increasing in the recent past. In the case of the British, a desire to respond has been hampered by a total aid program that was first cut sharply and has since been stagnant in real terms, although a modest increase was in prospect toward the end of the 1980s. American development assistance to Africa is in the worst condition, however. The U.S. Congress inflicted major cuts on the 1987 foreign aid bill, and these have had a particularly severe impact on BoP support for Africa. Conventional development assistance was also cut in real terms, although by a smaller proportion.

Taking these trends overall and bearing in mind that the World Bank's (understated) estimate of financing needs postulated a 20 percent increase in bilateral aid allocations over expected levels, there is likely to remain a substantial uncovered financing gap. Among the implications of this are that the viability of adjustment programs will remain at risk, the costs of adjustment will be increased, and the prospects for renewed growth will become even fainter. Deficiencies in aid programs could be made up by more generous debt negotiations. But although there have been some signs of movement along this line of approach it is most unlikely that these will provide relief on the scale necessary to close the financing gap. The prospect remains bleak.

FURTHER READING

Accelerated Development in Sub-Saharan Africa: An Agenda for Action. Washington: World Bank, 1981.

Africa's Priority Programme for Economic Recovery, 1986–90. Rome: Food and Agriculture Organization for the Organization of African Unity, 1985.

Bhatia, Rattan J. "Adjustment Efforts in Sub-Saharan Africa, 1980–84," *Finance and Development* 22 (September 1985).

The Critical Economic Situation in Africa. New York: United Nations, 1986.

Financing Adjustment with Growth in Sub-Saharan Africa, 1986–90. Washington: World Bank, 1986.

Financing Africa's Recovery. New York: United Nations, 1987.

Green, Reginald H. *The IMF and Stabilisation in Sub-Saharan Africa: A Critical Review.* Brighton, Sussex: Institute of Development Studies, 1986.

Helleiner, Gerald K., ed. *Africa and the International Monetary Fund.* Washington: International Monetary Fund, 1986.

Lancaster, Carol, and Williamson, John, eds. *African Debt and Financing.* Washington: Institute for International Economics, 1986.

AFRICA'S RESPONSE TO THE INTERNATIONAL MONETARY FUND- WORLD BANK PROGRAMS

BADE ONIMODE

INTRODUCTION

ANALYSIS of the African response to International Monetary Fund (IMF) and World Bank policies and programs is critical to understanding the dialectical relationship between these multilateral institutions and African countries in the 1980s. This is not only with respect to the evaluation of the impact of these programs on Africa, but also to assessing African initiative in coping with the desperate predicament of the continent and to gauging regional contribution to the emergent international consensus about the urgent need for the reform of these agencies.

In a more limited way this essay will also indicate the general background and salient features of these programs, their basic socioeconomic impact and the broad configuration of social forces that have been shaping Africa's response to them.

In this regard, Africa's response to fund and bank policies and programs has been a complex reflection of the nature of the programs themselves and the economic and political understanding of these programs and their sponsors by African governments, the changing tenor of the syndrome of underdevelopment, and the resonance of the increasingly hostile international environment. From the colonial era to the present, the real significance of these factors has been changing, but all of them have converged since the intensification of the African crisis in the 1980s. Thus, just as the fund and bank did not start paying any significant attention to Africa until the late 1970s, the African response to their programs did not become problematic until then. Hence the need for a brief discussion of the changing character of these policies and programs.

NATURE OF FUND AND BANK PROGRAMS IN AFRICA

Bretton Woods system

The exploration of the nature of fund and bank programs in Africa should be predicated on the global and historical contexts of the functioning of these institutions. Briefly, both agencies are the dominant institutions of an international monetary system set up at the Bretton Woods Conference in 1944.[1] Africa (still colonial then) and the rest of what is now called the Third World were not represented at the conference, and so their basic interests were not reflected in its proceedings. Essentially, the new monetary system was to achieve two explicit objectives—the reconstruction of Europe after World War II, which was to be the preoccupation of the International Bank for Reconstruction and Development (IBRD, or World Bank), and the expansion of free international trade and payments that was assigned to the IMF.[2] In reality, both objectives converged on a fundamental assignment, namely, the construction and maintenance of an international capitalist system in which multinational corporations can trade, invest and move capital without controls by national governments, and for the accumulation of private profits. Hence the ideology of the fund and bank is economic liberalism rooted in free international trade and capital movements.

Since its creation the Bretton Woods system has been dominated by American interests as the United States emerged from the war as the leader of world capitalism. This is why the president of the World Bank and the deputy managing director of the fund are always Americans, while the managing director of the fund is by agreement and tradition always a European. Though the fund and bank have passed through two main phases, from 1944 to 1971 and from 1971 to the present, their rules of operation have remained basically the same. In spite of the fact that the fundamental objective of these institutions is international, they give the false impression of concentrating on individual countries, which they treat unilaterally. This individual case approach is the source of their enormous power, deriving from the stringent constraint imposed on individual countries by their balance-of-payments and foreign-exchange requirements. This power over individual countries has shaped the roles of the two institutions in Africa as elsewhere in the Third World.

Fund and bank programs in Africa

The policies and programs of the IMF and World Bank in Africa span three broad periods: the colonial, the early postcolonial and the deep-crisis era, with the most decisive time being the 1980s. In the colonial period only the World Bank operated in Africa, on the invitation of individual colonial

---

[1] The other institutions of the Bretton Woods system are the International Development Association and the International Finance Corporation, affiliated with the World Bank; and the separate General Agreement on Tariff and Trade.

[2] For a good account of the Bretton Woods system, see Cheryl Payer, *The Debt Trap—The International Monetary Fund and the Third World* (New York: Monthly Review, 1974) and Payer, *The World Bank—A Critical Analysis* (New York: Monthly Review, 1982).

regimes. This was not due to the fact that these African countries had not yet joined the IMF as sovereign states, because their colonial administrations could have invited the fund just as they invited the bank. Rather, it was because the colonial system operated currency areas, like the sterling area and the franc zone, which meant in effect that the balance-of-payments stabilization role of the fund was played by the colonial powers with respect to each colony.[3] Thus, since the balance of payments of the colonies were integral parts of the balance of payments of their colonial rulers, any deficits in these colonial balance of payments were simply offset in the metropoles by adjusting the foreign-reserve accounts of the colonies—since their central banks were those of the colonial powers. Even the foreign loans of the colonies were guaranteed by the colonial administrations, which, therefore, kept such loans under severe limits. Just as the colonial monetary system was a kind of gold standard according to which domestic money supply was based on parity with external reserves, the associated colonial balance-of-payments adjustment was automatic.[4] A colony with a deficit lost foreign reserves and reduced its domestic money supply, which reduced aggregate demand, including import demand; the reverse held true for a colony with a balance-of-payments surplus.

The colonial era

In colonial Africa only the World Bank had programs; these were generally supportive of the colonial economic system. They consisted of two major activities, namely, the rationalization of the colonial capitalist division of labor and the initiative of sectoral programs.

Under terms of the first activity, the bank was invited by colonial governments to assist with the entrenchment of the colonial capitalist mode of production. This required the promotion of the production of mineral and agricultural raw materials for export, and the refinement of the mechanisms for colonial surplus extraction—for example, through "improved" tax and monetary arrangements for greater colonial exploitation in order to integrate the colonies more effectively into the world capitalist system; this is one of the explicit objectives of the current structural adjustment program (SAP) of the fund and bank. This streamlining of the colonial system by the bank involved World Bank missions to various colonies for comprehensive economic surveys; sometimes, only a sectoral survey was required. At the end of each of such surveys, the bank wrote a detailed report to the relevant colonial administration advocating new policies and programs as well as the modification of existing ones. Thus, on the invitation of the British colonial administration the World Bank sent a mission to Nigeria in 1953 and wrote a comprehensive report of their findings in 1954.[5]

[3] W. T. Newlyn and D. C. Rowan, *Money and Banking in British Colonial Africa* (Oxford: Clarendon Press, 1954)

[4] M.G. de Vries, *Balance of Payments Adjustment, 1945 to 1986—The IMF Experience* (Washington, D.C.: IMF, 1987), ch. 1.

[5] See World Bank, *The Economic Development of Nigeria* (Baltimore, Maryland: Johns Hopkins Press, 1954).

The second major activity of the bank in colonial Africa was the provision of loans to specific sectors, mainly agriculture and infrastructure, in different countries. These were usually project-tied loans whose repayment was guaranteed by colonial governments from the export earnings of their territories. The agrarian programs were usually for the promotion of so-called cash crops for export in the pursuit of an export-led growth strategy that considered foreign exchange as an indispensable requirement for growth. This export-as-engine-of-growth doctrine was inherited from the Latin American experience, especially during the export boom of the 1950s, and it has dominated development thinking in Africa since then.

The African response to these colonial bank programs was mediated by two factors: the dominant interests served by these activities, and the understanding of their technical character. As the colonial regimes invited the bank to consolidate its basic interests in political repression and surplus extraction, they naturally favored and encouraged these programs. But there were also marginal differences of technical detail and political expedience between the bank's perspective and that of the colonial governments. Thus, while the bank pushed for faster multilateralism and open-door policy, the colonial regimes, even after official adoption of the American-imposed open-door policy following World War II, were more monopolistic and restrictive. On the part of the indigenous Africans, even though their aspirations were not the same as the bank's preoccupations, their limited understanding of the essential logic and implications of these programs inhibited their explicit and sustained response to them. While the leadership of the nationalist movements might reject, or be unhappy with, specific aspects of the bank's activities, the mass of people involved in the anticolonial struggle lacked any deep understanding of these activities. Hence the nationalist response to the bank's programs tended to be muted, like the broader colonial struggle itself. In some instances the nationalist leaders even endorsed these bank programs, as demonstrated by their invitation to the bank to expand them after independence. This is the case with such bank policies as export-led growth, the primacy of the external sector, balance of payments and the promotion of primary exports to finance them.

Fund and bank programs in the early postcolonial era
By the early 1960s most African countries gained nominal or actual political independence, and joined the IMF after becoming independent members of the World Bank. Nigeria, for example, joined the fund in 1960–61 and Zambia in 1965. The period between the 1960s and 1978 can therefore be regarded as the second phase of fund and bank programs in Africa; and 1979 marked the beginning of the period when Africa became the major concern of the fund, as the continent started taking about 30 percent of the IMF's extended fund facility, which attracts stringent conditionality.[6] This later phase of fund and bank programs was characterized by four main features. One was a division of labor between the fund and bank in terms of their roles, not only in Africa but globally. The second

[6]See Lawrence Harris, "Conception of the IMF's Role in Africa" (1984, Mimeographed).

was the oil crisis of 1973–74, which aggravated the economic crisis that started in the 1970s in Africa, especially in oil-importing countries. This oil shock led, for example, to the establishment of an "oil facility" by the fund. The third feature of this phase was the general absence of conditionality in spite of the emerging economic and balance-of-payments deficits of some countries, which forced them to seek special facilities from the fund. As a fourth feature, the tail end of this phase of IMF and World Bank programs marked the beginning of critical relations between these multilateral institutions and Africa. This followed the "Second Slump"[7] in the economies of the major sponsors of the institutions.

In line with distinction between the functions of the fund and of the bank, the latter concentrated on its traditional involvement in agricultural or rural development, expansion of infrastructural facilities and general economic growth. These rural projects constituted the bank's "integrated rural development," or "green revolution," programs, which were usually generated in part from the reports of the bank's surveys of different countries. The technical design of these programs was done either by the bank or the relevant country.

For the practical execution of its policies and programs in Africa, the bank offers project-tied loans, as in the colonial era, and sends its own technical staff to participate in, or supervise, program implementation. As the expenses of the bank staff are charged to the project loans, recipient countries usually spend a sizable portion of bank loans on this very high, often excessive, remuneration.

Besides the funding of these programs, which constitutes the antipoverty rhetoric of the bank—especially of its former president, Robert McNamara—the bank has been playing a critical policy role in Africa. Through the reports of its invited missions for the economic survey of different countries, and through its publications (for example, its *Annual Report*; specialized occasional reports such as the Berg Report, *Towards Accelerated Development in Sub-Saharan Africa*; and its journal, *Finance and Development*), the bank wields tremendous influence on the policies of many, if not most, African governments. Policies like the now discredited integrated rural development, or green revolution; import-substitution industrialization; encouragement of cash crops; and export-led growth strategy were either developed by the bank or promoted by it in Africa and the rest of the Third World. Indeed, in the postcolonial era up to 1978, and even up to the present in some countries, many African governments would sooner solicit, accept and implement the bank's policies than those of national experts. This is because of the World Bank's alleged technical neutrality and the myth of expertise that the colonial regimes, the bank and its lobby in different countries have built for it. The policy influence of the bank is so pervasive that there is hardly any significant sector of these economies that has not been implementing some bank policies. In view of this long and pervasive influence of the bank, it is baffling to many observers of the

---

[7] E. Mandel, *The Second Slump* (London: Verso, 1978).

African scene in the 1980s that the bank and fund want to hold African governments alone largely responsible for the current crisis.

As for the distinctive roles of the IMF in Africa, these were clearly defined between 1960 and 1978. The preoccupation of the fund with balance-of-payments stabilization meant that its basic policies and programs in Africa at that time involved the funding of balance-of-payments deficits and crises, as well as the design of policies to facilitate balance-of-payments adjustment, to free international payments and to encourage the overall expansion of foreign trade. The funding activities of the IMF in Africa started with the regular borrowing by countries from its special drawing rights, under the first and second tranches. This was really the drawing down of member countries' quota contribution to the fund. In addition, the fund has also offered the following facilities, especially since the crisis of the 1970s:

1. Compulsory fund facility to Zambia in 1971
2. Extended fund facility, established in 1974 for balance-of-payments stabilization support
3. Oil facility, in 1975
4. Compensatory financing facility to Tanzania in 1976
5. Trust fund, in 1976, for concessional loans to low-income countries from the profits realized on its gold sales
6. Supplementary financing facility, 1979, which was replaced by the enlarged access policy to augment drawings from upper-credit tranches and/or the extended fund facility

The fund policies[8] associated with these lending facilities center around the restoration of balance-of-payments equilibrium, with the objective of facilitating the free international movements of goods and capital. In addition, the fund also claims that some of its policies are designed to promote economic growth,[9] but this is not convincing, especially in Africa. The main policies designed by the fund for these purposes favor currency devaluation, as in Zaire during 1972–76, Nigeria in 1973, Ghana under Busia (1969–72), Zambia in 1976, etc. Currency devaluation is suggested to eliminate overvaluation of currencies, promote exports by making them cheaper in foreign currency, and reduce imports by raising their domestic prices in local currency. In practice, however, things do not work out that way and countries have had to face persistent balance-of-payments deficits and cumulative devaluation as in Zaire, Ghana, etc. The removal of exchange control and multiple exchange rates is also an important IMF policy in Africa, and these imply an implicit drive toward a flexible exchange-rate policy. The other significant fund policies before 1978 were fiscal and credit policy designed to combat inflation, an open-door policy on foreign investment and an export drive in primary products.

[8] On this issue, see J. B. Zulu and S. M. Nsouli, "Adjustment Programmes in Africa," *Finance and Development* (March 1984): 6.
[9] S. Kanesa-Thasan, "The Fund Adjustment Policies in Africa," *Finance and Development* (September 1981).

In these ways the fund has been encouraging African countries to open up their economies to foreign trade and foreign capital, and make the balance of payments a major focus of national economic management. These are the major variables of external dependence in Third World countries.

Crisis programs in the 1980s
The crisis management of the 1980s is reflected partly by the fact that as of 1979, African countries started taking 30 percent of the IMF's total credit under its standby arrangements or extended fund facility, whereas they took only 3 percent during 1970–78.[10] Correspondingly, just as Third World countries started accounting for most of the fund's lending from the 1970s on, African countries became one of its major preoccupations in the 1980s. With the deepening of the current depression, export markets have become severely dislocated, with drastic shortfalls in foreign-exchange earnings causing widespread balance-of-payments deficits and crises among primary exporters, especially in Africa. These developments have been forcing more of these countries to seek fund accommodation and increased credit from the World Bank.

Thus, the 1980s have been dominated by three major developments in fund and bank programs in Africa.[11] One is the rapid expansion of these policies and programs in terms of the magnitude, variety and number of countries involved. The other is the increasingly stringent and pernicious conditions tied to these borrowings, which have given rise to such terms as "conditionality" and acronyms such as SAP, or Economic Recovery Program (ERP) in Ghana, and IMF into the daily vocabulary of most literate Africans. The third development is the convergence of fund and bank programs on a common theme of structural adjustment.

With regard to this third development, there exists hardly any African country that has not been implementing one fund or bank program or another. This is, of course, a reflection of the rapidly worsening crisis that has led to the total collapse of many African economies—those of Zaire, Sudan (under Nimeiry), Ghana, for example. A special concomitant of this escalating crisis has been the dominant position of Africa's external debt, which is partly the consequence of fund and bank policies in the region.

As Africa's borrowing from these multilateral institutions and other sources increased rapidly in the 1980s—to the tune of 228 billion nairas by December 1987—conditionality became a stringent aspect of these loans. While conditionality was associated only with the IMF's extended fund facility from 1977 to 1983, it has since become a feature of both fund and bank loans for structural adjustment. The associated tough conditions[12] include devaluation, trade liberalization, privatization of public enterprises, drastic subsidy withdrawals across the board, deep budget cuts with severe credit squeezes, foreign-exchange auctions or flexible exchange rates, open-door

[10] Lawrence Harris, "Conceptions of the IMF's Role in Africa" (1984, Typescript): 1.
[11] See Zulu and Nsouli, "Adjustment Programmes," and Payer, *The World Bank*.
[12] Cf. Tony Killick, *The Quest for Economic Stabilisation—The IMF and the Third World* (London: Heinemann, 1984).

policies on foreign investment, and debt-equity swaps. These are all characterized by classical economic liberalism or the free reign of market forces and monetarist demand management, à la Reagan—the globalization of Reaganomics.

Before the convergence of fund and bank programs in the early 1980s, the fund had since 1979 been concentrating on what was essentially emergency lending under its standby arrangements or extended fund facility, to which it attaches conditionality.[13] The supplementary fund facility of 1979, which later became the enlarged access policy, has also been introduced to deal with balance-of-payments crises. The main policies pursued under these programs are basically the fund's conditionality, otherwise called "the pill," or "IMF medicine." Their stated focus is balance-of-payments adjustment with sustainable growth, but this second goal has been widely contested, as shown below. The fund's conditionality became a requirement before the negotiation of rescheduling the external debts of poor countries.

Correspondingly, the bank has been sustaining its survey missions and project lending for its so-called antipoverty or rural development program, and infrastructural expansion. Both are designed to promote sustained growth with the usual emphasis on growth rather than development.[14] Then by 1980 it introduced structural adjustment lending, and followed this with policy-related lending. Both forms of credit are tied to the pursuit of specific policies, such as export promotion, land reform, economic diversification. Later, sector adjustment loans were added, especially in 1983, to underscore the necessity for addressing specific sectoral programs in such areas as agriculture, social services and even manufacturing.

Structural adjustment program (SAP)
The introduction of structural adjustment lending by the bank in 1980 led to the creation of SAP (ERP in Ghana). It is a synthesis of bank and fund policies and programs, especially in Africa. Because of its centrality to Africa's response to these multilateral activities, the basic features of SAP (or ERP) bear outlining.

After the bank's initiative, the fund created a structural adjustment fund in 1986 for concessional assistance to countries with protracted balance-of-payments problems. SAP unifies fund and bank programs in each country. Even though SAP (ERP) is usually a two-year shock treatment initially, it is envisaged to be followed by similar but milder programs, each of about three years' duration for a total of 25 years, so that each SAP is ultimately a quarter-century deal. SAP is designed to camouflage the increasingly unpopular conditionality of the fund; thus Nigeria rejected an IMF loan in December 1985, but started implementing a SAP by July 1986.[15] The

[13] J. B. Zulu and S. M. Nsouli, *Adjustment Programmes in Africa—The Recent Experience,* Occasional Paper no. 34 (Washington, D.C.: IMF, 1985) and World Bank, *World Debt Tables.*
[14] Indeed, the bank and fund tend to use the terms "growth" and "development" interchangeably, whereas Africa and the rest of the Third World want to liquidate underdevelopment, which requires more than growth.
[15] See Yusuf Bala Usman, *Nigeria Against the IMF* (Kaduna: Vanguard Publishers, 1986).

program provides for joint lending and monitoring by the fund and bank, and has become a precondition for debt-rescheduling negotiations by private foreign creditors. Besides being a certificate of merit, SAP is also a total program. Whereas fund and bank programs used to deal with individual projects or sectors, SAP controls and monitors the entire economy. It prescribes policies for all sectors; endorses budgets (both domestic and foreign exchange); imposes fiscal and credit limits, foreign exchange rates and regimes; and even posts fund and bank supervisory staff to the central bank, finance ministry and related sensitive institutions in each country. This is allegedly necessary because the objectives of SAP (ERP) are truly pervasive: economic recovery, balance-of-payments stabilization, debt relief, rapid and sustained growth, control of inflation, economic diversification and, of course, the firm integration of individual African countries into the international capitalist system—a neutral framework for the recolonization of Africa.

AFRICA'S RESPONSE TO FUND AND BANK PROGRAMS

The African response to these fund and bank programs, especially since the 1960s, has varied over the years. This is because the response has been a function not only of the specific policies and programs themselves but also of several other factors: the magnitude of the external debt associated with them, their socioeconomic impact, the collective understanding of these programs, the corporate interests of the African leaders, the trend of the African crisis, the export performance of the countries, and the overall external environment. As these factors changed from the 1960s through the 1980s, the African response to fund and bank programs also shifted over the two phases of the postcolonial era. Hence, in the first phase of 1960–78, as these factors were either generally favorable or mild, except for the second slump of 1974–78,[16] African response grew from warm during 1960–73 to suspicious or questioning during 1974–78. The generally poor understanding of the international roles of the fund and bank, together with the weak technical competence of the bureaucracy of most African countries at this time also encouraged a certain naive enthusiasm toward these institutions. This persisted even into the early 1980s in countries like Nigeria, Kenya, the Ivory Coast and Zaire, due partly also to the convergence of the national ideology of neocolonial capitalism and the corporate interests of the leadership of these countries (and those of most other African countries) on the capitalist and imperialist ideology of the fund and bank.[17]

Even though it is possible to trace an essentially collective African response at the level of the Organization of African Unity (OAU), especially in the 1980s, it is still necessary to note attitudinal differences involving three groups of countries. These are (1) the latecomers and marginal ones (marginal in the sense of hosting limited programs), embracing such Socialist-oriented states as Angola, Mozambique, Ethiopia, (2) the few tough

[16] Mandel *The Second Slump,* chaps. 1 and 3.
[17] On the ideology of the fund and bank, see Payer, *The Debt Trap.*

cases, namely, Zambia, Tanzania and Nigeria (until 1986); and (3) receptive countries that include Zaire as the softest host of fund and bank programs in Africa. For largely ideological reasons, the Socialist states of Africa have generally been more self-reliant and reluctant to borrow from the fund and bank until national emergencies like South African invasion in Angola and Mozambique, and famine in Ethiopia, forced them to negotiate limited programs with these institutions. The hard negotiators are also among the first countries to host fund programs in Africa. For example, Zambia was using fund facilities with a compensatory fund facility in 1971, while Tanzania got an oil facility in 1975 and a compensatory fund facility in 1976.[18] While Zambia scrapped its SAP with the fund and bank on 1 May, 1987, Tanzania resisted the fund from 1978 to 1980 before signing an agreement. Nigeria, in a national debate, rejected an IMF loan in 1985, though it capitulated to a SAP by 1986. By 1988 Zimbabwe was still resisting an IMF program. The other African countries fall somewhere between being soft and suspicious/angry hosts of fund and bank programs.

In the 1980s, however, African countries have been forced by the growing pressure of external debt service and internal crisis to take an increasingly collective stance on fund and bank programs under SAP. But each country still negotiates individually with the multilateral institutions. At the level of the OAU, there have been three major collective responses: those of Africa's Priority Program for Economic Recovery (APPER) and its U.N. associate the Program of Action for African Economic Recovery and Development (PAAERD); those of the Organization of African Trade Union Unity (OATUU), based in Accra; and those of the Institute for African Alternatives (IFAA), with its secretariat in London, and other nongovernmental organizations.

APPER, PAAERD and Abuja

In July 1985, during the trough of the current depression, African heads of state and government adopted APPER.[19] Scheduled to run between 1986 and 1990, it commits African countries at national, subregional and regional levels to the implementation of practical policies for durable structural change, rapid economic recovery, higher productivity and long-term development. Even though APPER was not directly addressed to fund and bank programs in Africa, its proposed policies and its demands on the United Nations as well as the international community indicate that it is such a response. At the national level, for instance, it commits African countries to policy reforms; agricultural development and elimination of the food crisis; rehabilitation of agro-allied industries, trade and finance;

[18] Economic Commission for Africa, *The Historical Profile of External Indebtedness of African Countries in Relation to the Economic Crisis of the Continent*, E/ECA/TRADE/102 December (Addis Ababa: ECA, 1987) and Organization of African Unity, *External Debt Crisis of Africa—Summary of Information, Statistical Data and Proposed Actions Communicated by the OAU Member States*, EAHG/EXP/FIN 111 (b) (Addis Ababa: OAU).

[19] United Nations, *Africa—UN Programme of Action for African Economic Recovery and Development, 1986–1990* (New York: United Nations, 1986).

control of drought and desertification as well as development of human resources. At the subregional level it focuses on the problems of refugees, drought and rising external debt burden. Its regional concerns include the strengthening of social and economic institutions, consolidation of African cooperation within the framework of the Lagos Plan of Action, and financial estimates for the implementation of APPER. APPER's estimates are that U.S. $128 billion would be required for it during 1986–90, of which African countries would provide $82 billion, or 64 percent, with the balance of $46 billion to be supplied annually from external sources.

APPER was used by the OAU to request a special session of the United Nations, May 27–31, 1986, to discuss the critical economic situation in Africa. This led to the adoption of PAAERD, which commits the international community to support the initiatives of African countries "to promote food production, build up agricultural industries and related infrastructure, reverse the effect of drought and desertification, and develop human resources through 'radical changes' in the education systems."[20] Thus PAAERD consists of two basic elements—the OAU's APPER of July 1985, and the response of the international community to complement the African effort, e.g., by mobilizing the estimated $46 billion in external resources for the funding of APPER. The specific assistance promised from the international community includes improvement in the quality and modality of external assistance and cooperation; improvement in the international environment with respect to the expansion of Africa's trade and the financing of commodity problems; support for Africa's policy reforms of economic recovery, through the elimination of debt constraints; increased south-south cooperation with a machinery for continuous follow-up; and evaluation at national, regional and global levels.

In effect, then, the OAU's APPER was expanded with an international commitment to implement PAAERD at regional, subregional and national levels, and the United Nations was to implement it at the international level. Besides the demands for additional external resources and debt restraint, both APPER and PAAERD effectively complement and reinforce fund and bank policies and programs. This is hardly surprising because, as many argue, PAAERD is essentially the reintroduction of the now discredited Berg Report of the World Bank.[21]

As the promised international support for Africa's internal efforts was not forthcoming two years after APPER, the Economic Commission for Africa (ECA), the OAU, the African Development Bank and Nigeria jointly organized an international conference at Abuja as one of the follow-up actions envisaged in PAAERD. Besides being an assessment of the prospects for economic recovery, "the main objective of the Conference was to assist the African countries and the international community to fully exploit the opportunities and advantages of APPER and the UN-PAAERD, and to

---

[20] *Ibid*, p. 1.
[21] For the critique of the bank's Berg Report, which undermines the OAU's Lagos Plan of Action, see *Africa Development*, Spring 1987.

ensure that a truly solid foundation is laid for the achievement of the longer-term goals of African development."

The Abuja statement itself, "Economic Recovery and Long-Term Development in Africa," consists of two parts, since the main title of the conference (held June 15–19, 1987) was "An International Conference on Africa: The Challenge of Economic Recovery and Accelerated Development." The first part of the statement was "Overall Assessment of the Situation" and the second consisted of "Conclusions and Recommendations." The assessment dealt with three themes: progress, problems and prospects of recovery; Africa and the international community; and long-term development prospects. The progress report noted that African countries were implementing internal reforms, including the execution of SAPs in 28 of them. At the subregional level, it indicated that the Economic Community of West African States, or (ECOWAS) and Southern African Development Coordination Conference (SADCC) had initiated plans to achieve food security and fight drought and desertification (in ECOWAS) as well as to counter the destabilizing policies of South Africa's apartheid regime (in SADCC).

At the international level, the conference estimated that in addition to the total external resource of $45.6 billion under PAAERD, an additional $14.6 billion would be required annually for external debt service, thus raising the total annual external resource requirement from about $9 billion under PAAERD to between $24 billion and $34 billion, assuming that community prices remained constant at the 1985 level.[22] The conference was also pleased with three positive international developments: the increase of International Development Association (IDA; a member of the World Bank group) resources by $12.4 billion, with a decision to allocate 45 percent of it to sub-Saharan Africa; an increase in the grant element in official development assistance (ODA) by some developed countries to desperate, low-income African countries; and the cancellation of ODA debts by some donor countries for some of the least-developed African countries. But the conference noted that these international concessions were ad hoc, partial and far below the external resource needs of Africa. This is in the main because of the dramatic collapse of export commodity prices, which caused Africa a loss of $19 billion in foreign-exchange earnings between 1985 and 1986, and the escalation of external debt obligations.

On Africa's long-term development prospects, the conference concluded that these "must be based on fundamental structural change," which has to be done by Africans themselves. This means that food and agriculture must be the base of this structural change and associated with the gradual reduction of the role of primary exports and the promotion of the significance of domestic and intra-African production relationships. The scientific and technological backwardness of the continent must therefore be remedied.

The conclusions and policy recommendations of the conference center on seven themes: (1) measures for accelerating the recovery process; (2) debt

---

[22] Economic Commission for Africa, *The Abuja Statement* (Addis Ababa: ECA, 1987), 7.

and debt-service payments; (3) development assistance; (4) commodities, trade and price stabilization; (5) effects of political and economic destabilization by South Africa, which cost SADCC countries an estimated $2 billion annually; (6) prospects for long-term development; and (7) economic cooperation within Africa as well as between Africa and the international community. The themes that dealt directly with fund and bank programs in Africa were the first, second and third.

As to accelerating recovery, African countries were required to ensure that SAPs were consistent with the needs of economic recovery and growth, and to exchange information on their negotiations over SAP and with foreign creditors. On the question of debt, the conference demanded lower interest rates, longer repayment and grace periods for existing debt, the possibility of repayment in local currency, and conversion of bilateral debt and interest payments from low-income countries into grants as well as debt-equity swap. With respect to development assistance, the conference sought more concessional resources through multilateral institutions, such as the tripling of structural adjustment facility and additional funds to IDA and to the African Development Fund for increased lending to Africa. It also canvassed for the issuing of new SDRs for development purposes. The follow-up actions required that these recommendations should be raised at appropriate international forums, and that the ECA should play a catalytic role in sustaining international public interest in Africa's development.

This conference, therefore, addressed fund and bank policies and programs more directly than APPER and PAAERD. It also dealt more explicitly than before with Africa's debt crisis. But its recommendations for dealing with the crisis were less comprehensive than the existing proposals on the problem at that time, and less radical than the options being raised in Latin America.[23] In particular, it is disturbing that on the basis of the promise of financial assistance in PAAERD, the African countries went to the conference to adopt SAP, agree on 30 percent debt-service ratio (which was what Nigeria announced in its 1987 federal budget, though it actually paid about 37 percent), and accept debt-equity swaps. These are mechanisms for the strengthening of fund and bank programs and for the re-colonialization of Africa.

Addis Ababa 1987
It was against this background that the OAU held its third extraordinary assembly on Africa's external debt crisis between November 30 and December 1, 1987 in Addis Ababa. The actual meeting was preceded by preparatory work by a committee of African experts. Its major conclusions are summarized in its draft declaration, which is an abridged version of its

---

[23] On these other debt options, see J. Schatan, *World Debt—Who Is to Pay?* (London: Zed Press, 1987) and K. J. Havnevik, *The IMF and World Bank in Africa: Conditionality, Impact and Alternatives* (Uppsala: Scandinavian Institute of African Studies, 1987, and P. Komer, et al. *The IMF and the Debt Crisis—A Guide to the Third World's Dilemmas* (London: Zed Press, 1986), chaps. 3 and 5.

"Draft African Common Position on Africa's External Debt Crisis."[24] The declaration stated that a lasting solution to the external debt problem of developing countries should be sought "in recognition of the interdependence among the external debt issues, flow of development assistance, improved international trading system, improved commodity prices and the reform of the international monetary system" (i.e., the Bretton Woods system).

Specific recommendations that relate to fund and bank policies and programs bear enumeration here:

- Increase resource flows to Africa through the increase in grants in bilateral assistance; increase in the grant element in the financing of international and regional financial institutions; and reduction in interest rates and extension of the repayment and grace periods of financial and commercial loans for all types of new loans
- Convert all past official bilateral loans into grants
- Reduce real interest rates on existing loans
- Grant 50-years' repayment period and 10-years' grace period for the repayment of all new loans
- The total amount of the debt service of a debtor country should not exceed a reasonable and bearable percentage of its export earnings as proposed in the Priority Programme for Africa's Economic Recovery (1986–1990)
- Pay part of official bilateral debt in local currency
- Suspend debt repayment during the remaining period of PAAERD
- Multiyear rescheduling, of a minimum of five years, should be the norm, with maturities of at least 50 years, 10 years' grace and zero rate of interest
- Convene an international conference of Africa's external indebtness[25]

This is the most specific response to fund and bank policies and programs by the OAU so far. Just as its focus is clearer than that of the Abuja conference, its demands are more concrete, even though conservative and, in some cases, not well informed. Its recognition of the interdependence between external debt and other external factors is very significant, though its call for the reform of the international monetary system will not solve the problem without a basic restructuring of the international capitalist system. The conversion of bilateral loans into grants gives some respite, but if this is associated with continued borrowing, it merely postpones the evil day. The call for lower interest rates, grace periods and longer repayment periods with rescheduling all assume that the Third World's external debts can and should be repaid. In spite of the call for an international conference on external debt, the declaration still falls far short of a clear recognition of the political character of the external debt crisis and the collective political initiatives required to resolve it as the Latin Americans have done.

[24] See Organization of African Unity, *Draft Declaration,* EAHG/DRAFT/DECL.1 (111) (Addis Ababa: OAU, 1987), and *Draft African Common Position on Africa's External Debt Crisis,* EAHG/2 (111) (Addis Ababa: OAU, 1987).
[25] OAU *Draft Declaration,* pp. 4–5.

Nongovernmental responses to fund and bank programs
The inadequacies of the OAU's response to fund and bank programs have prompted the intervention of African nongovernmental organizations. This has also been the result of the unacceptable fact that reactions to the fund and bank come from African governments and their agencies alone, neglectful of the input of other critical social forces like organized labor, African professionals, students, women and similar groups that bear the brunt of the unfair burden of adjustment in these programs. Two highly significant unofficial responses come from the IFAA[26] and the OATUU. The IFAA organized an international conference, "The Impact of IMF and World Bank Programmes on the People of Africa," in London September 7–10, 1987. The conference statement and report[27] summarized case studies of the impact of these fund and bank programs on 19 countries across Africa. These studies show that the policies and programs have failed in their basic objectives of rural development, balance-of-payments stabilization and economic recovery. Hence, the conference criticized the economic theories that inform bank and fund programs (one example: that poor countries must borrow or seek foreign capital to develop), the dominant roles of foreign trade, balance of payments and foreign exchange in Third World countries, the excessive external dependence of poor countries, and the imposition of development models on them by the fund and bank. The conference recommended that Africa's external debt should be canceled or repudiated collectively; all SAPs should be scrapped, as Zambia has done, and replaced with national recovery programs; all fund and bank monitoring staff in sensitive institutions in African countries should be withdrawn forthwith; African and other poor countries should stop all external borrowing and adopt an inward-looking development strategy with effective national self-reliance; alternative development models that address the basic needs of African countries should be promoted; fund and bank development principles should be replaced; control of both institutions should be democratized; African and Third World debtors' cartels should be formed to provide concerted response of the fund and bank, with an alliance of workers, peasants, students, etc., in each African country to press for the implementation of these demands.

Later in 1987 the OATUU, the World Federation of Trade Unions and the Ethiopian Trade Unions jointly organized an international conference, "Africa's Debt and Debt Servicing," in Addis Ababa from December 8 to December 10. The main objectives were to present the African workers' perspective on the debt crisis and offer political support for the efforts of African governments toward the resolution of the crisis and the development of Africa. While OATUU's basic document at the conference elaborated its views on the problem, the conference declaration demanded the conversion of Africa's external debt into grants, their cancellation, or their collective repudiation by African countries. It also called for the disman-

---

[26] The IFAA, a research and policy body of African social scientists, is located at 23 Bevenden Street, London N1 6BH.
[27] See IFAA, *The IMF, World Bank and Africa: Report of a Conference* (London: IFAA, 1987).

tling of all SAPs on the continent, noted the partial responsibility of African governments for the predicament of the continent and called for joint political action between Africa, Latin America and Asia on the external debt problem, with the formation of African and Third World debtors' cartels. It ended with a call for "international workers' solidarity" on the debt problem and the hosting of an international trade union conference on the issue.

CONCLUSION—PROBLEMS AND PROSPECTS OF AFRICA'S RESPONSE

From the colonial era to the present, fund and bank policies and programs in Africa have been preoccupied with the rationalization of the basic roles of the continent in its integration into the international capitalist system. This is because the consolidation of this global system is the real and central objective of the Bretton Woods international monetary system, of which the fund and bank are core institutions.

The responses of African countries to these multilateral programs have varied over the years with the changing fortunes of the continent, especially during the colonial, early postcolonial and crisis eras. These responses have been characterized by a governmental and highly centralized approach to the negotiation and evaluation of these programs, and by growing popular rejection of the programs—as reflected in sporadic demonstrations, riots and even coups in countries like Zambia, Sudan, Morocco, Ghana, etc. The nonviolent responses of African nongovernmental bodies to the programs have been of recent vintage and on a limited scale, and these have compounded the problems of a collective African response.

These problems center around the low sensitivity to and relatively poor understanding of the logic of these policies and programs. Thus, in spite of their marginal positive impact and their major traumatic effects on various economies, sectors and social groups, the official response to them has been embarrassingly mild. In spite of the huge external debt that has been associated with these policies, it took 27 years before African countries summoned a special conference on the debt crisis. Partly because of the severe political repression and pervasive illiteracy in most African countries, the broad masses of working people, who have been bearing most of the hardships associated with these policies, have also remained relatively acquiescent.

Moreover, African countries lack technically competent staffs that can analyse the implications of fund and bank programs and negotiate effectively with these institutions. Even in countries like Nigeria, where such personnel is available, they are ignored because they are not bureaucrats. This is one reason, for example, why it has taken Africa so long to grapple with the patently political character of fund and bank interventions and of the external debt crisis.

The vested corporate interests of some African leaders in seeking fund and bank loans also preclude any serious response to the activities of these institutions. This has been aggravated by the untying of the loans of these institutions, so that in many cases these foreign loans do not even get to Africa. Where they do, much of the funds are simply preempted by officials; the corruption associated with these foreign loans accounts largely for why they cannot generate returns for their repayment.

Such venality also ties in with the convergence of interests between the multilateral institutions and many African governments. This is especially true in relation to the naive preference of these countries to go it alone and negotiate individually with the fund and bank. While this offers good opportunities for swindling funds, it also strengthens the enormous power of the institutions over individual countries.

Judging from these experiences, the present African response to fund and bank programs presents rather dim prospects. This is in spite of the growing radicalism of the OAU, for example, from the setting up of APPER to the meeting in Addis Ababa in 1987. This pessimism derives from the basic attitudes of most individual African governments, which accept SAP, clamor for increased foreign loans, swindle much of these funds, and accept and promote the neocolonial status of their countries. The growing hostility of the international environment, the visible marginalization of Africa in the global scheme of things, the persistent decline of commodity exports and prices, as well as the essentially indifferent-to-callous posture of the fund and bank compel this inference.

However, if African countries can be urged to take collective action in their dealings with the fund, bank and private foreign creditors; demonstrate greater urgency and seriousness, backed with expertise; coordinate their efforts with progressive national social forces (trade unions, peasants, students, etc.); and link up politically with the rest of the Third World, then they can make great positive impact. The prospect of this alternative collective and political strategy could include the scrapping of SAP, better trading terms for Africa, effective national self-reliance, the reversal of net capital flows from Africa, and the cessation of increased foreign borrowing. These could even lead to the reform of the IMF and World Bank, together with the restructuring of the international capitalist system that they serve.

FURTHER READING

The Abuja Statement. Addis Ababa: U.N. Economic Commission on Africa, 1987.

The Economic Development of Nigeria. Baltimore: Johns Hopkins University Press for the World Bank, 1954.

Harnevik, K. J. *The IMF and the World Bank in Africa: Conditionality, Impact and Alternatives.* Uppsala: Scandinavian Institute of African Studies, 1987.

Kanesa-Thasan, S. "The Fund Adjustment Policies in Africa." *Finance and Development* (September 1981).

Killick, Tony, ed. *The Quest for Economic Stabilisation: The IMF and the Third World.* London and Exeter, New Hampshire: Heinemann, 1984.

Körner, P., *et al. The IMF and the Debt Crisis: A Guide to the Third World's Dilemmas.* London: Zed Press, 1986.

Mandel, Ernest. *The Second Slump: A Marxist Analysing Recession in the Seventies.* London: New Left Books, 1978.

Newlyn, W. T., and Rowan, D. C. *Money and Banking in British Colonial Africa.* Oxford: Clarendon Press, 1954.

Payer, Cheryl. *The Debt Trap: The International Monetary Fund and the Third World.* New York; Monthly Review Press, 1975.

————. *The World Bank: A Critical Analysis.* New York: Monthly Review Press, 1982.

Schatan, J. *World Debt: Who is to Pay?* London: Zed Press, 1987.

Usman, Yusufu Bala. *Nigeria Against the IMF.* Kaduna, Nigeria: Vanguard Publishers, 1986.

de Vries, Margaret Gerritsen. *Balance of Payments Adjustment, 1945 to 1986: The IMF Experience.* Washington: International Monetary Fund, 1987.

————. *The International Monetary Fund, 1972–1978: Cooperation on Trial.* Washington: International Monetary Fund, 1985.

Zulu, J. B. and Nsouli, S. M. "Adjustment Programmes in Africa." *Finance and Development* (March 1984): 6ff.

THE AFRICAN DEBT CRISIS

JOHN LOXLEY

IN the early 1980s it was widely believed that the "world debt crisis" was confined to no more than about 20 middle-income developing nations, largely in South America and Asia. These alone among Third World countries had been considered creditworthy enough to borrow from Western banks over the previous decade. More recently it has become apparent that there is an African debt crisis that, in several respects, appears to be even more intractable than that facing the world's major debtors. This crisis remained unrecognized for so long because it is not perceived as a threat to the stability of the world banking system. This perception may not be entirely well founded for, as will be seen, the search for a solution to Africa's debt difficulties poses dilemmas similar to those encountered in proposals for solving the problems of the major debtors, while a failure to deal effectively with Africa's crisis could well have spillover effects on the attitudes and behavior of the major debtors. What is less ambiguous is that in attempting to manage their debt crisis, African nations are encountering economic and political problems almost identical to those being experienced by large debtor nations, but, being much poorer, have even fewer resources to devote to them.

Comprehensive statistics on the size of Africa's debt are impossible to come by, since certain types of debt (e.g., short-term, private, arrears or International Monetary Fund/IMF) and certain regions and countries (North Africa, Nigeria or South Africa) are often excluded from published series. Total debt appears, however, to be well in excess of U.S. $200 billion, roughly broken down as follows:

Region	U.S. $ billion
Sub-Saharan Africa	135
(of which low-income countries)	(60)
North Africa	80
South Africa	25
	240

841

Sources: Reginald Green and Stephany Griffith-Jones, "External Debt: Sub-Saharan Africa's Emerging Iceberg," in *Crisis and Recovery in Sub-Saharan Africa*, ed. Tore Rose (Paris: Organization for Economic Cooperation and Development, 1985); Lawrence Harris, "South Africa's External Debt Crisis," *Third World Quarterly* 8 no. 3 (July 1986); Organization for Economic Cooperation and Development, *Financing and External Debt of Developing Countries: 1986 Survey* (Paris, 1987).

Nigeria is by far the largest debtor in sub-Saharan Africa, with an estimated $25 billion, or 18%, of that region's total indebtedness; five other countries (the Ivory Coast, Sudan, Zambia, Kenya and Tanzania) collectively account for $36 billion, or 27%, of the total.

In North Africa, Egypt ($32 billion) accounts for over 40% of that region's indebtedness, Algeria ($22 billion) for 28%, and Morocco ($15 billion) for 19%.

Total African debt represents about 20% of total Third World debt, a relatively small proportion but still much larger than is usually attributed to Africa.

Africa's relative debt burden is, however, in some respects much greater than that facing major debtors. The average ratio of total debt to annual income (GDP) for Africa as a whole, 54.4% in 1987, is the highest of any region in the world; that for sub-Saharan Africa is even higher, at 73.8% (according to the IMF, 1987). This compares with an average figure for the large global debtors of about 50% of GDP. For many individual countries of Africa, however, this ratio is well in excess of 100%—e.g., Gambia, 170%; Mauritania, 184%; Zambia, 181%; Zaire, 160%.

When total debt is measured against the annual earnings of foreign exchange in theory available to support that debt, Africa's debt burden (two times exports) is again comparable with that of the largest debtors (2.4 times exports). On this measure, some individual African countries have impossible debt burdens, e.g.: Somalia, over 15 times exports; Guinea-Bissau, 13 times; Sudan, nine times—while the 12 largest debtors in sub-Saharan Africa owe the equivalent of five times their annual export earnings.

For sub-Saharan Africa, the annual service payments for debt (principal and interest) average 31% of export earnings, which is about 50% less than that of large global debtors, reflecting the heavier reliance of Africa on concessional loans. Notwithstanding this, there are individual African countries whose debt-servicing ratios are in the same range as or higher than those of Brazil, Mexico, etc., at the height of their debt crisis in 1982. Thus the scheduled debt-service ratio for the largest debtors in sub-Saharan Africa was 62% in 1986–87. For Mozambique this ratio reached a staggering 250%; Sudan, 150%; and Somalia, 97%—implying, of course, completely unmanageable debt situations. In North Africa debt-servicing problems are not so acute, but even there three of five countries (Algeria, Morocco and Egypt) have servicing ratios in excess of 30% of exports. Unfortunately, for the region as a whole the debt-servicing problem is expected to become even greater over the next two years. The term *crisis* is not too strong a word, therefore, to describe the debt problem facing Africa (see Table 1).

There area number of reasons why Africa is now facing such large debt obligations. Many countries pursued very ambitious development plans in the 1970s, often funding them by credits from foreign governments. Many projects financed in this way did not prove to be self-sustaining in terms of foreign exchange, and hence have not proved capable of servicing their loans. In some countries, e.g., Zaire, corruption and the flight of capital seem to have been major factors in the nonproductive use of loans. More generally, many non-oil-producing African countries have suffered a severe deterioration in their terms of trade since the late 1970s, so that earlier forecasts of export-earning capabilities, on which decisions to borrow were made, have proved grossly overoptimistic. For poorer African countries the deterioration amounted to about 30% between 1970–75 and 1980–85. For some, of course, the decline was much greater—e.g., Zaire, 56%; Niger, 52%—as it was for some middle-income countries, e.g., Zambia, 72%; Mauritania, 47%; Liberia, 46%. Throughout the 1970s several African governments also neglected export activities by allowing real exchange rates to appreciate, and by allowing taxes and internal terms of trade to have a negative impact on export incentives. They therefore relied more heavily than was warranted on debt-financed imports, while discouraging the capacity to service that debt when it fell due. The recession in the early 1980s, and the collapse of export earnings it entailed, also led many countries to borrow even more in the form of payments arrears and credits from the IMF.

Oil-producing African countries fared much better than others until the collapse of oil prices in 1985–86, at which point their earlier borrowing became suspect and their need for short-term credit expanded greatly.

With the onset of global recession, African countries suddenly found it more difficult to gain access to trade credits, while private flows of capital, including bank credits, virtually ceased. This helped to reduce the level of economic activity (and exports) and put great pressure on the liquid foreign-exchange resources of African governments and businesses. Official financial flows to sub-Saharan Africa also stagnated during this time. Thus, the flow of new capital to the continent dried up at the very time that foreign-exchange earnings, domestic savings and investment collapsed—i.e., at the time of greatest need. For the handful of African countries that did have access to bank credits, e.g., Nigeria, South Africa, the Ivory Coast, Egypt, Algeria and Morocco, the large increase in real interest rates after 1981 was an added source of difficulty.

South Africa's debt-servicing problems had a somewhat special origin. They were caused primarily by the upsurge of popular opposition to the apartheid regime, which culminated in a state of emergency being declared in July 1985. This, and the mounting pressure on European and American banks to withdraw from that country, led to the threat of nonrenewal of short-term bank debts, which accounted for well over one-half of the total. The development to that point of a debt portfolio so heavily weighted with

Table 1
SUB-SAHARAN AFRICAN COUNTRIES' DEBT
POSITIONS, END 1987

Debt outstanding

	Total[1]		*Medium- and long-term publicly guaranteed debt, of which, in percent*			
	(billion U.S. dollars)	*Of which outstanding use of IMF credit (million U.S. dollars)*	*Multi-lateral creditors*	*Bilateral creditors*	*Financial institutions and others*	*Debt ratio*[2]
Market borrowers						
Congo	4.36	13.5	10.8	21.8	67.4	435.6
Gabon	1.64	60.3	11.3	78.4	10.3	114.2
Ivory Coast	10.11	576.7	25.7	32.2	42.0	296.2
Nigeria	26.65	—	7.9	49.1	43.0	352.7
Official borrowers						
Burkina Faso	0.72	—	67.1	31.2	1.7	300.8
Burundi	0.71	12.1	68.4	27.9	3.7	627.8
Cape Verde	0.11	—	58.9	38.4	26.8	250.0
Central African Republic	0.64	45.4	51.0	48.3	0.7	330.7
Chad	0.27	18.6	72.7	27.3	—	162.7
Comoros	0.15	—	59.6	40.4	—	704.2
Djibouti	0.15	—	43.5	54.4	2.0	109.5
Equatorial Guinea	0.15	7.7	21.9	75.2	2.9	483.9
Gambia	0.25	34.7	53.3	31.3	15.4	244.9
Ghana	2.78	836.5	48.7	39.9	11.4	318.4
Guinea	1.62	46.2	25.8	60.2	14.0	275.6
Guinea-Bissau	0.36	4.5	37.8	48.9	13.3	1,500.0
Liberia	1.30	291.4	36.6	45.8	17.6	328.3
Madagascar	3.14	223.0	28.3	64.0	7.7	754.8
Malawi	1.25	110.3	67.3	26.0	6.7	399.7
Mali	1.69	75.1	34.4	64.0	15.5	523.7
Mauritania	1.63	71.2	28.7	60.8	10.5	347.5
Rwanda	0.43	—	72.5	27.5	—	216.8
São Tomé and Príncipe	0.11	—	38.9	42.2	18.9	873.0
Senegal	3.53	327.2	30.2	57.2	12.6	290.3
Seychelles	0.13	—	26.5	37.9	35.6	152.9

Debt outstanding

	Total[1]		Medium- and long-term publicly guaranteed debt, of which, in percent			
	(billion U.S. dollars)	Of which outstanding use of IMF credit (million U.S. dollars)	Multi- lateral creditors	Bilateral creditors	Financial institutions and others	Debt ratio[2]
Sierra Leone	0.66	99.6	33.7	46.2	20.1	562.7
Somalia	1.80	166.2	32.6	63.7	3.7	1,428.6
Sudan	12.10	858.7	13.8	62.5	23.7	1,520.1
Swaziland	0.27	3.2	51.4	39.0	9.7	58.3
Tanzania	3.67	94.9	38.4	57.6	4.0	677.1
Togo	1.27	78.4	46.0	47.0	7.0	301.4
Uganda	1.82	257.1	63.5	33.8	2.7	497.3
Zaire	7.97	916.4	18.5	71.6	9.9	413.2
Zambia	6.51	956.9	23.5	57.6	18.9	915.5
Others						
Benin	0.84	—	34.9	14.7	50.4	371.4
Botswana	0.51	—	60.0	29.7	10.3	48.2
Cameroon	2.91	—	38.1	46.2	15.7	104.0
Ethiopia	2.33	62.7	36.1	53.1	10.8	385.6
Kenya	4.59	380.9	46.9	36.9	16.2	267.2
Lesotho	0.22	—	88.9	9.2	1.8	55.5
Mauritius	0.54	149.7	47.9	33.9	18.1	58.8
Mozambique	3.59	17.3	6.7	77.6	15.8	1,726.0
Niger	1.11	114.7	38.1	43.2	18.7	264.5
Zimbabwe	2.48	156.5	18.3	20.6	61.1	182.0

[1] Excludes arrears; includes short-, medium-, and long-term publicly guaranteed and unguaranteed debt, plus outstanding use of IMF-credit.
[2] Total debt outstanding plus use of IMF credit over exports of goods and services.
Source: IMF, country level data base, *World Economic Outlook*; IMF, *International Financial Statistics*; and IMF staff estimates; *IMF Survey*, June 1988.

short-term credits was itself a reflection of perceived underlying weaknesses in the South African economy and of persistent political instability. To meet the threat of bank withdrawals, the government placed a temporary freeze on the repayment of bank-debt principal until a settlement could be negotiated with the banks.

For the rest of sub-Saharan Africa, both bank debt and short-term debt are much less important. Bank debt is approximately one-third of total debt and less than 20% if Nigeria and the Ivory Coast are excluded, while short-term debt is under 10% and 5%, respectively (although this is probably an underestimate). Official debt and credits guaranteed by foreign governments account for about 70% of the total, 20% being multilateral; and a further 6% owed to the IMF. Concessional loans account for 30% of the total and for 42% of debt owed by the poorer sub-Saharan Africa countries. Sub-Saharan African debt is therefore cheaper and less volatile than that of South Africa.

The debt profile of North Africa falls midway between that of sub-Saharan Africa and that of South Africa. Bank debt is about 37% of the total, short-term debt about 15%. Official or officially guaranteed debt is just under two-thirds of the total; multilateral debt less than 10%; IMF credits, 1.5%; and concessional loans about one-quarter. Egypt and Morocco account for almost 90% of concessional debt outstanding, and for almost all the multilateral debt. Libya holds neither.

As will be seen, the composition of debt has implications for the manner in which debt problems are handled.

Coping with the burden of debt has posed considerable economic and political problems for many African countries. Debt payments have meant reduced living standards for large sections of the African population. Such payments have also diverted scarce foreign exchange away from the importation of goods vital for the maintenance of investment, production and consumption. For many countries this adds to pressures that have been felt for some years. In the poorer countries of sub-Saharan Africa, for instance, per capita income levels fell by an average of 0.5% per year between 1975 and 1980. Between 1980 and 1985 they fell by a further 11%. By 1980–82, real imports into this part of Africa were 26% below their 1970 level, and fell by a further 16% during the global recession. The debt crisis would have created serious difficulties had African economies been otherwise healthy; as it was, for many countries borrowing abroad had helped veil underlying weaknesses in the economy, weaknesses that became all too visible during the global recession, when many of the old debts also fell due for repayment.

It is clear from the figures above that for many countries in Africa the debt-servicing burden could not and cannot be met by import compression alone; the problem is simply too large for such a solution to be feasible. For this reason, import compression has been tempered by the rescheduling of debt-service payments and by the infusion of additional capital flows. The task of debt management has been handled primarily by the IMF through agreements with debtor countries in the form of stabilization programs. A typical IMF agreement provides governments with some balance-of-payments support in return for commitments to change policy in an effort to rectify macroeconomic imbalances and restore economic growth. On the basis of such an agreement, African governments can then approach other official agencies (including the World Bank) for balance-of-payments assistance and, more importantly, can negotiate a rescheduling of debt commitments. Official or officially guaranteed debt-service payments are re-scheduled in the Paris Club, which consists of a meeting of representatives of the Organization for Economic Cooperation and Development, the World Bank, the U.N. Conference on Trade and Development (UNCTAD) and, of course, the IMF. It is the fund that is the prime mover in Paris Club meetings, proposing the degree of relief and a program for nursing down payment arrears, based on its projections of likely flows of foreign exchange. Rescheduling of commercial bank debts takes place in the London Club, with the IMF again playing a leading role, or else, occasionally, under special ad hoc administrative arrangements (e.g., South Africa).

Since the onset of the global debt crisis there has been a significant increase in the number of rescheduling agreements. Between 1980 and 1982, 16 countries sought, successfully, bilateral debt relief from official creditors on a multilateral coordinated basis. Even at that time no fewer than 14 were African nations. Between 1984 and 1986 there were 51 official debt reschedulings, 33 of which were of African debt. Altogether, 23 African countries have been involved—all, with the exception of Morocco, in sub-Saharan Africa. Several countries have had more than one official rescheduling since 1980 (Central African Republic, three; Liberia, four; the Ivory Coast, three; Sierra Leone, three; Malawi, two; Senegal, five; Sudan, three; Zaire, four; Zambia, three; Niger, four; Togo, four). This indicates the recurring nature of their servicing difficulties and the fact that Paris Club reschedulings generally occur one year at a time, as a servicing problem is encountered. Rescheduling generally involves spreading debt payments out over nine or 10 years with a five-year grace period.

Between mid-1982 and early 1987, 36 countries rescheduled their repayments of commercial bank debt. Of these, 15 were African countries, including South Africa and Morocco.

For the most part, therefore, the African debt crisis is being tackled on an individual country basis, with debt reschedulings, capital inflows and policy adjustments being tailored to the needs of each specific debtor. African governments have argued, however, that current approaches are inadequate and that a systemic approach to African debt is required. They see three main weaknesses in the debt-management strategy to date. Firstly, debt rescheduling is seen as a relatively short-term palliative that is subject also to a number of technical shortcomings. It is regarded as a palliative because it simply delays the day of reckoning without avoiding it. Already, countries such as Zaire and Sudan are being called upon to repay debts that were rescheduled in the 1970s, and in a couple of years' time no fewer than 11 sub-Saharan African countries will be in this position. The Paris Club responded to this criticism in 1987 by allowing debtors with particularly acute economic problems to repay over as long as 20 years. Mozambique and Uganda were beneficiaries of this more liberal approach.

African governments also claim, quite correctly, that the Paris Club's insistence on year-by-year rescheduling prevents them from drawing up medium- and longer-term financing projections for stabilization and structural adjustment programs. Only one sub-Saharan Africa country has ever secured a multiyear rescheduling, the Ivory Coast in 1986, although a strong case could be made for extending this practice. Annual debt-rescheduling exercises not only prevent forward planning, they consume the time of scarce skilled personnel, are bureaucratic and generate uncertainty.

A further technical problem with current rescheduling practices is that they follow rather than precede negotiations for aid. This allows creditors to demand a portion of enhanced aid flows for the servicing of their debt—flows that were intended mainly to assist economic adjustment.

The main complaint of African governments is not so much over the mechanics of rescheduling as over its efficacy as a means of containing the debt crisis. On the basis of World Bank projections it appears that even after generous assumptions about the rescheduling of debt obligations, the poorer (IDA-eligible*) countries of sub-Saharan Africa will still pay, on the average, 25% of their export earnings in debt servicing. For 12 such countries this ratio will remain in excess of 35%. These are alarming figures, giving support to appeals by African governments for a systemic solution to their debt problems.

The second complaint with existing strategies is that stabilization and adjustment programs are grossly underfunded. In particular, there are inadequate flows of liquid, concessional support to allow African countries to raise significantly their real import levels and, therefore, domestic supply. The main sources of these funds are the IMF and the World Bank. Between 1981 and 1986 the approach of the fund to African adjustment programs was to demand high levels of policy conditionality (discussed below), while offering minimal short-run financial assistance on quite expensive terms. This heightening of conditionality and frugality was the international embodiment of monetarism, the dominant approach to economic policy in Europe and North America at that time. The principal instrument of IMF assistance was the one-year standby arrangement, which carried relatively high interest rates and, again, allowed no forward planning beyond the 12 months. At that time the fund considered that concessional long-term financial assistance, which it recognized was badly needed by poorer Third World countries, was outside its mandate. Notwithstanding several years of pressure from its poorer members and the publication of a number of studies indicating the relatively poor performance of IMF programs in Africa, the fund was reluctant to moderate its position on this issue. Only in 1985, when the severity of the African debt crisis became a cause of concern to the U.S. government, did the IMF consider altering its approach. In the following year, as Part II of the Baker (debt) initiative, it introduced a $3 billion structural adjustment facility (SAF), which provides to poorer countries funding over a three-year period on highly concessional terms, at 0.5% per year interest and repayable over 10 years. This represents a reconstitution of an earlier concessionary facility, the trust fund, repayment of which began falling due in the recent past, so adding to Africa's debt-servicing problems. It represents a net flow of IMF resources, therefore, only to the extent that the fund had earlier refused such recycling, and it

*Those countries eligible for concessional loans from the World Bank's International Development Association.

is best viewed as a turning over of a portion of Africa's IMF debt. The amount of SAF funding is, however, quite small, being limited to only 63.5% of a member's quota; and the SAFs, unlike trust fund loans, do carry policy conditionality embodied in a three-year policy framework paper (PFP) prepared jointly with the World Bank. To date (end 1987) 18 African countries have received these loans.

The World Bank is the other main source of balance-of-payments support for IMF-sponsored stabilization adjustment programs. It can provide liquid assistance in a number of ways—in the form of a structural adjustment loan, usually accompanying an IMF standby arrangement and involving quite comprehensive policy conditionality; or in the form of sector loans or export rehabilitation loans, which do not have the standby prerequisite and which carry more narrowly focused policy conditionality. IDA-eligible sub-Saharan African countries obtain such assistance on highly concessional terms, repayable over 40 years with a grace period of 10 years, and carrying only an annual fee of between 0.5% and 0.75%. In the financial year 1986–87 the bank advanced quick-disbursing loans to 16 African countries, totaling $1.4 billion. Of this amount Tunisia and Morocco received 40% and Nigeria one-third. To date, 25 sub-Saharan Africa countries have been involved in implementing reform programs with World Bank assistance.

Since July 1985 the bank has also administered a $1.2 billion special fund for special joint financing. This initiative also owes much to growing concerns among Western governments over the African debt problem, but was, in addition, a response to broader concerns about the economic health of the poorest countries in Africa. So far, 20 countries have drawn $600 million under this facility.

There is widespread agreement, however, that the current level of financial flows to Africa is quite inadequate to meet not only debt-servicing requirements but also the need for minimal growth. The eighth replenishment of IDA (IDA-8), for 1988–90, in the vicinity of $12.4 billion, will barely maintain the real flow of this form of assistance to sub-Saharan Africa. It will do nothing to fill the financing gap that African nations will face if they are to meet the World Bank's target of restoring their per capita incomes to their 1980–82 levels by the end of the decade (a minimal target indeed!).

It is for this reason that the World Bank has been seeking additional special funding for Africa's poorest countries as part of a special action program, discussed below. If this aid materializes, it will considerably ease the import constraint in sub-Saharan Africa; but it is unlikely to head off calls for debt relief, given the modest per capita income growth it is expected to support.

A not unimportant consideration in the efforts of the IMF and the International Bank for Reconstruction and Development (IBRD) to increase the flow of capital to Africa is the desire of these institutions themselves to avoid bad debt. Both institutions refuse to reschedule debts, and this is becoming a problem for a number of countries that borrowed heavily from the bank in the 1960s or borrowed from the fund earlier in this decade.

Indeed, the net flow of resources because of African transactions with the fund in 1986–87 was actually negative—to the tune of $400 million—while servicing IMF debt now accounts for fully 6.3% of Africa's total annual export earnings. It would, of course, be a mistake to see this as the sole motivation behind the search for expanded resource flows, especially given the size of those being sought by the bank, but it is a factor to be noted.

At the other end of the African debt spectrum, Nigeria, the Ivory Coast and Morocco were designated under the first part of the Baker Initiative as "highly indebted countries," among the 15 countries that were to be given large infusions of additional official and commercial credits to forestall the possibility of the global debt crisis coming to a head. In 1986 and 1987 they received $800 million and $1.3 billion, respectively, in additional funds from the World Bank; but this, apparently, has not been accompanied by the supporting inflows of additional commercial bank debt envisaged by Baker. In this respect the Baker initiative has been less than successful.

The third set of reservations of African governments about current debt-management strategies concerns the nature of the policy conditionality being imposed by the fund and the bank in return for the additional flows of capital they help secure.

Conditionality consists of a series of reforms of economic instruments and institutions designed to restore stability, efficiency and economic growth, and, of course, to ensure the orderly repayment of foreign debt. IMF conditionality focuses narrowly on monetary restraint and on improving the balance of payments by altering the relative prices of exports, imports and local goods through exchange-rate depreciation. It shares with the World Bank's conditionality a common emphasis on promoting the use of market forces and private enterprise as opposed to state intervention; but the bank tends to assume responsibility for detailed initiatives in this area. Likewise, the bank is active in helping determine specific producer prices in support of export promotion, and generally shores up the macroinitiatives of the fund by advocating reform at the sectoral and institutional levels. Since the introduction of the special African facility, the fund and the bank have a much closer, formal working relationship in formulating and monitoring reform programs and in ensuring their financing.

African governments have a variety of concerns about these programs, which go beyond the pivotal one of their frequent underfunding. The IMF emphasis on demand restraint, often in the form of a sharp shock, is often politically problematic. Restraint takes the form of cutbacks in state employment and in government spending on crucial services such as health or education; the abolition of revenue-draining subsidies on basic urban foodstuffs or other commodities; credit tightness; and reduced real incomes and consumption levels of some, primarily urban, sectors of society. Devaluation often compounds the impact of restraint, being designed to shift purchasing power from urban to rural sectors and, more specifically, from those producing for the local market to those producing for export. On a number of occasions the severity of cuts in the living standards of some urban groups has led to what have been termed "IMF riots." In recent years these have occurred in Zambia, Tunisia and Sudan, while less dramatic manifestations of political discontent have been quite widespread. Even where this has not been the case, some governments have expressed concern about the implication of IMF programs for income distribution and the provision of basic needs. It is for these reasons that many African governments are cautious in applying for fund assistance, doing so only when the economic situation is serious and when there seem to be no alternatives. Ironically, delaying resort to the fund in this way probably heightens the probability of tough adjustment measures being needed. It is, nevertheless, an indication of the seriousness of African economic problems that over three-quarters of the nations of sub-Saharan Africa have turned to the IMF for balance-of-payments assistance since 1980, and as a result have had their economic policies shaped by the fund. Over the same period African states have dominated the loan portfolio of the fund by number of loans, though not by amount of credit. In late 1987 they accounted for 17 out of the total of 23 standby arrangements and 17 of the 22 SAFs outstanding, but for only about one-quarter of total credit advanced under these agreements.

Other concerns about conditionality revolve around the seemingly ideological preference of the international financial institutions for market- and private-enterprise-oriented solutions to Africa's problems. State intervention in Africa is widespread and has complex historical origins, often rooted in perceived weaknesses in the market or in problems encountered with private enterprise. There may be no available alternative to some forms of state involvement, while, on occasion, there may be powerful vested interests in retaining it regardless of the cost to others. The fund and the bank are undoubtedly correct in emphasizing that inefficient state enterprises have on occasion led to small farmers receiving greatly reduced earnings from their crops, and have in some cases been a major drain on scarce tax revenues. Understandably, therefore, this area of adjustment programs is marked by tension and controversy.

Questions of economic strategy also arise, in particular that of the consistency between short- and long-term economic policies and goals. The relative emphasis on export crops tends to leave hanging in the air the question of food security, which is considered crucial by most African governments. Likewise, it tends to contradict the emphasis given to regional economic integration in the Organization of African Unity's (OAU's) Lagos Plan of Action, to which most African governments pay at least lip service.

Above all, there is the question of whether or not these programs actually work in Africa. Up to the present there has been no clear-cut evidence that they do. In the 1970s less than half of them met balance-of-payments, income-growth or inflation targets, and countries with programs did not seem to perform better than those without. There is, as yet, no published evidence of their performance since the global recession. Yet even if there were, measurement of country performance under conditionality is fraught with controversy. African countries would tend to argue that poor performance is indicative of design problems in programs. In particular, they would point to faulty assumptions about responsiveness of supply to price incentives and would question the wisdom of austerity. They would also claim that the fund places excessive dependence upon adjustment as opposed to financing, thereby inhibiting recovery in real imports, growth and price stability. For its part, the fund would counter that poor performance is often a reflection of governments being too weak to undertake the necessary policy adjustment steadfastly or quickly enough. These controversies can be judged only at the level of the experience of individual countries, and even then how the country would have performed in the absence of the IMF program cannot be known.

There are, therefore, acute problems with each aspect of the current three-pronged approach to the management of the African debt problem, with the result that extreme difficulties are being encountered by both large and small debtors.

What appears to be the overwhelming problem is that flows of foreign capital to support African adjustment efforts in the recent past have been grossly inadequate given the pressures of external debt servicing. Nowhere is this more graphically illustrated than in the case of Ghana, considered by the international financial institutions to be a success model to be emulated by the rest of sub-Saharan Africa. Unquestionably, Ghana's economy made a dramatic recovery between 1983 and 1987. In part this was due to improved weather conditions and a sharp recovery in the country's terms of trade, but policy reform undoubtedly helped to stimulate output and export growth. The huge inflow of foreign capital (about $1 billion) to support the program was almost exactly offset, however, by the repayment of debts and arrears. Bilateral donors have been slow to support the program, and repayment of earlier IMF loans is now only possible by additional borrowing from the fund. At some point soon, unless large inflows of concessional funds or more lasting debt relief can be obtained, Ghana may quickly encounter adjustment- and debt-servicing fatigue.

It is, however, the recent behavior of the especially large debtor countries that is worrying Western governments and banks. In response to its acute economic difficulties, Nigeria, the largest debtor in sub-Saharan Africa has followed the example of Peru and in 1985 unilaterally imposed a ceiling on debt servicing of 30% of its exports. This type of "conciliatory default" has the attraction to debtors of limiting their payments, while at the same time sending a signal to creditors that they remain willing to pay within the limits of their resources.

In the following year Nigeria went further and announced a three-months' moratorium on the repayment of principal on some $12 billion worth of medium- and long-term loans, in a bid to force its creditors to reschedule debts on terms consistent with its declared payments ceiling. There followed 18 months of bitter wrangling during which banks offered terms that even the IMF felt were too harsh, endangering Nigeria's recovery program. Perhaps it was this intransigence that led Nigeria to seek less confrontational ways of reducing its debt-servicing obligations; in any event, in 1987 it began to allow a limited form of debt-equity swaps. It is prepared to convert unguaranteed payments arrears on trade debts into prom-

852

issory notes redeemable in local currency. On redemption, the proceeds can be invested in Nigerian companies and, if these are located in sectors of national priority, the investment will be treated as if it had been a direct foreign investment for purposes of capital and dividend repatriation. To date, however, this type of swap is little more than a curiosity, as only about $70 million of debt has been converted. Indeed, so unattractive has Africa been to foreign investment in recent years that debt-equity swaps are unlikely ever to become significant even if they were considered desirable by African governments.

Other major sub-Saharan Africa debtors have had problems similar to those of Nigeria. In May 1987 Zambia went even further than Nigeria and limited its debt servicing to 10% of exports *after* making allowances for oil and other crucial imports. In effect, this puts the Zambian ceiling at much less than 5% of exports, and is tantamount to default. The irony is that its debt crisis is so acute that even if multilateral and some bilateral donors withdraw financial assistance, the loss to Zambia is likely to be no greater than the savings on debt servicing. It appears, though, that at least one of Zambia's motivations in taking this step is to highlight the monumental proportions of its debt problems in the face of a 70% decline in the price of copper, its major export, and to pressure the international community to take some imaginative remedial measures.

Also in May 1987, the Ivory Coast imposed a moratorium on its bank-debt repayments as its export earnings collapsed; and it informed the IMF that it could not force any additional austerity measures in support of debt servicing. Only in December 1987 was further rescheduling agreed upon. In the process, the Ivory Coast appears to have persuaded the World Bank that debt repayment should be contingent upon export market conditions—a position long advocated by President Houphouët Boigny and supported by other African heads of state. Given the difficulties experienced by Nigeria in this respect, it remains to be seen whether and how such contingency clauses will be inserted in African debt-rescheduling agreements. What is evident is that capital flows to the Ivory Coast were insufficient to stabilize its debt situation, notwithstanding the Baker initiative.

The threat of default by the Ivory Coast is best interpreted as a bargaining ploy to secure more resources. Such moves do, nonetheless, send shock waves through the system—especially since, between them, Nigeria and the Ivory Coast are responsible for at least $15 billion worth of commercial bank debt, fully one-half of the total outstanding to sub-Saharan African countries. In the rest of Africa, Algeria, Morocco, Egypt and South Africa are the only other countries with sufficient outstanding bank debts to cause concern in the international banking community, and it is worth noting that all of them have been involved in debt-rescheduling exercises in recent years. South Africa's debt moratorium caused particular anxiety and led to the first recorded rescheduling of interbank market loans. So sensitive was this case and so large was the number of bank creditors involved (262) that a special ad hoc mechanism of mediation was employed, drawing on the services of a prominent international businessman and banker. The rescheduling agreement achieved little more, however, than a temporary respite for bankers whose investments in South Africa are only as secure as the system of apartheid itself.

The international community has slowly begun to acknowledge that the debt problems of sub-Saharan Africa may require some systemic intervention. The establishment of the IMF's SAF under the Baker initiative was the first sign of a recognition that the case-by-case approach would not be sufficient within the institutional funding structure existing at that time. Yet, as has been seen, this was not much more than a token gesture. Recently, the managing director of the IMF has been seeking to triple the funds available for SAF, which would make a significant impact on resource flows to the poorest sub-Saharan African countries, as would the additional resources being pursued by the World Bank.

The proposal to increase the funding available under SAF was strongly endorsed by the Venice Summit in June 1987. It was also a recommendation of this meeting that gave rise to the Paris Club easing its rescheduling terms for sub-Saharan African debtors. The final recommendation of the summit—that consideration should be given to reducing the interest rates on outstanding sub-Saharan African debt—has, however, been received less enthusiastically. It is to be noted that the summit avoided recommending more substantial forms of debt relief and quite categorically emphasized its support for orthodox structural adjustment programs under the leadership of the IMF and World Bank. This amounted to an endorsement of the prevailing debt-management strategy, but with some concessions in terms of added financial flows from international institutions and the Paris Club. It also constituted a rejection of a more far-reaching plan for sub-Saharan Africa debt relief put forward at that meeting by Nigel Lawson, the British chancellor of the Exchequer. The Lawson plan proposed that all official loans should be converted into grants for those countries pursuing appropriate economic adjustment programs; that repayment periods on outstanding official debt should be extended to 20 years; and that interest rates should be reduced by about three percentage points below the market rate. It was estimated that these measures could save Africa some $25 million a year in debt repayments.

Following the Venice Summit, the World Bank drew up a special action program for 12 of the 22 low-income, debt-distressed sub-Saharan African countries. The object of this program was, first, to provide immediate relief from debt servicing so as to limit such payments to a maximum of 25% of exports; and, second, to provide for a growth in real per capita imports of 1% per year over the next three years. These are modest objectives but they would enable a slight growth in per capita income for countries that in general suffered further reductions in their standard of living in 1986. The bank calculated that this program would require additional financing of $1.5 billion per year in 1988–90. Extending the grace and repayment periods of Paris Club reschedulings, and reducing interest rates on rescheduled nonconcessional official debt by half would lower debt-service obligations by $350 million per year. The conversion of official loans into grants retroactively, as agreed at the 1978 UNCTAD Conference, would provide another $60 million per year. A balance of $400 million would be needed to reach the debt-ceiling target. In order to meet real import-growth objectives, an additional $7 million would have to be found. The bank proposed that these funds come from expanded IMF-SAF ($5–$9 million), IDA-8 and IDA flows to these specific countries ($0.2–$0.35 billion), and from an accelerated disbursement of adjustment financing from bilateral and other multilateral donors ($0.3–$0.5 billion).

It appears that the bank has had some success in raising additional funds, not only for these countries but for the other low-income, debt-distressed countries of sub-Saharan Africa. Bilateral donors are prepared, up to a point, to recognize that this part of the world does have unique problems requiring special solutions. The bank has had less success, however, in getting Western governments to agree to a debt-servicing ceiling relative to exports, presumably because they wish to avoid setting a generalized precedent for larger debtors elsewhere in the world. Moreover, while Canada, Britain and the Scandinavian countries have already taken up the Lawson proposal and canceled the official debts of low-income African countries, there is great reluctance on the part of Western governments to reduce interest rates on remaining debts or to extend write-offs to officially guaranteed export credits. This again is partly to avoid what could be interpreted as a precedent, which would be both expensive and destabilizing if applied to larger global debtors; but also it is partly because export-credit credit-guarantee agencies are supposed to be self-supporting commercial agencies.

Failure of the Western powers to accept even the modest debt-reform proposals of the Lawson plan and the World Bank special action program, together with the fact that not even these proposals address the other problems of such large debtors as Nigeria, the Ivory Coast or the countries of North Africa, seems to have helped galvanize African nations into collective action. In late 1987 the OAU called an extraordinary conference on debt and issued a declaration that contains proposals going well beyond the Lawson and World Bank plans. African nations are now calling for the conversion of all outstanding bilateral debt into grants; the supension of all payments on account of external debt servicing for 10 years; the payment of part of their debt in local currency; a reduction in real interest rates on their debt; the lengthening of the maturity and grace period of private debt; and the multiyear rescheduling of debts for a period of five years ahead of time, with maturities of at least 50 years, 10 years' grace and zero interest payments. They also wish to see debt repayment linked to export earnings in a proportion that is "reasonable and bearable;" enhanced flows of bilateral assistance; and an increase in the grant element of both bilateral and multilateral aid. Furthermore, they requested that Western governments take steps to improve the market environment for African exports. Finally, they called for a special international conference on Africa's external debt to be held, with creditors, sometime in 1988.

These requests are at one and the same time both radical and moderate. They are radical in that they envisage an effective write-off of much of Africa's debt and a considerable easing of the burden of servicing the balance. They are moderate in that there is no suggestion that private and bank debts be written off or that they not be serviced. Nor is there any suggestion that Africa make do without foreign assistance; rather, the emphasis is on diversifying that assistance, effectively reducing the influence of the IMF and IBRD, and on making it more concessional. Since African states seem to be unable to persuade the IMF and World Bank to take seriously their concerns about conditionality, they appear to have decided that the best approach is to minimize reliance on their funds. In calling for a conference to discuss these proposals, African governments are seizing the initiative and putting Western governments on the defensive. It is unstated, but understood, that should they be rebuffed, African heads of state, many facing increasing political pressure, might begin to consider more radical ways of dealing with their debt problems. There are many on the continent, including the much-respected Julius Nyerere of Tanzania, now chairman of the South Commission, who feel that Africa's debt cannot be repaid and that governments should simply cease attempting to service them, on the grounds that they are no more than the monetary reflection of the fact that the global economic system has in recent years worked systematically to the detriment of Africa. Since Western governments and international financial institutions wish, presumably, to avoid such a development, the suggestion of a debtor/creditor conference is likely to be accepted. By the time discussions start African governments may find their case strengthened by the report of the Advisory Group on Resource Flows to Africa, an international group of eminent persons appointed by the U.N. secretary general. This group is to examine the African debt problem, and its recommendations, due early in 1988, are likely to be that more substantial and permanent relief is required if the debt crisis is not to lead to widespread political turmoil in Africa.

FURTHER READING

African Recovery. New York: United Nations, 1987.

Culpeper, Roy. *Forced Adjustment: The Export Collapse in Sub-Saharan Africa.* Ottawa: North-South Institute, 1987.

Elements of a Special Action Program for Low-Income Debt-Distressed African Countries. Washington: World Bank, 1987.

Financing Adjustment with Growth in Sub-Saharan Africa, 1986–90. Washington: World Bank, 1986.

Financing and External Debt of Developing Countries, 1986 Survey. Paris: Organization for Economic Cooperation and Development, 1987.

Green, Reginald, and Griffith-Jones, Stephany. "External Debt: Sub-Saharan Africa's Emerging Iceberg." In Rose Tore, ed. *Crisis and Recovery in Sub-Saharan Africa.* Paris: Organization for Economic Cooperation and Development, 1985.

Harris, Lawrence. "South Africa's External Debt Crisis." *Third World Quarterly* 8 (July 1986).

Havnevik, Kjell, ed. *The IMF and the World Bank in Africa.* Uppsala, Sweden: Scandinavian Institute of African Studies, 1987.

Helleiner, Gerald K., ed. *Africa and the International Monetary Fund.* Washington: International Monetary Fund, 1986.

Lancaster, Carol, and Williamson, John, eds. *African Debt and Financing.* New York: Institute for International Economics, 1986.

Lawrence, Peter, ed. *World Recession and the Food Crisis in Africa.* London: James Currey, 1986.

Loxley, John. *The IMF and the Poorest Countries.* Ottawa: North-South Institute, 1984.

Martin, Matthew. "Crisis Management: Solving Africa's Debt Problem." In Olusola Akrinade and J. Kurt Barling, eds. *Economic Development in Africa: International Efforts, Issues and Prospects.* London: Pinter Publishers, 1987.

World Economic Outlook, Washington: International Monetary Fund, 1987.

BANKING INSTITUTIONS IN AFRICA

ANN SEIDMAN

BANKS play a major role in the accumulation and reinvestment of capital, financing and shaping the pattern of the development of a modern economy. In Africa, however, banks contributed to the growth of so-called modern enclaves geared to the export of crude materials produced by low-cost labor, the import of manufactured goods and the outflow of a major share of the investable surpluses generated in that process.[1] Following independence, African governments faced the challenge of reorganizing these institutions to finance more balanced, integrated development capable of providing productive employment and raising living standards for all their peoples.

Focusing primarily on southern Africa, this paper outlines the history of colonial banking institutions, reviews the consequences of the different postindependence government initiatives in three African countries, and suggests the implications for future strategies.

COLONIAL BANKING AND FINANCIAL INSTITUTIONS

Given the predominance of small-scale agriculture and handicrafts, operating at relatively low levels of productivity, African societies developed their own forms of money, but little in the way of sophisticated banking institutions. In some societies militarily strong groups captured peasants' agricultural surpluses to support relatively centralized states. Based on an emerging regional specialization of production, long-distance trade laid the foundation of extensive kingdoms. To facilitate this extensive trade, precolonial African traders devised a variety of media of exchange: cowrie shells, metal beads, gold dust, copper crosses.

The European colonizers destroyed these preexisting forms of money along with the extended trading systems that had introduced them. The need for cheap labor in the Americas led to the triangular slave trade, contributing to the primitive accumulation of capital that financed Europe's industrial

---

[1] Ann Seidman, *Money, Banking and Financial Institutions in Africa* (London: Zed Press, 1986).

revolution. The owner of a plantation in Jamaica maintained by slave labor invested his profits in British industry and laid the foundations of Barclays Bank. But in Africa, militaristic slave-trading states disrupted preexisting economies based on long-distance trade.

At the end of the 18th century, reinvesting their capital in rapidly growing industries and shipping at home, European industrialists penetrated more deeply into Africa to open up new markets and sources of raw materials. Using government power and superior military technologies, they carved the continent into separate colonies.

Despite differences in geographical and historical circumstances, southern Africa's experience illustrates how colonial governments imposed their own monetary systems and banking institutions. In the early 17th century the Dutch set up a trading post at South Africa's Cape of Good Hope, as a stop on the route to Asia; for two centuries, importing slaves from their possessions elsewhere and enslaving local inhabitants, they gradually expanded their land holdings. To prevent the French from capturing the Cape during the Napoleonic Wars, the British administered the colony. They imposed their own currency, tied to the British pound sterling, and encouraged private British banks to set up business.

To escape British pressures to end slavery, the descendants of the Dutch—today called Afrikaners—trekked inland to the Transvaal to build their own "republics." Living in predominantly agrarian subsistence economies dependent on slave labor, they paid officials and government debts with promissory notes called "good fors," since each was "good for" a given amount of state land. They thus created a paper currency backed by land rather than gold or silver. They set up state banks, offering foreign banks land in exchange for gold and silver. To acquire more land they fought the neighboring African peoples, borrowing from the British Cape commercial banks and imposing land taxes to pay for firearms and ammunition. Unable to pay the taxes, poorer Boer farmers abandoned their holdings, while the richer ones acquired thousands more acres.

In the 1860s the discovery first of diamonds and then of gold in the Transvaal made South Africa the continent's most attractive region for investment. Expanding world trade required an internationally accepted currency, multiplying the demand for gold. Although the Boer republics claimed the entire region, they could not muster sufficient capital to finance the new mining developments. From the outset, British banks provided the primary source of funds. At the turn of the century the British colonial officials sought to annex the Boer republics to facilitate British investment in the mines. When the resulting three-year war ended, the British-owned Standard Bank integrated the Boers' Transvaal banks into its South African banking system.

The 1910 Act of Union reunited the British and Afrikaners to rule a consolidated South Africa. The government used military power to subordinate the blacks, taking much of their land and taxing them to coerce them to work in the expanding mines and on settler farms. In 1920 the Currency and Banking Act unified all the preexisting currencies of the country into one backed by gold and linked to the pound sterling. The British

Barclays Bank took over two smaller South African banks to form its own South African branch, which, over the years, grew into Barclays' largest overseas affiliate.

Extending northward, the British South Africa Company spread the use of South African currency, issued through branches of these associated British-South African banks. In the British colonies of both central and East Africa, Barclays and Standard became the leading commercial banks.

Outside South Africa the British typically created currency boards that issued local currencies, backed 100 percent by British pounds sterling. These linked each colony's currency directly to its foreign-trade earnings.

POSTINDEPENDENCE BANKS

Even if space permitted, banking confidentiality traditions would render it difficult to detail the new banking institutions that more than 50 new African governments introduced after independence. Instead, to indicate the range of policies adopted, this section outlines the development of banking in Zimbabwe, Nigeria and Tanzania.

Zimbabwe's inherited banks [2]

The white regime that ruled Zimbabwe at the time of the Unilateral Declaration of Independence (UDI),[3] inherited the core of the Reserve Bank[4] from the Federation of Rhodesia and Nyasaland (1953–63), and issued its own pounds, later converted to Rhodesian dollars on a par with the South African rand. The Reserve Bank performed functions similar to those of most market-economy central banks. Throughout the UDI period it held the bank rate at a low 4.5 percent, spurring rapid expansion of bank credit and investment.

From 1963 to 1978, Zimbabwe's financial sector multiplied its annual contribution to the national product six times, and profits to its owners 12 times. Until the mid-1970s, when mounting guerrilla warfare and international recession hampered further growth, transnational corporations, together with the minority white community, annually invested about 25 percent of the GDP, spurring an annual GDP growth of 6 percent to 8 percent.[5] The manufacturing sector, mainly producing goods for the mi-

---

[2] The following information (gathered from Zimbabwe government statistics, annual company reports and interviews with relevant banking personnel conducted by the author together with students of the economics department, University of Zimbabwe, in 1981–83) provides a more detailed picture of banking structures than has been published for most African countries. In many, if not most, cases further research would help lay a sound basis for formulating more appropriate banking strategies.

[3] The Unilateral Declaration of Independence was made by the white minority to exclude black participation in government.

[4] Established to achieve greater control over local money supplies and increase the commercial banks' responsibility to the federated community. When it broke up, Zambia and Malawi set up their own central banks and issued their own currencies, called kwachas.

[5] Ten percent of the investments financed "whites only" residential housing in the few major towns.

nority in Salisbury (now Harare) and Bulawayo, doubled its output. South Africa's leading mining finance house, the Anglo American Group, working closely with the banks and other financial institutions, reinvested part of its locally generated profits and mobilized additional local investable surpluses to consolidate control over major enterprises in agriculture, manufacturing and trade, as well as mining.

Four foreign-controlled commercial banks—three of them closely linked to the Anglo American Group—handled all of Zimbabwe's commercial banking business. Barclays and Standard owned about two-thirds of the nation's commercial bank assets.[6] Standard's local board of directors included a representative of the Anglo American Group and local businessmen, and it held subsidiaries in the merchant banking, finance, trust and insurance business.[7]

Slightly smaller than Standard's Zimbabwe affiliate, Barclays' Zimbabwe branch had a network of some 10 branches, almost 40 fixed agencies and 100 "stopping points" throughout the country; a finance house; and the only equipment in the country for assaying the value of gold and minerals. An Anglo American Group representative also sat on the Zimbabwe Barclays Bank board.[8]

A South African bank, Nedbank, owned 62.2 percent of the capital of Zimbabwe's third largest bank, Rhobank. Local shareholders, including an affiliate of the Zimbabwe Anglo American Group, held the remaining shares. Other shareholders included several pension funds[9] and Old Mutual, the South African insurance firm that conducted about half of Zimbabwe's insurance business. During UDI, Rhobank increased its holdings from 11 percent to 16 percent of Zimbabwe's commercial bank assets, and acquired a merchant bank, a finance house and four insurance and financial firms.

The fourth and smallest commercial bank, National Grindlays, remained nominally British-owned. In reality, the U.S.-owned Citicorp, the world's largest bank, owned a controlling 49 percent; Lloyds Bank of Britain owned 41 percent.[10] In Zimbabwe, National Grindlays primarily financed associated transnational corporate affiliates' activities.

[6] Their South African affiliates likewise, between them, held about 60 percent of South Africa's assets.

[7] Its British parent had merged with the Charter Bank to become Standard Charter Bank. It has close ties with Chase Manhattan, the third-largest bank in the United States.

[8] The Anglo American Group also owned a major block of shares in the South African branch, and a representative sat on the board of directors of Barclays International. In 1987, as international anti-apartheid sentiment mounted, Barclays sold its South African branch to the Anglo American Group, which changed its name to the First National Bank of South Africa.

[9] About 40 percent of Zimbabwe's paid labor force paid into pension funds (although few received the benefits), which provided an important domestic source of capital for domestic economic expansion.

[10] In South Africa, Citicorp owned several branches and a representative office. In 1980 the chairman of Citibank (the U.S. wing of Citicorp) joined the board of the Anglo American Group's overseas investment arm, Minorco. In 1987 Citicorp sold its South African holdings to the Anglo American Group, which merged them with those of Barclays (see footnote 8).

Reflecting and reinforcing the dualistic nature of the national economy, most of the commercial bank activities concentrated around Harare and Bulawayo. As U.N. sanctions took effect, the government Agricultural Finance Corporation increased its loans to aid the farmers and commercial bank loans to commercial agriculture (about 6,000 white farmers) declined. Since their major working capital expenditure, wages, remained a relatively small percentage of total costs, mining firms borrowed less than 10 percent of the banks' loans. Whenever necessary, however, firms in the Anglo American Group drew on its extensive links with associated pension and insurance institutions to obtain longer-term funds. Since building societies—the largest ones closely interlinked with the banks and the Anglo American Group—mobilized most of the finance for residential housing and commercial structures, the banks provided relatively little credit to construction.

In contrast, the rapidly growing manufacturing sector received almost one-third of all commercial bank credit to finance its working capital requirements. Almost one-fourth of Zimbabwe's bank credit directly funded commerce—a smaller proportion than in many African states where, apart from producing exports, private enterprises primarily import and distribute goods manufactured abroad. However, a considerable share of Zimbabwe's commercial bank credit financed international trade indirectly through discount and accepting houses with which they, together with the Anglo American Group, maintained close ties.

During UDI the commercial banks collaborated with the white regime to set up an Export Credit Insurance Corporation to protect exporters against risks, including losses incurred when foreign governments enforced U.N. sanctions.

Initially, after independence, the Zimbabwe government made relatively few changes in this banking structure. Primarily, it Africanized the Reserve Bank, reduced direct South African involvement in the commercial banks and implemented training schemes for black African personnel. In 1983 it replaced the former Reserve Bank head, transferred from the South African Reserve Bank, with a black Zimbabwean who had worked for several years in New York for Citibank.

In the first postindependence years, three developments affected commercial banks. First, the new government bought the Nedbank's Rhobank shares, changing the latter's name to Zimbank. Initially it left the bank's management unchanged, and left open the question of whether it would sell the shares to Zimbabwe nationals or transform Zimbank into a wholly owned government bank.

Second, the government bought 47 percent of the shares of the Bank of Credit and Commerce of Zimbabwe (BCCZ), a newly created subsidiary of the Bank of Credit and Commerce, International (BCCI).[11] Four Pakistanis, one Indian and three Zimbabweans sat on the Zimbabwe board of directors. They announced plans to extend credit to peasants and small

---

[11] With headquarters in London, BCCI owned branches in 50 countries, including the Seychelles, Kenya, Zambia, Swaziland, Mauritius and Botswana.

African businesses in neglected rural areas, but as the BCCZ's lending criteria differed little from those of the other commercial banks, this seemed improbable.

Third, reflecting growing transnational corporate interest, several transnational banks established representative offices, providing international contacts to enable local banks to assist transnational corporate clients with international financial transactions. These offices represented the U.S. Citibank[12]; another one of the 20 largest U.S. banks with long-standing ties in South Africa, the Bank of Boston; and the Banque International Pour l'Afrique Occidentale, long a leading commercial bank in the former French colonies.

Immediately after independence, the Reserve Bank lifted the previous regime's prohibition on transnational corporate remittance of profits, permitting foreign firms to remit half their current after-tax profits to their home offices abroad. The net outflow of funds immediately increased and was, unfortunately, not offset by the anticipated inflow of new investment funds. Only several years later, however, did the government, confronted by severe foreign-exchange shortages, again reduce the percentage of profits firms could remit home.

Initially the Reserve Bank left the inherited foreign-exchange control system intact. In the context of its overall regulations, the commercial banks continued to make day-to-day decisions about the purposes for which their clients could obtain foreign exchange. The Reserve Bank began to train a team of monitors to supervise the system more closely.

Accepting International Monetary Fund (IMF) advice, the Reserve Bank raised the bank's rate of interest to 9.5 percent from the 4.5 percent that prevailed throughout UDI. This pushed up the cost of borrowing funds, hindering small (including new black African) entrepreneurs and peasants from obtaining essential finance. It did not, however, stem the inflationary pressures spurred by rising import prices (a consequence of IMF-recommended devaluation) and government borrowing.

Several years after independence the government established a development bank with foreign government equity participation; further research is required to assess its consequences in terms of securing and directing investments into new channels.

The available evidence shows that, having failed to obtain enough control to ensure that its financial institutions redirected locally generated investable surpluses to finance balanced national development, and being confronted with heavy expenditures for reconstruction, social welfare and defense, the new Zimbabwe government borrowed heavily both at home and abroad. By the mid-1980s it was spending about one-third of its foreign-exchange earnings to repay its foreign debt. To obtain IMF assistance it had ended serious land reform, cut back on government spending for social services and devalued the Zimbabwe dollar. Domestic prices rose. Unemployment mounted. By the mid-1980s the real incomes of Zimbabwe's lower-income urban and rural populations had fallen below 1980 levels.

[12] This was the case although Citicorp already owned controlling shares in National Grindlays; see above, p. 861.

The Nigerian banking system [13]

Nigerian commercial banking began back in 1894 when the Bank of British West Africa, now the First Bank of Nigeria (linked with Standard Bank), first opened its doors. Almost without government regulation in the colonial era, the banking system suffered instability, and smaller banks failed. Just prior to independence the British established the Central Bank of Nigeria, with features typical of market economies.

Nigeria's postindependence government adopted an approach similar to that initially introduced in Zimbabwe, but developed it further, over a much longer period. With the largest population in Africa, Nigeria enjoyed a major economic boost in the 1970s as a result of the exploitation of its rich oil wells and rising world oil prices. In this prospering environment, its banking and financial structure evolved rapidly.

As the federal government created new states after the civil war, the Central Bank established a network of branches, currency centers and clearing houses throughout the country. Total assets and the value of bank deposits outpaced the rapidly growing national product. By the end of the 1970s the number of banks had increased from 14 to 20. The number of banking offices almost tripled, to reach 740—each serving, on the average, 115,000 people. Reflecting and reinforcing the economy's characteristic dualism, however, about one-fifth of these offices remained concentrated in Lagos State.

The government imposed restrictions on foreign banks to accelerate Nigerianization of the financial system, and required transnational bank affiliates to incorporate in the country. A decade later, the Nigerian Enterprises Promotion Act stipulated a 60 percent minimum indigenous participation in the banking sector. A Quota Allocation Board determined the number and caliber of expatriate personnel the banks could employ. In practice, it limited them to top managerial and technical/professional positions. Nigerians soon held all the top executive and from 60 percent to 90 percent of the top managerial posts. They constituted 60 percent to 80 percent of the members of the Nigerian branches' boards of directors.

By 1980, Nigerian interests, including local state interests, owned 11 of the nation's 20 commercial banks. The federal government, transnational corporate banks and domestic private interests owned controlling shares in the remaining nine, called "joint banks." The two joint banks in which Barclays and Standard each owned about one-fifth of the equity dominated the country's commercial banking scene. With their ties to transnational firms, they controlled over one-third of all branches and deposits, and over one-fourth of the assets of the 20 banks.

The Central Bank of Nigeria relied primarily on aggregate credit ceilings, and cash and liquid asset reserve ratios to control the money supply. It kept the liquidity ratio at 25 percent, but varied the basket of qualified liquid assets. It manipulated the cash reserve ratio fairly frequently. It kept

---

[13] The data relating to the Nigerian financial system are from Okafor, *Transnational Banks in the Nigerian Economy* (Enugu: University of Nigeria, Faculty of Business Administration, 1982, Mimeographed).

the rediscount rate relatively low, raising it only from 4.5 percent in 1970–74 to 6 percent by 1980. It set minimum rates for bank loans, which rose only slightly, from 7 percent to 7.5 percent, over the decade, and held the maximum to less than 12 percent. More than the rest of the banking system, however, the joint banks tended to restrict their credit expansion.

The Nigerian Central Bank imposed a maximum annual percentage increase in the level of credit. It tried to stimulate a wider geographical spread of banking by tying approval of new urban branches to the opening of new rural branches. After this failed, it required joint banks to open a specified number of rural branches. It also tried to alter the sectoral distribution of credit away from trade. First, it specified permissible percentage increases in credit by sector—for example, by setting a minimum for industry at 45 percent, and a maximum for commerce at 10 percent. Up to 1980, even after the government acquired majority control, the joint banks responded less favorably to these requirements than did the rest of the banking system. After 1979 the Central Bank required commercial banks that did not attain the credit targets for housing and agriculture to deposit with it funds equal to the shortfall; it neither paid interest for these deposits nor counted them among the banks' liquid assets.

To remedy the widespread complaint that commercial banks discriminated against Nigerian borrowers, the Central Bank required them to allocate a gradually increasing percent of total credit (it reached 70 percent in 1980) to Nigerian business (defined as those in which Nigerians held 51 percent or more equity). In 1979 it required commercial banks to reserve 10 percent of the credit set aside for Nigerian business for small Nigerian-owned enterprises with an annual turnover of less than 500,000 nairas. In 1980 it raised this proportion to 16 percent.

As in Zimbabwe, the Nigerian Exchange Control Act empowered the commercial bank branches to act as agents in handling foreign payments by all firms, including repatriation of profits, dividends, interest and capital. The government imposed general exchange-control restrictions on profit remittance. In addition, the Banking Act restricted the banks' payment of dividends to their shareholders until all preproduction and other preliminary capitalized expenses were written off, and adequate provision was made for bad and doubtful debts. The Central Bank required each bank to transfer to a reserve fund 25 percent of its net annual profits, or 12.5 percent where the reserve exceeded the bank's paid-up capital. In 1976–77 the government income policy limited bank dividend payments, initially to 30 percent of profits, but rising by 1980 to 60 percent of after-tax profit or 25 percent of paid-up capital, whichever was higher.

The Nigerian Banking Act prohibited any commercial bank from engaging in wholesale or retail business, owning subsidiary companies not engaged in banking, conducting real estate business, or granting a single person any form of credit exceeding one-third of the bank's paid-up capital and reserves. Over the years, however, the banks expanded their activities, acting as agents for distribution of new securities and serving as registrars for public companies. By the 1980s, six merchant banks had begun operating in the country, primarily in the financial centers of Lagos, Kaduna and Port Harcourt. In addition, the federal government set up four national development banks, each of which specialized in a particular sector: the Nigerian Industrial Development Bank financed and provided supportive services for manufacturing, mining and tourism; the Bank for Commerce and Industry financed enterprises in most sectors, and conducted wholesale banking services for its clients; the Agriculture and Co-operative Bank extended loans to agricultural and allied activities; and the Federal Mortgage Bank provided credit for owner-occupied residential buildings and commercial estates. Development finance banks, set up by the State governments, financed and provided promotional services for deserving enterprises in their respective regions.

The collapse of world oil prices in the 1980s revealed the unfortunate consequences of Nigeria's failure to redirect the investable surpluses generated by its oil business to attain more balanced national economic development. Unable to earn the foreign exchange to finance its continued imports, or to repay the past debts it had incurred, Nigeria confronted a financial crisis. Its government proclaimed its resistance to IMF pressures to impose austerity and devalue the naira, but eventually it adopted policies similar to those promoted by the IMF.

Nationalization in Tanzania [14]

Tanzania's colonial history, first as a German colony then a British protectorate, bequeathed it a relatively underdeveloped economy, geared primarily to the export of sisal, coffee and cotton. At independence, the East African Currency Board still conducted the overall regulation of the regional money supply. The three biggest banks, Barclays, National and Grindlays, together with Standard, dominated the regional banking business—including Tanganyika's—from their European Community headquarters in Kenya.

In 1966, five years after independence, the government established its own central bank, the Bank of Tanzania. [15] Although the nation expanded agricultural exports, deteriorating terms of trade curbed its foreign-exchange earnings. Despite efforts to attract foreign investment, the net inflow of nonmonetary sector equaled only about one-third of the outflow of income payments abroad.

In 1967, after declaring at Arusha that they aimed to embark on a socialist path, Tanzania's political leadership increased state control of export-import trade, took 51 percent of the shares of the largest manufacturing firms and agricultural estates, and nationalized the commercial banks. By expanding banking facilities and offering attractive rates of return on savings deposits, the government anticipated that the new national banking system would help to mobilize domestic savings for more appropriate investments in both rural and urban areas.

[14] Unless otherwise cited, the material in the following section is drawn from T. Chimombe, "The Role of Banks and Financial Institutions" (Harare: University of Zimbabwe, Economics Department, M.A. thesis).

[15] The country's name changed when, shortly after independence, it joined together with Zanzibar.

The transnational corporate commercial banks immediately withdrew 52 bank managers and senior executives from Tanzania. They demanded about 15 times the compensation finally agreed to through arbitration; and they blocked the Tanzanian banks' access to their branch balances in England, although these far exceeded their net head-office investments in Tanzania.

A three-member management committee under the Ministry of Finance met almost daily to reorganize the new banking system. Local manpower and recruits from friendly countries, mainly Denmark and the Netherlands, helped to overcome the bank's personnel shortage. Combining the assets of all the commercial banks, they created the National Bank of Commerce (NBC) under a board of directors appointed by the minister of finance. The NBC closed down the least-effective urban branches and set up new ones along with agency units in previously unserved rural areas.

Debating the criteria for the new bank's credit policy, the board of directors concluded the national banking system "would be carried on, not with a view to make huge profits, but as an essential service to the people at large—which service would, while being completely self-supporting and offering reasonable surplus on the turnover, be run with the idea of service first and surplus next."[16]

The three criteria they established for making loans, related to: (a) the purpose; (b) the creditworthiness of the borrower; and (c) the security provided to ensure repayment. Since the government failed to formulate an overall national financial plan, however, bank officials apparently interpreted these on a rather ad hoc basis.

Set up only seven months before the Arusha Declaration, the Bank of Tanzania continued to function primarily as banker to the government and bank of last resort, along lines similar to the central banks in Zimbabwe and Nigeria. In the first four years it successfully reduced credit to the government from 12 percent to five percent of its annual revenues, and from one-fifth to two percent of its development expenditures. A temporary improvement in terms of trade and increased foreign development aid gave the nation a large inflow of foreign exchange.

In the 1970s, however, as Tanzania accelerated its *ujamaa* (familyhood) program,[17] it encountered worsened terms of trade and drought. The Ugandan dictator Idi Amin invaded this country, forcing Tanzania into a prolonged and expensive war. The government borrowed heavily from the central bank, aggravating inflationary pressures.

Throughout this period the central bank retained relatively low interest rates, ranging from 4.27 percent for 35-day treasury notes to 7.5 percent for 90- to 180-day nonagricultural loans. It did not, however, introduce more direct controls to enforce effective financial planning. In part, this reflected the government's failure to formulate and implement long-term physical plans to restructure the national economy.

The NBC successfully mobilized domestic savings and expanded credit.

---

[16] A. J. Nsekela, "The 1971/72 NBC Credit Policy," *The Standard*, 22 June 1971.

[17] *Ujamaa* villages represented an effort to bring scattered peasant families together to benefit from social services and increase productivity through cooperative cultivation.

From 1968 to 1979 its total deposits, 90 percent from nongovernment sectors, multiplied nearly ninefold. Loans and advances to the productive sectors, primarily in the form of relatively short-term credits, rose over sixfold. At the same time, the bank increased its purchases of government securities to almost one-fifth of its loans.

The bank sought to shift the inherited pattern of credit allocation by providing preferential treatment to specified sectors. It charged concessionary interest rates (0.5 percent to 1.5 percent below normal rates) to multipurpose cooperatives and *ujamaa* villages, marketing cooperatives, district development corporations, and firms manufacturing goods for export. It charged higher interest rates (1 percent to 2.5 percent above average) for personal consumption loans and to foreign-controlled firms. It limited foreign firms' borrowing to a maximum of 50 percent of paid-up capital, compared to 75 percent for local firms. As the public, parastatal and cooperative sectors expanded, credit to the private sector declined from over one-half to one-fifth of the total.

From 1970 to 1975, the state commercial bank's loans to mining and manufacturing increased sevenfold, from less than one-fifth to more than one-fourth of its total credit allocations. Most of these loans went to final rather than intermediate goods manufacturing, however, and hardly any financed capital goods production. In agriculture, most of its credit financed the estate sector, now largely state-owned. A relatively small share (less than 5 percent) went to *ujamaa* villages, but they had access to funds supplied by the Rural Development Bank.

The government created specialized banks for long-term loans and rural credit. The Tanzania Investment Bank (TIB) provided long- and medium-term finance to manufacturing industries and large-scale corporate agriculture. External sources provided almost two-thirds of its funds; the government provided about one-fifth; and the bank borrowed most of the remainder locally. However, the TIB loaned only about 45 percent of its funds on a long-term basis: about two-thirds to manufacturing, 10 percent to engineering, and the rest to miscellaneous activities. The investment bank retained over half its assets in liquid form, three-fourths of them in treasury bills, as an additional source of current government finance.

To promote rural development through medium- and long-term loans, provide technical assistance and facilitate the purchase of agricultural inputs, the government set up the Tanzania Rural Development Bank (TRDB). Rather than demanding collateral for loans, the TRDB focused on "technically and economically viable" projects. To ensure repayment it required potential borrowers to provide a history of technical success in the use of inputs to improve yields. Half its loans went to agricultural production— over half of those to small farmers through new *ujamaa* village institutions. The rest funded district development corporations, regional transport companies, national institutions and crop authorities.

The Rural Development Bank lent out about two-thirds of its funds in five regions that produced most of the nation's export crops. Over two-thirds of its funds financed inputs for tobacco cultivation. In part, this reflected a requirement of the World Bank (which provided much of its funds) that to ensure repayment the TRDB lend primarily to export-crop producers.

Apparently, however, the NBC did not exercise overall control over credit allocations as do most Socialist government banks. Parastatal organizations and other state agencies continued to extend credit outside of its jurisdiction. Even the specialized banks operated outside and sometimes in competition with it. This hindered the bank from exercising the monitoring role that most Socialist bankers consider essential.

Nationalization of the banks in Tanzania did not contribute much to a restructuring of its national economy, either. Even had they asserted more effective financial controls in the realm of finance, the banks could not offset the consequences of the government's failure to formulate and implement long-term physical plans to restructure the national economy. In the late 1970s and early 1980s, as the country's terms of trade deteriorated and its foreign debts mounted, Tanzania confronted a financial crisis. Although for several years it resisted IMF conditions, its neighbor's essentially competitive devaluation and its desparate need for foreign assistance ultimately forced it to accept their major thrust.

CONCLUSION

After independence, (inherited from a century of outright colonial rule) Africa's banks failed to halt the outflow abroad of a large share of locally generated investable surpluses in the form of profits, interest, fees or transfer pricing. Too often, they fostered reinvestment of the remainder in patterns perpetuating external dependence. Lack of credit, along with inadequate infrastructure, backward production technologies and weak marketing networks, hampered food cultivation by African peasants and the establishment of small-scale industries producing for domestic needs and providing jobs. Plans for larger, pole-of-growth industries, capable of taking advantage of regional resources and markets, never got off the drawing board.

Detailed postindependence research reveals some of the obstacles to reorganizing Zimbabwe's complex financial structure, which inherited direct links to foreign-owned transnational banks and the South African-based Anglo American Group. After independence, Nigerian bank policies, directed primarily toward Africanization accompanied by government participation in lead banks, contributed little to redirecting the huge financial surpluses generated by the nation's oil boom in balanced, integrated national development. Tanzania's experience suggests that state ownership of banks may facilitate accumulation of national savings, but, unless accompanied by carefully drawn physical plans and redrawn working rules, will probably not lead to a more appropriate pattern of reinvestment. Embroiled in the financial crisis of the 1980s, all three countries found themselves forced to adopt IMF policies that undercut, rather than reinforced, what ever efforts they had made to redirect locally generated surpluses to finance the restructuring of their national economies.

This analysis suggests, first, that to end the banks' role in fostering the lopsided growth that has impoverished the majority of Africans, African states must exert national control over their inherited banking and financial institutions. Secondly, however, state ownership of banks and financial institutions alone does not ensure the redirection of locally generated investable surpluses to achieve self-reliant, balanced, integrated national economic development. That requires careful formulation, and implementation of coordinated financial and physical plans monitored by well-trained financial personnel working in accord with appropriate criteria. African experience during the financial crisis of the 1980s underscores the need for further research to recommend changes in national and regional banking and financial institutions—changes that will reduce dependence on counterproductive IMF policies and foster their self-reliant national and cooperative regional development, in order to attain increased employment opportunities and raise living standards throughout the continent.

FURTHER READING

Amin, S. *Accumulation on a World Scale.* 2 vols. New York: Monthly Review Press, 1974.

Ayida, A. A., ed. *Reconstruction and Development in Nigeria.* London: Oxford University Press, 1976.

Ayres, R. L. *Banking on the Poor: The World Bank and World Poverty.* Cambridge, Massachusetts: MIT Press, 1984.

Brown, Robert, and Cummings, Robert. *The Lagos Plan vs. The Berg Report.* Lawrenceville, Virginia: Brunswick Publishing, 1984.

Jucker-Fleetwood, E. E. *Money and Finance in Africa: The Experiences of Ghana, Morocco, Nigeria, the Rhodesias and Nyasaland, the Sudan and Tunisia from the Establishment of Their Central Banks until 1962.* London: Allen & Unwin, 1965.

de Kock, G. *A History of The South African Reserve Banks, 1920–52.* Pretoria: J. L. van Schaik, 1954.

Newlyn, W. T., *Money in an African Context: Studies in African Economics.* Nairobi: Oxford University Press, 1967.

——— and Rowan, D. C., *Money and Banking in British Colonial Africa.* Oxford: Clarendon Press, 1954.

Nkrumah, Kwame. *Neo-Colonialism, The Last Stage of Imperialism.* London: Heinemann, 1965.

Nsekela, A. J., ed. *Southern Africa: Towards Economic Liberation.* London: Rex Collings, 1981.

Payer, C. *The Debt Trap and the IMF.* New York: Monthly Review Press, 1975.

———. *The World Bank: A Critical Analysis.* New York: Monthly Review Press, 1982.

Seidman, Ann. *Money, Banking and Public Finance in Africa.* London: Zed Press, 1986.

Terry, C. *The Desert Bankers: The Story of the Standard Bank of South West Africa.* Cape Town: W. J. Flesch, 1978.

THE AFRICAN UNDERGROUND ECONOMY

JANET MacGAFFEY

INTRODUCTION

A close look at the day-to-day realities of life for the inhabitants of Africa's towns, cities and rural areas leads to a different perspective on the economic decline reported for most of the continent. Few Africans are paid wages or salaries that can support them and their families; most farmers receive prices for their crops quite inadequate to purchase their needs. People in fact manage by resorting to the activities of what is variously referred to as the parallel, underground, second or informal economy. This sector of the total economy escapes the national accounts and official production figures. Two-thirds or more of the income of the average urban household is generally found outside the official wage and salary sector, most often in the underground economy. This situation indicates how significant the size of this economy is; by ignoring it, official statistics misrepresent the state of the economy as a whole.

The underground economy consists of activities that are unmeasured and unrecorded, and are either, in varying degrees, illegal or, if legal in themselves, carried out in such a way as to evade taxes or regulations. They all in some way deprive the state of revenue or involve misuse of state position.[1] It is increasingly recognized that this sector of the economy constitutes a growing share of the total economy of most countries in Africa, and indeed in the rest of the world. Its extent and the particular form it takes vary according to locally specific historical, geographical and sociopolitical factors.

The flows of underground trade ignore modern national boundaries. Ancient trade routes were originally established between natural regions offer-

[1] Keith Hart originally identified informal income opportunities outside the formal wage economy in Ghana. The informal economy has come to connote the small-scale enterprises of the urban poor. The term "underground" or "second" is used in this article in preference to "informal," because the article includes, as Hart did, activities that occur at all levels of society, on a large as well as a small scale, and that are sometimes very lucrative.

871

ing different resources. Colonial powers laid down national boundaries and imposed tariffs, trade restrictions and price controls. Smuggling and other forms of illegal trade, such as barter, sometimes reviving ancient routes, formed their own regional trading circuits, the real means by which many of Africa's seemingly disastrous economies manage to keep functioning. Very little information exists on these regional trading circuits, but one study has mapped them for West Africa and research in progress in Zaire reveals similar patterns in southern, eastern and central Africa.

This essay will look at some of these regional trade patterns, briefly surveying countries for which details of underground activities are known. The data all show the difficulties confronting people if they try to live within the official system, and the variety of solutions to which they resort. They appropriate resources from the official system, organize production and distribution themselves, import and export, make their own transport arrangements, and find ways of acquiring foreign exchange. The vast scale on which export, and even food, crops are smuggled out of some countries means that the economies are much more productive than appears in the official figures.[2] Some people merely engage in speculation and other activities that increase the inflationary trends of the economy; others accumulate considerable wealth by illicit means and invest it in the official system in productive enterprise.

West Africa will be considered first, then some countries of central (and adjoining) Africa.

O. J. Igue has mapped the illegal flows of trade for West Africa, describing the factors affecting their early development and the changes that have taken place since independence. During the colonial period a dualism developed between an official sector and a clandestine one that was no less organized but which escaped the control of the authorities. This parallel system of commerce revived precolonial trade patterns. After independence, with the expansion of the four monetary zones of the colonial period to 11, clandestine trade expanded enormously, fed by the disparity in currency values. Dynamic illegal trading sectors developed in the frontier zones of Benin-Nigeria, Niger-Nigeria, Ghana-Togo, Ghana-Ivory Coast, Ghana-Upper Volta (Burkina Faso) and Gambia-Senegal. In this trade kola cloth, shoes, and electronic goods go from south to north; smoked fish, animals and skins go from north to south. Fuel, roofing iron, kitchen utensils, soap, secondhand cars and spare parts are imported from Anglophone to Francophone countries; alcohol and printed cloth go in the reverse direction. Agricultural products are smuggled from Anglophone to Francophone

---

[2] Robert H. Bates shows that in Tanzania, for example, decline in food purchases by marketing agencies represented a flight from the government-controlled market and massive diversion into private channels of trade, rather than a decline in production.

countries—with the exception of peanuts, which move from Senegal to Gambia and from Niger to Nigeria.[3]

Ghana

The Ghanaian economy collapsed and went into a downward spiral from 1975 to 1981, resulting in huge budget deficits and shortages of foreign exchange, and thus of imported goods and essential industrial and agricultural inputs. This situation combined with drastic deterioration of the transport system and 100 percent inflation to produce an enormous expansion of *kalabule,* the Ghanaian term for black-marketing, corruption and profiteering.

Kalabule takes four main forms. The principal one is smuggling of agricultural products, mainly rice and cocoa, and of gold, diamonds, and timber. Rice is smuggled to the north to Burkina Faso, the Ivory Coast and Togo, but little is known about this trade. Cocoa is smuggled on a staggering scale to Togo and the Ivory Coast. According to one estimate, in 1980 four-fifths of cocoa production from the Volta region was smuggled to Togo or left unharvested while farmers turned to growing more profitable food crops. Twelve percent to 15 percent of gold production was smuggled annually in the 1970s and early 1980s, and a similar proportion of diamonds.

Increased smuggling to Togo and the Ivory Coast, as the real value of the cedi declined, was a primary cause of a drop in official cocoa exports, from an average of 430,000 metric tons in 1969–72 to 277,000 metric tones in 1977–78. During most of the 1970s Ghana's nominal producer price was below that of its neighbors, even at official rates of exchange; at the parallel rate it was four to five times higher in Togo, and seven to eight in the Ivory Coast. In 1978, even after doubling producer prices, relative prices for a load of cocoa in Ghana were 36.39 cedis, while in Togo they were ¢114.08, and in the Ivory Coast ¢211.54. Togo smuggles to Ghana tobacco, cigarettes, alcohol, printed cloth, etc. to the value of 4 billion CFA francs annually, as against the 1.7 billion estimate of imports by the Central Bank of West Africa. From 1969 to 1982 the amount of cocoa smuggled to the Ivory Coast alone is estimated to have ranged between 9.18 thousand and 37.83 thousand metric tons annually; in 1982 this smuggling fueled the black market trade in money to the value of ¢855.23 million. None of this production and trade, let alone similar activities across Ghana's other borders, appears in the official figures on the economy, which is thus considerably more productive than it appears to be.

Other forms of *kalabule* are hoarding or black marketeering, in which imported goods are often paid for with the profits of smuggling, corruption and embezzlement, and violent crime organized by gangs. *Kalabule* trade began to expand local regional economies by the mid-1970s, as profits from trade of the products of rural areas went not only to traders with transport

[3]O. J. Igue, "L'officiel, le Parallèle et le Clandestin: Commerces et Intégration en Afrique de l'Ouest," *Politique Africaine* 9 (1983):36–48.

monopolies, but also to producers who began to market their goods themselves and to local wholesalers who expanded their activities. Furthermore, this trade enabled farmers to evade the depredations and inefficiencies of the state as they marketed their produce through their own trade channels, setting up a "substitute marketing system which took full advantage of the inadequacies of formal mechanisms" and created "self-propelled enclosures autonomous of the state and as self-sufficient as possible."[4]

Guinea [5]

Liberalization of the economy, following the death of Sékou Touré in 1984 and the subsequent military takeover, led to a crisis in the Guinean economy. Production declined, except in the foreign-run bauxite sector. In 1983 this sector produced 97 percent of official foreign-exchange earnings, but by 1985 its profits were draining into private pockets and the economy was beset by shortages. Industrial production was almost at a standstill for lack of materials; money lost all real value, with the parallel rate of exchange standing at 10 times the official rate; and the banking sector foundered, lacking money even to pay salaries. In Conakry, at this time, salaries supplied on the average only 10 percent of household income. This meant that an official, for example, could only feed his family for the first three days of the month on his pay.

In such a situation, everyone has to have something either to barter or sell in order to survive. For Guinea, data are available for the ways in which officials and administrators managed to survive. Employment became important not for the money it could bring but for the social capital it represented. Jobs brought access to the profitable opportunities of a parallel commercial system developing in the heart of the state. From 1984 onward, citizens began to organize themselves around the pillage of the state and its enterprises, previously a privilege reserved for the president and his clan. Commerce flourished in the parallel marketing of goods produced or imported by the state, and distributed through vouchers and corruption. Any kind of official position brought the possibility of rendering services, creating obligations and receiving other services in return, in a system of reciprocal payments set in motion within the public sector. "Participation in trafficking is . . . a vital necessity for everyone, at the same time as it destabilizes the very social order that makes it possible."[6]

The means by which white-collar workers supplement their salaries are, first, through profits gained from corruption and favors, such as the extortion of additional customs dues and payments to the police to allow illegal passage of goods, to officials for an audience, to banks to obtain financial services, and to wholesalers to obtain purchase vouchers for goods. Sec-

[4]Naomi H. Chazan, *Development, Underdevelopment and the State in Ghana*, Boston University African Studies Center, Working Paper no. 8 (Boston, 1982), pp. 119, 122.

[5]Information in this section comes from Alain Morice, "Guinée 1985: Etat, Corruption et Trafics," *Les Temps Modernes* 42 (1985):109–36.

[6]Morice, "Guinée 1985," p. 115; translation of all quotations from the French are by the author.

ondly, salaries are supplemented through embezzlement of goods and equipment; thirdly, they may be increased by profits from trade. This trade consists of: illegal imports of goods and exports of food crops for higher prices across the frontiers; illegal sale of goods legally imported, especially through the voucher system; the black market in foreign exchange; and the profits made in commerce between the city and the rural areas. In the last, goods bought at low prices in the countryside are sold for large profits in the capital, and products bought at controlled prices in the city are sold for high prices in the hinterland where they are scarce.

These various forms of trade can be very lucrative, as shown by some examples of price markups. A length of cloth bought for 5,000 sylis at the factory could be sold for 40,000 sylis in the market. The construction industry is booming in Conakry; the official factory price for cement would be 6,500 sylis a metric ton, but much of the cement produced might be sold illegally from the factory at the same price as privately imported cement, about 28,000 sylis per metric ton. The price of rice in the market is three to five times the official price. Gasoline sells for a subsidized price in Conakry, derisory in relation to prices in neighboring countries; towns in the interior receive quotas, but most of the supply is sold on the black market. Thus gasoline bought at 30 sylis would sell for 100 sylis at Labé, the point of departure for the trade to Senegal, where the price is ten times as high. Profits made in this trade drain gasoline supplies from the city, creating scarcity and long lines at the gas pumps.

These activities, therefore, are not just the means whereby a poor population survives, but rather involve the circulation of very considerable amounts of money. The profits made in these activities are invested in real estate (the boom in the construction industry indicates their scale) and commerce, accentuating the speculative and inflationary tendencies of the economy. However, this opening up of the system beyond a small, privileged elite has only been under way for a few years. In other parts of Africa, when circumstances have been propitious, wealth accumulated in underground activities has been invested in productive enterprise, expanding the local economy. Given time, such investments may also occur in Guinea.

Senegal

In Senegal in 1965, "losses" and acknowledged fraud in the central marketing board were greater than annual net profits. Lax accounting, dishonest agents and inadequate supervision made possible a network of private appropriation in the nationalized marketing sector. By 1985, two-thirds of peanut production, the country's principal resource, were being smuggled to Gambia, and a highly organized illegal trade in medicines, arms and drugs was flourishing.

Sierra Leone

In Sierra Leone diamond smuggling, backed by illicit mining, accounts for an estimated two-thirds of annual production. This has deprived the banking system of foreign exchange, and has led to an intensification of parallel market activity and escalating prices for all commodities. Diamonds are primarily smuggled to Monrovia (in Liberia), where prices are higher than those offered by the Sierra Leone Government Diamond Office. From there they are sold to diamond cutting centers in Israel and Europe.

The expansion of these underground activities has had some beneficial effects on the economy, however. Although people condemn the diamond smugglers, they are ambivalent toward them because of a general awareness that "smuggling compels the Diamond Office to pay higher prices." The public sector is defrauded, but the economy in general benefits through redistribution of diamond earnings. Though profits go first to the big Lebanese dealers, competition forces the latter to pass most of the money on to the miners, directly or via other dealers.[7]

CENTRAL AFRICA

In central Africa, Zaire's border regions form part of flourishing trading zones with neighboring countries. Thus Kivu, in the east, has extensive illegal trade to Rwanda, Uganda and Kenya in gold, coffee, ivory, tea and foodstuffs, in return for fuel, vehicles and spare parts, construction materials, manufactured goods, medicine, and firearms. From Shaba, in the south, cobalt, ivory, spare parts stolen from the mining companies, and other goods go to Zambia and South Africa, in return for Zambian maize flour and other foodstuffs, fuel, stolen vehicles, and cement. Lower Zaire and Kinshasa are linked to Congo by a lively smuggling trade in gold, manufactured goods and food. These goods are sold for CFA francs, a source of hard currency for a flourishing and mostly illegal trade of manufactured goods from Europe and West Africa. To the north, upper Zaire is linked to Sudan and the Central African Republic by smuggling and the barter of ivory, gold and coffee in exchange for vehicles and spare parts, manufactured goods and electrical appliances.

Zaire

Data from Zaire reveal that underground activity may result not only in greater production than appears in statistics, but also in investment of illegally earned wealth in productive enterprise in the official economy.

Zaire has spiraled into economic crisis since the mid-1970s. Industrial and agricultural production decline; the national debt mounts; economic infrastructure decays; foreign exchange and the essential commodities it buys are in short supply. In this situation, prices have risen sharply while wages have remained derisively low. In 1979 an unskilled laborer needed five days' pay to buy a kilo of rice, seven days' pay for a kilo of dried beans and three days' pay for a loaf of bread. In 1982, 1,000 zaires were needed to purchase basic necessities for a month, but a clerk earned only Z115 and high administrators only Z832. A 1986 study of household budgets in Kinshasa found that on the average only 25 percent of income came from

---

[7] H. L. Van der Laan, *The Lebanese Traders in Sierra Leone* (The Hague: Mouton, 1975), 199.

wages and salaries; 29 percent came from unknown primarily underground sources; the remainder came from miscellaneous known sources.

In this situation, in order to survive and to find means to better their existence, everybody turns to *L'économie de débrouillardise*, as Zaire's underground economy is known locally. Some people become extremely wealthy in various ways: by smuggling coffee, ivory, cobalt, diamonds or gold; in the illegal export and import trade; through speculation and middleman activity; or through bribery and corruption. Others scrape out a meager living, which barely enables them to survive, through theft and petty unlicensed trade or small enterprise. Peasant farmers may sell or barter the food and export crops they grow, through smuggling across the frontiers or by unlicensed trade to the towns; hunters poach ivory and zebra and leopard skins, and kill other game for the trade in smoked meat to the cities.

So widespread and extensive is participation in these unmeasured and unrecorded activities that official figures on the economy seriously underestimate its size; some unofficial estimates calculate it to be, in fact, several times the reported GDP. As much as 40 percent or more of Zaire's coffee crop, its primary agricultural export, is smuggled out of the country annually. In 1979 diamonds were the country's fourth most valuable export, but diamond smuggling was estimated to equal 68 percent of official production. Massive quantities of cobalt, a primary mineral export, are smuggled and its revenues lost to the state. Zaire's majestic elephant herds have all but disappeared under the onslaught of poachers.

Clearly, the loss to the state's coffers of the foreign exchange that should be earned by these primary commodities, and the depletion of natural resources, create serious problems. But if one looks at the details of what is happening and who is carrying out these various activities, it is apparent that the consequences are sometimes beneficial. Foreign businessmen and traders, and those in powerful and unassailable positions have the easiest access to the most lucrative opportunities and are the biggest smugglers; their profits are mostly spent on consumption and overseas investment. But ordinary people also engage in many varieties of illegal trade. Some of those who have been successful are investing profits in official enterprises and becoming serious and substantial business owners; their efforts have resulted in expansion of the local economy in some regions.

In 1983 the production and sale of gold and diamonds was liberalized. Artisanal mining was legalized, and licensed purchase counters were set up. This measure significantly decreased diamond smuggling, and official exports of diamonds tripled.[8] Some smuggling continues alongside the legal trade, however, especially of the more valuable gem diamonds. Gold exports also rose, only to decline again because unlicensed dealers took advantage of the higher rate for the zaire on the parallel market. Furthermore, licensed gold buyers are too few and cannot respond as quickly as

[8] Zaire exported a total of 6,164 carats in 1982, 11,713 in 1983, 18,465 in 1984, and 20,159 in 1985; cf. *Conjoncture Economique* (Kinshasa: Département de l'économie nationale de la République du Zaire, 1986), 63.

illegal dealers to changes in price on the London gold market. Current research indicates that the quantity of gold being illegally exported may be considerably more than official exports.

Anyone can go out and pan gold in the rivers and forests; Zaire has experienced a gold rush reminiscent of that in the United States since the spectacular rise in the price of gold in the late 1970s. Workers from the towns and cities, teachers, and students have left for the gold-producing areas, seeking to better their miserable wages and prospects. Gold may be sold or directly bartered for goods in Zaire or across its frontiers, substituting for foreign exchange in the trade of the underground economy. In north Kivu "clothing, hardware, laundry and toilet material, jewelry, perfumes, medical products . . . are entirely paid for in gold," to the amount of four to five truckloads of goods every month.[9]

Kivu, in the east, and upper Zaire in the northeast, are the primary coffee-growing regions of Zaire, as well as major gold-producing areas. Farmers and traders smuggle and barter coffee to East Africa and Sudan. After the rapid price rise of 1976, those who went into coffee buying and transport made fortunes; they invested their profits first in trucks and then in plantations, ranches and commerce.

In north Kivu some of these very substantial business owners have cattle ranches that produce meat, milk and butter for the local town, and plantations that produce coffee, tea, cinchona and papain for export; maintain long-distance trading enterprises that send beans (a major staple) and other vegetables to Kinshasa; and own wholesale and retail businesses. Some own fleets of as many as five large trucks and several small trucks and cars; some employ over 300 workers. The illegal gold trade as well as coffee smuggling were in some cases the basis for the growth of these enterprises into substantial businesses, and thus for their expansion of the local productive base.

A wealthy commercial class has also grown up in Mbuji-Mayi on the basis of profits made illegally in diamonds before liberalization, but Kasai does not have Kivu's fertile volcanic soil and temperate climate; its people are not interested in agriculture, and their wealth is spent in high living or is invested in real estate and foreign bank accounts rather than productive enterprise. The big wholesale companies buy foreign exchange from diamond smuggling and use it to import consumer goods, in this way recycling illegally earned money into legal enterprise. As a result, Mbuji-Mayi stores have always been plentifully supplied with goods during periods when such items have been scarce in other regions. Traders do better than miners; they earn more money, and artisanal diamond miners work in appallingly dangerous and unhealthy conditions.

Official figures show declining food production, but much food that is produced is not reflected in these figures because rural producers smuggle food crops to neighboring countries or send them to relatives in town.

[9] Mukohya Vwakyanakazi, *African Traders in Butembo, Eastern Zaire (1960–1980): A Case Study of Informal Entrepreneurship in a Cultural Context of Central Africa* (Madison: University of Wisconsin, Ph.D. diss., 1982), 282–83.

Government and company reports and plantation owners complain that rural workers desert their jobs because they can make more money fishing and cultivating food for sale. In 1979–80 the amount smuggled daily to Burundi from Uvira zone in eastern Kivu averaged 70 bags of potatoes, 60 bags of beans and 50 piles of tobacco. A type of barter system is widespread, by means of which people send foodstuffs to their relatives in town for consumption or sale, and in return get manufactured goods that are scarce and expensive in the rural areas. If such production and distribution outside the official system is taken into account, the economy as a whole presents a less gloomy picture. Life for ordinary people may be a struggle, but is not as impossible as the figures on wages and prices indicate; nor is the decline in production so severe.

Uganda

Magendo is a Swahili word used to designate the black market, the illegal (or borderline illegal) economic sector by which the Ugandan population survived in the Amin period of economic change and political upheaval. The usage of the word spread to Rwanda, eastern Zaire, Kenya and southern Sudan, and its meaning broadened to signify "fending for yourself." For Europeans, *magendo* is synonymous with cheating, corruption and criminality; for Africans, it is a perfectly permissible form of economic activity that simply gets around state regulations perceived as oppressive.

In Uganda the *magendo* sector has become enormously large. In 1980 [10] it dominated the economy by one estimate, accounting for perhaps half of the total GDP and as much as two-thirds of monetary GDP. A rapid expansion of *magendo* followed the ruin of the economic, political and social system, which resulted both from the destructive policies of Idi Amin and from the decline of the international economy. Prior to 1970 smuggling had only amounted to about 3 percent of GDP. The primary cause of the expansion of *magendo* was physical, supply-side scarcity. Domestic industry was functioning at only one-third of the level of 1970; production of industrial and export crops was only one-quarter of this level; and the transport system was inadequate to move sufficient quantities of people and goods.

In this situation workers did not receive a living wage: A minimum-wage earner, if he received his pay at all, could buy only enough staple starch for his family for one week. A modest middle-class standard of living in Kampala in early 1980 required a pretax income of between 200,000 and 250,000 shillings, but a senior civil servant received a salary of only about Sh75,000.

Coffee smuggling intensified after 1975. In 1980, between 60,000 and 70,000 metric tons of coffee were smuggled: gold smuggling continues to average about three metric tons a year. The core of *magendo* activities lies in long-distance trade, exporting and importing, transportation, the food

[10] Information on Uganda is taken from Reginald Green, *Magendo in the Political Economy of Uganda: Pathology, Parallel System or Dominant Sub-Mode of Production?* (Brighton: Institute of Development Studies, University of Sussex, Discussion Paper no. 64, 1981).

trade, finance, wholesaling, construction, maintenance and manufacturing. Profits are invested in houses, commercial buildings and land. There has been some move into production: printing, construction, jaggery, illicit gin (*engulu*), vehicle repair. *Magendo* has been characterized as "a form of emergent, raw, grasping, growing capitalism, not so very unlike that of medieval Europe,"[11] Violence is an integral part of *magendo* in Uganda. A gun is as important as money; equity and justice are in abeyance.

Southern Sudan

In southern Sudan poverty and geography appear to be the root causes of *magendo*. Isolation, poor roads, ethnic rivalries and the north/south conflict combine to undermine the official economy. The 1955–72 civil war ruined the country's infrastructure; *magendo* represents an attempt to cope with an unreconstructed economy, and has become a mode of life. In the poorest region of the Christian south, the economy is controlled by northern Muslim interests perceived as alien by the local population. Trade between north and south is practically nonexistent for lack of transportation; almost all trade is with Kenya. Since Amin's ouster in 1979–80, the official route through Uganda has been closed, and illegal trade flourishes on an alternate route through northeast Kenya to the Sudanese border.

The trade from south to north is in beer, cigarettes, tea and spare parts; from north to south, trucks take machines for repairs, cannabis, qat (a stimulant that is cheaper in Sudan than in Kenya), and gold and mercury from clandestine mines in isolated areas on the way. The miners barter these minerals in direct exchange for potatoes, cooking oil, cigarettes and canned meat. Two types of traders carry on illegal trade; the agents of the big companies, driving big trucks, and independent traders with small trucks. A round trip grosses a profit for the latter of Sh20,000. Such profits can pay for a vehicle in 18 months; it will last for a maximum of five years, given the harsh road conditions. Owners of these small trucks are often former drivers of company trucks who have accumulated capital by trading on the side with goods hidden within legitimate company cargo. No clear distinction exists between official and illegal trade; the same people, the same enterprises and the same commodities are involved in both.

Angola

As a result of smuggling, official diamond exports in Angola dropped from 1.5 million carats in 1980 to 1.03 million carats in 1983. The recent huge expansion of the Angolan parallel market appears to represent a popular response to official scarcity and to the underpayment of labor. Neither workers nor high-ranking officials can support their families on their official earnings. In 1985 a few purchases on the parallel market would use up a whole month's wages. For a worker one egg cost half a day's salary; for an official the price of a chicken was the equivalent of six days' salary. In urban areas barter was the preferred means for obtaining foodstuffs; a bottle of whisky became the new measure of exchange.

[11] *Ibid.*, p. 22.

CONCLUSION

A realistic assessment of the state of African economies must include their underground sectors and set them in the wider regional context of illegal trade circuits. Such a perspective will give a more optimistic view of the real economic situation on the continent than is provided by national statistics. This situation, as one observer notes in Zaire, can be seen as the outcome of a struggle between the state and individuals: "Fraud in general is a manifestation of conflict between public powers and individuals. It is a sort of reaction against the rules of conduct imposed by the authorities, a reaction against what the citizens, rightly or wrongly, consider to be the increasing interference of public power in the economy."[12]

FURTHER READING

Bates, Robert H. *Markets and States in Tropical Africa: The Political Basis of Agricultural Policies*. Berkeley: University of California Press, 1981.

Bézy, Fernand, Peemans, Jean-Philippe, and Wautelet, Jean-Marie. *Accumulation et Sous-Développement au Zaire, 1960–1980*. Louvain-la-Neuve: Presses Universitaires de Louvain, 1981.

Cruise O'Brien, Donal. "Co-operators and Bureaucrats: Class Formation in a Senegalese Peasant Society," *Africa* 41, no. 4 (1971): 263–78.

Hart, Keith. "Informal Income Opportunities and Urban Employment in Ghana." *Journal of Modern African Studies* 11, no. 1 (1973): 61–89.

Jeffries, Richard. "Rawlings and the Political Economy of Underdevelopment in Ghana." *African Affairs* 81 (1982): 324.

MacGaffey, Janet. *Entrepreneurs and Parasites: The Struggle for Indigenous Capitalism in Zaire*. Cambridge and New York: Cambridge University Press, 1987.

May, Ernesto. *Exchange Controls and Parallel Market Economies in Sub-Saharan Africa: Focus on Ghana*. Washington: World Bank Staff Working Paper no. 711. Washington, 1985.

[12]Tshilombo wa Nshimba, "Libéralisation dans la Domaine des Matières Précieuses et Liquidité Monétaire au Zaire," *Zaire Afrique* 176 (1983): 340.

STATE-SECTOR POLICIES
IN AFRICA

BEN TUROK

AT the time of the establishment of independent states in Africa, it was a relatively simple matter to create a political image of an African state replacing the institutions of colonial rule. What role that state was to play in the economy was an altogether more difficult issue. The main function of the colonial state had been to facilitate foreign multinationals to exploit African economies. Newly established African governments had to determine whether they wished to continue with this or to initiate new policies.

Choices were partly governed by the nature of the inherited economy and partly by the ideological positions of those who came to power. Also important were the popular expectations of what independence might bring in the way of national control of the economy (nationalization) or control by nationals (indigenization), and also in the way of displacing expatriates (Africanization) and providing better living standards for the people.

Whatever motive predominated, changes in ownership followed after independence either by expropriation of foreign firms, forcing them to sell equity to nationals, or by heavy investment in public enterprises. Sanjaya Lall has noted that in Nigeria a decline of the share of foreign capital from 68 percent to 30 percent over two post-independence decades was exactly matched by the increase in the share of the public sector from 22 percent to 60 percent.

All the options were seriously constrained, however, by the knowledge that Africa's economies were sadly undeveloped, especially that sector which might be expected to lead the development of the rest, manufacturing industry. In 1965, sub-Saharan Africa low- and middle-income countries saw manufacturing making only a 9 percent contribution to GDP. In the low-income countries of sub-Saharan Africa, the share of value added by manufacturing in 1973 was only 9.3 percent, indicating the ineffectiveness of manufacturing as a source of new wealth creation. It should be noted in passing that performance has largely deteriorated since then, with even poorer results in many countries. Manufacturing value-added per capita in sub-Saharan Africa in 1983 was a mere U.S. $33 (compared with Brazil at $530).

What industry existed at the time of independence was almost entirely foreign-owned, so African governments set in motion a range of interventions to make some inroads on the enormous power of the multinational corporations. The early interventions were cautious enough, consisting of modest regulatory actions, imposition of increased taxation, and so on. State intervention was generally governed by the nature of the inherited economy. In Nigeria, for example, the essentially trading character of the economy and the existence of a large trading class placed a special stamp on what happened in the economy; it has been argued that the commercial class has been dominant and even runs the affairs of state. This class is made up of middlemen such as traders, contractors, currency dealers and their accountants, lawyers, and front men of all kinds, who constitute a major sector of compradors with international capital. There soon came into existence a commercial triangle made up of the middlemen from the private sector, the representatives of foreign firms, and government officials. These three parties collaborated fully, to the exclusion of all other sectors of business and production. Since control of and access to state positions was crucial for the triangle to operate smoothly, the role of the state as a positive instrument of Nigerian national policy was distorted, if not stifled.

Other African states, however, were not equally constrained, and they opted for more fundamental interventions such as nationalization of foreign industry, thereby laying the basis for a significant state sector in the economy. It has to be remembered that in the 1960s it was a commonly held view throughout the world that state intervention was a necessary part of development, and this policy was legitimated by volumes of advice from U.N. experts and from other development economists.

African leaders like President Nyerere justified nationalizations by arguing that there were no local capitalists who might represent local interests. President Kaunda argued that foreign corporations were responsible for an excessive expatriation of profits so that companies were undercapitalized, and there was excessive local borrowing, massive foreign-exchange expenditure on invisibles, transfer pricing, etc. He wanted to see that Zambians would "individually and corporately share in the commercial and industrial life of the country" (Kaunda 1968:v). He also argued that since individual Zambians lacked both the necessary skill and capital, the government would act on their behalf.

Tanzania's nationalizations began in February 1967 following the Arusha Declaration, which aimed at creating a dominant public sector; this was followed up in 1974 with new policies aimed at phasing out all large-scale private enterprise. By the end of 1974, about 80 percent of large- and medium-scale enterprises was in the public sector.

A similar process was under way in Zambia, where in a few years the state acquired a 51 percent holding in most large-scale enterprises, including the dominant copper industry, which was the hub of the whole economy. Soon the state came to control 80 percent of the economy and set up a large structure of parastatals to supervise its holdings.[1] Total government

---

[1] "A parastatal organisation is not an integral part of Government but an institution, organisation, or agency which is wholly or mainly financed or owned or controlled by the Government," according to the Mwanakatwe Commission of Zambia 1970.

controlled assets in Zambia were over U.K. £1.1 billion by the late 1970s, and employment in the parastatals stood at 140,000, or 30 percent of the work force (Parliamentary Debates 30 March 1979).

Like most other African governments, Zambia claimed that nationalizations were essential to Africanize top posts and pass on skills, a claim that was more than justified in view of the appalling record of the settler and colonial regimes in former Northern Rhodesia. However, larger claims were also made about socialist goals, and these have to be examined more critically not only in the case of Zambia and Tanzania but also elsewhere in Africa.

It soon became apparent that the enlarged role of the state in the economy was associated with large benefits for the state bureaucracy. Thus the Mwanakatwe Commission of Zambia reported in 1975 that superscale public-sector posts rose from 184 in 1962 to 1,116 in 1974—a sixfold increase in 12 years. Personal emoluments as part of government recurrent expenditures increased from 61.5 million kwachas in 1969 to K155.8 million in 1977 and have been increasing proportionally. The same phenomenon can be seen in most African countries. Yet, different from the early years of independence, expenditures on social services have stagnated and in most cases have declined seriously. These considerations prompt some crucial questions about the role of the state in the economy in postindependence Africa.

Looking at African economies over the whole period of independence, can it be said that state interventions, particularly those of nationalization, have made any material difference to the economy? Has nationalization been largely cosmetic, in that an appearance of nationalist or even socialist interventionism belied retention of the status quo? Have the new governments merely retained the role of colonial proxy for the former owners and controllers of important sectors of the economy? In other words, has state intervention changed the relations of production, and has it produced new class relations? Has state intervention led to redistribution of wealth and incomes, or to economic growth and development? Has it even led to the greater retention of economic surpluses within the country?

THE STATE AS INTERMEDIARY

The most common view on these questions is that the independent states of Africa have taken on the role of intermediaries between foreign multinational corporations and the domestic human and material resources, thereby ensuring the continuation of exploitation begun under colonialism. In some cases new multinationals have moved in, but the effect on Africa is the same. The reasons advanced are that external forces continue to control the economic system and even the political policies with the necessary help of the resident population in and around the state. The basis of the collaboration, called compradorism, is the coincidence of interests between the local and international forces. However, in this relation, domination appears as a function of an internal and not external force. Indeed it has to be recognized that the repressive institutions of the state—police, army, etc.—are staffed by nationals, and that day-to-day decisions are taken by the state, most commonly without reference to forces abroad, since the domestic ruling class has an interest in defending its survival on its own account. This is by no means to suggest that the system as a whole is not locked into a domination-subordination relationship based on the international capitalist system. "The critical issue for the imperial state is not the formal structure of government but access to the internally generated surplus and the creation of class relations which facilitate access." [2]

According to this view, as long as compradorism is the overriding consideration of state policy, whether sectors of the economy are nationalized or not is of little consequence. Indeed it is perfectly possible to conceive of state industries serving foreign not national interests. Everything, it seems, turns on the political orientation of the rulers.

It may also be argued, though, that the domestic rulers take on a comprador role not because of their ideological position nor because this is how they see their best interest, but because of the power of the multinational corporations, which forces them into compradorism. Even if the host countries wish to challenge the dominance of the multinationals they are unable to do so because of the stronger bargaining position of the latter. The state is compelled to play a facilitating and intermediary role by a form of coercion, direct or indirect.

The condition is illustrated by a crucial problem encountered in nationalized industries where the state has taken a majority share—say 51 percent—which is the most common situation in the Third World. Majority ownership allows the state to appoint a majority to the board, seemingly giving it control. In reality, however, majority ownership does not by itself give control and only does so exceptionally. In a penetrating study of nationalization, Penrose argued that 51 percent nationalization of foreign corporations was generally ineffective and could be an irrelevance, even as a beginning. This is especially the case if management is not taken over at the same time. In practice, however, a whole range of powers remains in foreign hands, which makes the nationalization largely token. Control remains with the multinationals since the new majority owners are unable to exercise their theoretical ownership powers effectively because of insufficient technical ability to monitor them. Penrose goes on to argue that where a crucial material resource, such as a basic industry, is at stake, a 100 percent ownership would be better, since this would give the state greater freedom to organize its control without hindrance from the previous multinational corporation. However, here again it would be essential for the state to be committed to the national as opposed to foreign interests.

SERVING THE PEOPLE

Even where the issue of ownership and control has been settled adequately, there remains the issue of the beneficiaries of nationalization. This is a

---

[2] James Petras, *Critical Perspectives on Imperialism and Social Class in the Third World* (New York: Monthly Review Press, 1978), p. 50.

thorny problem, and the aspirations of many nationalist movements lie in ruins as the interests of their supporters have been betrayed, either deliberately or by omission. Given that the class that has come to power in Africa has been petty bourgeois, nationalization has served the interests of this class rather than the interests of the masses. Even where attempts have been made to introduce some kind of popular participation in decision making, such as works committees or party work place committees, these have largely turned out to be cosmetic. In Zambia and Tanzania much lip service was given to this dimension of "democracy," but where workers have attempted to influence policy these committees have been silenced or worse. As a result, workers' remuneration is now often below subsistence, and dissatisfaction is acute. Only the repressive powers of the state keep the workers' anger at bay.

While few states in Africa can legitimately claim that nationalized enterprises serve the interests of their workers or of the people as a whole directly, there is little support for the denationalization of enterprises. This is because state industries do, on the whole, attempt to maintain job levels intact; there is a certain degree of protection of wage levels through state commissions and legislative supervision; and state subsidies are also often applied. Prices of mass consumption goods are held down so that workers can afford them. In many cases a form of trade unionism remains in place and wage exploitation is less acute than in the private sector. It is well understood by many wage workers that the option of small-scale private enterprises, so often advocated by international "experts," inevitably leads to much more fierce exploitation of labor through harsher conditions, longer hours and lower wages. Clearly, workers' protection is more difficult in the informal sector than in the larger state enterprises.

UNCLEAR GOALS

The ineffectiveness of state industries is often as much a function of unclear objectives as of malfunction because of inexperience or poor management. Many studies of the large parastatal enterprises in countries like Zambia have shown a crippling indecisiveness about production policies. Although these enterprises are meant to be in the public domain and managers are regularly lectured on their state's commitment to the public interest, these managers are also pressured to pursue commercial criteria in profit making. Torn between making products for the mass consumption market at a price the poor can afford, and manufacturing semiluxury goods that can be sold at profitable prices (and that often are not controlled), managers choose the latter road since this makes for a healthy balance sheet. Profit or loss often determines whether managers opt for high-technology production rather than labor-intensive but work-providing processes. Little attention is paid to the social cost of displacing labor by machines or to the cost in foreign exchange, import dependency, and dependency on foreign skills and management. Confusion about the social role of parastatals makes the integration of these enterprises into any system of central planning very difficult. Managers who see themselves as individual entrepreneurs rather than the agents of state policies, resist pressures from the center that might fit them into a chain of production linkages so necessary for the development of the economy as a whole.

Lall has highlighted the inadequate baseline of skills of all kinds and the meager industrial capabilities inherited from the colonial economy. He argues that state ownership has done nothing to improve matters and that the lack of industrial capabilities remains a major problem in Africa. Careful to show that there is no factor inherently responsible for this condition and that correct policies could lead to steady improvement, he nevertheless comes to conclusions that would not be acceptable to most people in Africa. He claims that the main determinant of industrial development in sub-Saharan Africa has been the success of each country in mobilizing and deploying non-African industrial capabilities; and he goes on to urge that nonindigenous "tutors" can play a critical role in enhancing indigenous capabilities. Indeed, he wishes to see "non-African communities" be allowed to have their head so that they can play a leading role in industrial development.

While it cannot be denied that expatriate capabilities have built up a significant amount of industry in Africa, it is also clear that the economies that have emerged have been grossly distorted, with benefits accruing not to the indigenous people but to the settlers or expatriate firms. Lall seems to be insensitive to the wage color bars and skills color bars practiced by white and foreign capital in southern Africa—which still persists in South Africa.

Although it may be the case that governments in Africa have given far too little attention to creating skills in the public enterprises over which they have control, this is not to say that the solution lies in turning the clock back to an enhancement of residual colonial powers or in dependence on expatriate skills. On the contrary, what is required is a massive effort to train indigenous skills and create the capacities necessary for industrial and other development. Furthermore, given the scale of the problem, it must be the case that it is primarily the state that can launch the kind of program that is needed. The indigenous private sector is far too small to be able to do so.

Whatever the difficulties state enterprises may meet—and the socialist countries have recently been open about the problems of controlled firms and central planning—African economies cannot conceivably leave their development to market forces and the decisions of individual entrepreneurs governed solely by the profit motive.

In any case, it is well known that foreign corporations are now reluctant to establish new ventures, while the campaign to reprivatize enterprises in Africa is moving ahead, but slowly. There are few local buyers with the necessary capital, with the possible exception of Nigeria. Studies of the potential of private business in Zambia showed that while there was plenty of zeal, real growth remained small. Lall confirms this finding in his recent study.

Paradoxically, although the International Monetary Fund and the World Bank are pressing forward with privatization as part of their structural adjustment programs, they seem to find their own interventions rather easier in countries with a large state sector. Since their new monitoring techniques involve locating senior personnel right inside the state apparatuses, they are able to manipulate industrial policy from the heart of the system, effectively intruding upon, and even seizing, the sovereignty of these countries. On the other hand, African governments sometimes seem to favor the debt-equity swop formula as a means of overcoming the debt crisis, an option that does not exclude the possibility of a future renationalization by a different government. This would be a neat way of eliminating a debt that is seen as unjust and unrepayable.

IMPLICATIONS FOR SOCIAL TRANSFORMATION

It is now clear that two decades of state-sector industrialization has failed in most of Africa. Enterprises are generally inefficient, and workers are badly paid and are denied both participatory openings and ordinary trade union rights. Central planning is practically nonexistent, and individual enterprises attempt to carry out their own programs of production under major constraints arising from external dependence and internal market considerations.

In Britain, postwar nationalization served the purpose of rationalizing capitalism. In Africa, postindependence nationalizations were meant to serve different purposes, as indicated above. But in the process, state legitimacy has come into question in many countries as a result of the poor performance of state industry and the evident benefits accruing to state personnel rather than to the public and the economy as a whole.

Nevertheless, the state will have to play a major role in Africa's economies if there is to be any opening to social transformation. And that role will have to go beyond the welfarism that was often the hallmark of postindependence state intervention. It must also go beyond redistribution, although that is an important consideration in the post-neocolonial period. The essential point is that there needs to be a new emphasis on production, not for itself or for export, but to satisfy need, which should also be the main criterion for the allocation of surpluses. Increased stress on production also implies greater productivity, which in turn depends on the faster creation of indigenous skills, and resources for education and welfare, and not simply intensified exploitation of labor.

Africa's economies must place the satisfaction of social need at the center of their concerns, and this can only come about through a strong lead from public enterprise. The aim must be to produce low-cost mass commodity goods using local raw materials to the best possible advantage. Central planning is essential, but it must be directed toward self-sustaining growth, and must use appropriate technology related to the intrinsic nature of the resources available.

Most important of all, there has to be a commitment to self-reliance and economic development that includes a perspective of ever-improving living standards for the mass of the people and the curbing of all tendencies on the part of the elite to cream off the surplus. Conspicuous consumption has to be publicly condemned and strictly controlled.

Lastly, the large state sector provides the opportunity for the state to lead in the field of worker participation. While the difficulties are immense, not least because workers can also fall into self-serving attitudes, there can be no advance toward social transformation without involving working people and their political organizations in decision making.

FURTHER READING

Bolton, Dianne. *Nationalisation, A Road to Socialism?: The Lessons of Tanzania.* London: Zed Books, 1985.

Green, R. H. "A Guide to Acquisition and Initial Operation: Tanzania." In Julio Faundez and Sol Picciotto. *The Nationalisation of Multinationals in Peripheral Economies.* London: Macmillan, 1978.

Lanning, Greg, and Mueller, Marti. *Africa Undermined: Mining Companies and the Underdevelopment of Africa.* Harmondsworth and New York: Penguin, 1979.

Oni, Ola, and Onimode, Bade. *Economic Development of Nigeria: The Socialist Alternative.* Ibadan: Nigerian Academy of Arts, Sciences, and Technology, 1975.

Onimode, Bade. *Imperialism and Underdevelopment in Nigeria: The Dialectics of Mass Poverty.* London: Zed Press, 1982.

Penrose, Edith. "Ownership and Control: Multinational Firms in Less Developed Countries." In *A World Divided: The Less Developed Countries in the International Economy,* edited by G. K. Helleiner. Cambridge and New York: Cambridge University Press, 1976.

Swainson, Nicola. *The Development of Corporate Capitalism in Kenya, 1918–77.* London: Heinemann; Berkeley: University of California Press, 1980.

Szeftel, M. "The Rise of a Zambian Capitalist Class in the 1970s," *Journal of Southern African Studies* 18, no. 2 (April 1982).

Turok, Ben, ed. *Development in Zambia: A Reader.* London: Zed Press, 1980.

———. *Africa: What Can Be Done?* London: Zed Books, 1987.

Williams, Mike. "Industrial Policy and the Neutrality of the State." *Journal of Public Economics* 19 (1982).

AFRICAN REGIONALISM

A. HAZLEWOOD AND P. ROBSON

INTRODUCTION

THE continuing interest and activity in regionalism and economic integration in sub-Saharan Africa arises from the fact that all but a very few of the states that have emerged into independence are small in population, in per capita income, and in the markets they afford. Indeed, many of these countries' domestic markets are no larger than those of several European cities. These facts encourage a belief that association in one form or another with other states, and particularly with neighbors, would increase their joint economic and political strength and foster economic development.

The formation of such associations in Africa is not a new phenomenon arising from independence, but was a prominent feature of colonial times. Various forms of association of territories existed in Anglophone East, central and southern Africa, as well as in the Francophone territories, some of which are described below. The motives of the colonial powers in forming these associations may not have been identical with those behind the integration initiatives of the independent states, but the arrangements have encountered many similar problems.

The conventional theory of customs unions, which suggests that the benefit derives from a shift of already-established production among the countries forming the union according to their comparative advantage, has little part to play in the analysis of African regionalism. Much of the economic benefit it is hoped will accrue from integration in Africa derives in one form or another from economies of scale. In the context of African development the most obvious, and most discussed, economy of scale is that available to new or potential producers, particularly in manufacturing, when they have free access to larger markets in the integrated area than are open to them in their small domestic areas. Production cost per unit of output can be greatly reduced in this way, and domestic production can become more competitive with imports from outside the area and its establishment therefore more attractive to local and foreign investors. But there are also, in other spheres, significant benefits to be gained from a larger scale of operations—in the provision of services, in food security arrangements, in

890

overcoming the many inefficiencies inherent in overlapping jurisdictions, and in international economic negotiations.

Despite the potential benefits, the experience of economic integration in Africa has been more often one of failure than success. Intrinsically defective mechanisms have played a part, but the failures are sometimes blamed on "politics." It is argued that political rivalries between and within states mean that integration cannot succeed. Certainly, the member-states' political commitment to the aims of integration is essential; it has often been weak, a weakness that was not irrational, given the experience of failure. Failure tends to feed on itself—as does success.

It may be presumed that a grouping of states will not be formed unless it is perceived to be in the interest of the ruling groups, and will not survive unless it continues to be perceived in that way. But such interests are more likely to be served if the economies of all the states are stimulated rather than stagnate. Hence, to suggest that it is all a question of politics is a statement of the obvious, and does not diminish the importance of devising conditions under which cooperation is likely to succeed rather than fail.

The difficulty is that, in the short term, the benefits may be less obvious than the costs, particularly in the more comprehensive scheme resting on trade liberalization. For instance, it is highly unlikely that there will be a general and speedy response to the establishment of an economic bloc, given the economic structure and degree of development of most African countries. The significant gains must be expected to arise in the longer term from the facilitation of development in the larger market, not from a reallocation in the shorter term of often nonexistent productive capacity. What is quite likely to occur in the short term, however, is that a more developed member of the group will appear to gain most of the benefit, finding a protected market in the other members that they do not find in the group. This perceived or real inequality in the distribution of benefits and costs is, if not remedied, a recipe for dissolution.

It must be acknowledged that although in the absence of specific measures to protect them, weaker states are unlikely to benefit, on balance, from integration because of the diversion of their demand from lower costs sources outside the area, they can still derive some offsetting benefits from the removal of the various obstacles to regional trade, which should accompany integration.

The basis for integration, and for a particular country's participation in any scheme, rests on the benefits that country itself will obtain. It was remarked at a 1987 African integration summit meeting that, unfortunately, what the members appeared to have most in common was national self-interest. But that is precisely the basis for integration, which is not based on helping others, but on helping oneself through the pursuit with others of common interests.

Integration will not, however, benefit one country, or at any rate not for long, unless it also benefits the others. The case for integration arises from self-interest, but the pursuit of self-interest requires that the interest of others be simultaneously served. Integration will not succeed unless every

891

partner benefits, because any who think they will not benefit will not participate or will soon withdraw, and there will then be no integration. The benefit is for everyone or no one.

Because of this fact, arrangements to ensure an acceptable distribution of the benefits are of fundamental importance. However, there exist no ready-made schemes that guarantee such an outcome. All kinds of devices have been tried to favor the weaker partners and to redistribute the gains so that all perceive that they gain—for instance, fiscal compensation, partial protection, preferential allocation of public investments—but without conspicuous success. No universally applicable package can be put together in advance to ensure that all partners remain satisfied. There will need to be frequent renegotiation of the terms of the partnership. The statesmanship of the cooperating states will be revealed by their flexibility and tolerance in such negotiations, and by their acceptance of constraints on their separate decision-making powers. Their willingness to compromise may be stimulated by the knowledge that they are faced with the choice of surrendering either some of their potential gains from integration—or all of them.

Most of the arrangements described in this article are, in U.N terminology, "subregional." The major "regional" organization is the U.N. Economic Commission for Africa (ECA), which was established by the U.N. Economic and Social Council in 1958. The ECA is one of the regional commissions of the United Nations and includes all of its African member states. It is not an association or grouping of states of the kind or with the purposes of the various subregional groupings and some all-Africa organizations. However, its secretariat has played a major role in the encouragement, establishment and monitoring of regional and subregional integration schemes. It was deeply involved in the formulation of, and can be said to be the brains behind, the Lagos Plan of Action (LPA) of 1980, which is discussed below.

If the term "integration" is allowed to refer to any cooperation arrangements between individual African states—and it is desirable that it should do so, because the scope for progress may lie in less comprehensive arrangements than those of the kind to which the term is sometimes confined—examples of integration abound. There are examples, existing and defunct, of comprehensive economic communities and unions on a subregional basis, and there are plans for an all-Africa common market. But many interstate arrangements deal only with particular products or services. Some are concerned with an individual export commodity. Others deal with transport and communications, and with services such as reinsurance and tourism. There are authorities concerned with the development of particular rivers and their basins, with membership drawn from the various riverine states. There is an association of central banks. There are monetary unions and clearing systems. And there are development banks and funds, which operate to a greater or lesser degree as instruments of integration according to the character of their investments; these include two pan-African institutions, the African Development Bank and its associated African Development Fund.

The institutions and arrangements existing under a broad definition of integration are too numerous even to list. There are more than 30 in West Africa alone. But the most important, including some that have disappeared, are listed in the Table below, and described and discussed in the course of this article.

AFRICAN REGIONAL ORGANIZATIONS*

Name and acronym	Date established	Membership population, 1985 (millions)	Total population, 1985 (millions)
U.N. Economic Commission for Africa (ECA)	1958	pan-African	555
African Development Bank (AfDB) and Fund (AfDF)	1963 1973	——— pan-African ——— (plus 25 non-African)	
East African Community (EAC)	1967 to 1976	Kenya (13.9), Tanzania (16.4), Uganda (11.9) (populations, 1976)	42 (1976)
East African Development Bank (EADB)	1967	See EAC	58
Federation of Rhodesia and Nyasaland (Central African Federation)	1953 to 1963	Northern Rhodesia (3.5), Southern Rhodesia (4.0), Nyasaland (3.8) (populations, 1963)	11 (1963)
Afrique Occidentale Française (AOF)		——— See CEAO ———	
Union Douanière de l'Afrique Occidentale (UDAO)		——— See CEAO ———	
Union Douanière et Economique de l'Afrique Occidentale (UDEAO)		——— See CEAO ———	
Communauté Economique de l'Afrique de l'Ouest (CEAO)	1973	Benin (3.9), Burkina Faso (6.6), Ivory Coast (9.8), Mali (8.2), Mauritania (1.9), Niger (6.1), Senegal (6.4). Observers: Guinea, Togo.	43

*Organizations are listed in order of appearance in text. (Other existing organizations, not referred to in text, are not included.)
Source for population figures: *U.N. Demographic Yearbooks.*

AFRICAN REGIONAL ORGANIZATIONS (*continued*)

Name and acronym	Date established	Membership population, 1985 (millions)	Total population, 1985 (millions)
Afrique Equatoriale Française (AEF)		———— See UDEAC ————	
Union Douanière Equatoriale (UDE)		———— See UDEAC ————	
Union Douanière et Economique de l'Afrique Centrale (UDEAC)	1964 (amended 1974)	Cameroon (9.9), Central African Republic (2.6), Congo (1.7), Gabon (1.2) Observers: Equatorial Guinea, Chad, Guinea	15
Mano River Union (MRU)	1973	Guinea (6.1), Liberia (2.2), Sierra Leone (3.6)	12
Economic Community of West African States (ECOWAS)	1975	Benin (3.9), Burkina Faso (6.6), Cape Verde (0.3), Gambia (0.6), Ghana (13.6), Guinea-Bissau (0.9), Ivory Coast (9.8), Liberia (2.2), Mali (8.2), Mauritania (1.9), Niger (6.1), Nigeria (95.2), Senegal (6.4), Sierra Leone (3.6), Togo (3.0)	162
Confederation of Senegal and Gambia (Senegambia)	1981	Gambia (0.6), Senegal (6.4)	7
Economic Community of Central African States (ECCAS)	1983	UDEAC members (see above) plus CEPGL members (see below), plus Chad (5.0), Equatorial Guinea (0.4), São Tomé and Príncipe (0.1)	77
Communauté Economique des Pays des Grands Lacs (CEPGL)	1976	Burundi (4.7), Rwanda (6.1), Zaire (30.4)	41
Union Monétaire de l'Afrique de l'Ouest (UMAO)		———— See CEAO ————	
Banque Centrale des Etats de l'Afrique Equatoriale et du Cameroun		———— See UDEAC ————	
Southern African Development	1980	Angola (8.5), Botswana (1.1), Lesotho (1.5), Malawi (7.1),	70

Name and acronym	Date established	Membership population, 1985 (millions)	Total population, 1985 (millions)
Coordination Conference (SADCC)		Mozambique (14.0), Swaziland (0.6), Tanzania (21.7), Zambia (6.7), Zimbabwe (8.3)	
Southern African Customs Union (SACU)	1910 (amended 1976)	Botswana (1.1), Lesotho (1.5), South Africa (32.4), Swaziland (0.6)	36
Eastern and Southern Africa Preferential Trade Area (PTA)	1981	Burundi (4.7), Comoros (0.4), Djibouti (0.4), Ethiopia (43.4), Kenya (20.3), Lesotho (1.5), Malawi (7.1), Mauritius (1.0), Rwanda (6.1), Somalia (4.7), Swaziland (0.6), Tanzania (21.7), Uganda (15.5), Zambia (6.7), Zimbabwe (8.3). Possible: Angola (8.8), Botswana (1.1), Mozambique (14.0)	135 (possible, 159)
Lagos Plan of Action (LPA)	1980	———— pan-African ————	

LIGHTS THAT FAILED

East African Community

The EAC was established by a treaty between Kenya, Tanzania and Uganda in 1967. It fell apart 10 years later. It was the most complete integration scheme that has existed between independent African states. It embraced a common market or customs union (though a union subject to certain restrictions in the short term), major transport and communications services owned in common, common research services, a development bank (the EADB), and elaborate arrangements for consultation and cooperation on planning and other matters. The treaty was designed to establish on a new basis, appropriate to the existence of independent states, the integration arrangements that had been inherited from the colonial past. It added new elements, particularly those designed to correct inequalities arising from the operation of the common market among the three countries. To this end, a member in deficit in intra-community trade was empowered to impose for a limited time a "transfer tax," or partial tariff, on the goods of the surplus partner.

Integration in East Africa had been more complete in the past. For instance, there had been a common currency, but that had been abandoned by the independent states. Prior to and following independence there had been a succession of disputes among the three countries on economic issues, centering on the predominance of Kenya, which was perceived by its partners to be benefiting from the common arrangements at their expense. Previous attempts to satisfy the three partners by modifying the arrangements had failed. The treaty of 1967 was the final attempt. It must be seen, therefore, not as a coming together, but as an attempt to prevent an established scheme from falling apart.

The mechanisms of the treaty failed to halt the movement toward dissolution. There was no single reason why the treaty failed; a number of interacting influences and issues, including some that could not have been foreseen by its framers, caused the member-states to lose interest in keeping the EAC alive. The mechanisms for dealing with the unequal effects of the common market proved inadequate; the differential effects of transport pricing policies were disruptive; the operations of state trading corporations were believed to be discriminatory; there were different attitudes toward development through transnational corporations; the fact that heads of state could be called upon to make decisions on contentious matters discouraged compromise at a lower administrative or political level. In addition, there was the disruptive effect of the Amin regime in Uganda.

In the end, the partner-states came to see no firm footing of mutual advantage in the continued existence of the community. Cooperation came to be seen not as a positive-sum, but as a zero-sum or even negative-sum, game, so that the members would be no worse off, and perhaps even better off, going it alone. The EADB, however, continues to operate, and has attracted increased donor backing.

The collapse of the EAC was a serious blow to those who saw the way to economic cooperation between African states as being through the establishment of such complex and comprehensive communities, having a customs union as a central feature. Its experience has encouraged the pursuit of more limited forms of cooperation not based on trade preferences, though attempts to follow different paths have not brought to an end the establishment of groupings resting on preferential trade. The various lines of approach are illustrated below.

Central African Federation

Still closer forms of cooperation than economic communities are confederations (in prospect in the Confederation of Senegal and Gambia, or Senegambia—see below) or federations, as experienced in colonial Francophone West and Equatorial Africa, briefly agreed upon in postcolonial East Africa, and actually established in the last decades of the colonial era in central Africa.

No one today can imagine the Federation of Rhodesia and Nyasaland, which comprised what are now the independent states of Malawi, Zambia and Zimbabwe, as showing the way forward. It was formed in 1953 as the outcome of a decades-long campaign by white colonials in the Rhodesias for "closer association." It is said that Nyasaland was attached at the insistence of the British government to relieve itself of responsibility for a "pauper state." The federation (which came to an end in 1963 after agitation and strife led by Nyasaland) was a barrier to the independence of the constituent territories under majority (i.e., black African) rule, and had been opposed from the start by blacks who feared the takeover of their land by whites. The ending of federation was followed by the independence of Malawi and Zambia; Southern Rhodesia became effectively an independent, white-run state under the terms of a Unilateral Declaration of Independence, and the establishment of Zimbabwe was delayed until 1980.

The distribution of powers between the territorial governments and the federal government, located in Southern Rhodesia, gave the territories control over functions that most directly affected the black African populations, such as agriculture and education. Other major functions of govenment were a federal responsibility. Customs revenue and more than 60 percent of the revenue from income tax accrued to the federal government.

In all the official discussions before and during federation, its economic advantages were more or less assumed. There was no serious analysis of its economic effects; in fact, the arrangements markedly favored Southern Rhodesia and the white populations of the federation.

For most of the federal period the price of copper was high, and there was a massive transfer to the federal government of revenues generated in Northern Rhodesia, and hence, through federal government expenditures, to Southern Rhodesia and to a minor extent to Nyasaland. The allocation of federal expenditure was biased both territorially and racially. Total federal expenditure in Southern Rhodesia was not far short of twice that in the other territories taken together, even though Southern Rhodesia had little more than one-third of the total population of the federation. But it had two-thirds of the whites. The federal protective tariff discriminated against the cheap imports that were a major element in Nyasaland's trade, in favor of the more costly products of Southern Rhodesian industry. It is likely that the rate of economic growth was higher than it would have been without federation, because there was a substantial inflow of capital, but it was mostly into Southern Rhodesia, which added to the economic inequalities.

In summary, the economic effects of federation were unfavorable to Northern Rhodesia, through both the fiscal and the tariff effects. Nyasaland gained from the first but lost from the second. Southern Rhodesia gained from both. But no improvement in the economic arrangements could have saved the federation, given its political function as a bulwark of colonial dominance in central Africa.

West African failures
There have been a number of failures also on the other side of the continent. The attempts of the majority of the states that succeeded the former Afrique Occidentale Française (AOF) federation to maintain and improve their previous economic links resulted in the establishment of the Union Douanière et l'Afrique Occidentale (UDAO) in 1959 and of the Union Douanière Economique de l'Afrique Occidentale (UDEAO) in 1966. Both federations failed. The reasons for their failure are numerous and complex,

and some are now mainly of historical interest. Technical, administrative, political and economic factors all played a part. But an overriding reason for the failure of these two initiatives was the inherent defectiveness of an orthodox customs union as an instrument of regional cooperation, given conditions in Africa in the 1960s. Some much-needed improvements were made in the provisions of UDEAO, notably in its acceptance of the necessity of intraregional tariff protection in a bloc that lacked a regional policy, and in the establishment of a permanent machinery of administration, previously lacking. In its almost exclusive concern with trade liberalization, however, UDEAO remained an expression of "negative integration." Its convention was hardly concerned at all with measures of "positive integration," of a kind designed to make the market area function effectively or to promote other broader economic policy objectives in the union. These omissions were to play a large part in the failure, in its turn, of UDEAO.

LIGHTS THAT SHINE: CONTINUING ASSOCIATIONS AND NEW
EFFORTS

Communauté Economique de l'Afrique de l'Ouest
The CEAO was established in 1973 under the Treaty of Abidjan, comprises the Ivory Coast, Niger, Burkina Faso, Mali, Mauritania, Senegal and, since its admittance at the summit meeting in October 1984, Benin. It is the successor to UDAO and UDEAO.

The CEAO treaty requires the establishment of a customs union, but a common external tariff is not yet in sight. At its present stage, CEAO is best described as a partial free-trade area in which trade is, in principle, free for unprocessed agricultural products and livestock, and is partially liberalized (through tariff preferences and the elimination of nontariff barriers, though some remain in defiance of the treaty) for some locally manufactured products.

The trade liberalization is buttressed by a scheme, the taxe de coopération régionale (TCR), which provides automatic compensation for losses arising from the tariff preferences according to objective criteria prescribed in the treaty.

Intracommunity trade is a relatively low proportion of total trade (12 percent in 1983), and only a proportion of it is in manufactures. Senegal and the Ivory Coast enjoy substantial surpluses with their partners, all the other CEAO members having deficits.

A valuable feature of the trade liberalization arrangement in CEAO is that each country effectively retains its policy flexibility and autonomy with respect to the protection accorded to new industries. Consequently, even before the industrial harmonization envisaged by the treaty is attained, a participating country's interest is unlikely to be damaged, and there is a workable basis for limited economic cooperation, which minimizes distributional difficulties and harmonization problems. But a corollary is that the opportunities for generating economic gains are likely to be modest by comparison with those that would in principle be available from more ambitious schemes.

CEAO has made substantial progress toward implementing its treaty provisions in customs affairs. It has adopted a common customs and statistical nomenclature. Agreement has also been reached on a simplified and harmonized structure of customs and internal indirect taxes. An absence of exchange problems because of the common currency (except for Mauritania) is also a favorable factor for economic integration in the subregion. In other fields of cooperation, such as agriculture and transport, progress has been less obvious, though steps have been taken to develop regional training and research institutes, and several useful community projects, e.g., fisheries.

The big deficiency of the community is that it does not seem to have encouraged a rationalization of industrial production. There is little national specialization with respect to particular products and little intra-industry trade. In numerous sectors of industry, plants are replicated, despite the fact that they are branches of the same multinational, and production takes place on a smaller scale than the size and structure of the regional market should permit. The advantages of integration are thereby dissipated insofar as they derive from specialization and the exploitation of scale economies. Industries in which uneconomic replication has occurred include textiles, pharmaceuticals, plastics, food products and electrical products.

This plant replication is not to any significant extent an inheritance from a preintegration era. It has largely grown up and continues to develop despite the arrangements for integration. It has been buttressed by a failure to harmonize national investment incentives, and it reflects, in particular, the absence of any regional industrial development program or any concerted regional approach toward foreign investment and multinational enterprises. The effect is to rob integration of much of its hoped-for benefits, and to hinder the attainment of important subsidiary objectives of development policy, such as the creation of interindustry linkages.

CEAO has so far had a limited impact on development. And there are few signs that the factors that impede a greater impact are currently accorded much attention by policy makers and politicians in the participating countries. Nevertheless, despite its limitations, the CEAO approach has two important merits that are capable of being built upon: (a) it is capable of avoiding the distortions that would otherwise be produced by trade liberalization undertaken against the background of initially very diverse tariffs; (b) it provides a workable basis for cooperation in the stage prior to industrial harmonization. Of course, even with policy reforms, the CEAO market is probably too small to produce really significant benefits anyway. In this respect, the attraction of a broader grouping such as the Economic Community of West African States (ECOWAS), discussed below, is undeniable.

Union Douanière et Economique de l'Afrique Centrale
As had happened in AOF, the states that succeeded the Afrique Equatoriale Française federation opted to continue economic and some political links after independence. The establishment of the Union Douanière Equatoriale in 1959 was the result. In 1961 Cameroon became associated and in 1964,

under a new treaty, became a full member of a modified union, UDEAC. In 1968 Chad withdrew.

The system established has many similarities to CEAO. A preferential free-trade area was established, with the taxe unique performing a similar function to TCR in the CEAO. A solidarity fund was established, to which after political negotiation ad hoc contributions were made annually for compensation purposes. In 1974, a revised UDEAC treaty was signed, formally widening the scope of cooperation to cover agriculture, transportation and other areas, and emphasizing balanced development to "compensate" the least-developed members; but no new policy instruments on institutional mechanisms were created to realize these new objectives.

The experience of UDEAC in intragroup trade has even been even less favorable than that of CEAO, and the two arrangements have similar defects. A major defect of the union is that it too has failed to encourage rationalization of industrial production, the fragmentation of the market being permitted and encouraged by the operation of the single-tax system and the absence of any concerted regional approach to industrial development, foreign investment and multinational enterprise.

Mano River Union

The MRU was inaugurated in October 1973 between Liberia and Sierra Leone. These two countries had previously been involved, in 1964, together with the Ivory Coast and Guinea, in an initiative to set up a West African free-trade area; but this became a victim of political conflict between their prospective Francophone partners. Current arrangements for economic integration between the two founding members of the MRU have their roots in initiatives going back to 1967, which had envisaged limited trade preferences for the products of several existing industries, and cooperation to promote new industries to serve the combined market. These initiatives eventually led to the signing of the Mano River Declaration. The original declaration made provision for the later adherence of other West African states, and in October 1980 Guinea acceded to the union.

The 1973 declaration called for the establishment of a customs union and trade liberalization, but its most notable provisions relate to cooperation for the creation of new productive capacity and the need to secure a fair distribution of the benefits from cooperation. The subsequently adopted Protocol 12 on union industries, i.e., those depending on the combined market, was intended to have an important role in their promotion, and envisaged influencing their location in the interests of balanced development through the provision of financial incentives, the cost of which was to be borne equally by member-states.

Despite this sensible emphasis, in practice the evolution to date of the MRU has mirrored features that, elsewhere in Africa, have produced largely ineffectual arrangements for cooperation and integration. In particular, there has been a familiar preoccupation with purely technical aspects of negative integration and with trade liberalization. Although the MRU, uniquely in current schemes, did succeed in arriving at a common external tariff for its two founder-members, it has had virtually no impact on either trade or industrial development.

Economic Community of West African States (ECOWAS)

ECOWAS is without doubt the most ambitious grouping in sub-Saharan Africa. The 15-country grouping—larger in area than Western Europe—was inaugurated in 1975, and includes the member-states of the MRU and CEAO, together with Nigeria, Ghana, Gambia, Benin, Togo, Guinea-Bissau and Cape Verde. ECOWAS includes some of the richest and most populous countries in Africa, several of which possess immense mineral resources. It also includes half of the least-developed countries in Africa, and only five of its members are not in that category.

ECOWAS is governed by the Treaty of Lagos, which includes a timetable of commitments with respect to (1) a tariff standstill; (2) trade liberalization; (3) fiscal harmonization; and (4) the introduction of a common external tariff (CET). Since 1981 ECOWAS has been endeavoring to implement the second of these commitments. The timetable of commitments is coupled with unscheduled obligations to adopt wider policy measures of positive economic integration, including industrial cooperation.

The ECOWAS Treaty is very elaborate (modeled on the Treaty of Rome), but it left most substantive issues—including the CET—to be resolved subsequently. The treaty requires trade liberalization to take place in advance of tariff harmonization, unlike the procedure followed in most other groupings where either liberalization was made conditional on prior tariff harmonization (so providing a stimulus to the formation of a common external tariff and avoiding possible misallocations of resources that might otherwise be produced), or other devices were adopted to avoid distortions (as in CEAO and UDEAC).

In itself, the implementation of a timetable of trade liberalization measures could be expected to operate adversely to the interests of the least-developed members. The treaty does, however, contain provisions designed to ameliorate these problems, which, if left unchecked, would certainly result (as they have elsewhere in Africa) in a maldistribution of the costs and benefits of integration, and in ultimate collapse. The principal provision, which is to come into force synchronously with trade liberalization, provides for fiscal compensation, to be paid through the ECOWAS fund, for revenue losses incurred in the process.

The treaty also contains other provisions that are designed to ensure that the interests of the community's less-developed members are protected. For instance, the ECOWAS fund is required to lay special emphasis on the promotion of projects in less-developed member-states. This provision has yet to be implemented. If the experience of other African groupings is any guide, it will not prove easy to do so.

With respect to policies about foreign direct investment, ECOWAS has sought to develop a more positive and radical approach than those of the CEAO and MRU. Indeed, bargaining with multinationals appears to have been very much in the minds of those who devised the provisions of the ECOWAS treaty. Ultimately, any useful policy in this field will have to rest on a prior harmonization of investment incentives and of industrial development programs, since it is basically the lack of harmonization of these key policy areas that accounts for many of the effects or abuses of which ECOWAS countries (in common with other developing countries) complain, and which may tip the balance of benefits unduly in the favor of the foreign investor. So far, however, the principal step taken within ECOWAS has been to add a local participation provision on its rules of origin. In itself that is likely to exacerbate the problems of less-developed members, and without a prior harmonization of investment incentives cannot be expected to ameliorate significantly the problems posed by foreign direct investment (of which ownership is only one aspect). For the time being, indeed, the provision simply has the effect of rendering any trade liberalization commitments ineffective, since those member-states (e.g., Nigeria and Ghana) that can meet the participation requirement are unable to export competitively in West Africa, whereas those other member-states that account for the bulk of intra-ECOWAS exports (e.g., the Ivory Coast and Senegal) cannot meet the ownership requirement.

Since its establishment, the principal achievement of ECOWAS has been to create the institutional framework for a customs union. A common tariff nomenclature has been adopted and common customs documentation has been developed. A range of protocols needed to give effect to treaty provisions with respect to trade and customs has also been adopted, thus giving operational content to some of the more general provisions of the treaty. In its fund, the community possesses an institution of potential importance for promoting positive integration, development and balance. Nevertheless, ECOWAS displays crucial weaknesses that have so far prevented it from making the treaty effective.

There are basic problems of compatibility between ECOWAS and the other smaller West African groupings, all of whose members also belong to ECOWAS. There are differences in rules of origin, trade liberalization procedures and compensation, to cite only three important areas. Strictly, some CEAO procedures are in contravention of the Treaty of Lagos. In an attempt to deal with these and other problems, the Adewoye Report [1] recommended a concentration of effort toward promoting integration and development through smaller and more intimate communities that would be closer to the interests of members than ECOWAS itself. The attraction of the smaller communities is certainly underlined by the adhesion of Benin to the CEAO. But the problem of delineating the relations of the smaller groups and of ECOWAS has not been tackled so far. These weaknesses substantially contribute to one of the most widely criticized aspects of ECOWAS, namely that the decisions it adopts at the level of heads of state or ministers almost invariably fail to be implemented by action at national level.

Other weaknesses of ECOWAS stem from many factors, of which two are closely connected with the integration strategy laid down in the treaty:

[1] United Nations Economic Commission for Africa, *Proposals for Strengthening Economic Integration in West Africa.* (Addis Ababa, 1984).

(1) the priority accorded to trade liberalization and the automaticity of the process; and (2) the lack of simultaneity in the obligations and benefits implied by the community's program.

Although sole reliance on trade liberalization as a means of integration among developing countries has long been discredited, the ECOWAS treaty nevertheless gave priority to trade liberalization on an obligatory, automatic, across-the-board basis; and its explicit economic strategy emphasizes the liberation of competitive forces. There is no agreed general structure of protection—to be provided ultimately through the adoption of a common external tariff and harmonized investment incentives. The ECOWAS program of automatic trade liberalization would thus come into effect, if it does, against the background of national protective structures that are diverse and generally very high, but that in any case have not been constructed with the needs and opportunities of a regional market in mind. There are no grounds for supposing that the effects of such liberalization would be favorable. Although any adverse distributive effects resulting from trade liberalization should be largely offset by the community's compensation scheme, this in itself cannot justify the pattern of trade that might result.

The second weakness of ECOWAS is one that primarily concerns its less industrially advanced members, although to some extent it affects all. Despite the treaty's emphasis on protecting the interests of the less-advanced members, it cannot be said to offer any very firm prospect of doing so adequately. The timetable of obligations of the treaty concerning the customs union and trade liberalization constitute measures that are likely to affect adversely the interests of the industrially less-advanced members through the resulting trade diversion. The measures from which such members might hope to benefit—in particular, differential action through the fund to promote their industrialization, and perhaps fiscal and industrial harmonization—are not on a timetable, and no specific proposals have yet been considered to give them operational content.

In any case, little can be expected of the trade liberalization program in itself, even if it were to be implemented, since "most countries of the region have nothing to trade with anyway."[2] The development of well-justified productive capacity is one of the most pressing problems of integration—in West Africa and elsewhere.

Senegambia
Initiatives for Senegambian economic cooperation and integration date back as far as 1960, but they found little real support from the Gambian side until 1981. In that year an attempted coup d'etat in Gambia led President Jawara to invoke the defense agreement with Senegal. The coup was thereupon suppressed by Senegalese forces and the outcome was that the presidents of the two countries agreed to establish a political confederation. The 1981 Confederation Agreement provides that this is to be based on the development of an economic and monetary union. To date, little progress toward confederation has been made. The development of such a union of

[2] *Ibid.*

the two countries evidently comes up against many problems involving their disparate sizes and levels of development. Moreover, Gambia's revenues rely heavily on customs duties on goods that are subsequently smuggled to Senegal. If economic union were to entail a simple customs union or other forms of integration hitherto favored by Senegal, it could hardly be intrinsically attractive to Gambia. In the light of the different interests of the two parties—that of Gambia in the maintenance of the status quo and that of Senegal in encouraging union—it is not surprising that to date implementation of the Confederation Agreement has been slow. A free-trade area, however, could be of some mutual interest, and is likely to be introduced shortly. Monetary aspects of a Senegambian union may turn out to be the least troublesome of the many issues surrounding the confederation, since options exist that would not adversely affect Senegal's interests, but which could be at the same time be beneficial to Gambia, such as the latter's participation as an independent member in the West African monetary union.

Implementation of different aspects of the confederation must in any case proceed with an eye on both countries' commitments to ECOWAS, and the adherence of Senegal to CEAO.

Economic Community of Central African States

ECCAS was set up in 1983, and is still in its preliminary stages. All of its members are also members of either UDEAC or of the Communauté Economique des Pays des Grands Lacs. ECCAS is likely to face problems of compatibility similar to those that have frustrated ECOWAS.

Monetary cooperation and monetary unions in West and central Africa

Currency inconvertibility and widespread controls and restrictions on exchange transactions in sub-Saharan Africa constitute powerful nontariff barriers, and are a major obstacle to trade expansion and production coordination. This is a dimension of economic cooperation to which too little attention has been given in recent years.

There do, in fact, exist two conspicuously successful examples of monetary cooperation in the shape of monetary unions that have operated in Africa since independence. The Union Monétaire de l'Afrique de l'Ouest (UMAO) and the Banque Centrale des Etats de l'Afrique Equatoriale et du Cameroun are largely coterminous with respectively, CEAO and UDEAC. In discussions of cooperation in Africa they are frequently ignored or criticized—in part because of the extra-continental dependence they are perceived to embody. The unions involve membership in the franc zone, and a French guarantee and some French participation in policy making. The exchange rate of the currency—the Communauté Française Africaine (CFA) franc—has remained in a fixed relationship to the French franc since independence. Though this fixity is not formally required, it has remained—from the African side—a practical necessity. The CFA franc has become the preferred currency of informal and cross-border trade throughout much of West and central Africa. Although the unions have attracted one or two small non-Francophone territories, and in the case of West Africa have proved to be sufficiently attractive to induce one country, Mali (which had established its own currency) to reenter the union, and although they may yet undergo some modest extension—perhaps by the entry of Gambia to the UMAO—anything more seems unlikely.

Southern African Development Coordination Conference

SADCC, embracing Angola, Botswana, Lesotho, Malawi, Mozambique, Swaziland, Tanzania, Zambia and Zimbabwe, came into being in 1980. In that year the members held what was primarily a pledging meeting with donor agencies, which became an annual function. The pledging of funds in the framework of the SADCC program was a significant support for the integration movement, and the pledging and coordination of aid continues as a major activity.

SADCC's integration aims were adopted in the context of the dependence of most of the members in one way or another, particularly in terms of transport, on South Africa. The pressure for cooperation came from the felt need to diminish that dependence. The funds pledged in 1980 were to a very large extent for transport, though they amounted to no more than one-third of the estimated total need of funds for transport and communications projects; and 80 percent of that total was for rehabilitation and upgrading, not for new developments. A Southern African Transport and Communications Commission (SATCC) was established in Maputo to manage the transport program. The importance of further transport development to reduce dependence on South Africa remains evident. At the 1987 meeting it was estimated that 60 percent of the members' external trade was either directly with South Africa or went in transit through South African ports.

In 1987 the value of projects being pursued by SADCC totaled U.S. $6.4 billion. The bulk of this amount was for transport and communications projects, the value of which amounted to 66 percent of the total. The other large sectors were industry and trade, with 19 percent; and food, agriculture and natural resources, with 10 percent. It was planned to raise 86 percent of the total from foreign sources. Although nearly $2.2 billion had already been secured, that sum covered only one-third of the total program, with a further 5 percent of the total under negotiation with donors. The financing gap amounted to 61 percent of the total. In transport, nearly one-half of the financing required had been secured, the gap being no more than 56 percent, but in industry and trade the gap was as large as 79 percent. Nevertheless, considerable donor support has been mustered through SADCC. The United States and Britain, in particular, cite their support for SADCC in countering criticism of their continuing involvement in South Africa.

SADCC, though potentially a comprehensive scheme, not confined to a particular aspect of economic development, has a distinctive approach. It is not built around a preferential trade area, and it is notable for allocating responsibility for particular functions to particular members: for instance, transport and communications to Mozambique, food security to Zimbabwe, and industrial development to Tanzania. A small secretariat, under an executive secretary, has been established in Botswana, but the individual member-states are responsible for pursuing the activity in the sphere (or spheres) they have been allocated. The summit of heads of state is the supreme body of SADCC, and under this a ministerial council is responsible for policy and for the coordination of activities.

A major feature of SADCC's activity in food and agriculture has been the development of a food security strategy, and in transport the development and defense of access routes outside South Africa. In industry there has been a recent emphasis on the involvement of the business community in proposals for investment and production; and SADCC studies and ministerial discussions have had beneficial effects in rationalizing plans and pointing to industrial development potential. It remains true, as the Tanzanian representative to SADCC is reported to have said, that "it is one thing for heads of government to agree to increase inter-regional trade, but if there are no goods to trade and no investment for the enterprises that will create the trade, what use is the agreement?"[3] Research projects to examine schemes for the development of intra-SADCC trade, including one concerned with direct trade measures and bilateral trade agreements, and another concerned with a system of general preferences for SADCC firms, have received donor support.

SADCC undoubtely has its achievements. It has raised substantial aid funds for its programs, though a large part of these funds is likely to have been available on a purely bilateral basis. It has concentrated on the major issues in the region's development; and the worsening transportation and food situations in the region are created by political and military circumstances that SADCC and its SATCC cannot be expected to overcome.

SADCC has avoided a likely field of conflict by not seeking to establish a preferential trade area. But the absence of this is a glaring gap in the organization's integration plans. The gap may not present a barrier to progress until perhaps a somewhat distant future, but once progress has been made with the more immediate problems of food security and transport, and such matters as coordinated industrial development become of greater importance and relevance, then the need for preferential trade will become apparent. It would not be impossible in the longer run to provide it by negotiation on a product-by-product basis, rather than by broader-based preferences. By then, of course, the progress and extension of the Eastern and Southern Africa Preferential Trade Area/PTA (see below) may have gone a long way toward dealing with the matter.

Southern African Customs Union

One obstacle to SADCC's becoming a preferential trade area would arise from the fact that three of its members, Botswana, Lesotho and Swaziland (BLS), are joined with South Africa in SACU. This customs union is the contemporary form of a long-established trade and customs relationship

---

[3] *African Business* (February 1987).

among the four territories, dating from 1910, which forbids BLS from making trade agreements without the consent of South Africa.

SACU is, in principle, an area of internal free trade with a common external tariff and common excise and sales taxes. Until 1969 the revenues from these duties were allocated on the principle of derivation, with no account being taken of the constraints and losses the union imposed on BLS. In that year the agreement was revised to provide BLS with a measure of fiscal compensation for such disadvantages as the price-raising effect of the tariff, resulting from the diversion of their consumers' expenditure on cheap imports from outside the union toward more costly South African goods, and for their loss of fiscal discretion.

The agreement was further amended in 1976. The previous amendment had "enhanced" the revenue paid back to BLS by 42 percent of the "derived" amount. The 1976 amendment provided substantial revenue benefits, but made them more dependent on the condition of the South African economy. The amendments to the 1910 agreement, in addition to providing fiscal compensation, allowed for some protective duties to be imposed by BLS to assist minor industrial developments in those countries, designed to fill gaps in the South African industrial structure. However, nontariff barriers are more important obstacles to BLS entry to the South African market than are tariffs, and this detracts from the significance of the customs union.

Since a substantial part of BLS public revenues is obtained from the SACU allocation, on balance it would seem to be advantageous for the time being to continue membership. For South Africa, membership in SACU has political advantages, and without it it would be impossible to control smuggling along BLS-South Africa borders. South African business interests complain that cheap foreign goods enter South Africa via BLS, where nontariff barriers are fewer.

The customs union has facilitated the development of sanctions-busting operations in BLS, particularly in Botswana and Swaziland, as the sanctions campaign against South Africa has gained momentum. Goods from South Africa are packaged, processed or relabeled for export. The Swaziland and Botswana governments have had to tread carefully in restraining these operations without discouraging the welcome investment they bring.

Eastern and Southern African Preferential Trade Area
The PTA began as an initiative of ECA, and came into formal existence when nine countries—about half the total potential membership—signed a treaty in 1981.

PTA is based on the concept of market integration through the establishment of preferential trade relations among the members. All barriers to trade are planned for removal by 1996. A PTA clearing house, operating in the Reserve Bank of Zimbabwe, was set up in 1984, and a development bank was established in 1986.

The rule of origin, which products have to satisfy if they are to qualify for preferential treatment, is a technical matter, involving political and ideological issues. To obtain preferential treatment as local products, goods

907

must be produced by firms that are managed and owned by nationals of the country in which they are located—a firm being counted as locally owned if not less than 51 percent of its equity is in the hands of nationals. A great deal of manufacturing, particularly in the more industrially developed PTA countries, is undertaken by transnational corporations whose products do not satisfy this rule of origin. Although Zimbabwe was allowed an adjustment period for companies to become localized, it was feared that the rule would constrain investment in industry and the growth of intra-African trade. The constraint was eased by the decision in 1986 to amend the "all-or-nothing" rule by allowing the degree of preference accorded a product to vary with the degree of local participation in its manufacture. The products of enterprises with at least 51 percent localization would continue to enjoy a 100 percent preference; in addition, there would be a 60 percent preference for the products of enterprises having between 41 percent and 50 percent local ownership, and a 30 percent preference for products of enterprises with a local participation of between 30 percent and 40 percent.

PTA, as a trade-focused, comprehensive integration scheme, is in contrast to SADCC's cooperation in a number of specific development and investment projects. PTA relies more on its bureaucracy to implement the provisions of a formal agreement, whereas SADCC is driven by, and depends for its progress on, regular decisions by the constituent governments. But there is no incompatibility in membership in both organizations. And two members of SACU, Lesotho and Swaziland, have joined PTA.

PTA has progressed in its membership, and includes all but a few of the potential member-countries. In other respects progress has been slow. The clearing house exists, but has been used for only a small part of the transactions arising from trade within the area. The development bank has not attracted a full membership, though it is too early yet to expect great activity. There have been reductions in customs charges to establish preferences within the area, but nontariff barriers in the form of licensing, exchange controls and bureaucratic administration remain. Enthusiasm for the scheme among the governments does not seem to be great, if that may be deduced from the small attendance of heads of state at summit meetings. Only four attended the meeting in Lusaka, Zambia, at the end of 1985, and decisions on important matters had to be deferred. It is true that in contrast with SADCC, for instance, PTA can make progress through the actions of civil servants, without ministerial action, and as a result may be less disturbed by political problems. Nevertheless, a firm commitment to the implementation and extension of integration by governments is ultimately essential for success, and one may wonder if at present such commitment exists among the members of PTA.

LIGHTS ON THE HORIZON: THE LAGOS PLAN OF ACTION

The most ambitious scheme for the development of intra-African trade, as well as for other elements of economic integration, is contained in the LPA, which looks forward to "the eventual establishment of an African Common

Market leading to an African Economic Community." Industrialization is a central feature of the LPA, with a "fundamental role" for "intra-African industrial cooperation" in the establishment of "major industrial complexes" and "multi-national industries in Africa."

Intra-African trade expansion "is meant to constitute the mainstay for the present strategy," and the LPA document presents a long list of the measures proposed. Existing preferential areas are taken into account; nontariff barriers are allowed for; the need for improved transport is recognized. These measures are all sensible enough, though there may well be incompatibilities within such a comprehensive list of desiderata. And the proposals are all at a high level of generality, without reference to specific policies or political obstacles and with a totally unrealistic timetable. In the list of aims and mechanisms there is also the surprising omission of any reference to the less-developed members of preferential areas and to mechanisms for dealing with their problems. True, "the least developed African countries" have a chapter to themselves, but this does not deal with their position in a preferential area via-à-vis more-developed countries, although this has always been the Achilles heel of integration schemes. There is, indeed, a reference to "ensuring that no undue advantage is taken of the liberalisation process," but if that is meant to refer to the process of "cumulative causation," which benefits the more developed, it is an unusually noncommittal way of doing so, and it is not linked to any proposals for corrective mechanisms. Nor does there seem to be even a hint of the problem, let alone a solution, in the chapter dealing with industry, which is the sector in which the problem is most likely to be generated.

But even if the proposals were entirely comprehensive and totally compatible, there would remain the question of realism. The LPA sees the way toward an Africa-wide common market and economic community as being paved by the establishment of preferential trading areas on a narrower geographical basis. But it does not examine the problems faced by the associations that already exist or have existed, nor does it suggest how their activities can be made to succeed. Governments have committed themselves to the Lagos Plan, it is true, but they have committed themselves in the past to other arrangements for economic integration without properly pursuing their commitments.

Despite all its deficiencies, the LPA points in the right direction. Africa's development will require a greater mobilization of its own resources combined with domestic policy reform and donor support. The balkanization of Africa is certainly a major constraint on its development. Donors must support attempts to ease this constraint, which has not always been the effect of economic aid. Correspondingly, the relations of African states with the outside world must not militate against intra-African cooperation. Above all, there must be the political will to succeed.

IN THE LIGHT OF EXPERIENCE: THE FUTURE

The community approach has been dominant in the attempts at economic cooperation among African states. There is good reason to fear that this approach is not constructive given African conditions, a fear that will almost certainly be confirmed if there is no redirection of effort coupled with institutional reform in existing schemes, and no determination to avoid over-ambitious strategies in schemes now in their formative stages. The following initiatives have been suggested as necessary for cooperation.

First, emphasis needs to be given to the development of a suitable infrastructure for regional economic cooperation. This has been a constant theme of analysis and policy declarations for 25 years, but it bears repetition since it remains so basic. Transport and other forms of communication between African countries after more than a quarter of a century of postindependence initiatives still frustrate trade and wider forms of cooperation. Postal service and telecommunications are often much worse than at the time of independence. In financial transactions, intra-African clearing arrangements can involve almost unbelievable delays: delays of up to four to six months before final payment have been reported in West Africa. The costs involved in delay and lack of prompt information constitute a major obstacle to intraregional trade.

The development and use of more effective instruments and arrangements for industrial cooperation is a second vital requirement, and is likely to be the single most crucial determinant of the future contribution of integration to sub-Saharan economic development. It is necessary to be realistic about what can be achieved, and which paths can be followed. In East Africa, for instance, just three countries, countries that had many affinities, found it impossible to implement even a very limited industrial "plan."

To make progress in Africa, it may be necessary to think in terms of much more limited and flexible arrangements for industrial cooperation than have hitherto been envisaged: perhaps overlapping groupings (involving smaller groups of as few as two or three countries), and possibly resting on joint financial participation in capital, profits, tax revenues and even staffing. Modification of established treaties of cooperation may be needed to facilitate such initiatives, and perhaps the creation of smaller subgroups, such as the Benin Union that has been proposed within ECOWAS. Initiatives of this kind would have to be handled cautiously if the process were not to be ultimately counterproductive in a regional or even subregional context. Guidelines that looked toward some longer-term rationalization of production on a regional basis, with fiscal incentives to follow them, would be essential.

Guidelines for industrial development initiatives should be based on a realistic appraisal of the strengths of the subregion (or smaller areas) and of the comparative strengths of the individual countries, and on some very broad agreement on the level and structure of protection toward which it would be reasonable for the region to work. Operationally adequate data on the basis of which such guidelines could be formulated have not been collected or evaluated, and the lack of such studies in Africa is currently an important constraint to constructive negotiation and decision making in this field. Integration agreements that are not well grounded will either be counterproductive or will fail to be implemented.

A fourth requirement is for payments reforms. For most African countries outside the monetary unions of West and equatorial Africa and SACU, such reforms are indispensable if trade cooperation is to be feasible, although perhaps new forms of industrial cooperation might circumvent some existing payments problems. The problem in the short term is to administer payments restrictions in a way that does not discourage intraregional trade; in the longer term the problem is to reduce the need for the restrictions themselves. There is mounting evidence that African countries that have undertaken policy adjustments to restore equilibrium in their balance of payments during the past decade have not suffered in terms of growth rates of real GDP or consumption. Limited convertibility—the currently peddled nostrum—would appear only to introduce further distortions into situations in which price systems are already so riddled with distortions that they cannot, without major policy reforms, provide a dependable guide to intraregional specialization and rationalization. A solution involving a major extension of existing monetary unions is unlikely, but small extensions have taken place in the Equatorial African Union, and others in prospect may help modestly.

Finally, to take another dimension altogether, the structures within member-states for reacting to and for developing integration initiatives need to be strengthened. It cannot be overemphasized that development projects are, and will long remain, largely the responsibility of individual member-states. Those states must therefore be involved initially, continuously and intimately in any workable integration program. Attempts to integrate from above are unlikely to make a significant impact.

FURTHER READING

Guillaumont, Patrick. *Zone Franc et Développement Africain.* Paris: Economica, 1984.

Hazlewood, Arthur, ed. *African Integration and Disintegration.* London: Oxford University Press, 1967.

————. "The East African Community." In *International Economic Integration*, edited by Ali M. El-Agraa. London: Macmillan, 1982, 2nd ed., 1987.

Robson, Peter. *Integration, Development and Equity: Economic Integration in West Africa.* London and Boston: Allen & Unwin, 1983.

————. "The West African Economic Community." In *International Economic Integration*, edited by Ali M. El-Agraa. London: Macmillan, 1982; 2nd ed., 1987.

United Nations Economic Commission for Africa. *Report of the ECA Mission on the Evaluation of UDEAC and the Feasibility of Enlarging Economic Cooperation in Central Africa.* Libreville, Gabon, 1982.

AFRICAN INDUSTRIAL DEVELOPMENT

DERRICK CHITALA

INTRODUCTION

Since the early 1970s Africa has experienced a steadily mounting socio-economic crisis. Statistics attest to the unsatisfactory trends in industrial performance.[1] This paper provides an analysis of the industrial crisis in Africa since the 1970s. The first part discusses Africa's experience and provides data on the prevailing situation in the industrial sector. The section following assesses the main features of the industrial conundrum, showing the major causes of the crisis. Another section discusses other external factors that have continued to aggravate the crisis. The conclusion suggests possible areas of reform and the nature of the possible alternatives.

INDUSTRIAL STRUCTURE AND PERFORMANCE

Africa's industrial structure and role in the international division of labor continues to be dominated by the production of consumer goods, with light industries playing the primary role while the share of heavy industry is low. In 1980, for instance, light industry accounted for an average of 77 percent of manufacturing value-added (MVA).[2] Furthermore, Africa's industry in general has been marked by industries based on the processing of raw materials and by import-substitution. This is reflected in the high rate of food processing and textiles, which in 1980 accounted for 56 percent of the total manufacturing output. The other consumer goods (principally beverages and tobacco products) accounted for 14 percent of the total manufacturing output. The basic-industry sector continues to be of a secondary character, contributing very insignificantly to output. Statistics for 1980 showed that production of chemicals accounted for only 9 percent of the total industrial output, metal-based engineering and wood-based industries

---

[1] *Economic Commission for Africa Report.* E/ECA/LDCS, March 4, 1985.
[2] U.N. Industrial Development Organization, *Industry in the 1980s* (1985), 196.

912

accounted for 6 percent, nonferrous metallic minerals comprised 4 percent, and all other basic industries made up 5 percent.

In general terms, Africa's industrialization record during the past two and one-half decades has, by and large, been one of blighted hope. Instead of the hoped-for industrialization after the conquest of the colonial oligarchy, the continent's industrial development has continued to be sluggish, and became particularly so in 1980 when the crisis reached alarming proportions. Table 1 shows the percentage contribution of manufacturing to gross domestic product (GDP) at a constant (1970) factor cost. As this table demonstrates, the manufacturing sector recorded not very significant growth rates in most African countries.

Table 1
PERCENTAGE CONTRIBUTION OF MANUFACTURING
TO GDP AT CONSTANT (1970) FACTOR COST

Country	1970	1975	1980
Algeria	11.16	7.75	8.12
Angola	5.18	4.04	2.58
Benin	8.36	9.30	5.21
Botswana	7.84	8.12	5.24
Burkina Faso	10.88	14.45	14.57
Burundi	6.77	11.32	10.39
Cameroon	10.02	9.44	9.64
Cape Verde	5.23	6.45	5.52
Central African Republic	13.09	12.32	13.99
Chad	5.49	10.76	9.14
Comoros	6.69	8.05	5.22
Congo	10.39	6.26	7.81
Djibouti	6.09	7.47	8.96
Egypt	19.60	17.77	14.02
Equatorial Guinea	3.77	6.97	5.22
Ethiopia	9.55	10.54	10.64
Gabon	4.17	4.89	7.66
Gambia	5.10	5.66	8.58
Ghana	12.15	14.19	9.16
Guinea	2.89	3.65	3.10
Guinea-Bissau	1.07	1.32	1.75
Ivory Coast	11.40	11.85	10.82
Kenya	17.13	12.02	13.24
Lesotho	2.71	5.70	4.93
Liberia	4.00	4.60	4.98
Libya	1.75	1.77	2.35
Madagascar	11.51	11.28	11.49
Malawi	15.36	13.23	15.16
Mali	9.26	9.07	7.65
Mauritania	4.90	4.86	6.39

Table 1 (*Continued*)
PERCENTAGE CONTRIBUTION OF MANUFACTURING
TO GDP AT CONSTANT (1970) FACTOR COST

Country	1970	1975	1980
Mauritius	16.09	18.25	15.25
Morocco	15.86	19.78	18.92
Mozambique	5.89	9.37	8.65
Niger	6.04	8.10	5.31
Nigeria	4.45	5.45	5.44
Rwanda	3.47	11.75	12.84
São Tomé and Príncipe	4.81	7.05	4.74
Senegal	15.93	14.52	15.05
Seychelles	1.56	5.29	6.20
Sierra Leone	6.45	5.59	4.81
Somalia	6.49	9.56	8.61
Sudan	10.18	8.59	7.01
Swaziland	12.35	13.97	23.54
Tanzania	10.08	10.44	10.01
Togo	10.34	7.59	5.70
Tunisia	9.22	10.13	10.03
Uganda	7.45	6.05	4.76
Zaire	7.55	8.58	2.62
Zambia	6.53	15.38	15.95
Zimbabwe	21.30	23.33	25.45

Source: Economic Commission for Africa National Accounts Computer Printouts (Table 3C 12/30/82).

The same is true for the share of MVA to the GDP. Table 2 shows the growth of the MVA by subregions of Africa, and shows that since 1980 it has generally decelerated.

Data on the contribution of the manufacturing sector to real GDP of the least developed countries in Africa is even more vexing. Table 3 presents statistics of real GDP arising in manufacturing in the 26 African nations designated by the United Nations to be among the 37 least-developed countries.[3] The average annual growth rate at constant prices of these countries was a meagre 1.9 percent.

The growth of investment in the manufacturing sector has, since the 1970s, also followed a downward trend. This declining trend led to a declining output/capital ratio in most countries—which, in turn, meant that the sector's share in total employment could not increase appreciably. Table 4 shows the levels of capacity of utilization for some countries between 1981 and 1982—which averaged 30 percent to 50 percent. For some countries, such as Tanzania, the industrial malaise since 1980 reduced industrial

[3] U.N. Conference on Trade and Development, *The Least Developed Countries—1986 Report* (New York, 1978), 31. See also U.N. Industrial Development Organization, *Industry and Development: Global Report* (1986).

Table 2

GROWTH OF MVA BY SUBREGION OF AFRICA
(%)

	Share of MVA in GDP		Annual average		
	1970–77	1977–82	1970–77	1977–82	1981–82
North Africa	12.5	12.8	6.6	6.5	4.4
West Africa	6.7	7.8	7.8	3.5	−1.7
East Africa	11.1	11.3	3.8	2.0	2.8
Central Africa	8.0	7.9	3.4	1.6	0.6
Total Africa	9.9	10.6	4.6	1.5	—

Source: Economic Commission for Africa, E/ECA, Change 11/32, Annex 11: 3.

output by more than 70 percent.[4] In order to raise capacity of utilization from the low level of between 20 percent to 30 percent (in 1986) to 60 percent, great sacrifice and innovation would be required.

The industrial sector generally failed to create a positive impact on the development process. It failed to influence and integrate the traditional sector, and it failed to stimulate the growth of other sectors (such as agriculture and the tertiary sector) to act as suppliers of machinery, which could have meant the manufacturing sector's contributing positively to the establishment of intra- and inter-sectoral linkages. A clearer picture of the inability of the industrial sector to act as the key link in the overall economic development of Africa becomes possible when a general characterization of some countries is analyzed.

EXPERIENCES AMONG THE COUNTRIES

Broadly speaking, country experiences can be divided into two groups: the industrial experiences of nonmineral producing countries and of mineral producing countries. The development strategy followed has generally conformed with this categorization.

Nonmineral producing countries
The group of nonmineral producing countries is broadly defined to constitute such countries as Ghana, Tunisia, the Ivory Coast, Kenya, Malawi, Tanzania, Egypt, Senegal, Ethiopia, Somalia, and others—countries that were compelled by economic reasons to stress agriculture and industry as a basis for accumulating investable surpluses.

One subgroup of nonmineral producing countries includes Ghana and Egypt, among others. Ghana's strategy during the rule of Kwame Nkrumah was to engage in building up the industrial sector, with relative neglect of agriculture. The same was true for Nasser's Egypt, although there some land reforms were attempted.

A second subgroup of nonmineral producing countries included Kenya,

[4]*Ibid.*, pp. 279–80.

Table 3
REAL GDP ARISING IN THE MANUFACTURING
SECTOR OF 26 OF THE LEAST-DEVELOPED
COUNTRIES IN AFRICA

Country	Levels in U.S. dollars per capita (1984)	Share in total GDP (1984)	Annual average growth (1980–84) Value-added at constant prices
Benin	24	10	24.2
Botswana	73	7	8.2
Burkina Faso	20	15	2.8
Burundi	19	9[c]	5.7[d]
Cape Verde	15	5	4.7
Central African Republic	19	8	−3.2
Chad	11	9	−8.1
Comoros	12	6	5.0
Djibouti	57	10	0.6
Equatorial Guinea	11	5	1.7
Ethiopia	13[c]	11[c]	4.1[f]
Ghana	29	10	11.2[b]
Guinea	7	2	0.6[f]
Guinea-Bissau	7	4[c]	—
Lesotho	14	7	3.7
Malawi	21	12	3.3
Mali	10	7	—
Niger	11	4	−1.6
Rwanda	51	18	5.5
São Tomé and Príncipe	39	10	−3.3
Sierra Leone	17	6	−3.1
Somalia	16	6[a]	−0.8[g]
Sudan	33	9	3.3
Tanzania	18	7	−4.7
Togo	16	7	−5.2
Uganda	9	4[e]	3.6[f]

[a] 1979. [b] 1978. [c] 1983. [d] 1982. [e] 1981. [f] 1980–83. [g] 1980–82.
Source: U.N. Conference on Trade and Development, *The Least Developed Countries—1986.*

Malawi and the Ivory Coast, among others—countries that put emphasis on agricultural development as the overall strategy, attempting to accumulate investable surpluses on this basis. This subgroup made deliberate policy attempts to facilitate the transportation of rural production, for export and/or for urban consumption. Colin Leys has shown, in respect to Kenya, that in spite of relatively heavy infrastructural development of the rural areas, what resulted was a warped export-oriented development that

916

Table 4
LEVEL OF CAPACITY OF
UTILIZATION FOR SELECTED
COUNTRIES, 1981–82
(%)

Country	Capacity of utilization
Liberia	50
Morocco	60
Somalia	40
Sudan	50
Zaire	30

Sources:
World Bank Economic Memorandum, 1981, 1982.
World Bank Policy Measures for Rehabilitation, 1983.
World Bank Investing for Economic Stabilization and Structural Change, February 16, 1982.

exacerbated the flight of investable surpluses from the rural areas.[5] The aggregate result of this was a deepened pauperization of the rural areas.

A third subgroup, comprised of such nonmineral producing countries as Tanzania, attempted to institute balanced growth by paying equal attention to both agriculture and industry. The *ujamaa* (familyhood) experiment (representative of the efforts of this subgroup and its failure) resulted in widespread resentment against "socialist" experiments.[6]

In general terms, the countries that emphasized the development of agriculture (Kenya, Malawi, the Ivory Coast, etc.) were also the countries that instituted liberal attitudes toward foreign capital. Various investment codes were enacted that were aimed at encouraging foreign investments. Attractive inducements (such as tax exemptions or repatriation of profits) were offered to foreign investors. Coupled with the fact that these countries stressed primary production relative to processing, they received relatively higher foreign capital, primarily in the form of "aid"—and so were able to enjoy a period of relative growth.

On the other hand, the countries that stressed the development of the manufacturing sector (such as Nkrumah's Ghana, and Egypt) not only suf-

[5] Colin Leys, *Underdevelopment in Kenya: The Political Economy of Neo-Colonialism* (London: Heinemann, 1975).
[6] Dan Nabudere, *Imperialism in East Africa* (London: Zed Press, 1981), 97–108. See also: Lionell Cliffe and John Saul, eds., *Socialism in Tanzania* (East African Publishing House, 1972) and T. F. Rweyemamu, *Underdevelopment and Industrialization in Tanzania* (Nairobi: Oxford University Press, 1973).

fered from the undesirable consequences of overdependence on foreign capital and markets, and the acknowledged long-term decline in the terms of trade, but also received relatively less aid—and so were unable to accumulate sufficient investable surpluses to facilitate expanded production and development.[7]

Mineral producing countries

The experience of the mineral producing countries, in real terms, has not been any different from the experience of the nonmineral producing countries. A relatively large proportion of African countries is dependent on the export of base metals to earn foreign exchange. Table 5 records the mineral and metal exports of each African country as a percentage of their total merchandise exports, and shows that almost half of the countries were dependent on mineral exports for their foreign-exchange earnings.

One subgroup of mineral producing countries (comprised of Liberia, Sierra Leone and Mauritania, among others) concentrated solely on the production of minerals for export; another subgroup (comprised of Algeria, Libya, Nigeria, etc.—producers of hydrocarbons) and a third subgroup (Zaire, Zambia, Zimbabwe, etc.—base metal producers) have engaged to some degree in local processing before export, as a way of procuring some MVA. In general, however, none of these countries has succeeded in making the transition to the production of import-substitution products. They still remain import dependent for a whole range of essential inputs, as Table 6 (the percentage of imports by broad economic category) shows.

The effects of the global economic crisis that started in the 1970s have been most severe on the mineral producing countries. Three factors in particular have been contributory to this.

First, most of the mineral producing countries tended to neglect agriculture, particularly peasant agriculture. As a result of this neglect in Zambia, for instance (as an International Labor Office JASPA report showed), the rural terms of trade, in relation to the urban terms of trade, continued to deteriorate.[8] The barter terms of trade started declining in 1975, when they averaged 84 percent. It is clear that real resources moved from the rural areas to the urban areas, with the result that these countries tended to be dependent on foreign imports.

Second, the overreliance on mineral exports to earn foreign exchange and tax revenues tended to be dependent on the fortunes of the world economy, to which these countries were linked in a crisscross of relationships. This largely explains the crises of Zambia and Zaire following the fall of the world market prices of copper.

Third, by using imported technology as the foundation of the import-substitution industries, the mineral producing countries were integrated into the world economy as importers of technology, and became more vulnerable to inflationary pressures of that market.

Nigeria's experience is a good, instructive example of the general prob-

[7] Third World Forum, Africa Office. *Bulletin No 3* (Feb. 1984): 34–58.
[8] ILO/JASPA. *Basic Needs in an Economy Under Pressure*. (Addis Ababa, 1973), 46.

Table 5
EXPORTS OF MINERALS AND METALS
AS PERCENTAGE OF ALL MERCHANDISE EXPORTS

Country	1966[a]	1970[a]	1975[a]	1980	1984
Algeria	1.8	2.5	1.2	89.5	63.9
Angola	2.7	12.1	8.2	—	—
Benin	0.4	0.1	0.4	2.4	1.6
Botswana	—	—	24.7	27.1	12.2
Burkina Faso	1.4	0.1	—	0.1	—
Burundi	0.7	3.7	0.8	0.6	0.2
Cameroon	14.7	9.6	7.5	30.7	—
Cape Verde	10.0	10.8	3.0	9.5	20.0
Central African Republic	—	—	—	26.2	—
Chad	0.6	0.2	0.5	0.2	—
Comoros	—	—	—	—	0.5
Congo	1.8	—	1.7	93.7	—
Djibouti	0.4	0.5	1.0	2.1	0.8
Egypt	1.2	0.6	0.5	57.9	47.2
Ethiopia	0.6	0.5	0.4	—	0.1
Gabon	40.1	13.7	10.2	100.0	83.1[b]
Gambia	—	—	—	—	—
Ghana	14.6	12.0	7.4	24.4	18.4
Guinea	64.0	66.1	85.4	90.2	92.2
Guinea-Bissau	—	0.1	0.8	—	—
Ivory Coast	1.9	1.1	0.5	0.2	0.1
Kenya	1.0	0.5	0.8	—	—
Liberia	73.0	73.5	79.3	57.3	64.3
Libya	—	—	—	100.0	—
Madagascar	3.7	5.0	6.5	3.4	3.9
Malawi	0.2	0.3	—	—	0.2
Mali	0.6	0.5	0.1	0.3	0.9
Mauritania	74.7	73.3	78.0	64.0	43.5
Mauritius			—	1.3[b]	1.1
Morocco	36.6	32.6	56.7	40.5	30.5
Mozambique	4.7	2.1	2.7	8.8	—
Niger	0.1	—	61.0	83.2	72.1
Nigeria	6.3	4.2	0.5	94.7[c]	—
Reunion	0.5	0.5	0.2	0.3	0.1
Rwanda	35.9	34.4	15.9	10.5	9.9
São Tomé and Príncipe	—	—	—	—	—
Senegal	7.6	9.8	24.1	20.0	15.5
Seychelles	5.6	4.8	1.5	1.1	0.4

[a] Excluding major petroleum exporters.
[b] 1983.
[c] 1979.

Table 5 (*Continued*)

Country	1966[a]	1970[a]	1975[a]	1980	1984
Sierra Leone	17.6	19.0	16.4	76.6	74.7
Somalia	0.1	0.1	—	0.0	—
Sudan	0.8	0.4	0.6	0.5	0.3
Tanzania	1.0	0.7	0.4	7.9	10.1[d]
Togo	42.6	24.7	64.9	40.3	55.1
Tunisia	26.3	19.0	16.0	52.6	43.7
Uganda	7.8	7.9	3.7	0.7	—
Zaire	76.2	73.2	74.8	59.2	54.8
Zambia	97.3	98.4	96.9	96.7	98.0
Zimbabwe	—	—	—	—	—

[d] 1981.
Sources: U.N. Conference on Trade and Development, *Commodity Year Book*, 1986. 16–17. UNO, *1985 International Trade Statistical Yearbook*, vol. 1.

lems of Africa's industry. Almost one-third of Africa's MVA (excluding South Africa) is located in Nigeria. Before the indigenization decree of 1974 Nigeria's economy was quite diversified, with the various arms of the government paying equal attention to agriculture and industry. After the oil boom of 1973–82 Nigeria realigned its policies and looked upon the oil revenues as a source of income for general modernization. The oil revenues jumped to about 90 percent of the state revenues during that period. At the same time food production dropped—which necessitated the importing of food to feed the population. The value of food imports rose from 1.2 billion nairas to 12 billion over the same period. The disquieting factor, however, was that in spite of the investable surpluses created by oil exports, these surpluses were used largely for luxury consumption instead of for profitable investments; this accounts for why the industrial share of GDP has remained virtually the same.

When the oil glut of the 1980s came Nigeria experienced a severe economic crisis. It was forced by the Organization of Petroleum Exporting Countries cartel to reduce its oil production from 2.8 million barrels per day (b/d) in 1973 to 1.3 million b/d in 1981. The oil asset that could easily have become a key instrument in industrializing Nigeria became a key factor of national distress, reinforcing the country's dependent status. In 1982 Nigeria's balance-of-payments deficit exceeded 5 billion nairas, and Nigeria was forced to negotiate with the International Monetary Fund for a standby arrangement.

EXTERNAL FACTORS AGGRAVATING THE PROBLEMS

The problems experienced in Africa's industrial development process illustrate the features and characteristics of a self-sustaining process—that of the ever-increasing weaknesses of the economies of African countries. The problems represent a disturbing feature that is a result of imbalances in the international division of labor and Africa's failure to devise appropriate development strategies. A few features may be pointed out that illustrate the evolution of Africa's development problems.

First, in almost every African country the state has been the key instrument for accumulation and investment. In all the countries there has generally been an absence of a private industrializing bourgeoisie (in the Western European sense) to act as the industrializing agent; and there has not been the self-reliance of socialist countries. The postcolonial state (a dependent institution insofar as its social forces are aligned to foreign interests in dominating the economy) has maintained and reproduced the status quo. In other words, the state has been used not as an industrializing instrument but as a tool to enrich itself.

The second feature is that the two industrial development strategies that African countries adopted failed to generate the dynamics needed for the structural transformation of industry toward the attainment of self-sustaining economies. Almost all of the countries employed the import-substitution industrialization strategy. The argument for adopting this strategy was that it would orient African industrial activities into processing for the domestic market, and hence ease balance-of-payments pressures. This, however, has not been the case. Almost all the countries that applied this strategy failed to stimulate the development of key industries with strong domestic linkages. The production of consumer goods (which constitutes about 60 percent of Africa's total MVA) was heavily oriented toward the production of food, beverages and tobacco (see Table 6). Basic consumer goods, like clothing, pharmaceuticals, paper, etc. are still being imported. Furthermore, apart from failing to induce desired industrial development, the import-substitution industrialization strategy raised a number of unsettling structural problems, such as the installation of capital-intensive import-substitution industries, with a high cost of investment and large production strategies disadvantaged by economies of scale. This led to considerable drain on the scarce foreign-exchange reserves, owing to the excessive dependence on imported inputs. Furthermore, the nature of investment has not created extensive employment opportunities or facilitated technological development. It is because of this that a new export-led strategy along the lines of the new industrializing countries of Southeast Asia has been suggested and adopted.[9]

The export-led growth strategy has also met with limited success. In almost no country in Africa has the practice of domestic processing for exports led to an overall industrialization, that is, to developing a dynamic comparative advantage so as to be competitive on the international market. Africa's manufactured exports have been subjected to severe competition from other countries in terms of quality and prices, the high import content of goods produced for export, the low levels of capacity utilization, and so on. Furthermore, the recession in the developed countries—the countries that were supposed to provide the export market—has resulted in their adopting protectionist prices and quota restrictions on products from the developing countries in general. It is therefore not surprising to

[9]G. Frank "Export Led Growth," *IFDA Dossier No 33* (Jan.-Feb. 1983).

Table 6
IMPORTS BY BROAD ECONOMIC CATEGORY
(Percentage of Total Value of Imports)

Country	1970			1978			1984		
	Consumer goods	Inter-mediates	Capital goods[a]	Consumer goods	Inter-mediates	Capital goods[a]	Consumer goods	Inter-mediates	Capital goods
East and Southern Africa									
Kenya	31.5	46.5	22.0	20.7	48.6	30.7	20.7[a]	48.6[a]	30.7[a]
Tanzania	32.0	45.6	22.4	6.9	46.1	47.0	12.1[b]	51.9[b]	37.0[b]
Malawi	30.9	49.5	19.6	23.3	48.3	28.4	14.7[b]	51.2[b]	34.5[b]
Madagascar	33.4	45.8	21.8	26.4	48.4	25.2	21.5[c]	27.4[c]	31.1[c]
West Africa									
Ghana	—	—	—	—	—	—	14.9	55.1	29.8
Senegal	40.9	41.0	18.1	36.7	42.3	21.0	33.6[b]	48.2[b]	18.3[b]
Ivory Coast	34.7	41.4	23.9	28.7	39.5	31.8	30.4[d]	44.4[d]	35.3[d]
Liberia	39.1	35.7	25.2	34.5	41.7	23.8	45.9	37.0	26.9

Niger	30.0	49.3	20.7	24.9	35.2	38.3	31.3[a]	42.3[a]	26.4[a]
Nigeria	—	—	—	24.9	35.2	38.3	—	—	—
Central Africa									
Congo	42.2	34.4	23.4	35.9	39.0	25.1	31.0[e]	51.0[e]	18.0[e]
Rwanda	20.0	58.6	21.4	20.3	58.5	21.2	18.1[e]	61.5[e]	20.4[e]
Central African Republic	37.1	37.5	25.4	31.7	39.1	29.2	46.3[e]	33.3[e]	20.4[e]
Zaire	30.5	42.0	27.5	29.0	44.9	26.1	—	—	—
North Africa									
Egypt	23.5	55.1	21.4	14.2	—	—	32.5	41.6	27.5
Morocco	35.3	49.4	15.3	35.9	59.8	26.0	21.5	58.1	20.4
Sudan	18.5	59.9	21.6	19.2	36.5	27.6	26.4	50.2	23.4
Tunisia	20.6	47.6	31.8	16.7	51.4	29.4	19.9	48.8	31.2
Algeria	—	—	—	—	41.6	41.6	23.5	42.6	33.9

Source: U.N. *Yearbook of International Trade Statistics.*

[a] 1981 figure.
[b] 1982 figure.
[c] 1983 figure.
[d] 1985 figure.
[e] 1980 figure.

see Africa's exports of its processed material since the 1970s growing more slowly in relation to imports of manufactured goods. Lawrence Cockroft, for instance, noted that though foreign companies were most effective in boosting industrial growth in Kenya and the Ivory Coast to an annual rate of 100 percent in the 1960s and 1970s, such industrial growth was, however, dependent on imports.[10] Industrial growth failed to establish local linkages with agriculture, did not create appreciable employment opportunities (only 12,000 jobs in Kenya during the period 1964–70), and relied heavily on expatriate labor. Furthermore, Cockroft observed, for Kenya and the Ivory Coast, in most recent years, the total value of foreign investment has been less than the combined value of repatriated profits and fees—themselves severely underrepresented by overinvoicing on imports and underinvoicing on exports to parent companies.

The export-led growth strategy is inherently limited. Taking the newly industrializing countries in Asia—Taiwan, Hong Kong, South Korea and Singapore—as models is not only ahistorical but strategically untenable. The historical circumstances under which these Asian countries amassed surpluses are different from the circumstances of African countries. Hong Kong and Singapore are city-states, while Taiwan and South Korea were created as fringe economies as a result of the cold war against China and the Soviet Union. Furthermore, the supposition that export-led growth generates foreign exchange and provides employment as it attracts foreign capital is questionable, looked at from the point of view of African experience.

Far from improving the balance-of-payments problems, export-led growth worsens them because, in order to export, an export-led economy must import raw materials and machinery; this not only reduces its foreign-exchange earnings but, in fact, drives it to borrow more from foreign money markets in order to enable it to finance its import programs. This is the key to understanding the source of the external debt burden that most African countries are currently carrying.

CONCLUSION: THE NATURE OF POSSIBLE ALTERNATIVES

It has been observed above that the failure of African countries to industrialize is rooted in their stultifying structures and in the roles they have continued to play in the international division of labor. Tackling the problems therefore means that fundamental changes have to be brought about in the whole complex of relations, both at the national and international levels. Ingredients of such alternatives must include the following:

1. On the national level, it will be necessary to change the postcolonial state in order to enable it to perform such functions as

   • Building industry around agriculture to reduce import dependence
   • Selective delinking from the world economy
   • Promoting small-scale industries

[10] Lawrence Crockroft, "Is Africa's Industry Beyond Hope?" *Africa Analyst* (May 1, 1987): 4.

- Mobilizing and redeploying domestic finances and foreign exchange
- Recycling of materials
- Stamping out corruption

2. At the international level, African countries could consider the strategy of using collective self-reliance, on the basis of regional cooperation, to create an enabling environment to facilitate accumulation of resources for expanded production. Such already existing institutions as the Economic Community of West African States, the Eastern and Southern Africa Preferential Trade Area and the Southern African Development Coordination Conference, among others, could exchange information on industry-related matters such as local technologies, raw materials, energy and spare parts; they could establish cooperative agreements to deal with such issues as market access and joint purchases; they could pool resources when national actions might not be very effective; and they could jointly mobilize resources for investment (see the chapter "African Regionalism" in this Handbook). Furthermore, the international community could also facilitate Africa's industrial development by providing grants, canceling debts, and actively assisting in managerial and technical training.

The solution to Africa's industrial malaise lies first in the creative articulation of internal capacity within countries (because it is at the nation/state level that resources can best be harnessed). Then, together with regional cooperation and multilateral assistance acting as stimulants, it will be possible for Africa to move closer to industrial self-sufficiency and economic independence.

FURTHER READINGS

Adedeji, A. and T. Shaw, *Economic Crisis in Africa*. Boulder, Colorado: Brenner, 1985.

Cliffe, Lionell, *et al.,* eds, *Socialism in Tanzania*. Dar-es-Salaam: East African Publishing House, 1972.

Fransman, Martin ed. *Industry and Accumulation in Africa*. London: Heinemann, and Exeter, New Hampshire, 1982.

Leys, Colin. *Underdevelopment in Kenya: The Political Economy of Neo-Colonialism, 1964–1971*. London: Heinemann, 1975.

Nabudere, Dan Wadada. *Imperialism in East Africa*. London: Zed Press, 1981.

Ravenhill, John. *Africa in Economic Crisis*. Basingstoke, Hampshire: Macmillan; New York: Columbia University Press, 1986.

Rweyemamu, T. F. *Industrialization and Income Distribution in Africa*. Dakar, Senegal: Codesria, 1980.

———. *Underdevelopment and Industrialization in Tanzania*. Nairobi: Oxford University Press, 1973.

Shaw, Timothy M. *Towards a Political Economy for Africa: The Dialething Dependence* New York: St. Martin's Press, 1985.

———. and Olijide, Aluko, ed. *Africa Projected*. New York: St. Martin's Press, 1985.

Timberlake, Lloyd. *Africa in Crisis: The Causes, the Cures of Environmental Bankruptcy*. Philadelphia: New Society Publishers, 1986.

AFRICA'S AGRARIAN MALAISE

MICHAEL F. LOFCHIE

INTRODUCTION

The ominous recurrence of famine in Ethiopia underscores once again the perilous fragility of Africa's agricultural sector and the bitter paradox of an agricultural continent periodically unable to feed its own population. The imagery is cruelly familiar: painful news photographs of starving children; weary mobilization of private voluntary organizations, many of whose workers and staff have seen it all before; quick, fleeting involvement of media personalities, some of whom unscrupulously exploit the situation to increase their personal fame; and a belated response by various official agencies, both national and international, too easily criticized as "too little, too late"—as if any governmental reaction could be either timely or adequate.

According to a recent U.N. study, Ethiopia is only one of a number of African nations where the problem of food supply has once again become desperate. A severe food crisis continues, for example, in Mozambique, primarily because of war-related disruption and turmoil. Its long-standing civil war, pitting the Frelimo government's forces against a resistance movement calling itself the Mozambican National Resistance (Renamo), has for several years not only prevented normal cultivation in the countryside, but also severely restricted the distribution of food and vitally needed agricultural inputs. Political instability is so severe and the destruction of the country's rural infrastructure is so advanced that Mozambique is unlikely to receive more than a small fraction of the grain it requires to feed its rural population.

For similar reasons, the food situation in Angola is also desperate. Because of disruptions to the country's food supply, resulting from armed conflict between the MPLA government and the UNITA resistance movement, the food requirements of the country's urban population of approximately 2,000,000 and its displaced population of approximately 700,000 will have to be met almost entirely by imports. Even if the remainder of the country is self-sufficient, Angola's import needs for 1988 may well

926

exceed 350,000 tons. Because of serious balance-of-payments difficulties arising from lowered oil prices and the prodigious hard-currency costs of the ongoing war, two-thirds of this amount will need to be provided on concessional terms by donor nations. Desperate as this situation may seem, Angola's food needs appear almost manageable by comparison with those in Mozambique, where 750,000 tons of food aid were required in 1988 to prevent further starvation in the countryside.

The list of African countries presently threatened by dire food emergencies is almost the duplicate of the list of those affected by ongoing civil wars. The most serious situations exist in Ethiopia, Mozambique, Angola, Sudan and Chad. Because the evidence linking civil war with famine is so compelling, it may be useful to establish a basic analytic distinction between famine and poor agricultural performance. Contemporary famines in Africa do not typically result from inadequate food production but, rather, from the immense difficulty of delivering food relief to politically disturbed regions. Indeed, famines sometimes occur in countries that are enjoying unprecedentedly high levels of food production.

This is the case, for example, in both Chad and Sudan. In Chad total grain production for 1986–87 approached 700,000 tons, a near-record level, and included record levels of millet and sorghum. The country's acute food deficits principally affected the northern regions, where refugees from the civil war had to be supplied with external food aid. During the past two years Sudan has also enjoyed bumper crops, especially of its principal food staple, sorghum. The country's total grain production during the two-year period 1985–86 and 1986–87 approached 8 million tons. By the end of 1987 Sudan enjoyed a grain surplus of nearly 1 million tons, and the Agricultural Bank of Sudan was searching for ways to export about three-fifths of this surplus. Indeed, the food supply in northern Sudan was so ample that many farmers were beginning to reduce the area sown to sorghum and millet. In the southern regions of the country, however, the civil war severely affected both transportation and production, and ongoing military activity prevented distribution of food aid.

If the list of countries suffering food shortages were confined to those racked by civil war, an analysis of cause and remedy would need to proceed little further. The principal issue for debate would be the direction of causality: does civil war result in regionalized pockets of deprivation or do regionalized pockets of deprivation result in civil war? A search for the causes and effects of African hunger cannot rest on this issue, however, for the list of countries that presently face food emergencies is not confined to the five mentioned above, and includes societies long considered politically stable and virtually immune to famine conditions. At the head of this list are Botswana and Malawi.

In Botswana, serious food shortages appear to be principally the result of a prolonged drought. Six consecutive years of unusually low rainfall levels have reduced grain production to only about 50 percent of its long-term average. As a result, nearly two-thirds of the country's total population (about 700,000 of a total of 1.2 million) have had to be supported by food relief. This has necessitated annual grain imports of approximately 200,000

927

tons. A similar situation exists in Malawi, where domestic grain shortfalls that also amount to about 200,000 tons have required the importation and distribution of food relief. Much of Malawi's food relief has been directed to camps in the southern part of the country housing refugees from the Mozambique civil war.

The critical difference between Bostwana and Malawi, on the one hand, and Angola and Mozambique, on the other, lies in the fact that, owing to the greater political stability of the first two, it has been possible to import and distribute the requisite amounts of food assistance. Botswana and Malawi are far more typical of the majority of African nations in being able to compensate for domestic food deficits through successful programs of food imports than are war-torn countries such as Mozambique and Angola. For vast numbers of African countries, such imports have now become relatively routinized. The list of these countries includes nations as politically, geographically and economically disparate as Cameroon, Congo, the Ivory Coast, Ghana, Lesotho, Madagascar, Nigeria, Senegal, Zaire and Zimbabwe. The routinization of food aid suggests that the continent's chronic food deficits cannot be adequately understood as the result of episodic factors such as civil war or drought, but must be interpreted as the outcome of longer-term structural factors. Civil wars may produce localized famines by disrupting the importation and distribution of food aid; Africa's pandemic food shortages are far better understood, however, as the symptomatic outcome of a continent-wide tendency toward inadequate agricultural production.

The table below helps to confirm, in very crude numerical terms, that this tendency has a long-term character.[1] During the three-year period 1966–68, per capita grain production for the countries of independent black Africa averaged approximately 262 pounds/199 kg. per person per year. During the three year period 1982–84, average per capita grain production had fallen to only about 216 pounds/98 kg. per person a year. These figures corroborate a 1981 study by the U.S. Department of Agriculture that showed that per capita food production in sub-Saharan Africa was falling by about 1 percent per year.[2] By the late 1970s per capita food production had fallen to less than 80 percent of its 1961–65 average, and the statistical trend appeared unambiguously on a continuing downward trajectory. Significantly, Africa was shown to be the only one of the world's developing areas where this was the case. In both Asia and Latin America, for example, per capita food production has risen steadily since the early 1960s, and both of these regions are now significant food exporters.

Declining per capita food production is only one dimension of poor agricultural performance in Africa. The most common misunderstanding of the continent's agricultural difficulties is to view the problem in narrow terms as a matter of rebuilding the food sector. This is a regrettable over-

[1] The author is grateful to the Developing Economies Branch of the U.S. Department of Agriculture for this table.
[2] U.S. Department of Agriculture, *Food Problems and Prospects in Sub-Saharan Africa: The Decade of the 1980's* (Washington, D.C.: Economic Research Service, 1981), 2.

TOTAL SUB-SAHARAN AFRICAN GRAIN
PRODUCTION, 1966–85

Year	Production (million tons)		Population (000s)		Percent production (kg)	
	With S.A.	Without S.A.	With S.A.	Without S.A.	With S.A.	Without S.A.
1966	35.776	29.758	273,468	253,201	131	118
1967	44.948	33.331	280,563	259,742	160	128
1968	36.361	29.562	287,952	266,569	126	111
1969	41.299	34.425	295,592	273,631	140	126
1970	41.181	33.244	303,093	280,550	136	118
1971	44.920	34.067	311,197	288,096	144	118
1972	46.463	34.691	319,412	295,740	145	117
1973	38.238	31.953	328,044	303,791	117	105
1974	50.133	36.700	336,819	311,968	149	118
1975	49.279	37.929	345,786	320,316	143	118
1976	48.078	38.174	355,452	329,349	135	116
1977	50.831	38.761	365,523	338,791	139	114
1978	53.488	40.851	375,886	348,518	142	117
1979	50.383	39.531	386,717	358,687	130	110
1980	53.026	40.007	398,068	369,345	133	108
1981	61.822	44.186	409,616	380,170	151	116
1982	53.846	42.691	421,891	391,704	128	109
1983	43.955	37.717	433,808	402,870	101	94
1984	45.297	38.020	445,759	414,061	102	92
1985	60.712	50.407	458,769	426,304	132	118

simplification, for Africa has also performed badly with respect to the production of exportable agricultural commodities. The World Bank has summed up this dimension of the problem in succinct terms:

> By the end of the 1970s, agricultural exports were no greater than in the early 1960s. In fact, a modest rate of increase of 1.9 percent a year in the 1960s was offset by an equal decrease in the 1970s. As a consequence, Africa's share of world trade declined for most of these commodities. While world trade in those commodities exported by sub-Saharan countries grew in volume by 1.8 percent a year, and 3.3 percent in value (constant prices) over the two decades, the growth rates of exports from Africa were zero and 1.8 percent respectively.[3]

The following figures may help indicate the extent of this decline. Between 1970–72 and 1982, Africa's share of the world market for cocoa declined from 80 percent to 65 percent; for groundnuts, from 54 percent to 27

[3] The World Bank, *Accelerated Development in Sub-Saharan Africa: An Agenda for Action* (Washington, D.C.: The World Bank, 1981), 46.

percent; for groundnut oil, from 55 percent to 42 percent; and for palm oil, from 21 percent to 3 percent.[4]

It does not require a sophisticated exercise in the theory of comparative advantage to appreciate the impact of stagnation in the export sector. If Africa had merely been able to maintain its 1960s share of world trade in agricultural commodities, the difference in the level of export earnings would amount to several billion dollars per year. Since food grains have become an abundant and inexpensive item in the contemporary international marketplace, it would have been a relatively easy matter to finance the food imports necessary to make up for domestic shortfalls.

Taken together, declining per capita food production and stagnating levels of agricultural exports constitute Africa's agrarian malaise. The causes of this malaise are by no means simple, and any single-factor analysis is likely to overlook critically important dimensions of the problem. To understand the roots of this malaise, it is useful to distinguish at least four patterns of causality: (1) episodic factors; (2) environmental degradation; (3) adverse aspects of the international economic environment; and (4) inappropriate policy frameworks implemented by African governments.

EPISODIC FACTORS

As the close correlation between civil war and famine in Africa demonstrates, the impact of transitory factors such as domestic insurgency cannot be overlooked. Wars diminish agricultural production not only by disrupting planting, harvesting, the maintenance of infrastructure and the delivery of inputs, but by generating an atmosphere of economic unpredictability and extreme personal insecurity. Civil wars create refugee populations and thereby lessen the number of persons who are productively engaged in agriculture, while at the same time increasing the number of those who are a burden on already fragile food delivery systems. Where agricultural production has already been reduced by the operation of other factors, civil war can make the difference between a crisis and a disaster. As Ethiopia and Mozambique illustrate, civil war is not the cause of poor agricultural performance, but it is the cause of death due to famine.

Drought may also be included in the list of episodic events that have contributed to the poor performance of the agricultural sectors of African countries. Africa has experienced two particularly severe droughts during the past 20 years. The first was the Sahelian drought of 1968 to 1973, which severely affected the West African countries lying along the southern border of the Sahara Desert. The impact of this drought was so severe that it stimulated an outpouring of international assistance to the Sahelian countries and the formation of the Club du Sahel, a multinational donor organization devoted to redevelopment of the region. The second drought, centered closer to the Horn of Africa in Sudan and Ethiopia, occurred between

---

[4]John Sender and Sheila Smith, "What's Right with the Berg Report and What's Left of Its Criticisms?" in *World Recession and The Food Crisis in Africa,* ed. Peter Lawrence (London: James Currey, 1986), 118.

1983 and 1985 and may still be affecting parts of southern Africa, including Botswana and the Republic of South Africa.

The critical question is whether Africa's recent droughts are part of a long-term shift toward a more arid climate. The Sahelian drought was initially interpreted as a unique event, and the resumption of more abundant rainfall in 1974 as a return to "normal" conditions. Climatologists analyzing the 1983–85 drought concluded, however, that the low levels of mean annual rainfall during the 16-year period of 1970–85 were unprecedented in this century, a finding that suggested the possibility that a new, more arid era, was under way. The evidence for this point of view is unpersuasive, however. Historical rainfall data for Africa is fragmentary at best, and much of the case rests on flimsy archaeological evidence about the incidence of drought in previous centuries.[5] The weight of expert opinion views climate change as an extremely gradual process extending over several millennia and one that would, therefore, allow much time for human adaptation (see accompanying maps, Vegetation and Mean Annual Precipitation).

This suggests that the critical factor is not rainfall patterns alone, but rather the interaction between rainfall patterns and changing patterns of human settlement. Africa has experienced massive population growth since the beginning of the colonial era during the last quarter of the 19th century. This population growth is itself the product of numerous factors, most notably the end of the slave trade, generally dated around the 1880s for West Africa and slightly later for East Africa, and, as importantly, the introduction of bioscientific medicine, which drastically reduced infant mortality and has helped extend life expectancy. The result of population growth, however, has been enormous pressure on the continent's high-potential agricultural areas, some of which have begun to experience population densities as high as any in China, India, or Western Europe.

As population has grown, some proportion has been compelled to seek economic opportunity in agriculturally marginal areas, principally semiarid regions where rainfall has always been less in volume and more unpredictable in pattern. In many African countries, agricultural communities have been established in areas that were traditionally occupied only by nomadic pastoralists whose need for water was substantially less and who customarily traveled vast distances in order to find it. Since agriculture has been carried out to a greater and greater extent in drought-prone areas, it is not surprising that drought has periodically had a significant effect on agricultural production. This is to be expected where intensive agriculture is attempted in regions climatically unsuitable for it.

Population growth may also have exacerbated the effects of climatic irregularity by necessitating a changeover from patterns of cultivation that were suitable for low-rainfall conditions to agrarian systems that are dependent upon more abundant rainfall and more predictable patterns of precipitation. Historically, much of African agriculture was carried out on the

[5] The author is indebted to Michael Glantz of the National Center for Atmospheric Research for his assistance on these points.

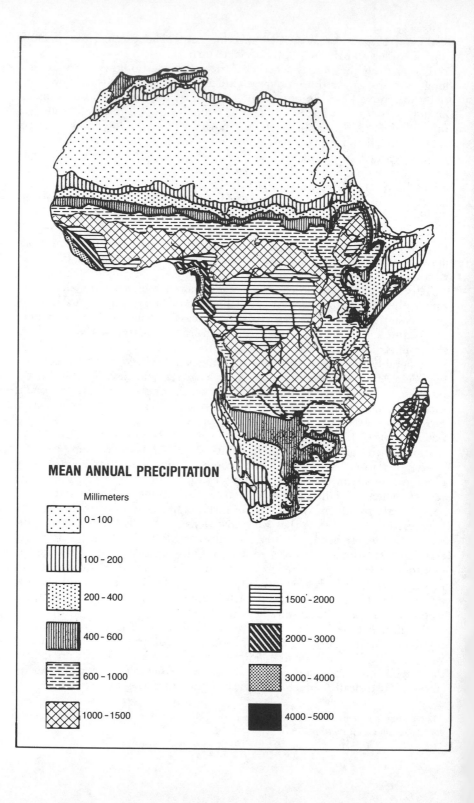

MEAN ANNUAL PRECIPITATION

Millimeters

0 - 100	
100 - 200	
200 - 400	
400 - 600	
600 - 1000	
1000 - 1500	

1500 - 2000	
2000 - 3000	
3000 - 4000	
4000 - 5000	

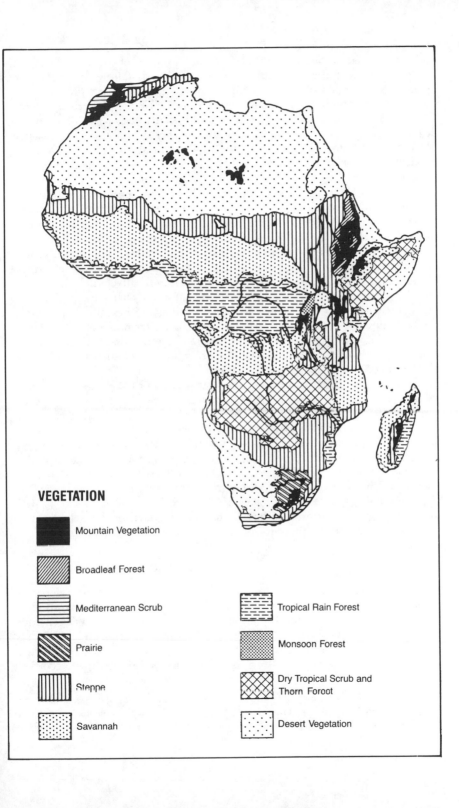

VEGETATION

- Mountain Vegetation
- Broadleaf Forest
- Mediterranean Scrub
- Prairie
- Steppe
- Savannah
- Tropical Rain Forest
- Monsoon Forest
- Dry Tropical Scrub and Thorn Forest
- Desert Vegetation

basis of shifting cultivation. Individual families or localized communities typically carried out agricultural activity in a number of scattered locations, leaving certain of these, as their fertility declined, fallow for fairly long periods. Since much of Africa is highly microclimatic, with growing conditions often varying greatly within very short distances, there was a reasonable chance that even if a drought should occur, one or two of a family's fields would yield a crop. So long as the supply of arable land was fairly plentiful in relation to the population, there was always the possibility of moving to a more distant location if dry conditions continued to prevail in a particular area.

As Africa's population has increased, the escape mechanisms that permitted localized adjustment to drought conditions have been eliminated. Shifting cultivation is now extremely rare inasmuch as, in most regions, there is simply not enough land available to permit significant portions to be left fallow for extended periods; and, more importantly, population growth has increasingly cut off the possibility of cultivating more than a single piece of farmland. If this is located within a drought-affected climatic zone, there is no backup provided by virtue of the family that owns it having other agricultural plots in less-affected locations. It has also become virtually impossible for the vast majority of African farmers even to contemplate moving their farms to regions where drought conditions are not so severe, if for no other reason than that the majority of such regions are in all likelihood already densely populated.

Explanations of agricultural decline that focus on drought alone, without taking these additional factors into account, miss the complexity of the problem. Part of that complexity lies in the fact that rainfall patterns are simply one feature of the physical environment within which agriculture in Africa must be carried on. If it is difficult, on the evidence available, to make the case that Africa's rainfall levels are undergoing a long-term shift in a downward direction, there is compelling reason to believe that other features of the continent's natural environment have, in recent generations, been intensely subjected to processes of physical depletion. There is little doubt that broad patterns of environmental degradation have had a profound effect on the productivity of the continent's agricultural system.

ENVIRONMENTAL DEGRADATION

In searching for explanations for Africa's deteriorating agricultural performance, it is essential to take into account the effects of the continent's rapidly deteriorating physical environment. The relationship between these phenomena, though extremely complex, is now well established.[6] To understand the nature of the environmental constraints on African agriculture, it is useful to begin by dispelling the myth of tropical fertility. According

[6]The analysis that follows owes much to Antoon de Vos, *Africa, The Devastated Continent?* (The Hague: Dr. W. Junk b.v. Publishers, 1975). The author is also indebted to Professors Dean Freudenberger, Claremont School of Theology, and Antony Orme, University of California, Los Angeles.

to this myth, the dense green cover found in many tropical regions is evidence of the rich arability of their soils and of a capacity to sustain lush cultivation of a wide variety of grains and horticultural products. There is even a popular form of racist thought about Africa that asserts that the continent's lack of economic growth is because natural resources are so abundant there is little incentive for human efforts toward further development.

As a factual corrective to this myth, it is useful to recall that Africa's initial physical endowment was not conducive to agricultural development. Although African soils vary greatly in depth and nutrient content, they are generally unsuitable for intensive agricultural production. According to Antoon de Vos, "sandy soils deficient in important elements preponderate over clay and limestone soils and there are proportionately fewer young, rich alluvial soils than on any other continent."[7] The majority of West African soils, for example, are highly weathered, deficient in humus and, because of their claylike character, extremely difficult to cultivate. In many regions of Africa the soils are also highly lateritic and therefore susceptible to the formation of a hard iron pan at levels sufficiently close to the surface as to severely reduce the nutrient uptake of both ground and tree crops. Because of their abrasive effects on iron and steel implements, lateritic soils also present especially severe problems of agricultural management.

With an initially poor endowment, Africa's physical environment has been subjected to a variety of pressures that have resulted in worsening its capacity for sustained agricultural production. The factors that have contributed to environmental deterioration are not difficult to discern. The starting point is the extreme fragility of tropical soils, their high degree of susceptibility to such damaging processes as erosion and leaching. Before the modern era of intensive agricultural production and growing population, African soils were largely protected from these processes by a widespread cover of forests and perennial grasses. The forest cover performed several critical functions. Leaf litter from the trees provided a protective mulch on the surface of the soil, insulating the ground beneath from the baking action of the sun and the bombardment effects of intense tropical rains. As the leaf litter decomposed, it contributed humus content to the subsurface soil layers, and this, in turn, was of vital importance in furnishing nutrients and retaining moisture to sustain plant life. In addition, the root systems of the trees were vitally important in helping to stabilize the soil and retain it in place.

No single process has contributed so greatly to Africa's environmental deterioration as deforestation. It is the result of numerous factors. In many regions of the continent forests were simply cleared away to make room for large-scale plantations devoted to such crops as cotton, tobacco and groundnuts. In other countries, including most notably the Ivory Coast, acute pressure on foreign-exchange reserves has led to massive and unplanned harvesting of the forests as a source of timber for exports. One expert estimates that more than two-thirds of the Ivory Coast's forest has been re-

---

[7] De Vos, 20.

moved for this purpose.[8] Virtually everywhere in Africa, charcoal remains the most common cooking fuel, and this factor as well contributes heavily to the process of deforestation.

In numerous countries the forests are being further denuded by contemporary forms of slash-and-burn agriculture. Madagascar offers an excellent example. Because of the declining quality of the country's existing farmland, peasant farmers clear new areas for cultivation by burning sections of forest. The residual ash provides temporary nutrients, but when the burned areas have lost their fertility, usually after four or five years, the farmers move on to burn fresh areas. It is presently estimated that Madagascar may have lost more than one-third of its forested area to this practice alone. Overgrazing has also contributed to the depletion of Africa's forests, as rural populations, hard pressed to survive on agriculture alone, increase their animal herds as a survival strategy.

The results of deforestation are disastrous. Without protective layers of mulch and humus above and just below the surface of the topsoil, the land has no protection from natural elements. Rainfall, for example, can percolate rapidly through the upper layers of soil, leaching the nutrients down to levels where they are not available for food or export crops. Soils that are directly exposed to the sun become brittle and cracked and are much more susceptible to erosion when rainfall does occur. Without constant replenishment of its humus content, lateritic soil becomes far more prone to the formation of an iron pan layer just below the soil surface, because the more rapid evaporation of rainwater causes the iron to precipitate in solid pieces. More importantly, removal of the principal source of humus contributes directly to the loss of nutrients, thereby triggering additional cycles of forest removal.

The end product of these processes is desertification, the conversion of once arable land to desertlike conditions. This process is most dramatically under way in the Sahel countries, where the southern movement of the Sahara Desert has sometimes been estimated in the magnitude of miles per year. According to a 1987 article in *National Geographic* magazine, desertification in this region has consumed nearly 250,000 sq. miles/647,500 sq. km., an area the size of France and Austria combined, during the past 50 years.[9] Desertification is by no means confined to the Sahel, however. It can be observed in every major region of the continent, including eastern and southern Africa as well. Indeed, desertification is so widespread that its effects are virtually impossible to measure precisely. But the cumulative impact of various processes of environmental deterioration is certainly enormous. If so, Africa's prospects for agricultural recovery are all the more bleak, because the process of environmental decay is seemingly irreversible.

According to one theory, desertification may even have contributed to changing Africa's rainfall pattern, since an area that is vegetated is more likely to receive rain than one that is not. Ellis states the relationship in the following way:

[8] Howard Schissel, "Forest Cover Blown," *The Guardian* (London), 29 April 1981.
[9] William S. Ellis, "Africa's Sahel: The Stricken Land," *National Geographic* (August 1987), 144.

Vegetation blankets the soil—retaining solar heat at night, releasing it during the day. With the normal seasonal monsoon, air containing moisture from plant transpiration rises during the day and condenses to form clouds. With denuded land, no cycle occurs. . . . no clouds form because solar energy is immediately reflected back into space.[10]

If correct, this theory suggests that Africa's droughts are of human origin and emanate from the destructive manner in which human populations have interacted with their physical environment.

The portentous implication of the environmental factor is that it appears to rule out so many frequently suggested solutions to the continent's ongoing agricultural crisis. A readaptation of certain historical forms of agricultural production would be wholly impractical, for example. Traditional agricultural practices would be completely incapable of supporting today's population levels; also, they were dependent upon ecological systems of soil preservation and replenishment that, in many areas, have all but ceased to be a part of the physical environment. Africa's unique environmental problems also cast doubt on the viability of further developing scientifically based agricultural production systems, for these could have disastrous effects on the continent's fragile topsoils and further accelerate the tendency toward desertification. It seems imperative that future attempts to solve Africa's agricultural crisis be based on sound environmental as well as economic principles. Neither the African governments nor donor organizations, however, seem to know exactly how this may be accomplished.

EXTERNAL CIRCUMSTANCES

Declining terms of trade.
A third point of view about Africa's agricultural crisis holds that the difficulties besetting independent Africa's agricultural economies must be understood in terms of the impact of a number of exogenous factors, most notably the adverse features of the international economic system. By far the most commonly cited of the outside economic forces that intrude upon the continent in ways that lower its standard of living and reduce the well-being of its peoples is the terms of trade. Among numerous observers it is virtually an article of faith that Africa has suffered severely from the declining purchasing power of its exportable agricultural commodities vis-à-vis the goods it needs to import, and that this factor alone helps explain the crippling foreign-exchange constraint that seems to be the root of its current economic crisis. For those who emphasize the importance of declining terms of trade, it is axiomatic that the real price levels of Africa's exports have not risen nearly as fast as those of the industrial and other goods it must import, and that this is the basic cause of the continent's inability to finance food imports out of its own resources.

Although a decline in the terms of trade may have been harmful to Africa, especially in recent years, it is important to approach this issue with

[10] Ellis, 145.

great caution, for the economic evidence is by no means unambiguous. One complication is the fact that Africa has failed so dramatically to maintain its earlier share of the world market for critical agricultural exports. In the World Bank's Berg Report, this factor is held to be far more accountable than declining terms of trade for the continent's balance-of-payments difficulties. Analyzing the two decades from 1960 to 1980, the report states the following:

> In brief, past trends in the terms of trade cannot explain the slow growth of Africa in the 1970s because for most countries—mineral exporters being the main exception—the terms of trade were favorable or neutral. . . . The main cause of rising current account deficits and shortages of foreign exchange in the 1970s was not the terms of trade but the slow growth of exports. [11]

To substantiate this position the report presented evidence showing that Africa's agricultural exporters had, in fact, enjoyed a slight positive shift in the terms of trade during the 20-year period between 1960 and 1979.

The World Bank has since modified this harsh position and now acknowledges a substantial decline in the terms of trade of Africa's low-income countries for the first half of the 1980s. According to a more recent report, these countries suffered a fall in their terms of trade of about 14.5 percent between 1980 and 1982, and the continent's middle-income countries sustained a drop of about 11 percent during this same period. [12] The report also states that during this same period the real prices of Africa's non-oil exportable commodities fell by about 27 percent, and that this drop alone caused real GDP for these countries to fall about 2.5 percent. A precipitous drop in Africa's terms of trade after the oil price increase of 1979 was further documented in the bank's *World Development Report* for 1984, which showed that Africa's low-income countries experienced a net fall in their terms of trade of nearly 15.5 percent between 1980 and 1983. [13]

Development economists are now in general agreement that Africa has suffered a serious drop in the international terms of trade since the early 1980s. This is due principally to a continuing decline in the real prices of both mineral and agricultural primary commodities. Between 1984 and 1986, for example, the prices for nonfuel primary commodities fell to record lows. [14] Because of a worldwide commodities glut there is little hope that this downward trend will reverse itself in the near future. Results of this trend have been disastrous. Skyrocketing debt-service ratios, for example, are a direct reciprocal of falling export earnings, as is the continent's paralyzing shortage of foreign exchange. This, in turn, has had all-pervasive economic consequences. It has contributed directly to the low rate of

[11] *Accelerated Development*, 19.
[12] The World Bank, *Toward Sustained Development in Sub-Saharan Africa: A Joint Program of Action* (Washington, D.C.: The World Bank, 1984), 12.
[13] The World Bank, *World Development Report 1984* (New York and Oxford: Oxford University Press, 1984), 25.
[14] The World Bank, *World Development Report 1987* (New York and Oxford: Oxford University Press, 1987), 17.

capacity utilization in the industrial sector, since Africa's industries are almost entirely dependent upon imports of capital goods, spare parts and raw materials to maintain their productivity. More importantly, the scarcity of hard currency has made it all but impossible to stimulate an agricultural recovery, because so many of the needed inputs, including mechanized equipment and chemical fertilizers and pesticides, must also be imported.

Low demand elasticities for agricultural exports
Africa's prospects for economic recovery are also diminished by a second adverse feature of the international economic environment, low demand elasticities for its principal agricultural exports. The relationship between price and demand for agricultural goods on the world market is very different than that for industrial products. In the case of industrial products such as automobiles, consumer electronics or other finished goods, demand generally rises in response to falling prices. As a result, countries that export these items can often expect to improve their foreign-exchange earnings even as the real prices of their exports fall; they can take advantage of more robust demand at the lower price level—a situation of high demand elasticity. Agricultural commodities, on the other hand, are typically characterized by low demand elasticity, i.e., world demand does not generally increase significantly if prices drop. Indeed, world demand may fall dramatically if prices increase.

Countries that are dependent upon the export of primary commodities such as coffee, tea and cocoa are thus in an unenviable position as they seek to remedy their balance-of-payments deficits by increasing their level of exports. They may simply confront glutted markets in which oversupply causes price levels to fall to such a degree that the potential gains from increased export volumes are entirely eroded. Sudan's cotton exports offer an excellent illustration of this phenomenon. One World Bank report summarized the country's plight as follows:

> In Sudan, major changes in macro and sectoral policies have been introduced by the government in recent years to improve cotton production. These policy reforms contributed to a 35 percent increase in output in 1981 and to a further 10 to 20 percent increase in 1982. However, due to a fall in the world market price, the gains which could have been expected . . . have essentially been wiped out.[15]

This phenomenon raises serious doubts about the export-led growth strategy. While any single country might be able to help itself by improving its export levels, this approach would probably not work for agricultural exporters as a group, since increased volumes of any commodity would simply bring about an offsetting drop in price.

This problem of low demand elasticity for agricultural goods is unlikely to lessen in the foreseeable future. Indeed, the factors that are causing

[15] The World Bank, *Sub-Saharan Africa: Progress Report on Development Prospects and Programs* (Washington, D.C.: The World Bank, 1983), 3.

downward pressure on agricultural prices are more likely to intensify between now and the end of this century. One such factor is the widespread introduction of synthetic substitutes for agricultural products. The lowered price level for Sudan's cotton exports, for example, was in part the outcome of the growing use of polyester and substitutes. Many other critically important African exports also compete directly with synthetic alternatives: beverages like coffee, tea and cocoa with soft drinks and processed juices; rubber with several synthetic alternatives; sugar with artificial sweeteners and corn fructose, a substitute manufactured in temperate-zone countries. For still others of Africa's agricultural exports, the prospective availability of inexpensive substitutes is a kind of background threat to any serious prospect of price increases.

A second major cause of the problem of low demand elasticity is the disappearance, in recent years, of some of the world's most important markets for agricultural goods, including India and China. Until relatively recent times (India through the 1950s and China through the late 1970s), both these countries were high-volume importers of a wide range of agricultural commodities. Their participation in the international marketplace as high-demand consumers helped to buoy up a wide range of prices. Within a remarkably short period of time both of these countries have not only attained a marked degree of agricultural self-sufficiency but have emerged in the world marketplace as high-volume sellers. China, for example, is now not only virtually self-sufficient in rice and other grains but, during the past decade, has managed to capture about 15 percent of the world cotton market. Similarly, India is now not only virtually self-sufficient in foodstuffs but, through its low-cost textile industry, an important world exporter of cotton products.

Low demand elasticity for agricultural exports has the most serious implications for the prospect of Africa's long-term economic recovery. Even the best-case scenario is far from optimistic. If Africa were to recapture its former share of world trade in agricultural goods, the impact of this factor is such that the effect of this improvement on the balance-of-payments position of most countries might be negligible. The most likely scenario is much more bleak than this. According to a World Bank study of Africa's future trade prospects, the continent's economic crisis has become so entrenched that it is likely to suffer a continuing decline in world market shares for many agricultural products through the mid-1990s. The author of the bank's study, Shamsher Singh, has forecast that Africa will continue to experience a diminishing share of the world market for such diverse products as cocoa, palm oil, sisal, cotton and rubber.[16] If this should occur, there is virtually no likelihood whatever that agricultural exports will generate sufficient hard-currency earnings to finance needed programs for economic recovery.

[16] Shamsher Singh, *Sub-Saharan Agriculture: Synthesis and Trade Prospects* (Washington, D.C.: The World Bank, 1983), Table 17, p. 48.

INAPPROPRIATE POLICY FRAMEWORKS

The fourth source of agrarian malaise in Africa is the fact that numerous African governments have, since independence, pursued a set of economic policies the long-term effects of which have been adverse to agricultural growth. The most influential formulation of this position may be found in Robert Bates's book, *Markets and States in Tropical Africa*. Bates's work found powerful corroboration, three years later, with the publication of John C. de Wilde's *Agriculture, Marketing and Pricing in Sub-Saharan Africa*. These authors believe that a common feature of agricultural policies in African countries has been an attempt to use the agricultural sector as a source of economic resources to be dispensed elsewhere in the society. In their view, Africa's agricultural crisis is a direct result of the fact that African governments have intervened in rural markets in ways that pose serious constraints on agricultural production.

It would be impossible, in a brief essay, to summarize the various policies that have had this effect. But it may be useful, for illustrative purposes, to select two: currency overvaluation and price suppression.

Currency overvaluation
A policy of great importance in contributing to the present agricultural crisis has been the widespread tendency toward currency overvaluation. The nearly ubiquitous practice of setting official exchange rates at higher levels than would prevail under conditions of free convertibility sets in motion a whole set of powerful disincentives to agricultural production.[17] Currency overvaluation tends to lower the cost of living of urban consumers by cheapening the process of imported goods, including foodstuffs. But it does so by lowering the real return to agricultural commodities. Since the producer price of an export crop is necessarily a function of the conversion rate between foreign and domestic currencies, overvaluation functions exactly like a tax on export-oriented agriculture: the greater the overvaluation (fewer units of local currency per dollar) is, the less the payment, in local currency, to the farmer.

If the policy of overvaluation thus provides a compelling explanation of the tendency toward stagnating export volumes and, hence, of Africa's loss of world market share for agricultural exports, it also provides a partial explanation of the tendency toward declining per capita food production. To prevent farmers shifting from export crops to growing the food staples, African governments must maintain some sort of a ratio between the price levels of exportable commodities and domestically consumed food items. Overvaluation thus indirectly compels governments to lower the prices for food items as well. It also lowers the prices received by food producers in a secondary way, by cheapening the cost of imported goods; including

[17] For one discussion of this process, see Ravi Gulhati, *et al.*, *Exchange Rate Policies in Eastern and Southern Africa 1964–1983*, World Bank Staff Working Papers, no. 720 (Washington, D.C., 1985).

foodstuffs. It has become increasingly commonplace for Western grains, including corn, wheat and rice, to be less expensive in African markets than the same or equivalent items produced by local farmers. To compete in their own markets, African farmers must be prepared to offer their goods at price levels designed to subsidize urban consumers.

Price suppression

By far the most common form of governmental intervention in the agricultural sector is direct regulation of producer prices. In their books on the pricing policies of African governments, both Robert Bates and John de Wilde present convincing evidence that, since independence, African governments have used their authority to set producer prices in ways that suppress farmgate prices to levels far below what they might have been under freer market conditions. De Wilde believes that this policy has had particularly marked effects in regard to food prices.

> Government intervention in the marketing and pricing of food products has probably been marked by the most serious deficiencies. In this field, governments have been caught up in a conflict between the political necessity they have evidently felt to keep food prices lower for urban consumers and the need to stimulate domestic production of food. Reconciliation of this conflict has been virtually impossible.[18]

If de Wilde is correct in asserting that food pricing policy in Africa is typically motivated by the concern of African governments with the political volatility of urban consumers, the implications are disturbing. Since urban coalitions have great potential to threaten the stability of governments whose policies are not to their liking, it may well be extremely difficult for African states to piece together a politically effective combination of social groups favorable to reform of this critical policy area—that is, to increasing producer prices as a means of stimulating heightened domestic production. Short of such a reform, the prospects of a long-term turnaround in the continent's food sector are virtually negligible.

CONCLUSION

It has been the purpose of this brief essay to demonstrate the complexity of Africa's contemporary agrarian malaise. No single-factor explanatory model can even begin to offer an adequate approach to the problem. Nor is it possible, given the state of knowledge at the moment, to assign degrees of weightiness to the various strands of causality. Africa is unlikely to begin to recover economically unless there is dramatic turnabout in the character of its international economic environment. But it seems equally clear that countries that have not adjusted such important policies as currency exchange rates and producer prices, to name only two, would be in no position to take advantage of a more favorable world environment, should one

---

[18] John de Wilde; *Agriculture, Marketing and Pricing in Sub-Saharan Africa* (Los Angeles: Crossroads Press and African Studies Center, 1984), 118.

come into being. There is no simple recipe for agricultural recovery. In a particularly illuminating essay of Africa's agricultural crisis, Jonathan Barker warned against the danger of an analysis that "presents its recommendations as if they were verified applications of an established economic science to a well-understood situation."[19] Though directed against the World Bank's early emphasis on the primacy of inappropriate policies, Barker's structure could easily be taken as a warning against any monistic analysis.

FURTHER READING

Barker, Jonathan, ed. *The Politics of Agriculture in Tropical Africa*. Beverly Hills, California, and London: Sage Publications, 1984.

Bates, Robert H. *Markets and States in Tropical Africa: The Political Basis of Agricultural Policies*. Berkeley: University of California Press, 1981.

Glantz, Michael H., ed. *Drought and Hunger in Africa: Denying Famine a Future*. Cambridge and New York: Cambridge University Press, 1987.

Hansen, Art, and McMillan, Della, eds. *Food in Sub-Saharan Africa*. Boulder, Colorado: Rienner, 1986.

Lofchie, Michael, and Commius, Stephen K. *Food Deficits and Agricultural Policies in Sub-Saharan Africa*. San Francisco: The Hunger Project, 1984.

Mellor, John W., Delgado, Christopher L., and Blackie, Malcolm J. *Africa's Agrarian Malaise: Accelerating Food Production in Sub-Saharan Africa*. Baltimore: Johns Hopkins University Press for the International Food Policy Research Institute, 1987.

[19] Jonathan Barker, "Politics and Production," in *The Politics of Agriculture in Tropical Africa*, ed. Jonathan Barker (Beverly Hills and London: Sage Publications 1984), 13.

AFRICA'S ENVIRONMENTAL CRISIS

JIMOH OMO-FADAKA

INTRODUCTION

THE African tragedy is not simply economic but is essentially ecological and environmental, with all that that implies.

Is Africa being turned into a permanent cripple, unable to stand, let alone move forward, without massive outside assistance? The present crisis, of which famine is only the most dramatic manifestation, should force both Africans and others to face this question head on.

The facts of the crisis are as follows:

- One hundred and fifty million people suffer from chronic malnutrition.
- Thirty million people face actual famine.
- The continent's population in 1984 was 400 million; with a population growth rate of between 2.8 percent to 3.0 percent per year, it will be 800 million by the year 2000.
- Food production fell from 353 pounds/160 kg. per capita in 1970 to 220 pounds/ 100 kg. in 1984 for all Africa. The rate of increase in food production from 1977 to 1980 was 1.5 percent, while (as stated above) the population growth rate was 2.8 percent to 3.0 percent.
- Cereal imports rose from 3.8 million tons in 1965 to 11.0 million tons in 1976 and to 20.0 million tons in 1980, and is still rising.
- Over 80 percent of Africa's rain-fed cropland and rangeland, and 30 percent of its irrigated lands are at least moderately affected by desertification; i.e., they have lost up to 25 percent of their productivity.
- Africa's use of fertilizers (11 pounds/5 kg. per acre; 26 pounds/12 kg. per hectare) is the lowest in the world.
- Africa's 1.754 billion acres/710 million ha. of pastureland (the major source of crops to feed cattle) has shrunk by an estimated 25 percent since 1986.
- Every day, 16,062 acres/6,500 ha. of slightly productive savanna are cleared.
- Over the past century a 93-miles/150-km. belt on the southern edge of the Sahara has turned to desert.
- Africa is losing its tropical forests at a rate of 3.2 million acres/1.3 million ha. per year. The Ivory Coast has lost 70 percent of its forest cover since the turn of the century.

944

Of course, conditions vary from country to country, and even within countries, and attempts are being made by the governments to come to grips with the problem as it relates to the conditions in each country.

Some advances have been made in the last six years. These include the setting up of new institutions (and the strengthening of existing ones) within Africa to help combat desertification, increase awareness of the problem and generate increases in donor assistance. However, despite these developments, the record of success in the fight against desertification is at best mixed.

A few battles have been won, as in Kenya, Lesotho and Senegal, but on the whole the situation cannot be said to be improving. In many countries, especially in the Sahel, including Northern Nigeria, the problem is judged to have become worse in the last six years. This is not an unexpected finding, for even if all the projects attempted in all the countries had been well focused, completed and successful, they would have addressed only a small part of the problem in this short time period.

INTERNATIONAL AND REGIONAL RESPONSES

Within the international community, for at least the last 20 years, there has been an awareness of the problems of drought and desertification due to unreliability of rainfall. Drought has occurred frequently (at an average of 10-year cycles) in recent times and is the underlying cause of most famines in Africa.

Previously, the effects of these droughts was not serious because of the limited population of the rangeland areas, but with population growth and increasing pressure on dry grazing lands, drought is now a serious problem that claims the lives of both livestock and people.

There have been various international and regional responses to the problem of drought and desertification. The major drought of the 1970s in the Sahel led to the setting up of various new agencies or the reorganization of existing ones to study the problem and come up with effective solutions.

At the international level, the first main, key conference was the U.N. Conference on Desertification held in Nairobi in 1977, organized by the U.N. Environment Program (UNEP). It brought together some 500 delegates, including policymakers and scientists from as many as 94 countries around the world.

The delegates unanimously adopted a comprehensive Plan of Action to Combat Desertification (PACD) with a view to arrest the problem by the year 2000. The plan was endorsed by the U.N. General Assembly in 1978.[1] According to the plan, "Desertification is the diminution or destruction of the biological potential of the land, and can lead ultimately to desert-like conditions." Again according to the plan, the status and trend of desertification can be measured by the following indicators:

---

[1]United Nations 1978. *United Nations Conference on Desertification 29th August–9th September, 1977. Round-Up Plan of Action and Resolutions*, United Nations, New York (page 4).

1. Encroachment and growth of dunes and sand sheets
2. Deterioration of rangelands
3. Deterioration of rain-fed croplands
4. Waterlogging and salinization of irrigated lands
5. Deforestation and destruction of woody vegetation
6. Declining availability and quality of groundwater and surface-water supplies

Broadly speaking, the PACD can be summed up under three main headings: national priority measures, general priorities, and the formulation of an improved development plan.

Governments are to set up national machinery to assess and monitor desertification, prepare national plans of action and start such action. They are to cooperate on the wise management of shared resources, especially through six major transnational projects. U.N. agencies, other intergovernmental organizations and nongovernmental organizations are to participate in the plan, and consider its recommendations in their programs.

General priority measures include sound land-use planning, improved livestock raising, improved rain-fed farming techniques, rehabilitation of irrigated lands, environmentally sound management of water resources, protection of existing tree cover, establishment of woodlots, conservation of flora and fauna—with public participation in all measures.

An improved development plan is to include investigating the social, economic and political factors connected with desertification; expanding awareness of desertification and the skills with which to combat it; assessing the economic impacts of settlements and industries on desertification; introducing appropriate measures to control population growth; and improving scientific capabilities and health services.

Four main priorities were also listed for the period 1977–84. These were:

1. Establishment by each government of a national body to assess, monitor and combat desertification, and prepare a national plan
2. Organization of regional workshops and seminars to discuss and coordinate technical activities of the plan
3. Preparation for setting up research, development and demonstration centers for rain-fed cropping, irrigated cropping, livestock and rangeland management, and afforestation/revegetation
4. Organization of the six transnational projects to help coordinate action and allow nations to pool their experiences

UNEP was charged with the follow-up on the implementation of the plan. Part of the 12th Governing Council of UNEP, in May 1984, was set aside to assess seven years of antidesertification efforts. Delegates were told by the executive director of UNEP, Dr. Mostafa Tolba, that the number of people threatened by severe desertification had by then increased from 57 million in 1977 to 135 million, rural population only—or from 80 million to 230 million, urban and rural population combined.

Council delegates were also told that every year 15 million acres/6 million ha. of land continued to be lost lost irretrievably through desertification or because of degraded or desertlike conditions, while the amount of the land reduced to zero economic productivity increased from 49 million to 52 million acres/20 million to 21 million ha. per year.

The most affected areas are the developing countries and especially those belonging to the group of least-developed countries, several of which have suffered from the serious international and economic situation and from adverse climatic conditions. The increasing land deterioration caused by desertification has had severe effects on agriculture and therefore on domestic food supplies, on exports, on the balance of payments and on economic growth.

The Organization of African Unity (OAU) and the Economic Commission for Africa (ECA), have from time to time over the past six years held joint meetings on the general economic situation in Africa. The end result of these meetings was the The Lagos Plan of Action for the economic development of Africa up to the year 2000, published in 1980. So far, very few of the recommendations of the report have been implemented, because of African countries' lack of funds and as a result of poor donor response due to the world economic situation.

Not deterred by this, the OAU and ECA wanted to try again. This time, because of the worsening environmental situation in Africa, the first African Ministerial Conference on the Environment was held in Cairo in December 1985; it was organized by UNEP, in cooperation with the OAU and ECA.

Regional cooperation was high on the agenda, and each minister outlined his country's environmental problems, progress towards solving them and priority areas for action. The ministers adopted a plan of action, the Cairo Program for African Cooperation,[2] which outlined how to stop the misuse of Africa's natural resources and how to work for their rehabilitation in order to solve the continent's food crisis.

Among the main elements of the Cairo Program were the institutionalization of the African Ministerial Conference on the Environment, normally to meet once every two years. A permanent secretariat under the auspices of UNEP, in close cooperation with ECA and the OAU is to be provided. Its brief is to perform the functions entrusted to it by the conference. Committees are to be set up on four areas of priority environmental concern: deserts and arid lands; river and lake basins; forests and woodlands; and seas. These committees would function between the conference sessions. Each committee is to be composed of a small number of African experts who are specialists in the respective priority area, to assist the secretariat to carry out its functions. The conference also proposed that the African Non-Governmental Organizations Environment Network should be represented on each of these committees.

Further, eight specialized regional technical-cooperation networks on environment and ecodevelopment are to be established. These specialized re-

[2] Report of the First African Ministerial Conference on the Environment, Cairo, 16–18 December 1985, UNEP, Nairobi (page 6).

gional networks are in the field of environmental monitoring, climatology, soils and fertilizers, water resources, energy, genetic resources, science and technology, and education and training. The networks are to concentrate their efforts in the first place on:

(a) Adoption of comprehensive soil and water development, and conservation measures in irrigated and rain-fed agricultural areas in Africa
(b) Improvement and protection of rangelands, and the introduction of better rangeland, livestock and wildlife management in Africa
(c) Protection of the existing vegetation, and replanting denuded areas in Africa
(d) Reforestation and the use of alternative energy sources as means of combating desertification

These networks will also assist the conference secretariat, in collaboration with the four committees, in carrying out its functions.

Regional pilot projects are to be set up. All available African skills and experience will be sought in order to apply economically feasible, environmentally sound and socially acceptable solutions to the complex problems of grassroots development, in 150 villages (three per country) and 30 semi-arid stock-raising zones (one in each of 30 countries).

The goal is to assist those 180 communities to become self-sufficient in food and energy within five years, by having the villages and stock raisers themselves utilize local traditional skills and experience. Another objective is to improve conditions in these villages and areas as a way to check the drift to urban centers, with its consequent problems.

Also under the Cairo Program for African Cooperation, a trust fund to finance a Five-Year Plan is to be set up. The fund—estimated to be around U.S. $55 million to 60 million, and to be contributed to voluntarily by African governments—broadly follows the lines of the U.N. Development Program (UNDP) scale of assessment, with a few modifications.

The executive director of UNEP was asked by the ministers to seek additional funding from other sources, such as the World Bank and donor countries, to supplement the resources earmarked from UNDP sources.

In June 1986, the U.N. General Assembly in New York held an emergency session on the critical economic situation in Africa. The main conclusion of the session (no plan of action drawn up) was that the main responsibility for solving Africa's problems lies with African governments, and that the donor countries will help as much as they can without making any financial commitments.

There has recently been, however, a resurgence of concern and reawakened interest among bilateral and multilateral donors concerning the problem of desertification. A major achievement has been the very considerable increase in donor assistance to Africa countries.

Before 1975, development assistance to African countries was about $1.7 billion annually. In 1980, assistance to these countries totaled over $4.7 billion. Within this major donor effort, there has been some focus on issues related to desertification and drought. Out of the total of $4,700 million received in development assistance, an estimated $150 million, or about 3.5 percent, is allocated directly to desertification control. Despite this increased effort, the dearth of financing for antidesertification activities is still a major constraint, however.

Nevertheless, Africa has the potential to recover and end the crisis. There are 544 million acres/220 million ha. of arable land in Africa, of which only 289 million acres/117 million ha. have been sown and harvested. Forty-eight percent of total arable land still lies in reserve.

Some 148.3 trillion cu. feet/4,200 billion cu. m. of fresh water flow out of Africa into the oceans every year. Ten percent of this water would increase Africa's food production by 10 percent over that produced by the 289 million acres of land currently under crops.

The efficiency of wood used for fuel is currently 8 percent to 10 percent; it could be 20 percent to 30 percent. Only 3 percent of Africa's hydroelectric potential has been harnessed. There are 200 million potentially useful draft animals in Africa (horses, donkeys, camels, cattle). If one out of three of these animals was put to work for four hours a day, 13 million units of horsepower per year would be produced.

OVERALL ASSESSMENT

As a result of the various regional and international responses, there has been an increased awareness of the problem of desertification during the 1980s. Analyses of speeches by presidents and senior government officials in African countries, and of their country-planning documents, make it clear that at this level the importance of the problem is understood and is frequently well articulated.

There are shortcomings, however, in the present response. PACD, while recognizing desertification as a global problem that must have a place on the agenda for international endeavors, makes it clear that action against desertification must be carried out by those countries themselves that are now, or are likely to be, affected by desertification.

Because many African countries face chronic budget deficits and have limited financial resources to carry out or keep supporting basic development, desertification control activities are allocated minimal amounts. And immediate financial returns are not as great as those for more conventional development activities. Governments usually have other priorities, such as industrial development, transportation, construction and education, in mind. Grassroots development activities included in most desertification control activities have often taken a back seat in national financial allocation or priorities submitted to donors.

The bodies usually responsible for national plans and financial matters are the ministries of planning and finance, which typically do not place high priority on projects to combat desertification and instead emphasize projects, often in urban areas, that yield early financial returns.

It is therefore essential, in the coming years, to increase the flow of national resources for desertification-control activities in order to reach a threshold where the accumulative positive impact of desertification-control activities can stop, if not reverse, the accelerating degradation of the natural-resources base of these countries.

On the funding side, donor priorities and policies are often reflected in allocations. Most of the countries affected have found it very difficult to interest donors in antidesertification. Many donors have not been prepared to earmark resources for this type of activity, and while allocating large amounts of funds to the countries under review, have stayed with more conventional high-profile projects.

Kenya is one of the few African countries that has succeeded in attracting major donor investments for antidesertification projects. This may be not unconnected with the fact that nationals of donor countries regard Kenya as a paradise for wildlife and game viewing—apart from its healthy climate—which every year attracts them to visit.

At UNEP, the one U.N. organization charged with follow-up on the implementation of the PACD, a special Desertification Control Program Activity Center was set up to oversee and coordinate at the global level, the implementation of the plan of action. Also established to coordinate and promote international efforts in mobilization of resources against desertification was a special mechanism, the Consultative Group for Desertification Control (DESCON). The total financial requirements for implementing the PACD were estimated at $320 million annually in 1980.

Beginning in 1985, DESCON held five sessions at which 62 antidesertification projects were proposed by some of the affected countries. Necessary financial support for 48 project proposals, as presented to the group at the second, third and fourth sessions, came to an estimated $528 million. Only 12 projects were fully financed and seven partially financed, however, through DESCON. Of the $102 million additional funds needed for the full financing of these 48 projects, after commitments by the governments of the affected countries, only $26 million was secured, a success rate of only 25 percent.

Foot-dragging and poor coordination on the part of the donor community in the follow-up on their expressed support for DESCON project proposals is yet another major hindrance to the effective and timely implementation of DESCON projects.

Nevertheless, donor assistance has on the whole been helpful. However, there should be an expanded role for the Desertification Branch of UNEP, UNSO, the European Development Fund, FAO, ODN (UK), UNDP, UNESCO, IFAD, the World Food Program, the Organization for Economic Cooperation and Development, the African Development Bank and the U.S. Agency for International Development; and for the bilateral assistance programs of Canada, Australia, New Zealand, Great Britain, Denmark, Finland, Italy, Norway, Sweden and the Netherlands.

After its first meeting the Cairo Program for African Cooperation set up a permanent secretariat at UNEP's headquarters in Nairobi in August 1986. The implementation of the program started in January 1987, as most of the countries had started contributing to the trust fund.

If desertification control is to be successful, there are certain constraints that have to be overcome. The first is the lack of indigenous professional scientific and technological capability, institutions, infrastructure, equipment, and running costs to engage in research and development (R&D). This restraint is the result of low investment in R&D (only 10 percent of the global R&D expenditure is extended to the less-developed countries), and the decline in investments in real terms over the past 10 years in Africa—mainly due to the economic and environmental crisis. As a consequence, African countries have experienced a massive brain drain of professional scientists and technologists; escalating attrition of skilled R&D personnel; lack of equipment and supplies for R&D; and/or the want of leadership for attracting youth into science and technology.

A shortage of trained manpower exists at all levels, but the middle professional levels appear to have the greatest needs. Professional ecologists, specialists in remote sensing techniques, foresters and water resource managers are still found only in limited numbers in most countries.

Middle-level professionals in these and other fields are numerous, but they are usually not fully trained and have only a few years of practical field experience. It is of vital importance to strengthen basic science education.

The wide range of technical and scientific personnel needed includes laboratory and field assistants; research teams; and experts in law, economics, demography, sociology, urban planning, ecology, geography, geology, soil science, agricultural sciences, hydrology, climatology, remote sensing, statistics and cartography. Education and training should be geared to these various needs.

Where such training is not available locally, arrangements should be made to train the people elsewhere until the required training facilities are established locally.

Education and training is here conceived in its broadest sense: formal and nonformal, conventional and nonconventional. There is the need for public awareness, to inform citizens and pursuade them to cooperate meaningfully and effectively in national programs to combat desertification.

The various national, regional and international responses have not paid as much attention as they should to the question of finance, to strengthening scientific and technical capabilities, and to education and training for desertification control. It is in these areas that intervention is needed urgently.

Finance focused on the full range of desertification activities is still a problem, and will need a special and perhaps differently organized effort in the coming years—as is the case too with the need to strengthen national scientific capabilities in order to generate and apply innovations for the development and management of resources; and with the need for training and education of requisite personnel.

The mass media—radio, television, newspapers, magazines—can play a vital role in the process of transformation, if they are flexible and can respond quickly to the real and varying needs of people in different parts of a country. The mass media perform a nonformal educational role, complementary to that of the formal educational system. Literacy campaigns and training can be carried out via the mass media, which can also be used to introduce new ideas, attitudes, skills and knowledge into the various communities.

FURTHER READING

African Environmental Conference, Cairo, 16–18 December 1985. Nairobi: United Nations Environment Program, 1986.

Ahmad, Yusuf J., and Kassas, Mohamed. *Desertification: Financial Support for the Biosphere.* London: Hodder & Stoughton, 1987.

Land Use Policy (special issue on desertification) 4, no. 4 (October 1987).

Our Common Future. Oxford and New York: Oxford University Press for the World Commission on Environment and Development, 1987.

Voices from the Desert. Nairobi: United Nations Environmental Program, 1985.

Yeager, Rodger. *Africa's Conservation for Development.* Hanover, New Hampshire: African-Caribbean Institute, 1984.

———, and Miller, Norman M. *Wildlife, Wild Death: Land Use and Survival in Eastern Africa.* Albany: State University of New York Press for the African-Caribbean Institute, 1986.

ROAD TRANSPORTATION
IN AFRICA

PETER GUTHRIE

INTRODUCTION

Transportation in Africa is beset by the full range of problems and difficulties facing the continent. National boundaries drawn in colonial times now inhibit trade and communication; infrastructure has been built without the corresponding capacity to maintain it; skill shortages chronically inhibit institutional development; and in some countries all this is compounded by political instability and upheaval.

Transportation, particularly by road, is traditionally perceived as the motor for development; the more ambitious the scheme, the more spectacular is the envisaged growth. The major projects, such as the African east-west highway, the Cape to Cairo route and the premier national schemes, have generally failed to fulfil the expectations of consequent growth. At the same time huge programs of feeder roads in many countries have faltered because of the enormous difficulty of managing such scattered resources. Communications development does not determine the rate of development, but without communications there will be no development. Reasonable physical links in a country are a necessary but not sufficient condition for the economic growth.

The raw statistics on Africa's road infrastructure are startling. Sub-Saharan Africa has a land area of very roughly 18 million square kilometers, and a population of 350 to 400 million. Without regard to quality of road, there is thought to be approximately 1 million kilometers of road, of which 15 percent are paved. For comparison, the United States has only half the area, three-quarters of the population and six times the length of roads, only 15 percent of which are *not* paved. The indicative (weighted mean) Gross National Product per capita for Africa is under U.S. $500; for the United States, it is over $14,000. Whether the relationship between road infrastructure and national wealth is cause or effect, the broad correlation is indisputable.

In the light of these stark figures, it seems natural to seek to promote economic growth by increasing the road network in a country. Without roads it is difficult, for instance, to see how agriculture can progress from

953

subsistence to surplus, and the same applies to the extension of health and education provision. But it is in maintenance and its lack that the process breaks down. Without regular and effective maintenance, any part of a country's infrastructure will decay and become unserviceable prematurely, and capital investment will fail to provide the return on the service allowed for. This means, furthermore, that the debt incurred for the capital outlay will not be covered by the income or benefit from the asset. Roads are no exception to this economic rule. Countries in Africa generally look to external funding for their road construction programs; and even when they finance projects internally, these consume large amounts of scarce foreign exchange. Either way, road programs are assessed critically and roads are built only when their economic feasibility can be demonstrated. Into this feasibility is written an estimate of road life and necessary maintenance inputs. These estimates often prove overoptimistic and the actual life of the roads is generally far less, at least at an acceptable level of service.

The countries in this position are caught in a downward spiral. Faced with a network of substandard roads, road authorities are forced to divert limited resources from periodic, routine and recurrent maintenance to emergency operations to keep roads open. This is because previous lapses in maintenance have resulted in failures. Culverts, for instance, which are not cleared out regularly become blocked, are eventually washed away, and the road is cut; a lack of simple patching of sealed roads may cause major potholes and finally complete washouts; neglect of erosion protection around piers and abutments can lead to the catastrophic failure of bridges. The resources allocated to planned maintenance become hurriedly reassigned to emergency remedial operations. This in turn results in shortfalls in planned maintenance activity which leads to more "black spots" requiring emergency inputs, and so the downward spiral continues.

The tempting response to the perilous state of roads in many African countries is to increase the funds for maintenance or construction. Until relatively recently, it was the policy of the international agencies to give or lend money only for capital investment, arguing, with good logic, that to fund recurrent elements of a country's expenditure would be to increase dependency on external finance. Accordingly, money was largely confined, in the roads sector at least, to construction or reconstruction. Unfortunately, the consequence of this policy was that maintenance was increasingly neglected in favor of more glamorous externally funded construction programs.

There were two largely inevitable results of this process. First, roads were built, not adequately maintained, then rebuilt within only a few years. There is a road in southern Sudan which, in 1985, was being built for the third time in 12 years. Many, of course, have been built just once, merely as temporary arteries of growth, trade and development. The second result was that the number and total length of new roads constructed in some countries exceeded the sustainable network for the economic activity in the countries. Far from having too few roads, several African countries have networks of roads which are too extensive, placing an intolerable burden on the economies.

Maintenance expenditure can be expressed as a percentage of GNP. In the United States, to take the previous example, 0.61 percent of GNP is spent on road maintenance, only twice the arithmetical mean of the percentage expended in sub-Saharan African countries (based, however, on incomplete data). However logical this may be, the actual expenditure is correspondingly less in Africa than in America. In the United States, over U.S. $3,000 per kilometer is spent on maintenance, while a typical figure in Africa is nearer $500 and, in several countries, around $200 (see Table 1).

CASE STUDIES

Road transportation in Zimbabwe

Several African countries have special transportation requirements, and it is worth mentioning some of them. Zimbabwe's position and geography in the continent give rise to some unique problems.

Zimbabwe is being drawn into the war in Mozambique, and its troops are defending the strategic corridor of rail, road and oil links to the eastern seaboard port of Beira, an outlet vital to Zimbabwe's efforts to reduce trade and transport links with South Africa. Looming over Zimbabwe is South Africa's destabilizing presence. Implicated with the rebels in Mozambique and suspected of links with the Matabeleland dissidents, Pretoria is ready to retaliate by means of trade and transport should Zimbabwe apply selective economic sanctions against South Africa.

The boom years of the early 1980s are emphatically over for Zimbabwe. Inflation is running at around 15 percent. Servicing the country's external debt required 32 percent of export earnings in 1987. The tight foreign-exchange position (import allocations in real terms are only 40 percent of peak 1982 levels) have left much of the country's industrial and manufacturing sector in no position to replace aging plant and equipment. At the same time, population growth is running at around 3 percent annually.

Zimbabwe urgently needs to reopen, and keep open, the Beira corridor to give access to seaports independent of South Africa. Twenty years ago, this route carried 4 million tons of goods a year. In 1984 and 1985, this figure fell to 1.4 million tons. The massive international effort announced in 1987 seeks to restore the strategic oil pipeline, railroad and road. If it is successful, Malawi, Mozambique, Zambia and Zimbabwe will reduce their almost total dependence on exporting and importing through South African ports. New troops and maintenance crews are trained to minimize rebel attacks and to effect repairs within hours to keep the route open. Although an isolated and extreme example, this demonstrates the difficulties faced by some African governments in maintaining infrastructure.

Southern Sudan: gripped by war

Civil war has raged with greater or lesser intensity in southern Sudan since 1956. Despite the accord signed in 1973, the hosilities now again cripple the economic life of the region. Indeed, in eastern Equatoria province, in the southeast corner of the country bordering Kenya, Uganda and Ethiopia,

955

Table 1

ROADS AND ROAD MAINTENANCE IN SOME SUB-SAHARAN AFRICAN COUNTRIES

Country	Km. of road	Km. per 100 sq km.	Maintenance expenditures as % of GNP	GNP per capita	Expenditure per km. ($)	Maintenance expenditure per capita ($)	Km. per 1,000 population	Population density	Paved roads as % of total
Benin	7,200	4	0.3	250	240	0.6	2	30	11
Botswana	18,000	3	0.8	480	370	8	21	1	6
Burkina Faso	11,000	4	0.3	180	260	0.5	2	20	8
Burundi	3,000	10	0.4	180	870	0.6	0.8	142	10
Cameroon	59,000	12	0.3	560	247	1.8	4	17	4
Ethiopia	40,000	3	0.4	130	410	0.5	1.3	25	8
Gambia	3,100	27	1.2	180	390	2.2	6	48	9
Ghana	31,400	13	0.15	400	220	0.6	3	47	15
Guinea	13,300	5	0.15	280	170	0.4	2.5	22	8
Kenya	51,000	9	0.4	380	470	1.6	3.3	26	9
Lesotho	3,450	11	0.4	340	570	1.5	2.7	43	7
Malawi	13,300	14	0.2	200	260	0.6	2	140	18
Liberia	7,300	7	0.2	500	220	0.9	4	16	5

Mali	13,200	1	0.3	140	230	0.4	2	5	12
Mauritania	7,000	0.7	0.3	320	230	1	4	1.5	7
Niger	11,000	0.9	0.3	270	445	0.9	2	4	12
Rwanda	6,300	24	0.18	200	280	0.35	1.3	188	6
Senegal	13,750	7	0.5	430	370	0.9	2.5	28	21
Somalia	17,700	3	0.2	130	54	0.3	5	6	8
Swaziland	2,700	16	0.6	600	610	3.3	5	29	8
Tanzania	45,000	5	0.5	260	540	1.4	2.5	19	7
Togo	7,400	13	0.45	350	510	1.6	3	42	22
Zaire	145,000	6	0.3	250	150	0.8	5	12	1.5
Zambia	35,000	2.5	0.3	500	230	1.5	3	7.5	13
Zimbabwe	85,000	22	0.8	470	350	4	12	18	14
Average	—	5	0.39	—	350	1.1	3.5	—	—
Britain	351,000	153	0.5	6,320	5,250	33	6	228	96.4
West Germany	482,000	194	0.27	11,730	4,062	32	8	245	87

Source: G. A. Edmonds and J. J. Deveen, *Road Maintenance: Options for Improvement*, Geneva: International Labor Office, 1982.

the government has been unable to service infrastructure, health or education on anything like an adequate level. International agencies such as Norwegian Church Aid (NCA) have given considerable assistance. Although there is now a reasonable network of main roads in easter Equatoria thanks to the NCA program, the real cost has been enormous.

Tanzania

Unstable government has certainly not been a problem for Tanzania. Julius Nyerere was president from 1961 to 1985; even in semiretirement as chairman of the ruling party, he continues to influence government policy. Tanzania's development has been obstructed rather than assisted by its doctrinal stance. Several aid donors have selected the country as a model for ambitious and often grossly inappropriate projects. The British government's massive program for groundnut production in the late 1940s set the scene for subsequent schemes that owed more to extravagant hope than sustainable development.

China's railway from Dar es Salaam to Zambia, the Tanzam line, was completed over a decade ago but the line works at all only because almost a thousand Chinese engineers and technicians still operate it, and it receives special support from several developed countries.

Tanzania's agricultural policies, including collective farms and cooperatives, have been failures. The economy had been in decline for years when, in 1986, the International Monetary Fund's conditions for a financial rescue were accepted by President Mwinyi, newly installed. Floating the currency, easing restrictions on foreign transactions, and dismantling some of the national corporations have encouraged foreign trade, revived the failing cotton export industry, and allowed more goods into shops throughout the country.

The challenge now is to revitalize Tanzania's infrastructure. The World Bank's current sixth highway project is only part of the massive amount of money needed to get the country's transportation network into adequate condition. It is not merely a question of producing roads of useable standard. The revitalization of the nation's road network needs to address the question of whether the existing lengths of road of primary, secondary and tertiary standard are in fact needed—not whether they are sufficient. There would be no point in rehabilitating roads for which there is neither money nor sufficient institutional capability to maintain. In countries across Africa, external aid is being pumped into rehabilitating roads whose reopening is expected to spur development. Not enough is being done to nurture the institutions back to health so that they can oversee the useful life of the roads and maintain them to an adequate standard. These institutional difficulties in Tanzania, as elsewhere, are deeply rooted and cannot be solved in isolation: skill shortages, for instance, are both a national and a continent-wide problem. Salary levels in government departments in many countries have fallen far behind private-sector and international opportunities. This virtually imposes corrupt practices on the incumbents in road maintenance departments who may earn the equivalent of as little as U.S. $100 a month. At the same time, prices of basic commodities spiral upward as the national currency is allowed to float toward a realistic level against hard currencies. Training and improved secondary and tertiary education would help, but not alone. Once trained, engineers urgently needed in government departments must have the support, the salaries and the prospects to keep them in place.

TRANSPORTATION: ALL ROAD AND RAIL?

International agencies such as the World Bank, the African Development Bank and others, in talking about overland transportation, are invariably referring to roads or railways as the means. Natural though this is, some important work commissioned by the International Labor Office has shown that in rural areas the great majority of journeys are on foot. The findings of one study in rural Tanzania showed that for the sizable community in question, 98 percent of all journeys involving carriage of goods were on foot. These journeys represented the necessary activities for daily living: fetching and carrying water and fuelwood, carrying grain to and from the local mill, and carrying exportable goods to the collecting points for vehicles.

At first sight, such pedestrian journeys do not seem to have any impact on the potential for a country's growth. They also seem largely independent of the issues facing planners who decide on the necessary roads in a region. However, journeys on foot are often made over difficult routes and over long distances. As a result, journey times for daily activities are frequently several hours. If people spend eight hours a day on survival, there is little opportunity for any real progress. The priority is to reduce these pedestrian journey times before improving the lot of the motorized traders, who represent the next level up in the economic life. In other words, more accessible water and fuelwood, or alternative sources of energy, are prerequisites for progress.

One aspect of making water more accessible, apart from making more water points (either wells or springs) available, would be to improve the tracks to the water sources. Providing footpaths in countries like Nepal, where terrain is severe, is not uncommon, but similar provision on an institutionally organized basis is rare in Africa. While the vast open spaces of the African plains do not require the elaborate engineering of suspension footbridges, much could be done to reduce journey times for people on foot. Such measures include cutting grass, which may be higher than a person and infested with tsetse fly, snakes, and so on, clearing ways through thorn bush and scrub, removing boulders where these present an obstruction, and providing pathways down steep inclines.

Many thousands of kilometers of road in Africa were originally built with vehicles in mind, but their greatest contribution to the surrounding communities has been the pedestrian access provided. If pedestrian traffic had been originally perceived as their primary function, they could have been built at a fraction of the cost and, more significantly, they could have followed the route best suited to foot travel rather than having to be constrained by the much more demanding standards imposed by motor traffic.

ROADS: STANDARDS OF DESIGN

A massive program of road building and rehabilitation is needed throughout the countries of sub-Saharan Africa. In countries where large areas of agricultural land remain inaccessible, new roads are needed to provide the conduit for economic growth. In many more cases, existing roads have deteriorated to a point where they can no longer be maintained without reconstruction.

The key features of road design standards are vertical alignment, horizontal alignment, cross section of the road, and drainage. These features are all geared to a national design speed, an indicator of comfortable traveling speed along the road. The vertical alignment is the design of the rise and fall of the road; in design standards there are, necessarily, maximum gradients imposed—a road may not climb at a steeper grade than that limit. The horizontal alignment is the design of the bends in the road; design standards stipulate the minimum radius of the road's curvature, which determines the sharpness of the worst allowable corner. The cross section of the road defines its width (carriageway and shoulders) and the camber, as well as the materials used and their density and strength. The drainage covers the side drains running parallel to the road, their size, shape, depth, lining and so on, as well as the cross drainage (culverts, fords, bridges) in terms of their sophistication and frequency of placement along the road. Road design requires many more factors than these to be taken into account, but these are the main elements.

Traditionally, in developing countries and almost universally in Africa, design standards for roads have been taken from standards in use in Europe and America and adapted only insofar as is necessary to cater for local tropical or subtropical conditions. For primary roads, and for secondary roads with high traffic levels, this is not an unreasonable approach. A road needs to have a certain strength, drivers need minimum safety and comfort levels, and vehicles have the same turning radii in Europe and Africa.

But most African roads are not primary or well-trafficked secondary roads; they tend to be low-volume roads on the secondary and tertiary networks. Hundreds of thousands of kilometers of roads have traffic levels below 50 vehicles per day. Many carry less than 10 or even 5 vehicles daily. Below about 50 vehicles per day, the validity of extrapolated design standards breaks down. It is foolish to design a road to geometrical standards with design speeds of 40 or 50 km/h when only 50 trips are made on the road in a week. The imposition of such standards means the road will be uneconomical to construct and impossible to maintain.

For very low-volume roads new approaches are needed. If access to an area is required, the need for vehicular access should first be established. The maximum acceptable journey time to a more major road should be realistically assessed, along with the requirements for seasonal and year-round access. If, for example, a road 20 kilometers long is needed to allow cash crops to be exported from a fertile area, the trucks may need to be sure of completing the journey in less than two hours so they can reach the area from the market and return in one day.

960

The constraint on the road's geometry is then the realistic one, not one based on some national design speed. The steepest grade should be that which a truck can negotiate without danger; the sharpest corner should allow a truck to negotiate it without reversing; the camber should be steep enough to drain the road efficiently without presenting a hazard by being too severe; the road's width should allow two trucks to pass, if that is likely to be a common occurrence, or there should be passing places if not; the cross-drainage should be largely fords, unless access is critical during rains. In other words, road design should be user-driven, not imposed by a hierarchy of standards and constraints invalid for low-volume rural roads.

In Britian, indeed throughout Europe, are many thousands of kilometers of roads that do not conform to the national standards in force because they follow old cart-tracks which would be too expensive to widen or straighten, or because they are too steep and the volume of traffic does not justify the earthworks needed for improvement, or because they are too narrow and widening would entail excessive disruption or land acquisition. In the highlands of Scotland, for example, single-track roads are commonplace. It seems unrealistic to impose higher standards on roads for countries far less able to pay for the extra capital or maintenance costs involved.

Road design standards almost invariably presuppose that the method of construction will be by mechanical means. Two examples will make this point. First, earthworks and haulage along the route of a new road are efficient operations by machine. Design takes this into account—larger cuts and fills are preferred to a route which may be longer but which minimize earthworks by following the terrain more closely. Second, cross-sectional shapes of roads are designed to suit the output of graders—ditches are usually gradual slopes which can be formed by the grader blades rather than more well-defined geometrical shapes suited to manual methods.

CHOICE OF TECHNOLOGY IN ROAD PROJECTS

For too long, labor-based methods have been assumed to be applicable only to roads where traffic is light and where access is the only requirement. Labor-based methods have been largely confined to those roads which would not have received attention from a governmental roads department in any case. Changing this view will be a difficult, slow process. Politicians and economists will be among the first to be converted, but convincing the great majority of engineers that manpower is a serious alternative to scrapers, dozers and graders will require a dramatic transformation in attitude. Manpower is viewed here not in terms of its social benefit or moral advantage, but as an efficient, versatile and readily available resource requiring only management and a change of design approach to provide a serious alternative to heavy equipment.

Studies of manual methods have produced a system of dividing construction work into a series of tasks, which are then subdivided into activities. Examples of tasks are road formation, graveling and bridge construction; examples of activities are excavating soil, loading gravel, mixing concrete and hauling aggregate. Activities are simple, repeatable operations comparable from one site to another. Estimation and on-site control can thus be implemented, and laborers can see that the work they are given to do is consistent from day to day. An unskilled workforce is better suited to work arranged so that each laborer has a single function to perform. Even so, the term *unskilled* is misleading. Every construction activity, whether excavating with pick and shovel, loading gravel on to a trailer or truck, or mixing concrete by hand requires technique and ability. This can be demonstrated by the increase in productivity during the early stages of a new labor-based project as the laborers develop simple systems and methods to achieve daily tasks.

Manual methods are obviously better suited to some activities than others. One inherent disadvantage of labor is its inability to be highly energy intensive, and compaction of materials is an energy-intensive operation. Clearly there are ways of achieving a degree of compaction by hand, and animal-drawn smooth- and square-wheeled rollers can give good results, but in general the compaction is less than that achieved by mechanized equipment. Excavation of soil and weathered or fractured rock is amenable to manual methods. Excavation of solid rock is more marginal, although for limited volumes excavation by hand is quite feasible. Mixing of concrete can be done manually, but for high-strength structural concrete manual methods are not efficient because the low water content required makes mixing by hand very difficult. Haulage of materials is more complex. The relative efficiencies of manual haulage is efficient only over relatively short distances up to 200 meters. Simple animal haulage can be competitive up to perhaps two kilometers; beyond this only mechanical methods (tractor-trailers, truck) can be considered. Table 2 summarizes the activities and the suitability of manual methods to accomplish them. The relative strengths and weaknesses of labor and equipment should also be considered (see Table 3). Equipment is not best suited to countries with shortages of foreign exchange and lack of skilled mechanical ability. Also, where labor wage rates are high (more than about U.S. $7 per day) labor is not generally competitive with equipment. Where high-quality finishes are required on large projects, equipment-intensive operations are efficient and effective. However, the more often labor rates fall below the break-even level, the more labor-based methods become competitive, always given that the requisite quality is achieved by employing the right equipment for the required finish. Labor-based programs are well suited to remote projects where backup in the form of spares and fuel would be difficult or expensive. The social benefits of labor-based programs are obvious but continue to be overlooked, because their benefits accrue to a sector of society with almost no lobbying power.

The choice has been so far presented as a clear one between labor and equipment, but this is misleading. Labour-based projects can be thought of as those using labor as a power source in a constructive and well-managed way instead of as a necessary evil. But a labor-based technology does not need to exclude equipment. The *appropriate* technology should be used; this will almost always be a mixture of labor-intensive techniques and mechanical methods. The idea of labor-based programs sometimes conjures up

962

Table 2
MANUAL, ANIMAL AND MECHANICAL SUITABILITY
FOR ROAD-BUILDING ACTIVITIES

Activity	Manual			Animal	Mechanical
	Very suitable	Suitable in some cases	Not effective	Suitable	Cannot be done
Bush clearing	•				
Excavation of soil	•				
Excavation of weathered rock	•				
Excavation of rock		•			
Loading/Unloading	•				
Hauling up to 200 meters	•				
Hauling up to 2,000 meters			•	•	
Hauling more than 2,000 meters			•		
Spreading	•				
Watering	•				
Compaction			•	•	
Mixing mass concrete	•				
Mixing structural concrete			•		
Masonry/stone pitching/stone paving	•				•
Aggregate production		•			
Spray and chip surface dressing		•			
Premix surface dressing			•		

images of small-scale projects undertaken by a local communities with inadequate technical support, which achieves poor-quality, ineffectual results. But labor-based methods can and should be applied to full-scale engineering projects. To do so requires an understanding of what labor can achieve and how to amend design and contract procedures to neutralize those factors militating against labor in conventional projects. Taking road projects as an example, Table 4 presents the suitability of various degrees of labor input in labor-based programs for projects of different types.

Design has developed, naturally, in line with available technology and current practice. Hence almost all road design now assumes an extensive use of equipment. Those operations in which equipment is inefficient are modified to suit these capabilities. For instance, if frequent changes in subbase material thickness are indicated by the design, the engineer will usually reduce the number of changes of thickness, because the additional cost of materials will be offset by a more efficient use of the plant. Such a choice

Table 3
ABILITIES OF MECHANICAL EQUIPMENT VS.
MANUAL LABOR IN ROAD BUILDING

Mechanical equipment

For	*Against*
High output/unit	Highly capital intensive
High quality finish	Requires foreign exchange
Accepted practice	Requires high-tech supervision
Familiar to engineers	Does not use local skills
Familiar to clients	Requires fuel brought to site
Avoids labor problems	
Generally single-function	

Manual labor

For	*Against*
Divisible into small units	Requires effective management
Versatile, multifunction	Innovative
Selective, nonwasteful	Not suited to some activities
Comes to site ready-fueled	May cause trouble
No spares/maintenance	May be seen as second best
Very low capital outlay	Critically dependent on wage rate
Cash enters local economy	
Uses locally available skills	
Provides employment	

would generally be made with no detailed cost comparison because the awareness of equipment's potential is so much a part of an engineer's training. To take another example, on rural secondary roads with moderate traffic, conventional high-level bridge design would be the engineer's instinctive response to river crossings. Such a design would undoubtedly comply with accepted standards and would use proven methods and materials. It would be most unusual for the engineer to question the necessity of 365-day-a-year access, or to consider a bridge design that might be submerged for no more than a few hours in a year. Few road or bridge designers ever inquire about the locally available skills for a proposed project.

Against this background of accepted practice, the engineering of projects to suit labor-based methods obviously threatens many sacred cows. The process, however, is simple: designing to suit labor-based methods requires the engineer to match as far as possible the construction operations to tasks for which labor is suitable and to minimize those operations where equipment would have to be used. As seen in Table 2, haulage over 200 meters should be minimized and geometric design can be amended to accommodate this. Compaction generally is inevitable and equipment must be used to achieve adequate results. Structural concrete cannot be properly mixed by hand, but designs can be changed to use masonry and mass concrete.

964

Table 4
SUITABILITY OF LABOR BY PROJECT TYPE

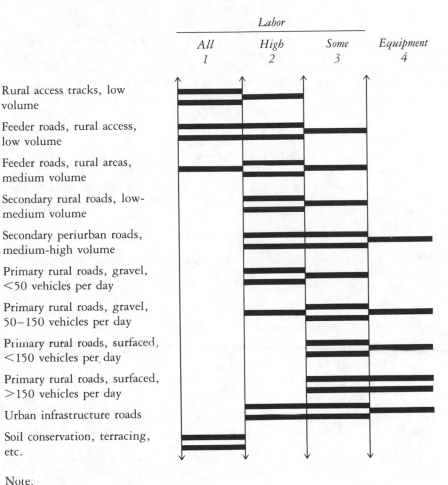

Note:
1 = All labor, no equipment
2 = High labor, simple equipment
3 = Labor-based, some equipment
4 = Equipment-based

▬▬▬▬▬   very suitable

▬▬▬▬   marginally suitable

Such design changes, far from requiring less engineering expertise, in fact require of the engineer imagination, innovation, and fundamental understanding well in excess of that called for on conventional design.

Producing designs amenable to labor-based methods entails first considering what activities such methods are best suited to, then designing the project with these in mind, while at no time compromising the quality actually required. Where a certain result is required and labor cannot effectively or efficiently produce it, equipment must be introduced. The mix of labor and equipment on any job will depend on the standard of product required. For normal-access tracks carrying fewer than 10 vehicles a day, no equipment at all would be required. For feeder or secondary roads, trucks or tractor-trailer combinations might be necessary to haul gravel, and rollers would be required. For primary roads and highways, considerable plant and equipment would be needed. But operations efficiently done by labor could remain as manual operations, and the project could remain as a labor-based operation.

FURTHER READING

Allal, M., *et al.* "Development and Promotion of Appropriate Road-Construction Technology." *International Labor Review 116* (September–October 1977): 183–95.

————.*Manual on the Planning of Labor-Intensive Road Construction.* Geneva: International Labor Office, 1977.

Costa, E., *et al. Guidelines for the Organization of Special Labor-Intensive Works Programs.* World Employment Program Research Working Papers. Geneva: International Labor Office, 1977.

Coukis, Basil. *Labor-Based Construction Programs: A Practical Guide for Planning and Management.* Oxford and New York: Oxford University Press for the World Bank, 1983.

Edmonds, G. A. *The Institutional Aspects of the Construction Industry in Developing Countries.* World Employment Program Research Working Papers. Geneva: International Labor Office, 1980.

Lal, Deepak. *Men or Machines.* Geneva: International Labor Office, 1978.

McLeary, W. A., *et al. Equipment versus Employment.* Geneva: International Labor Office, 1976.

Phan-Thuy, Nguyen. *Cost Benefit Analysis of Labor-Intensive Public Works Programs.* World Employment Program Research Working Paper. Geneva: International Labor Office, 1978.

PART THREE

SOCIAL AFFAIRS

AFRICA'S POPULATION

JOHN I. CLARKE

AMONG the many problems besetting the continent of Africa, not least are those concerning the growth, structure, distribution and redistribution of population. The continent is experiencing the most rapid population growth rates of all the world's regions, having made much less progress than other regions in demographic transition from high to low birth and death rates. Although there are regional variations in demographic transition within Africa, the continent as a whole now lags well behind other parts of the so-called Third World, or developing world, much of which by the middle of the 20th century had rates similar to those of Africa. Furthermore, the rapid growth rates are increased by youthful age structures and by the severe economic and political problems prevailing in many parts of the continent, which provoke large-scale migrations of workers and refugees. Also, population distribution is becoming ever more uneven because of rapid urbanization. The population problem, therefore, has varied aspects.

POPULATION SIZE

Although it incorporates 22.3 percent of the world's land area, Africa does not contain one of the major concentrations of humanity. With 580 million people in 1987, it has only 11.7 percent of the world's population—more than Europe (excluding the USSR) but only a little over half the population of China and three-quarters that of India. This contrasts, however, with 222 million people in 1950, just 7.8 percent of the world's population, and with a projected total of 869 million at the end of the century, when Africa will probably contain 14.2 percent of the world total. In short, although not densely inhabited, it comprises a rapidly growing proportion of humanity.

One of the ironies of Africa is that although it experienced very early human habitation, it never witnessed large concentrations of population until the 20th century. The reasons are manifold and include a variety of environmental and human factors. Certainly, large areas of the continent have not been favorable to the emergence of dense populations of peasants, as known in China, India and Europe; the Nile valley is of course a notable exception. Vast expanses of desert, semidesert, savannas, clay plains and tropical forest lent themselves more to pastoral nomadism, hunting and

969

gathering, and slash-and-burn agriculture than to sedentary cultivation; consequently there were low densities of population and only limited and localized development of urban settlement. Difficulties of climate, vegetation and soils have long provoked drought, flood and famine; and these disasters have been exacerbated by diseases such as malaria, sleeping sickness, yellow fever, schistosomiasis and river blindness, which have wreaked further ravages upon human population growth.

Among the many human factors restricting growth is the persistence of an enormous number of different peoples with distinct languages, customs, traditions and economies, especially in the vast zone of cultural fragmentation stretching from Senegal through West Africa, western central Africa and southern Sudan to Ethiopia. The cultural complexity of Africa is reflected in the fact that some 2,000 languages have been identified, some widespread (e.g., Swahili, Arabic, Hausa), others local dialects. Such ethnic diversity was associated with relatively closed subsistence economies in the past, and with intertribal conflicts and warfare. Undoubtedly, these conflicts were used to the advantage of the slavers from the Arab world and Europe who caused such demographic disaster to so many black African populations, particularly in the above-mentioned zone of cultural fragmentation. Moreover, the situation was not alleviated by the early impact of European colonizers, whose conquests and diseases were to lead to much loss of life in all parts of the continent, from Algeria to South Africa. Obviously, the introduction of the modern sector in the 20th century, with the growth of mines, industries, communications, cities and ports, as well as considerable, though uneven, improvements in medicine, sanitation, hygiene and nutrition, has done much to offset the earlier impact, and has contributed markedly to the upsurge of population.

POPULATION GROWTH

Africa's population growth rate is currently about 2.9 percent per year; that is to say, it will double in about 24 years. For purposes of comparison, the average growth for the world as a whole is 1.7 percent, for the less-developed countries 2.0 percent, and for the more-developed countries 0.6 percent, so it can be seen that Africa is exceptional. Naturally, the situation is not the same everywhere; indeed, the range is very wide: from 1.5 percent in Mauritius, and other low rates in Indian Ocean islands like Réunion and the Seychelles, to 4.1 percent in Kenya, which has probably the most rapid growth rate in the world (Map 1). No African region has yet managed to reduce its population growth rate to lower levels, as has been done in China, Taiwan, Korea, Hong Kong and Singapore. Indeed, only a handful have annual growth rates less than 2 percent (Guinea-Bissau, Mauritius, Réunion, Saint Helena and the Seychelles).

Before embarking on an explanation of the rapid population growth, it should be emphasized that in Africa data on population is generally much less profuse than elsewhere. With a few noteworthy exceptions (in Egypt, Algeria, Tunisia, South Africa), the gathering of population data is recent, particularly in tropical Africa, and often does not involve universal enu-

970

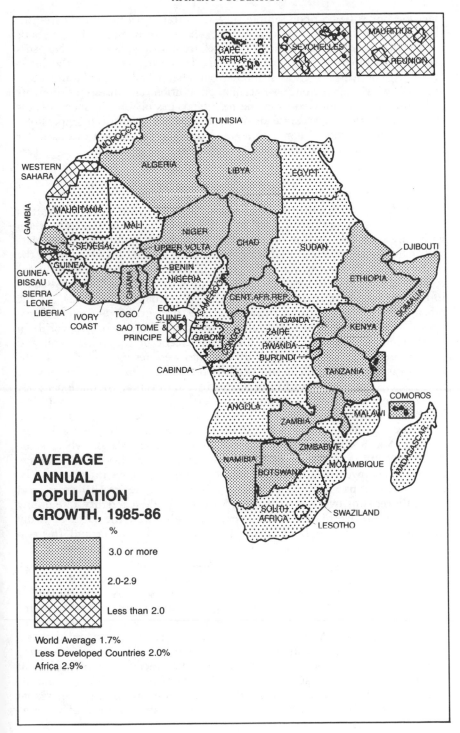

**AVERAGE
ANNUAL
POPULATION
GROWTH, 1985-86**

%

3.0 or more

2.0-2.9

Less than 2.0

World Average 1.7%
Less Developed Countries 2.0%
Africa 2.9%

meration but is based upon sample surveys. Vital registration data are usually far from complete, and consequently a series of demographic methods have been devised to determine vital rates from inadequate data. Not surprisingly, population rates and ratios are least satisfactory for the least-developed countries, such as Ethiopia, Somalia, Chad, Uganda and Mozambique, which, apart from poor economic conditions and disastrous droughts and famines, have suffered from the recent ravages of war. In such circumstances, collection of accurate demographic data is well-nigh impossible. Consequently, it should not be imagined that the population estimates for African populations (Table 1) have a high degree of reliability.

HIGH POPULATION FERTILITY

It is quite apparent, however, that the rapid population growth in Africa since mid-century has been caused by sustained high fertility in comparison with only a modest decline in mortality—the result being substantial natural increase. Birth rates in Africa have remained high, the average for the continent in 1985 being about 46 per 1,000, compared with a world average of 27. Comparison of average birth rates for 1960–65 and 1980–85 in the various world regions is particularly illuminating (Table 2). As the other regions have decreased their birth rates to a greater or lesser extent, Africa is accounting for an increasing proportion of births in the world. In 1970, Chinese births accounted for 19.0 percent of the world total and African births 13.9 percent; by 1985 the roles were reversed, African births accounting for 19.5 percent and Chinese births 12.6 percent. Africans are now responsible for one in five of all births, and even at the national scale the continent stands out with almost uniformly high birth rates; in 1980–85 some 30 countries had birth rates of 45 or more per 1,000, and 42 countries had 40 or more per 1,000, the only exceptions being Egypt, Tunisia, South Africa, Gabon and the Indian Ocean islands where some decline results from family planning programs and socioeconomic change (Map 2). The average number of children born to women in most of sub-Saharan Africa has not fallen substantially during the last 30 years, and generally remains over six. In Kenya, with the highest fertility rate of any country in the world, it is just over eight, although the rates of many Muslim countries like Bangladesh, Pakistan, Saudi Arabia and the two Yemens are over seven per woman.

Factors influencing high fertility in Africa are numerous. Early marriage of women is particularly important; for example, in Kambia district in Sierra Leone in the 1970s, 38 percent of girls were married by the age of 13, 55 percent by 14, and 71 percent by 15. Early marriage is more prominent in rural areas than in towns, but everywhere a high proportion of women are married. Moreover, recent fertility surveys have revealed that a striking majority of women want more children, even among the relatively few who practice modern contraception. The uncertainty of successful childbearing because of sterility, the high rates of infant and child mortality, and the fear of divorce mean that many women abstain from sexual relations until their latest-born child has been weaned, a form of self-reg-

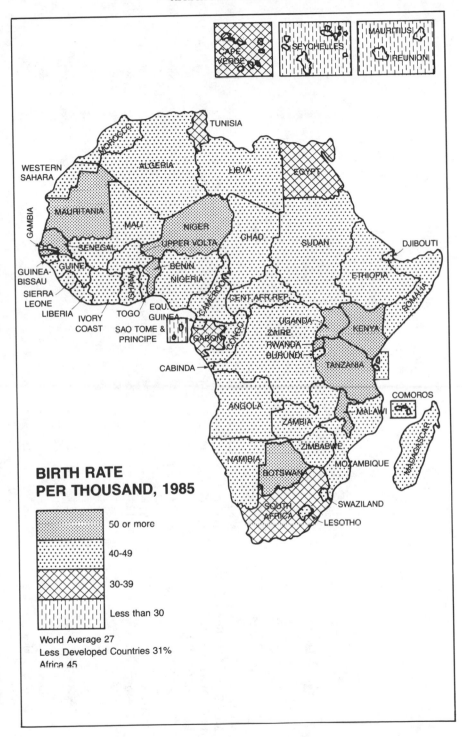

**BIRTH RATE
PER THOUSAND, 1985**

50 or more

40-49

30-39

Less than 30

World Average 27
Less Developed Countries 31%
Africa 45

Table 1
THE POPULATION OF AFRICA

	Population estimate mid-1985 (millions)	Crude birth rate	Crude death rate	Natural increase (annual, %)	Population doubling time (at current rate)	Population projected to 2000 (millions)	Population projected to 2020 (millions)	Infant mortality rate	Total fertility rate	% Under age 15/over age 64	Life expectancy at birth	Urban population (%)	Per capita GNP (US $)	Total area (000 sq. miles)/ percent cultivated
WORLD	4,845	27	11	1.7	41	6,135	7,760	81	3.7	35/6	62	41	$2,760	51,720/11
MORE DEVELOPED	1,174	15	9	0.6	118	1,271	1,351	18	2.0	23/12	73	72	9,380	21,344/12
LESS DEVELOPED	3,671	31	11	2.0	34	4,863	6,409	90	4.2	39/4	58	31	700	30,375/10
LESS DEVELOPED (Excl. China)	2,629	36	12	2.4	29	3,666	5,121	101	5.0	41/4	56	34	880	26,670/10
AFRICA	551	45	16	2.9	24	869	1,433	110	6.3	45/3	50	31	750	11,716/6
Northern Africa	128	41	12	2.9	24	190	282	97	6.0	43/4	56	42	1,190	3,291/4
Algeria	22.2	45	12	3.3	21	35.5	53.5	109	7.0	46/4	60	52	2,400	919.6/3
Egypt	48.3	37	10	2.7	26	67.3	94.2	80	5.3	40/4	57	44	700	386.7/2
Libya	4.0	46	11	3.5	20	6.7	11.5	92	7.2	46/2	58	64	7,500	679.4/1
Morocco	24.3	41	12	2.9	24	37.5	58.8	99	5.9	46/3	58	42	750	172.4/19
Sudan	21.8	46	17	2.9	24	33.2	51.3	118	6.6	45/3	48	21	400	967.5/5
Tunisia	7.2	33	10	2.3	30	9.7	12.9	85	4.9	40/4	61	52	1,290	63.2/31
Western Africa	166	48	18	3.0	23	272	454	118	6.4	47/3	48	29	580	2,372/10
Benin	4.0	51	23	2.8	25	6.3	10.9	149	7.0	49/5	43	39	290	43.5/16
Burkina Faso (Upper Volta)	6.9	48	22	2.6	27	10.5	17.7	149	6.5	44/3	44	8	180	105.9/10
Cape Verde	0.3	36	9	2.7	26	0.4	0.5	77	4.5	31/4	57	20	360	1.6/10

Country													
Gambia	0.8	49	29	2.0	35	1.0	1.6	193	6.4	43/3	35	21	290	4.4/14
Ghana	14.3	47	15	3.2	22	22.9	36.5	107	6.5	46/3	52	40	320	92.1/12
Guinea	6.1	47	23	2.4	29	8.9	14.3	147	6.2	43/3	40	22	300	94.9/6
Guinea-Bissau	0.9	41	22	1.9	36	1.2	1.8	143	5.4	44/5	43	27	180	13.9/8
Ivory Coast	10.1	46	18	2.8	25	16.0	29.0	122	6.7	45/3	47	42	720	124.5/12
Liberia	2.2	46	15	3.1	22	3.7	6.9	112	6.7	47/3	49	39	470	43.0/3
Mali	7.7	49	21	2.8	25	11.4	19.2	137	6.7	46/3	42	18	150	478.8/2
Mauritania	1.9	50	21	2.9	24	3.0	5.3	137	6.9	46/3	44	35	440	398.0/2
Niger	6.5	51	23	2.8	25	10.5	18.4	140	7.1	47/3	43	16	240	489.2/3
Nigeria	91.2	48	17	3.1	22	156.5	258.0	105	6.3	48/2	50	28	760	356.7/33
Senegal	6.7	50	19	3.1	22	10.5	17.9	141	7.1	45/3	43	42	440	75.7/27
Sierra Leone	3.6	47	30	1.7	41	4.9	7.3	200	6.1	41/3	34	28	380	27.7/25
Togo	3.0	45	17	2.8	25	4.7	8.3	113	6.1	44/3	49	20	280	21.9/25
Eastern Africa	159	48	17	3.1	23	258	452	109	6.8	47/3	49	17	300	2,454/7
Burundi	4.6	48	21	2.7	26	7.0	10.4	137	6.4	44/3	44	7	240	10.7/47
Comoros	0.5	46	16	3.0	23	0.7	1.0	88	6.3	46/3	50	19	—	0.8/42
Djibouti	0.3	46	20	2.6	27	0.4	0.7	122	6.8	45/3	47	74	—	8.5/0
Ethiopia	36.0	43	22	2.1	33	54.8	88.5	142	6.7	45/3	43	15	140	471.8/11
Kenya	20.2	54	13	4.1	17	37.3	68.0	82	8.0	52/2	53	16	340	225.0/4
Madagascar	10.0	45	17	2.8	25	15.6	26.8	67	6.4	44/3	50	22	290	226.7/5
Malawi	7.1	52	20	3.2	22	11.4	20.5	165	6.9	48/2	45	12	210	45.7/20
Mauritius	1.0	21	7	1.5	47	1.3	1.6	26.9	2.7	33/4	67	43	1,150	0.7/58
Mozambique	13.9	45	17	2.8	25	21.4	36.0	110	6.1	46/5	49	13	—	309.5/4
Réunion	0.5	23	6	1.7	42	0.7	0.8	14	2.6	33/5	66	41	3,710	1.0/22
Rwanda	6.3	53	17	3.6	19	10.7	20.3	110	7.3	46/3	49	5	270	10.2/39
Seychelles	0.1	26	7	1.9	37	0.1	0.1	14.4	4.1	37/7	70	37	2,400	0.1/21
Somalia	6.5	47	21	2.6	27	9.1	14.1	143	6.5	44/4	43	34	250	246.2/2
Tanzania	21.7	50	15	3.5	20	37.3	70.7	98	7.1	46/4	50	14	240	364.9/6
Uganda	14.7	50	15	3.5	20	24.5	43.7	94	6.9	48/2	52	14	220	91.1/25
Zambia	6.8	48	15	3.3	21	10.9	20.7	101	6.8	47/3	51	43	580	290.6/7
Zimbabwe	8.6	47	12	3.5	20	14.5	28.1	70	6.6	48/3	56	24	740	150.8/7

Table 1 (continued)
THE POPULATION OF AFRICA

	Population estimate mid-1985 (millions)	Crude birth rate	Crude death rate	Natural increase (annual, %)	Population doubling time (at current rate)	Population projected to 2000 (millions)	Population projected to 2020 (millions)	Infant mortality rate	Total fertility rate	% Under age 15/over age 64	Life expectancy at birth	Urban population (%)	Per capita GNP (US $)	Total area (000 sq. miles)/ percent cultivated
Central Africa	62	45	18	2.7	26	95	163	119	6.1	44/3	48	34	420	2,553/4
Angola	7.9	47	22	2.5	28	12.0	20.2	149	6.4	45/3	42	24	—	481.4/3
Cameroon	9.7	44	18	2.6	27	14.4	23.1	117	6.5	43/4	48	42	800	183.6/15
Central African Republic	2.7	46	22	2.4	29	3.9	6.3	143	5.9	43/4	43	41	280	240.5/3
Chad	5.2	44	23	2.1	33	7.6	12.4	143	5.9	42/4	43	22	—	495.8/2
Congo	1.7	44	19	2.5	28	2.6	4.5	124	6.0	44/3	47	48	1,230	132.0/2
Equatorial Guinea	0.3	43	21	2.2	32	0.4	0.6	137	5.7	41/4	44	60	—	10.8/8
Gabon	1.0	35	18	1.7	41	1.6	2.8	112	4.7	36/6	49	41	4,250	103.3/2
São Tomé and Príncipe	0.1	39	10	2.9	24	0.1	0.1	69.2	5.4	38/6	65	32	310	0.4/38
Zaire	33.1	45	16	2.9	24	52.4	93.3	106	6.1	45/3	50	34	160	905.6/3
Southern Africa	37	36	14	2.2	31	53	82	94	5.2	39/4	53	52	2,280	1,040/6
Botswana	1.1	50	13	3.7	19	1.8	3.5	79	6.6	50/2	54	16	920	231.8/2
Lesotho	1.5	42	16	2.6	27	2.3	3.7	110	5.8	42/4	49	6	470	11.7/10
Namibia	1.1	45	17	2.8	25	1.7	2.8	115	5.9	44/3	48	51	1,760	318.3/1
South Africa	32.5	35	14	2.1	33	46.5	70.1	92	5.1	38/4	54	56	2,450	471.4/11
Swaziland	0.6	48	17	3.1	22	1.0	1.8	129	6.5	46/3	47	26	890	6.7/8

From 1985 World Population Data Sheet. Prepared by Mary Mederios Kent and Carl Haub for Population Reference Bureau.

Table 2
CRUDE BIRTH RATES OF WORLD REGIONS,
1960–65 TO 1980–85

Region	1960–65 (per 1,000)	1970–75 (per 1,000)	1980–85 (per 1,000)
Africa	48.3	47.0	46.4
Latin America	41.0	35.4	31.8
Asia, excluding Japan	42.1	37.7	21.8
Less-developed countries	42.8	38.7	31.2
More-developed countries	20.3	17.0	15.5
World	35.9	32.7	27.3

ulation to enable the child to survive. Women also rearrange the timing of childbearing through fostering, a very common practice in black Africa. Recent surveys of numerous ethnic groups have revealed that one in seven to 10 of children aged from five to 14 are not living in the same household as their mothers—the proportions being much higher in West Africa than in East Africa. Other checks on high fertility include the high incidence of (a) venereal disease in certain areas; (b) male labor migration, which interrupts family building; and (c) polygamy, which is widespread, especially in rural areas—for example in the above-mentioned Kambia district in Sierra Leone where 58 percent of all women are in polygamous marriages.

In contrast, the use of contraception is low by world standards. In sub-Saharan Africa very few women practice contraception; only four countries (Botswana, Mauritius, Zimbabwe and South Africa) are reported to have prevalence rates of 25 percent or more among married women. But North Africa, Tunisia and Egypt have relatively high rates, especially among young educated women living in cities. Undoubtedly, the very low levels of literacy and education of females, particularly in the least developed countries of tropical Africa, are important deterrents to lowering both fertility and infant and child mortality rates. It is found that family planning services are more successful in countries where there has been more socioeconomic development of women, as in northern and southern Africa and the Indian Ocean islands. Until the 1980s, governmental interest in family planning programs was not widespread, but since then many countries have shown interest in integrating such programs with those of mother and child health services, which aim to generally reduce fertility, infant and child mortality, and maternal mortality and morbidity rates, as well as to improve birth spacing. Naturally, these programs are in various stages of development, and are mostly moderate or weak in comparison with the strongly effective programs in East Asian countries.

HIGH MORTALITY

Blessed with the highest human fertility rates of all world regions, Africa also has the less enviable status of being the world leader in mortality, though the difference from the rest of the world is less striking. Africa's average crude death rate is 16 per 1,000, compared to the world average of 11. Nevertheless, the world map of crude death rates reveals that most of the countries with rates of 20 or more per 1,000 are in Africa; and in 1980–85, 34 countries in the continent had rates of 15 or more per 1,000 (Map 3). Once again, the major exceptions are in the north and south, especially Tunisia, Egypt and South Africa, Mauritius, Réunion and the Seychelles. In these latter countries life expectancy at birth has progressed to 60 to 65 years, not as high as the more-developed countries where life expectancy almost everywhere exceeds 70 and in Scandinavia is approaching 80 for females. In contrast, in much of tropical Africa life expectancy has progressed much less, and is not more than 40 years (Map 4). Infant mortality (i.e., death in the first year of life) affects one in eight babies born in sub-Saharan Africa—compared with one in 65 in Europe—although the range is considerable: from one in 70 in Réunion to one in five in Sierra Leone. Of course, to this appallingly high infant mortality rate must be added very high child mortality rates (i.e., deaths of children aged one to four), caused by measles, dysentery, gastroenteritis and many other killers associated with poverty, malnutrition and lack of hygiene—which have been largely eliminated from the more-developed countries.

It is mostly in the poorest countries that the gains in mortality reduction have been least: in the countries of the Sahel zone from Mauritania across to Ethiopia; in Uganda, Angola and Mozambique—countries devastated by recent environmental and human disasters, which as always tend to affect most the most disadvantaged. Famine in Africa, now depicted regularly on the television screens of the world, is killing millions of people and affecting many millions more. In Ethiopia alone during the 1984–85 famine it is said that 8 million were malnourished and 1 million may have died— just one country among many to be seriously affected by a disaster that is certainly as much a result of political and social causes as environmental ones.

To these calamities in recent years there has been added the scourge of AIDS. In 1987 it was estimated that 10 million people were affected, 17 percent of some Ugandan towns and eight out of 10 female prostitutes. East Africa appears to be particularly affected, though the disease is spreading fast.

DEMOGRAPHIC TRANSITION

It follows that most African populations have experienced little demographic transition from high to low birth and death rates. Many of the least-developed countries of tropical Africa may be described as being in a pretransitional stage of high rates, while the countries of the north and south and the Indian Ocean islands are in an intermediate stage of generally lowering birth and death rates, although the latter have declined more markedly than the former. The countries that have progressed the most in this respect are the small island populations of Mauritius and Réunion, but

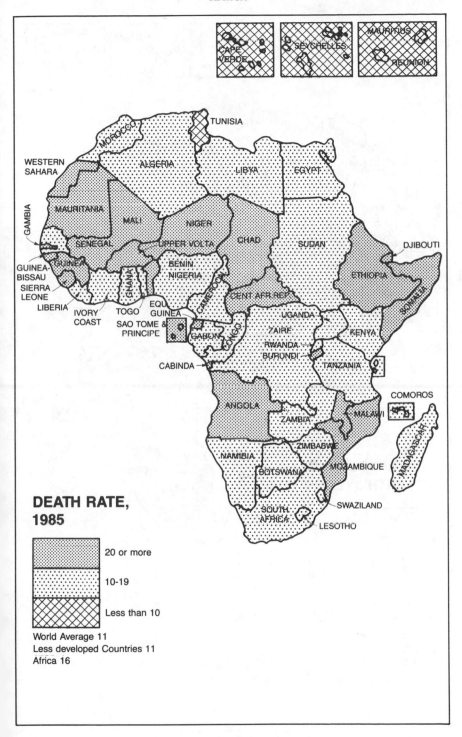

CAPE VERDE

SEYCHELLES

MAURITIUS
REUNION

TUNISIA

WESTERN
SAHARA

MOROCCO

ALGERIA

LIBYA

EGYPT

GAMBIA

MAURITANIA

MALI

NIGER

CHAD

SUDAN

DJIBOUTI

SENEGAL

UPPER VOLTA

GUINEA-
BISSAU

GUINEA

BENIN

SIERRA
LEONE

GHANA

NIGERIA

CENT. AFR. REP.

ETHIOPIA

SOMALIA

LIBERIA

IVORY
COAST

TOGO

EQU.
GUINEA

UGANDA

KENYA

SAO TOME &
PRINCIPE

GABON

CONGO

ZAIRE

CAMEROON

RWANDA

BURUNDI

CABINDA

TANZANIA

COMOROS

ANGOLA

ZAMBIA

MALAWI

MADAGASCAR

ZIMBABWE

NAMIBIA

MOZAMBIQUE

BOTSWANA

SWAZILAND

SOUTH
AFRICA

LESOTHO

DEATH RATE,
1985

20 or more

10-19

Less than 10

World Average 11
Less developed Countries 11
Africa 16

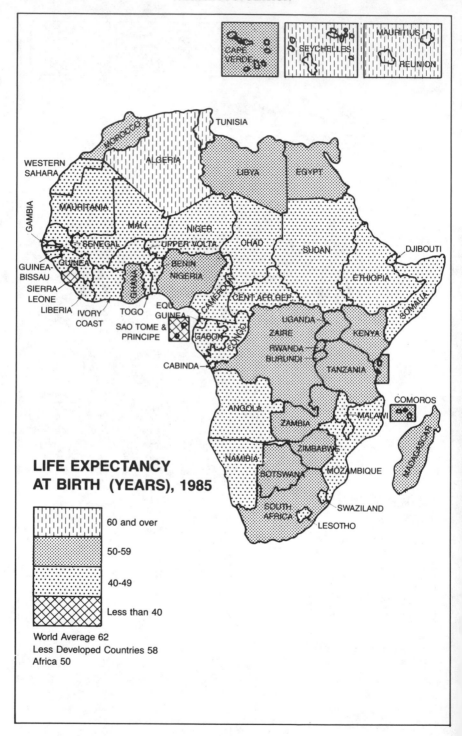

LIFE EXPECTANCY AT BIRTH (YEARS), 1985

60 and over

50-59

40-49

Less than 40

World Average 62
Less Developed Countries 58
Africa 50

their birth and fertility rates are still well above those of the more-developed countries.

One characteristic feature of African populations, arising from the prevailing birth and death rates, is their youthfulness. On the average, about 45 percent of the total population of Africa is aged under 15 (over twice the proportion of Europe's population), and only 3 percent are aged 65 or more (compared to 13 percent in Europe). In Kenya the young account for as much as 52 percent—perhaps the highest percentage in the world—and the elderly only 2 percent. Such youthful populations naturally cause very different social conditions and demands from those in more developed countries, where the growing proportion of the elderly is a key problem.

It will be apparent that although most African countries are faced with rapid population growth, few have effective policies to bring about any reduction in the rate of growth. There is more effort in lowering mortality than fertility, which for a variety of religious and traditional values is not greatly affected by the government objectives.

POPULATION DISTRIBUTION

Any glance at a population distribution map of Africa will reveal marked spatial unevenness, with patches of very high density (e.g., the Nile Delta, Nigeria) and large areas of moderate or low density. This patchiness of population distribution is not new, but it has intensified during the 20th century.

Factors influencing population distribution in Africa are numerous. They include in particular:

1. The diversity of environments, ranging from Mediterranean zones, steppes and deserts through the Sahel and savannas to tropical forests, and from coastal swamps and clay plains through gravel plateaus to high mountains
2. The bewildering ethnic complexity, with different groups practicing varied modes of life and types of economic activity
3. The long and varied impact of alien peoples who have affected the continent as slavers, conquerers, colonists, traders, industrialists and various technological experts.

Much of the 20th-century development has been localized, and associated with the development of modern agriculture, mining, industries, commerce and service functions that tend to be concentrated in economic cores, or islands, of economic development, with better infrastructures, more-developed city systems and higher population densities. Given the external orientation of African economies, many of these economic cores are focused upon coastal zones and port-capitals, which are so prominent in Africa. The coasts of the Maghreb and West Africa are the most obvious examples; and generally the patterns of migration have been from the less-developed parts of the interior toward the more-developed peripheral cores, which have become poles of population concentration largely through the greater economic opportunities they offer.

Different economic cores attract different types of migrants. Mining regions, usually dominated by multinational corporations and characterized by company towns with expatriate managerial staff, attract contract labor forces coming from long distances away. Regions of agricultural development often attract much more seasonal labor, which is often less controlled.

URBANIZATION

The most polarizing aspect of Africa's population distribution has been the growing concentration of people in towns and cities. Although it is the least urbanized of the continents, Africa has the fastest urbanization rate in the world, currently about 5 percent per year. In 1950, its urban population was about 32 million, less than 15 percent of the total population. By 1985, about 170 million people, 31 percent of the total population, were living in towns; and by the end of the century it is expected that 350 million people, or more than 40 percent of the total, will be urban. In half a century, the urban population will have multiplied more than 10 times, an astonishing transformation. On the whole, the levels of urbanization are highest in northern and southern Africa, and higher in West Africa than East Africa and in coastal countries than landlocked ones (Map 5; Table 1).

Moreover, much of the urbanization has been localized in larger cities, so that by 1985 Africa had five cities with 2 million inhabitants or more (Alexandria, Cairo, Casablanca, Kinshasa and Lagos); and it is forecast that this number may increase to 29 cities by the year 2000. Many of these larger cities are capitals, which since independence have acquired expanded administrations, industries, and commercial, educational, health and many other facilities, as well as an increasing concentration of communications.

In consequence, many African countries exhibit strong urban primacy, i.e., their urban systems are markedly dominated by the largest cities—as for example in the Ivory Coast, Ethiopia, Zaire and Sierra Leone, though less so in Nigeria, Zimbabwe and Zambia. However, urban primacy is not as prominent in Africa as it is for example in Latin America, because with the exception of Cairo no African city can compete with some of the giants of that continent, such as Mexico City and Buenos Aires. The reasons are the recent nature of urban growth, the rudimentary transportation networks and the extreme political fragmentation of the African continent, which means that the average population size of an African state is less than 10 million.

POPULATION AND THE POLITICAL MAP

There are 45 independent states and three dependent territories on mainland Africa, to which must be added six independent island-states and eight dependent island groups, a total of 62 countries containing 580 million people in 1987. Many of these areas are very small. Seven independent states are smaller in area than Wales; and in the mid-1980s, 12 had pop-

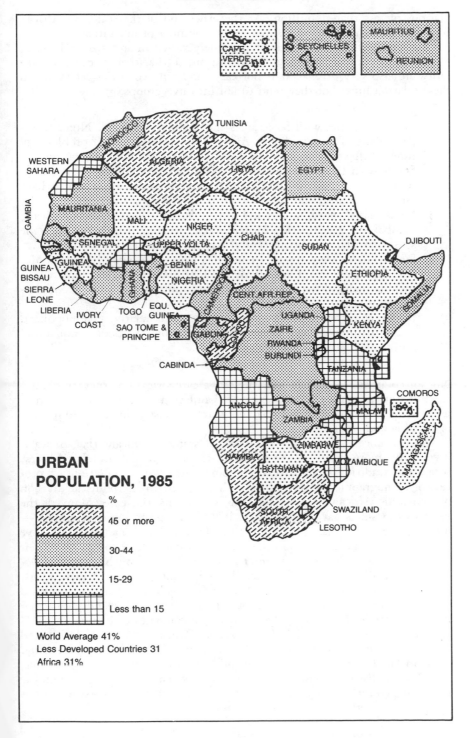

URBAN POPULATION, 1985

%

45 or more

30-44

15-29

Less than 15

World Average 41%
Less Developed Countries 31
Africa 31%

ulations of less than 1 million. At the other end of the scale, no African country rivals the giants of Asia in area or number of inhabitants.

Of course, African countries are extremely varied in area size and shape, as well as in population size and distribution, so that their population-area ratios are also very diverse. It is not easy to classify countries according to these relationships, but they tend to fall into five groups:

1. Major countries with large areas and populations (e.g., Nigeria, Sudan, Zaire, Ethiopia, South Africa), which tend to face problems of internal diversity and demands for decentralization or separation
2. States with large areas and relatively small populations (e.g., Mauritania, Mali, Niger, Libya, Chad, Botswana), many of which have large desert areas and very uneven population distributions
3. Middle-sized states, in area and in population (e.g., Cameroon, Ghana, Zimbabwe, Madagascar, Mozambique, Kenya), which can in some senses lay claim to being typical African countries.
4. Small but densely peopled countries (e.g., Rwanda, Burundi, Malawi, the Comoros, Cape Verde Islands, Mauritius, Réunion), which include many of the islands and many countries that suffer from population pressure
5. Minor countries that are small in area and relatively unpopulated (e.g., Guinea-Bissau, Benin, Togo, Gabon, Djibouti, Equatorial Guinea)

Not all countries fall neatly into these five categories, but they emphasize the differences in spatial complexity of population distribution. The problems facing countries like Nigeria and Zaire are vastly different from those of Gambia and Swaziland.

The existence of this complex jigsaw of states has meant that Africa is divided by more than 50,000 miles/80,450 km. of political boundaries, separating traditional population groupings into state populations, a process of demographic nationalization. This has led to the political division of numerous African peoples, like the Somali and the Ewe. Many of the new African states have found themselves with a profusion of neighbors—for example, Zaire has 10; and Sudan, Tanzania and Zambia each have eight—and 14 states are landlocked with no direct access to the sea. Their need for access emphasizes the internationalization of much human movement, especially as many of the landlocked countries (e.g., Niger, Chad, Burkina Faso, Lesotho, Swaziland) are less developed than the seaboard states and so tend to be sources of migrant labor. Most migrant labor moves up the economic scale, particularly to countries benefiting from oil and mineral wealth, such as Libya, Nigeria, Zambia and South Africa; and of course millions of Egyptians, Sudanese, Somalians and others have found work in Saudi Arabia and the other oil-rich Gulf states. Some countries, like Burkina Faso and Lesotho, have become extremely dependent upon the remittances of their migrant workers, a fact that makes these countries extremely vulnerable.

African countries find it very difficult to control migration across their borders, although they are anxious to do so by means of passports, visas, customs regulations and work permits. Their inability to do so means that there are millions of illegal or clandestine migrants in Africa who are sometimes subject to expulsions; countries like Nigeria, Ghana and Zambia have all expelled other Africans at one time or another so that they could offer more employment opportunities to their own nationals.

Another aspect of the effect of the political map upon population is the huge numbers of refugees now found in Africa. In the late 1970s they exceeded 4 million, but by December 1985 their numbers had been reduced to just below 3 million—about 28 percent of the world total—found mainly (in order of numbers) in Somalia, Sudan, Zaire, Burundi, Tanzania, Algeria, Uganda and Angola, with lesser numbers in more than 10 other countries in all parts of the continent (Table 3). The major receiving countries are among the poorest on the continent, and the refugees are among the poorest and most vulnerable people. Victims of wars, revolutions and the regimes of one-party states, they tend to concentrate along the border areas of the receiving countries where many integrate spontaneously among friendly peoples. Others relocate to organized settlements, some of which have been integrated into national development schemes. Repatriation is the preferred solution, but is not always possible unless political situations change. Very few Africans find third-country asylum, and unfortunately too many are living in long-term holding camps, as found in Algeria and Somalia. The work of the U.N. High Commissioner for Refugees is vital in this field.

It should also be mentioned that apart from the international refugees, there are large numbers of intranational refugees who flee within their countries, as in Sudan and Ethiopia. In addition, from time to time, there are the so-called economic refugees, fleeing from drought and famine; the Sahel drought brings to mind the plight of such migrants.

Table 3
REFUGEES IN AFRICA ACCORDING TO U.N.
HIGH COMMISSIONER FOR REFUGEES,
DECEMBER 1985

Algeria	167,000	Rwanda	49,000
Angola	92,200	Somalia	700,000
Burundi	256,300	Sudan	690,000
Cameroon	13,700	Tanzania	179,000
Central African Republic	42,000	Uganda	151,000
Djibouti	16,700	Zaire	317,000
Ethiopia	59,600	Zambia	96,500
Lesotho	11,500	Zimbabwe	46,500
	Rest of Africa	42,200	

POLICIES OF POPULATION REDISTRIBUTION

Most African governments are faced with population distributions, urban hierarchies and migration patterns that they find unsatisfactory; generally, however, they have no strong policies to deal with them, being usually much more concerned with the problems of social and economic development than with the spatial patterns of population. However, almost every government policy, directly or indirectly, affects population growth and distribution.

What sorts of policies have been implemented to affect population distribution and redistribution in Africa? They are varied, some being urban oriented and others rural oriented. Among the former are accommodational policies to improve housing and employment conditions in cities, but these are most evident in countries that can afford them, like Libya. Perhaps more common in the past have been closed-city programs to deter incursions of migrations, as in South Africa and many colonial countries that endeavored to plan their urbanization. Sometimes the policy has been even more authoritarian and drastic, sending rural migrants back to their homelands, a form of urban rustication or reversal designed largely to reduce the problems of rapid urban growth. Another policy employed is that of dispersed urbanization, where there is an attempt to develop dormitory towns and satellite new towns, as around Dakar and Cairo. Some countries have, for various reasons, attempted to relocate their capitals, as in Nigeria, Tanzania and the Ivory Coast—but with limited success so far. More effective are decentralization policies designed to develop regional centers and medium-sized cities—a growth-pole strategy, which has been particularly effective in Nigeria (where the federal structure lends itself to this sort of policy) and to a lesser extent in Algeria, Morocco and Tunisia.

Many governments are anxious to develop their rural areas and thereby stem the tide of rural-urban flows. Land colonization of the sparsely peopled zones is practiced in many African countries, like Kenya, Zimbabwe and Mali. In the countries that formerly were quite intensively colonized, such as Algeria, Kenya and Mozambique, resettlement and redistribution of colonized lands has had an important effect. This has been intensified in Mozambique as in neighboring Tanzania by major programs of forming villages and collectives of rural populations, moving, and transforming the lot of, millions in East Africa—not always for the better. Capital-intensive agricultural development schemes, as along the Nile in Sudan and Egypt and the Volta in Ghana, have also had dramatic effects upon population redistribution. However, such schemes are now often regarded as being too alien and too dependent on substantial external finance. In consequence, many African governments (as for example those of Botswana, Swaziland and Zambia) are more concerned with integrated or comprehensive rural development, reducing rural-urban disparities by greater investment in rural areas and by improving the infrastructure and facilities.

Unfortunately, many of the policies have been devoted to only one aspect of population distribution, especially the excessively rapid growth of capital cities, and their impact has been limited. Generally, their effect has been most marked where they have reflected overall government policies, as in Nigeria where federalism has meant that there are now 19 state capitals plus Lagos and the new Federal Capital Territory at Abuja.

CONCLUSIONS

It is evident that the population of Africa is in an extremely unstable condition—growing rapidly and changing its distribution—over which the governments of the numerous countries have only limited influence. Only in a few countries, mostly in the north, the south and the islands, do population policies have any effect upon population dynamics. Indeed, in most countries it is only in recent years that population problems have been seen to be important, there being so many other apparently more pressing problems facing governments. Population problems are seen as long-term ones, but they must not be ignored for they will impose themselves increasingly upon the map of Africa.

FURTHER READING

Caldwell, J. C., and Okonjo, C., eds, *The Population of Tropical Africa.* London: Longmans, 1968.

Clarke, J. I., and Kosiński, L. A., eds, *Redistribution of Population in Africa.* London: Heinemann, 1982.

Clarke, J. I., Khogali, M. and Kosiński, L. A., eds. *Population and Development Projects in Africa.* Cambridge: Cambridge University Press, 1985.

Demographic Handbook of Africa. Addis Araba: United Nations Economic Commission for Africa.

Griffiths, Ievan L. *An Atlas of African Affairs.* London and New York: Methuen, 1984.

Hance, W. A. *Population, Migration and Urbanization in Africa.* New York: Columbia University Press, 1970.

Moss, R. P. and Rathbone, R. J. A. R., eds. *The Population Factor in African Studies.* London: University of London Press, 1975.

O'Connor, Anthony. *The African City.* London: Hutchinson, 1983.

Oliver, R. and Crowder, M., eds. *The Cambridge Encyclopaedia of Africa.* Cambridge: Cambridge University Press, 1981.

Population Studies Series. Addis Araba: United Nations Economic Commission for Africa.

Prothero, R. Mansell, ed. *People and Land in Africa South of the Sahara.* Oxford: Oxford University Press, 1972.

Udo, Reuben K. ed., *Population Education Source Book for Sub-Saharan Africa.* Nairobi: Heinemann, 1979.

REFUGEES IN AFRICA

BARBARA HARRELL-BOND, KARIM HUSSEIN AND PATRICK MATLOU

INTRODUCTION

DESPITE wide discrepancies in estimates, it is agreed that African states host the largest refugee population in the world (see Table 1). Even by the most conservative estimate provided by the U.N. High Commissioner for Refugees (UNHCR), 3.7 million people as of the mid-1980s have crossed African state borders to seek asylum. This represents nearly 1 percent of the total population of the continent. This figure does not include the even

Table 1

NUMBERS OF AFRICAN REFUGEES
BY HOST COUNTRY*

Country	Number of refugees	Country	Number of refugees
Algeria	167,000	Lesotho	11,500
Angola	92,000	Malawi	100,000
Benin	3,700	Morocco	800
Botswana	4,600	Mozambique	700
Burundi	267,500	Nigeria	4,700
Cameroon	53,600	Rwanda	19,400
Central African Republic	13,000	Somalia	700,000
Congo	1,200	Sudan	974,000
Djibouti	16,700	Swaziland	12,100
Egypt	1,100	Tanzania	220,300
Ethiopia	132,400	Zaire	301,000
Ivory Coast	900	Zambia	138,300
Kenya	8,000	Zimbabwe	65,200

*These figures, compiled from UNHCR statistics, are mainly those provided by governments, and are based on their own records and estimates. Figures for countries that host fewer than 500 refugees are not included.
Source: *Refugees* 48 (December 1987).

vaster numbers of people who have been internally displaced by civil wars and other man-made disasters.

Although the phenomenon of both voluntary and involuntary migration in Africa is not new, the first occasion on which African refugees came to international attention was the Algerian war for independence. Such anticolonial wars in Africa created large numbers of refugees, but the vast majority of these were accommodated in neighboring countries that sympathized with these struggles against a common enemy. Thus, during the early postcolonial period, African states viewed refugees as temporary, a "problem" that would disappear once Africa was rid of European domination. It was in this political climate that the 1969 Organization of African Unity (OAU) Convention Governing the Specific Aspects of the Refugee Problems in Africa was promulgated.

THE DEFINITION OF REFUGEES AND STATE INTERESTS

The OAU convention expanded on the definition of a refugee laid down by the United Nations in 1951, which it adopted, by including—in addition to those who were subject to individual persecution—those who seek asylum as a result of external aggression, occupation, foreign domination or events seriously disturbing public order. For UNHCR, which since 1956 had been campaigning to stretch the definition beyond the confines of its 1951 convention, and which advised and participated in the drafting, the OAU convention was regarded as an achievement, a model that should be applied outside the region. It permitted the practice of accepting refugees en masse on prima facie evidence. It also defined the granting of asylum to refugees as a peaceful and humanitarian act that should not be regarded as an unfriendly one.

This convention was written, however, against the background of the formation of newly independent states that were seeking to establish legitimacy and consolidate internal control, and this influenced its content. The cornerstones upon which the OAU had been built were the sanctity of borders existing on the attainment of independence, as well as the principles of "territorial integrity" and "noninterference in the internal affairs of member states." Just prior to the founding of the OAU, Eritrea had been annexed by Ethiopia and there were already refugees in Sudan as a result of the Eritrean war for independence. Other refugee-producing conflicts, such as the civil war in Sudan and uprisings in what is now Zaire, also influenced thinking about the administration of refugee populations by host governments.

While the OAU definition of a refugee may be seen to be more liberal than that of the U.N. convention, the caveats that were included could be used to undermine its stated purpose: the protection of refugees. The effect of these caveats was to place an overriding priority on the protection of the rights and interests of the state. First, and perhaps most dangerous of all if it were implemented, the convention gives the host state the power to determine when those circumstances in the country of origin that caused it to give refugee status have ceased to exist. It denies refugee status to any person who has been "guilty of acts contrary to the purposes and principles of the OAU or the UN." In the interest of interstate relations, it requires that refugees be settled away from the frontier of their country of origin. It forbids any action that could be defined as subversive against any member of the OAU. Finally, the convention gives the state of asylum the prerogative of defining who is a refugee.

DEPOLITICIZING REFUGEES

Signatories to the convention (see Tables 2 and 3) undertake the responsibility of ensuring that refugees are prohibited from attacking any member of the OAU "through subversive activities, especially through arms, press, and radio, which may cause tension between Member States." Thus if states strictly observe the convention, refugees will only be tolerated if they are politically passive. Consequently, despite refugees, by their very nature, desiring political change in their country of origin so that they can return, states have agreed to support each other in the prevention of such activity. If a host state were to follow the convention, refugee status would not be accorded to "freedom fighters" who are seeking to overthrow the government of another member-state.

THE CAUSES OF REFUGEES

Refugees have been created by a multiplicity of factors. The most obvious immediate causes have been civil, interstate, or anticolonial conflicts; governmental oppression, political upheavals and the persecution of particular political, ethnic or religious groups within states; and environmental disasters such as drought and famine—all of which have been exacerbated and complicated by the cold war politics, economic underdevelopment, particular government-directed development policies, and increasing arms sales to African governments and liberation movements.

The two regions that continue to produce the majority of refugees in Africa are the conflict-ridden Horn and southern Africa—where the white-minority regime of South Africa continues its policy of destabilizing neighboring states.

Given the poverty and the structure of the economies African states inherited from colonial regimes, few governments have been able to meet the expectations of their populations for development, which had been so long denied them by their colonial overlords. More to the point concerning the creation of refugees, even the scarce resources available to African states have only benefited certain regions or groups within their societies. The resulting inadequacies in technology and infrastructure, and the unequal methods of distribution within countries have left large sections of the population without the basis for sustaining even a minimal level of subsistence. Such disparities have become the basis for internal challenges to state authority. These issues are compounded by the absence of solutions to the nationalities question, which continues to plague most independent African states and provoke power struggles. The ability of states to enforce the

Table 2
AFRICAN STATES PARTY TO 1951
U.N. CONVENTION AND/OR 1967 PROTOCOL
RELATING TO STATUS OF REFUGEES

Algeria	Liberia
Angola	Madagascar (C)
Benin	Mali
Botswana	Mauritania
Burkina Faso	Morocco
Burundi	Mozambique (C)
Cameroon	Niger
Cape Verde (P)	Nigeria
Central African Republic	Rwanda
Chad	São Tomé and Príncipe
Congo	Senegal
Djibouti	Seychelles
Egypt	Sierra Leone
Equatorial Africa	Somalia
Ethiopia	Sudan
Gabon	Swaziland (P)
Gambia	Tanzania
Ghana	Togo
Guinea	Tunisia
Guinea-Bissau	Uganda
Ivory Coast	Zaire
Kenya	Zambia
Lesotho	Zimbabwe

(C) Party to 1951 convention only.
(P) Party to 1967 protocol only.

Table 3
STATES NOT PARTY TO 1969 OAU CONVENTION
GOVERNING THE SPECIFIC ASPECTS OF
REFUGEE PROBLEMS IN AFRICA
(AS OF JANUARY 1987)

Botswana	Madagascar
Cape Verde	Malawi
Djibouti	Mauritius
Guinea	Mozambique
Guinea-Bissau	São Tomé and Príncipe
Ivory Coast	Sierra Leone
Kenya	Swaziland
Lesotho	Uganda

apparent stability previously enjoyed by colonial regimes through state monopoly of violence is frustrated by international involvement—for instance, in the transfer of arms to insurgents. However, the monopoly of force held by the colonizers should not be seen as positive; it contained in the short term, and exacerbated in the long term, the root causes of most of the refugee problem in Africa today.

REFUGEES: THE STATE AND INTERNATIONAL INVOLVEMENT

The major host governments in Africa are among the poorest states in the world and the least economically developed in Africa. The reception of large numbers of refugees has increased their already great dependence upon external aid, which in general can be shown to threaten national sovereignty, i.e., the control and allocation of resources within territorial boundaries.

In crisis situations such as large influxes of refugees represent, there is an even greater tendency among donors of aid to give control over the administration of funds to external agencies rather than host governments. This approach has been legitimized on the grounds that all African states lack the administrative capacity to cope with a disaster, and that emergency programs are particularly prone to financial mismanagement—a euphemism for the perception that all Third World governments are corrupt. This is in despite of what experience has so often demonstrated: that *no* governments are adequately prepared for emergency situations and *all* lack systems of accounting for funds derived from diverse sources spent under such conditions.

Even in an emergency the availability of external assistance to African states is conditioned by the political interests of the primarily Western donors and their clients, the intergovernment and nongovernmental aid agencies. Thus aid will be more forthcoming in situations where the interests of these bodies will be enhanced. For example, Sudan's ability to attract sufficient external funding to assist the several refugee nationalities within its borders has always been affected by the attitudes of Western governments both toward the Sudanese government itself and its relationships with the governments of the countries of origin; and, most recently, by the West's warming relations with Sudan's neighbor Ethiopia, which is itself actively supporting the civil war in southern Sudan.

On the other hand, there is considerable humanitarian concern behind the assistance given by some external donors, which aim to make available resources that will alleviate suffering and promote more democratic forms of government. Such donors face a dilemma. To establish a presence in a country in order to give assistance to the needy who are also subjects of an oppressive government lends credibility to such a government. Conversely, supplying aid through liberation movements implies political commitment to efforts to overthrow recognized regimes—and often commitment to particular ideological positions. The dilemma is not so great for those donors and agencies that support the work of the African National Congress (ANC) or the South-West Africa Peoples' Organization, because of U.N. support for these two organizations and general international condemnation of apartheid. But many other situations are less clear cut, especially when agencies want to work on both sides of a border. One example occurred during the period between 1979 and 1985 when Milton Obote was once again in power in Uganda. Many armed groups were fighting to overthrow this regime, which was producing far more refugees than did Idi Amin's government; and some of these refugees received international humanitarian aid. Although Yoweri Museveni recognized the great support his own movement received from humanitarian agencies during this struggle to overthrow Obote, now that he is in power his government is exceedingly wary of the activities of humanitarian agencies.

The presence of refugees may also provide the occasion for outsiders to undertake activities that threaten the security or compromise the foreign relations of the host government. Southern African states are continually threatened by the espionage activities of South African agents. An example of the use of a refugee situation to further the political interests of states outside Africa was the case of the Falasha. The existence of refugee camps in eastern Sudan provided the cover for the movement of this group out of Ethiopia. On arrival in Sudan the Falasha were put into camps that were largely under the control of external aid agencies. The U.S. and Israeli governments were then able to use bribes to persuade certain Sudan government officials to cooperate in the smuggling of the Falasha out of Sudan, an exercise that began in the 1970s and was first exposed in the international press in 1983. This not only had serious implications for Sudan's relations with Arab states at the time, but once Nimeiry's government was overthrown there was a tendency for the new government to equate all refugees with this regime and with corruption. The result was the dramatic deterioration of security for refugees.

African states cannot adequately control international aid policy. Even if funds for refugees were provided bilaterally between governments, states would still be faced with constraints. However, funds from Western sources are normally channeled through intergovernmental or international voluntary agencies, which assume primary responsibility for implementing aid programs in the field. The determination of aid strategies and the allocation of resources, as well as the planning of specific projects, are controlled by these external agencies without reference to overall national planning. Funds are normally earmarked for refugees, excluding the (sometimes poorer) host communities. For example, during the 1985 famine in Sudan, humanitarian agencies had a surplus of food earmarked for refugees that had to be distributed before it rotted. Instead of giving it to the starving Sudanese villages nearby, the refugees received extra rations.

The Sudanese experience shows how increasing levels of refugees, rising from a small number in the 1960s to an estimated 500,000 in 1982 and to over 2 million in 1987, have eroded the sovereignty of a state through international involvement. In an attempt to combat this, the Sudanese government had set up its own Commission for Refugees as early as 1967 to coordinate and organize the relief given to refugees. It is no wonder that the government tried to restrict aid organizations' activities when they proved reluctant to consult with local officials. However, the vast increases of ref- ugees forced Sudan to submit to external forces, and its battle for sover- eignty began to be lost in 1979 when it joined in the demand for more funds for African refugees.

It is estimated that, at most, no more than 40 percent of Africa's refu- gees are recipients of international assistance; the majority in Africa are, as UNHCR describes them, "spontaneously settled." They depend for their survival on the willingness of the local people among whom they live to provide them employment and access to land, and to share their meager resources. For social services such as transportation, housing, education and health care, these refugees depend entirely on the host's already inadequate resources.

Despite this, efforts by African governments to situate refugee assistance within national planning have not been successful. Renewed efforts—by requests for additional funding—were made through first and second inter- national conferences on assistance to refugees in Africa (ICARA I, 1981; ICARA II, 1984). The very poor response by Western donor governments to these requests demonstrates the vulnerability of host governments vis-à- vis the international community.

Today, UNHCR is the conduit for most international funds for assisting refugees. This office was established in 1951 with a global mandate to protect refugees. Even when it had become clear that its sphere of action would be outside Europe, in Asia and Africa, it was necessary for UNHCR to overcome reluctance within U.N. circles to allow this office to extend its activities beyond its major function of protection and to become in- volved in implementing assistance programs for refugees.

Despite its international mandate to protect all refugees, UNHCR can only provide its services to refugees with the permission of the host govern- ment (and even in protection, its powers are limited to persuasion and diplomacy). Such permission may not be forthcoming, particularly in cases where states are not parties to the international refugee conventions. Assis- tance programs can, however, be used to legitimize its presence in a par- ticular state in order that it may also carry out its protection work. Today, assistance programs are the main focus of UNHCR's work in Africa, and its staff and budget have dramatically expanded over the past decade. In the interests of protecting refugees, UNHCR has found it necessary to solicit invitations to provide assistance.

Such attempts have not always been successful, as is illustrated by at least one case in Africa where a state actually rejected aid and managed to cope with a very large influx of refugees without resorting to requesting assistance from outside its borders. During the war against the Portuguese in Guinea-Bissau, refugees fled both to Senegal and Guinea. While UNHCR established a presence and administered assistance in Senegal, Sékou Touré not only failed to invite UNHCR to establish an office in Conakry, he actually rejected its offers of assistance for the refugees. Even though there was no evidence that refugees were either unprotected by the host state or needed material assistance, the then high commissioner undertook a special mission to Conakry to try to persuade Sékou Touré to reverse his decision.

994

This displays a general tendency within all organizations to cultivate opportunities for widening their sphere of activity, enhance their prestige and serve their own interests as an expanding organization.

Another example of an African state that did not request international assistance for refugees is Sierra Leone. During the regime of Sékou Touré, tens of thousands of Fula-speaking people fled Guinea and were, for the most part, peacefully received by Sierra Leone. The government permitted their integration into the national economy. Their leadership was absorbed into the Islamic religious community, where they were held by Sierra Leonean imams in very high esteem. Significantly, there was no involvement of international agencies and as a result, in this instance, refugees were integrated with no perceptible threat to national sovereignty.

REFUGEES: INTERSTATE RELATIONS

At the time of the founding of the OAU, pan-Africanism was an ideal espoused by some prominent African leaders. It stressed that ultimately there should be one united African state rather than a continent artificially divided by the state boundaries of the colonizers. The ideal was rendered impracticable as the governing elites sought to preserve their independent authority and status. However, the establishment of the OAU in 1963 aimed to provide a mechanism for some unity of action, with the emphasis on finding African solutions for African problems.

In 1979 the Conference on the African Refugee Problems was held in Arusha, where state representatives discussed ways of dealing with the continent's increasingly severe refugee situation. At this conference the principle of states sharing the burden caused by refugees was emphasized. But, as would appear self-evident, most African states lack the resources either to give direct assistance to host governments or to resettle within their own boundaries refugees from countries of first asylum. Moreover, by 1979 refugees had become a source of extreme tension in interstate relations in Africa.

As noted earlier, according to the OAU refugee convention, in interstate relations the granting of asylum to refugees should be regarded as a peaceful and humanitarian act and not as an unfriendly, i.e., political, act. In reality, of course, refugees symbolize the character of the enemy across the border, and the attitude has been that whoever gives asylum to an enemy is himself an enemy.

REFUGEES AND INTERSTATE TENSIONS

In order to avoid interstate tensions over refugee issues, at times states have simply ignored the presence of refugees on their soil. For example, although refugees fleeing from Portuguese colonial oppression in Guinea-Bissau received considerable international attention, at the same time the Ivory Coast government kept very quiet about the refugees they were hosting who were part of the numbers flooding out of independent Guinea. In deference to good relations with Rwanda, Burundi agreed not to publicize the presence of Rwandan refugees on its territory. Little information is available concerning the very large numbers of Oromo refugees from Ethiopia who live in Kenya and Sudan. Not only have the latter two governments appeared to ignore their presence, they are also not recipients of international assistance. It is quite possible that these governments and international agencies are collaborating in silence in order to maintain the legitimacy of the government of Ethiopia in the face of opposition from the largest nationality within the state: the Oromo.

Despite the rules of the OAU refugee convention, which aimed to prevent state support of subversive activities by refugees, and despite the OAU principles of noninterference in the internal affairs of member states, state interests have generally overridden pressures to comply. This has had serious consequences for interstate cooperation, in one case leading Morocco to walk out of the OAU. It has also raised serious tensions, in some cases leading to war.

In 1975, instead of granting independence to the people of the Spanish Sahara, Spain, the colonial power, handed the territory over to Morocco and Mauritania in a secret agreement. The war of independence, which had already begun, now involved OAU member-states. Algeria, which supported the right of the Sahrawi people for self-determination, provided asylum for the civilians who fled across its borders. Further, it has recognized the Sahrawi Arab Democratic Republic (SADR) as a nation in exile, has given its civilians autonomy in the region where they have settled and has overtly provided assistance for its military struggle. When the majority of member-states recognized SADR, which should have given it automatic OAU membership, Morocco withdrew from the organization.

Such support for refugees who are actively engaged in armed resistance against the state that caused their expulsion can, as noted, lead to war between states. Tanzania's antagonism toward Amin's brutal regime in Uganda had a moral flavor to it. Yet its overt support for the subversive activities of Ugandan refugees, which included armed raids inside Uganda, justified Amin's military foray into Tanzania. This in turn justified the Tanzanian army, in conjunction with Obote's forces, launching an invasion of Uganda in 1979, which brought down the Amin government.

There has always been considerable sympathy among the Sudanese people for the cause of the Eritreans who are fighting for independence. From the perspective of the average Sudanese, this, like the war in Western Sahara, is an anticolonial war. In addition to the Eritrean refugees, Sudan also hosts refugees from two other Ethiopian groups: the Tigre, who are fighting for local autonomy, and the Oromo, who are seeking to set up an independent state. These groups are actively involved in an armed struggle against the Ethiopian government. The Sudanese government has never officially supported any of these armed groups, but it is an open secret that it allows its territory to be used for the transport of arms and other supplies needed inside the liberated areas. Somalia has also allowed the leadership of Eritrean and Ethiopian liberation organizations considerable freedom of movement in its territory, exacerbating its already tense relations with the Addis Ababa government.

That the Sudanese government has given official recognition to the humanitarian wings of more than one political front should not be construed as overt political support. This recognition, which accords these various organizations with the same privileges as other humanitarian agencies—such as the duty-free importation of material assistance—was prompted by the realization that these organizations were efficient and in a better position to organize aid for their peoples than were many outside agencies.

Not surprisingly, this support has aroused more than indignation within the Ethiopian government, and Sudan has paid a heavy price for its efforts to provide security for its now nearly 1 million refugees from Eritrea and Ethiopia. Not only has Ethiopia regularly carried out raids against refugees inside Sudan, it has provided asylum for Sudanese refugees and given active support to the Sudan People's Liberation Army, which since 1982, under the leadership of Dr. John Garang, has used Ethiopian territory to train its army to carry out a war to liberate Sudan.

Even if a state does not give overt support to liberation armies, the mere presence of a refugee population in its territory can lead to military incursions originating from the refugees' home state. There are numerous examples of situations where the state that has created the refugees launches military expeditions into its neighbor's territory to attack them. For example, from 1982 on there were regular incursions into southern Sudan by the Uganda National Liberation Army, which resulted in the death and abduction not only of refugees but of local Sudanese. The best-known examples, however, have been the regular incursions of the South African military forces into neighboring states, killing refugees under the pretext of eliminating ANC terrorists. These incursions are an ever-present threat to the security of the front-line states, even though several of them, as well as Lesotho, have complied with South Africa's demand that all known ANC supporters be resettled elsewhere. Although the causes of the flight of refugees from Angola are somewhat different, in 1985 Angolan government troops attacked some of the estimated 400,000 refugees who had sought asylum in Zambia and Zaire.

The potential of such incursions to cause wars has in fact been diffused by states. The most typical response has been both to protest the incursions through diplomatic channels and to remove refugees into camps away from the border areas so that the states of origin have less reason to perceive them as a direct threat. In 1971 Sierra Leone received a demand for the return of a refugee the Guinea government accused of having been involved in "the aggression of 22nd November 1970," which was intended to topple that government. The request that led to this *refoulement* referred to the "existing cordial relationship between the two Republics" and reminded the host government "that any enemy of Guinea is also an enemy of Sierra Leone."

There have been other cases of *refoulement*, either in compliance with demands from a more powerful neighboring state of origin or in the interest of peacekeeping. For example, Botswana has repatriated refugees to South Africa and has also returned armed freedom fighters to Lesotho and Zimbabwe. In these ways, refugees have served as political pawns both for their

997

hosts and states of origin. Indeed, too often refugees are the expendable pawns, because in addition to being the cause of interstate tensions they are also viewed as economic burdens.

Ironically, as the Sierra Leone example illustrates, the security of refugees may be more at risk when friendly relations exist between states or when states are looking for ways to demonstrate good will after a period of alienation. For example, when, during Obote's rule, there were attempts by the governments of Uganda, Kenya and Tanzania to revive the East African Community, one of the first signs of cooperation was the return of refugees from Tanzania to their state of origin: Kenya. Even before this, Ugandan refugees in Kenya were abducted, apparently with the connivance of Kenyan security services. Tanzania was also involved in efforts to secure the removal of many Rwandan refugees; these people were victims of an earlier expulsion exercise implemented by Uganda.

The promotion of voluntary repatriation can be a feature of state cooperation over the refugee issue. Although the possibility of returning home would, of course, be the solution most likely to be desired by refugees themselves, this can only be the case if the situation at home has changed so that they need have no fear of returning. The fact that refugees have been repatriated despite unsafe conditions prevailing in their home states, points to the ways in which states, with the support of UNHCR, fulfill their own interests over and above the interests of the refugees. For example, in 1983 a tripartite agreement was signed between UNHCR and the governments of Ethiopia and Djibouti to facilitate the return of refugees living in Djibouti. Ethiopia greatly depends on the rail link that passes through Djibouti to the sea; moreover, given its serious need for food aid from Western sources, international approval for the return of its refugees helps to alter its human rights image. Djibouti, on its part, depends on this transport system for much of its income; moreover, it lacks the resources to provide any future for the refugees who have sought asylum within its borders. In this instance, the repatriation solution has clearly served both the resource and the political interests of the contracting states. It is also in the interest of the international donors to lessen or terminate their financial responsibilities for assisting refugees.

REFUGEES AND INTRASTATE TENSIONS

As should already be clear, the presence of refugees has serious repercussions for internal stability, resource distribution and the economic development of the host state. However, the general misconception of refugees as a "problem" tends to ensure that they become one. That is, rather than focusing on the economic contribution refugees might make to their host state, at both the state and international level, refugees are seen as a short-term problem that can be resolved by short-term solutions.

One of these solutions has been to hive refugees off into camps, a policy that has been supported by UNHCR and other international humanitarian agencies that have responded to requests by states for external assistance, and that are only willing to provide assistance when the recipients can be clearly demarcated from the local population. Moreover, as noted, the failure of international donors to provide assistance to refugees within the overall development plans of the host government, which would ensure that aid resulted in lasting benefits to the economy, has contributed to tensions between hosts and refugees.

The peoples of Africa have a long tradition of receiving the stranger. In fact, as noted above, most (an estimated 60 percent) of the refugees in Africa are what UNHCR calls spontaneously settled. In reality, these refugees are depending on the generosity and sacrifices of their hosts. States have relied on the hospitality of their people rather than on the availability of resources to cope with sudden refugee influxes. At a certain point, however, hospitality becomes a function of resource availability. The increased demand on already scarce resources, such as fertile land, health care, food, education, paid employment, fuel, housing, and even water for both people and livestock, is bound to lead to tensions between local and refugee populations. Hence, near a refugee camp in Sudan locals have been fighting with refugees from Tigre over the issue of cutting down trees for fuel. Refugees, who compete for all scarce resources, have also been blamed for inflating the costs of accommodation. Conflicts over water have occurred during a drought in Sudan; and similarly, during a drought in Zaire in 1977–78, Angolan refugees were seen as an unnecessary burden and were expelled by their hosts.

In many cases refugees are in direct competition with locals for extremely scarce employment opportunities. As a result, daily wage rates have been driven downward to the detriment of the poorest hosts. The tensions that can result from this situation are graphically illustrated by the situation that developed in the Sudanese city Gedaref, which hosts huge numbers of refugees. In October 1979 there was an uprising during which some of the inhabitants of the town destroyed the huts and belongings of refugees.

Tensions between local people and refugees are not only created by direct competition for the scarce resources of the state, they are also the result of jealousies that arise because in some cases assisted refugees in camps enjoy superior medical and educational facilities, and, as already noted, may become better off than their hosts.

An approach to assistance generously supported by international donors, concentrating on the already existing long-term developmental infrastructural needs of the host economy, and benefiting the entire population without discriminating between the recipients—whether refugees or locals—holds more promise than existing approaches to assistance.

REFUGEES: THE LABEL

In spite of some of the recent expulsions that have occurred, the record in Africa of a willingness to accommodate strangers, whether the cause of their movement was voluntary or involuntary, has generally been exemplary. The idea of large numbers of people, labeled refugees, who have not been incorporated into the host society in Africa is relatively new.

It has been deduced from this analysis that the international system of states is in itself a major factor making and perpetuating refugees as a problem in Africa and elsewhere. As has been noted, *refugees* are outside the state-centered concept of international law. Indeed, refugee is a concept, a label, that has been created to serve the purposes and interests of states. Refugees have been defined as noncitizens, and those who have been "captured" by the state-sponsored assistance program have been frozen in a permanent state of marginality in their host societies. As nonpersons they are not consulted in the development of policies that affect their futures. Those who manage to settle within the existing host community have a greater chance of retaining some freedom of action and of contributing to the host economy.

Although the conventions were designed to ensure protection by the host state, in reality refugees are people without rights and are therefore the victims of the very institution—the state—that was created to guarantee their survival. UNHCR, the institution created to uphold the conventions, is itself a creature of states in its very conception, bound to serve their interests.

It is not surprising, in this context, that international organizations, the instruments of states, have confirmed this status. Thus individuals who are forced to cross state boundaries find themselves rendered useless by the definition of their status as refugees, a status forced upon them through the act of receiving aid. Even they themselves may agree to adopt the role implied in the term *refugee*, in order to gain access to assistance. The danger is that they become useless to themselves or to the state of asylum.

The dependent and passive role into which refugees have been cast was pointed out in 1984 by Mark Malloch-Brown, at the time a UNHCR official, at the Oxford Refugee Studies Programme's International Symposium, "Assistance to Refugees: Alternative Viewpoints." This symposium was, as he observed, notable because it included a large number of African refugees among the participants:

> . . . . what excites me most about this conference is the presence of refugees amongst us who have arrived here straight from refugee camps. It strikes me as quite extraordinary that we should be hailing this as such an innovation. But innovation it is. I would hope that experts will never again have the effrontery to sit down together to discuss refugees without refugees being present, but I doubt it. Refugee work remains, perhaps, the last bastion of the ultra-paternalistic approach to aid and development. It is hard to think of another area where the blinkered nonsense of the "we know what's best for them" approach survives so unchallenged.

CONCLUSION

As has been shown throughout this discussion of refugees in Africa as a problem of the state, refugees are a symptom of much deeper problems: a complex of interlinked dilemmas facing states and international organizations, which ultimately results in systems of coping with refugees that perpetuate their suffering.

Some would argue that until the structural defects of the world states system have been corrected, African states will continue to be overwhelmed by refugees. There is no sign of the world system being changed in the near future; rather, there is more and more evidence in Africa of an escalation of the retrogressive process, the seeds of which were sown centuries ago. However, the root cause of refugees in Africa is the failure of states to satisfy basic needs of their populations.

Thus, in order to prevent refugee flows—that is, to resolve the causes of their exodus—states must, in exchange for the allegiance of their citizens, provide them the guarantee of physical security and the elements of a minimal subsistence, i.e., unpolluted air and water; adequate food, clothing and shelter; essential preventive health care; and liberty of political participation and physical movement. "No reasonable person should be expected to be satisfied with less. Beneath this threshold the social compact has no meaning."* The failures of states, which result in refugee movements, are potentially within the control of African states even without greater resources than are already available.

No effort to sustain a minimal level of subsistence necessarily requires extensive capital investment, specialized knowledge, heroic governmental efforts or saintly sacrifices by the local affluent. A hoe may be an altogether satisfactory tool for processing a resource, and a footpath may suffice as a conduit for commerce. Similarly, a minimally satisfactory method of food distribution (where no one suffers from a severe protein/caloric deficiency) is consistent with extensive inequalities of wealth. In situations where subsistence is threatened because of inadequacies in technology, infrastructure or distribution—all factors within human control—the state has failed to perform its basic duty to protect its citizens from the actions of others.

FURTHER READING

Brooks, Hugh C., and El-Ayouty, Yassin, eds. *Refugees South of the Sahara: An African Dilemma.* Westport, Connecticut: Negro Universities Press, 1970.

Erikson, L., Melander, G., and Nobel, P., eds. *An Analysing Account of the Conference on the African Refugee Problem, Arusha, May 1979.* Uppsala: Scandinavian Institute of African Studies, 1981.

Hamrell, Sven, ed. *Refugee Problems in Africa.* Uppsala: Scandinavian Institute of African Studies, 1967.

Hansen, A., and Oliver-Smith, A., eds. *Involuntary Migration Resettlement: The Problems and Responses of Dislocated People.* Boulder, Colorado: Westview, 1982.

Harrell-Bond, Barbara E. *Imposing Aid: Emergency Assistance to Refugees.* Oxford: Oxford University Press, 1986.

————, and A. M. Howard. *Community Leadership and the Transformation of Freetown, 1801–1976.* The Hague: Mouton, 1978.

Kibreab, Gaim. *African Refugees: Reflections on the African Refugee Problem.* Trenton, New Jersey: Africa World Press, 1985.

United Nations High Commissioner for Refugees. *Refugees,* nos. 35 (November 1986), 46 (October 1987) and 48 (December 1987).

* A. Shakenove, "Who Is a Refugee?" *Ethics* (January 1985): 280–81.

AFRICAN HEALTH AND MEDICAL SERVICES

COLE P. DODGE

INTRODUCTION

AFRICA'S health crisis is most tragically understood from its infant mortality rate (IMR)—which is higher than that of any other continent—and from its life expectancy, the lowest in the world. The causes, while historical in large part, are complex, ranging from the very evident emergencies of drought, famine and civil war to more subtle economic problems of constant growing of single crops and economic underdevelopment to rapid population growth, while budget allocations for health services have declined. Issues of ideological commitment, international emphasis on macroeconomic adjustment policies, the accountability of health workers, and the continent's brain drain all contribute in varying degrees from country to country to this human health tragedy.

COLONIAL MEDICAL LEGACY

Western medicine introduced to Africa[1] during the colonial period was directly related to medical discoveries in Europe and applied by colonial administrators who recognized the need for improved health, first for their armies and administrative services and gradually for the African people who congregated around colonial outposts. Similarly, missionaries brought not only Christianity but also education and curative health services to the continent. Little or no attention was given to traditional medical beliefs or practice, as both missionary and government promoted entirely Western models of medicine. Colonial contact, however, also brought diseases (such as smallpox) previously unknown to Africa, diseases which were introduced to a susceptible population that had no resistance to them, and which resulted in massive epidemics that cost hundreds of thousands of lives.

Medicine, like other technologies, was linked directly to colonial power. In Europe rapid economic development occurred side by side with major advances in technology and so medical technology evolved rapidly, following new scientific breakthroughs. The discovery and use of vaccines and

---

[1] The 45 countries of sub-Saharan Africa are the principal concern of this chapter.

antibiotics followed improved standards of living to dramatically decrease infant mortality in industrial Europe between 1850 and 1950, while life expectancy correspondingly rose in the same period.[2] However, the colonial system did not produce a similar development spurt in Africa, where the IMR in 1950 stood at 197 per 1,000 live births.[3] Meanwhile, the original purpose of bringing Western medicine to Africa by colonial administrations—to provide health care for their administrators and army—remained the same. The health professionals who headed the medical services of both the colonial and the missionary health care systems were also drawn from the colonial powers and applied the same medical technologies. When schools to train paramedics and eventually doctors were established, these were strictly tied to the professional standards of developed countries. As the disease patterns of the West changed from infectious diseases to chronic illnesses, such as those associated with old age, so did the character of the mainstream of medical practice. This mainstream of Western medicine carried doctors from Africa, trained in the West or indoctrinated with Western concepts, models and practices, along with it and away from concentration on the infectious diseases that accounted for the high infant mortality of the African population.

By the time the colonial era came to an end in the early 1960s, an educated African elite took over from their European predecessors. Medical schools at such places as Makerere were engaged in cancer research, a reflection of Western influence, while Uganda's Mulago Teaching Hospital was a 1960s version of the state-of-the-art hospitals in Manchester and Liverpool and more suited to the practice of medicine in England than to tackling the endemic infectious diseases of Africa. Similarly, the multistoried hospital design proved a major obstacle to inpatient care by the 1970s, when electrical failures and water shortages became chronic. Nonetheless, these universities and hospitals were serving the professional interests not only of the doctors, but also of Africa's elite, whose health problems were comparable to those of their contempories in Europe.

MEDICAL MANPOWER AND THE BRAIN DRAIN

Doctors trained in Western models of medicine are seldom equipped to care for the infectious diseases suffered by rural Africans. Doctors in Africa are generally inadequately trained to work in rural settings, where even the hospitals sometimes lack running water and sewage disposal systems. Overcrowded wards, backlogs in surgical cases, and poorly paid and unmotivated support staff make their job an uphill battle from the outset. Lacking public-health experience and with unrealistic expectations aroused by their Western training, many of these doctors become frustrated and return to urban practice or emigrate for more lucrative positions abroad.

[2] Jon Rhode, "Why the Other Half Dies: The Science and Politics of Child Mortality in the Third World," in *Assignment Children 61/62* (Geneva: UNICEF, 1983), 35–68.
[3] Leo Goldstone, "Statistical Review of the Situation of Children in the World" (Geneva: UNICEF, October 1986.)

Another major problem is the internal distribution of doctors. Whereas 75 to 90 percent of Africa's population is rural, only 40% of doctors work in rural areas; and 60% are urban-based, serving only 10 percent to 25 percent of the population.

In Uganda, for example, in addition to nearly two decades of civil war, budget cuts and run-down and poorly administered hospitals, galloping inflation has eroded salaries to the point where doctors are not paid enough even to feed their families, let alone live up to their supposedly prestigious position in society. Between 1972 and 1985, almost 50 percent of medical doctors and 80 percent of the country's trained pharmacists fled the country in search of more professionally satisfying and better paid jobs.[4] However, it is not merely monetary reward or the Western influence of medical school that drives professional health workers from Africa, but also threats to human rights, restrictions on freedom of expression and, occasionally, fears of personal safety. Unfortunately, many countries in Africa do not tolerate, let alone encourage, freedom of ideas and expression. Medical personnel, being part of the educated elite, are aware of these constraints and quickly move to more developed countries, where they are able to enjoy more freedoms.[5]

This brain drain, frequently from the poorest African countries, has a double disadvantage for the country concerned. First, it is expensive to train doctors in terms of both professional and monetary resources. Second, it deprives the health services of medical professionals, since usually the brightest and most highly motivated are the first to leave. This out-migration is not limited to doctors alone: nurses, pharmacists and scientists are also susceptible.

POSTINDEPENDENCE OPTIMISM

Independence brought a wave of nationalism; development plans were made, budgets established and an optimism about improving the predominantly rural citizenry was pervasive.[6] Ministries of health were created or expanded, while infrastructure was built more rapidly than at any time in history. The number of hospitals, health centers and dispensaries increased dramatically in the postindependence period. Medical schools were opened and doctors trained, but even so the medical profession remained doggedly committed to the major trends in Western countries. Led by doctors, hospitals took precedence over rural facilities, and the training of doctors over paramedics in much of postcolonial Africa.

Nonetheless an impact was seen. Infant mortality generally declined between 1960 and 1970, while life expectancy edged upward from 38 years

---

[4]Cole P. Dodge, and Paul D. Wiebe, *Crisis in Uganda: The Breakdown of Health Services* (London: Pergamon, 1985).
[5]F. M. Mburu, "Scholarship, Freedom and Brain Drain in Africa" *Social Science and Medicine* 19, no. 11 (1984), 1127–29.
[6]Goran Hyden, *No Shortcuts to Progress: African Development Management in Perspective.* (London: Heinemann, 1983).

to 51 years between 1950 and 1986.[7] The 1960s model of health was an outgrowth of the colonial health-service structure, including that of the mission hospitals, except that independence saw an overall expansion of services. Basically, hospitals formed the center of expansion, with satellite referral health centers or dispensaries at the periphery. Mobile services filled the gaps between regularly established units and provided specialized services. In a "growth" environment, where newly independent countries were committed to expansion of services, this approach made considerable headway. However, as political will waned and was replaced by factional infighting and regional interest groups in the late 1960s, nationalistic goals were abandoned for more narrowly defined regional and tribal gain; and with this, the commitment to an equitably distributed network of social services also faded. Similarly, new facilities and programs required more and more money, while the economy of much of Africa stagnated and then declined. By the time the oil crisis of the early 1970s hit African countries, there were paralyzing developments. Fuel and other import bills doubled, which not only reduced fuel availability but also reduced budget allocations for the social services sectors, particularly health services. Mobile health services ground to a halt, accompanied by reduced supervision, a collapse of the referral system, and decline of specialized services such as malaria control and immunization.

ECONOMIC CRISIS

The economic crisis of stagnating and declining growth was further worsened by oil price increases, and was also related to cash cropping, which formed the bulk of the raw material exports from African countries to markets concentrated in the industrialized North. World prices of such standard African exports as coffee, cotton, cocoa, tea and tobacco fluctuated widely between 1960 and 1988 and in general fared much more poorly than the price of manufactured goods, which relentlessly escalated. Africa is dependent both for a market and for essential imported manufactured commodities, with the consequence that world trade is heavily biased against both the producer and the consumer in Africa. The low, and at times sporadic, earnings from raw-material exports were accompanied by disproportionate increases in the import bill for manufactured goods.[8]

To stimulate development and lessen the impact of the trade imbalance, many African countries borrowed from financial institutions during the 1970s. The debt burden mounted as donors encouraged borrowing in the decade's global environment of excess money and low interest rates. African countries, increasingly strapped for money to sustain services and finance development programs, turned readily to these lenders. But the years of low interest, excess money and a stable world economic order soon gave way to high interest rates, galloping inflation, a decline in raw-material prices,

[7] J. P. Grant, *The State of the World's Children Report 1987* (London: Oxford University Press, 1987).
[8] John Ravenhill (ed.), *Africa In Economic Crisis* (London: Macmillan, 1986).

and global recession. With the loans came conditions. Of importance and concern here was the eventual demand to apply adjustment policies to reduce spending for "soft" social services in favor of investment in such "hard" economic areas as agriculture (particularly cash cropping), but also light industry and energy, communication and transportation. Country after country in Africa was faced with a heavy debt burden and had to reschedule payments under tough International Monetary Fund adjustment policies, which threw the optimism of independence into disarray as social-services spending was slashed in the worst-hit countries such as Ghana, Uganda and Sudan.[9] An absolute decline in per capita GNP further reduced the ability of individuals to provide for themselves. There was a fall in absolute terms, from modest gains to a negative decline between 1960 and the mid-1980s. The average growth in per capita GDP in Africa between 1960 and 1970 was 1.4 percent per year, declined to just 0.4 percent from 1971 to 1979, and was a negative 3.6 percent early in the 1980s.[10]

POPULATION GROWTH

The demographic profile of Africa is one dominated by children, with nearly half the population being under the age of 15, and 19 percent under the age of five. Half of the total population, therefore, have no vote and no economic power of their own; and the youngest ones are completely dependent and hence the most vulnerable members of the society. If a single age-specific group most affected by the crisis in Africa can be identified, it is the children under five years of age. If an African child lives to reach his or her fifth birthday, that child's life expectancy is only a few years less than the life expectancy of a child in Europe or North America. On the other hand, the life chances of that same child at birth brings the average African life expectancy down to only 50 years, as compared to 70 in most developed countries.

Viewed from an economic perspective, Africa has the highest dependency ratio of all the continents. Young and elderly or nonproductive dependent persons place extraordinary strains on the bankrupt economies of countries and households alike. Between 1960 and 1987, the population of Africa nearly doubled, and while there are only 18 persons per square kilometer, the carrying capacity of the land is not as much as in other continents. In 1960 Africa was self-sufficient in food, but by the mid-1980s one-third of the population was dependent upon food imports.[11]

Human fertility in Africa is double the world average, at 6.6 pregnancies per each woman of childbearing age—with Kenya topping the list at 8.8. Population growth stands at 3.2 percent per year and again leads the world—

[9] U.N. Children's Fund, *Within Human Reach: A Future for Africa's Children* (Geneva: UNI-CEF, 1985).

[10] Fred T. Sai, "Population and Health: Africa's Most Basic Resource and Development Problem," in *Strategies for African Development*, ed. Robert J. Berg and J. S. Whitaker (Berkeley: University of California Press, 1986), 129–54.

[11] Peter Lawrence (ed.), *World Recession and The Food Crisis in Africa* (London: James Currey, 1986).

with Kenya again in first place with the highest population growth rate. Simply stated, Africa's rapid population expansion has far outstripped the farmers' capacity to grow food, national economic growth, and governmental provision of essential basic services such as health care, water supply, sanitation and schools.

CASH CROPS AND NUTRITION

While the economies of most African countries labor under the international economic order that is biased against them in favor of the industrialized countries, there are severe problems that go beyond terms of trade.

Single-crop agriculture and preferential investment in cash export crops, such as coffee, tea, tobacco, sugarcane, groundnuts and cotton, often push subsistence crops, produced largely by women, onto poor marginal land—especially as population expansion works simultaneously to increase the pressure on limited arable land. The result in Sudan, for example, has been lower yields per acre and lower overall harvests despite roughly twice the area under cultivation between 1964 and 1984.[12]

Because of the heavy reliance by government on the income from raw-material exports, and because of an overall breakdown of the rural tax base in many countries, central governments sometimes pay low farmgate prices for cash crops, pocketing the difference to pay the civil service and run the government. Thus, even when coffee prices soar, as they did in 1986, for example, the real price paid to the producer is often only a small portion of the price received in the international market. Cash cropping has therefore not had the desired impact on the nutritional status of the population. In Malawi, for example, where maize has been the principal cash crop, the nutritional status of young children has actually declined as exports have climbed.[13] What is required is a food and nutrition policy that gives proper weighting to the food needs of the people, rather than favoring the colonial legacy of dependence on raw-material exports of cash crops. In addition, more equitable internal redistribution mechanisms are essential in countries that have food surplus and deficit areas. Farmers should be paid a fair share of the world price for their cash crops. More adequate attention should be given to small farmers in the form of credit, access to markets and productive inputs, which, at present, are frequently monopolized by large farmers. Women are the principal farmers in much of Africa, and more attention must be paid to their needs.

Another problem has to do with the intrafamily distribution of cash income. Increased incomes are frequently monopolized by men who spend it on such consumer goods as transistor radios, bicycles, clothes and alcohol, leaving little for their wives for the feeding, clothing and education of

[12] Jay O'Brien, "Sowing the Seeds of Famine: The Political Economy of Food Deficits in Sudan," in *World Recession and Food Crisis in Africa,* ed. Peter Lawrence, (London: James Currey, 1986); Nick Cater, *Sudan: The Roots of Famine* (London: Oxfam, 1986).
[13] Victoria J. Quinn, "Malawi: Agricultural Development and Malnutrition" (UNICEF, ESARO, Nairobi, 1986, Mimeographed).

their children. Therefore, even where cash crops bring more disposable income to the rural family, this does not necessarily have an immediate or direct beneficial impact on the health and well-being of the people, or on society as a whole.[14]

The past decade has witnessed major catastrophes across Africa. Drought has taken its toll most recently in 1984–85 in Ethiopia, Sudan and the Sahelian countries; a decade earlier the Sahel drought wiped out crops and livestock that sustain life for the subsistence farmers of these arid and semi-arid countries. Drought, often but not invariably followed by famine, is caused by poor, sporadic or untimely rainfall. The Sahara desert moves south each year as average rainfall has consistently declined in some areas over the past 30 years—as in Darfur in western Sudan, where average annual rainfall has declined from 26 in./650 mm. in 1928 to 12 in./300 mm. in 1985. But declining rainfall is not the whole picture. Governments and aid agencies have turned their backs on time-honored traditional food security systems and subsistence farming, in favor of rapid agricultural growth. Deep bore holes have been drilled in grazing areas, allowing rapid expansion of livestock herds beyond the carrying capacity of the pasture in dry years; this leads to overgrazing, impacted soil and desertification around such watering points. Mechanized farming has displaced subsistence farmers and pastoralists, forcing them onto marginal land where yields per acre are less, causing larger areas to be cleared and planted or grazed, which in turn increases soil erosion and causes ecological degradation.[15] Meanwhile, the population explosion continues placing even more pressure on fragile agricultural resources, the ecology and environment.

Pictures of severely malnourished Ethiopians, Sudanese or Karamojong tribesman were flashed from remote villages across television screens worldwide, and have brought this African catastrophe into the homes of people around the world. While the world community responded to the great emergency of 1984–85 with millions of dollars of relief food, this was not enough to tackle Africa's development problems. A silent emergency, meanwhile, rages on—taking the lives of the rural and urban poor—the result of ill-conceived national development programs, inadequate policies and misdirected strategies. The "social periphery"—young children, women, the elderly, the landless and the unemployed—show the consequences of the silent emergency in exactly the same way as the victims of drought, with starvation, disease and premature death.[16]

[14] Virginia Lee Barnes Dean, "Social Change and Lugbara Subsistence Agriculture in West Nile District," in *Crisis in Uganda: The Breakdown of Health Services.*
[15] Cater.
[16] F. M. Mburu, "The African Social Periphery," *Social Science and Medicine* 22, no. 7 (1986): 785–90.

CIVIL WAR

As if the ravages of climate were not enough, civil war has beset many of the most drought-affected countries. Civil war engulfed nine African countries in the mid-1980s, political instability many others, while drought and famine have taken their toll on 16 countries since 1970. More than any other continent, Africa has borne the brunt of these life-threatening events in the 1980s.

Civil war has multifaceted impacts on African countries. First, if the evolution of war is traced in relation to its impact on civilians, an alarming trend becomes evident. In World War I only 10 percent of casualties were civilian, but by World War II this figure had escalated to 50 percent; and in all wars after 1960 the civilian toll has been upward of 80 percent.[17] The overwhelming majority of the civilian victims are women and children. While few reliable statistics are available, mention of the civil war in Nigeria (Biafra) or Uganda alone conjures up the worst images of death, deprivation and human suffering. One example from Uganda demonstrates this: from 1981 to 1985 the Luwero Triangle, with a population of 750,000, was engulfed in guerrilla war between the Uganda National Liberation Army (UNLA) of Obote and the National Resistance Army (NRA) led by Yoweri Museveni. When the NRA defeated the UNLA, stacks of human skulls, mass graves and entire fields covered with skeletons—of women, children and the elderly—were revealed. They are still there. It is estimated that between 200,000 and 500,000 people were killed in this period in Uganda.[18]

Second, civil war also demands huge financial resources, especially scarce foreign exchange. Forty percent of Uganda's budget in the early 1980s went to "security," while the war in southern Sudan took an estimated additional 25 percent of that country's already severely strained resources.[19] Money spent on war deprives Africans of health care, education and other basic services, and contributes to the overall crisis.

Third, civil war totally disrupts what meager health services the rural population has. Outright destruction and looting at worst, neglect of the health facilities at best, lead to decline and eventual collapse of physical infrastructure and medical services. In Mozambique, 482, or 42 percent, of the country's health centers were destroyed between 1982 and 1986 in the civil war.[20] Rural health workers, whether they are loyal to the government or are antigovernment guerrillas, are among the first to flee civil war, while medicines are frequently the target for raids by the fighting factions. Food supplies, local agriculture and livestock are similarly devastated, with corresponding rises in malnutrition and death. For example, the Red Cross

[17] Cole P. Dodge and Magne Raundalen (eds.), *War, Violence and Children in Uganda.* (Oslo: Norwegian University Press, 1987).
[18] Paul Wiebe, and Cole P. Dodge, *Beyond Crisis: Development Issues in Uganda* (New York: M.I.S.R./African Studies Association USA, 1987).
[19] Ruth Leger Sivard, *World Military and Social Expenditures 1986* (London: World Priorities, 1986).
[20] U.N. Children's Fund, *Children on the Front Line* (Geneva: UNICEF: 1987).

found that infant mortality in the Luwero Triangle in 1983 was 305 per 1,000 live births, while one of the few studies of infant mortality during the civil unrest and drought of 1980 and the anarchy following the 1979 Ugandan liberation war that toppled Idi Amin, showed one of the highest IMRs ever recorded—609 deaths per 1,000 infants.[21]

While most countries have managed to reduce their IMR in the past decade, there are two examples where the IMR has increased as a result of civil war: Mozambique and Angola. As front-line states with South Africa, both countries are the target of destabilization and are fighting major civil wars within their borders. The result: the world's highest IMR, estimated to be 200 per 1,000 live births in 1986. As a direct impact of war and destabilization an estimated 500,000 or more infant and child deaths occurred in Mozambique and Angola between 1980 and 1986. Meanwhile, other front-line states (Zambia, Zimbabwe, Botswana, Lesotho and Swaziland) have all suffered adversely from cross-border raids and economic pressure by South Africa and the increase of resources being devoted to military security, thus weakening health and other social services.[22] (See the chapter on South Africa's war on its neighbors in this Handbook, pp. 748ff.)

AIDS: AFRICA'S NEWEST DISEASE THREAT

Acquired Immune Deficiency Syndrome (AIDS), first reported widely in the United States, is the latest pandemic[23] besetting many countries in Africa. Twenty-nine sub-Saharan countries have reported cases of AIDS, and the list continues to grow.[24] AIDS, a sexually and blood transmitted disease, is transmitted in Africa the same way as elsewhere in the world. This major new killer, caused by Human Immune Virus (HIV) in the blood, has a growing incidence in many African as well as other countries. With no cure in sight, this new disease only compounds the health crisis in Africa, since the cost of treatment and loss in economic income due to disability and premature death will further cripple health-care budgets and overall health status.

Africa has been hit especially hard. "At least one million Africans, mostly in central Africa, will probably die of AIDS in the next decade. This simple statement, probably a considerable underestimate, cannot do justice to the complexity, variety and urgency of the AIDS situation in Africa."[25] However the Panos Dossier goes on to report that "the facts of HIV in Africa are fragmentary and incomplete . . . from . . . unsystematic testing . . ." and concludes that "the statistical picture of AIDS in Africa is still a sketchy one."[26]

[21] Robin J. Biellik and Peggy L. Henderson, "Mortality, Nutritional Status and Diet During the Famine in Karamoja Uganda," in *Crisis in Uganda: The Breakdown of Health Services.*
[22] *Children on the Front Line.*
[23] World Health Organization, "Special Programme on AIDS: Guidelines for the Development of National AIDS Prevention and Control Programme (Geneva: WHO, October 1987).
[24] Renée Sabatier, *AIDS and The Third World,* Panos Dossier, no. 1 (Paris: Panos Institute, 1987), 35.
[25] Ibid.
[26] Ibid.

Dr. Lobe Monekaso, African director of the World Health Organization (WHO), has commented that "AIDS represents not only a health problem but a serious economic problem."[27] Half of the per capita health budgets in Africa would be required just to carry out the simple testing for HIV, while hospital-based care of AIDS suffers is simply impractical. When the potential impact of AIDS on the economy is considered, the picture is even more grim. It is young, educated and skilled breadwinners—in the prime of life—who are predominantly infected with HIV. "AIDS in Africa does not only threaten individual lives. The survival of whole industries and national economies may be at stake."[28]

The only control mechanisms so far recognized are the screening of blood used for transfusions, and public information advising that intravenous drug users should not share or reuse needles, that sexual promiscuity is dangerous and that use of condoms may help to reduce transmission. Unfortunately, medical equipment to screen blood and the means to disseminate health-education programs in much of Africa are severely limited; and in many countries condoms are not readily available or widely used. Resistance to family planning (use of condoms) is commonplace, especially in rural communities where large families are desired. For many of Africa's Roman Catholic population, contraception is still discouraged. The AIDS pandemic will therefore strike another blow to Africa. However, it is important to recognize that the AIDS epidemic is no different as an epidemic in Africa from elsewhere, and in the words of a WHO report: "AIDS cannot be stopped in any country until it is stopped in all countries."[29]

CONCLUSION

Many questions remain unanswered: What does the future hold? What trends can be identified? Is the situation improving or getting worse? Using total infant and child deaths as a yardstick, Africa's health crisis, compared with the rest of the world, reveals improvement, but at a slower rate than the rest of the world. UNICEF compiled a ranking of 25 countries whose combined cumulative total infant and under-five deaths account for over 80% of all such deaths throughout the world. In the 1960–65 period eight out of 25 were African countries, compared to 11 of 25 in 1980–85, and this is projected to increase to 14 of 25 by 2000–05. Clearly, the situation is improving for other continents while in relative terms the situation in Africa is worsening.[30]

With international satellite news coverage beaming images throughout the world from remote villages in, for example, northern Ethiopia, governments have been pressured into providing emergency assistance despite major political differences, e.g., American support to the pro-Soviet govern-

[27] Lobe Monekaso, "Medicine Now—AIDS in Africa," BBC Radio Four, 20 October 1987.
[28] Sabatier, p. 41.
[29] WHO, p. 3.
[30] Leo Goldstone, "Infant and Child Deaths: Top Twenty-five Countries" (Geneva: UNICEF, April 1986, Mimeographed).

ment in Ethiopia. Out of this a new international ethic can be seen to be emerging, stimulated by the emergency of drought and famine initially, but increasingly directed toward the ongoing silent emergency. Individuals, agencies, religious leaders and governments increasingly recognize that the high infant mortality of Africa is simply not acceptable given the technological advances of the past 20 years, which enable the saving of lives through inexpensive techniques such as immunization and oral rehydration therapy. The major killer diseases that are preventable by the use of vaccines are pertussis (whooping cough), measles, diphtheria, tuberculosis, polio and tetanus. Diarrheal diseases, malaria and acute respiratory infection can also be controlled through public health measures and good case management, while scientific breakthroughs in oral rehydration have dramatically reduced infant and young child mortality as a result of dehydration caused by diarrheal diseases.

Gradually too, local models of health care delivery are emerging from the diversity of indigenous African traditions. Hospitals and local health programs in many parts of Sudan have begun to solve their financial problems through a wide variety of innovative strategies. For example, in Wad Medani the Health Scouts project managed to persuade local government to levy a 10-piaster (four U.S. cents) tax on all bus tickets, which financed their project. Traditional birth attendants are being trained to provide health care at low cost in remote villages throughout much of Africa. Indigenous food security systems are increasingly considered before "development" projects are implemented, and environmental impact studies are now required by some aid donors. Boy Scouts and Girl Guides earn merit badges in child survival in Uganda, and Red Cross/Red Crescent workers promote a global program—Child Alive. Rotarians have joined the battle against polio in their Polio 2001 Project, and the Organization of African Unity declared 1987 as the year of immunization.

Local accountability is important to the success of health programs. For example, in Tanzania, essential drugs are turned over to local dispensaries at regional depots so that communities, rather than the government, are responsible for costly and difficult logistics arrangements. The radio broadcasts information about which local councils have drug kits at regional stores, so that everyone in the community knows the status of "their" medicines. Through such local cost-sharing mechanisms, the sustainability of health care is being tackled and solutions found.

Local organizations are also emerging, as well as professional organizations such as the African Medical and Research Foundation headquartered in Nairobi, to help governments in the fight against ill health, disease, and high infant and child mortality. Universities are beginning to revise their curricula to address the health problems of their countries, while some governments require minimum national medical service for new graduates, thus slowing the brain drain. Gradually, governments are reorganizing their health services, setting achievable priorities and distinguishing between cost-effective primary and costly specialized tertiary care.

Out of the crisis come some remarkable achievements in many different countries. But a sustained improvement in the health of the people of Africa will depend upon hard choices, involving political as well as technical commitment to public-health interventions, such as immunization, as well as a variety of micro-responses to underdevelopment—with a keen eye to sustainability built on the strength of local traditions. People are, after all, the most valuable asset of any nation, and therefore health must be established as a complementary priority to economic development. Thus, while there is a long way to go to reverse the health crisis in Africa, there are nonetheless reasons for hope.

FURTHER READING

Bennett, F. J., ed. *Special Edition on Medicine and Social Sciences in East and West Africa.* Kampala, Uganda: Makerere Institute of Social Research, 1973.

Buhrmann, M. Vera. *Living in Two Worlds: Communication between a White Healer and Her Black Counterparts.* Cape Town: Human & Rousseau, 1984.

De Beer, Cedric. *The South African Disease: Apartheid, Health, and Health Services.* London: Catholic Institute for International Relations, 1986.

Dodge, Cole P. and Raundalen, Magne, eds. *War, Violence and Children in Uganda.* Oslo: Norwegian University Press, 1987.

———, and Wiebe, Paul D. *Crisis in Uganda: The Breakdown of Health Services.* London: Pergamon, 1985.

Feierman, Steven. *Health and Society in Africa: A Working Bibliography.* Waltham, Massachusetts: Crossroads Press, 1979.

Jansen, G. *The Doctor-Patient Relationship in an African Tribal Society.* Assen, Holland: Van Gorcum, 1973.

Janzen, John M. *The Quest for Therapy in Lower Zaire.* Berkeley: University of California Press, 1978.

Last, Murray, and Chavunduka, G. L., eds. *The Professionalisation of African Medicine.* Manchester, England and Dover, New Hampshire: Manchester University Press in association with the International African Institute, 1986.

Makhubu, Lydia Phindile. *The Traditional Healer.* Kwaluseni, Swaziland: University of Botswana and Swaziland, 1978.

Monqbet-Lamare, Marc. *La médecine bamoun: étude d'anthropologie.* Lamare. Yaoundé, Cameroon: Lamaro, 1975.

Njogu, A. R., Tukei, P. M., and Roberts, J. M. D., eds. *Recent Developments in Medical Research in Eastern Africa: Proceedings of the First Annual Medical Scientific Conference of Kenya Medical Research Institute and Kenya Trypanosomiasis Research Institute.* Nairobi: KEMRI and KETRI, 1982.

Sofowora, Abayomi. *Medicinal Plants and Traditional Medicine in Africa.* Chichester, Sussex and New York: Wiley, 1982.

Ulin, Priscilla R., and Segall, Marshall H., eds. *Traditional Health Care Delivery in Contemporary Africa.* Syracuse, New York: Maxwell School of Citizenship and Public Affairs of Syracuse University, 1980.

LABOR ISSUES AND TRADE UNIONISM IN AFRICA

NICHOLAS VAN HEAR AND TAFFY ADLER

With the exception of South Africa, considered separately later in this chapter, Africa has not witnessed the acceleration of industrialization seen over the last two or three decades in parts of the developing world, notably east Asia and Latin America. Nor has Africa experienced the expansion of unionism that has recently accompanied rapid economic change in some of the newly industrializing countries.

Wage earners still make up a relatively small proportion of the labor force in Africa. In West Africa, for example, they probably represent only about one-tenth of the economically active population. Although the proportion is higher in some countries, such as the Ivory Coast and Ghana, wage earners probably do not exceed 15 percent of the work force in any African state. Many of them work in small- and medium-scale owner-operated and family businesses. Probably no more than half work in the so-called modern sector of government enterprises, public corporations and large private companies. Relatively few are employed by multinational corporations, which have received a disproportionate amount of attention from commentators on labor and trade-union affairs.

The number of wage earners belonging to unions is even smaller. Union organization is usually only viable in larger enterprises. It is often concentrated in the public sector, although large-scale private enterprises may be organized. Large sections of the labor force are not unionized. In agriculture, the informal sector and the household—in which most of the economically active population are engaged—unions are usually absent.

All figures must be treated with caution, but Zambia probably has the largest proportion of unionized workers in sub-Saharan Africa. In the mid-1970s, the 17 unions affiliated with the Zambia Congress of Trade Unions were said to have a membership totalling 205,000, the number of these organized workers having doubled since independence. Even this number, however, represented only 30 percent of the country's waged and salaried workers. The proportion is smaller in Africa's most populous country, Nigeria. The Nigeria Labour Congress, the country's central union body, and

1014

its 42 constituent unions claimed a membership of around 1.5 million in 1984, out of an estimated 6 million wage and salary workers and a total population of around 100 million. In a country where reliable statistics are especially difficult to come by, other estimates have put the total number of wage earners in recognized employment—the modern sector—at between 3 and 5 million, with the number unionized correspondingly lower. Union membership, moreover, has dwindled rapidly with the mass redundancies of recent years.

Nevertheless, African unions have an importance and an influence far greater than their membership numbers might suggest. They frequently played a substantial part in independence struggles, and have been a significant force since, often despite considerable obstruction by the state.

The characteristic African regime has become the one-party or military state, featuring political demobilization, authoritarianism and a strong intolerance of independent organization by social classes and interest groups. Corporatism has been a very strong trend. Like other interest groups, unions have been sanctioned, subsidized and supervised by the state in an effort to neutralize competing power centers. Not all unions, however, are hopelessly compromised. Some have managed to retain independence and effectiveness, often despite repression or legislation designed to render them impotent. In many states they are the only voice through which opposition or dissent can be channeled. Increasingly, in the austere conditions of the 1980s, African unions have taken up issues that go beyond the immediate concerns of their members.

We here examine the organization of unions, considering their emergence, their relations with the state, and their organizational problems. We then scrutinize the issues currently giving rise to labor unrest, including new pressures on African unions arising from the austere conditions of the 1980s. Unions' international relations are considered next, then we look at the prospects for trade unionism to the end of the century. Finally, we examine the many distinct problems facing trade unionism in South Africa and Namibia.

ORGANIZATION OF TRADE UNIONS

The emergence of unions

Such workers as dockers, railway personnel, miners, clerks and teachers formed unions quite early in the colonial period. Strikes and other forms of industrial action have been traced to the 19th century, and unions from the early 20th century. In Sierra Leone, the Gold Coast (later Ghana) and Nigeria, a number of unions were well established by the early 1930s. While these early unions were formed on the initiative of African workers, official intervention shaped the subsequent emergence of labor organizations. The colonial state was often prominent in overseeing the emergence of unions, and they consequently often bore the mark of formation under official supervision.

Prompted by labor unrest in other colonial territories, British administrations in Africa sought to establish orderly and controllable systems of industrial relations. Early unions were encouraged to take the shape of British urban labor movements, which indeed sometimes contributed specialists to advise on their formation. In 1930, the British government decreed that trade unions should be recognized and encouraged, and subsequently legislation was passed to provide for their establishment on the British model, but with compulsory registration and restrictions on strikes. Colonial development and welfare legislation during the 1940s further encouraged the formation of "responsible" unions. Yet British attempts to form African unions according to a nonpolitical mold could not prevent their support for emergent nationalist movements.

In the French colonies, union emergence followed the metropolitan French pattern even more closely. They developed first in Algeria and Tunisia, but unionism was exported from France into tropical Francophone territory from about the late 1930s, particularly to such west African cities as Dakar. A labor code of 1952 brought the unions into line with French legislation, but, as in the British territories, strikes were restricted by means of an obligatory arbitration system. The unions were often dominated by expatriates and were subordinated to metropolitan political interests and labor groupings. Yet they rapidly took root among African workers, who began the struggle for autonomy from metropolitan unions; these struggles became part of nationalist campaigns against French rule. In other colonies, including those under Belgian and Portuguese rule, more repressive conditions meant that unions emerged later and were placed under greater constraints.

Colonial regimes tried to manage unions and labor relations with a mixture of institutionalization and suppression. There were nevertheless intermittent waves of strikes and protests throughout the colonial period, as workers, particularly in the public sector, pressed for better pay and conditions. After World War II, much labor unrest was linked with rising nationalist protest.

Union-state relations and problems of organization

After independence, relationships between unions and nationalist organizations diverged fundamentally from their alliances forged during the anticolonialist struggles. As the new governments monopolized power, they pushed hard to maintain and extend their control over union movements. Although the unions were not remolded wholly according to the wishes of the new governments, many union organizations became compromised by or even incorporated into the state or ruling party.

The pace of the transformation of union-state relations varied considerably. Some new governments moved rapidly to change industrial relations substantially. In Ghana, the Industrial Relations Act of 1958 restructured numerous unions into a smaller number of industry-wide unions affiliated with a strongly centralized organization, the Ghana Trades Union Congress. This reform strengthened the influence of organized labor, but there was the loss of the right to strike and the loss of autonomy because of the GTUC's links to the ruling party and government. This was the pattern followed in many other independent states. In Tanzania, the ruling party rapidly brought to heel unions formed during the 1950s under the Tanganyika Federation of Labour as it strove for a monopoly of power. After a wave of labor and political unrest during the early 1960s, the TFL was abolished in 1964 and the National Union of Tanganyika Workers was established. It was a completely centralized organization, with nine industrial sections rather than member unions, and with virtually all posts appointive.

In Francophone countries, the alliance between nationalist parties and independently organized labour did not long survive after 1957, when semiautonomous governments were established in each French territory. In Guinea, where union leader Sékou Touré had spearheaded the movement for autonomy from French unions, the Confédération Nationale des Travailleurs Guinéens became the sole union organization, strongly integrated from the start with the ruling party. After full independence from France in 1960, the drive by the new governments to bring unions under official control accelerated, as it had in the former British territories.

The transformation of industrial relations was more gradual in other states, particularly where former trade unionists held positions of power or where the new regimes relied heavily upon union support. In Sierra Leone, where the union leader Siaka Stevens became president, and in Kenya, where the union leader Tom Mboya became a minister, legislation covering union organization followed fuller consultation with organized labor, and single-union centers were established later. In Nigeria, although for different reasons, a single-union organization did not emerge until the late 1970s.

Countries which gained independence later than most other African states—the Portuguese colonies in the mid-1970s and Zimbabwe in 1980—have deviated little from the familiar pattern. In Angola, Mozambique and Guinea-Bissau, single-union organizations were formed shortly after independence and were strongly integrated into the ruling party. Zimbabwe followed the precedent of other Anglophone states by merging numerous small unions linked to a number of central organizations into new industrial unions affiliated with the Zimbabwe Congress of Trade Unions.

While many African states have ratified International Labor Office conventions on the right to organize, official interference constraining free organization and activity has been commonplace through legislation or other means. As well as obligatory affiliation of unions to state-sponsored federations or centrals, methods applied to control trade unions include registration, the removal or registration of the right to strike, and the cooperation of leaders through financial inducements or office. Removal of government subventions and the revocation of state-sanctioned checkoff agreements are powerful threats to assure union compliance. Appeals to nationalist and antiimperialist sentiments and the invocation of development ideology are regularly made to induce unions to sacrifice their members' interests in the name of national development or a supposed common good.

The one-party states' armories of repression also include preventive detention acts and brute force. Although preventive detention has often been used, although the armed forces and police have frequently been deployed to quell labor unrest, and although there have been political murders of

1017

unionists, yet state terrorism on a large and systematic scale, as seen in other developing countries, has so far not been deployed against trade unions in black Africa. While union organizations have in some states succumbed to state control, in others they have proved remarkably resilient. Union-state relations in Africa therefore differ substantially. Union organizations in Francophone Africa include those fully controlled by the state and barely distinguishable from the ruling party or junta, those cooperating with the government but with a degree of autonomy, and, rarely, those possessing full autonomy. Unions sometimes exist, usually clandestinely, as opposition groups. In a few more pluralistic states, such as Senegal, more than a single-union organization has been tolerated; in such circumstances unions may have more freedom to pursue their interests independently, although they may be tied to political parties.

Various degrees of union incorporation are also apparent in Anglophone countries. Ghana under Nkrumah and Tanzania after the Arusha declaration offer the clearest examples of incorporation of unions into the ruling party. In Ghana subsequently, and in Nigeria, Kenya and Zambia, unions have had some room for maneuver, although they are circumscribed by government control of registration, by the threat of the removal of official subsidies, and by the threat of revocation of checkoff and other concessions. Where unions are relatively independent, their vitality is often derived from special circumstances. In Zambia, the government has not been able to coopt the mineworkers' union, although it has created the central Zambia Congress of Trade Unions and has the usual battery of legislation and administrative procedures regulating labor relations. This union's relative strength is largely due to the miners' strategic role in the economy, but even after its position was eroded during the 1970s by the collapse of the price of copper, the union resisted incorporation and retained considerable vigor.

Pressures from below

Labor leaders have encountered pressures not only from the state, but also from below. Leaders of central union organizations have encountered demands for accountability from their constituent unions. Leaders of these constituent unions have in turn faced similar pressures from the rank and file. Union leaders, therefore, often act as brokers between the state and employers, on the one hand, and the rank and file they are representing on the other.

Rank-and-file organizations, or those more responsive to their pressure, have been an intermittent feature of recent African labor history. The *autogestion* movement in Algeria during the early 1960s, workers' committees in Tanzania during the early 1970s, the proliferation of local unions in Nigeria during the 1970s, and the workers' committees formed in Ghana and Burkina Faso during the early 1980s are evidence, in different ways and under different circumstances, of the currents of rank-and-file democracy, which is often opposed to official organizations.

1018

Workers' self-management appeared in Algeria after independence during the early 1960s, when industrial and agricultural workers took over the factories and farms deserted by the *colons*. The *autogestion* movement was at first endorsed by the ruling party and state and then neutralized by bureaucratic obstruction. In Tanzania, workers' committees largely independent of NUTA, the official union organization, emerged during the early 1970s and took at face value government guidelines stressing workers' self-management of factories and workplaces. After several years of industrial unrest, including many workers' takeovers, they were dissolved in 1976 and replaced by compliant NUTA branches.

In Ghana, the upheavals following the seizure of power by Jerry Rawlings and the Provisional National Defence Council late in 1981 led to a radical shakeup of the structure of the country's labor movement, which had been in existence continuously since the late 1950s. In 1982, the leaders of the GTUC and the 17 unions affiliated with it were overthrown by an ad hoc rank and file body, and interim management committees were elected to run the unions. Meanwhile, workers' defence committees (WDCs), at first encouraged by the government, were formed in many enterprises and took over management, often in the face of vigorous employer opposition. The WDCs also came into conflict with the restructured unions, for their respective spheres of influence were never properly decided. Eventually, while the government sought support from the International Monetary Fund, it progressively restricted the autonomy of the WDCs, which became effectively an arm of government, and were renamed Committees for the Defence of the Revolution. Ghana's trade-union movement has since recovered to become one of the few forces of opposition to the PNDC regime. A decline in autonomous rank-and-file labor organizations appears to be the trend throughout much of Africa in the straitened conditions of the 1980s, as workers have put their faith in more conventional unionism to defend their interests.

LABOR DISPUTES AND PROTEST: CURRENT ISSUES

As well as having a prominent role in union formation and regulation, the state has intervened strongly in other aspects of industrial relations. Labor-relations structures inherited from the colonial era have often been maintained after independence. In Anglophone states, labor departments, the roles of labor officers and inspectors, labor legislation, conciliation and arbitration procedures, as well as industrial tribunals and courts have often remained substantially the same. Francophone states adopted national labor codes during the 1960s, modeled on the code for French colonies introduced in 1952. This and other legislation have survived long after independence.

In most African countries, state intervention into industrial relations has increased. Pay levels are often officially determined. Where collective bargaining exists, agreements are usually made subject to official approval. Official dispute-settlement procedures are often compulsory. Unions are the junior partners in such consultative bodies as governmental tripartite committees—comprising the government, the employers and the unions—which decide industrial-relations issues. Yet despite the trend of increasing bureaucratization of industrial relations, labor has moved away from presenting its grievances, let alone settling them, through official channels. Mechanisms for resolving disputes are frequently so restrictive as to make any such procedure unworkable. Because the cumbersome procedures for settling disputes are rarely exhausted, strikes and other forms of labor protest are seldom legal; volatile unofficial actions are commonplace, often organized in defiance of government and union leadership. Here we outline the principal issues giving rise to labor disputes, official and unofficial, in recent years.

Pay

Wage regulation has been a main imperative for governments eager to accumulate surpluses for national development, redistribution or, often, for official or illicit appropriation. The impetus for wage control is increased by the large number of workers in government employment who draw directly on the state purse, as well as the workers in economic sectors owned, wholly or in part, by the state. Wage restraint has been accomplished in a number of ways. Collective bargaining may be acknowledged in principle, but it is frequently subject to official restraint which may effectively negate it. Agreements usually require government approval, governments may impose upper limits to any collective bargaining, or they may by decree freeze wages or even cut them. In many countries, pay levels are determined not by collective bargaining, but by official minimum wages set by the governments. Negotiations among the government, employers and unions are conducted at the national level and are frequently highly politicized. Even if the minimum wage is not officially applicable to the private sector, it often establishes a base level for negotiations at the plant or company level, and large-scale private employers frequently reflect changes in the public-sector minimum wages in the wages they pay. In Nigeria, for example, general wage adjustments occurred after the reports of official wage commissions—including the Morgan commission of 1963–64, the Adebo commission of 1970–71 and the Udoji commission of 1975—appointed in recognition of the erosion of the real value of wages. Strikes and disputes have followed such adjustments, with workers pressing for payment of the raises. A brief general strike in 1981 secured a further 25 percent improvement in the minimum wage after another such upward adjustment occurred in 1980.

In Francophone states, pay levels have similarly been determined by reference to officially guaranteed fixed hourly minimum wages, the SMIG for industry and the SMAG for agriculture, both modeled on the French SMIC (Salaire Minimum Interprofessionnel de Croissance). The minimum wage is supposedly linked to the cost-of-living index, but the way in which this is determined is frequently disputed, because the official cost-of-living data are usually inaccurate and out of date. In such countries as Gabon and the Ivory Coast, which, until recently at least, have had the resources, the

1020

purchasing power of wages has generally been maintained. In poorer states, wages have lagged behind the cost of living, particularly during the high inflation of the 1970s. As in Anglophone countries, an increase in the minimum wage signals a rise in other salary levels.

Since the 1970s, the collapse of commodity prices on world markets, the increased cost of oil imports, and the rising debt problem have increased pressures on governments to economize by holding down wages, particularly in the public sector. An ILO study in 1984 found that the situation of minimum-wage earners had become extremely precarious. The minimum wage was reported to have declined in real terms by more than 18 percent in the Ivory Coast during the early 1980s, and wages of low-income earners in Liberia were cut by 17 percent at the beginning of 1983. Similar trends were evident in Congo, Sierra Leone, Tanzania, Zambia and Zimbabwe.

Official austerity measures have often been linked to intervention by the IMF, which has demanded wage restraint as a condition for granting financial support. In Ghana, where an economic recovery program overseen by the IMF has been implemented, increases in the minimum wage following large currency devaluations have failed to maintain even the wage's current level, which has for a long time been recognized as inadequate by the World Bank. This has led to strong protests from Ghana's unions, which have until recently given only grudging support to the government program, and has sparked off large demonstrations in some of the country's major industrial centers. Some modification of the country's pay structures has followed these protests.

As many African countries implement similar "structural adjustment" programs, there have been indications that the era of government-determined wage levels may be coming to an end. A four-year wage freeze in Nigeria was lifted in the 1988 budget, apparently signaling the return of free collective bargaining and reflecting the deregulatory strategy pursued under the government's structural-adjustment program. It was, however, a selective deregulation. The state still intended to oversee agreements negotiated between workers and employers; agreements had to be approved by the ministry of employment, and the Productivity, Prices and Incomes Board was to monitor pay agreements among large employers and to use them as models to advise smaller and medium-scale employers. Further, and most disturbing from the unions' point of view, a ban on strike action during pay negotiations greatly constrained the unions' capacity to exert pressure on employers.

Benefits and allowances
With the impact of inflation on money wages, other components of workers' remuneration—so-called fringe benefits—have assumed increasing importance. These include allowances for, or access to, transport, housing, meals, medical treatment and other welfare benefits. These allowances have partly offset decreases in the real value of the money wage caused by inflation. Grievances over such benefits, the social or welfare components of pay, are often more frequently the causes of industrial disputes than straightforward wage disagreements. This has recently been the case in Ni-

geria. It was the withdrawal of such allowances in the public sector that sparked the general strike of 1981. Since then, cuts in allowances, as well as in pay, by the federal and state governments implementing austerity programs have prompted strong protests from organized labor, although often with few results. Many private employers have, meanwhile, increased the benefits and allowances paid to their employees. Mindful of these increases, as well as stagnating pay and falling morale among public-sector workers, and recognizing the falling real value of wages, the government introduced a package late in 1987 increasing benefits and allowances paid to civil servants.

Nonpayment of wages and allowances

As the worldwide recession has deepened and public resources have dwindled sharply, another issue has become prominent: the actual nonpayment of wages and allowances due. In Nigeria, by the early 1980s, the federal and state governments were in grave financial trouble, partly as a result of the slump in the country's oil earnings, but also because of mismanagement. Seven of the 19 states could not pay their employees, and pay arrears accumulated rapidly. Only by striking or threatening strikes did workers force payment of some of these arrears, marking the beginning of a long struggle by public-sector employees to be properly paid. Unrest has arisen for similar reasons in Ghana. Nonpayment of wages by that country's largest exporter of timber products, a state-owned company, led to serious labor protest in 1986, with workers claiming they had not been paid for up to ten months. A committee of enquiry set up to examine the grievances failed to alleviate the unrest, which eventually erupted into violent confrontations with the police. Although not so frequent, similar disputes over nonpayment of wages in the private sector have also occurred recently in a number of countries.

The social wage

Subsidies on food, fuel, transportation and other necessities, as well as health, education and other welfare provisions—the broader "social wage"—have recently become the focus of attention in many African countries. Subsidies may be in the form of direct government subventions or in the maintenance of overvalued exchange rates. Hence the removal of subsidies and the devaluation of currencies—like cutbacks in welfare, frequent features of structural adjustment—have become another arena of contention between unions and governments. In Nigeria, union agitation late in 1987 against a substantial upward adjustment of petroleum-product prices following a fourfold depreciation of the currency led to the arrest and detention of 13 trade-union leaders for alleged sedition. Zambia has also recently seen popular protest, supported by unions, against the removal of subsidies. Such struggles, as well as those over the diminution of health, education and other services, have pushed unions further into the wider political arena. In the absence of opposition parties or organizations, unions became the focus for opposition to such measures, and there are some signs that governments and their economic advisers may be beginning to heed them.

Unemployment

Another major grievance, directly related to the recession and indirectly to structural adjustment, is the level of redundancies. Terminations and lay-offs are currently probably the most pressing problem for labor and unions. Mass redundancies are routine consequences of austerity measures implemented in conjunction with economic programs overseen by the IMF and the World Bank. They have affected public-sector employment particularly, but the private sector has also been hit by the general economic contraction wrought by austerity measures. An ILO study in 1984 highlighted an alarming decline in modern-sector employment in Africa. In the Ivory Coast, such employment was reported to have fallen by 12 percent annually between 1979 and 1981. Construction has been hit worst by reduced government expenditure; jobs in this sector declined by more than 18 percent in Zimbabwe between 1979 and 1982 and by more than 55 percent in Zambia between 1975 and 1983. Government employment has also been under serious pressure: early in 1986 the Zambian government announced it was aiming to reduce its civil-service staff from 80,000 to 60,000.

The pattern is similar elsewhere. The Nigerian Labour Congress estimated that around 1 million workers were laid off between 1981 and 1983. After the military took power at the end of 1983, purges of the public sector accelerated, and perhaps another 250,000 lost their jobs. The severe squeeze on employment was part of a stringent austerity program imposed to revive the ailing economy without recourse to loans from the IMF. Largely as a result of curbs on importing raw materials, retrenchment in the private sector has also been very extensive. Hundreds of thousands of workers have been laid off, particularly from construction, textiles, vehicle assembly, light manufacturing and the ports. Redundancies have continued to gather pace since a more radical structural-adjustment program was introduced in 1986 under IMF surveillance. In Ghana, the reduction in employment has been proportionately even more drastic: about 30,000 public-sector employees were made redundant in 1985 alone, 27,000 of them from one employer, the Cocoa Marketing Board.

Such mass redundancies have led to protests from organized labor. But because their bargaining power has been so reduced in recent years—not least because of the slump in membership as a result of relentless layoffs—unions have been unable to mount much resistance to the redundancies in either public or private sectors. Governments have instigated employment or redeployment programs in several countries, but these have had little real impact on levels of unemployment. Plans to create 40,000 jobs in Ghana and similar undertakings in Nigeria are unlikely to make more than a dent in unemployment, even if they become fully implemented.

Workplace discipline

Control of work and the workplace is another source of labor dispute and protest. As in fully industrialized countries, the hours and speed of work are a major area of contention between management and labor; timekeeping and the length of the working day are frequently disputed. Securing full

1023

days of work from all workers may be as important for management as the level of pay. Efficiency is another arena of struggle. Low utilization of plant capacity, due in part to low worker productivity, is a common management complaint. In Nigeria, capacity utilization in many plants has dropped to 20 percent in recent years; in Ghana, it has been as low as 10 percent, with similar poor performance reported by many other countries.

Attempts by management to extend control over the production process and work patterns in pursuit of greater productivity have led to frequent disputes. Workers are naturally reluctant to concede to management whatever control they may have over their work. Attempts to introduce new shift patterns often give rise to worker protest. Authoritarian or abrasive supervision may be as common a source of disputes as pay and benefits. As in industrialized countries, management's assertion of the "right to manage" is a common expression of this tension between labor and management. In current conditions of recession and austerity, managements have found it easier than in the past to assert such control. As in the fully industrialized world, they have been able to impose substantial measures of restructuring and "rationalization," usually to the great disadvantage of the work force.

INTERNATIONAL RELATIONS

Foreign influence over African trade unions has long been a source of contention, both between unions and governments and among the different labor organizations themselves. Both before and after independence, many African unions looked to European labor organizations and the international federations for financial support, and affiliations to international organizations—principally the Brussels-based International Confederation of Free Trade Unions (ICFTU) and the Prague-based World Federation of Trade Unions (WFTU)—grew substantially. But the growth of pan-Africanism and the nonaligned movement gave rise to misgivings about such affiliations and pressure to dissolve them. An early effort, during the 1950s, to assert African union autonomy from foreign influence was the Union Générale des Travailleurs de l'Afrique Noire (UGTAN), led by Sékou Touré of Guinea with a wide base in Francophone Africa. The main international federations responded by establishing continentally-based organizations, while UGTAN was succeeded by the independent All-African Trade Union Federation (AATUF), formed by unionists from Ghana, Guinea, Mali, Morocco and Egypt. In addition to these organizations, which underwent numerous realignments during the 1960s, were a number of other foreign-funded agencies with interests in African trade unions, the most prominent being the African-American Labor Center (AALC) funded by U.S. unions and other American sources.

Hopes that the creation of the Organisation of African Trade Union Unity (OATUU) in 1973 on the initiative of the OAU would overcome problems arising from affiliation with the various international labor confederations have been disappointed. The OATUU, like its predecessors, has been dogged by financial, organizational and leadership problems; by Afro-Arab, Anglophone-Francophone, national and personal rivalries; and by allegations of foreign interference.

Within a few years of the foundation of the OATUU, most national unions in Africa had joined. Union centers in 52 countries were affiliated by 1976, and the membership has until recently remained at around that figure. Voting rights, which have proved contentious, are dependent on the fulfillment of three criteria: member union centrals should be fully paid up; they should be the only national trade union central in their country; and they should not be affiliated to any international trade-union organization. Based in Accra, Ghana, the OATUU has regional sections covering southern, western, central, eastern and northern Africa, and sectoral suborganizations covering unions of mining, agricultural and industrial workers.

The OATUU's fragility was highlighted at conferences in Lagos and Accra in 1985 and 1986, when major divisions came into the open. Amid allegations of interference by the AALC and the U.S. Central Intelligence Agency, criticisms of the performance of the secretariat, a vote of no-confidence in the secretary-general, and acrimonious disputes over voting rights, election of new officers, financial irregularities and ideological differences, the OATUU split into two groups. One was headed by the incumbent president, Ali Nafashi of Libya, and the other, the majority comprising 28 countries' union centrals, by the former president of the Nigerian Labour Congress, Hassan Sunmonu. The majority faction emerged with eventual control of the OATUU. By late 1987, the organization had regained sufficient cohesion to organize a conference and issue a cogent statement on the African debt problem, following an assembly of the OAU heads of state on the debt crisis. Despite this apparent progress, however, the issue of foreign interference in African unions remains unresolved and the prospect of real pan-African trade union unity stills seems remote.

PROSPECTS FOR ORGANIZED LABOR IN AFRICA

African workers suffer from the effects of austerity measures accompanying structural adjustment programs: removal of subsidies, imposition of charges for health, education and other services, other reductions in the social wage, and mass redundancies. The deregulatory impulse instigated under such programs has recently been extended specifically to the labor sphere. The squeeze on labor imposed over the last few years in austerity programs is being intensified in a number of countries by the dismantling of gains, however limited, made by labor since independence and formalized in labor legislation. Advances made in pay and working conditions have come under threat, as has the very right to organize.

The outlook for organized labour in the face of such changes seems very gloomy. Weakened by falling memberships as a result of mass redundancies, unions hardly seem in a position to challenge such developments. Deregulation, moreover, is being selectively applied. While the resumption of collective bargaining has apparently been sanctioned in Nigeria, for example, the unions' bargaining power has been weakened by bans on strikes during pay negotiations. Zambian unions have likewise been hamstrung by recently enacted statutes barring strikes and restricting free collective bargaining; this legislation has remained in force despite the government's break with the IMF. If such developments continue, some African states could conceivably follow the course of deregulated, cheap-labor nations elsewhere in the Third World. Faced with weakened bargaining positions, trade unions, it has been argued, should form alliances with the so-called new social movements—community groups, cooperatives, women's organizations, agricultural workers' associations and other popular pressure groups. Such alliances might enhance efforts to mitigate the worst effects of recession and structural adjustment on Africa's poor. Such a process is already under way to some extent, with unions calling for better education and health and welfare services, among other issues of concern to the general populace. The contrary view is that such a strategy would dilute the defense of specific worker interests.

Organized labour has occasionally shown itself able to mount strong resistance to retrenchment policies. In Ghana, the government had to back down from its curtailment of allowances and redundancy payments in 1986–87. Following trade-union and popular pressure early in 1987, the Nigerian government rescinded an amendment to legislation that would have effectively abolished the minimum wage. Throughout Africa, simply maintaining workers' purchasing power has been no mean achievement in the face of rampant inflation and retrenchment. Such limited successes testify to the continuing resilience of African unions, whatever their limitations. There is also evidence suggesting that some governments recognize the wisdom of maintaining reasonable relations with union organizations in order to avoid the explosions of popular discontent against austerity that have recently occurred in Tunisia, Egypt, Sudan and Zambia. An uneasy, ambivalent relationship between government and unions, rather than confrontation, may be the developing pattern. There is an increasing official recognition at both governmental and international levels that structural adjustment must be accompanied by measures ameliorating the consequent socioeconomic damage. Yet the precariousness of union activity was amply demonstrated in Nigeria in 1988 when the government dissolved the executive of the Nigeria Labour Congress. This was ostensibly done to halt the bitter infighting between rival factions of the NLC, but the intervention occurred after effective union agitation against austerity measures accompanying the government's structural adjustment program.

African trade unionists hope such interventions do not become the norm. Unions' survival over the coming years is important not just for their members but for the population at large. For all their shortcomings, unions are often the best-organized interest groups and frequently the only voice of opposition in many African states. They are often the only bodies with the capacity, however tenuous, to defend human rights in an increasingly bleak political and economic landscape.

CONTEMPORARY TRADE UNIONISM IN SOUTH AFRICA AND NAMIBIA

Trade unions have emerged as a major political and economic force in South Africa over the past 15 years. Growing from a series of spontaneous strikes in the early 1970s, the contemporary black trade-union movement has consolidated itself into a formidable opponent of apartheid. With a membership of around 1.5 million, the roots of the unions now extend through all the major urban and periurban industrial areas. The domestic and agricultural sectors of the economy, historically notoriously difficult to organize, are now also increasingly being penetrated.

The emerging trade unions have been responsible for important improvements in the living standards of their members. These include the massive increases in wages that have occurred since 1973, as well as the initiation and design of such new forms of social-security benefits as provident funds and maternity leaves. The nonracial trade-union movement can also claim responsibility for the dismantling of a paternalistic and racist industrial-relations structure, which has now been replaced by a negotiating framework recognizing democratic, shop-floor unions as partners in industrial bargaining. At a political level, the black trade unions have organized the largest protest demonstrations against the apartheid system, including the creation of "people's holidays," de facto holidays created as a result of union-sponsored work stoppages on such important occasions as International Workers Day (May 1) and the June 16 day of commemoration—the anniversary of the 1976 uprising in Soweto.

We shall present a brief history of the development of trade unionism in South Africa and Namibia and chronicle some of its achievements, particularly over the last decade. While mention will be made of the role of white workers, the major focus will be on the most important actors of the past ten years, the black trade unionists.

White trade unions

Trade unionism is not a new phenomenon in South Africa. Immigrant white workers from the British, American and Australian mining industry brought with them a tradition of craft-based trade unions. From the early 1890s, white workers attempted to form racially exclusive craft unions whose major campaigns for wages and recognition led to the formation of a hierarchy of color in both mining and manufacturing. This division of skill and privilege, forged during the first years of industrializing South Africa and consolidated by the accession to power of governments voted in by white workers (blacks were excluded from voting), remained until economic forces, creating a need for black skills in the economy, forced the abandonment of job reservation and the color hierarchy from the late 1960s.

The alliance of white workers and the white-controlled state served to create a trade-union tradition based on race, craft and government support. The achievements of white trade unions occurred not as a result of shop-floor militancy, but because of their influence as an important constituency in the political domain. After an initial militancy during the first two decades of this century, when strike action by white workers was not uncommon and led even to the failed workers' revolt of 1922, white workers used their voting power to oust the procapital South African party of General Jan Smuts and install instead a coalition government of the National party with the South African Labour party as a junior partner. The Industrial Conciliation Act of 1924 provided the major vehicle for white trade-union activity. While the industrial council system introduced by the act served well the interests of white workers over the next 60 years, in the long run the bureaucratic practices it encouraged gave the white trade-union movement a passivity that undermined any serious ability to defend its parochial interests after the 1970s. During this time the black work force, growing in skill, confidence and size, began to take center stage in the struggle for a just South Africa.

Three waves of unionization
Black workers first joined trade unions in South Africa during the second decade of the 20th century. The first known trade union to organize black workers was the Industrial Workers of Africa, organized under the auspices of the Socialist League in 1915. This shortlived organization was soon superseded by the spectacular growth of the Industrial and Commercial Workers Union (ICU), led by Clements Kadile. Born during a strike of dockers in Cape Town in 1919, during its life span of some 15 years the ICU became the largest mass movement of its time, rising to a membership of 100,000. Spurred by low wages and poor working conditions in the urban areas, severe overcrowding and land dispossession in the rural areas, and the general political oppression of blacks, membership in both town and country soared. Yet the very mass nature of the organization, its failure to consolidate organizational structures, its very wide base among both workers and peasants, as well as its failure to make significant political gains in the face of intransigent capital and state, led to a demise that was swifter and more spectacular than its rise. By 1930 the ICU was a spent force, and it left behind disappointment and division. To its credit, however, it formed a tradition of organizing blacks into trade-union structures—a tradition that had at least some practical experience of success and failure. This legacy was a crucial backdrop to the next wave of black trade-union organization.

Encouraged by the industrialization of South Africa from a mining to a manufacturing economy (a structural change which has its origins in the isolation of South Africa from the world economy during World War I), black workers and some of their white colleagues organized themselves into new industrial trade unions. Unlike the ICU (which was a widespread mass movement not necessarily based in factories) and unlike the craft unions (whose basis was the skill of their members), this second wave of unions organized all workers in the industries in which they operated. Some unions, such as those affiliated to the Communist-led Federation of Non-European Trade Unions (FNETU), which grew to a membership of 10,000 workers, were predominantly black but recruited all workers into the same unions. The successor to FNETU, the Council of Non-European Trade Unions (CNETU), was formed in November 1941. By the end of the war, CNETU was a national federation claiming 150,000 members in 119 unions.

While some of the industrial unions practiced nonracial organization, others, such as the Garment Workers Union, organized on a parallel-union basis—so that separate union branches of workers based on color existed within the same union. The important development, however, was that black, Coloured, Indian and white workers would be organized into the same union in the same industry. Industrial unionism, based on organization of all workers on the shop floor, would eventually predominate over craft-based traditions. The industrial unions grew strong and by 1947 came to control the largest trade-union federation of the time, the South African Trades and Labour Council (SATLC).

Despite the growth of industrial unions, racist practices continued, and tensions within the trade-union movement, which had grown dramatically during the industrialization of the war years, split it asunder. By the end of the war, the SATLC could no longer contain the various tendencies within it. Conservative craft unions, white racist industrial unions, racially mixed industrial trade unions organizing black workers on a parallel basis, and nonracial industrial trade unions sat increasingly uneasily within the same organization.

During the postwar period, restructuring took place. The SATLC split; in 1947, seven unions protesting the affiliation of African unions with the SATLC broke away to form the Co-ordinating Council of South African Trade Unions (CCSATU). In 1950, a more important split occurred in the course of debates within the SATLC over whether to mobilize members for the passage of the Suppression of Communism Act, which contained important implications for trade unions. The conservative craft unions and the white industrial unions supported the bill, and eventually left the SATLC to form the South African Federation of Trade Unions (SAFTU). In 1954, the remaining unions within the SATLC decided to attempt to reestablish links with the craft unions at the expense of the black trade unions within the organization. While not successful in attracting back the right-wing unions, the result nonetheless was a racially exclusive South African Trade Union Council (SATUC, later the Trade Union Council of South Africa, TUCSA). TUCSA's major contribution to the history of trade unionism in South Africa was its vacillation, which at times admitted black trade unions on a parallel basis, only to exclude them later. These exclusions would occur whenever the government attempted to suppress the black trade union movement and at the same time to create a racially exclusive union organization. TUCSA's inability to take a stand one way or the other on the issue of racially integrated unions finally led to its demise some 33 years later when, unable to satisfy both left- and right-wing unions, it disbanded.

The SATLC unions, committed to nonracialism, were left out in the cold in the reshuffling that occurred during the early 1950s. In May 1954, CNETU called a conference to discuss unity among black trade unions and to organize opposition to the proposed Industrial Conciliation Act, which promised to entrench racial separation within registered trade unions. Fourteen SATLC unions attended these talks and, together with the CNETU unions, formed the South African Congress of Trade Unions (SACTU) in 1955. SACTU represented the third wave of black unionization: while it was the smallest of the federations operating at the time (representing at its height 53,000 workers in 51 unions), it had the largest effect on African workers. Not only did it bring to the work force an industrial militancy, it also argued that politics and economics could not be separated in the workers' struggle against exploitation.

A major part of the strategy of the SACTU affiliates was their attempt to build effective national industrial unions. They were involved in a number of factory-bound struggles to improve the wages and working conditions of their members. In the main, however, shop-floor activity was smashed by a combination of employer intransigence, police action and a weakening of the black trade-un')n movement as a whole in the face of increasingly stringent state action. Of the SACTU unions, only one or two survived into the 1960s.

Because of SACTU's lack of success at the factory level, and given its commitment to linking political and economic issues, it worked with other organizations opposed to apartheid, and in particular became part of what was known as the Congress Alliance, which combined the major opposition groups of the time, the African National Congress (ANC), the South African Indian Congress (SAIC), the predominantly white Congress of Democrats (COD), and the South African Coloured Peoples Organisation (SACPO). As part of the Congress Alliance, SACTU organized the 1957 pound-a-day campaign and participated in a number of calls for protest stoppages and national strikes. Over its first five years, however, SACTU faced a massive onslaught unleashed by the newly elected Nationalist government. Alongside their Congress allies, SACTU leadership was arrested, detained and banned. SACTU members involved in strikes and demonstrations were similarly harassed, physically assaulted and detained. Given the inability of SACTU unions to consolidate their shop-floor structure in the face of such massive repression, SACTU faded from existence in the early 1960s and joined other sections of the alliance, in particular the ANC, which was banned in 1961, in exile. (SACTU itself was never actually banned.)

Black workers therefore entered the 1960s with their organizations destroyed and their leaders either in exile or in jail. They faced a militantly right-wing government determined to impose apartheid and to smash any opposition with a zeal previously unknown in South Africa. Employers were generally sympathetic to the crushing of black trade-union organization, and their hostility in the work place was a further barrier which black workers found it difficult to overcome. The decade was a dismal one for black workers, and it was fully ten years before they recovered sufficiently to begin again the long march toward organization. During the early 1970s, organization of workers recommenced and worker militancy reemerged with strike action in Johannesburg and Durban.

The latest wave
The first indication of this new stirring was the strike by black bus drivers in Johannesburg in 1972, followed by a massive strike involving 60,000 workers in Durban in 1973. These strikes were accompanied by the organization of workers, at first, into such service organizations as the Urban Training Project and the Industrial Aid Society in Johannesburg, the General Factory Workers Benefit Fund in Durban, and the Cape Town-based Western Province Workers Advisory Board. Often initiated and led by

white students and academics, these groupings soon gave way to more permanent union structures, and by 1979 the emergent unions had consolidated into three distinct organizational thrusts. The largest of these groups was the Federation of South African Trade Unions (FOSATU), which at its launch in 1979 claimed 12 unions and 45,000 members. FOSATU's guiding policies were a commitment to nonracialism, shop-floor leadership, and a style of organization which promoted shop-floor militancy. FOSATU was followed in 1980 by the launch of the Council of Unions of South Africa (CUSA), with 9 affiliates and 30,000 members. CUSA differed from FOSATU in stressing black leadership and a more decentralized form of organization. CUSA unions were also noticeably less militant on the factory floor. The third organizational thrust could be perceived in those black trade unions which chose to remain outside the two major federations, notably the Cape Town-based Food and Canning Workers Union (one of the SACTU affiliates that survived the 1960s) and the Western Province General Workers Union. Both unions were committed to nonracial union organization, but differed from FOSATU affiliates in their commitment to a more overt link between politics and economics. FOSATU's insistence on concentrating organizational effort on the shop floor before engaging in direct political confrontation with the state was the major difference between the two groups. During the early 1980s, the independent unions were joined by the South African Allied Workers Union (SAAWU), which organized mainly in the East London and Durban areas.

Political events during the early 1980s set the scene for a consolidation of these groups. Amendments to the Industrial Conciliation Act, a result of a recognition by both capital and the state that black workers and their unions could no longer be ignored, for the first time legally recognized black and nonracial trade unions and created a space within which newly established unions could develop. Not only did membership grow, but worker militancy, as evidenced by a growing number of strikes, also increased. According to official figures, there were 276 strikes in 1973 involving 98,029 workers; by 1985 this had jumped to 389 strikes involving 239,816 workers.

The new legislation initially was cause for a major division among the various union groups. FOSATU unions agreed to register with the Registrar of Trade Unions, arguing that registration, by conferring legal recognition, gave considerable room to strengthen worker organization without imposing any major constraints. The independent unions, on the other hand, argued that to accept registration was to accept state control. The bitterness created by this division, however, soon gave way to a unity forced by the state's action against a Food and Canning organizer, Neil Aggett. Found hanging in his cell in February 1982, Aggett was the first trade-union leader to die in detention. A national day of protest mobilized 100,000 workers throughout the country to stop work for periods varying from ten minutes to a whole day. It was the first major national demonstration called by the unions since the stoppages of the 1950s. Called and supported by all the emerging black trade unions, the Aggett stoppage furthered the unity process and culminated four years later in yet another restructuring of the black trade-union movement.

1031

Between 1981 and 1985, representatives of the various union groups met on several occasions to discuss the elusive goal of unity. At the end of the process, two formal organizations were born. In November 1985, the Congress of South African Trade Unions (COSATU) was inaugurated. Comprising 33 unions and claiming a membership of 500,000, COSATU could justly claim to be the most representative organization of workers in South African history. Size was not the only criterion here, for the new federation also embraced the largest unions organizing in the most important sectors of the economy. Endorsing the policies of nonracialism, democratic worker control, and industrial unionism as well as a commitment to take up campaigns to defend and advance the political and economic demands of the working class, the new federation clearly intended to be a force to reckon with.

Two early actions by COSATU had important consequences. Criticism by its newly elected president, National Union of Mineworkers leader Elijah Barayi, of Chief Buthelezi, the leader of the Inkatha movement and chief executive of the KwaZulu homeland, prompted Inkatha to launch its own union federation, the United Workers Union of South Africa (UWUSA). Militantly procapitalist as well as antisanctions, Inkatha and UWUSA have been accused of acts of violence, including murder, against COSATU members in Natal, where Inkatha has its strongest base. The second initiative, taken within weeks of COSATU's launch, was a meeting between the newly elected general secretary, Jay Naidoo, and senior members of SACTU and the banned ANC in Harare. These talks were followed in March 1987 by a meeting of the senior officials of all three organizations, which concluded with a communiqué noting that "lasting solutions can only emerge from the national liberation movement, headed by the ANC, and the entire democratic forces of our country, of which COSATU is an important and integral part." COSATU clearly meant to be no stranger to controversy.

Unwilling to join COSATU, those unions involved in the unity discussions who remained committed to a policy of black leadership formed the National Council of Trade Unions (NACTU) in 1986. Claiming a signed-up membership of 400,000 and a paid-up membership of 250,000, NACTU comprised ex-CUSA unions who joined up with unions affiliated to the Azanian Congress of Trade Unions (AZACTU), a small grouping of unions explicitly identified with the black-conciousness movement. At its inaugural congress, NACTU adopted a policy of worker control, black working-class leadership and nonaffiliation to political organizations. Smaller than COSATU, NACTU and its affiliates also have a less prominent industrial and political profile. In general, NACTU affiliates have been less involved in industrial action. NACTU's major political initiative was a meeting with the banned and exiled Pan-African Congress (PAC), the black-nationalist rival of the ANC, held in Tanzania during 1987.

Major campaigns
A major reason for the growth of trade unions in South Africa over the past decade has been their ability to deliver material goods to their members. The living-wage campaign, initiated in 1979 with industry-wide strikes by

the National Automobile and Allied Workers Union and subsequently taken up by the union movement as a whole, has resulted in a considerable upward movement of wages. For reasons not entirely clear, the South African government has seen the living-wage campaign pursued by COSATU affiliates as dangerous to state security. A number of rallies to discuss and publicize the campaign have been banned, as well as several COSATU publications dealing with the issue.

Other working conditions have also come under scrutiny. Hours of work, fixed at a maximum of 46 per week in 1941, have increasingly come down as a result of union demands. Unions have demanded a 40-hour week, insisting at the same time that the reduction in hours should not result in any loss of income. Unheard of before 1980, industrial agreements incorporating these demands have dramatically increased in number. Shifts, shift premiums, overtime and overtime rates, discipline and fair disciplinary procedures have all become part of most union-company negotiations. The important point here is that both in terms of the power achieved by unions on the factory floor and increasingly in terms of decisions handed down by the Industrial Court (an institution born of the new industrial-relations dispensation), conditions affecting workers can no longer be arbitrarily decided by employer or government fiat.

Social-security issues have also been in the forefront of union demands. An ill-conceived attempt in 1981 by the government to retain pension contributions in a national fund until a worker reached pensionable age resulted in major industrial unrest. As a result, the government withdrew the bill, one of only two occasions when the Nationalist government backed down on a proposed law. Unions have gone on to negotiate provident funds as alternatives to pension schemes. Union representatives now sit on the boards of a number of pension and provident funds, controlling large amounts of money. In the case of the Metal Industries Pension Fund, its assets are in excess of R250 million. The political muscle of the unions is increasingly being applied in the financial sphere, a development with important consequences for the future.

Housing has also become a major issue for unions. With a national shortage of at least 500,000 units and much resultant overcrowding and squatting in the urban areas, unions have increasingly used their financial muscle on pension and provident fund boards to finance more housing. Building cooperatives for unemployed union members are also currently being discussed as a method of not only overcoming the housing shortages at relatively reasonable cost but also of combating increasing unemployment in the country.

The black unions' ability to achieve this progress is the more impressive given the political environment in which they have had to work. It is to a consideration of this environment that we now turn.

Unions and politics
We need to examine the South African government's attempts to control the growth of the trade unions within its so-called reform program. In

addition, we must take account of the internal political dynamics of the union movement. A full picture requires understanding both elements.

In 1979, the Nationalist government introduced an amendment to the Industrial Conciliation Act, which for the first time in South African history gave legal recognition to trade unions with black membership. Seen by the government as part of its newfound "reform" strategy, the amendment unleashed a storm of controversy among the black trade unions. The FOSATU unions, as we have seen, agreed to register with the government. The requirements of the new act, such as the submission of a union constitution for approval, the annual submission of financial reports, and the regular updating of the names of national office holders, FOSATU argued, placed no new restrictions on trade unions. They were already operating in an environment where the state had the license to acquire whatever information it needed. The new legislation, FOSATU argued, provided a space within which emergent unions could grow. The independent unions— SAAWU, the General Workers Union and the Food and Canning Workers—argued that to register was to agree to state supervision. Registered unions would inevitably become collaborators in the state strategy of reform.

With hindsight, FOSATU's argument has proved correct. Union militancy increased after 1979. Indeed, the unions that registered, notably the Metal and Allied Workers Union and the National Automobile and Allied Workers Union, became responsible for the largest number of days lost consequent to strike action. Because of a further amendment to the labor legislation which required unregistered unions to supply exactly the same information to the Registrar of Trade Unions as registered unions, and because of the increasingly obvious fact that registration had not adversely affected the militancy of the registered unions, the majority of black trade unions have now registered.

The state has recognized that its strategy of union registration to curb their militancy has failed. Indeed, the black unions have made innovative uses of their legal status. Rather than accept the state's version of a union constitution, generally modeled on those of white trade unions, the FOSATU unions forced the registrar to accept a new model enshrining shop-floor participation and nonracial membership. Instead of agreeing to the strike clauses of the legislation, intended to impose long cooling-off periods in industrial disputes, the unions took employers to the new Industrial Court. This court began convicting employers of unfair labor practices, an entirely novel concept provided for in the amended labor legislation. The court handed down several decisions reinstating many workers dismissed in the course of labor disputes. The Court's decisions raised howls of protest among employers. In response to employer pressure, and reacting to the black unions' increasing industrial militancy and political strength, the state has launched new attacks on the movement.

The employers, aided by the recession which has increased unemployment by some 18 percent over the past three years, have increased their resistance to the unions' demands. Over the same period, wage increases have been contained at around the 12 percent level, well below the inflation rate of 15–20 percent. In addition, employer caution in handling recent industrial disputes has tended to protect them from union-sponsored unfair labor practices suits. The most dramatic example so far was the 1987 mineworkers' strike, in which 100,000 members of the National Union of Mineworkers struck for six weeks over the percentage difference between their demands and the employers' offer. Employers refused to budge in the face of the largest strike in the history of the mining industry; miners returned to work, having demonstrated to the employers an ability to organize industrial action on a massive scale. Yet workers' demands were not achieved.

State policy has been threefold. First, the government has served notice of its intention to curb "political unionism"; the most prominent example of this determination is the long trial (1987–88) of National Union of Metal Workers general secretary, Moses Mayekiso. Charged with treason, he is being tried for helping establish the so-called street committees and people's courts, alternative local-government institutions established in the black township where he lives. Less dramatic has been the refusal to permit overseas travel to union leaders who have been outspoken in their criticisms of the government and who have met with officials of the ANC. The state has increasingly prohibited meetings to consider issues it considers "political." May Day rallies and general meetings to consider COSATU's living-wage demands have been forbidden. There has also been a noticeable increase in harassment and detention of union leaders. During the first quarter of 1988 COSATU union offices were searched and union officials arrested in ten separate incidents.

The second part of the state's strategy is to undermine union organization by deregulating the economy. Policy now permits the deregulation of designated geographical areas. The effect of this policy, recently applied to an urban industrial area in Johannesburg, has been to nullify any statutes regarding wages and working conditions and to allow employers to regulate them at will. This strategy has been highly successful in the tribal homelands and in those industrial areas that border on them. Wages and working conditions in these notoriously antiunion areas are appalling, and an increasing number of employers have been encouraged to move there. But such moves will no longer be necessary now that the homelands, because of the deregulation policy, have come to the towns.

The third part of state strategy, which was before parliament in 1988, is a series of amendments to the Labour Relations Act. This amendment is designed to curb union militancy in a way that the current state of emergency, so successful in suppressing black political and community organizations, has signally failed to do for the unions. The amendment provides, in the first place, for far more stringent regulations regarding strike action; employers may sue unions for damages in the event of illegal strikes. Unfair labor practices are more strictly defined, removing the court's discretion to interpret such practices. Sympathy strikes are henceforth specified as unfair labor practices, and individual union organizers may be held liable for the actions of their members.

Allied to this strategy of containment was the promulgation, in March

1988, of regulations forbidding COSATU to undertake any "political" campaigns. At the same time, administrative action all but banned the most prominent of the black political organizations still operating legally in South Africa. The trade-union movement is considering its response to these restrictions. A campaign against the amendments has resulted in a number of demonstrations: in one incident, in Johannesburg, 300 members of three unions undertook a protest march; it was broken up by the police and 21 workers were arrested. The state is clearly determined that its reform policy shall be narrowly conceived—limited to allowing workers "economic" rights, and sternly forbidding any concessions in the "political" field.

It is sometimes argued that South African black trade unions have been politicized because they represent the only available channel for black protest. The state is certainly worried about the increasing politicization of black trade unions and the measures described above are an attempt to curb this trend. To understand the nature of this politicization and the roots of various union actions, we should describe the current ideological currents within the unions. Three of these are discernible: a black-consciousness ideology associated with NACTU; the procapitalist moderation of UWUSA; and the so-called populist vs. workerist tendencies within COSATU. While only the contemporary forms of these debates can be described here, they all have long histories within the South African context.

NACTU's black-consciousness ideology expresses itself primarily in a commitment to black leadership of the NACTU unions. The major result of this is the absence of any white officials or members in NACTU unions, with no other substantial practical consequence. This has not resulted in more militant stances by the unions either inside or outside the factory. Indeed, the activities of NACTU's unions are relatively insignificant when compared with their COSATU rivals. The political implications of black consciousness, however, are important. In deciding against nonracialism, NACTU has placed itself in opposition to those antigovernment organizations, currently in the majority in South Africa, who subscribe to a nonracial policy. Because these include such major groupings as the United Democratic Front and the ANC, such a policy has driven NACTU closer to a political alliance with the ANC's rival, the PAC. While the PAC is currently not a major force either inside or outside South Africa, this has not always been the case, and it may change in the future. The appeal of black nationalism in a situation as racially polarized as South Africa is a powerful one and may well reassert itself. Should that happen, NACTU would offer an established union wing to any political party which then might emerge.

UWUSA now exists more as an appendage of the Zulu Inkatha than as an independent trade union. On an ideological level, its main interventions have been to support the Inkatha antisanctions position and to argue that socialism is not an appropriate ideology in the South African context. At a practical level, UWUSA's activities have not resulted in a growing union presence or a large number of recognition agreements with employers. One of the few such agreements was with BTR Sarmcol, a British-owned rubber manufacturer, involved in a bitter dispute with COSATU's Metal and Allied Workers Union, in which the entire work force was dismissed. UWUSA's recognition at this Natal-based company, following the dismissals, cast the union in the role of strikebreaker. In other situations, such as the dispute at the Marievale mine, UWUSA members have been accused of picking fights with members of rival unions, a recurrent accusation leveled at the union. UWUSA's importance thus lies not in its size or industrial muscle, but in its tactics in the factories and townships, predominantly in Natal. Its future depends very much on the place of Inkatha in South Africa's unfolding political drama.

An important political division in unionism has been that between "populists" and "workerists," a division which predates COSATU but which has now come to reside within it. The debate is occurring among those unions having the largest presence in the country, the largest number of shop stewards, the most recognition agreements, unions responsible for the majority of strikes and the most impressive political demonstrations. At the debate's heart lies the political disagreement over which group should lead the struggle for liberation in South Africa and should then take power once the struggle is concluded. The populists believe that such leadership should be exercised by the United Democratic Front and by implication the ANC. Accordingly, the political strategy to be followed would entail a two-stage liberation: first, liberation from apartheid (the so-called bourgeois democratic revolution) by an alliance of popular opposition groups headed by the ANC, followed by a socialist revolution when issues of economic equality (as distinct from political equality) would be addressed. Workerists, on the other hand, argue that the massive development of the working class demanded by the South African economy have long obviated the need for a bourgeois democratic revolution. The workerist view provides for the apartheid regime to be replaced by a socialist one, headed by a working-class party. The current alliance between the ANC and the Communist party (one of the oldest Communist parties in existence) is not seen as leading to this future, and while there is no evidence of an alternative party structure emerging, certainly the workerist emphasis on building leadership from the factory floor is seen as a prerequisite for the establishment of a democratically controlled workers' party. At the same time, workerists argue that experience in other newly developing countries, especially African ones, has shown that unless the workers' movement is strong and rooted in the factories, it will be suppressed by its former allies in the struggle for independence. Trade unions in Africa have not shown any marked ability to defend worker interests after independence. An independent trade union movement in the liberation struggle is therefore a necessary prerequisite for the defense of worker interests after liberation has been achieved.

Differences in political world views have led to very different practices on the ground. Populist-led unions have emphasized political struggles, and have been more evident in high-profile political debates and demonstrations. Workerist-led unions have continued to consolidate their presence in the factories. The question of which element will dominate COSATU very much depends on events within the South African political environment as a whole. During the mass mobilizations in the black townships, which led to the imposition of the states of emergency in 1985 and 1986 (the latter is still in force), populist groupings held the upper hand. COSATU held high-level talks with the ANC, and participated in a number of mass stoppages whose initial effectiveness diminished as the state of emergency took hold. Workerists have increased their influence recently as the retreat into the factories has taken place in the face of the state and employer offensives. The final outcome of this struggle, part and parcel of the outcome of the greater liberation struggle in South Africa, is likewise entirely unpredictable.

Namibia

Namibia remains very much in the shadow of developments in South Africa. In many respects, developments in the union field have mirrored South African events. Labor began to stir in 1971: in that year the South-West African People's Organisation (SWAPO) activists helped organize a general strike in which more than 12,000 people in 12 towns stopped work for three months. Their protest was against wages, working conditions and the so-called wire system, the contract-labor system which dominated the Namibian labor economy. In 1973, a further massive wave of strikes took place. Some saw these events in Namibia influencing South Africa's wave of strikes in the same year. While these displays of solidarity eventually led to the formal abolition of the wire system in 1978, they did not consolidate into lasting union structures. Worker organizations collapsed because of inexperienced leaders, insufficient factory- and mine-based organization, and most importantly state repression. An attempt by SWAPO's internal wing to set up the National Union of Namibian Workers (NUNW) in 1978 failed within a few months.

During the mid-1980s, coinciding with SWAPO's decision to build internal organizations parallel to its armed struggle waged from Namibia's borders, the NUNW was relaunched. Influenced by events within South Africa, the union grouping decided to abandon its status as a general union and set up industrial affiliates in the main sectors of the economy. Mindful of its earlier collapse, NUNW embarked on a shop-steward training program to develop leadership at the factory level. The union then began a massive recruiting drive throughout the economy and has over the past few years established an impressive presence in Namibia. It showed its organizational ability on May Day, 1987, when more than 35,000 workers, almost 16 percent of the work force, arrived at union-organized rallies. May Day was followed by a spate of strikes in the major sectors of the economy, including the meat-processing plants, the fish-packing factories and the copper mines. Union membership has also increased: the main NUNW affiliates—the Mineworkers Union of Namibia, the Namibian Food and Allied Workers Union and the Metal and Allied Namibian Workers Union—numbered an estimated 32,000 members throughout the country by early 1988.

The state has not remained passive in the face of this challenge. Police action has resulted in raids on union offices, detention of union members and officials and confiscation of documents. A more long-term response is the establishment of a commission of enquiry into the territory's labor legislation under the chairmanship of Professor Nic Wiehan, who was chairman of the similar commission in South Africa that set the stage for the labor reforms occurring there. The establishment of the new Wiehan Commission is an attempt by the state to counter and control the developing labor movement in Namibia.

FURTHER READING

On African trade unionism in general:

Ananaba, Wogu. *The Trade Union Movement in Africa: Promise and Performance*, London: C. Hurst, 1979.

Effects of Recession in African Countries: Synthesis Report. Jobs and Skills Program for Africa (JASPA). Addis Ababa: International Labor Office, 1984.

Freund, W. "Labour and Labour History in Africa: A Review of the Literature." *African Studies Review* 27, no. 2 (1984).

Labour Relations in Africa: Proceedings of a Symposium Held in Nairobi, November 1982. Labour-Management Relations Series. Geneva: International Labor Office, 1983.

Report of Activities of the OATUU by the Secretary-General to the Fourth Congress, Lagos, Nigeria, January 1985. Accra: Organization of African Trade Union Unity, 1985.

Sandbrook, Richard, and Cohen, Robin, (eds.) *The Development of an African Working Class: Studies in Class Formation and Action.* London: Longmans; Toronto and Buffalo: University of Toronto Press, 1975.

Southall, Roger J., ed. *Labor and Unions in Africa and Asia.* London: Macmillan, 1988.

———. *Trade Unions and the New Industrialisation of the Third World.* London: Zed Books; Ottawa: University of Ottawa Press; Pittsburgh: University of Pittsburgh Press, 1988.

On South African trade unionism:

Adler, Taffy. "The Extent of Shiftwork in South Africa." *South African Labour Bulletin* 12 (October 1987).

———. "Social Welfare and the Democratisation of the Economy." *South Africa International* 17 (October 1986).

Callinicos, Luli. *A People's History of South Africa.* Vol. 1, *Gold and Workers, 1886–1924.* Johannesburg: Ravan Press, 1980. Vol. 2, *Working Life, 1886–1940.* Johannesburg: Ravan Press, 1987.

Davis, R. *Capital, the State and White Wage Earners.* London: Harvester Press, 1979.

Friedman, S. *Building Tomorrow Today: African Workers in Trade Unions, 1970–1984.* Johannesburg: Ravan Press, 1987.

Graaff, Janet, and Maree, Johann. *Residential and Migrant African Workers in Cape Town.* Cape Town: Southern Africa Labour and Research Unit, 1977.

Lewis, Jon. *Industrialisation and Trade Union Organisation, 1925–1955: The Rise and Fall of the South African Trades and Labour Council.* Cambridge and New York: Cambridge University Press, 1984.

Lodge, Tom. *Black Politics in South Africa since 1945.* London and New York: Longman, 1983.

Luckhart, K., and Wall, B. *Organise or Starve: The History of SACTU.* London: Lawrence & Wishart, 1980.

Maree, Johann, ed. *The Independent Trade Unions, 1974–1984.* Johannesburg: Ravan Press, 1987.

Roux, Edward. *Time Longer than Rope.* Madison: University of Wisconsin Press, 1972.

Simons, Jack and Ray. *Class and Colour in South Africa, 1850–1950*. London: International Defence and Aid Fund for Southern Africa, 1983.

Webster, Eddie. *Cast in a Racial Mould: Labour Process and Trade Unionism in the Foundries*. Johannesburg: Ravan Press, 1985.

————, ed. *Essays in Southern African Labour History*. Johannesburg: Ravan Press, 1985.

Wickens, Peter. *The Industrial and Commercial Workers Union of South Africa*. London and New York: Oxford University Press, 1978.

WOMEN IN AFRICA

EFUA GRAHAM AND WENDY DAVIES

WHAT part do women play in the socioeconomic life of Africa, and in the political, religious and cultural systems of the continent? What do they contribute today to the development of agriculture and industry, education and health, law and government, and what could their potential contribution be? How are their lives affected by national and global economic systems? These are questions that have long been neglected by commentators and development planners alike, but that are gradually being recognized as crucially important.

It has been pointed out that the terms adopted in the dialogue on international development are revealing of the status bestowed on women. For a long time women were conspicuous by their absence as a focus of interest in such discussions; in the 1970s there was increasing talk of "women *and* development," a description that by the mid-1980s had been largely replaced by "women *in* development." In June 1985 the U.N. Decade for Women culminated in an international conference in Nairobi, attended by 15,000 women. There, African women, alongside women from every other part of the world, made known their legitimate demands for a radical transformation in the conditions of their lives. The "Forward-Looking Strategies" document adopted by the conference represented an important step in the struggle of women to gain control over their own lives, a struggle in which African women are playing an increasingly prominent part.

DEFINITION OF "AFRICAN WOMEN"

There are obvious dangers in generalizing about African women—just as there would be in speaking about "European men" or "Latin American children." Consider, for a start, the enormous size of the continent and the wide range of geographical and climatic conditions it embraces. The historical and political contexts are equally diverse; it is only comparatively recently that nation-states as political entities have existed in Africa, and more recently still that any notion of shared continental identity and concerns has emerged. Although external influences tend toward the creation of a uniform materialistic culture, which is particularly evident in the cities, traditional forms of culture and social organization remain a dominant force in many communities. Here, too, there is very great diversity.

An important general distinction can be drawn between matrilineal and patrilineal societies. In those societies where descent is reckoned in the female line, women tend to have rather more rights and freedom than they do in patrilineal communities. In matrilineal Akan society in Ghana, for example, girls are highly valued. When an Akan woman marries she retains a considerable amount of independence and can normally rely on continuing support from her mother's side of the family. She is not obliged traditionally to move in with her husband, and she can inherit property and gain access to land through her mother's family. In Ewe society, which is patrilineal, a woman is expected to move into her husband's compound when she marries, and is dependent on her husband to allow her access to land.

Other factors are equally important in shaping women's lives. Political systems—from the egalitarian forms found, for example, in Eritrea and Tigre, to the repressive apartheid regime in South Africa—as well as religion and social class all have an impact on both men and women, but affect women in particular ways.

WOMEN IN TRADITIONAL RURAL SOCIETY

Even in traditional matrilineal society, women were not on a par with men, but it is important to point out that in all traditional societies women have enjoyed a respected status as mothers. Older women were accorded particular respect after their long years of bearing and rearing children. Women not only exercised considerable control in the domestic sphere, but in some societies could enjoy positions of power and authority as healers and priestesses.

Ifi Amadiume has described how in traditional Igbo polity, gender construction was flexible and separate from biological sex.[1] Women who were able to take on male roles and responsibilities were viewed, to all intents and purposes, as male. Although these women were the exception, and the majority of African women were accorded a lower status, nevertheless the flexibility that existed in some societies is noteworthy.

Important female power bases were built up in some societies, partly as a safeguard for women's interests. In Sierra Leone women's secret societies are to this day extremely powerful. Traditionally, women have been able to use these bases as a means of pressing for their rights and winning some concessions from a male-dominated society. However, they represent negative as well as positive elements since, as in most social situations, contradictions abound. It could be claimed that older women in these secret societies are in control of younger women's fertility, which coincides with men's interests, and can therefore be seen as a reactionary force in modern times. The most glaring example of the harmful use of such powers is the practice of female genital mutilation.

[1] Ifi Amadiume, *Male Daughters, Female Husbands: Gender and Sex in an African Society* (London: Zed Press, 1987).

THE ROLE OF WOMEN IN FOOD PRODUCTION

Despite rapid urbanization, Africa is still a predominantly agricultural continent. Yet its ability to supply food to a growing population has been steadily deteriorating, to the point that when drought also occurs, widespread famine follows. This tragic fact can to a large extent be explained by the distortion of agricultural production (begun in colonial times and continued since) as a result of which cash crops for the global market have severely undermined food crops for local consumption. Africa finds itself trapped in a situation where it has to raise foreign exchange to service its debts and is denied the possibility of diversifying its economy in ways that would be more appropriate to the needs of its people. All efforts on the part of African governments to improve food production have to be seen within the context of this global economic stranglehold. Falling food production is also aggravated by the neglect of women in the planning and implementing of agricultural development programs. As recently as 1976 the U.S. Department of Labor could issue a statement that only 5 percent of African women worked,[2] whereas the reality is that women make up half the agricultural labor force and contribute between 60 percent and 80 percent of labor hours. In the production of food they are estimated to provide 90 percent of the labor.

Farm tasks traditionally assigned to women are planting, hoeing and weeding, harvesting, transporting crops home from the fields, and collecting water and fuel. Women are very often solely responsible for processing, storage and preparation of food and for marketing any surplus. This already onerous work load has to be seen alongside women's reproductive role. Not only do they bear children, but as in every other part of the world they also have the major responsibility for the care of children. This combination of reproductive and productive roles has given rise to what E. Boulding terms the concept of the "triple burden" borne by women, that of "breeder-feeder-producer"; as she puts it: "Within the rural and non-industrialized parts of the fifth world, women breed babies, produce milk to feed them, grow food and process it, provide water, fuel and clothing, build houses, make and repair roads, serve as beasts of burden, and sit in the markets to sell the surpluses."[3]

Particularly in the savanna regions, women spend many hours and expend much physical energy in collecting water. In rural Ethiopia, for example, women may travel at least six miles/10 km. a day to fetch water in pots that, when full, weigh up to 88 pounds/40 kg.[4] Both in the fields and at home women continue to use very basic tools and utensils. They urgently need access to the technology that would lighten their work burden.

[2] Heather M. Spiro, *The Fifth World: Women's Rural Activities and Time Budgets in Nigeria*, Queen Mary College, Occasional Paper no. 19 (London, 1981).
[3] E. Boulding, *Women in the Twentieth Century World* (New York: John Wiley & Sons, 1977).
[4] Tsehai Berhane Selassie, *In Search of Ethiopian Women*, International Report no. 11 (London: Change, n.d.).

The development programs implemented since the 1950s, far from improving conditions for women, have generally tended to make their lot harder. The penetration of capital into the rural areas has led to great emphasis being placed on cash-crop production. As food crops have been undermined, women's decision-making power, which was traditional in the area of food production, has been eroded. Much of the best land has been claimed for cash crops and women have had to work less fertile land, further away from their villages. Within cash-crop production it has generally been the male-identified tasks that have been more frequently mechanized, creating more rather than less work for women. Mechanical technology introduced for swamp rice cultivation in Sierra Leone reduced men's work, but increased women's by 50 percent because the amount of cultivable land increased.[5] Female tasks have often not been improved by technical inputs. Fertilizer, for example, stimulates growth and therefore increases the amount of weeding women have to do. In some cases fertilizer has even been thrown away by the women when they have seen the men collect extra payment for increased yields while their own work burden has become intolerable.[6] Acceptance or rejection of modern inputs by women is frequently related to financial factors. Fertilizer and high-yield seeds are much more likely to be welcomed if they are made available to women to use on their own fields and thereby increase their own income.

Women have tended to have much less access than men to agricultural credit and to miss out on extension schemes that are directed at the men. In Ghana it was found that only 6.7 percent of women had been granted credit to help improve their farms, compared with 26.7 percent of the men.[7] Banks tend to underestimate women's productivity, whereas it has consistently been shown that women's output can be as high as, or higher than, men's when they have access to the same inputs and services. Where low productivity occurs it is almost always because of a lack of these advantages and because women are forced to take on too many roles—spending more time on their husbands' fields and engaging in a variety of income-generating activities in order to meet their familial obligations.

Measures to improve rural development include the establishment of rural banking services. For these to benefit women, who traditionally remain in the background, specially targeted backup services are needed to mobilize and train women, and to give them the confidence to make use of these services. A further problem is that men may act as an obstacle, preventing their wives from utilizing these services for fear of losing control and influence over the women as they gain greater economic independence. Female extension workers could play a very important role in this respect, provided that they are sensitive to the sexual politics of the situation. These are aspects that have been frequently neglected by development programs.

Land-reform programs, for example, have frequently paid no regard to women. In countries like Kenya and Tanzania women traditionally had

[5] *World Survey on the Role of Women in Development* (New York: United Nations, 1986).
[6] Ibid.
[7] Ibid.

usufructuary rights to some of the land owned or controlled by their husbands, fathers or brothers. However, land-reform programs have ignored women's rights and have established exclusive male ownership.

Male migration from rural areas has had a significant impact on many women farmers. In some areas, especially in East and southern Africa, 30 percent to 50 percent of rural households are headed by women. The apartheid system in South Africa depends to a great extent on men serving white industry and commerce in the cities, while the majority of women are left in the Bantustans or other impoverished rural areas to shoulder the responsibility of raising their families and looking after the old.

WOMEN IN THE URBAN ECONOMY

Industrialization in Africa has proceeded at a much slower rate than in Asia and Latin America, but its effects have nevertheless been profound. Among these has been the creation of gross inequalities along lines of class, race and sex.[8] In the textile, garment, food-processing and electronics industries, transnational companies frequently employ women because of stereotypical notions—which can be traced back to industrialization in Western countries—about female manual dexterity and preference for routine work. Women are employed at lower wages than men in some instances, particularly by agro-industries with monopoly control, such as the sugar industry in the Ivory Coast. A survey of manufacturing industries in Kenya and Tanzania revealed that women's wages were approximately 75 percent of male earnings, and that in many cases they worked longer hours.[9] Owing to large-scale unemployment, women may be forced to take jobs where no maternity benefits or child-care facilities are provided. In an unusual case, that of Ghana, despite the country's economic problems some positive steps have been taken in giving women in the civil service the right to three months' maternity leave, followed by six months during which they can take one hour out of the working day for nursing their babies. In Botswana this period is twelve months.

Urbanization has far outstripped industrialization in Africa. Large-scale male migration to the cities has imposed on women who remain in the rural areas the burden of running households without the support of their husbands, although usually with the wider support network of the extended family and community. As men's wages only go a short way because of high inflation, the women in the villages bear a heavy burden in trying to support their families, and they are expected to provide a source of subsistence and security that migrant males can fall back on. Often, though, the very different life-style in the cities makes for male infidelity, neglect of the women left behind in the villages, and marital breakdown.

Women, too, are increasingly migrating to the cities. Some accompany their husbands, others are single women in search of an independent in-

---

[8] See Filomina Chioma Steady, "African Women, Industrialization and Another Development," in *Another Development with Women*, Development Dialogue 1982:1–2 (Uppsala: Dag Hammarskjöld Foundation, 1982).

[9] *World Survey on the Role of Women in Development.*

come and better life-style, both of which may be elusive. Whatever their reasons for moving to an urban area, women inevitably encounter a fresh set of problems, though there may be gains for them too.

In the cities women often lose the support of the extended family that helps sustain them in the rural areas. They may be forced to employ someone to look after their children. They may be restricted to occupations that will let them remain at home and combine child care with work. They have no access to land that would allow them to grow some food to help feed the family or that could be sold for extra income. Impoverished governments and municipal authorities are unable to provide adequate housing, medical care and other facilities, and social class structures become sharply defined. Women who find themselves in the sprawling slum areas are particularly vulnerable. Separated from kinship support, living in crowded, unhygienic conditions, unable to provide adequately for their children, they are literally at the bottom of the social heap.

Women who have been able to reach a reasonable educational level have access to a restricted range of jobs within the formal employment sector. They tend to gravitate toward service jobs, working as teachers, nurses, secretaries and receptionists. Dependent on men for job security and promotion, they are a prey to male manipulation, and sexual harassment in the work place is a growing problem. The majority of female migrants from the rural areas, lacking education beyond the primary level and without formal qualifications of training, have no access to the regular job market and turn instead to a variety of activities on a self-employed basis within the informal sector. These include market-trading, brewing and selling beer, preparing and selling cooked food, dressmaking and hairdressing. The harshness of life in the cities has driven many women into prostitution, a problem that is also aggravated by the increase of tourism and by the growth of Western materialism and objectification of women. With the rapid spread of the AIDS epidemic, more and more women are at risk.

Women engaged in the informal sector can often earn a better income than many who are employed in the formal sector, and some run very successful enterprises. In her study of women in urban areas of Uganda and Kenya, Christine Obbo found that the most important gain for women was the independence and initiative they were able to exercise; the great majority of women she interviewed expressed positive feelings about being self-employed.[10] The illegality of much of their work (many women operate without trade licenses, for example) has also strengthened women's solidarity and encouraged them to set up informal associations and unions to safeguard their interests and protect themselves against the police.

For all its precariousness, the informal sector can bring considerable benefits to women if it is combined with strengths drawn from the traditional background. The Asante market women in Ghana, for example, are able to combine independence gained from the matrilineal system with economic freedom in the modern economy, and could be seen, in some re-

[10]Christine Obbo, *African Women: Their Struggle for Economic Independence.* (London: Zed Press, 1980).

spects, as among the most independent and emancipated women in the world. They are able to buy property, educate their children, move around freely and exercise considerable autonomy, even if they belong to polygamous households.

WOMEN AND HEALTH

An improved health status for African women is a crucial need, for many reasons. On the question of numbers alone, the population of the 42 countries of sub-Saharan Africa is approximately 434 million, of which slightly over 50 percent is female and 14.8 percent is in the childbearing age-group, from 15 to 44 years old.[11] The health status of mothers is closely linked to the health and welfare of the family because of their multiple roles in reproduction and in nourishing and caring for the young and old, as well as their major contribution to food production. The struggle to survive severe economic pressures causes widespread male migration in large parts of Africa, leaving many rural households consisting of women, young children and the old. This situation puts tremendous pressure on the mental and physical health of women in maintaining their households.

Available statistics show maternal mortality rates in excess of 500 per 100,000 births, reaching over 1,000 deaths per 100,000 births in some areas.[12] In developed countries the rate is of the magnitude of five to 30 deaths per 100,000 live births. In many African countries maternity-related causes are among the five leading causes of death for women of childbearing age. The World Health Organization estimates that in the areas with highest maternal mortality (most of Africa and Asia) about half a million women die each year from maternity-related causes, leaving behind at least 1 million motherless children of various ages.[13] The majority of women do not have access to modern health care services despite the growth of mother-child health clinics.

Good nutrition, required throughout life, is vital for the female because of her added role in reproduction. In common with women in other developing countries, African women face major problems caused by nutritional anemia. This is further aggravated by parasitic infections. It is estimated that in developing countries, two-thirds of the pregnant women are anemic.[14] This has deleterious consequences for mother and child during pregnancy, childbirth and nursing.

Child marriage persists in Africa. Often, complications during pregnancy and childbirth, such as obstructed labor caused by cephalopelvic disproportion in the adolescent, are associated with malnutrition in early childhood. Nutritional anemia among women remains a largely unrecognized problem contributing to chronic ill health. This should be of more

[11] *Population* Newsletter No. 11 (2). UNFPA, February 1985.
[12] *Health and the Status of Women,* Document FHE/80.1 (Geneva: World Health Organization, 1980).
[13] Ibid.
[14] *Women and Health in Africa*, EPC Publications no. 6 (London, 1985).

concern to both health and economic planners and should feature more in the current debate on crises in Africa, particularly in view of women's heavy daily work load and their contribution to food production. Unfortunately, women in general are socialized from early childhood to expect to put their own needs last. When there is a shortage of food in the household they are the last to eat.

A variety of factors affects women's health status. In addition to heavy work load, continuous childbearing and lack of health care, certain social customs may add to the general morbidity rates. A case in point is female genital mutilation, said to be practiced in more than 20 African countries from the west to the Horn of Africa and in parts of North Africa such as northern Sudan and Egypt.

Female genital mutilation, commonly known as female circumcision, involves amputation to some degree of the woman's outer genitalia. In its most extreme form, practiced on over 80 percent of the female population in Somalia and northern Sudan, and to a lesser extent in parts of Ethiopia, Egypt, Kenya and Mali, two-thirds of the outer genitalia is amputated. The remaining tissue is pulled together and stitched, leaving a small aperture for urination and for the passage of menstrual blood. In such circumstances the aperture has to be widened at the time of marriage in order for sexual intercourse to take place, albeit very painfully. The practice of female circumcision is derived from a complex set of societal ideas and beliefs, but a recurrent theme running through these is that of maintaining the chastity and fidelity of women. The operation, in particular the extreme form, has been associated with a range of short- and long-term complications, such as hemorrhage, infections and childbirth difficulties, quite apart from coital problems and pain. Ironically, women themselves are often in the forefront of the resistance to abolition of the practice, since they are conditioned to believe it has a value on which their survival and status depend. It is estimated that 70 million women and girls are affected by this practice in one way or another.

With the emphasis placed by international agencies on population control in Africa, the problem of infertility tends to be an obscure and neglected one. It is the much-debated issue of population growth and its control, on the other hand, that has become a troublesome question for many Africans. Despite the emphasis on family planning in some areas, nothing much has been achieved in reducing population growth. Kenya, for example, was one of the first sub-Saharan countries to adopt a national policy favoring family planning as a means of controlling population growth. Today it has the fastest growing population in the world—a growth rate of 4 percent per year.[15] Family planning in the absence of socioeconomic development has been shown to be ineffective in controlling population growth. For the African poor, a large family unit is seen as a safeguard for future security. In areas where there is high infant mortality it is extremely difficult, not to say inappropriate, to push through family planning.

[15] "Women of the World: The Facts," UNICEF News.

THE EDUCATIONAL NEEDS OF AFRICAN WOMEN

Education is seen as crucial to the emancipation of women. It can provide women with alternatives and choices in their lives, help them become aware of their own value, and increase their self-confidence in challenging their subservient role in society. Today, however, 85 percent of the female population of Africa is illiterate (the percentage for men is 67 percent).[16]

In general, colonialism widened the gap in educational levels between men and women. The gap is still very evident today; for example, the percentage of males between the ages of 12 and 17 enrolled in school in 1975 was 40 percent, while that of females in the same age-group was 24 percent.[17] Embedded deep in European educational systems was a set of values that accorded low status to women, as well as an inferior position to other races. Education came first to men, who were trained to take on junior clerical roles serving the white administration. The initial formal education given to women or girls was provided largely by missionaries, who taught their charges how to be good Christian wives for the up-and-coming black clerks. Girls learned needlework, cookery, etiquette and other such "female" subjects (within a white middle-class set of values). Up to today, the colonial system of education predominates in Africa, and girls attending school still gravitate toward subjects like home economics rather than technical or science subjects. When they leave school they are much more likely to take jobs of a service nature—secretarial work or nursing, for example—than to take managerial positions and higher-paid jobs. A few women who have managed to break away from traditional female subjects have done well for themselves, gaining employment in high-status professions as lawyers, accountants, university lecturers and bank managers, sometimes with more gains than their Western counterparts. To the vast majority of African women, though, formal education brings very few benefits.

In many African countries mass literacy campaigns have been conducted, literacy being seen as the key to liberation, development and freedom from poverty. But very often these campaigns have been ill conceived, ill suited to the needs of the people they purported to serve, leaving them with expectations that cannot be fulfilled rather than with skills by which to improve their lives.

There are, however, a few success stories. The liberation movements in Eritrea and Tigre have carried out widespread literacy campaigns that have been closely integrated with the teaching of relevant skills. Of the 450,000 people who learned to read and write in Tigre in 1984, 53 percent were women.[18] In Burkina Faso, too, literacy has been used as an important tool in bringing about revolutionary changes. At only 10 percent of the popu-

[16] Ibid.
[17] Ibid.
[18] "The gains of women in the revolution in Tigray" [Interview with Besserat Asfaw] *Sister Links* 1, no. 2 (June 1985). *Sister Links* is published in London by FORWARD (Foundation for Women's Health Research and Development).

lation, the literacy level there was one of the lowest in Africa. Materials were produced in nine of the main national languages and, as in Eritrea and Tigre, focused on the acquisition of practical skills, such as the prevention of serious illnesses and new methods of agricultural production. The policy has been to give intensive literacy training to groups of villagers—half of them women—who then pass their knowledge on to others.[19]

As the majority of women are going to remain in the informal sector for a very long time, the importance of informal education—and the need for resources in this area—cannot be overemphasized.

THE NEED FOR LEGAL REFORM[20]

The duality of legal systems in Africa poses serious problems for women. Colonial administrations superimposed European legal systems on customary law, and in some countries the situation was rendered even more complex by the simultaneous existence of Islamic law. The source of most legal problems for African women is the interaction between customary and received law. There is no uniformity in the way that African states have dealt with this duality. In the Ivory Coast, for example, polygamy has been made illegal, whereas in Ghana all marriages are recognized as legal provided they are registered.

The health of women is in many ways contingent upon legal reform. In patrilineal societies a woman is subordinated under customary law to the position of a minor, under the guardianship of her husband, father or another male relative whose consent is required before the woman is given certain types of medical treatment or services. For this reason women are frequently barred from access to contraceptives and to abortion, hospitals and clinics believing the male relative's consent to be a legal requirement. Women are also often unaware of their rights even when these have been sanctioned by law.

Opposition to change runs deep, as women's rights are often perceived as being alien to African culture. Positive strides have been made, however. In Zimbabwe, for example, the perpetual minority status of women was abolished by the Legal Age of Majority Act of 1982, which conferred majority status on all people over the age of 18. During the U.S. Decade for Women, many African countries became signatories to the U.N. Convention on the Elimination of All Forms of Discrimination Against Women, but the legal advances have still to be fully put into practice.

Besserat Asfaw, of the Tigre People's Liberation Front, has described graphically the difficulties faced by a hierarchical feudal society, and the strategies adopted for solving these problems.[21] Food taboos for women

---

[19] Daouda Api, "The Magic Word," *New Internationalist* no. 180 (February 1988). This issue was devoted to education.

[20] Much of the information here is drawn from the section by Jane Connors on the legal position of African women in the forthcoming report, *Women in Sub-Saharan Africa*, Minority Rights Group Report no. 77. To be published in 1988.

[21] "The gains of women in the revolution in Tigray."

have been abolished, female circumcision outlawed and child marriages, too, made illegal. The minimum age for marriage is now 15; before the revolution 98 percent of girls were married before the age of 12. Legal reform has been seen as part of a comprehensive process of socioeconomic reform, in which the education of the people has been of central importance. Thus, women have been given land—in a society that previously denied them this right—as men were able to respond favorably to the argument that female ownership of land would mean more food for the family, and that with their own form of economic security women would not be forced into prostitution in order to earn a living.

CONCLUSION

For the majority of African women the U.N. Decade for Women came and went without making any difference to their lives. Meanwhile, the situation of the masses of women and men has steadily worsened, and the future looks no less bleak. Since women constitute half the population and are so crucial to the welfare of the next generation, it is essential that they be brought right to the center of economic, political and social development, and that their creativity and potential be released. The best of traditional society, such as in matrilineal Akan Ghana, gives women strength, confidence and independence, qualities that could be a tremendous asset in the modern world. As long as women are seen as marginal to the political and socioeconomic process, an enormous resource remains untapped. There is a vital need both for the mobilization of women at the grassroots level and for strong female leadership. The inappropriateness of many development programs, despite the rhetoric of "integrating women into development," has denied women the ability to decide on priorities themselves and to shape their own destiny. Field-workers in many development agencies have in fact come to recognize the need for flexibility and community participation but the question always needs to be asked: "Who is participating in whose development?"

Several African countries have made attempts to support women by establishing women's bureaus. Some of these have fallen into the trap of becoming a tool for the ruling party, unable to operate fully independently and to delve into sensitive areas of importance to women. Others have achieved a considerable amount despite underfunding and understaffing. There is always the danger of marginalization from the main governmental processes, and that other government ministries will fail to take on board the needs of women.

Nongovernmental women's organizations are essential to the process of change and can be complementary to government agencies, but at the moment the majority of these lack a progressive perspective and concern themselves with very restricted welfare activities. With training and politicization, they could be a formidable force for change. Unfortunately, there are severe limits to the growth of such organizations in countries that are not ruled democratically. Given the right environment, women organizing at the grassroots can transform the conditions of their lives. According to

1051

Asfaw, "all the economic and social benefits that . . . women have today are as a result of their own organisational strength and dedication for democracy and justice."[22]

FURTHER READING

Callaway, Helen. *Gender, Culture, and Empire: European Women in Colonial Nigeria*. Basingstoke, Hampshire: Macmillan in association with St. Antony's College, Oxford, 1987.

Davies, Miranda, ed. *Third World—Second Sex: Women's Struggles and National Liberation: Third World Women Speak Out*. London: Zed Press, 1983.

El Dareer, Asma. *Women, Why Do You Weep?: Circumcision and Its Consequences*. London: Zed Press, 1982.

Hay, Margaret Jean, and Stichter, Sharon, eds. *African Women South of the Sahara*. London and New York: Longman, 1984.

Mickelwait, Donald R., Rugelman, Mary Ann, and Sweet, Charles F. *Women in Rural Development: A Survey of the Roles of Women in Ghana, Lesotho, Kenya, Nigeria, Bolivia, Paraguay, and Peru*. Boulder, Colorado: Westview, 1976.

The WIN Document: Conditions of Women in Nigeria and Policy Recommendations to AD 2000. Samaru, Zaria, Nigeria: Women in Nigeria, 1985.

Women in Nigeria Today. London: Zed Press, 1985.

[22] Ibid.

RELIGION AND SOCIAL FORCES IN AFRICA

ALI A. MAZRUI

INTRODUCTION

KWAME NKRUMAH once described the African conscience in terms of three strands of moral thought: first, the traditional indigenous heritage of Africa; second, the impact of Islam; third, what Nkrumah called "Euro-Christian influences." Faced with these three strands of moral thought, contemporary Africa had to find not only a compromise among them, but a synthesis of all three. In the words of Nkrumah:

> Our society is not the old society but a new society enlarged by Islamic and Euro-Christian influences. A new ideology is therefore required, an ideology which can solidify in a philosophical statement, but at the same time an ideology which will not abandon the original human principles of Africa. Such a philosophical statement will be borne out of the crisis of the African conscience confronted with the three strands of present African society. Such a philosophical statement I propose to name *philosophical conscientism*, for it will give the theoretical basis for an ideology whose aims shall be to contain the African experience of Islamic and Euro-Christian presence as well as the experience of traditional African society, and, by gestation, employ them for the harmonious growth and development of that society.[1]

But until such a cultural synthesis takes place one day, the relations between Islam and Christianity are likely to remain basically competitive. The rivalry is partly a continuation of their past history, and partly a logical consequence of the fact that both religions are ambitious enough to want to convert the whole world to their own view of ultimate reality.

However, one of the most remarkable aspects about *indigenous* religion is that it is relatively neutral in politics and an active force in war. Because traditional religion is not universalist like Christianity and Islam, traditional religion is not competitive. The gods of the Yoruba and the Kikuyu are not seeking to convert the whole of the human race to their creed. Mainly because of these considerations, politics in Africa have not been torn

[1] Kwame Nkrumah, *Consciencism: Philosophy and Ideology for Decolonization*. Rev. ed. (New York: Monthly Review Press, 1970). Consult also Mazrui, *The Africans: A Triple Heritage* (London: BBC Publications; Boston: Little, Brown, 1986).

1053

by indigenous sectarianism. Where religion has been a divisive factor in Africa, it has been the imported religions of the Middle East—Christianity, Islam and their own internal variations.

So tolerant is indigenous religion that it moderates even the tensions of Christian-Islamic rivalries. These religions of Middle Eastern origin are sometimes more tolerant of each other within Africa than outside. The population of Senegal is over 80 percent Muslim, and yet the country had a Roman Catholic president (Léopold Sédar Senghor) for approximately the first two decades of its independence. Tanzania has a plurality of Muslims over Christians, and yet the country had a Roman Catholic head of state (Julius K. Nyerere) from 1961 to 1985.

Many ordinary African families are multireligious (Muslim, Christian, traditionalist, etc.) without acrimony or rancor. Nor is it unheard of for highly visible political figures in Africa to change their religion in the glare of national or international publicity. The conversion of President Omar Bongo of Gabon from Christianity to Islam was one case in point. The changing religious affiliations of President Dawda Jawara of Gambia was another case. The late President Yusufu K. Lule of Uganda was a Christian who had once been a Muslim. President Diouf of Senegal, who succeeded Léopold Senghor, is a Muslim with a Roman Catholic wife. When Idi Amin was president of Uganda he declared his intention to have one of his sons trained for the Catholic priesthood. Idi Amin himself was a Muslim and has always remained one. These conversions, with high political visibility, are a measure of the basic ecumenical spirit of indigenous religious attitudes in Africa. It is partly for this reason that differences in indigenous religion have not been especially subject to politicization in Africa.

It has been said that war is the continuation of politics by other means. In traditional Africa, war is sometimes the continuation of *religion* by other means. The same indigenous religion that has tended to be relatively unpoliticized in peacetime has sometimes been mobilized for combat purposes in war. Indigenous religions have been used in warfare not as part of a crusade to convert others but as sacred weapons for attack or sacred shields for defense. Indigenous religions have been a source of spiritual ammunition against "the enemy" or part of the fortress of invincibility.

The most dramatic African Joan of Arc of the 1980s was Alice Lakwena of Uganda. She arose out of northern Uganda's resistance to the rule of Yoweri Museveni. In 1987 she inspired thousands of Acholi and mobilized them for combat with very few weapons. Like Joan of Arc before her, Lakwena claimed to have visions and communicate with spiritual forces.

RELIGION, SEX AND WAR

Religion has sometimes been the bridge between conventional feminine virtues and masculine roles in combat. In cultures that are otherwise vastly different from each other, the military profession has been a man's preserve. Women as a rule have not been expected to kill for their country. They have not even been expected to die for their country. Armed patriotism has usually been a male preserve.

But from time to time religion has played a part in militarizing women. In Uganda 1987 was such a year, with the aforementioned phenomenon of Alice Lakwena as a female warrior with supernatural powers, engaged in combat against Museveni's forces. As an instance of using traditional religion for military purposes, Lakwena's approach was often reminiscent of the Maji Maji war against German rule in Tanzania in 1904–05. Tanganyikan warriors had immersed themselves in sacred water in the expectation that it was bulletproof. Similarly, Alice Lakwena convinced many Acholi warriors in 1987 that carrying a particular leaf or artifact would make them bulletproof. Both in Tanganyika at the beginning of the 20th century and in Uganda in 1987 this faith in the protection of indigenous religion against bullets proved disastrous for the warriors. The faithful died in large numbers.

But Alice Lakwena's movement not only illustrated a link between war and indigenous religion, it also illustrated how religion can make it possible for a woman to break the male monopoly of military command. At the beginning of this century a Muslim holy war in the Horn of Africa included women crusaders against European invaders and their local allies. Somalia produced its own African "Maid of Orleans," Hawo Osman Tako, who was pierced by an enemy's arrow and still continued to fight. A statue stands in her honor in today's Muqdisho. It symbolizes armed patriotism with a female face. But her valor also symbolized religious inspiration at work in remilitarizing women. Joan of Arc, Hawo Osman Tako and Alice Lakwena are all historic fusions of priestess and female warrior.

Elsewhere from to time, religion has fused priestess and politician. Alice Lenshina in Zambia has been leader of the Lumpa church, which has on several occasions clashed with government authorities and its supporters. Strictly speaking, the Lumpa church was antipolitical from the outset and did not want its members to join any political party. But to be antipolitical was itself a political statement. The clashes between the church and the ruling party of Zambia in the mid-1960s resulted in President Kenneth Kaunda's authorization of the security forces to "shoot to kill" in efforts to control Lenshina's uprising of 1964–65. The tradition of priestesses had in that period escalated into violence. And even a good Christian like Kaunda— a devout disciple of Mahatma Gandhi—could be driven to a response of counterviolence.

But the confrontation between Alice Lenshina and Kenneth Kaunda had more symbolic contradictions as well. Lenshina was a woman who, by leading her men into violent political battle, seemed to have assumed a role normally associated with men. In his Gandhian days, on the other hand, Kenneth Kaunda was opposed to the use of violence in any of its forms, and seemed inclined toward expressions of compassion usually more associated with women.

In Africa the admonition "Turn the other cheek!" could be viewed as the most feminine imperative of them all. Only a woman turned the other cheek upon being punished by her man. And even a submissive African woman attempted as a rule to shield herself with her arms. Yet the principle of turning the other cheek was part of the baggage that came with Christianity.

Kenneth Kaunda in his younger days was close to this kind of ethic. To his critics from within Africa's warrior tradition, he exemplified how Christianity had softened Africa's masculinity. Brought up in a highly devout Christian home, Kaunda exhibited early his abhorrence of fist fights and the readiness of his tears of compassion. Critics saw this as part of the process of emasculation under Christian missionary tutelage. Although much later, as head of state, Kenneth Kaunda surrendered to the economist Max Weber's definition of the state as institutionalized monopoly of physical force, his tendency to compassion persisted and came to embarrass many an international conference when (as president) he sometimes broke down in tears in the middle of a speech.

It is against this background that Kaunda's confrontation with Alice Lenshina soon after independence was so remarkable. In the mid-1960s either Lenshina had to retreat into feminine compassion and nonviolence or Kaunda had to respond with macho toughness. Kaunda decided to be ruthless. He declared that he did not care if he was called a savage. Alice Lenshina's followers had started killing innocent citizens of independent Zambia. Kaunda decided that only using force would stop carnage by members of the Lumpa church. Kaunda's Christian compassion had given way to the demands for toughness; state machinery prevailed.

RELIGION AND ETHNICITY

In contemporary Africa, tensions between religious groups are never purely religious. They are usually an aspect of either ideological conflict between militants and moderates (as in parts of Ethiopia), racial conflict between white and black (as in southern Africa), ethnocultural conflict between different African "tribes" and communities (as in Uganda), or class conflict between the haves and have-nots (as illustrated in virtually all cases).

At least three major civil wars in Africa within the last two decades have had a religious dimension. For 17 years (1955 to 1972) southern Sudan waged war against the government in Khartoum for reasons that included religious differences between the Muslim north and the Christian-led south. (The southern leaders were indeed mainly Christian, but the majority of their followers were neither Christian nor Muslim; they were still adherents of local ancestral religions of their own communities.) In the 1980s the Sudanese civil war was reactivated—compounded for a while by the legacy of President Jaafar Nimeiry's adoption of the *Sharia* (Islamic law) for both north and south.

In the case of the Nigerian civil war (1967–70) the north was identified with Islam while "Biafra" (or the east) was identified with Christianity. In reality, the Nigerian civil was was mainly ethnic, but Biafra's public relations machinery successfully created the impression among many in the Western world that Ibo Christians were fighting a war in defense of Christianity. In spite of the fact that General Yakubu Gowon, the head of the federal government of Nigeria, was a Christian, and that much of his support came from other non-Muslims, Biafra brilliantly managed to suggest that a jihad was being waged against the Ibo. Even the Vatican seemed for a while to have bought that version.

The third major civil war with a religious dimension is still under way. This is the struggle by Eritrea to break away from Ethiopia. The majority of Eritreans are Muslim, and this has enabled them to secure support from the Arab states. There are large numbers of Muslims in the rest of Ethiopia as well, but the country has had many centuries of Christian theocracy.

The military rulers of Ethiopia since the fall of Emperor Haile Selassie have gone further than their predecessors to concede that Ethiopia is not a purely Christian country. After the revolution of 1974 the Muslim festival of Idd el Haj was celebrated as a national holiday throughout the whole of Ethiopia. That would have been inconceivable under the late emperor.

But while the new military rulers have made concessions to Islam, they have simultaneously cut the Coptic Christian church in Ethiopia down to size. Indeed, the Marxist-Leninist orientation of the rulers has paradoxically been at once more tolerant of Muslims (outside Eritrea) and more suspicious of Christian church leaders as potential sources of "ideological reaction." Ethiopia is certainly one case where religious tensions are interwoven with the tensions of secular ideology—as well as with the tensions of ethnic separatism in Eritrea.

The class dimension is also persistent all over Africa. Sometimes new military rulers are opposed to older church leaders, partly because the religious leaders once belonged to the political establishment whereas the soldiers were recruited from some of the poorest strata of the old society. The soldiers in power in African countries are often essentially "lumpenmilitariat," disorganized recruits from sectors of society that were once disadvantaged and often uneducated, and have since become callous and insensitive.

The class dimension has also been relevant in race relations. In southern Africa it has certainly not been easy to determine where race differences end and class distinctions begin. In the words of the late radical black thinker Frantz Fanon, who has long been popular among many liberation fighters in southern Africa: "You are rich because you are white—but you are also white because you are rich." The Japanese (who are rich) after all are honorary whites in the Republic of South Africa. Meanwhile, the churches have become more important than ever as the regime has become more repressive and the society more polarized. Archbishop Desmond Tutu and Rev. Alan Boesak are leading the Christian opposition.

But the most perennial problems in Africa may well turn out to be ethnic ones involving blacks against blacks. When, therefore, it is learned that a black cleric has been killed, it would be important to investigate not only issues of religion, class and ideology, but also issues of ethnic affiliation and "tribal" origins.

In the 1970s a number of Christian church leaders and missionaries were killed in Africa in rather violent circumstances. For example, the month of February 1977 witnessed two highly publicized acts of brutality reportedly committed by black Africans. First came the news that seven white Roman Catholic missionaries, including four nuns, had been gunned down in Southern Rhodesia. The sole survivor, Father Dunstan Myerscough, was convinced that the murderers were nationalist guerrillas. The second event, less than two weeks later, was the apparent murder of the Most Reverend Janani Luwum, Anglican archbishop of Uganda, while in custody on the charge of plotting to overthrow the government of President Idi Amin. Amin's government claimed that the archbishop and two of Amin's own cabinet ministers held on a similar charge were killed in a car crash, but most of the world was understandably skeptical.

In the case of the murder of the seven missionaries in Southern Rhodesia, it was assumed that they died as casualties of a racial war, rather than as martyrs in a religious crusade. But in the case of the Ugandan archbishop, the world jumped to the conclusion that he was a martyr to his faith as a Christian. Was the world justified in assuming that Archbishop Luwum died for religious reasons and not as a victim of ethnic strife? After all, cabinet minister Oryema who was killed with the archbishop was also an Acholi. Before long, further news seemed to validate ethnic factors rather than religious ones as dominant behind the new atrocities in Uganda. Leading Langi and Acholi, including some at Makerere University, were rounded up, brutalized or at least briefly subjected to harassment. Hundreds of refugees from Lango and Acholi were soon reported to be pouring into Tanzania and Kenya.

But while ethnicity is indeed more highly politicized in Africa than religion, there are occasions when religion is explosive in its own right. The Maitatsine Islamic movement in Nigeria—regarded as heretical by other Muslims—has been at the center of violent political confrontations a number of times in the 1980s. Both the movement and the security forces have at times goaded and provoked each other, with great loss of life.

In Nigeria, tensions between Christians and Muslims are more generally just below the surface for a variety of historical, economic and theological reasons. Once again, religion in Nigerian politics is not an isolated force but has remained inseparable from the politics of regionalism and ethnicity. President Ibrahim Babangida's hesitant move to make Nigeria a full member of the Organization of the Islamic Conference in 1986 infuriated large sections of the Christian population of the country and was interpreted as a violation of Nigeria's constitution as a secular state. But behind the Babangida move and the response it provoked were the wider politics of relations between north and south in the political equation of Nigeria.

RELIGION AND DISEASE

Historically, international missionary work has included a concern for the sick and the disabled. Christian missionaries especially have helped to build clinics and hospitals, and to nurse the aged and the infirm. Albert Schweitzer's controversial work as a Western doctor in the African wilderness used to symbolize this commitment and dedication. In this volunteer work to help the sick, both Islam and indigenous African culture have lagged behind Christian medical efforts.

But more enduring than the link between Church and clinic as institutions is the link between religion and disease as human experiences. In the 1980s a particularly compelling issue has been the new affliction of AIDS.

AIDS as an issue has interacted with religion at a number of levels. There is first the level of theories of causation. A mysterious disease that kills relentlessly, and hits young people at the prime of life, is bound to generate new speculations about its cause. In Africa, as elsewhere, there have been religious theories. Conventional Christians have speculated about "the wages of sin" and about the wrath of God. AIDS has almost become the equivalent of the plague in Biblical accounts of divine disapproval.

In Africa the "sin" associated with AIDS is not homosexuality, as it is in the United States, but heterosexual promiscuity. Prostitutes are major carriers in African cities. African writers, such as the Ugandan poet Okot p'Bitek or the writer Okello Oculi, who have in the past often idealized the prostitute may now have to reevaluate this.

In situations of urban loneliness, the prostitute provided much the same sanctuary as the traditional one of the cathedral.[2] Today more than half the prostitutes of Kampala and Jinja, Uganda's largest cities, are believed to be carriers of the AIDS virus. Far from the prostitute providing the sanctuary of a cathedral, the brothels in Uganda are becoming an ominous war zone of disease—and theories of the wages of sin are once again reinforced.

Beliefs from indigenous African religions have also played a part in speculations about the causes of AIDS. Sorcery directed against individual sufferers has often been blamed for the affliction. Sexual jealousy, economic envy and other rivalries have been held accountable for "slim" (the popular name for AIDS in some parts of East Africa, because of the emaciation resulting from the disease) when the disease has hit a particular person.

In Islam, adultery can, in certain circumstances, carry the death penalty under the *Sharia*. The most highly publicized death penalty for adultery in recent times was carried out not in Africa, but in Saudi Arabia, on a Saudi princess. In Africa, President Jaafar Nimeiry, who introduced the *Sharia* in Sudan, carried out amputations of hands for stealing and, in one famous case, for heresy and apostasy. The penalty for adultery was definitely available for implementation also, but no conviction occurred in the short period from Nimeiry's adoption of the *Sharia* to his overthrow in 1985.

There is a school of thought, however, in orthodox Muslim circles that AIDS has been sent by Allah because adultery was going unpunished all over Africa and in the Muslim world. In reality, there are fewer cases of AIDS in Muslim Africa than outside the lands of Islam. On the other hand, there may be less adultery in Muslim Africa than outside. At any rate, this line of speculation among Muslim fundamentalists turned AIDS into an extension of the *Sharia*. What human beings have failed to implement through the law of God (the death penalty for adultery), Allah himself has intervened to implement through the laws of epidemiology (AIDS).[3]

Because all three religious traditions of Africa (indigenous, Islamic and Christian) have speculated about the causes of AIDS, they have inevitably

[2] Cf. Okello Oculi, *Prostitute* (Nairobi: East African Publishing House, 1968).
[3] This line of thought has been heard among the more orthodox in Tunisia following the discovery of a number of AIDS cases in 1987. The theory has also been heard in eastern Africa. The author is indebted to discussions with, among others, Stanbul Fadhl Allah, and to the press-clipping collection on "The Socio-Cultural Context of AIDS in Africa," Center for Afroamerican and African Studies, The University of Michigan, Ann Arbor.

also played a part in experimenting with the treatment of AIDS. The most ambitious attempts have been on the part of indigenous religion, which in different parts of the affected countries of Africa has tried to cure the afflicted. Where the disease has been attributed to sorcery, traditional healers and diviners have attempted countermeasures of witchcraft. But sometimes the techniques of sorcery have been combined with the use of traditional herbal medications. Religion and traditional healing have jointly attempted to cure AIDS—and one more paradigm of treatment has failed.

Muslim healers in black Africa are popular even among non-Muslims. Indeed, in parts of Zaire, the overwhelming majority of the patients of Muslim healers are often Christians or followers of traditional religion. Some of the recent patients in Zaire are sufferers of AIDS.

A popular technique of Muslim healers in Africa is to write an appropriate verse of the Koran in ink made from an appropriate medical herb. The verse is written on a slate and then carefully washed away into a cup or bowl. The bowl now contains liquid Koran. The patient then drinks the holy potion.

In Africa areas of more orthodox Christianity, AIDS has resulted in a renewed search for miracles. Zaire is the largest Roman Catholic country in Africa. It also has the largest concentration of AIDS sufferers on the continent. (But when Pope John Paul II visited Zaire the country was not yet in the AIDS-limelight; the Pope therefore did not embrace a Zairean AIDS sufferer, as he did when he visited the United States.)

Faith healing is still important, however, to many African Christians, as Archbishop Emmanuel Milingo demonstrated in Zambia in the early 1980s. The archbishop was subsequently transferred by the Vatican to what was regarded as a more harmless occupation in Rome. The assumption was that faith healing was less close to "superstition" in Italy than it was in Zambia. Again, the controversy just preceded the recognition of the AIDS crisis in Zambia. Since then, no less a person than the son of President Kenneth Kaunda himself has died of AIDS. The search for a religious cure includes the search for faith healing and miracles. Middle-class African Roman Catholic sufferers of AIDS have almost certainly tried the cure at the Shrine of Lourdes, in France. French-speaking African patients, however, are more likely to know about the record of miraculous cures there than are other Africans. Portuguese-speaking African Catholics are more familiar with the miraculous stories of the sanctuary of Fatima, in Vila Nova de Ourém, in Portugal. Like other AIDS sufferers elsewhere, African patients have had to resort to prayers for miracles. Where science has failed, humans poignantly continue to turn to religion as the court of final appeal.

RELIGION AND SEXUALITY

Should AIDS in Africa be studied in a wider context? One premise is that there are three major sexual cultures at work in contemporary Africa. These are: the indigenous legacy of Africa's own sexual mores; the legacy of Islam and its sexual culture; the impact of Western sexual mores, both Christian and secular.

The second premise is that AIDS (whatever its origin) is affected by cultural variables in a society, and spreads faster or more slowly partly in response to cultural habits.

Were AIDS primarily confined to homosexuals, there would be very little of it in sub-Saharan Africa outside the areas of high tourist activity. Indigenous African culture is (presumably) less prone to homosexual tendencies than either Western culture or those versions of Islamic culture that segregate the sexes too rigidly.

AIDS in Africa seems to be primarily confined to heterosexuals and affects women in numbers that are comparable to those of men. What religious and cultural factors have played a part in this?

In Uganda, since Idi Amin, the soldiers have probably been both the most sexually promiscuous and the most geographically mobile professional group. Civil conflict (even when ethnic and religious) has weakened moral restraint. Soldiers could potentially become major agents for the spread of AIDS in such strife-torn countries.

So far there seems to be limited AIDS in Muslim Africa generally, in spite of the fact that some Muslim societies are more prone to homosexuality than other African societies. Is there a cultural explanation for this apparent anomaly? Marriage habits may be connected with this.

African men legally monogamous are more likely to be promiscuous outside marriage than African men legally polygamous. A legally polygamous African may be less tempted to stray casually. Based on such actualities, polygamous households may be less affected by AIDS than monogamous families in Africa, but it is too early to be sure.

South Africa's work policies in the mines are based not only on racial apartheid but on sexual apartheid. Miners are generally separated from their families for a year at a time, and quite often get cut off from their churches as well. Resort to prostitution and to homosexuality does occur among the miners. What are the implications of these realities for the spread of AIDS?

The African preference for having large families has created a distaste for the use of condoms. Condoms are also too closely associated with prostitutes in Africa to be acceptable. The Roman Catholic church has been watching with unease the new efforts to introduce more Africans to condoms as a protection against AIDS. Islam is more neutral on this issue.

Are women who have been circumcised at a higher risk in relation to AIDS than other African women? Female circumcision is indigenous and not Islamic, even when practiced by Muslims. There is of course the new risk of AIDS in the actual surgical operation itself. But for circumcised women there are also the long-term implications of lacerations during sexual intercourse.

Has Western culture increased prostitution in Africa? Almost certainly. Is Muslim Africa less prone to prostitution? That is also probable. What are the AIDS implications? That is an ominous issue yet to be fully explored. Are African men becoming less sexually promiscuous than they have traditionally been? Is AIDS promoting the fear of casual sex? Religious and moral leaders may be pleased with this trend, but much more research needs to be conducted to ascertain the full extent of sexual reform.

Two factors should guide the choice of geographical areas in which to do research on AIDS generally. The first consideration is how many cases of AIDS seem to have occurred in a given area. The other consideration is the cultural and religious pattern of the particular community. What is the interaction among the legacies of the triple heritage (indigenous, Islamic and Western) in the particular geographical area?

The countries where all three legacies are strong are not necessarily, however, those where the incidence of AIDS is the most pronounced. Indeed, one of the questions worthy of research is whether Muslim Africa has so far been less prone to AIDS than non-Islamized communities in Africa. Testing such a hypothesis empirically will pose both theoretical and geographical problems. Research may need to be done in countries in which Muslims and non-Muslims live in regionally distinct locations. But such studies may also need to consider countries where Muslim and non-Muslims are intermingled.

Is there enough incidence of AIDS for research among the Yoruba in Nigeria? In the Yorubal region, Muslims and non-Muslims are intermingled; is there a statistically significant difference there in the incidence of the AIDS virus among Muslims and non-Muslims? Some Yoruba clans practice both male and female circumcision (though with some variation geographically); what relevance have these practices for the HIV spread?

The other comparative divide in Nigeria might be between Muslim northerners (mainly Hausa) and non-Muslim southerners (ethnically mixed). Is there enough incidence of AIDS in the two parts of the country to permit comparative research? In this case Muslims and non-Muslims would be studied in regionally distinct contexts (unlike the intra-Yoruba case of close proximity).

Countries with higher incidence of the AIDS virus than Nigeria include Zaire, Rwanda, Uganda, Tanzania and Kenya. There are considerable religious and cultural variations in these countries—including differences between one indigenous culture and another within each country. AIDS as a phenomenon may be caught up in the full diversity of Africa's cultural experience.

RELIGION AND THE DRUG CULTURE

As for the link between religion and the drug culture, the interactions are still obscure questions for researchers in Africa. It is known that there has often been a cultural transition from the consumption of traditional alcoholic beverages like *waragi*, *marwa* and *mwenge bigile* to gin and whisky in Uganda; from palm wine to Western-style beer in Nigeria and Ghana. Traditional religion has had many roles for alcohol in rites from birth to death. Christianity has had its ritual wine, sometimes leading to consumption of other drinks in Africa.

One question that arises is whether a similar transition is in prospect from the use of traditional African narcotics and stimulants to use of cocaine and heroin, complete with Western-style needles. Are there new cults

1062

on the horizon, dependent on ritual uses of drugs? There is no evidence of such so far.

There is reason to believe that qat and marijuana originally spread in Islamic Africa as a functional substitute for alcohol, which is more clearly forbidden in Islam. In eastern Africa qat has particularly prospered in the Horn. In a small country like Djibouti, according to some estimates, about half the population (men, women and teenagers) have begun to chew it.

In Somalia qat was well institutionalized long before Europeans established control. The British tried to stamp out the addiction to it both in Yemen and in Somalia, but with little success. President Mohammed Siad Barre has been the latest crusader against qat in Somalia. In March 1983 he imposed a formal ban. A year later the National Qat Control Commission announced that it had captured 300 truckloads, confiscated 122,000 kilos of qat, collected over 9 million shillings in fines, arrested thousands of people and succeeded in creating enough of a shortage to put up the price of qat in Muqdisho to 3,000 shillings a bundle. But in due course smuggling helped to bring the price down.[4]

In Kenya (mainly the coast and the northeast), qat sometimes goes under the name of *miraa*. As the hold of Islam has weakened, use of marijuana has also become quite prevalent along the Kenya coast. As it happens, the coast is also one of the most popular attractions for Western tourists in black Africa. Local marijuana and qat addicts may well be among the most vulnerable to the temptations of the stronger drugs like cocaine and heroin, which have come with Western cultural influence and the tourist subculture. The evidence from the Rastafari movement and its use of ganja in the African diaspora is ambiguous in its implications.

Marijuana grows wild in Uganda, but its use was not a traditional addiction before the impact of alien cultural influences. Now marijuana is indeed widely smoked there, but may well be more of a rural phenomenon than an urban one. Sometimes it does have a ritual role, though less explicit than ganja does in the Rastafari movement.

In terms of social class, marijuana in rural Uganda is sometimes smoked by those who cannot afford cigarettes. Moreover, some rural people believe it has medicinal properties since it seems to cure ailing chickens who eat the weed. Traditional religion and indigenous science merge. Such beliefs carry the risk of popularizing marijuana further for humans.

The kola nut in West Africa has been much less of a risk. It comes from the trees of *Cola acuminata* and *Cola nitida* of the cacao family. The nut contains caffeine, and can become addictive. But it seems unlikely that it could enable a transition from traditional addiction to modern—from kola to cocaine. However, a variety of religious and cultural beliefs do continue to surround the kola nut.

Parts of Muslim Africa have of course had an older tradition, the use of hashish, derived from the female hemp plant (*Cannabis sativa*). (It is ironic that the English word *assassin* comes from the Arabic for *hashish eater* originally referring to the Nizari Ismaili, an Islamic political movement

---

[4] See "Horn of Africa: Smugglers Beat Khat Ban," *Africa Now* no. 38 (June 1984): 27.

operating from the 11th to 13th centuries.) Has there been a Westernization of hashish through cocaine and heroin? Were the new cases of AIDS diagnosed in Tunisia in the summer of 1987 narcotics-connected? The evidence is not conclusive.

Hard drugs have indeed arrived in Africa. Nigeria, under Gen. Muhammad Buhari's administration, even turned drug trafficking into a capital offense. Sometimes drug possession was treated as evidence of drug trafficking—with public execution as the ultimate penalty. Both Christian and Muslim leaders in Nigeria have been uneasy about this.

Underlying all these patterns of indulgence in drugs is the threat of greater use of needles in societies where such needles are bound to be expensive and in short supply. Multiple use of needles results in the spread of disease, particularly AIDS. In Africa, needle-utilizing narcotics are still a minor problem, however. The compelling question, on the other hand, is whether the threat is growing in demographic scale and geographic distribution as the restraints of traditional religions weaken and new cults threaten to emerge.

RELIGION IN ECONOMIC DIPLOMACY

Partly linked to all these developments is the interplay between the legacy of colonialism, the political resurrection of Islam, the rise of the Organization of Petroleum Exporting Countries (OPEC) and Africa's entry into the mainstream of economic diplomacy.

OPEC in composition is an overwhelmingly Muslim institution. The largest oil-exporting country is Saudi Arabia, the custodian of the holy cities of Makkah and Madinah, and one of the more fundamentalist of the Muslim countries on the world scene today. The second-largest oil-exporting country, when at peace, is Iran, another major Muslim country, perhaps with potentialities for considerable expansion as an influential power in world politics following the end of the Gulf war. If it is accepted that Indonesia is the most populous Muslim country since the collapse of old Pakistan, then Indonesia as a member of OPEC is also part of its Islamic composition. Fourthly, there are the Gulf states, most of them very small; but precisely because they are small and with enormous financial resources, they have surpluses capable of being mobilized for political and economic projects in different parts of the world.

Black African members of OPEC at the moment are Nigeria and Gabon. In the case of Gabon, the leader, President Omar Bongo, is a convert to Islam. In the case of Nigeria, there is an African country that best encompasses within itself Nkrumah's three parts of the soul of Africa. The indigenous, the European Christian and the Islamic forces are strong there. What is more, the Islamic factor has been growing in national influence since independence.

If OPEC as a whole is analyzed, it can be said that it is virtually two-thirds "Islamic" in terms of quantity of oil production, and over two-thirds in number of states. Thus the emergence of OPEC and petroleum on the world scene signify the beginning of the political resurrection of Islam.

A related issue is the nature of the regimes in power in these resource-rich Muslim countries. It just so happens that the country with the largest known reserves, Saudi Arabia, is also the most strongly Islamic in tradition. And it also so happens that Iran still has a fundamentalist system in a revolutionary Iranian-Islamic context. Along the Arab/Persian Gulf there are also traditionalist rulers. There is a tendency to regard this as a cost in the equation, but it is possible to examine it as a benefit in global terms. The influence within OPEC is not exerted merely by Westernized or relatively secular Muslim countries like Algeria. It comes even more from countries where Islam has been less diluted by Westernism.

From the point of view of the Muslim world as a whole, there is now a dialectic between underpopulated but very rich and Islamically traditionalist countries on one side, and more populous, more secular and less wealthy Muslim countries on the other. A dialectic between resource-poor populations on the one side and resource-rich traditionalists on the other could change the balance between the forces of secularism and the forces of traditionalism in the years ahead. Muslim Africa is caught in between.

New possibilities arise, however. Africa's most natural allies consist of the black diaspora and the Arab world. Nearly two-thirds of Arabs live within Africa. The bulk of Arab land is there. Black and Arab states share in the Organization of African Unity; this organization and the Arab League have overlapping membership. There are possibilities of exploiting this relationship—in which Islam features—to the mutual advantage of both peoples.

Before the end of this century African Muslims will probably outnumber the Arabs and will be making a strong bid for shared leadership of Islam. It would not be surprising if, within the next generation, black Muslims from Africa are seen establishing schools and hospitals in New York's Harlem and preaching Islam to black Americans. The funding for this Islamic counterpenetration will probably come from the oil producers of the Arab world. But since African Islam is distinctive from Arab Islam, and carries considerable indigenous culture within it, counterpenetration into the United States would also be, in part, a process of transmitting African indigenous perspectives as well. Islam has in any case been spreading significantly among black Americans in the last two decades.

But at least as important as Muslim money for African cultural entry into the West is the sheer potential of the black American population. Black America is one of the largest black nations in the world and is situated in the middle of the richest and mightiest country of the 20th century. At the moment, black American influence on America's cultural and intellectual life is much more modest than, say, the influence of Jewish America. But as the poverty of black America lessens, its social and political horizons widen, and its intellectual and creative core expands, black American influence on American culture is bound to rise. And the links between Africa, the Muslim world and the black diaspora may in turn find new areas of creative convergence.

These trends, however, have been interrupted by the oil glut and the decline of OPEC in the 1980s. A resurrection of demand for oil is forecast in the 1990s, and Arab and African producers will continue to feature prominently, though controlling a smaller share of the market. Prospects for Islam and prospects for oil are interlocked: a kind of "petro-proselytism" in a world of competing visions and rival ideologies.

The gods of Africa preside over these trends—and Jesus and Allah are supreme in the pantheon. The ecumenical miracle of Africa's religious diversity is about to step into the glare of global history.

FURTHER READING

Dawisha, Adeed, ed. *Islam in Foreign Policy.* Cambridge and New York: Cambridge University Press for the Royal Institute of International Affairs, 1983.

Lewis, I. M., ed. *Islam in Tropical Africa.* London: International African Institute; Bloomington: Indiana University Press, 1980.

Mazrui, Ali A. *The Africans: A Triple Heritage* (London: BBC Publications; Boston: Little, Brown, 1986.

Nkrumah, Kwame. *Consciencism: Philosophy and Ideology for Decolonization.* New York: Monthly Review Press, 1970.

Paden, John N., *Ahmadu Bello, Sardauna of Sokoto: Values and Leadership in Nigeria.* London: Hodder & Stoughton, 1986.

Pipes, Daniel. *In the Path of God: Islam and Political Power.* New York: Basic Books, 1983.

Ruthven, Malise. *Islam in the World.* New York and London: Oxford University Press, 1984.

Sanneh, Lamin. *West African Christianity: The Religious Impact.* London: C. Hurst, 1983.

Taha, Mahmud Muhammad. *The Second Message of Islam.* Translated by Abdullahi Ahmed An-Naim. Syracuse, New York: Syracuse University Press, 1987.

Third World Quarterly 10 (April 1988). Special issue, "Islam and Politics."

Trimingham, J. Spencer. *Islam in Ethiopia.* London: Frank Cass, 1976.

ISLAM IN AFRICA

GEORGE JOFFE

INTRODUCTION

ALTHOUGH Islam is normally considered to be the dominant religion of the Middle East, there are in fact many more Muslims in Africa. Indeed, Africa has the second-largest Muslim community in the world, with an estimated 236 million Muslims out of a world total of 840 million in 1986 (see Table). This is just under half the number of Muslims found in South Asia (535 million)—the area that contains the world's largest Muslim communities and that, according U.N. definitions, comprises both the Middle East and Southeast Asia with its massive Muslim populations in Indonesia, Malaysia, the Philippines and the Indian subcontinent. In Africa itself, the Muslim communities in 1986 were almost equal in number to the largest religious denomination—Christianity—which had 260 million adherents.

Even more significant is the fact that most observers believe that it is Islam that is currently attracting adherents at the fastest rate, even outstripping Christianity. In 1966, for example, a study of Islam south of the Sahara suggested that the Islamic population of the region was 50 million, with a similar number of Muslims residing in North Africa itself.[1] Thus, in two decades the Muslim population of Africa has more than doubled, an increase that cannot be explained simply by demographic increase. It is, indeed, a reflection of the success of Islamic proselytization in recent years.

Islam in Africa is also uniquely varied in the way in which it is manifested, for, as one noted Muslim commentator on African affairs has pointed out, "Every African Muslim has four religions: Islam, Christianity, Judaism and the legacy of his own ancestors. . . . All these combinations of values and beliefs have helped to make Africa a peculiarly fascinating theatre of cultural exchange, a melting pot of standards and values."[2] Indeed, it is the syncretic nature of African Islam that gives it its unique character. At the same time there are significant variations in doctrine and practice, in both geographic and sociological terms, which contribute to this uniqueness.

---

[1] I. M. Lewis (ed.), *Islam in Tropical Africa* (London: Oxford University Press, 1966), 1.
[2] Ali A. Mazrui, *The African Condition*, Reith Lectures (London: Heinemann, 1980), 55.

AFRICA'S MUSLIM POPULATIONS, 1986

Country	Muslims (millions)	Total population (millions)	Percentage
Algeria	22.36	22.56	99
Angola	—	8.82	—
Benin	0.54	4.13	13
Botswana	—	1.13	—
Burkina Faso	3.49	8.12	43
Burundi	0.24	4.83	5
Cameroon	2.17	9.87	22
Cape Verde	—	0.34	—
Central African Republic	—	2.71	—
Chad	2.26	4.14	55
Comoros	0.41	0.41	100
Mayotte (Comoros)	0.69	0.69	100
Congo	—	2.10	—
Djibouti	0.43	0.46	95
Egypt	39.27	48.01	82
Equatorial Guinea	—	0.32	—
Ethiopia	14.08	43.19	33
Gabon	—	1.29	—
Gambia	0.65	0.77	85
Ghana	2.06	13.14	16
Guinea	4.30	6.23	82
Guinea-Bissau	0.27	0.90	22
Ivory Coast	2.57	10.69	24
Kenya	1.27	21.14	6
Lesotho	—	1.59	—
Liberia	0.35	2.31	15
Libya	3.83	3.95	96
Madagascar	—	10.29	—
Malawi	1.18	7.27	19
Mali	7.61	8.45	90
Mauritania	1.68	1.68	100
Mauritius	0.13	1.03	13
Morocco	22.16	22.45	99
Mozambique	2.33	13.83	17
Namibia	—	1.20	—
Niger	6.26	6.42	98
Nigeria	44.15	98.10	45
Rwanda	0.17	6.34	3
São Tomé and Príncipe	—	0.11	—
Senegal	6.10	6.70	91
Sierra Leone	1.47	3.73	39
Somalia	5.98	5.98	100

Country	Muslims (millions)	Total population (millions)	Percentage
South Africa	0.36	36.72	1
Sudan	17.96	24.61	73
Swaziland	—	0.86	—
Tanzania	6.74	22.46	30
Togo	0.52	3.07	17
Tunisia	7.28	7.32	99
Uganda	2.47	15.64	16
Zaire	—	31.07	—
Zambia	—	6.94	—
Zimbabwe	—	8.41	—
	235.79	571.11	41

Source: *Encyclopaedia Britannica Book of the Year* 1987.

Islam in North Africa, for instance, is very different from its counterpart in the Sahel, while the similarities of orthodox Islamic practice throughout the continent only serve to emphasize the great differences in popular belief. There, pre-Islamic practices have been integrated into Islam, such as the *Zar* cults of Somalia and Sudan or the Hausa *Bory* cults of West Africa, which find their echo in some of the popular Sufi orders (*Tariqas*) in North Africa. In addition, it is the central role played by the Sufi *Tariqas* in African Islam that distinguishes it from Islam elsewhere. This is particularly important in Senegal and in Sudan, but it has also played a significant role in the Maghreb. Nonetheless, the differences are generally most easily identified in geographic and historic terms. These, in any case, reflect the way in which Islam spread into Africa. It is in Africa north of the Sahara desert that the most intense Islamization of Africa has taken place. Islam is the religion of over 95 percent of the populations of Libya, Tunisia, Algeria, Morocco and Mauritania—the Maghreb. In Egypt 82 percent of the population is Muslim, with virtually all the remainder being Coptic Christians.

Only nine other African states or territories have a similar proportion of Muslims in their populations, and their location reflects the ways in which Islam is concentrated in Africa—on the east coast (the Comoro Islands [including Mayotte], Djibouti and Somalia), in West Africa (Gambia, Guinea and Senegal) or in the Sahel region (Mali and Niger). Only two other states have Muslim majorities in their populations (Chad and Sudan), while in Nigeria, normally considered to be a major Muslim influence, only 45 percent of its population is Muslim. Nonetheless, of Africa's 52 states and territories, only 15 have no Muslims in their populations at all. The role played by Islam in the continent is thus highly significant.

1069

ISLAM IN PRECOLONIAL AFRICA

The Islamic presence in Africa is, of course, a direct reflection of the way in which Islam spread throughout the continent before the advent of colonialism. As with the spread of Islam throughout the Arabian peninsula and into Asia, the agent for Islamization was the Arab armies that were created in the wake of the initial successes of Islam in the Hijaz. The dynamism unleashed by that early success was sufficient to create an irresistible wave of conquest that swept through the peninsula and into the Persian Sassanid and the Greek Orthodox Byzantine empires that surrounded it.

The initial conquest

Within a few years of the death of the Prophet Muhammad in A.D. 632, Arab armies began to appear in Africa, conquering the Byzantine province of Egypt in 640. A year later, the first attempts began to extend Muslim influence with military probes south toward the Christian state of Nubia and west into Cyrenaica, still under the control of Byzantium. Neither attempt at expansion proved easy. In the south, Nubia resisted the Arab military advance in 641 and, again, in 651. To the west, the collapse of Byzantium brought the Arabs into conflict with a far more tenacious opponent—the Berber populations of North Africa.

In North Africa, however, the Berbers, sensing the advantages that Islam could offer them, soon became enthusiastic converts and by the 10th century had become the demographic springboard from which the Fatimid dynasty reconquered Egypt and founded the city of Cairo. By the 11th century, the Fatimid caliph in Cairo, irritated by North African independence, ordered the troublesome nomads of the Banu Hilal and the Banu Sulaim, who had moved from the Levant into the Nile Delta region, to migrate into North Africa. Over the next 50 years the region underwent a social and political upheaval that not only entrenched Islam but began the process—still uncompleted—of converting the indigenous Berbers into using Arabic as their daily language.

Islam in East Africa

In northeast Africa, however, ideas of military conquest were abandoned in favor of peaceful penetration through trade and migration. Indeed, it was only in 1317 that the Mamluks eventually took over the small states of Dongola and Soba, which had been formed in the 7th century from the Christian kingdom of Nubia (ruled from Meroë), thus completing a process that they had started with the invasion of Dongola in 1276. They then began the formal process of Islamizing and Arabizing what is today all of northern Sudan. Of the many populations there, only the Nubians and the Beja have managed to preserve their own languages while accepting Islam. Indeed, Islamization was to be a process that continued to be dominated by influences from Egypt to the north. It developed gradually over the next 600 years, reaching its apogee in the 19th century, in the Mahdist movement. It was Egypt, after all, that bequeathed to Sudan its adherence to Malaki *Sharia* in the 16th century and—as a result of the Turco-Egyptian

1070

conquest at the start of the 19th century—its use of the Hanafi legal school in its religious courts.

Islamic Egypt was not the only influence leading to the growth of Islam in Sudan. There was also the effect of direct contacts with the Hijaz and the wider Arabian peninsula. These developed as an independent sultanate grew up in northern Sudan under the Funj at the start of the 16th century. For the next 300 years, Islamization was carried out by individual holy men and by the growing numbers of Sufi *Tariqas* that began to appear as the result of contacts across the Red Sea. Over 20 separate orders have been identified, of which the most important were the Shadiliyya (which is also the earliest) and the Khatmiyya (one of the two dominant orders in Sudan today).

Despite the initial Arab invasions of Eritrea in the wake of an Abyssinian attack on Makkah in 702, the Christian populations of present-day southern Sudan and Ethiopia resisted Islamization, although some groups in Eritrea and in the Horn of Africa proved less resistant. In any case, the dominant influence here came not from Egypt but through the later growth of trading links along the coast created by Arab merchants from the Arabian peninsula and the Gulf, and even by Persian traders who also set up trading posts along the Gulf. The growth of Islamic influence along the coast was not solely pacific, however, and military might often accompanied trade. More importantly, over the years, the intermingling of Arab or Persian culture with indigenous African traditions produced the distinctive cultures that characterize East Africa today. Both the Malaki and Hanafi legal schools are predominant and, like Sudan, the Horn region has always been one of adherence to a wide range of Sufi *Tariqas*, particularly the Qadiriyya (the oldest in Islam, founded in the 12th century) and the 18th-century Ahmadiyya order.

The one great success for Islam was the conversion of the Somali pastoralists through the Arab trading center of Muqdisho. The nomads carried Islam into the hinterland of the Horn from the 10th century onward. The great failure, however, was the inability of the Somalis or the small trading sultanates of Ifat in eastern Shoa, Dawaro, Hadiya and Bali to crush the Christian kingdom of Abyssinia. After the final Muslim defeat in 1542 Abyssinia was itself transformed from being a defensive barrier against Islamic expansionism into an aggressive threat to its survival, one which has lasted through until modern times—with Somali jihads against Ethiopia at the start of the 20th century and with the Somali struggle against Ethiopia over the Ogaden in recent years.

Further south, Islam was basically confined to the coast, with the first physical evidence of Islamic settlement at the important trading settlement of Kilwa only occurring at the start of the 12th century—although there is literary evidence to suggest that the town itself was probably founded in 957. Once again, the agents for the propagation of Islam were Arab and Persian traders from the Hadramaut and the Gulf. There was little opportunity for the penetration of Islam inland, however, because of Galla and Zimba migrations to the coast; and from the 16th century onward, Portuguese commercial and military competition along the coast virtually destroyed the links with Persia. Islamic influence was left to groups from Oman who settled on offshore islands such as Zanzibar and the Comoros, and at Kilwa (which controlled the gold trade from the interior of Zimbabwe via Sofala) and, eventually, Mombasa on the coast of Kenya. By the 15th century, there were apparently 37 coastal trading towns between Kilwa and Muqadisho to the north.

Trade involved gold, ivory and slaves, but Muslim traders rarely penetrated into the interior until the 19th century. This was due not only to the hostile environment in the African interior, but also to the fact that the centralized political structures typical of northeastern Africa—which facilitated trade and Islamic proselytization—did not exist in East Africa. Nonetheless, the coastal trading settlements in Kenya began to create their own unique fusion of Arab and Bantu culture that, by the 17th century, became embodied in Swahili culture around the town of Mombasa. Mombasa became the cultural and commercial center of the coast until the growth in influence of Zanzibar in the 19th century, as the result of renewed Omani interest in the region. As a result of the Omani presence, Shafism and the Ibadi rite are still dominant influences, particularly in Zanzibar, which was controlled by an Arab elite until its integration into Tanzania two decades ago. Sufism has less of an influence than further north, but the Qadiriyya is still the most important *Tariqa*.

Central Africa

It is in central and southern Africa that Islamic influences have been the weakest. Indeed, in southern Africa there were no Muslims at all until the advent of emigrant groups from India under colonialism. Further north, in modern Zimbabwe, Zambia and Zaire, there is little evidence of a substantial Islamic presence today, although it appears that there may have been many more Muslims there up to the 15th century. Two factors seem to have limited the spread of Islam: the growth of Portuguese control along the East African coast and in the interior, and the waves of indigenous migration from the north and the west.

Nonetheless, between the 10th and the 16th centuries there seems to have been a substantial commercial presence that started in the Zimbabwean kingdom of Karanga and extended to Sena on the Zambezi river. After Portuguese commercial activities displaced the Arab traders, Islamic influence declined until the start of the 19th century. It then began to grow again as a result of the growth of Zanzibari trade, as Omani traders based there began to compete effectively with Portuguese traders in Mozambique. By the 1830s, Arab traders were seeking slaves and ivory among the Luanda tribes, and by the 1880s they had spread into Zaire. Some observers have linked this commercial expansion with religious concerns by pointing out that it was also stimulated by the extension of Egyptian influence in East Africa and by the Mahdist movement in Sudan. However, both developments were rapidly checked by the growth of British colonial interests; and the recrudescence of Islam in central Africa in the 19th century has left its mark only in Tanzania and in Malawi.

North Africa

After the Hilalian invasions of the mid-11th century, North Africa began slowly to come to terms with its twin legacies of Islam and Arabic culture, and to create its own synthesis of them. Even before this, however, Islam had begun to penetrate across the Sahara, as Arab and Berber traders sought access to West African gold. The Sanhadja Berbers of the Sahara also began to seek political power, and it was from them and, later, from the Masmouda Berbers of the High Atlas mountains that the two great Berber dynasties of North Africa—the Almoravids (1042–1145) and the Almohads (1145–1269)—were derived in the 11th and 12th centuries. Both intensified Islamic influence southward into West Africa and northward into Spain, as well as reasserting control of the North African littoral against caliphal and dynastic pressures from Cairo and Baghdad.

After their disappearance, however, Maghribi interest in controlling events in West Africa began to diminish. Although trans-Saharan trade links continued to be vital up to the end of the 19th century, and the Saadian dynasty in Morocco actually attempted to control Timbuktu in the 16th century, events in the Mediterranean diverted attention away from West Africa. The growth of European power in the Mediterranean itself, first with the Normans in Sicily in the 13th century and then with the *reconquista* in Spain, which expelled the last Muslim ruler from Grenada in 1492, meant that Islam in North Africa was increasingly mobilized to counter the Christian threat.

By the 16th century, Spanish and Portuguese coastal settlements began to appear in the Maghreb and corsairing began—that is, legalized, state-controlled piracy that embodied the confrontation between European Christianity and Maghribi Islam. As a result, by the 1520s, North Africa found itself under alien, albeit Muslim, control once again, in the form of the Ottoman Turks. A series of small Turkish states, based on corsairing appeared along the Mediterranean coastline. Although within 150 years of their being created, the Barbary States had broken their links with Constantinople, their maritime concerns nonetheless continued to force Maghribi attention toward Europe and away from sub-Saharan Africa.

As piracy declined from the 18th century onward, in the face of Europe's greater naval strength in the Mediterranean, the Barbary States found a new role for themselves as suppliers to Europe's armies and navies. This reached its apogee at the start of the 19th century during the Napoleonic Wars. Once the wars had ended, European commercial influence had become so pervasive that North Africa had little time to consider its relations with the wider Islamic environment in Africa and the Middle East in the face of the inevitability of colonial occupation, which began in 1830 in Algiers.

In Egypt the 19th century had seen the collapse of the Mamluks, who had survived there through Ottoman support, and their replacement by a modernist statesman, Muhammad Ali. His advent to power had been the result of the profound upheaval created in Eyptian society by the French invasion of Egypt in 1792. Egyptians—and Muslims elsewhere in Africa and the Middle East—had come to realize through that event the degree to which Europe had seized the initiative in world affairs. Muhammad Ali was anxious to modernize Egyptian society and the state along European lines, but failed to provide the financial basis that was required. As a result, his modernization program also began the process of economic collapse that was to end in massive debts to Europe and, eventually, in British occupation.

West Africa and the Sahel

In West Africa and the Sahel region, the initial spread of Islam reflected the role of commerce as an agent of proselytization. Indeed, up to the 11th century the role of mainly Berber traders (together with a few Arab merchants) from the Maghreb, and of the Saharan tribes that controlled the trans-Saharan trade, was crucial. A considerable number of trading settlements grew up in the great medieval empires of Songhai, Mali and Ghana, and acted as centers for the dissemination of Islam.

However, Islam was not/adopted as the official religion of any of these major political entities until the Almoravids extended their political control southward toward Ghana. The Almoravids conquered Ghana in 1067 and then pushed eastward toward Mali (which soon afterwards adopted Islam) and even as far as Songhai. At about the same time, Islamic influence percolating southward from Libya and Egypt in the wake of Arab-controlled trade led to the conversion of the rulers of Kanem-Bornu to Islam.

Islam soon became firmly entrenched in the western Sahel region where, by the 15th century, Songhai had come to dominate the region until its power was destroyed by the Saadian military push southward toward Timbuktu from Morocco. This, in turn released a further wave of migration, as Fulani pastoralists from Senegal began to spread southward into the Fouta Djallon region and eastward toward the great Hausa trading states in what is today northern Nigeria. The Hausa had already been exposed to Islam from Mali and Kanem, and thus became the agents for the spread of Islam southward through trade. The Fulani themselves reached Lake Chad, where they came into contact with a similar migration by the Shuwa Arabs moving westward from Sudan and bringing Islam into the eastern Sahel.

Although the Fulani were not Muslims, they were later to become the agents of Islamization when, after conversion in the 18th and 19th centuries, they sparked off a series of jihads throughout the Sahel—such as that started in 1804 by Shehu Usumanu Dan Folio from Fouta Toro against the Hausa states of Gobir, Kano, Katsina, Zaria and Daura. By the 19th century, the Fulani jihads created a major wave of Islamic purification throughout the Sahel, in which the accretions of traditional African belief on Islamic doctrine were to be swept away. At the same time, the jihad movement extended Islamic influence in the greatest wave of Islamization since Islam had first appeared in West Africa or the Sahel. Its spread was embodied in a series of theocratic states from Senegal to northern Nigeria, including Fouta Djallon, Fouta Toro, Sokoto and Bornu. By the end of the 19th century, however, many of these new theocratic states had begun to decline and were unable to resist the pressure of colonial occupation. In any case, the underlying interrelation of Islam with trade, particularly in Senegal, reasserted itself. There, the Tijaniyya *Tariqa* (founded at the start of the 19th century in North Africa) linked commercial and religious concerns north and south of the Sahara, and confronted the Quadiriyya *Tariqa*, which had been introduced in the 16th century.

The Fulani jihads were only part of the great Muslim revival movement of the 19th century, however. North Africa began to feel the winds of the Salafiyya movement, started by al-Afghani in the latter part of the 19th century in order to resist European penetration into the Islamic world by revitalizing Islam through a return to its original doctrinal purity. In East Africa, the pressure of the Turco-Egyptian occupation of Sudan stimulated the Mahdist movement in Sudan that, in 1881, created a theocratic state based in Khartoum—which was only overthrown by an Anglo-Egyptian force after the battle of Omdurman in 1898. The Mahdist movement was both a search for the purification and revivification of Islam, and an attempt to create an Islamic and indigenous alternative to colonial occupation, whether by Egypt or, ultimately, Great Britain. Its effects were felt to the west and to the south, where it served as the inspiration for the Somali jihad in 1900–02.

To the west, its influence fused with that of the Sanusiyya, a reforming Sufi *Tariqa* that had grown up during the 19th century in Cyrenaica in eastern Libya, where it dominated the local tribes and the trans-Saharan trade routes to such an extent that it rivaled the Ottoman administration created there after 1835. In addition to expanding into Tripolitania and southern Tunisia, the Sanusiyya had been drawn into the Sahara and the Sahel to oppose French moves into equatorial Africa toward the end of the 19th century. There, Sanussi resistance to French occupation at the start of the 20th century fused with Mahdist-inspired attempts to prevent French occupation of Chad. All three movements also clearly had contacts with the West African jihad movement, and all of these movements represented the most significant revival of Islamic sentiment in sub-Saharan Africa since Islam had first appeared. It is notable that these movements, moreover, were closely related to established Islamic states and thus implied a quite different awareness of Islam than that found further south in East Africa, where Islam had relied on trade for its dissemination.

AFRICAN ISLAM UNDER COLONIALISM

One of the great ironies of African Islam under colonial occupation was the fact that, rather than being forced into decline, Islam experienced its greatest rate of expansion. This was due to two factors that appear to have been mutually exclusive but which were, in fact, mutually reinforcing. On the one hand, Islam acted as a vehicle of opposition to colonial occupation and as an organizational base for movements of national liberation. It thus acquired renewed support by the example, it provided to indigenous populations. On the other hand, Islamic proselytizers and traders rapidly learned to exploit the vast improvements in communications wrought by colonialism, and thus contacted potential converts in increasing numbers.

There was a further opportunity that was exploited by certain elements of the African Islamic community. This was to integrate into the new colonial societies that had been formed and to capitalize on the opportunities they offered to strengthen the role of Islam in the new communities. In this they were often helped by colonial administrations that frequently came to appreciate the modernizing effects of Islamic social organization in circumstances where provision by metropolitan colonial authorities rarely corresponded to local needs. In those areas, such as northern Nigeria and Sudan, where "indirect rule" was applied, this approach was particularly important. It also applied in Eritrea and in parts of West Africa, under Italian and French colonial administrations where "direct rule" was not applied.

Islam as a vehicle of opposition
The initial colonial occupations were often resisted by organized Islamic groups. Although they were unsuccessful at preventing European states from realizing in practice the division of Africa that had been sanctioned by the Congress of Berlin in 1880, they nonetheless left a memory of resistance that was to help to fuel national liberation movements later on. Indeed, this phase of "primary resistance" was to play a crucial role in formulating the way in which colonial occupation was eventually ended.

In Sudan the Mahdist state created in the latter part of the 19th century was only crushed in 1898, when the Anglo-Egyptian Condominium was established. Even after the death of the Mahdi and the subsequent defeat of the Mahdiyya under his Khalifa Abdallah, sporadic Mahdist revolts spluttered on into the 20th century. Indeed, it was only with the British occupation of the formerly independent Muslim state of Darfur in 1916 that the danger of Islamic revivalist rebellions finally receded. The same was true in Libya where the Italian occupation, which began in 1911, was forced into a series of wars, first with the Sanussi order until 1927, and later against individual local leaders claiming an Islamic justification—which continued until 1927.

Even earlier France had run up against the same type of ferocious opposition in Algeria. Here the initial ease of the French occupation of Algiers was soon transformed into increasingly tenacious resistance in western Algeria under the Qadiriyya leader Emir Abd al-Qadr. The resistance was only finally crushed in the mid-1840s. Another revolt in eastern Algeria in 1871 also seriously threatened the French presence in Algeria, at a time when France was weakened by its defeat in the Franco-Prussian war. Other rebellions laying claim to Islamic legitimization continued sporadically up to World War I.

Perhaps the most striking example of the resilience of Islam occurred in Morocco. Although France was able to suborn the Moroccan sultanate into accepting its "protection" in 1912—with Spain hastening to carve out its own protectorate in northern Morocco—it took a further 22 years before colonial authority was effectively established there. Yet even before this occurred, the colonial presence was seriously threatened between 1921 and 1926 by the Rif war. The war, which began in the Spanish zone of Morocco with a catastrophic defeat of the Spanish army by the Rifi tribes under Muhammad bin Abd al-Karim at Anual in 1921, eventually involved the French army as well when Rifi forces invaded the French zone in 1925 and threatened Fez. Although a combined Franco-Spanish army eventually suppressed the Rifi tribes, it was not able to erase the popular memory of an anticolonial war that also reformed Rifi society along the lines of the Salafiyya vision and, equally, sustained the nascent Moroccan nationalist movement.

Similar, albeit less dramatic, examples of Islamic resistance to colonialism occurred in West Africa and the Sahel. Mahdism—the millenarian belief in a leader who would both establish the ideal Islamic society on earth and thereby be able to lead a successful jihad against European occupation—appeared throughout the western Sahel and in West Africa, particularly in Guinea, Mauritania and Senegal between 1906 and World War I. After the War, two *Tariqas* also appeared in the same region to lead an anticolonial struggle—the Muradiyya in Senegal and the Hamalliyya in Senegal, Mali, Niger and Mauritania. At the end of the 19th century, resistance to French occupation in Upper Volta (Burkina Faso) was organized by Muslims, and the Mahdist movement led by Rabih Fadl Allah in southern Chad tried unsuccessfully to prevent French penetration into central Africa. A similar movement developed in Somalia, under Sheikh Muhammad Abdille Hassan; it resisted British and Ethiopian encroachment for 20 years after 1900.

Islam and collaboration

The Islamic response to colonialism was not simply one of rejection, however. After the first phases of opposition, Muslims had to come to terms with the fact that colonial powers had established their authority and control throughout Africa. As a result, Muslims and Islamic institutions learned to live with and even to exploit the colonial presence. Even former opponents—the Muradiyya in Senegal, for instance—became integral and cooperative elements within the community. In many cases, this was made relatively easy by the policies introduced by colonial powers. In both French and British colonies, local administrators often preferred a Muslim political presence because it provided those generalized institutions of control that obviated major colonial administrative costs. In some cases this was the result of local decision—as in many parts of West Africa where it often ran counter to declared government policy. In other places, however, this attitude of colonial tolerance was a deliberate act of policy.

The British authorities in northern Nigeria quite deliberately opted for a policy of indirect rule whereby Muslim states such as Kano were preserved, once the Sokoto caliphate had been broken up. A similar policy was followed in Sudan after World War I. This led to the growth in political influence of the Ansar movement—a *Tariqa* that claimed legitimization by lineal descent from the old Mahdi of precolonial days. Similarly, in Chad, the sultanates of Biltine, Abeche and Kanem were preserved under French control, while military government was installed in the Tibu-dominated north of the country. Perhaps the chief examples of this fostering of Islamic authority were in North Africa, where the French policy of "association"—

the equivalent of British indirect rule—sustained the political structures of the Moroccan sultanate and the Tunisian beylik.

Of course, this policy of preservation went hand in hand with one based on the policy of "divide and rule." Just as Britain deliberately undermined the Sokoto caliphate, France encouraged the collapse of the Tukulor empire and the growth of *Tariqas* throughout West Africa in order to split its opponents. The Anglo-Egyptian administration in Sudan (which became virtually a British-controlled administration after Egypt was granted effective independence in 1922) also used the Ansar and Khatmiyya *Tariqas* (the Khatmiyya was pro-Egyptian and anti-Ansar) to preserve its control. Later on, when political parties began to be formed in Sudan—with the Umma party associated with the Ansar and the Ashigga party (later to become the National Unionist party/NUP, and today known as the Democratic Unionist party/DUP) associated with the Khatmiyya—the British were able to play off one *Tariqa* against the other. It was only when both *Tariqas* and the associated political parties were able to fiind common ground that Britain was obliged to agree to independence in 1956.

From the Muslim point of view, however, the stable political conditions created by colonialism favored the spread of Islam—already seen by many non-Muslims as an integral part of the African scene. Trade and communications improved, colonial authorities encouraged submissiveness among their Muslim subjects by the provision of Islamic schools and mosques, and new Islamic groups entered the African world. They included Syrian and Lebanese trading communities in coastal West Africa, but the most important development in this respect was the arrival—principally in East Africa—of migrants from the Indian subcontinent. They brought with them Shia (Ismaili) Islam and at least one other *Tariqa*, the Ahmadiyya, which was also to contribute significantly to the eventual struggle for independence.

Islam and the struggle for independence

Indeed, many Muslims found the colonial presence to be an intolerable interference with the Muslim world in which they lived, and were thus predisposed to support the growth of "secondary resistance" to colonialism. However, except in areas were Muslims were in the majority, one of the consequences of colonial policy (which had tended to favor Christian groups in educational provision, while preserving Muslim communities in relative isolation) was that national liberation movements were dominated by the secularized or Christian products of the missionary system. It was only in North Africa and in the Sahel and northern Sudan that Muslims controlled the struggle for Africa.

Elsewhere, the role played by Muslims depended heavily on how Islam had been treated by colonial powers. Wherever Muslim institutions and states had been preserved or favored—as in, for example, Zanzibar and northern Nigeria—Islam tended to take on a conservative aspect and to resist the modernizing force of national liberation movements, which thereby threatened its privileges. However, when Islam had suffered from colonial repression—as in Mali particularly and, to a lesser extent, in Guinea and

Senegal—it either dominated the national liberation movements involved or played a very significant role within them. Even the Muradiyya movement in Senegal abandoned its quiescence and turned to support Léopold Senghor's Bloc Démocratique Sénégalaise—partly, no doubt, because it feared the threat to its support base offered by the more radical Hamalliyya.

In those states where Islam had been the dominant ideological force, the national liberation movements were controlled by Muslims. In Sudan this was the case, as it was in Somalia where nationalism and Islam were very closely identified. In Francophone North Africa, this was a particularly important aspect of the movement toward independence. Although the national liberation movements in Tunisia and Algeria were formally secular, their legitimization among the population at large, particularly in Algeria, depended very strongly on the Islamic connection. Indeed, in every case, the movements began as explicitly Islamic in character: the Destour party in Tunisia under Sheikh At-Taalbi, the ulama movement under Ibn Badis in Algeria, and the reform movement led by Allal al-Fassi in Morocco. This was hardly surprising, given the fact that North African populations were in the vast majority Muslim, and that the colonial presence—including sizable settler communities—were Christian. Indeed, in Morocco, the religious status of the sultanate was a crucial factor in legitimizing the struggle of the Istiqlal nationalist movement for independence.

ISLAM IN THE INDEPENDENT AFRICAN WORLD

Since independence was achieved by most African states between the mid-1950s and the mid-1960s (Egypt had achieved independence except for the Canal Zone in 1936 and Libya had been granted independence by the United Nations in 1951), the major issue for Islam in Africa has been its relationship with the institutions of the independent state. Nine African states—Egypt, Libya, Tunisia, Algeria, Morocco, Mauritania, Sudan, Djibouti and Somalia—are members of the Arab League. In this respect, they provide Africa with a significant connection with the Middle East.

At the same time, African Islam has had to cope with exogenous factors such as the Arab/Israeli conflict. In the 1960s, most African states that were predominantly Muslim or that had sizable Muslim minorities broke off relations with Israel because of its occupation of the West Bank, the Gaza Strip, the Golan Heights, Jerusalem and Sinai after the 1967 war. In recent years, however, African solidarity on this issue has begun to wane, and several important African states south of the Sahara, including the Ivory Coast, Nigeria and Liberia, have renewed links with Israel.

There has also been the growth of Islamic fundamentalism in Africa as elsewhere in the Muslim world. This has affected the structures of states such as Sudan, as well as leading to considerable popular unrest over the political structures of several other states, such as Egypt and Nigeria. In addition, there has been a striking growth in the mobilization of Islam at a popular level as a means of articulation of opposition to economic decline and neocolonialist influences, particularly in Francophone Africa.

1079

These factors have produced a series of differentiated responses in which the North African states have played a major role, led by Egypt. Indeed, the Egyptian role in the wake of the Nasserist revolution in 1952 was particularly important. President Nasser's vision of the three circles affected by the revolution over which he presided—Africa, Islam and the Arab world—acted as a beacon to many Africans. It ensured the predominant role of Egypt until President Nasser died in 1970. It also linked many African states into the Non-Aligned Movement, which had been founded by Egypt, Yugoslavia and India. The Egyptian role in this respect has, however, been vastly reduced by the far more moderate policies followed by President Nasser's successors.

There have also been significant developments elsewhere, from the Libyan attempt to create Islamic hegemony in the Sahara and the Sahel to the grotesque Ugandan manipulation of Islam in the Idi Amin regime or the distortions of the Nimeiry regime in Sudan. In Chad and Nigeria, Islam has played a significant role in civil war. Islam is, in short, a powerful and dominant influence in large parts of Africa today.

Islam and the nation state
One problem that faced many states on achieving independence was that of creating a nation that would thus legitimize the state that it inhabited. The problem often existed because independent African states were colonial constructs in which administrative borders paid little attention to ethnic community. African leaders realized the dangers inherent in this situation early on and, in the Cairo Declaration in 1964, the Organization of African Unity decided that national boundaries inherited from colonialism would be retained so as to avoid endless disputes between states and between communities within specific states. In consequence, the issue of creating a sense of national identity has become a major preoccupation for African states today, as has that of avoiding interstate conflict over border issues.

Islam has played an important role in two ways. On the one hand it has been used—generally unsuccessfully—as a conduit for defusing border disputes through an appeal to the wider Islamic vision of the *umma*, the Islamic community that supersedes the nation-state. On the other hand it has been used as the catalyst for creating a sense of national identity within a particular state. This latter use is rather surprising, since the very essence of political ideologies derived from Islam (as is typified by Islamic fundamentalism today) is supranational. However, the homogeneity and universality of the Islamic vision is an ideal tool for overcoming the regional particularism that has often characterized African states, or for sustaining the sense of identity between different political units, which may eventually lead to regional political structures.

One of the best examples of this is Somalia, where ethnic homogeneity and cultural identity are integrated through Islam. Indeed, ever since Islam first came to Somalia it has acted as an integrating force. This tendency was reinforced by the 1900–20 jihad against Britain and Ethiopia, and then by the division of Somalia during the colonial period between Britain, Italy and France. There were further irridentist demands on the Ogaden in

Ethiopia and on northern Kenya. Independence brought together British and Italian Somaliland, but French Somaliland has become the independent state of Djibouti. Claims on northern Kenya have never been resolved, while the Somalian attempt to recover the Ogaden failed in the face of Soviet-backed Ethiopian resistance in 1977–78. However, despite this failure, the Somali state has maintained its cohesion, in no small part as a result of the integrating influence of Islam.

A similar role has been sought for Islam in two nearby regions. The Eritrean dispute, in which indigenous national liberation movements have contested Ethiopian control ever since 1961, has been seen by some moderate Islamic states as a struggle of Muslims against Christian or atheist domination by Ethiopia. As a result, they have funded the Eritrean resistance over many years. In Uganda, Idi Amin was able to portray his rule as an Islamic regime, thus countering growing Christian and missionary influence. This enabled the regime to obtain some support from other Islamic states, particularly Libya, but few of them ultimately accepted its Islamic credentials, particularly after its excesses became public.

North Africa has also been an arena in which Islam has played a vital role in guaranteeing the nation-state. In the case of Morocco, for example, the identity of the monarchy with the caliphate, in which the king claims descent from the Prophet Muhammad has been vital in legitimizing the political system. It has also provided the monarchy with an essential technique for rendering palatable a whole range of policies that otherwise would never have been accepted by the population at large. Its role is enshrined in the slogan that is omnipresent throughout the country: *Allah, al-watan, al-malik* (God, country and king)—which neatly elides the essential elements of the Moroccan political system.

In Algeria, the government has deliberately sought to legitimize its austere socialist system through Islam. Algeria is, it repeatedly claims, an Islamic and Arab state that practices Islamic socialism. In Tunisia the situation is more complex, for the Bourguiba regime resolutely sought a secularist complexion, an approach that, formally at least, has been sustained by its successor under Zine el-Abidine Ben Ali. However, President Habib Bourguiba was certainly not averse to justifying his actions through an appeal to Islam, even though he rejected certain key elements, such as the Ramadan fast. Indeed, even here he was careful to ensure that his rejection of the fast-month tradition was justified in Islamic terms, by pointing out that the fast was suspended during jihad and that national development was itself a prolonged form of jihad.

Indeed, Islam is so deeply woven into the fabric of daily life, custom and culture that North African governments could not ignore it even if they wished to do so. The resurgence of Islamic sentiment since the mid-1970s at least, and particularly after the Iranian revolution in 1979, has also caused many governments to adopt policies so as to integrate growing fundamentalist sentiment and defuse popular protest. In Egypt, for example, many professional organizations are dominated by fundamentalist elements, particularly in the wake of the assassination of President Sadat in 1981 and the subsequent riots in Asyut; and this is reflected in the increasing role of *Sharia* law in government policy and of Islamic banking procedures in local finance. Algeria has engaged in a major program of mosque construction in order to satisfy popular religiosity, and even Tunisia has reversed some of the secularist policies of the former regime.

Perhaps the most striking and catastrophic example of these attempts to mobilize Islam to support the structure of the state occurred in Sudan. In September 1983, in the midst of a profound economic crisis and a growing constitutional crisis as the non-Muslim south of the country sought to split off, President Nimeiry introduced full-blown *Sharia* law into Sudan. It was a move that reflected the growing chaos within the regime itself for, although it represented the culmination of a process of reconciliation between Nimeiry and the three major religious groups in the north—the Khatmiyya under Muhammad Uthman al-Mirghani, the Ansar under Sadiq al-Mahdi, and the Muslim Brotherhood (*al-Ikhwan al-Muslimin*—which dated back to 1978) under Dr. Hasan al-Turabi, it inevitably hastened the fission between the predominantly Muslim north and the non-Muslim south.

Over the next 18 months, until Nimeiry was overthrown in April 1985, the intensifying Islamic nature of the regime also led to splits in regime support within the north. The rigid and excessive application of *hadd* punishments under *Sharia* law, the collapse of the tax system through Islamic-style tax reforms and the increasing intolerance of the regime toward its opponents—which ultimately climaxed in the execution of the moderate Republican Brothers leader, Mahmoud Muhammad Taha, in January 1985—coupled with Nimeiry's decision to proclaim himself imam alienated the Ansar and Khatmiyya. The *Ikhwan* soon fell under suspicion and, as a result, the Islamization process undertaken by Nimeiry's regime for the sake of its own legitimization only led to its isolation and collapse. The legacy has been a divided state, a civil war and a weak northern-based government that can neither resolve the civil war nor reform or abandon its Islamic legacy.

It is in Libya, however, that Islam has had the most profound effect, for the Qadhafi regime makes explicit reference to Islam to justify its policies. The *Green Book*, Colonel Qadhafi's own political testament, exemplifies this for, although Islam is rarely mentioned in its pages, its ideas are entirely Muslim in inspiration. The same sentiment permiates the "Third Universal Theory" (the theoretical construct that underpins the *Green Book*) and legitimizes the political system of popular committees and congresses that is the formal essence of the Jamahiriya (the state of the masses). However, the Libyan Islamic vision is very much Colonel Qadhafi's own. He has rejected the formal intermediaries of the ulama, imams and fiqhs in institutionalizing Islam after a major argument with them in 1978. Instead he argues that there should be no intermediary between Allah and man, that the Koran is the sole source of religious legitimization and that the individual may constructively interpret the Koran in order to deal with the problems of the modern world.

All these claims are regarded by most Muslims as heterodox. Nonetheless, they are also innovative and have gained a considerable populist support for the colonel. They also legitimize Libya's intrusive foreign policies, for they are called upon to justify anti-imperialism, regional unification (not just of the Arab world but also of the Islamic world) and rejection of other regimes in the region. Islam has played an explicit role in Colonel Qadhafi's endemic quarrels with moderate Arab states, particularly Saudi Arabia, Egypt and Morocco, in promoting breaches in diplomatic relations between African states and Israel in the 1960s and 1970s; in relations with other Islamic states such as Iran and, notoriously, Uganda under Idi Amin where Libya supplied troops and military aid; and in religious proselytization, particularly in the Sahel where the activities of Libya's ad-Da'wa al-Islamiyya (Islamic Call) society have been particularly noticeable. In the early 1980s, in fact, Libyan interest in Sahel states such as Niger, Mali, Mauritania and northern Nigeria was so striking that many observers believed that Tripoli was attempting to construct a Libyan-led Islamic federation of the Sahara.

Islam and protest

Perhaps the most important role for Islam in Africa today, however, is as a means of populist articulation of protest and resentment toward established government. In this respect it has played a particularly important role in the Maghreb and in Nigeria. In the Maghreb this populist protest has been stimulated by events elsewhere, particularly in the Arab Middle East and in Iran during the 1970s. In northern Nigeria, however, the primary causes have been indigenous. They have either reflected the massive ethnic conflicts in what is an ethnically composite state (particularly between the Hausa and other groups) or they have symbolized the growing social problems linked to economic and social development—as in the Yan Tatsine riots of the early 1980s. In Chad, Islam played a simlar role in the start of the civil war in 1965 and the eventual success of northern Muslim tribal communities in dominating the state.

Islamic fundamentalism first became a significant movement in North Africa in colonial times, with the development of the Muslim Brotherhood (*Ikhwan*) in Egypt under Hassan al-Banna in 1921. The movement continued to be of considerable importance until it was crushed in the 1950s by President Nasser. It has reemerged since the mid-1970s as a result of the strains imposed on Egyptian society by the demographic explosion and economic stagnation. In its modern forms, fundamentalism in Egypt ranges from the relatively moderate version now practiced by the *Ikhwan* and tolerated by the regime, to the extremist and violent rejectionism of groups such as Takfir wa'l-Hijrah and Jihad. Nonetheless, the modern hydra of fundamentalism in Egypt has so far been successfully curbed by government, albeit at the cost of political concessions to fundamentalist sensitivities.

In the Maghreb, fundamentalism first became a significant movement in Tunisia in the post-1973 period. By the start of the 1980s it had been organized into a clandestine political movement, the Mouvement de la Tendance Islamique (MTI), under Rached Ghannounchi and Sheikh Mourou. The movement sought legitimate participation in the formal political arena as provided for by the constitution. This was rejected by President Bourguiba, who was not prepared even to allow formal registration, let alone open participation, to the MTI, even though the Tunisian Communist party, a socialist movement and the Social Democrat movement were permitted to register after 1983. The MTI was kept beyond the political pale, however, and accused of being responsible for the abortive fundamentalist rebellion at Gafsa in January 1980, which had had Libyan backing, and for the bread riots in January 1984.

In fact, the Tunisian authorities persisted in confusing the essentially moderate MTI with the growing radicalism of various extremist fundamentalist offshoots. Although some of these were linked to the mysterious Islamic Liberation party, which sought a return to the political purity of the period of the "four rightly guided caliphs," or to the *Ikhwan*, many of them had no links at all and were genuine vehicles of populist protest. Nevertheless, the Tunisian government insisted that all Tunisia's fundamentalist movements were essentially a threat to the state and were linked to Iranian radicalism. It was a view that became increasingly untenable, and in late 1987 a conflict between the hawks around President Bourguiba, who wanted to execute leading fundamentalists, and moderates in the government who rejected such policies led to President Bourguiba's being removed from power. The new authorities are expected to come to terms with the moderate fundamentalist movement, thus providing for it to be integrated into the national political process.

The situation in Algeria and Morocco has been far less serious, although both countries have also had to face a surge in fundamentalist support in the early 1980s. In Algeria this culminated in a conflict within the educational system that was linked to the parallel issue of whether French should continue to play a dominant role in national life. In April 1980, the government's Arabization and Islamization policies came under sustained attack in demonstrations and riots in Kabylia. The official response was twofold; while crushing the riots, it also turned against the fundamentalist movements that had become active both within the university system and inside the industrial labor force in towns such as Hussain Dey, Blida and Laghouat, or the Vieux Kouba district of Algiers itself. The situation quieted down, although a violent clandestine movement had to be liquidated in the Blida region in 1986.

The Moroccan authorities were able to handle the fundamentalist problem with greater expedition because of the competing role of the monarchy to religious authority. As a result, the mainstream fundamentalist tendency, led by Abdeslam Yacine, was cut off by his imprisonment in February 1983. More extreme and clandestine movements, such as those led by Muhammad Naamani and Abdeslam Mutai, have been severely damaged by the activities of the security services, and many of their militants were arrested in the wake of the January 1984 riots throughout the country. There seems little likelihood that fundamentalism will pose a serious threat in the medium term.

In sub-Saharan Africa, Islamic protest seems to relate far more directly to indigenous causes only. In Nigeria, for example, the Yan Tatsine riots in Kano (1980), Kaduna (1982), Bulum-Ketu (1982), Jimeta (1984) and

Gombe (1985) were clearly movements of protest over economic disadvantage among local Muslim groups derived from traditional-style populist movements, which suffered increasing economic disadvantage in the modern world. The movements are believed to have been connected to the religious leader Alhaji Muhammad Marwa Maitatsine, who was killed during the Kano riots in 1980. Most observers consider that their protest was due to the fact that those involved claimed to be *gardawa*—peripatetic Koranic scholars who also acted as a substantial seasonal labor force of Hausa and Fulani origins. These groups had become seriously disadvantaged by the changes in the Nigerian economy during the oil boom years of the late 1970s. They had responded to their social and economic marginalization by seeking a millenarian ideology that rejected the material benefits to which, in any case, they had no access.

The result was a series of movements of fanatical commitment to the ideas put foward by Maitatsine. When the *gardawa* were confronted by the authorities, whom they saw as brutal and oppressive, the consequent riots were horrendously violent and led to profound disruption inside northern Nigeria. Despite claims by the Shagari government that they were inspired by Libyan propaganda, there appears to have been no significant external influence at all. Indeed, in their violence, the Yan Tatsine riots recall the communal riots of 1966, and the massacres of Ibos in the north and of Hausa and other Muslims in the south of Nigeria that led to the Nigerian civil war in 1967. In these events, after all, Islam was the common identifier of those, particularly the Hausa, who confronted the perceived threat from the south—itself also originally conceived in economic terms.

In fact, Islam has also played an incidental role in another major civil conflict in Africa, that in Chad, which has still not been fully resolved. The civil war broke out in 1965 as the result of maladministration by the southern-dominated government created by France from the Sara populations after independence in 1960. This political dispensation reversed the original political structure of Chad, in which the central Muslim sultanates had controlled the acephalous Sara society of the southern part of the country, while the Sahara fringe had been controlled by the Tibu nomads who paid a titular respect to Islam. By 1968 the Tombalbaye government had also managed to cause the north of Chad to join the rebellion, and over the next decade the rebellion, although nominally in the hands of a national liberation movement, FROLINAT, came to be dominated by the Tibu and thus to become effectively a Muslim movement. This tendency was increased by the growth of Libyan involvement, first because of Libya's claims to the Aozou Strip region in northern Chad, and then because of Libya's role in supporting one Tibu group against another.

Since 1980 the Chadian civil war has essentially degenerated into a factional struggle between the supporters of Goukouni Oueddei and Hissène Habré, with the latter receiving Egyptian, Sudanese, U.S. and French support to counter the aid provided by Libya to the former. The role of Islam here is now clearly marginal, but it is significant that originally the struggle was seen by many of its participants in religious terms, thus encapsulating the way in Islam has become a potent element within the political and cultural fabric of much of Africa today. It is a tendency that the increasing rate of proselytization of Islam throughout the continent must inevitably stimulate.

FURTHER READING

Adu Boahen, A., ed. *Africa under Colonial Domination 1880–1935.* London: Heinemann; Berkeley: University of California Press, 1985.

Curtin, T., Feierman, S., Thompson, L., and Vansina, J. *African History.* London: Longmans, 1987.

Fage, J. D. *A History of Africa.* London: Heinemann, 1978.

Haseeb, Khair El-Din, ed. *The Arabs and Africa.* London and Dover, New Hampshire: Croom Helm; Beirut: Centre for Arab Unity Studies, 1985.

Lewis, I. M., ed. *Islam in Tropical Africa.* London: International African Institute; Bloomington: Indiana University Press, 1980.

Mazrui, Ali A. *The African Condition: A Political Diagnosis.* London and New York: Cambridge University Press, 1980.

———, and Tidy, Michael. *Nationalism and New States in Africa from about 1935 to the Present.* Nairobi: Heinemann, 1984.

Niane, D. T., ed. *Africa from the Twelfth to the Sixteenth Century.* London: Heinemann; Berkeley: University of California Press, 1984.

J. D. Y. Peel, and Stewart, C. C. *Popular Islam South of the Sahara.* Manchester: Manchester University Press, 1985.

EDUCATION IN AFRICA

LALAGE BOWN

POLICIES AND PROBLEMS

SINCE independence, education has been an article of faith with African governments and many of their citizens. It has been seen to be a good in itself, a means to national integration in multiethnic countries, and generally the key to catching up with and asserting independence from the developed world. Investment in education was seen, in the words of Dr. O. Ikejiani, a political notable of the first Nigerian republic, as "an investment in the future, because the national security, economic and technological growth, and the whole strength of Nigeria entirely depend on this investment." Leaders with a more specific vision of social transformation have seen education as the key to attitude change. In his 1967 policy document, *Education for Self-Reliance*, Julius Nyerere said that education "must encourage the growth of the socialist values we aspire to. It must encourage the development of a proud, independent and free citizenry which relies upon itself for its own development and which knows the advantages and the problems of cooperation."

Postindependence aspirations were expressed in concrete terms by African education ministers meeting in Addis Ababa in 1961, when they undertook to introduce universal primary education (UPE) by 1980 and to provide by the same date an entry into secondary education for at least 30 percent of primary leavers. Most countries failed to achieve these targets, as we shall see, but there has been very general expansion and a willingness to spend quite heavily. Overall, expenditure on education absorbs one-fifth of national budgets in Africa. Education is usually the largest budget sector, only exceeded, sometimes, by defense.

Worldwide disillusionment with education has not yet occurred in Africa and the political impetus, within both local and national communities, continues to press African governments to keep up educational expenditure and widen opportunities. Vigorous growth of school-age populations means added effort to maintain even a constant proportion of the relevant age groups within reach of education, while the attainment of UPE has turned out to be an enormous task. Philip Coombs in 1985 suggested that whereas African school systems had created 55 million new primary-school places between 1960 and 1980, they would have to provide another 116 million between 1980 and 2000 if UPE were to be realized. At the same time, there is an inbuilt dynamic to increase provision from one level to another: UPE inevitably generates a greater demand for secondary schooling, as the 1961 Addis Ababa conference foresaw.

In opposition to these pressures for more education and more resources for education is the long slow undertow of economic crisis. Hard times have forced educational policy makers into hard decisions about quality, years of schooling, curricula, rate of progress through the system, community contribution and alternative forms of provisions. Policy makers have also been forced into greater recourse to foreign aid. An Ethiopian educationist recently explained the dilemma: "Our own resources are stretched to the utmost in running the infrastructure we have managed to develop and in securing budgetary increases for new infrastructure. The development discussion—and its internal priorities—is therefore inevitably the aid discussion."

In 1987 there were serious differences of opinion on educational priorities between African authorities and the World Bank, particularly over teachers' salaries and higher education. Ironically, education, originally seen as the major means to full independence, is thus now in danger of contributing to a continued dependency.

PARALLEL SYSTEMS

"Education" in most African contexts means the systems inherited and in some measure adapted from Europe—systems involving literacy, schools and the paraphernalia of examinations and qualifications—but with only minimal commitment to the education of age-groups past adolescence. A system may operate variably, with reliance on Christian religious agencies for supervision and management, as is the case in Lesotho, or with devolved responsibility for inspection and some financing, as in Nigeria through the state governments, or with some obligation on parents and local communities to provide textbooks and equipment, as in Zambia. In all cases there is national regulation.

Most African countries also have parallel systems, which function at much less cost and usually without much governmental intervention. Every ethnic group has its own mechanisms, often complex and sophisticated, for cultural transmission, teaching social norms and providing training in general skills such as agriculture and specialist skills such as smithing, music or medicine. In countries or areas where a large proportion of children do not go to formal school, these systems are still substantially in place. Where formal schools predominate, elements of these indigenous and community-based systems coexist with them. In Zambia, for instance, it is quite common for parents to use the school holidays to send their children to the traditional training programs for initiation into adulthood. Occasionally, without any external stimulus, the systems intermingle: long-established, precolonial modes of apprenticeship are now widely used to transmit car-repair skills; where the apprentices are literate, as in Ghana and Nigeria, they may supplement what they learn from their masters with correspondence courses in simple mechanical engineering.

Another parallel system exists in Islamic societies. It has a component of literacy and is based on an international network of scholarship. It also has a procedure for accrediting teachers and a hierarchy of institutions, from the Koranic school through the university. The Islamic system is, however, more flexible than the Western, with no age limit or formal admission qualifications and less dependence on certification. In Mauritania, there are still more pupils in the Koranic than the official schools and in some of the northern states of Nigeria young children may go for a year or two to the *malam*, the Islamic teacher, before moving into the government school. Several governments have attempted to ingegrate Islamic and Western systems, often by founding or strengthening higher-education institutions to bridge them, such as the Islamic Institute in Dakar, Senegal.

On the whole, the contributions of indigenous and Islamic systems are underrated by Western-educated functionaries and their Western advisers. A Hausa in northern Nigeria, for instance, who had been to an Islamic teacher and writes his own language using the Arabic script will probably be officially classified as illiterate because he is unfamiliar with Roman script. Much still remains to be done to bring the various systems together.

One attempt might mitigate the rigidness which keeps the mainstream system too closely imitative of Western models. Most formal school curricula have been conscientiously Africanized, but the educational structures are questioned only seldom. The educational calendar, for instance, in many African countries continues to follow the rhythm of the European academic cycle, without regard to different harvest times and climates.

ACHIEVEMENTS SINCE 1961

Problems of cost or structure should not obscure the very substantial achievements in African education in the decades since the Addis Ababa conference.

UNESCO has assessed that in 1960 there were 21.4 million pupils/students enrolled in all levels of education in sub-Saharan Africa, representing an age-participation rate of 20 percent—that is, out of every 100 young people of school and university age, 20 were benefiting from formal education. By 1982, there were 87.1 million enrollments and this represented an age-participation rate of 44 percent. There remain differences reflecting the various colonial legacies, as Table 1 shows.

In Francophone Africa there remain significant expatriate populations with middle-level skills as well as French functionaries, including secondary teachers; consequently there has been less effort to train indigenous technicians and teachers.

Expansion, however, has been impressive. The average annual increase in primary school enrollment between 1970 and 1980 was 7.3 percent and according to the 1987 *World Development Report*, 16 African countries out of 47 are known to have achieved or to be approaching UPE, as shown in Table 2. Zimbabwe's place on this list dramatically exemplifies the enthu-

Table 1
AFRICAN ENROLLMENT RATIOS AND LITERACY RATES 1984

| | Enrollment ratios | | | Literacy rate |
	Primary	Secondary	Higher	
Francophone Africa	46	14	2.4	18
Anglophone Africa	77	17	1.2	40

Source: Bray et al., *Education and Society in Africa*, 1985.

Table 2
PRIMARY SCHOOLING: AFRICAN COUNTRIES WITH AGE PARTICIPATION RATE OF 80% OR ABOVE
(1985 or nearest year for which figures available)

Country	Percentage of age cohort in primary school
Angola	134
Botswana	97
Cameroon	107
Egypt	84
Lesotho	111
Madagascar	121
Mauritius	106
Morocco	80
Mozambique	83
Nigeria	92
Tanzania	87
Togo	97
Tunisia	116
Zaire	98
Zambia	100
Zimbabwe	131

Source: World Bank, *World Development Report* (New York: Oxford University Press, 1987). N.B.: Figures above 100 are the result of various factors, including a timelag since the last census and an influx of immigrants—refugees, for example.

Table 3
SECONDARY SCHOOLING: AFRICAN
COUNTRIES WITH AGE
PARTICIPATION RATE OF 25%
OR ABOVE
(1985 or nearest year for which figures
available)

Country	Percentage of age cohort in secondary school
Botswana	25
Egypt	58
Ghana	36
Madagascar	36
Mauritius	51
Morocco	31
Nigeria	29
Zaire	57
Zimbabwe	29

Source: *World Development Report* 1987.

siasm for education apparent in newly independent states. During the first two years after independence in 1980, primary school enrollment there rose by 168 percent.

The growth in secondary enrollment has also been particularly impressive. In 1960 there were 1.9 million young people in secondary institutions in sub-Saharan Africa, representing an age-participation rate of 5 percent; in 1982 the figures were 17 million and 25 percent. Since 1970 secondary enrollments have been increasing in number by over 13 percent a year; for the continent as a whole, the 1987 *World Development Report* lists nine countries at or above the 25 percent age-participation level, as shown in Table 3.

What about higher education? The 1961 Addis Ababa target was an intake of 6 percent of eligible population, a goal attained by only a handful of countries. There has, however, been an overall increase in enrollments in higher education of 11 percent since 1960. The average age-participation rate is still 1 percent. Twenty-one countries appear in the *World Development Report* with enrollments in higher education of 2 percent or over of the relevant age groups. These are shown in Table 4.

A final set of statistics is included in Table 5, indicating the dimensions of achievement relating to adult literacy.

This rate should cross the 50 percent line by 1990. It must be understood, however, that whereas the *percentage* of illiterates in the population may have declined substantially, the *absolute number* of illiterates is still rising—a reflection of population increase. It is estimated that the 124

Table 4
HIGHER EDUCATION: AFRICAN COUNTRIES WITH AGE PARTICIPATION RATE OF 2% OR OVER
(1985 or nearest year for which figures available)

Country	Percentage of age cohort in higher education
Angola	2
Benin	2
Botswana	2
Cameroon	2
Congo	6
Egypt	21
Ghana	2
Guinea	2
Ivory Coast	2
Kenya	2
Liberia	2
Libya	11
Madagascar	5
Morocco	8
Nigeria	3
Senegal	2
Sudan	2
Togo	2
Tunisia	6
Zambia	2
Zimbabwe	3

Source: *World Development Report* 1987.

Table 5
ADULT LITERACY RATE IN SUB-SAHARAN AFRICA

Date	Percentage of adult population reported as literate
1960	19
1970	29
1985	46

Source: Bray et al., *Education and Society in Africa*, 1985.

million illiterates in Africa in 1960 increased to 156 million by the mid-1980s.

What do such statistics really mean? Overall, they stand for great achievement in terms of quantitative expansion, implying large numbers of new teachers and new buildings, the latter ranging from simple mud-walled classrooms with plain openings for windows and doors to extremely expensive scientific and technical complexes with sophisticated equipment, which often consume expensive materials as well. Vigorous efforts have also been made to improve the quality of education, both by more effective teaching and more relevant curricula. Teacher qualifications have increased throughout Africa, although there are still countries with many untrained teachers; there have been several imaginative efforts to help teachers in the field to upgrade themselves, such as the Teacher In-Service Education Programme in the northern states of Nigeria during the early 1970s and the current Zimbabwe Integrated National Education Course.

Curriculum reform was attempted by Kwame Nkrumah's government in Ghana during the late 1950s; almost all African countries have since tried to devise and develop curricula featuring social studies and basic science that explain the pupils' own environment and stress the history and cultural heritage of their own nation and the African continent. Long gone are the days when a Nigerian child was taught that the River Niger was discovered by Mungo Park; gone also, if not so long ago, are scenes once universal in Francophone classrooms from Senegal to Gabon in which black-haired, brown-eyed African children learning history chanted in unison, "Our ancestors were the Gauls, with blond hair and blue eyes." African specialists have worked to prepare textbooks and to Africanize the substance of examinations; African scholars have supported the use of the various mother tongues in education, and there has been a trend toward their use.

These are some of the attempts to improve what the pupils and students receive in their education. What has been the impact on society of increased access to formal education and of the changed curricular shape of that education? Perhaps the most fundamental is the emergence of "schooled societies," with psychological changes brought about by literacy and a change in traditional power balances. It is still possible in some parts of Africa for persons with little formal education to arrive at success and influence as businessmen or businesswomen, but substantial economic power is now on the whole accessible only to the educated. Certainly it is now difficult to imagine a politial regime made up of unschooled people.

This transformation has occurred gradually over the last 25 to 30 years. Some may argue that it is not necessarily an achievement, but the point here is that efforts to enlarge the *amount* of education have resulted in a *qualitative change* in society. As to more specific effects, there is good evidence that school education or literacy acquired outside school are accompanied by improved family nutrition, lower infant mortality and smaller family size. They are also accompanied by higher earning capacity, both in formal sector employment and in the urban informal sector; in rural areas a "critical mass" of educated farmers may encourage greater productivity. Higher levels of education have contributed to the indigenization of senior positions in government and the private sector. In Zambia, for instance, the proportion of non-Zambians in formal sector employment went down from 12 percent in 1964 to 4 percent in 1984. Where education has been used for "nation-building," there is anecdotal evidence that in some countries it has increased national awareness.

The full effects of a greater diffusion of formal education can still only be speculated on, because it takes a long time for them to work their way through the economy, the polity and society. Human maturation, it has often been said, cannot be accelerated.

LIMITATIONS, COSTS AND DIFFICULTIES

The generalizations enunciated above may hide several limitations in provision. There are various inequalities of access to education: over geographical areas, as in Ghana, where the primary school enrollment rate in the northern parts of the country is half that in the south; between different levels of the educational system, as in Sudan, where only about 12,000 out of every 100,000 taking their school certificates can move on to any form of tertiary education; and between the sexes, because a balanced enrollment between males and females has only been achieved by ten countries at primary level and two at secondary level. Furthermore, there is universal inequality in provision for different age groups. Very few countries commit serious money to the education of adults, even though the correlations between literacy, especially among females and improved health and nutrition seem clear. Yet it is the adult population who shoulder the expense of all educational services, both as taxpayers and through community and parental contributions.

This brings up again the question of costs. African governments' financial outlays on education are heavy and incremental. Education becomes more expensive at higher levels, and tertiary education, at present reaching only 1 percent of the age group, already absorbs one-fifth of education budgets. Even with no population change, commitment to UPE followed by increased secondary education are bound to generate more expenditure, and efforts at increased cost-effectiveness are unlikely to outweigh the effects of population growth.

Except for Tunisia and Egypt, no African country is expected to achieve a steady-state population before the year 2025 and the large majority will not reach it until 2035 or 2040. Until the end of this century, the population bulge will be in the younger age groups, so that in the year 2000 there will be in Africa 122 people under the age of 19 for every 100 adults. Any education budget is bound to assume additional payments per adult taxpayer to keep the system going at all. Commitments even to maintain existing quality will also demand further expenditure on certain components of the service. The enhancement of teachers' qualifications has been mentioned, but there are still countries where many teachers are unqualified. In Sierra Leone, 60 percent of primary teachers are untrained. In Nigeria, teachers trained for the upper primary level are having to be used in the secondary system because of the shortage of trained secondary teachers, so their qualifications are misapplied.

Citizens may well begin to ask whether such expenditure is worth it. We have examined some of the reasons why Africans have supported educational growth and some of its positive social effects. But what about its negative effects? While education is a tool for change and development, it is not self-propelled; its efficacy may be helped or hindered by other social forces. It has obviously been hindered in some countries by political upheaval and war. In parts of Uganda almost every educational institution was damaged or looted during the early 1980s: school libraries were left empty because soldiers made cooking fires with the books; headmasters' offices were bombed to get at the school safe; teachers fled. Other less visible factors may also affect educational progress. The state of a national economy may limit the absorptive capacity of the formal sector, so that school leavers with expectations of wage employment may be balked and disillusioned, and official rhetoric often vaunts the links between education and that type of employment. Education cannot itself invent or create employment; if it becomes a mechanism for producing greater competition in a job-market which is not increasing at any notable rate, then it will effectively add to urban unemployment.

There is a connection here to the kind of value system reflected by education. While education is seen as a good, unevenness of access has usually made it a scarce good for which competition has become necessary. The desperation in that competition can be seen in the crowds besieging the Nigerian Joint Admissions and Matriculation Board at examination time; Dr. Ikejiani's vision of education as a means to greater cooperation is trampled underfoot in such melees. Individual success tends to result from having parents educated and affluent enough to pay for kindergarten, extra coaching and sometimes education in separate schools. (Private schools still exist even in Tanzania, with its officially socialist values.) Not only may education in Africa thus promote social stratification, it may also promote dependency, even without the compromises resulting from direct foreign aid. There is an uncomfortable truth in the harsh assertion that the educational system encourages an unhealthy consumer attitude, in that the output of our schools tend to consume, sometimes uncritically, knowledge, skills, values, attitudes, goods and services produced in other countries; they have not developed what might be called production ethics.

THOSE LEFT OUT

We have presented a picture of the formal system outrunning resources, not attaining announced goals, becoming divisive and promoting dependency. Two additional issues must also be raised relating to quantity and quality. First, increased quantity of educational provision has still largely left some people out. Most obviously, as we have indicated, females have considerably less access than males to education in most countries, and participate only in small numbers in secondary and higher education. They also have little opportunity for any form of technical training, and this inevitably reduces their chances for modern sector jobs. It is estimated, for instance, that in Kenya, Ghana and Zambia, women form only about 15

Table 6
PERCENTAGE OF AFRICAN POPULATION
ILLITERATE, BY SEX

Date	Percentage of males illiterate	Percentage of females illiterate
1960	73.4	88.5
1970	58.3	82.4
1980	48.0	72.8

Source: *Journal of East African Research and Development*, 1985.

percent of the wage-paid work force. Furthermore, the majority of African illiterates are women: a greater proportion of adult females than adult males is illiterate—and this gap is widening (see Table 6). Nonformal education, especially for women, has been touted as an alternative to the formal system, but this has been largely ineffective. It does, however, have potential for reaching adults and has often proved successful in providing educational opportunities for adult women, helping them to achieve literacy, save time and labor in their ascribed tasks, learn skills that generate cash income, and gain greater confidence in facing personal and community problems. But when women have limited access to education in schooled societies, their roles are generally limited to social decision making.

Others edged out or kept out include members of ethnic, linguistic or religious minorities. In South Africa it is government policy to offer different types and a different quality of education to different racial groups (see below).

A particular challenge is posed by the educational needs of refugees. While there is no accurate estimate, the Organization of African Unity in 1982 suggested that there were about 4.5 million refugees in African countries other than their own and another half-million internally displaced within their own countries; most authorities believe that these figures are now substantially higher. Refugee populations usually include a high proportion of children. Researchers in the refugee camps of southern Sudan found, furthermore, that 10 percent of the children were orphans and that more than two-thirds or all the women over 14 years of age had had no schooling at all. Host countries, struggling to finance education for their own people, are usually not in a position to help and relief organizations are unable to provide secondary or postsecondary schooling. Exceptions are the special secondary institutions for South African refugees in Zambia and Tanzania and the Namibian experiment in distance learning for people in camps in Angola and Zambia.

THE VOCATIONAL FALLACY

An important quality issue relates to the curriculum. Periodically it becomes fashionable to plan education against manpower targets and to devise curricula to prepare pupils for specific types of jobs. One problem with this approach has already been mentioned: schools tend to become linked to urban formal sector employment. Another problem is that even when educational programs are devised for the rural sector, the young people who go through them may react against them. The vice-chancellor of the University of Ghana has crisply stated that it is not possible to predispose pupils to agricultural or other technology "so long as selling dog-chains or imported apples along the streets of Accra, or opening a kiosk anywhere, proves more lucrative and requires less capital outlay than farming or tool making." The fundamental point was, however, made more than 20 years ago by Philip Foster: "Those who criticise the 'irrational' nature of the African demand for 'academic' as opposed to 'vocational' education fail to recognise that the strength of academic education has lain precisely in the fact that it is prominently a *vocational* education, providing access to those occupations with the most prestige and, most important, the highest pay." Sociologists have often noted that education has remained more open in Africa than it is in other continents, offering greater chances for social mobility, with relatively large numbers of the underprivileged gaining access to its higher levels. As long as this remains the case, or is perceived to be so, it will be very difficult to persuade the public to accept curricula that limit possibilities of access to these higher educational and hence occupational levels. The revival of outside pressures for the greater vocationalization of African education needs to be weighed against these sociological phenomena.

HIGHER EDUCATION AND THE WORLD BANK

A Zambian policy document of the 1970s compared education as a whole to a long train, off of which most passengers fall before the end of the line, but whose whole energy is directed toward getting to the final station: the education system is thus distorted by concentrating on the needs of higher education. Both African governments and outside aid agencies are concerned to change this perception. Some governments have attempted to change the nature of primary education. Some others have tried to make up for the imbalance between the privilege given to a few university students as against the relatively little education given to the majority of young people by imposing various schemes of national service—as in the use of students in such literacy campaigns as the National Youth Service Corps in Nigeria, compulsory for all higher-education graduates, whether educated at home or abroad. A vibrant current issue, however, is whether higher-education spending should be rechanneled into increased primary education, a course strongly advocated by some employees of the World Bank. There are good arguments for this, but they leave out of account the peculiar importance of universities as creators of national intellectual communities and as the only possible means of ending scientific and technological dependency. Universities produce national self-confidence in African societies, as well as being sources of high-level professionals. Reacting to what seems to be this dismissive approach to universities, Dr. Kamba, head of the University of Zimbabwe, has said, "We would be colonies for all time—this is what the World Bank is trying to do to us. Whatever the deficiencies of our universities, the answer will not be to succumb to them, but to find solutions." His remark could apply to the whole of African education. To avoid dependency while enlisting outside cooperation requires facing up to deficiencies and looking for solutions engendered within the continent.

THE CASE OF SOUTH AFRICA

We have largely concentrated on the educational policies, achievements and predicaments of the member countries of the OAU. The points made here do not apply to South Africa, where educational policy is framed by a white minority for itself and, separately, for a black majority and is based on two sets of premises: that the education made available to blacks should fit them for subordinate roles in society; but that the performance of blacks within the system should be based on criteria derived from whites' education. The country, in education as in most other matters, is therefore an aberrant case.

Education for different racial groups has been largely segregated in South Africa, and one of the most highly contentious political issues of recent years has concerned the language of instruction. Government policy has been to limit it to mother tongues and Afrikaans for nonwhites, whereas parents and children, especially in the periurban areas, see English as the vehicle of access to quality schooling. While the myth of equal "separate development" will always be so as long as there is inequality in the amount of per capita resources put into each system, some of the so-called homelands have attempted limited innovations, such as upgrading teachers with nongovernmental help. For instance, the Bophuthatswana department of education during the 1970s provided an interesting in-service training program designed to help teachers enhance their basic academic qualifications. At higher levels, also, blacks have made use of the opportunities offered within the white system by the University of South Africa, one of the world's oldest correspondence universities.

In general, however, the education made available to blacks is underresourced and seems to fail the children. Well over half of all black children "fail" at least once during their first four years of schooling. The reasons for this may well include such noneducatonal factors as malnutrition, but the South African government's ideology attributes it, without any evidence whatever, to home and parental deficiencies. Until there is a change of regime, therefore, the best antidote to the system within South Africa must lie in maintaining educational opportunities for blacks outside it, whether in independent black Africa or on other continents.

CONCLUSION

With the exception of South Africa, the story of education in Africa since 1960 has been one of expansion of the whole of education and of considerable achievement in building up systems. While this has led to increased expenditure, the amounts spent are small compared to those spent on other continents—$18.85 million in 1985 out of a world expenditure of $689.64 million. African governments' expenditure on education as a proportion of GNP is comparable to the world average; although education bulks large in national budgets, it cannot be said to have led to an overextended public sector, since average overall budgets make up about the same proportion of GNP as in other parts of the world.

The difficulties encountered in education can be largely seen as the result of major economic decline—lack of resources and of import capacity, so that there is often even a shortage of such basic educational equipment as writing materials and desks. As a result, the quality of education and the morale of teachers and students is likely to suffer.

Education is an important factor in national development, and higher education should help to provide internal solutions to both educational and developmental problems. But external pressures on the economy and imposed external solutions by aid agencies cannot easily be averted by individual nations. The question is, do the African nations have any room for maneuver with regard to their education systems? One answer may lie in concentrating not upon expenditure but upon cost. The World Bank approach is valid insofar as it emphasises the need to look at areas of waste and possibilities of cost saving. Organization could be improved and ways, for instance, of reducing class repetition and the dropout rate could be found. Even such a simple change as an academic calendar in tune with the climate might increase efficiency.

At the same time, new methods of education still have potential. UNESCO has been touting "innovation in education" for so long that it has become a stale idea, but there are possibilities, such as closer links with traditional forms and means of education as well as the greater use of such inexpensive newer media as the transistor radio, which merit consideration. Another approach may be to see education itself generating alternative resources. Some countries have made fairly serious efforts to develop schools as productive units—school farms and school craft enterprises—but there has often been a lack of motivation and skill among teachers. There are surely ways of making educational innovations of this type both challenging and rewarding. But these are all merely suggestions. Decisions on educational policies at all times, even in the face of severe economic problems and challenges, are the absolute prerogatives of the African governments and peoples themselves.

FURTHER READING

Bray, Mark, et al. *Education and Society in Africa*. London: Arnold, 1986.

Cameron, John and Hurst, Paul. *International Handbook of Education Systems*. Chichester, Sussex: Wiley, 1983.

Harrell-Bond, Barbara. *Imposing Aid: Emergency Assistance to Refugees*. Oxford: Oxford University Press, 1986.

Hawes, Hugh, et al. *Education Priorities and Aid Responses in Sub-Saharan Africa*. London: Office of Development Assistance and University of London Institute of Education, 1986.

Hinchliffe, Keith. *Higher Education in Sub-Saharan Africa*. London and Wolfeboro, New Hampshire: Croom Helm, 1987.

Ikejiani, Okechukwu. *Nigerian Education*. Ikeja, Nigeria: Longmans, 1964.

Nyerere, Julius K. *Education for Self-Reliance*. Dar es Salaam: Tanzanian African National University Press, 1967. Reprinted in Resnick, A. *Tanzania: Revolution by Education*. Arusha, Tanzania: Longmans, 1968.

Psacharopoulos, George, and Woodhall, Maureen. *Education for Development: An Analysis of Investment Choices*. New York: Oxford University Press, 1985.

Thompson, A. R. *Education and Development in Africa*. London: Macmillan; New York: St. Martin's Press, 1981.

World Bank. Various publications, including *Accelerated Development in Sub-Saharan Africa*. Washington, 1981; *Toward Sustained Development in Sub-Saharan Africa*. Washington, 1984; and *World Development Report 1987*. New York: Oxford University Press for the World Bank, 1987.

LITERATURE AND POLITICS IN AFRICA

NEIL LAZARUS

It is appropriate to begin this general commentary on the politics of African literature since independence with a citation from Basil Davidson's *The Liberation of Guiné*. Writing in 1969, Davidson observed that

> It was clear to most observers in 1968 that the reformist régimes of the "decolonisation" period had largely failed to solve the basic problems of development: the problems, that is, of uniting and enthusing the efforts of Africa's rural millions so as to realize those human and productive potentials whose deployment can alone make good the hopes of independence. As things stood, much of independent Africa was in deepening confusion. Only new approaches, new policies, new leaderships could . . . now expect to find the mass response that was required.[1]

The significance of this passage rests in its identification of a historical crisis of consciousness in radical African theory and politics toward the end of the 1960s. The "reformist régimes of the 'decolonisation' period" to which Davidson alludes were those that had acceded to power at independence in such states as Nigeria, Zambia, Senegal, Kenya and the Ivory Coast. These nationalist regimes had been swept to power in the years of decolonization on the basis of the revolutionary rhetoric of their anticolonial campaigning. Identifying "freedom" with the overthrow of colonialism, the leaders of nationalist parties in colony after colony had spoken of unity, of emancipation, of African control of African resources. "The support of the masses" for their cause had been secured, as Peter Worsley has noted, "by telling them that independence was the precondition for economic expansion which would benefit everyone."[2]

In his famous essay "The Pitfalls of National Consciousness" (1961), Frantz Fanon suggested that the aspirations of reformist nationalists in the decolonizing years extended only to a vision of "the transfer into native hands of those unfair advantages which are a legacy of the colonial pe-

---

[1] Basil Davidson, *The Liberation of Guiné: Aspects of an African Revolution* (Harmondsworth: Penguin, 1971), 158–59.
[2] Peter Worsley, *The Three Worlds: Culture and World Development* (Chicago: University of Chicago Press, 1984), 2.

1101

riod."[3] Whether or not this statement accurately addressed nationalist sentiments is debatable; even in retrospect, the reformist sensibilities of a good many individual nationalists appear principled and unassailably sincere. Yet as a statement about nationalist ideology, Fanon's formulation seems incontrovertible. For it is undeniable that, having captured what Kwame Nkrumah called the "political kingdom" of the colonial state, nationalist parties throughout the continent failed spectacularly to implement most of the reforms about which they had been so fulsome in their campaign speeches. The colonial state apparatus was not only not dismantled in the years following independence, it was actively consolidated. After the fact, it is difficult to resist Fanon's argument that anticolonial nationalism was animated above all by frustration. All along, it was aimed not at national liberation but at securing for its constituents (the national middle classes) the political power that, under the colonial system, was unattainable. Its project was framed by the desire to "inherit" the colonial state apparatus. Its goal was not, therefore, the overthrow of the colonial state, but, on the contrary, its capture and appropriation. Certainly it is clear that, despite their rhetoric, it was not capitalism as such but only foreign capitalism that reformist nationalists in Africa were eager to contest.[4]

Throughout Africa, reformist nationalist parties acceded to political power at independence on a swell of goodwill, only to embrace policies that served to harden and entrench the fundamentally authoritarian and exploitative tendencies of the colonial state. Far from ushering in an era of unity, strength and humane government, independence paradoxically bore witness to stagnation, elitism and class domination, and to the intensifying structural dependence—economic, political, cultural and ideological—of Africa upon the imperial Western powers. "Reformist" policies failed precisely because they were merely reformist, precisely because they were premised upon presuppositions that took the character of the "territorial-bureaucratic State . . . inherited from the colonial powers"[5] entirely for granted. The reformist era would be better represented typographically as (post)colonial than as postcolonial, for its horizons remained indissolubly bound by colonialism.

"In an under-developed country," Fanon wrote,

an authentic national middle-class ought to consider as its bounden duty to betray the calling fate has marked out for it, and to put itself to school with the people; in other words to put at the people's disposal the intellectual and technical capital that it has snatched when going through the colonial universities. But unhappily we shall see that very often the national middle class does not follow this heroic, positive, fruitful and just path; rather, it disappears with its soul set at peace into the shocking ways— shocking because anti-national—of a traditional bourgeoisie, of a bourgeoisie which is stupidly, contemptibly, cynically bourgeois.[6]

[3] Frantz Fanon, The Wretched of the Earth, trans. Constance Farrington (Harmondsworth: Penguin, 1977), 122.
[4] See Worsley, p. 2.
[5] Anthony D. Smith, State and Nation in the Third World: The Western State and African Nationalism (New York: St. Martin's Press, 1983), 51.
[6] Fanon, pp. 120–21.

In ex-colony after ex-colony throughout Africa, "reformist régimes" not only "failed to solve the basic problems of development," they also refused to recognize this central failure as such. Ultimately, they could not acknowledge the failures of reformism without jeopardizing the political power that, as ruling elites, they had won at independence. The longer they remained in power the less attractive the prospect of relinquishing it began to seem. The longer they remained in power the less it could plausibly be maintained that independence had benefited the nation as a whole. But, increasingly committed to the safeguarding of their own political power at all costs, these ruling elites increasingly gave over to the politics of class—as distinct from national—interest. Realizing that wealth and power and privilege meant more to them than social justice—realizing, in fact, that a precondition of their own wealth, power and privilege was social injustice—they moved to consolidate what independence had bestowed upon them. In ex-colony after ex-colony, such consolidation was seen to entail security, not social democracy; and, in the name of national security, new rulers from Malawi and Zaire to Kenya, Somalia and Cameroon began to move against the popular forces massed against them. Gradually, at first, and then more and more rapidly, their "nationalism" stood unmasked in its true historic guise, as profoundly dominative. This sequence of events has been lucidly chronicled by Claude Ake:

> The reaction of the new rulers was all that could reasonably be expected of anyone in their situation. They decided to maintain the exploitative relations and a stratification system which they dominated. They decided to firmly discourage demands for redistribution of wealth and for mass participation. Having made these commitments, they were obliged to use coercion to solve the problems of authority and integration and to initiate the process of depoliticization.[7]

So swiftly effected, and so unexpected, was the "transformation" of reformist nationalist parties into reactionary, neocolonial regimes in the years following independence, that radical elements in the leadership, among the intelligentsia, or in worker- or peasant-based groups found themselves at first outflanked and unable to counter the demobilizing initiatives of the state. This is the precise context of the quotation from Davidson, which begins this article: a crisis of consciousness on the part of progressive thinkers in Africa toward the end of the 1960s, reflecting the failure of reformism, the emergent authoritarianism of the postcolonial state and the apparent strength of this repressive polity, as measured by its ability to enforce the depoliticization of popular movements and to secure the marginalization of the leaders.

The wonder of 1968, as Davidson addresses it, is that it was in just "this unpromising situation"[8] that struggles for national liberation elsewhere in Africa—and, crucially, in the most viciously policed and administered colonies, those of Lusophone Guinea-Bissau, Angola and Mozambique—were gathering momentum. In these latter struggles, it was not

[7] Claude Ake, *Revolutionary Pressures in Africa* (London: Zed Press, 1978), 90.
[8] Davidson, p. 159.

only the political superstructures of colonialism that were repudiated by the national liberation movements of PAIGC, FRELIMO and MPLA, but, very clearly and self-consciously, the economic basis upon which these superstructures rested. In the policy deliberations of these liberation movements, as Emmanuel Ngara has written,

> the question . . . was not just "independence" but "what form of independence?" This was the question posed by those countries which gained their freedom through protracted armed struggles in the seventies and eighties—Mozambique, Angola, Guinea-Bissau and Zimbabwe. When they acquired their freedom, these countries had a different concept of independence from the countries which had acceded to sovereignty in the previous two decades. Their long struggle for independence, and the experience of independent African countries now under the grip of neo-colonialism taught them to look at national independence from a radical ideological point of view, and they consequently chose the socialist path to development.[9]

The successes of these militantly anti-imperialist movements exercised a profound effect upon radical thought elsewhere in Africa. Confronted by the setbacks and repression of the postcolonial years, by the failure of reformist regimes to forge cogent and effective strategies for development, progressive African thinkers had, by the late 1960s, come to take up a rhetoric that was both abstractly totalizing and, despite itself, politically disenabling. All too often they tended in their theories to cast Africa as the passive victim of an imperialist "world system" so implacably powerful that resistance to it seemed futile. This defeated and defeatist line of thought was exploded by the revolutionary developments in the Lusophone colonies; by 1968 the PAIGC was already winning major battles against the Portuguese colonial forces, liberating and placing under its jurisdiction large sections of the interior of Guinea-Bissau. Hence Davidson's recognition that these developments provided an urgently needed "solution" to the crisis of reformism elsewhere on the continent:

> No doubt it is true that we are only at the beginning of a long development. Yet it will be hard to think that political approaches, methods and solutions such as those adopted by the PAIGC and their companions of the MPLA and FRELIMO may not prove decisive in tackling the rugged problems of achieving self-sacrifice and unity during the years ahead. . . . What the leaders of the PAIGC say, in effect, is that they took the road of radical structural change, of revolutionary politics within the context of their own country, because no other road lay open to them except continued surrender; that having taken this road they laboured for years among the rural people of Guiné until these hard-bitten farmers had made the PAIGC their own movement, their own vehicle to the future; that with this achievement the PAIGC have been able to evoke and canalize mass unity and individual sacrifice—not only and not even mainly towards fighting the Portuguese, but above all towards opening the way for basic and far-reaching mental and political adjustment to the needs and opportunities of the modern world.[10]

[9] Emmanuel Ngara, *Art and Ideology in the African Novel: A Study of the Influence of Marxism on African Writing* (London and Exeter, New Hampshire: Heinemann, 1985), 36.
[10] Davidson, p. 159.

The trajectory that Davidson charts with respect to African politics in the 1960s—from the "hopes of independence" to the reality of reformist nationalism, to neocolonialist reaction and consequent crisis, and finally to the reaffirmation of revolution in the practice of the PAIGC—is precisely replicated in the development of African literature during the same years. The dominant ideological trope of the first years of independence was that of the writer as teacher. Speaking in 1965, the Nigerian writer Chinua Achebe declared that "I would be quite satisfied if my novels (especially the ones I set in the past) did no more than teach my readers that their past—with all its imperfections—was not one long night of savagery from which the first Europeans acting on God's behalf delivered them." [11] Representing the views of a generation of African writers, Achebe spoke of his desire to contribute to the decolonization of the mind in Africa:

> Here then is an adequate revolution for me to espouse—to help my society regain belief in itself and put away the complexes of the years of denigration and self-abasement. And it is essentially a question of education, in the best sense of that word. Here, I think, my aims and the deepest aspirations of my society meet. For no thinking African can escape the pain of the wound in our soul. . . . The writer cannot expect to be excused from the task of re-education and regeneration that must be done. In fact he should march right in front. For he is after all . . . the sensitive point of his community. [12]

Increasingly, however, in the years after independence, the question of "re-education" began to seem an indulgence in face of the glaring persistence of structural inequalities deriving from the colonial era, and in the light of new abuses daily being added to these inequalities. Although they had tended to experience independence as a time of massive transformation, writers were quick to appreciate in its aftermath that something had gone terribly wrong. There could be no tranquility in the face of such recognitions. In his seminal novel *A Man of the People* (first published in 1966), accordingly, Chinua Achebe moved to abandon the formally assumed role of teacher and to adopt a more openly political stance, directly opposed to the perceived corruption and elitism of the African political classes in the postcolonial era. Portraying one such class in his novel, Achebe had his narrator describe it unforgettably as a

> fat-dripping, gummy, eat-and-let-eat regime . . . a regime which inspired the common saying that a man could only be sure of what he had put away safely in his gut or, in language evermore suited to the times: "you chop, me self I chop, palaver finish"; a regime in which you saw a fellow cursed in the morning for stealing a blind man's stick and later in the evening saw him again mounting the altar of the new shrine in the presence of all the people to whisper into the ear of the chief celebrant. [13]

[11] Chinua Achebe, *Morning Yet on Creation Day* (London and Exeter, New Hampshire: Heinemann, 1975), 45.
[12] Ibid., pp. 44–45.
[13] Chinua Achebe, *A Man of the People* (London: Heinemann, 1975), 149.

Nor was it only Achebe whose outlook changed during these years. One after another, writers as different in other respects as Wole Soyinka, Ayi Kwesi Armah, Okot p'Bitek and Ngugi wa Thiong'o began to turn their attention to the stagnation of postcolonial society, and to attempt to account for it. Typically they addressed themselves to the parasitism of the African political elite, exposing this elite in all its ruthlessness and vulgarity. There was its ethic of conspicuous consumption, its corruption, its greed and crass materialism, and above all there was its atrocious lack of vision. In such works as Ayi Kwei Armah's *Fragments* (1970), Kofi Awoonor's *This Earth, My Brother* (1971), Cyprian Ekwensi's *Beautiful Feathers* (1963), Gabriel Okara's *The Voice* (1964), Lenrie Peters' *The Second Round* (1965), Robert Serumaga's *Return to the Shadows* (1969) and Wole Soyinka's *The Interpreters* (1965)—to list only writers publishing in English—the African political class was portrayed as a murderously hypocritical social fraction, a kleptocracy, living not only beyond its own means but beyond the means of society as a whole. In these works, and many others like them, writers very movingly identified and deplored social injustices in postcolonial societies, and even, on occasion, called for the revolutionary transformation of these societies. Achebe and Soyinka, the most "visible" of this group of writers during the 1960s, also wrote extensively about African literature and society, calling explicitly for a literature of social engagement.

For all the manifest progressivism of this writing of the 1960s, however, it remained caught up, in ideological terms, within the class project of the national bourgeoisie of the various postcolonial societies. It was not only that, despite its patent commitment to questions of intellectual accountability and social regeneration, the writing tended to focus centrally (and often exclusively) on the situation of intellectuals and other members of the political elite in the postcolonial universe; it was also that, in the literary and critical works even of authors like Soyinka and Achebe, no matter how admirable or ideologically progressive, it was always possible to discern a residual strain of class arrogance, a strain that might usefully be interpreted as a cultural analogue of nationalism in its reformist idiom.

Starting in the mid-1960s, however, this "reformist" address of most of the writing of the first years of independence began to be subjected to radical critique. In an important article of 1966, for example, entitled "Wole Soyinka, T. M. Aluko and the Satiric Voice," Ngugi wa Thiong'o argued that despite the breadth of Soyinka's social canvas and the integrity of his denunciation of political abuses, the Nigerian author's work was marred by stasis and abstraction—defects, Ngugi maintained, that derived from the marginalization of "ordinary people" in Soyinka's drama and in his 1965 novel, *The Interpreters:*

Confronted with the impotence of the élite, the corruption of those steering the ship of State and those looking after its organs of justice, Wole Soyinka does not know where to turn. . . . Soyinka's good man is the uncorrupted individual: his liberal humanism leads him to admire an individual's lone act of courage, and thus often he ignores the creative struggle of the masses. The ordinary people, workers and peasants, in his plays remain passive watchers on the shore or pitiful comedians on the road.

Although Soyinka exposes his society in breadth, the picture he draws is static, for he fails to see the present in the historical perspective of conflict and struggle. It is not enough for the African artist, standing aloof, to view society and highlight its weaknesses. He must try to go beyond this, to seek out the sources, the causes and the trends of a revolutionary struggle . . . which, though suffering temporary reaction, is continuous and is changing the face of the twentieth century.[14]

The central problem with the type of sympathetic, expressive postcolonial writing of which *The Interpreters* was such a prime example, Ngugi suggested (the same argument could have been made with respect to Achebe's *A Man of the People*), was that it was only able to pose the question of the failures of the reformist regimes. It was not able to suggest ways of reversing these failures.

Of great importance, in Ngugi's critique, was his identification of a class distance between Soyinka as intellectual and the "ordinary people" represented not only marginally but as marginal in his work. In all of Soyinka's writing of the 1960s, "creative" or "critical," there is encountered what (following Ngugi's lead) might be described as an elitist and self-justifying conceptualization of intellectualism. Such a conceptualization received manifest formulation in 1967 when, in a celebrated address delivered at a conference in Sweden, Soyinka spoke of the historic role of the African artist as "the record of the mores and experience of his society *and* as the voice of vision in his own time."[15] Soyinka was immediately and appropriately criticized at this conference for rather grandiosely overestimating the significance of writers in society. Lewis Nkosi argued that it was quixotic in the context of postcolonial Africa to attempt to retrieve or revive an essentially romantic (not to say Western) conception of artists as the "unacknowledged legislators" of the world. Writers, Nkosi mused drily, "can have a fantastic capacity both for self-deception and for sheer inability to understand what is very clear."[16] To Nkosi, it seemed merely tautological to urge writers to be the bearers of a vision. "Every writer," he stated, "has a vision. Otherwise I do not see what he is doing writing."[17]

Beneath the ultimately rather trivial matter of Soyinka's hypostatization of cultural creation, however, lay the more weighty question of the social assumptions borne by African writers in social situations similar to Soyinka's own during the 1960s. For Soyinka was by no means alone in retaining throughout the decade an elitist presumption as to the uniquely privileged, hence uniquely portentous and significant, role of intellectuals in the postcolonial social process. Achebe's conception of the writer as "the sensitive point of his community" has already been referred to, for example. It was precisely against such representations that Ngugi moved to take up

[14] Ngugi wa Thiong'o, *Homecoming: Essays on African and Caribbean Literature, Culture and Politics* (London: Heinemann, 1972), 65–66.

[15] Wole Soyinka, "The Writer in a Modern African State," in *The Writer in Modern Africa,* ed. Per Wästberg (New York: Africana, 1969), 21.

[16] Lewis Nkosi, response to Soyinka's "The Writer in a Modern African State," in Wästberg, p. 56.

[17] Ibid., p. 57.

a revolutionary position on the place of the writer in postcolonial society. Responding to Soyinka's Swedish address, Ngugi spoke of the need for African writers not merely to speak on behalf of the people but, more concretely and decisively, "in the terms of" the people. As he put it, "When we, the black intellectuals, the black bourgeoisie, got the power, we never tried to bring about those policies which would be in harmony with the needs of the peasants and workers. I think that it is time that the African writers also started to talk in the terms of these workers and peasants." [18]

This declaration proved to be of the greatest significance in the development of African literature. Well in advance of the majority of his fellow African writers, Ngugi had diagnosed the crisis of consciousness in progressive African thought in the late 1960s for what it was, and moved to take the measure of liberation struggles in the Lusophone African colonies and elsewhere in the world—Indochina, Southeast Asia, Central America—by advocating a "(re)turn to the people" on the part of radical intellectuals. Such a "(re)turn," he argued, could not possibly be grounded on the reformist and implicitly elitist terrain of middle-class intellectualism. Where Chinua Achebe, thus, had spoken of the responsible intellectual as an educator, whose task it was to guide "the people," Ngugi now called upon intellectuals not only to act in solidarity with "the people's" interests, but to position themselves directly among these "people"—and not, as though that were an entitlement, at their head. For he argued that African intellectuals could only truly hope to serve their greater communities if they first "unclassed" themselves. The conscious repudiation by intellectuals of their class of ascription was an indispensable precondition of their legitimacy as representatives of "the people's" interest; only through means of such a repudiation could the forging of "a regenerative link with the people" [19] be consolidated.

Ngugi not only declared his commitment to a revolutionary conception of intellectualism; he attempted to put it into practice. He was increasingly convinced of the need to address the failures of postcolonial government in Kenya in terms of a class conflict between an indigenous bourgeoisie buttressed by and representing the interests of metropolitan capitalism, on the one hand, and the masses of the peasant and working classes, on the other. And he also sought to forge and institutionalize alliances between workers, peasants and radical intellectuals in the general cause of anti-imperialist struggle. While still teaching at the University of Nairobi, he helped to found the Kamiriithu Educational, Cultural and Community Centre, which devoted itself to programs of community development, adult literacy and the like. Gearing his literary production to the needs of the center's membership, Ngugi resolved to write not in English but in Kikuyu and to turn his hand from the form of the novel to that of workshop theater. In this he was following the general lead of other radical African writers who had begun in the late 1960s to ask themselves fundamental questions about the

[18] James Ngugi [Ngugi wa Thiong'o], response to Wole Soyinka's "The Writer in a Modern African State," in Wästberg, p. 25.

[19] Ngugi wa Thiong'o, *Detained: A Writer's Prison Diary* (London: Heinemann, 1981), 160.

nature and effectiveness of their cultural practice. Sembene Ousmane of Senegal, for instance, had very successfully embraced the medium of film in an attempt to democratize the base of his audience; and the Ghanaian writer Ayi Kwei Armah had attempted to have his fourth novel, *Two Thousand Seasons* (1973), serialized in newspapers in East and West Africa.

Since Ngugi and other radical writers were moving precisely to overturn the romantic conception of the writer as a privileged and uniquely sensitive member of society—since, in fact, they were attempting to demolish the ideologically constructed gaps, not only between mental and manual labor but, even more narrowly, between intellectual labor and creative writing— it is perhaps not surprising that they should have incurred the wrath of the postcolonial authorities. Throughout the immediate postcolonial era, African writers, with rare exceptions, had indeed been viewed as a breed apart and had tended to escape the repression that had been visited upon other sectors of their societies and even on other branches of the national intelligentsias. In the territories still struggling for national liberation, of course— South Africa, Mozambique, Angola, etc.—no such privilege had been enjoyed. The names of Dennis Brutus, Jose Luandino Vieira and Luis Bernardo Honwana testify to the fact that writers were as subject to detention and persecution as other categories of activists. In independent Africa, however, the politics of reformism seemed to dictate a differentiation between "creative writing" and other species of intellectualism. In Ghana, for instance, Kwame Nkrumah's Convention People's party shut down *Drum,* a cultural magazine, in 1960; it banned the *Ashanti Pioneer,* a newspaper, in 1962, and passed the restrictive Newspaper Licensing Act in 1963; and it outlawed and suppressed the dissemination of numerous popular high-life songs from the early 1960s onward. But even though it contrived through informal means to prevent the publication of much literary work it considered bothersome, it seldom moved to take direct action against Ghanaian creative writers.

This type of "repressive tolerance" was shattered throughout the continent in the late 1960s, as Ngugi and other radical writers began to contest the elitism of the national culture in country after country. The response of the various postcolonial states was quickly forthcoming, and brutal. In Malawi, for example, where Hastings Banda had wasted no time since independence in 1964 in establishing a one-party state, enacting repressive legislation, eroding still existing legal rights and institutionalizing detention without trial, torture and police violence, a Censorship and Control of Entertainments Act was passed in 1968. Despite its evocations of "public safety" and "public order," the purpose of this bill was plainly to render illegal and therefore punishable even the semblance of dissent. Under the provisions of the act, works by such writers as Samuel Beckett, George Orwell, Doris Lessing and Paul Theroux were banned. More pointedly, so too were works by Achebe, Soyinka, Armah, Ngugi and Mbella Sonne Dipoko. Even so, the act was itself a cover, beneath which the Malawian state legitimized its intent to act against Malawian writers. Nor has the state since scrupled to take such action. Without exception, every significant Malawian writer of the past 20 years has been subjected to harassment and persecution at the hands of the state. Some, like Legson Kayira and Frank Chipasula, have been driven into exile; were they to attempt to return to Malawi today, it is certain that they would be detained, and not unlikely that they would be murdered. Others, like Steve Chimombo and Jack Mapanje, who had resolved to remain in Malawi, have had their work seized and banned. Felix Mnthali was imprisoned during the 1970s. On September 25, 1987 Jack Mapanje was arrested. He has still not been released. As the Nigerian writer and critic, Chinweizu, recently reported,

> It is still unclear why [Mapanje] . . . was detained, or where exactly he is being held, or on what charges, if any. . . . [There is] speculation that it may all have to do with how politicians, who are jockeying to succeed Malawi's president-for-life, Dr. Hastings Kamuzu Banda, may have interpreted those of Mapanje's poems which could be seen as critical of government policies.[20]

The situation in Malawi is dismal and extreme, but it is not exceptional. Very much the same narrative, with a similar catalogue of names, could be produced with respect to any number of postcolonial African states: Mali, for instance, or Somalia or Cameroon. All of Mongo Beti's works written since independence have been banned in his native Cameroon by the regime of Ahmadou Ahidjo, and Beti himself has been obliged to live in exile since 1959. Similarly, Nuruddin Farah's work has been suppressed in his native Somalia, and he too has been driven into exile. Camara Laye, a Guinean, died in exile in Senegal. But Senegalese writers have themselves been persecuted: Ousmane Sembene's film *Xala* was cut without his knowledge before being distributed in 1977, and all of his more recent films have been censored or banned outright, as has been his latest novel, *The Last of the Empire* (1981).

With grim irony Ngugi wa Thiong'o has pointed out that it is today dangerous for African writers to attempt to represent the reality they daily encounter. In terms of the official ideology, it would seem the task of the African writer is to criticize colonialism and euphamize the tyranny of postcolonialism under the rubric of "nation building":

> When I myself used to write plays and novels that were only critical of the racism in the colonial system, I was praised. I was awarded prizes, and my novels were in the syllabus. But when toward the seventies I started writing in a language understood by peasants, and in an idiom understood by them and I started questioning the very foundations of imperialism and of foreign domination of Kenya[n] economy and culture, I was sent to Kamiti Maximum Security Prison.[21]

The transformation of consciousness to which Ngugi refers here is a significant one. In its terms not only has the distinction—previously useful to the established order—between writers and other intellectuals been obliter-

---

[20] Chinweizu, "The Detention of Jack Mapanje," *Times Literary Supplement*, no. 4423, January 8–14, 1988, p. 36.

[21] Ngugi wa Thiong'o, *Barrel of a Pen: Resistance to Repression in Neo-Colonial Kenya* (Trenton, New Jersey: Africa World Press, 1983), 65.

ated, but there is a move to define the situation of writers along the axis of class solidarity rather than, romantically, through reference to the mysteries of "vision" or "imagination." The plight of writers cannot be assessed separately from that of other categories of intellectuals; and the plight of intellectuals cannot be assessed without addressing the larger and more embracing questions of national culture and political justice.

It seems obvious that the silencing of writers in Africa must be represented as one strand within a wider crisis of legitimacy in the era of postcolonialism, and that this crisis not only cannot be "done away with" through repressive state measures, no matter how terroristic, but is actually intensifying through every resort to such measures. As Ngugi notes,

> Today questioning the presence of foreign military bases and personnel . . . on Kenyan soil is disloyalty. Questioning colonialism is sedition. Teaching the history of the Kenyan people's resistance to colonialism is sedition. Theatrical exposure of colonial culture is sedition. Questioning the exploitation and oppression of peasants and workers is Marxism and hence treason. Questioning corruption in high places is sedition.[22]

Imprisoned for almost a year without charge in 1978, stripped of his position as chairperson of the department of literature at the University of Nairobi, and subsequently forced into exile in Britain, Ngugi is exemplary of the new generation of African writers because he is, characteristically, able to draw defiant lessons from his experience. It is not, as he has repeatedly pointed out since his detention, that he would "wish the experience of prison" on any other writer. And yet, "To be arrested for the power of your writing is one of the highest compliments an author can be paid. . . ."[23] The point is that, in a neocolonial state such as Kenya, it is often only through persecution or imprisonment that a writer can indeed forge a "regenerative link with the people." In his prison memoir, *Detained*, Ngugi recalls that upon his incarceration in 1978, he encountered Wasonga Sijeyo, a fellow inmate at Kamiti Prison, who told him: "It may sound a strange thing to say to you, but in a sense I am glad they brought you here. The other day . . . we were saying that it would be a good thing for Kenya if more intellectuals were imprisoned. First, it would wake most of them from their illusions. And some of them might outlive jail to tell the world."[24] Certainly, Ngugi has lived to "tell the world." And, as he would be the first to insist, he is not alone.

FURTHER READING

Achebe, Chinua. *Morning Yet on Creation Day*. London and Exeter, New Hampshire: Heinemann, 1975.

Cabral, Amilcar. *Return to the Source: Selected Speeches*. London and New York: Monthly Review Press, 1973.

---

[22] Ibid., p. 2.
[23] See Sasha Moorsom, "No Bars to Expression," *New Society*, 19 February 1981, p. 334.
[24] Ngugi, *Detained*, 8–9.

Davidson, Basil. *Let Freedom Come: Africa in Modern History*. London: Methuen; Boston: Little, Brown, 1978.

Fanon, Frantz. *Wretched of the Earth*. Harmondsworth, Middlesex: Penguin; New York: Grove, 1968.

Gugelberger, Georg, ed. *Marxism and African Literature*. London: James Currey; Trenton, New Jersey: Africa World Press, 1986.

Harlow, Barbara. *Resistance Literature*. London and New York: Methuen, 1987.

Irele, Abiola. *The African Experience in Literature and Ideology*. London and Exeter, New Hampshire: Heinemann, 1981.

Ngara, Emmanuel. *Art and Ideology in the African Novel: A Study of the Influence of Marxism on African Writing*. London and Exeter, New Hampshire: Heinemann, 1985.

Ngugi wa Thiong'o. *Decolonising the Mind: The Politics of Language in African Literature*. London: James Currey; Portsmouth, New Hampshire: Heinemann, 1986.

———. *Homecoming: Essays on African and Caribbean Literature, Culture and Politics*. London: Heinemann, 1972.

Nkosi, Lewis. *Tasks and Masks: Themes and Styles of African Literature*. London: Longmans, 1981.

Soyinka, Wole. *Myth, Literature and the African World*. Cambridge and New York: Cambridge University Press, 1978.

AFRICAN TOURISM AND BUSINESS TRAVEL

LINDA VAN BUREN

INTRODUCTION

SPLENDID scenes of lions basking in the warm light of an East African savanna are now well known to most European and North American television viewers. And in the second half of the 1980s, more of them than ever before spent their vacations in sub-Saharan Africa recording this aspect of the continent with their own cameras.

Tourism in Africa enjoyed something of a boom, made possible by relative economic prosperity in the industrialized nations in the mid-1980s, further stimulated by the popularity of the 1985 Oscar-winning motion picture *Out of Africa,* filmed on location in Kenya. Kenyan critics panned the film for, among other things, presenting a rosy view of a colonial Kenya that never was; but the Western public seemed to flock straight from movie house exits to travel agencies to book their package tours. In tourism, image is all-important.

Around the world those tourist attractions with enough money spend millions every year promoting themselves, cultivating their images and keeping their names before the public's eye. African destinations, however (with the exception of South Africa)—even the ones most successful in tourism—have nowhere near enough money to build or protect their images with expensive advertising campaigns. They are, therefore, much more at the mercy of happenstance; an *Out of Africa* does not come along every year, nor does it come along at all for many destinations. It offered Africa a level of exposure it could not possibly have bought.

On the minus side, Africa does find itself before the public eye almost daily on TV evening news programs in the main tourist market countries. Here the publicity is much more likely to be negative. If it is not famine yet again in Ethiopia, then it is clashes between police and blacks in South Africa under apartheid. The latter have had a particularly potent effect. Ten years ago, an *Out of Africa*-engendered yen to go to Africa would have brought many more people to South Africa; by the late 1980s that country's tourism arrivals from overseas had slowed to a trickle.

Neither famine in Ethiopia nor riots in South Africa have much real relevance to the other tourism destinations of Africa, of course, but they do influence the often distorted image many Westerners have of the continent. Other, more isolated news items have a more direct bearing on that image—for example, a kidnapping or massacre in some dissident-held area, or an Amnesty International report of torture or other infringement of human rights in any of a number of countries. And coups in Burkina Faso and Burundi in 1987 served to reinforce Africa's image of political instability, though neither of these two countries ranks high on the list of African tourism destinations, and several other African countries have never had a violent change of government in their entire 20 or 30 years of independence.

Early misinformation about AIDS also caused African tourism officials to tremble, but saturation media campaigns in the industrialized countries have made considerable headway in dispelling some of the more unfounded fears. "AIDS does not," in the words of one AIDS expert, "jump out of trees at visiting tourists." And those tourists who go to Africa specifically for sex are rethinking their sexual habits on vacations as well as at home. Another, more realistic fear about AIDS concerns the possibility of receiving AIDS-contaminated blood through transfusion, should tourists have an accident or fall ill during their African vacations. Many areas of Africa, it is true, do not yet have the expensive screening equipment necessary, but Kenya and Zimbabwe, to name only two of several countries, are well ahead of the game on this score; all blood is screened at any hospital equipped to carry out transfusions.

Tourism is one of the most competitive sectors in the world economy. Africa has scenery of undeniable beauty, some of it yet to appear in any travel literature—but then, so do many other competitor destinations. In tourism, then, there is plenty of supply. Yet demand is highly elastic. Jitters have hit the sector worldwide since the stock market shock waves of October 1987, because when times are tight people forgo vacations long before they give up more essential purchases. The upmarket destinations—and with the exception of North Africa, all African countries must consider themselves such—are the most nervous of all. Their clients are the ones with a bit of extra, discretionary income; after they have housed, fed and clothed their families, they have sums left over to spend on nice vacation trips and to invest in stocks and bonds. Now that some of that discretionary income has disappeared and what remains is perceived as under threat, these families may either stay home or else go somewhere nearer and cheaper.

MASS TOURISM

For some years, in several of the more northerly destinations in Africa, a debate has raged as to whether mass tourism would bring in more revenue or not. The debate does not occur much south of the equator (except in the case of southern African destinations hoping to tap the South African market), since the great distance between major tourism markets and the host country makes the air fare alone prohibitively expensive for all but the fairly affluent. Most hotels are packed (if not overbooked) at Christmas time, but they lie empty for many months during the rest of the year. Lower room rates and air fares during low season fill only a few of these rooms. Those tourists who are able to take time off during low season often find that they have the beaches or the game reserves to themselves, and that they receive much more individual attention from their hosts.

All destinations acknowledge that they have to keep their revenue above their costs if they are to make any of the "easy money" that the more inexperienced seem to think flows freely from tourism. What is less clearly understood by some is that it has to be the other way around: they have to keep the costs below the revenue. Global market forces determine the revenue they can get, and there is little the host country can do about that. Tourist destinations therefore have to take a long, hard look at their costs.

Tourism can be a bona fide sector of the local economy, as it is in Kenya, for example. Kenya has to import many, but not all, capital goods when new hotels are built; but when it comes to the variable costs of hosting each visiting tourist, the list stops with fuel, some alcoholic beverages, the less-obvious imported components of locally assembled vehicles and other equipment, and a few other smaller items. Instead, the wide variety of foods tourists eat (from the standard bacon, eggs, cornflakes and tea to more exotic comestibles like mushrooms, artichoke hearts, *viande séchée* and smoked sailfish), the beer they drink, the beds they sleep in and blankets they sleep under, the vans that take them out to view the animals, the paper products and soap they use, the brochures and other literature, the postcards and toiletries they may purchase, many medications and (from 1987 on) even the glassware they use, are all made in Kenya. These are items that, where they do have to be imported, bite deep into the net amount of foreign exchange a country earns from a tourist's dollar.

The volume of tourists coming to Kenya—an estimated 750,000 in 1987—means that the sector makes a viable contribution to the treasury, that it is well integrated into the other sectors of the economy, and that it sustains jobs for Kenyans in brewing, agribusiness, farming, textiles and other industries. In turn, all these sectors back up the tourism sector. Tourists in Kenya seldom experience shortages of the amenities they are used to, like bread or soap or toilet paper or electricity. Several other African destinations, of course, also keep tourists well supplied, for example, the Ivory Coast, Togo, Zimbabwe, Botswana, the Seychelles and Mauritius, to name a few. But some others do not.

One of the arguments that always emerges in the debate over whether to opt for mass tourism, concerns the licensing of charter flights from European cities. In the classic situation, the flagcarrier African airlines—more often than not loss-making parastatals—are vehemently opposed, since they cannot cope with the competition. Some countries use other means to protect their flagcarriers; Zimbabwe, for example, does not permit some European carriers to fly wide-bodied aircraft to Harare. Many African airlines have aging fleets (the loving care given to these veteran aircrafts' maintenance varies widely, with Ethiopian Airlines invariably earning top marks) because they cannot afford to replace them. New noise regulations that came into effect in EC countries in 1988 have effectively barred several African carriers from landing their Boeing 707s or 720s in Europe. A few lines have managed to buy new-generation, low-noise and (while they are at it) wide-bodied jets. Among these are Ethiopian Airlines, Kenya Airways, Zambia Airways, Cameroon Airlines, Nigeria Airways and Air Afrique; but they have taken on heavy debt burdens to do this. Others, such as Air Seychelles, have opted for "hush kits" to reduce the noise made by their existing jets, with these, they meet the noise regulations and beat the ban on landing at European airports, and they avoid the really big debts—but they have to operate some rather lengthy flights (eight hours or more) with single-aisle planes.

PACKAGE TOURS

Most tourists to Africa choose package-tour vacations. This way, someone else makes all the arrangements for them in advance for a destination they probably know very little about; and they also assume that all package tours are cheaper than individually booked trips. A problem for many African host countries has been that tourists pay the tour operators in their own countries, and rather little of that money ever makes its way down to the host country. Kenya, in particular, has made some headway in closing this loophole; for example, many package tours use Kenya Airways or Kenyan-owned hotels. In return, the burden is on the hotels and the airline to keep their standards high.

The vast majority of package tours to Africa fall into either of two categories: wildlife safaris or beach vacations. Some combine both. Almost all the major European tour operators include several packages to Kenya, and some combine Kenya in two-center vacations with Egypt, the Seychelles or Tanzania. Also popular is a two-center vacation entirely within Kenya, with one week on photographic safari in any of several game reserves and the other week at one of the dozens of hotels along the country's spectacular Indian Ocean beaches.

BUSINESS TRAVEL

Business travelers choose their destinations for entirely different reasons, of course. Facilities vary enormously from place to place, e.g., from the utterly Spartan in Beira to the downright sumptuous in Nairobi or Abidjan. Francophone Africa by and large keeps the standards up to a certain minimim level, though one does not expect to find all the luxuries of Abidjan or Lomé when one is in Ndjamena or Conakry. In Anglophone Africa, things are much more uneven, while in Lusophone Africa one fares worst of all.

Throughout the 1980s, new hotels—the vast majority of them with African owners but under contract with well-known multinational hotel groups as managers—have proliferated. The cities that already had the best facilities, like Nairobi, went from strength to strength. Others, which previously had had woefully inadequate accommodations, like Lagos, saw major improvements. Some which had been far off the beaten path—Bissau, for example—suddenly found themselves part of the international network of a major hotel chain.

Still other cities, though, have no international-standard hotels. Some of these simply have never had the wherewithal to build. Others have hotels that once were quite adequate, but which now function as little more than empty shells, having fallen into decay after years of economic collapse. A few of these, it must be said, hang onto their internationally known names even though they fall far below standards, because if a hotel group from country A drops a hotel in country B from its catalogue, then B denies A's airline landing rights.

WEST AFRICA

The pulsating drumbeat so often heard in West Africa sets the pace for this colorful, steamy, animated part of the continent. Teeming markets, voices raised in haggling, the din of car horns, the smell of cassava cooking, and the blistering heat make a formidable assault on one's senses. Some capital cities offer the tourist or the businessperson islands of calm in the form of lavish resorts or high-rise, business travelers' hotels. Some do not.

The West African countries geared up for tourism are Senegal, Gambia, the Ivory Coast and Togo. Gambia hosts sun-worshipping Swedes and Americans keen to reexperience Alex Haley's *Roots*. Togo allows tourists to go upcountry to see its rural cultural variety without having to cover great distances. The Ivory Coast, the most industrially developed of the tourism-oriented countries in the region, offers the visitor a chance to see an African rural economy that works, and to see coffee, cocoa, palms, pineapples and rubber trees growing. Cameroon and Gabon host organized groups of tourists—those to Gabon invariably eager to see the hospital at Lambarené that Albert Schweizer built in 1926; and those to Cameroon being invited to experience the country's diverse cultural variety as well as to view its wildlife in the north. But Cameroon's omnipresent local police and its bureaucracy inhibit tourist's movements where Socatours is not there to run interference for them.

For beach vacations, Gambia, Senegal, the Ivory Coast and Togo are the main destinations. Countries with considerable tourism potential as yet undeveloped are Liberia, Sierra Leone, Ghana and Nigeria. Of these, Ghana is most likely to begin realizing some of that potential. Its economy has recovered significantly from a low point in the late 1970s, and it is now rehabilitating some hotels and building new ones. Ghanaians have a knack for making guests feel welcome, which will stand them in good stead when tourists begin to return in any numbers. With too little money, however, to launch a marketing campaign, Ghana may have trouble finding a place for itself on the world tourism map. This would be unfortunate for host and would-be visitor alike, for Ghana offers much to see of historical interests, some gorgeous beaches, a rich cultural heritage and a communicative, English-speaking populace from whom tourists could learn a great deal.

Nigeria is always West Africa's great paradox. Pandemonium at airports, lack of electricity and water even in Lagos's top hotels (though the opening of the fully self-contained Lagos Sheraton has now helped), legendary traffic jams, piles of rubbish, pressing throngs and unfathomable red tape have given rise to horror stories that not only rule out any hope of world tourism in Nigeria, but also put some people off the idea of going to Africa at all. In this country of 100 million people, some entrepreneurs no doubt would like to realize some of the country's tourism potential—but generally, Nigerians are not interested in coddling foreigners. And after all, for the most part, the traveler is free to choose. If comfort and pampering are wanted, the tourist can forget about Nigeria. But if travelers have plenty of time and the open-mindedness and the stamina to meet Nigeria on its own terms, it will never fail to fascinate. Despite all the insults foreigners have hurled at the place, few have ever called it boring. The Nigerians one encounters on the tourism front line—airport personnel, customs officials, policemen at roadblocks, et al.—give Nigerians a reputation for unfriendliness that most of them do not deserve.

Guinea-Bissau, heretofore not equipped to cope either with tourists or business travelers, now has a new hotel, part of an international chain, which will make life easier for the latter.

The Central African Republic, while not on the beaten path of tourism, does have some repute as a preserve for big-game hunting, mostly attracting French VIPs, with mollycoddling on an individual basis and at a price.

SOUTHERN AFRICA

Here, Zimbabwe presents a strong case for tour operators to use Harare as a gateway for the region as a whole. Zimbabwe has added to the ample tourism infrastructure it inherited in 1979 from white rule, with several new tourist and business-travel facilities. Smaller towns also have small, family-run hotels.

Zimbabwe has no fewer than three noteworthy sights to make a tourist's journey worthwhile, not to mention many interesting places one can enjoy along the way. Victoria Falls, the world's biggest cataract and certainly one of the world's most famous natural wonders by all accounts, lies about three quarters in Zimbabwe and one quarter in Zambia. Tourists can stand close enough to the falls to be doused with spray, they can fly over it in small aircraft, or they can go whitewater rafting nearby on the Zambezi River. Further downstream lies the man-made wonder of the Kariba Dam and the lovely Lake Kariba it forms. A boater's paradise, the lake has many lodges and campsites along its shore. South of Harare, near Masvingo, lie the ruins of Great Zimbabwe, a rare surviving remnant of an African civilization that flourished here 700 years ago. Air connections from Europe to Harare are good, and it is no longer necessary to use Johannesburg as a gateway for the region.

From Harare, tourists can take the train south to Botswana, although and road links also exist. Botswana's primary tourist area is the swampy Okavango Delta in the north, where unique climatic conditions in this otherwise desert country support species of wildlife found nowhere else. Botswana is expensive but is well equipped to look after tourists in style.

Zambia, cohost for Victoria Falls, has several game reserves and is eager to attract tourists, but the country's economic difficulties make it hard for tour operators to keep everything running smoothly. Some seem to manage, however; others can not.

Wars against South African-backed guerrillas render both Mozambique and Angola off limits to tourists, and in fact tourist visas are impossible to get, with one exception. In the late 1980s Mozambique developed some tourist facilities on islands offshore from Maputo, in the south, geared mainly toward attracting South African tourists. In Angola, business-travel facilities in Luanda are extremely expensive, without the excellence one would expect at these prices; at Mozambique's two main destinations, conditions are described as difficult in Maputo and as very difficult in Beira. In Beira's best hotel, according to one frequent business guest, some days it is "eggs for breakfast, eggs for lunch and eggs for dinner. Other days, it's prawns for breakfast, prawns for lunch and prawns for dinner. . . . You see people coming down to breakfast carrying their own supplies of jam, bread, butter, coffee and so forth."* Conditions in Lesotho, Swaziland and Malawi are comfortable for business travelers; South African money and clientele dominate the first two, with emphasis on gambling and other vices the South African authorities do not consider wholesome enough to permit inside the republic (except for the so-called homelands). Lesotho offers sub-Saharan Africa's only alpine environment and scenery (apart from a few isolated peaks in East Africa). Malawi treats tourists to its lengthy lakeshore, with optional cruises on lake steamers.

EAST AFRICA

It is here for a variety of reasons, that African tourism has flourished most. Nairobi, with its air links to just about every capital in Europe and some Asian cities besides, is the region's gateway. Kenya is by no means the only place of interest to see in East Africa, yet it will continue to draw more tourists than its neighbors until the latter overcome their economic difficulties. Kenya has several large game reserves, each of them rather different from the others and all of them with good, comfortable, well-managed facilities offering every necessary comfort. The visitor may stay in a lodge or in a tented camp; either way, amenities are available: hot and cold running water, good meals with nothing lacking, excellent tea from the country's own high-quality gardens, soap, toilet paper, clean linens, ice-cold beer, wine and soft drinks, and a radio to summon the Flying Doctors if necessary. Nairobi's Wilson Airport, the busiest small-craft airfield in Africa, provides regular, dependable air links to dozens of remote landing strips in game-viewing areas all around the country. For beach enthusiasts, Kenya's north coastal area or the snow-white sand of Diani Beach south of Mombasa are unsurpassed, and the resorts on them offer

*Business traveler quoted in *African Business* (November 1987): 27.

every type of atmosphere from the all-frills gathering places to secluded surfside quiet—yet the comfort standard is high throughout. A coral reef offshore shelters a variety of interesting sea creatures.

Besides these two well-known types of vacations, Kenya offers tourists a chance to see snow all year round on the equator, on the twin-peaked 17,058 -ft/5,199-m. high Mount Kenya (higher than any of the Alps); the remote Lake Turkana, in the far north; tea, coffee, sugar and pineapples growing; and Lake Victoria (Africa's largest lake, which offers huge un-tapped tourism potential for the three countries that share it—the other two being Tanzania and Uganda). Visitors can also glimpse the various Kenyan cultures at first hand in different parts of the country or in micro-cosm in Nairobi's *bomas*; or they can explore the narrow streets of Mom-basa, East Africa's largest port, with its distinctly Arab air.

South of the Kenyan border, Tanzania, with its legendary Serengeti Plain and its Ngorongoro crater, boasts even more wild animals than Kenya; and though one can see Mount Kilimanjaro from Kenya, it actually lies in Tanzania. Its snowy peak, at 19,340 ft/5,895 m., is the highest in Africa; and unlike many mountains of its height, it has slopes gentle enough for anyone who is reasonably fit to hike up. Offshore, the islands of Zanzibar and Pemba boast lovely but now decaying remnants of a long-established Arab presence.

Tanzania has some guest lodges that were once quite comfortable and could be so again, but—owing again to economic difficulties in the coun-try—during the 1980s they started to suffer from neglect. By the mid-1980s, some tourists who had been rather tolerant of the lack of water, electricity or variety at mealtimes found that their patience ran out when lack of gasoline prevented them from driving out to view the game they had come so far to see. In 1988, foreign private investors were brought in to spruce up several hotels and lodges.

For business travelers, Dar es Salaam fell on very bad times in the mid-1980s, when it was a case of bring your own everything (even light bulbs at one stage, it was reported). International Monetary Fund-induced eco-nomic reforms have since made more consumer goods available, at a price, but guests find that plenty of room for improvement remains. The coun-try's main conference venue is Arusha, in the north near the Kenyan border and near the main game-viewing areas. Transport in Tanzania is a chal-lenge, whether across potholed roads, through disorganized airports, via equally chaotic boat passage from Dar es Salaam to Zanzibar, or by rail. It is possible to take the famous Chinese-built Tazara railway from Dar es Salaam to Zambia's copper belt, but one needs plenty of time, as the "schedules" bear little resemblance to what happens in practice.

Rwanda is visited by a small number of enthusiastic upmarket tourists who come to see the mountain gorillas. Only a few guests can be accom-modated at a time, though, so it is important to make reservations well in advance. Air links from Nairobi are good. Rwanda and Burundi both have adequate hotel facilities in their capital cities.

Uganda's many spectacular sights—Queen Elizabeth National Park, Lakes Edward and George, Murchison Falls and the Ruwenzori Range (the

"Mountains of the Moon")—are for all practical purposes off limits to tourists. Accommodations for tourists are badly in need of renovation, for a start, but efforts got under way in 1987 to spruce them up. More significantly, until the security situation in Uganda improves—and, indeed, until tourists begin to feel confident that it has improved—few if any will take the risk of going to the country. The good news for business travelers to Kampala is that a renowned old hotel in the city center has reopened as a part of a modern international chain.

Ethiopia is one of the world's tourism treasures, but it too is now virtually closed to tourist travel. Ethiopia has its own language, its own alphabet, its own culture, its own cuisine and its own unique branch of Christianity that dates directly back to New Testament days and was never part of the Roman Catholic Church. Priceless early Biblical manuscripts lie in cupboards in the rock-hewn churches of Lalibela, carved by hand out of the surrounding sandstone. Ethiopia is, as well, the source of the Blue Nile. But a protracted guerrilla war makes it impossible to move about much. Air services are good when the destination airport—which often is a dirt landing strip on a mountain top—is safely in government hands. Hotel accommodation in Addis Ababa is surprisingly good, considering the country's economic situation.

INDIAN OCEAN

Four countries along the Indian Ocean offer themselves on the tourism market. The largest is Madagascar, which has a curiously South Pacific air about it and which has several species of wildlife (for example, lemurs) not found anywhere else on earth. Antananarivo has a modern hotel. The Comoros have recently been developed by South African investment. But the region's big two in tourism are Mauritius and the Seychelles. Despite some shared cultural and economic links, the two are quite different from each other in appearance. Mauritius is a single volcanic island, a microcosm of the whole Indian Ocean, with African, Indian and Far Eastern peoples and language all well represented. Several large hotels are owned by South Africans, but other investors are also present in abundance in this relatively open economy, where sugar is king. Both Mauritius and the Seychelles offer a range of accommodations from top luxury hotels to small guest houses, and have adequate air links to Europe and the Far East.

The Seychelles, on the other hand, consist of hundreds of islands, of which only a few are inhabited; the main ones are of granite, while most of the others are low-lying sandy atolls. The scenery is unsurpassed. Air links between the main islands developed for tourism are excellent; on Bird Island, for example, the landing strip runs coast to coast. The main island, Mahé, has several big-name hotels. But any Seychelles vacation, whether at the top or the bottom of the range, is expensive. Nearly everything tourists consume has to be imported.

Africa, with its 52 countries, its hundreds of languages, its great variety of peoples and culture, its wealth of wildlife and its abundance of natural beauty, offers much more to the tourist than most people in the West realize. Not all of the continent is ready to receive them, but as the Kenyan example has shown, the more tourists who do visit the better prepared the hosts become, to the mutual benefit of both.

FURTHER READING

Africa Calls from Zimbabwe. Harare: Zimbabwe Tourist Board. Bimonthly.

Africa South of the Sahara, 1988. 17th ed. London: Europa Publications, 1987.

African Business. London: IC Publications. Monthly.

Botswana: An Economic Survey and Businessman's Guide. Gaborone: Barclays Bank of Botswana, 1985.

Hancock, Graham, Pankhurst, Richard, and Willetts, Duncan. *Under Ethiopian Skies.* London: Editions HL, 1983.

Hildebrand's Travel Guide Seychelles. Frankfurt: Karto + Grafik Verlag, 1985.

Jewell, John H. A. *Mombasa and the Kenya Coast: A Visitor's Guide.* Nairobi: Evans Brothers, 1987.

Kenya: A Land of Contrasts. Nairobi: Kenyan Ministry of Information and Broadcasting, 1981.

Macintyre, Kate. *The Nairobi Guide.* London: Macmillan, 1986.

Mountjoy, Alan B., and Hilling, David. *Africa: Geography and Development.* London: Hutchinson, 1988.

Rake, Alan, ed. *New African Yearbook, 1987–88.* London: IC Publications, 1987.

————. *Traveler's Guide to Central and Southern Africa.* London: IC Publications, 1988.

————. *Traveller's Guide to East Africa and the Indian Ocean.* London: IC Publications, 1988.

————. *Traveller's Guide to West Africa.* London: IC Publications, 1988.

République Centrafricaine. Paris: Agence de Coopération Culturelle et Technique, 1984.

Tomkinson, Michael. *The Gambia: A Holiday Guide.* Banjul: Gambian Ministry of Information and Tourism, 1983.

Tourism in Cameroon. Yaoundé: General Delegation for Tourism, 1977.

UTA Africa Travel Guide, 1988–1989. Puteaux, France: UTA, 1988.

Van Buren, Linda, ed. *Traveller's Guide to North Africa.* London: IC Publications, 1988.

THE MEDIA IN AFRICA

SEAN MORONEY

IN many ways the state of the media in each African country reflects its level of political and economic development. The sad fact is that the press is not free in most parts of the continent and that in many cases press freedom has been reduced since independence. There has been an overwhelming trend of increased state control and ownership of newspapers, and most radio and television development has been by government broadcasting authorities. The much-heralded new era of free enterprise for Africa is unlikely to be allowed to encompass the press for decades to come.

In a recent report on the African press, the right-wing New York-based Freedom House judged only three sub-Saharan African countries to have a "generally free" press: Gambia, Mauritius and Botswana. The press in another 11 countries was classified as "partly free," while 30 have a "generally not free" press. Dr. Raymond G. Gastil, who conducted the survey, said that "sub-Saharan Africa and the Middle East are the worst in the non-Communist world" in terms of harassing the press.

Despite this depressing overall picture, there are exceptions that point the way to a far more diverse, dynamic African press in years to come.

THE ROLE OF THE PRESS

African governments have rationalized their ownership of national newspapers as a means to ensure national development and unity. In reality, what has happened is that the papers have become, to varying degrees, government mouthpieces. The independence, creativity and individualism of editors and journalists has been stunted. The credibility of the papers has declined, and readers have turned to alternative sources of information, particularly overseas radio broadcasts and international magazines, when they can obtain them, for independent perspectives.

Baffour Ankomah, writing in the *Index on Censorship*, has defined the dilemma of African journalists as follows: "In Cameroon, the press is torn between the conflicting roles of mobilising the people for national development, and playing an independent watchdog role. Government officials like the first role and are doing everything in their power to suppress the second." [1] In reality, of course, the two roles are not conflicting. One of

[1] Baffour Ankomah, "Cameroon's Forbidden Topics," *Index on Censorship* (February 1988).

1123

the major contributions the press can make toward national development is to act as watchdog against state excesses, corruption and sheer stupidity. But state officials invoke the urgency of national unity to justify their actions in preventing the press from playing a watchdog role.

Referring to the postindependence trend for governments to bring the press under their own control, Niyii Alabi writes:

> The result has been disastrous: Governments who pay the piper expect to call the tune. The press has been reduced to a mere marionette which can only respond to the whims and caprices of the governments of the day, leaving the public it is supposed to serve in the lurch.
>
> In the Francophone countries in particular, the press has become an organ of propaganda for the various governments and parties. Even in Senegal, which practises a multi-party system, Le Soleil serves the interest of the ruling Socialist party and the Government of President Diouf.[2]

CONTROL MECHANISMS

Various mechanisms are used by African governments to control the media: outright purchase, in the case of Zimbabwe; complicated censorship procedures in Cameroon; highly sophisticated campaigns of legislation and regulation in South Africa; a combination of security police harassment of individual journalists and subtle and informal pressures on editors in Kenya.

Abodel Karimou, editor of La Gazette, one of several privately owned weeklies in Cameroon, describes the tortuous prepublication censorship rigmarole all material has to go through:

> When an edition of La Gazette is ready for press [I send] a photocopy of each page to the Ministry of Territorial Administration in Yaoundé, the capital, which is three hours by bus from Douala, where La Gazette is printed.
>
> At the Ministry in Yaoundé, the newspaper pages go through the bureaucracy—from the Reading Bureau, to the Director for Public Freedoms, to the Deputy Director for Political Affairs. Each official is permitted by law to make notes on the articles which are finally presented in resume form to the Minister for Territorial Administration.
>
> The big man goes through the resume, if he has time to spare. He orders each approved page to be stamped and signed by the Deputy Director for Political Affairs.
>
> Printers in Cameroon are not allowed to print material without the censor's stamp. From the printers, 10 copies of the approved newspaper pages are sent back to the Ministry for final approval and a second stamp. Newspaper vendors are forbidden to distribute any publications without the censor's second stamp.[3]

"The censorship which I exert leaves me at ease because I know it is an action necessary for our democracy," the deputy director for political affairs, Mr. Eric Sousse, told participants at a seminar in Yaoundé in 1987. "In the great democracies whose example we follow," he continued, "we know very well that censorship exists under many forms."

[2] Niyii Alabi, "Publish and Survive," New African (May 1988).
[3] Quoted in Ankomah, "Cameroon's Forbidden Topics."

South Africa provides probably the continent's most extreme example of press control. Pretoria's unremitting campaign against press freedom has been far more sophisticated than those encountered elsewhere on the continent, and has included a wide range of control mechanisms.

South African officials and ministers often boast that the country has the "freeest press" in Africa. And indeed the newsstands display probably the continent's most lively and critical papers, possibly rivaled only by Nigeria in their diversity and controversy. But the newsstands do not reveal the wide range of material that is not published, and the long-running battle between the state and the independent press.

The South African media reflect the sharp divisions within a society based on apartheid. Of crucial importance to the government, the latter have retained control over all television and most radio broadcasting. The South African Broadcasting Corporation is an effective and sophisticated propaganda machine, which broadcasts in English, Afrikaans and all the major indigenous African languages, as well as in Portuguese, Swahili and other languages in its external radio services. Government personalities, policies and actions are positively portrayed by a staff selected for their sympathy with the government position.

The press, like society, is ethnically divided, with very little cross-flow of ideas and perspectives. The Afrikaans newspapers, although mostly privately owned, strongly support the government, with some liberal or conservative nuances. The English-language papers, some of which would be regarded as the "opposition press," reflect the free enterprise liberalism of their owners, but in fact support the status quo and have generally accepted the controls and self-censorship that the government has imposed. In the words of Irwin Maniom, coeditor of the *Weekly Mail:* "It would be unfair to say that mainstream South African newspapers ignore events in the black townships and rural areas. They are conscious of injustice and have spoken out strongly often enough in the past. But they tend to cover the townships as if they were foreign lands: exotic, remote, of sporadic interest."[4]

The major black newspapers, although owned by the white-controlled press giants—Argus or SAAN (South African Associated Newspapers)—have over certain periods demonstrated strong independence, and have accurately reflected the concerns of and events in the black community. *The World*, under the editorship of Percy Qoboza, rose to the challenge of the national crisis in 1976, when children were being shot wantonly by the police and thousands were detained without trial. The paper was soon banned, but was revived as the *The Sowetan*, which has become a shadow of its former self.

These major-circulation black newspapers, owned by the white press giants, to a large extent toe the state's line, although their content is of a fairly high standard when compared with the rest of the continent. The *Golden City Post*, published by Jim Bailey, founder of *Drum*, in the late 1970s and early 1980s, provided a strong black voice, combined with highly profes-

[4]Irwin Maniom, Skirmishes on the Margins: The War Against South Africa's 'Alternative Press,' *Index on Censorship* (April 29, 1988).

sional investigative reporting. But it succumbed to market forces and was eventually sold to the Afrikaner-controlled *Nasionale Pers.*

On the fringe of the mass circulation press is South Africa's small but increasingly important "alternative press." It consists of a handful of tabloids, some weekly, some monthly, ranging from the high-profile *Weekly Mail*—with a sophisticated, urban readership—to little known *Saamstaan*, a working-class paper in a tiny, remote township. Some, like *Saamstaan*, are ardently and openly partisan; others, like the *Weekly Mail*, prefer to keep a critical distance, however difficult it is for its government critics to perceive that. What these papers have in common, according to Irwin Maniom, is a concentration on political news, primarily news of labor and township unrest, of activist groups and community organizations, of security crackdowns and detentions. At their worst they can be turgid and monotonously "preachy"; at their best they push back the edges of what can still be published in South Africa, exposing issues the mainstream press has long ignored. Most of these publications struggle to find revenue, for newspapers that write unflatteringly of the rich, and are read largely by the poor, do not meet with favor in advertising agency boardrooms.

The *Weekly Mail* heads the field, in terms of its professionalism, production quality and hard-hitting editorials. It has a highly dedicated and determined staff, which has battled against great financial and legal odds to survive since its launching in 1985. It was formed by a group of journalists who pooled their redundancy money following the closure of SAAN's pioneering *Rand Daily Mail*. The *Weekly Mail* remains under continued threat of closure, and its journalists and editors have to survive a minefield of restrictions and regulations.[5] This requires constant legal advice, and risks have to be weighed on virtually every news item.

Its possible fate was demonstrated by that of the *New Nation*, a weekly paper largely staffed by black journalists and financed by the Roman Catholic Church. Its editor, Zwelakhe Sisulu, has spent most of its short two-and-a-half-year life in detention. Eventually the paper was "suspended"—a move calculated to kill it off without attracting the international condemnation that an outright ban would. Having received the statutory "warnings" that precede a "suspension," by mid-1988 the *Weekly Mail* staff feared the final blow in what they have termed "death by a thousand pinpricks." Unlike the *New Nation*, they would not have the financial backing to sustain them through any long suspension. As Irwin Maniom writes:

> One man who has chosen to make a mission out of silencing the alternative press once and for all is the Minister of Home Affairs. But unlike some of his colleagues, Stoffel Botha has chosen to work slowly, discreetly, with the scalpel, not the bludgeon. . . . Suspension will indeed mean death . . . commercial death. And the minister will be free to protest: "My hands are clean. I didn't close them."

Other members of the South African alternative press have been subject to the same warnings procedure and are liable to be suspended. They in-

[5] For a detailed description of the laws and regulations restricting the press in South Africa, see J. Collinge, et al., "What the Papers Don't Say," *Index on Censorship* (March 1988).

clude *South*, *Grassroots*, *Work in Progress* and *Out of Step*, an anticonscription journal. In Namibia, *The Namibian* is the leading alternative newspaper, partly funded by the European Community. In mid-1988 its editor, Gwen Lister, was detained.

IMPACT OF THE NEW TECHNOLOGY

Desktop publishing (DTP) has had a dramatic impact in South Africa, where it has allowed low-cost production for the alternative press. The *Weekly Mail* played a pioneering role in introducing DTP, and has introduced systems comparable with the rest of the world. Material is keyed in directly by the journalists on personal computers, thus avoiding time- (and money-)consuming typesetting, and laser printers are used to generate page layouts from which the newspaper is printed.

In Kenya, too, desktop publishing has grown in popularity as publishers of smaller publications have realized its cost-saving virtues.[6] One such publication was *Beyond*, published by the National Council of Churches. But it was banned on March 15, 1988, just a few weeks short of its second anniversary, for its coverage of the national elections. The editor, Beden Mbugua, was detained after the magazine reported that the nominating primary elections results had been tampered with in several regions. The public interest in the report was demonstrated by the fact that 40,000 copies of the offending edition were snapped up, compared with the magazine's normal circulation of 15,000.

New technology may help reduce costs and will eventually help wrest publishing monopolies away from the large government-controlled or large corporate publishers. But editors are still faced with authoritarian one-party or military governments, whose paranoia and insecurity lead to actions of the sort outlined above.

A NEW ERA FOR PAN-AFRICAN PUBLISHING?

During the 1970s there was a rapid increase in the number of pan-African magazines, published either from Paris for the Francophone countries, or from London for the Anglophone nations. Their development was stimulated, in part, by the lack of a sophisticated internal press that could satisfy readers' demands for good quality, independent editorials, and by the development of international advertising budgets for marketing consumer goods to Africa, requiring high-quality magazine production and continent-wide distribution. And the English-language magazines were also substantially stimulated by Nigeria's oil boom. This became the continent's major publishing market, to which the pan-African magazine publishers hitched their stars.

Their bases in Paris or London allowed them the freedom to publish without state harassment or censorship. "We are still in business simply

---

[6] See Julie Whipple, "DTP Transforms Publishing in Kenya," *Computers in Africa* (March/April 1988).

because we are not operating on Africa soil," said Alan Rake, one of the doyens of the African press, currently managing editor of *New African* and *African Business* in London.[7] But in reality, substantial self-censorship was exercised, particularly in relation to the major markets, where the publishers did not want to risk thousands of magazines being stopped at the airport by the government censors. In most countries, distributors are required to submit all international publications for approval before releasing them to the newsstands.

The oil slump of the 1980s spelled disaster for the pan-African publishers.[8] In 1986 and 1987 four out of the seven largest mass-circulation pan-African magazines went into liquidation: *Africa, Africa Now, AfricAsia* and *Afrique Asie.* The first two had been owned by Nigerians, Ralph Uwechwe and Peter Enahoro, respectively, and they had developed a strong dependency on the largesse doled out by their contacts in the Nigerian state and federal governments in the form of state-sponsored supplements. A new discipline and austerity imposed by Babangida's regime cut this lifeline. In addition, budgets for international consumer advertising directed at Africa were dramatically cut in response to the general slump in Africa, and in Nigeria in particular. And finally, the growth of a range of sophisticated indigenous weekly magazines in Nigeria reduced the demand for the pan-African ones.

The demise of *AfricAsia* and *Afrique Asie,* both published by Simon Malley in Paris, was also rooted in the oil price slump, but with additional complications. Malley had pursued a strong socialist-oriented editorial policy and had benefited from substantial "solidarity advertising" from state corporations in Angola, Algeria and Madagascar. The oil prices, combined with Angola's state of war, meant that these corporations could no longer support him, and he could attract very little advertising from other sources. The liquidators were called in in mid-1987.

So by 1988 the only pan-African newsstand magazines remaining were *New African* and *African Business*, both published in London by IC Publications; *Africa Events*, a pro-Islamic magazine that appeared to be heavily subsidized because of the little advertising it carried (also published in London); and *Jeune Afrique*, published in Paris.

Following this shakeout, African periodical publishing is expanding in four new areas: indigenous news magazines, particularly in Nigeria; subregional magazines; business newsletters on Africa; and special interest magazines. No longer can Africa be treated as an undifferentiated market by publishers or advertisers.

NIGERIA: A BOOM MARKET

Despite its successive economic crises and military regimes, Nigeria, Africa's most populous country, has the continent's most vibrant press. And during the 1980s privately owned newspapers and magazines mushroomed.

[7] Quoted in Albert Sam, "Gloomy Future for Journalists?" *Index on Censorship* (October 1987).
[8] See Andrew Weir, "Pulp Harvest Blighted," *The Guardian* (London), December 11, 1988.

Until 1980 there were only two privately owned newspapers, the *Nigerian Tribune* and *The Punch*. Two Nigerian millionaires then launched their own publishing empires: Alex Ibru set up the *Guardian* group and Moshood Abiola established the *Concord* group. Both launched weekly magazines as spin-offs, and this led to others being established in competition: *This Week*, *Newswatch*, *Hotline* and *Times International*. By 1988 there were 21 national dailies, 25 weekly newspapers, seven newsmagazines, three financial newspapers, four evening papers, six vernacular papers and at least 20 community papers.[9]

Most Nigerian publications are still owned by federal and state governments: 13 of the 21 dailies and 13 of the 25 weeklies. In addition, the governments own all of the country's 36 television and 25 radio stations. But it is the privately controlled publications that the public prefers and are most profitable and viable. There has always been strong resistance against government attempts to interfere with press freedom, and Nigerian editors probably have the most independence on the continent. But in 1984, two *Guardian* journalists were detained for a year and fined by the Buhari regime for publishing generally accurate stories that the government said caused embarrassment. And according to one editor, the government continues to take steps "clearly aimed at influencing, controlling, intimidating or coercing the press."[10] In October 1986, Dele Giwa, editor in chief of *Newswatch*, was killed by a letter bomb suspected of being planted by state security agents. In 1987 the magazine was suspended by the government for six months for publishing what it said was classified material—a report of the political bureau set up by the government to draw up guidelines for the return to civilian rule. In May 1988 Ray Ekpu of *Newswatch* was honored as international editor of the year by *World Press Review* and the Overseas Press Club in the United States. In his speech at the presentation ceremony he said that although Nigeria's press was "the freest in Africa," it was nevertheless threatened by arbitrary government actions. "The press in most parts of Africa is an endangered species," he added.

But Nigeria's crop of news magazines now constitutes the most dynamic sector of the media, offering readers a sophisticated mix of news analysis, business news, personality gossip and sports.

SUBREGIONAL MAGAZINES

Africa's longest-surviving magazine, if not publication in general, is *West Africa*, founded in 1917. It is published in London and is currently owned by the Nigerian government through its 60% control of the *Daily Times* group. It covers the entire West African region, although Nigeria is its major market. It has become a publication of record and is not noted for particularly pioneering or investigative journalism.

In March 1988 the first edition of the *Southern African Economist* was published—the first time a substantial magazine had been published for

[9] Jato Thompson, "Nigeria: Mushrooming Media," *New African* (May 1988).
[10] Ibid.

another subregion (*Drum East Africa* having retreated to more or less exclusive coverage of the Kenyan market, following economic chaos in Uganda and Tanzania in the late 1970s and early 1980s.) The *Southern African Economist* had been proposed for several years as a publishing project for the nine-member Southern African Development Coordination Conference (SADCC), as a medium for promoting its objective of stimulating economic development independently of South Africa, and for contributing toward the development of a regional, rather than exclusively national, perspectives, particularly among business and political decision makers. Eventually, the Scandinavian countries committed U.S. $4 million to back the project, to be based in Harare and staffed by journalists from the SADCC countries. Dominic Mulaisho, a former economic adviser to President Kaunda of Zambia, was appointed editor in chief. Its first editions in 1988 attracted substantial advertising support from within the SADCC countries.

Also in 1988, a group of South African and Zimbabwean journalists based in Harare were planning to launch the following year a regional magazine that would cover the SADCC countries, South Africa and Namibia. Its proposed title was *Africa South*. It was also pledged start-up money by various donor countries.

BUSINESS NEWSLETTERS ON AFRICA

Inversely to the demise of the pan-African magazines, the second half of the 1980s witnessed a boom in the publication of newsletters covering Africa. Since the 1960s the only authoritative newsletter on Africa had been *Africa Confidential*, a fortnightly published in London; it covered mostly political and diplomatic news. Then, in the late 1970s, *Africa Economic Digest* was launched as a weekly business-intelligence publication; although in the format of a magazine it was essentially a high-priced newsletter.[11] Since then, others have been launched, including *West African Hotline, Front File: Southern Africa Brief, Africa Analysis, EASA: Trade & Investment in Eastern & Southern Africa*[12] (all published in London); and *Indian Ocean Newsletter* (published in French and English in Paris).

Richard Hall, editor of the £185-a-year *Africa Analysis*—the most successful of the new crop—attributed much of the success of these newsletters to the "almost goulish interest" in Africa's economic troubles. "Business may be bad there but there are many people who have to know how bad—banks, multinational corporations, exporters who are owed money, embassies and so on. In some degree, Africa's misfortunes are the secret of our success."[13]

---

[11] *Africa Economic Digest* was originally launched as part of the MEED Group, modeled on their highly successful *Middle East Economic Digest*. However, it never achieved the high levels of advertising support enjoyed by MEED, and in 1988 was bought by Chief Abiola's *Concord* Group.

[12] Published by the author.

[13] Quoted in Weir, "Pulp Harvest Blighted."

SPECIAL INTEREST MAGAZINES

As the African market becomes increasingly sophisticated, readers demand more specialized media. Publishers within the major countries have started to respond to that demand, particularly in Zimbabwe, Kenya and Nigeria. South Africa already has a well-developed specialist press. However, it will be interesting to see to what extent a pan-African specialist press will develop. By 1988 there were several specialist magazines for Anglophone Africa: *African Health*, *Computers in Africa* (published by the author), *African Farming* and *African Technical Review*.

These are all trade publications, although *Computers in Africa* does serve the interests of computer hardware and software consumers. The development of more consumer-oriented publications for Africa is inevitable; the timing, however, will be determined by the pace at which Africa recovers from its current economic crisis.[14]

FURTHER READING

The African Book World and Press: A Directory. 2nd ed. Munich: K. G. Saur; Detroit: Gale, 1980.

Harrison, Paul, and Palmer, Robin. *News Out of Africa: Biafra to Band Aid.* London and Wolfeboro, New Hampshire: H. Shipman, 1986.

The Index on Censorship. London: Writers and Scholars International. Monthly.

"Publish and Survive." *New African.* London: IC Publications, May-July 1988.

[14]See *Consumers in Africa: A Growing Voice,* The Hague: International Organization of Consumer Unions, 1988.

INDEX

AALC (African-American Labor Center), 1024, 1025

AATUF (All-African Trade Union Federation), 1024

Abbas, Ferhat, 6, 7

Abbud, Ibrahim, 509

Abdallah, Ahmed, 115-16, 120

Abdelaziz, Mohammed, 358

Abdi, Abdesalam, 359

Abdou, Abdelrame, 29

Abdou, Ahmed, 117

Abéché (Chad), 102

Abibi, Daniel, 131-32

Abidjan (Ivory Coast), 45, 235, 237, 240, 243, 1116

Abiola, Moshood, 1129

Abuja (Nigeria), 403

Abuja Conference, 833-35

Abyssinia, 1071. *See also* Ethiopia

Accra (Ghana), 202, 1025

Acheampong, I. Kuta, 206-7

Achebe, Chinua, 1105, 1106; *A Man of the People*, 1107

Acholi people, 563, 567, 571, 1054, 1055, 1058

ACP (Africa, Caribbean and Pacific) Group, EC, 771, 772-82

Acquired Immune Deficiency Syndrome. *See* AIDS

Act of Union, South Africa, 859

Adamawa Massif, 67

Adams, Pita, v

Addis Ababa (Ethiopia), 169, 172, 177, 1121; education meeting, 1087; OAU conference, 688, 835-36

Addis Ababa Agreement, 509, 510, 516, 700

Adedeji, Adebayo, 676-77

Adewoye Report, 902

Adja people, Benin, 25

Adler, Taffy, v; "Labor Issues and Trade Unionism in Africa," 1014-40

ADMARC (Agricultural Development and Marketing Corporation), Malawi, 322

Adouma people, 181

Adrar des Iforas mountains, 327

Adult education, 1094; Angola, 22; for women, 1096

Adultery, Islamic law, 1059

AERP (African Economic Recovery Program), 690, 691

Afar people, 133, 135-36

Afghanistan, 709

AFRC (Armed Forces Ruling Council), Nigeria, 404-5
Africa Analysis, 1130
Africa Confidential, 1130
Africa Economic Digest, 1130
Africa Events, 1128
Africa South, 1130
African Business, 1128
African Development Bank, 549, 574, 593, 833, 892, 893
African Development Fund, 892, 893
African National Congress. *See* ANC
African Non-Governmental Organizations Environment Network, 947-48
African-American Labor Center (AALC), 1024, 1025
Africanization, 882
Afrikaans language, 378, 476, 477
Afrikaner, Jonker, 380
Afrikaner National party, 476
Afrikaners, 734, 859
Afro-Asian People's Solidarity Organization, 708
AG (Action Group), Nigeria, 406-7
Agacher strip, 331
Agadez (Niger), 393
Agalega Island, 347
Age at marriage, of girls, 1047
Age of population, 670, 981, 1006; Algeria, 4
Agee, Phillip, 708
Aggett, Neil, 1031
Agriculture, 675-77, 791-92, 815, 926-43; development, 916-17, 986; employment figures, 630-31; IMF and, 827; Lomé Convention and, 775-76; military spending and, 719, 725; mineral producing countries, 917; minimum wage, 1020; smuggling, 872-73, 877; state control, 805-7; women's role, 1043-45. *See also* Economy
Agriculture, Marketing and Pricing in Sub-Saharan Africa (John C. De Wilde), 941, 942

Ahidjo, Ahmadou, 71-72, 79-80, 1110
Ahmadiyya *Tariqa*, 1071, 1078
Ahmet, Acyl, 698
Ahomadegbé, Justin Tometin, 28, 29, 32
AIDS, 978, 1010-11, 1046, 1058-62; Cameroon, 78; and drug abuse, 1064; Kenya, 264; Malawi, 323; Rwanda, 421; and tourism, 1114
Aikhomu, Augustus, 414
Aikpé, Michel, 32
Air France hijack affair, 568
Aïr Massif (Niger), 393, 397
Airlines, 1115-16; Ethiopia, 176; Mauritius, 352; São Tomé and Príncipe, 428
Airports: Cameroon, 77; Cape Verde, 85; Equatorial Guinea, 165; Kenya, 1119; Liberia, 286; Malawi, 321, 322; Niger, 398; Senegal, 439; Sierra Leone, 457; Zaire, 590
Ait-Ahmad, 5
Ajuran people, 249, 259
Akan people, 202, 204, 237, 1042, 1051
Ake, Claude, 1103
AKFM (Madagascar), 305
Akosombo Dam (Ghana), 201, 206, 211, 548
Akouta (Niger), 397
Akuffo (Gen., Ghana), 207
Akur people, 563
Akwapim mountains, 201
Alabi, Niyii, 1124
Alaouite dynasty, Morocco, 357
Albania, Ivory Coast and, 240
Albert Nile River, 561
Alcohol consumption, 1062
Alemaya (Ethiopia), 177
Alexandria (Egypt), 142, 143, 982
al-Fatah Revolutionary Council, 294
Algabid, Hamid, 396
Algeria, 2, 3-12, 684; agriculture, 646, 650; Arab League, 1079; diplomatic relations, 103, 294, 295, 331, 341, 358, 509, 555; education,

664; food production, 648, 652; health figures, 658, 662; liberation movement, 1079; military spending, 717, 724; Muslims, 1068, 1069, 1076, 1081, 1082, 1084; population, 626, 660, 974, 986; refugees, 985, 988, 991, 996; Saharan warfare, 695-97; trade relations, 206, 359, 440; trade unions, 1016, 1018-19; *economy*: 8-11, 628, 644, 654, 656; currency, 642; employment figures, 630; foreign debt, 842, 843, 853; foreign trade, 632, 634, 636, 638, 640; imports, 923; industry, 913, 918; mineral exports, 919

Algerian League of Human Rights, 5

Algiers (Algeria), 4, 5

Algiers Agreement, 341

Ali, Moses, 571

Ali, Muhammad, 1073-74

Ali, Zine el-Abidine Ben, 1081

Alier, Abel, 700

Alimadi, Otema, 569, 570

Ali-Yahia, Adbennoûn, 5

Al-Khums (Libya), 291

Alladaye, Michel, 29, 32

All-African Conference, 206

Alley (Benin Lt. Col.), 28

Alliance Démocratique Sénégalaise, 434, 436

Allowances to workers, 1021-22

Almohad Berbers, 1071

Almond production, 557

Almoravid Berbers, 1073, 1074

ALN (Armée de Libération Nationale), Algeria, 6

Alternative press, 1126-27

Aluminum production, 77, 153, 211, 225

Alves, Nito, 18

Amadiume, Ifi, 1042

Amambo, Dimo, 385

AMD (Alliance pour une Mauritanie Démocratique), 339, 345

Amhara people, 170, 682

Amin, Idi, 259, 534, 564, 566-68, 574, 575, 577, 1054; and EAC treaty, 896; invasion of Tanzania, 867; and Islam, 1081; Qadhafi and, 293; and Rwanda, 420; and underground economy, 879

AML (Friends of the Freedom Manifesto), Algeria, 6

Ammonia production, Libya, 297

Amnesty International, 258, 430, 468, 546, 586

ANC (African National Congress), 18, 40, 382, 383, 486, 611, 612, 681, 717, 1030; and Commonwealth group, 763; and Communist party, 1037; Freedom Charter, 743; headquarters, 602; Kaunda and, 606; Mozambique and, 369-70; publications, 502; refugee assistance, 992-93; and South Africa, 479, 484-89, 521, 751, 758, 744-46, 747; Zimbabwe and, 614

Ancestor workship, 304

Andom, Aman, 702

Andriamanjato, Richard, 305

Anemia, nutritional, 1047-48

Anglican Church, 192, 202, 249, 258, 379, 404, 445, 477, 563, 609

Anglo American Corporation, 495, 496

Anglo American Group, 861-62

Angola, 13-24, *14*, 384-87, 680-81, 751, 802; agriculture, 646, 650; armed forces, 493; Cuban troops, 694; diplomatic relations, 127, 427, 534, 585, 587; and EC, 770; education, 664, 1090, 1092; famine, 926-28; food production, 648, 652; health figures, 658, 662; life expectancy, 978; military spending, 717, 722; Muslims, 1068; population, 626, 660, 976; refugees, 985, 988, 991; and SADCC, 749, 750, 905; and South Africa, 187, 489, 492, 754-55, 757, 758; super-power relations, 711; trade relations, 86, 428, 429; trade unions, 1017; travel facilities, 1119; *economy*: 19-22, 628, 644, 656, 804; currency, 642; employment figures, 630; foreign trade, 632, 638, 640; manufacturing, 913; mineral exports, 919; underground economy, 880; *warfare*: attacks on refugees, 997; civil war, 1010; with South Africa, 693, 703-4, 748-49, 751-52, 760-61

Anjouan (Comoros), 113, 117, 119

Ankole people, 564, 565

Ankomah, Baffour, 1123

Ankrah, Joseph, 206

Annaba (Algeria), 4, 10

Annan, D. F., 204

Annobón (Pagalu), 159

ANR (Assemblée Nationale Révolutionnaire), Benin, 27, 28

Ansar *Tariqa*, 1077, 1078, 1082

Antananarivo (Madagascar), 303, 304, 307, 1121

Anti-imperialism, 1104

Anticlericalism, Burundi, 62

Anticolonialism, 708

Antidesertification program, Burkina Faso, 52

Antseranana (Madagascar), 304

Anyanya (Sudanese guerillas), 509, 699, 700

Aouzou Strip, 103, 106-7, 109, 295, 697, 699, 1085

Apartheid, South Africa, 476, 485-93, 499-501, 670, 680, 733-34, 747, 757-59; Commonwealth countries and, 762-64; EC and, 776, 779; Namibia, 381-82; trade unions and, 1027; women and, 1045

APC (All-People's Congress), Sierra Leone, 453, 454

Apithy, Sourou-Migan, 28, 29, 32

APPER (Africa's Priority Program for Economic Recovery), 832-35

Arab conquest, 1070-75

Arab Fund for Economic and Social Development, 470

Arab League, 151, 293, 467, 470, 555, 1065, 1079

Arab people, 115, 133, 143, 292, 339, 342, 356, 507, 528, 553

Arab Republic of Egypt, 141, 149. *See also* Egypt

Arab rule, Zanzibar, 529, 530

Arab states: and Libya, 294, 295; and Uganda, 567

Arabic language, 1070. *See also* Languages

Arab-Israeli conflict, 148-51

Arabization programs, 7, 342

Arafat, Yasir, Qadhafi and, 294

Archaeological sites, 35, 607, 1118

Areas of countries, 626-27

Aref Bourhan, Ali, 139

AREMA (Avant-Garde de la Révolution Malgache), 305, 306

Arlit (Niger), 397, 398

Armah, Ayi Kwesi, 1106; *Two Thousand Seasons*, 1109

Armed forces: and national economies, 724-25; super-power relations, 713; *by country*: Algeria, 8; Angola, 19; Benin, 29; Botswana, 39, 40; Burkina Faso, 52; Burundi, 62; Cameroon, 74; Cape Verde, 84; Central African Republic, 94; Chad, 107; Comoros, 118; Congo, 127; Djibouti, 136; Egypt, 151-52, 707; Equatorial Guinea, 165; Ethiopia, 174-75, 702; Gabon, 185; Gambia, 196; Guinea, 220-21, 224; Guinea-Bissau, 231; Ivory Coast, 240; Kenya, 259-60; Lesotho, 273; Liberia, 284; Libya, 295, 296; Madagascar, 307-8; Malawi, 320, 321; Mali, 329-30, 331; Mauritania, 341, 342; Morocco, 358, 359, 696; Mozambique, 366, 369-70; Namibia, 387; Niger, 396; Nigeria, 410; Rwanda, 419; São Tomé and

Príncipe, 427; Senegal, 437; Seychelles, 446; Sierra Leone, 456; Somalia, 467, 469; South Africa, 493-94, 734; Sudan, 512; Swaziland, 521; Tanzania, 534; Togo, 546-47; Tunisia, 556; Uganda, 568, 572; Zaire, 587; Zambia, 602; Zimbabwe, 614

Armée Patriotique Lumumba, Zaire, 582

Arms deliveries, 716-17

Arts, postcolonial, 684

Arusha (Tanzania), 746, 1120

Arusha Declaration, 531, 883

Aruwimi River, 579

Asamoah, Obed, 204

Asante empire, Ghana, 204-5

Asante people, 202, 1046-47

Asbestos production, 495

Asfaw, Besserat, 1050-51, 1052

Ashanti Pioneer, 1109

Ashigga party, Sudan, 1078

Asia: birth rates, 977; food production, 928; industrialization, 924

Asian people, 304, 314, 366, 476, 477, 499-501, 528, 530, 563, 567, 575, 598, 609

Asmera (Ethiopia), 169, 170, 177

ASP (Afro-Shiraz Party), 529, 530-31

Assassie (Lt. Col., Ghana), 204

Assegai River, 517

ASU (Arab Socialist Union), Egypt, 144, 147-48, 149, 150

Aswan (Egypt), 142, 143

Aswan High Dam (Egypt), 141, 146-47, 153; funding, 707

Asylum for refugees, 989-90, 995

Asyur (Egypt), 143

Atacora Mountains, Benin, 25

Atakpamé (Togo), 544

Atchade, André, 29

Atim, Chris, 207, 208

Atlas Mountains, 3, 355, 356, 551

At-Taalbi, Sheikh, 1079

Aubame, Jean-Hilaire, 183, 188

Australia, 763, 767

Authenticity policies, 546, 584-85

Autogestion movement, 1018, 1019

Automobile industry, 153, 233, 262, 438-39, 496, 538, 573, 576

Averages, economic survey, 787

Awash River Basin, 169

AWB (Afrikaanse Weerstandsbeweging), 481, 492, 731

Awolowo, Obafemi, 406, 408, 409

Awoonor, Kofi, *This Earth, My Brother*, 1106

AZACTU, 1032

Azanian Congress of Trade Unions, 743

Azapo (Azanian People's Organization), 480, 492

Azhari, Ismail al-, 509

Azikiwe, Nnamdi, 406, 407, 409, 687

Azouzou Strip, 296, 105

Az-Zawiyah (Libya), 291

Baardheere Dam, Somalia, 469

Babangida, Ibrahim, 74, 404, 409-10, 414, 1058

Babu, Abdoula Rahman Mohamed, v; "The Superpowers and Africa," 706-15

Bafatá (Guinea-Bissau), 227

Bafoussam (Cameroon), 67

Baganda people, 561, 563-66

Bagaza, Jean-Baptiste, 61, 62, 65, 66

Baghdad Pact, 146-47, 707

Bagisu people, 563

Bagré Dam (Burkina Faso), 53

Bahir Dar (Ethiopia), 177

Bailey, Jim, 1125

Baker, James, 816

Baker Initiative, 848, 850, 854

Bakgatla people, 36

Baking industry, Chad, 109

Bakongo people, 123

Bakota people, 181

Bakwena people, 36

Balance-of-payments, 718, 811-15; colonial period, 825; EC support funds, 778-79; and economic reform, 818; and export-led growth, 924; IMF and, 828-30; and military spending, 722. *See also* Economy

Balante people, 229

Balewa, Abubakar Tafawa, 406, 407, 688

Bali, Domkat Yah, 414

Bamako (Mali), 327, 328, 329

Bamalete people, 36

Bamangwato people, 36

Bambara people, 327, 328

Bamiléké people, 69

Banana, Canaan Sodindo, 619-20

Banana production, 76, 85, 224, 241, 469, 470, 561, 575, 588, 780

Banda, Aleke, 318, 319

Banda, Hastings Kamuzu, 252, 314, 317-21, 325, 370, 687, 1109

Banda people, 89

Bandama River, 235

Banfora (Burkina Faso), 53

Bangui, Sylvestre, 92

Bangui (Central African Republic), 89, 93

Bangura, John, 454

Bangwetse people, 36

Bangweulu Lake, 597

Banjul (Gambia), 191, 192, 193, 197

Banks, 136, 874, 904-5; colonial, 858-60; Nigeria, 864-66; and productivity of women, 1044; regional, 78, 399, 428, 440, 863, 893, 896; Tanzania, 866-69; Zimbabwe, 860-63. *See also* IMF; World Bank

Banna, Hassan al-, 1083

Bantu Authorities Act, South Africa, 485

Bantu people, 15, 67, 248, 366, 507

Bantu-speaking people, 161, 378, 476, 563, 581, 692

Bantustans (homelands), 381-82, 476, 477, 478, 485, 486, 489-90, 494-95

Banyankore people, 563

Banyoro people, 563, 564

Baptist church, Nigeria, 404

Barakana, Fr. Gabriel, 65-66

Baralong people, 36

Barayi, Elijah, 1032

Barbary States, 1073

Barclays Bank, 860, 861, 864, 866

Bariba people, 25

Baringo Lake, 247

Barite mining, Tunisia, 558

Barker, Jonathan, 943

Barley production, 8, 296

Barlow Rand, 496-97

Barre, Abdul Rahman Jama, 468

Barre, Ahmed Sulayman Abdulla, 468

Barre, Khadija, 468

Barre, Mohammed Siad, 465, 466-68, 471-72, 1063

Barre, Raslah Masleh Siad, 468

Barter system, 879

Bash-Taqi, Ibrahim, 454, 455

Basil production, Comoros, 118

Basoga people, 563

Bassa people, 279

Basters, 378

Basuto people, 269

Basutoland, 269. *See also* Lesotho

Bata (Equatorial Guinea), 159, 161, 162

Batawana people, 36

Batéké people, 123, 181, 183-84, 188

Bakéké plateau, 121

Bates, Robert, *Markets and States in Tropical Africa*, 941, 942

Bathily, Abdoulaye, 434, 436

Bathurst. *See* Banjul (Gambia)

Batlokwa people, 36

Batoro people, 563

Batswana people, 36

Battle of Adwa, 701

Battle of Omdurman, 509, 1075

Bauchi (Nigeria), 723

Bauxite: deposits, 77, 109, 128, 211, 232, 285, 333, 451; production, 225, 457, 458, 874

Baye, Berhanu, 178

Bazeye, Fatimata, 394

BCEAO (Banque Centrale des États de l'Afrique de l'Ouest), 399, 440

BCM (Black Consciousness Movement), 480, 488-89

BCP (Basuto Congress Party), Lesotho, 269, 271-72

BDG (Bloc Démocratique Gabonais), 183

BDP (Botswana Democratic Party), 36, 37, 38, 40

Beach vacations, 1116, 1117; Kenya, 1119-20

Bean production, 45, 85, 152, 232, 538, 575

Beau Bassin/Rose Hill (Mauritius), 347

Beautiful Feathers (Cyprian Ekwensi), 1106

BEC (Bureau Exécutif Central), Mali, 328-29

Bechuanaland. *See* Botswana

Bedié, Henri Konan, 240, 244

Bedouins, Egypt, 143

Beef production, 41, 522. *See also* Livestock production

Beer, underground economy, 880

Beira (Mozambique), 365, 366, 750, 753, 755, 955, 1116, 1119

Beja people, 507, 1070

Belgian Congo, 417, 583. *See also* Zaire

Belgium: colonialism, 61, 417, 418, 583, 708, 771; diplomatic relations, 62, 420, 585, 587, 770; trade relations, 63, 95, 333, 459, 593

Belier oil field, 241

Bello, Ahmadu, 406

Bemba people, 598

Ben Ali, Zine El Abidine, 553, 556, 560

Ben Bella, Ahmed, 5, 6-7, 11-12

Ben Khedda, Ben Yusuf, 6

Ben Salah, Ahmad, 553, 555

Ben Yousouf, Salah, 554

Benefits for workers, 1021-22

Benelux countries, 286-87, 429

Benghazi (Libya), 291, 295, 299

Benguela (Angola), 15

Benguela Railway, 587, 590, 755

Benhamouda, Boualem, 12

Benin, 25-33, *26*, 678, 802; agriculture, 646, 650; CEAO membership, 898; currency, 643; diplomatic relations, 52, 184, 546; economy, 29-30, 628, 644, 654, 656, 804; ECOWAS membership, 901; education, 664, 1092; employment, 630; food production, 648, 652; foreign debt, 845; foreign trade, 632, 634, 636, 638, 640; health figures, 658, 662; manufacturing, 913, 916; mineral exports, 919; Muslims, 1068; population, 626, 660, 974; refugees, 988, 991; road system, 956

Benjedid, Chadli, 7-8, 12, 359, 696

Benoit, E., 719-20, 722, 723

Bentiu (Sudan), 510

Benue River, 67, 401

Berber people, 4, 7, 291, 356, 553, 695; and Islam, 1070, 1073, 1074

Berbera (Somalia), 463, 467, 468, 470

Berbérati (Central African Republic), 89

Berenger, Paul, 349, 353

Beriberi-Manga people, 393

Bernstein, Lionel, 486

Bestman, John G., 283

Beti, Mongo, 1110

Betsileo people, 304

Betsimisaraka people, 304

Bette Peak, 289

Beverage production, 21, 398, 428, 438, 921

Beyond (Kenya), 1127

Bhekimpi, Prince of Swaziland, 521

Biafra, 408, 1056

Bidonvilles, 674

Biko, Steve, 480, 488-89

Bilateral aid, 821, 855

Binaisa (Atty. Gen., Uganda), 569
Bintimani Mountains, 451
Bioko Island, 159, 161, 162-63, 166
Birds, Gambia, 191
Birth rates, 788, 972-77, 1006-7
Bissa people, 47
Bissau (Guinea-Bissau), 227, 233;
    travel facilities, 1117
Biya, Paul, 69-74, 80
Bizerte (Tunisia), 551, 554-55, 557
Black markets, 155, 206-7, 373, 591,
    807, 873, 875, 879. *See also*
    Underground economy
Black people, South Africa, 476, 477,
    495, 499-501, 733, 737-47;
    newspapers, 1125-26; trade unions,
    1028-38
Blanche River, 45
Blantyre (Malawi), 314, 322
Blida (Algeria), 1084
Bloc Démocratique Sénégalaise, 1079
Blockades, South African, 753
Bloemfontein (South Africa), 477, 482
Bloom, Tony, 736
Blue Nile, 169, 505, 1121
BNF (Botswana National Front), 36,
    37, 38, 40
BNP (Basuto National Party),
    Lesotho, 269, 271
Bo (Sierra Leone), 452, 460
Bobo Dioulasso (Burkina Faso), 45
Bobo people, Burkina Faso, 47
Bodelswart people, 703
Boer War, 483, 859
Boers, South Africa, 270, 482-84
Boesak, Alan, 492, 1057
Boganda, Barthélémy, 91
Bogoria Lake, 247
Bogou scarp, 543
Bogué (Mauritania), 337
Bokassa, Jean-Bedel, 91-92, 93, 97,
    670
Boky Mena (Red book), Ratsiraka, 311
Bolama (Guinea-Bissau), 229
Bondelswart people, 380, 381

Bongo, Omar (Albert-Bernard),
    183-84, 188, 427, 1054, 1064
Bongor (Chad), 99
Bophuthatswana (South Africa), 40,
    476, 477, 486, 489, 494, 501, 503;
    education, 1098
Boran people, 249
Bornu, 1074
Bory cults, 1069
Botchwey, Kwesi, 204
Botha, Louis, 484
Botha, P. W., 117, 272, 482, 490,
    491-93, 503, 749, 751, 758, 763
Botha, Roelof Frederik, 503
Botha, Stoffel, 501
Botswana, *34*, 35-44, 680, 748, 802;
    agriculture, 646, 650; and ANC,
    745; Commonwealth aid, 768;
    contraception, 977; drought, 931;
    education, 664, 1090-92; food
    production, 648, 652; food
    shortages, 927-28; free press, 1123;
    health figures, 658, 662; Muslims,
    1068; population, 626, 660, 976,
    986; refugees, 988, 991; road
    system, 956; and SADCC, 749,
    905-7; South Africa and, 486, 752,
    753, 763; tourism, 1115, 1118-19;
    trade relations, 119, 617; *economy*:
    40-42, 628, 644, 654, 656, 804;
    currency, 642; employment figures,
    630; foreign debt, 845; foreign
    trade, 632, 638, 640;
    manufacturing, 913, 916; mineral
    exports, 919
Botswana Meat Commission, 41
Bouabid, Maati, 356
Bouaké (Ivory Coast), 235, 237
Bouar (Central African Republic), 89
Boubacar, Toumba, 396
Bougeaud, Gilbert. *See* Bob Denard
Boulding, E., 1043
Boumedienne, Houari, 6, 7, 12
Boundaries, 693-94, 872, 984, 1080;
    and defense, 726-27
Boundou, 431

Bourguiba, Habib Ben Ali, 553, 554, 559-60, 1081, 1083-84
Bourguiba, Habib, Jr., 556
Bouri oil field (Libya), 298
Bown, Lalage, v; "Education in Africa," 1087-1100
Boy Scouts, 1012
Boycotts, South Africa, 740-41
BPP (Botswana People's Party), 37, 38
Brain drain, medical, 1004
Brazil: foreign debt, 794; trade relations, 20, 21, 614
Brazzaville (Congo), 121
Bretton Woods Conference, 824, 838
Brewing industry, 53, 94, 109, 233, 285, 496, 573, 576
British Cameroon, 407
British East Africa Company, 565
British Indian Ocean Territory. See Seychelles
British people, Zambia, 598
British South Africa Company (BSA), 38, 600, 601, 610, 869
Broadcasting. See Mass media
Broederbond (Fellowship of Brothers), South Africa, 487
Brown, Irving, 708
Brunei, education plan, 769
Brutus, Dennis, 1109
Bubi people, 161, 163
Buchanan (Liberia), 285
Buddhism, Mauritius, 348
Budget deficits: comparative figures, 796; reductions, 814. See also Economy
Buffalo husbandry, Egypt, 152
Buffalo River, 475
Buganda Kingdom, 561, 564-66
Bugosa people, 564, 565
Buhari, Muhammad, 404, 409, 1064
Building materials: imports, 119; production, 153. See also Cement production
Bujumbura (Burundi), 59
Bukoba (Tanzania), 568
Bulawayo (Zimbabwe), 607, 609, 862

Bulgaria, aid to Congo, 128
Bunjur (Gambia), 192
Bunyoro Kingdom, 565
Burco (Somalia), 468
Bureaucracies, 147-48, 361, 399, 806; and state-control of economy, 884
Burkina Faso, 45-57, 46, 678, 802; agriculture, 646, 650; CEAO membership, 898; diplomatic relations, 208-9, 331, 546; education, 664; food production, 648, 652; health figures, 658, 662; literacy campaign, 1049-50; Muslims, 1068, 1077; population, 626, 660, 974; refugees, 991; road system, 956; smuggling, 873; trade unions, 1018; economy, 52-54, 628, 644, 654, 656, 804; currency, 643; employment figures, 630; foreign debt, 844; foreign trade, 632, 634, 636, 638, 640; manufacturing, 913, 916; mineral exports, 919
Burundi, 58, 59-66, 417, 802; agriculture, 646, 650; education, 664; food production, 648, 652; health figures, 658, 662; Muslims, 1068; population, 626, 660, 975; refugees, 985, 988, 991, 995-96; road system, 956; tourism, 1120; underground economy, 879; economy, 62-64, 628, 644, 654, 656, 804; currency, 642; employment figures, 630; foreign debt, 844; foreign trade, 632, 634, 636, 638, 640; manufacturing, 913, 916; mineral exports, 919
Bush, George, 396
Bush, James, 283
Bushmen, 35, 377, 476, 482
Busia, Kofi, 206, 674
Business newsletters, 1130
Business travel, 1116-17
Butare (Rwanda), 415, 421
Buthelezi, Mangosuthu Gatsha, 481, 489-90, 503, 738, 739, 740, 1032
Buyoya, Pierre, 60, 62

Bwaka people, 581
Bwanausi, Augustine, 317, 318

Cabinda province (Angola), 13, 16
Cabo Delgado (Mozambique), 368
Cabral, Amilcar, 84, 230, 234
Cabral, Luiz de Almeida, 230-31, 234
Cacheu (Guinea-Bissau), 229
Cacheu-Farim River, 227
Cacine River, 227
Cadmium deposits, 377, 589
Cahora Bassa Dam, 365, 371, 493
Cairo (Egypt), 142, 143, 156, 982, 1070; riots, 150
Cairo Declaration, 1080
Cairo Program for African Cooperation, 948, 950
Caledon River, 267, 475
Camara, Assan Musa, 196
Camdessus, Michel, 821
Camel husbandry, 137, 341, 469
Cameroon, 65-80, 66, 546, 802; agriculture, 646, 650; education, 664, 1090, 1092; food imports, 928; food production, 648, 652; health figures, 658, 662; Muslims, 1068; population, 626, 660, 976; press freedom, 1123, 1124; refugees, 985, 988, 991; repression, 1110; road system, 956; tourism, 1117; UDEAC membership, 899-900; economy: 74-78, 628, 644, 654, 656, 804; currency, 643; employment figures, 630; foreign debt, 845; foreign trade, 429, 632, 634, 636, 638, 640; manufacturing, 913; mineral exports, 919
Cameroon Airlines, 77
Cameroon Democratic Front, 73
Camp David accords, 150
Canada, 74, 386, 593, 763, 855; aid from, 397, 767
Cancelling of debts, 855
Cannabis, 880
Canning industry, 398, 438, 470
Cap des Biches (Senegal), 439

Cape area (South Africa), 473-75, 477
Cape of Good Hope, 859; oil route, 708, 710
Cape Town (South Africa), 476, 477, 482, 490, 497
Cape Verde Islands, 81-87, 82, 681, 802; ECOWAS membership, 901; Guinea-Bissau and, 230-31, 233; health figures, 658; Muslims, 1068; population figures, 626, 974; refugees, 991; economy: 85-86, 628, 644, 656, 804; currency, 642; employment figures, 630; foreign debt, 844; foreign trade, 632, 638, 640; manufacturing, 913, 916; mineral exports, 919
Cape Verdean people, 229
Capital flows, 820-21, 843
Capital formation, and military spending, 724
Capital goods, imports, 922-23
Capitalism: Inkatha and, 738; and military spending, 719; nationalism and, 1102; international, 824, 836, 838; and colonialism, 825
Capitals, relocation, 986
Caprivi Strip (Namibia), 377, 378, 380
Cargados Carajos Island, 347
Caribbean Basin Initiative (CBI), 772
Carter, Jimmy, 709, 711
Casablanca (Morocco), 355, 356, 357, 361, 362, 982
Casablanca group, 688
Casamance (Senegal), 431, 435
Cash crop economy, 675, 1043-45; and nutrition, 1007-8; see also Agriculture
Cashew nut production, 232, 233, 371, 535, 536, 538
Cassava production: Benin, 30; Burundi, 63; Cameroon, 76; Cape Verde, 85; Central African Republic, 94; Congo, 127; Ghana, 209; Liberia, 284; Madagascar, 309; Mozambique, 371; Rwanda, 419; Sierra Leone, 456; Tanzania,

538; Togo, 543, 547; Uganda, 575; Zaire, 588

Cassinga (Angola), 384

Cattle. *See* Livestock production

Caucasian Berbers, 356

Cavally River, 235, 279

CCM (Chama Cha Mapinduzi), Tanzania, 528, 529, 531, 532-33

CCSATU (Co-ordinating Council of South African Trade Unions), 1029

CEAO (Communauté Economique de l'Afrique de l'Ouest), 893, 898-99

Cement industry, 30, 225, 262, 285, 343, 371, 398, 470, 538, 548, 573, 575-76, 590; underground economy, 875, 876

Censorship of press, 79, 157, 215, 226, 324, 390, 559, 1109-11, 1123-27, 1129; South Africa, 501-2, 733

Central Africa: imports, 923; Islam, 1072; military spending, 717; population figures, 976; underground economy, 876-80

Central African Federation, 317, 600, 611-12, 893, 896-97

Central African Republic, *88*, 89-98, 183, 670, 802; agriculture, 646, 650; education, 664; food production, 648, 652; health figures, 658, 662; Muslims, 1068; OAU and, 690; population, 626, 660, 976; refugees, 985, 988, 991; tourism, 1118; *economy*: 94-95, 628, 644, 654, 656, 804; currency, 643; employment figures, 630; foreign debt, 844, 847; foreign trade, 86, 632, 634, 636, 638, 640, 923; manufacturing, 913, 916; mineral exports, 919; underground economy, 876

Central America, EC and, 781

Central Treaty Organization, 709

CEPGL (Communauté Economique des Pays des Grands Lacs), 420, 894

Cereal imports, 944

Cereal production, 41, 342

Césaire, Aimé, 688

Cetewayo (Zulu leader), 483

Ceuta (Morocco), 355

CFA franc, 78, 164, 399, 440, 632, 642, 780, 904-5; underground economy, 876

CFTC (Commonwealth Fund for Technical Cooperation), 766, 768

Chad, 99-112, *100*, 183, 683, 802; agriculture, 646, 650; civil war, 295, 697-99, 1085; colonialism, 1077; diplomatic relations, 72, 93, 293, 295, 296, 395, 436, 546, 587, 696; education, 664; famine, 927; food production, 648, 652; health figures, 658, 662; military spending, 722; Muslims, 1068, 1069, 1075, 1080, 1083; population, 626, 660, 976; refugees, 991; UDEAC membership, 900; warfare with Libya, 693-94; *economy*: 107-9, 628, 644, 654, 656, 804; currency, 643; employment figures, 630; foreign debt, 844; foreign trade, 632, 636, 638, 640; manufacturing, 913, 916; mineral exports, 919

Chagga people, 528, 675

Chaillu Massif, 181

Chakuamba, Gwanda, 316, 319

Chambeshi River, 597

Chan, S., 720

Charcoal, 936

Chari River, 89, 99

Charter of People's and Human Rights, 690

Chase Manhattan Bank, 861n

Cheapoo, Chea, 281

Cheikh, Moustapha Said, 116

Cheikh Anta Diop University (Dakar), 441

Cheliff River, 3

Chemical industry, 285, 297, 371, 438-39, 496, 590, 616, 654-55, 912

Chevron, Sudan oil, 700

Chewa people, 314, 316, 325, 609
ChiChewa language, 314
Chiepe, Gaositwe K. T., 36, 44
Child marriage, 1047
Child mortality, 658-59, 797-98, 972, 978, 1006, 1011
Childbearing, 1047
Children, military training, 94
Chilembwe, John, 317
Chili pepper production, 557
Chimombo, Steve, 1110
China, 771, 788, 805; agriculture, 940; aid recipients, 17, 164, 286, 369, 537, 612; birth rate, 972; foreign relations, 52, 74, 127, 206, 306, 329, 331, 534, 602, 615; and South African political parties, 480; Tanzam railway, 958; trade relations, 198, 333, 558, 614
Chinese people, 304, 348, 349, 445
Chingola (Zambia), 598
Chinguetti (Mauritania), 339
Chinweizu (Nigerian writer), 1110
Chipande, Manuel Joaquim, 367
Chipasula, Frank, 1110
Chipembere, Henry, 317, 318
Chirac, Jacques, 117, 240
Chirwa, Edward Yapwantha, 316
Chirwa, Orton, 316, 317, 318, 320
Chirwa, Robson, 315
Chirwa, Vera, 316, 320
Chisano, Joaquim, 493
ChiShona language, 609
Chisiza, Dunduzu, 317
Chisiza, Yatuta, 317, 318, 319
Chissano, Joaquim Alberto, 367, 368, 370, 374, 704
Chitala, Derrick, vi; "African Industrial Development," 912-25
Chitungwiza (Zimbabwe), 609
Chiume, Kanyama, 315, 317, 318
Chobe National Park (Botswana), 35
Chokani, Willie, 318
Chokwe language, 15
Cholera, Mali, 333
Chopi people, 366

Chott El Jerid, 551
Choua, Lol Mohamed, 104
Christian Democratic Union (Madagascar), 305
Christianity, 1055-56, 1067; and AIDS, 1058-60; Coptic, Egypt, 143; and education, 1088; and ethnicity, 1057-58; and Islam, 1053-54, 1056-58, 1081; and medical services, 1002; nationalist movements and, 1078; ritual wine, 1062. See also Religion
Chrome deposits, 30, 475
Chrome production, 309
Church, conflict with, 62, 568
Church schools, 1088; Ghana, 214-15; Liberia, 287; Mali, 334; Zaire, 594
CIA (Central Intelligence Agency), U.S., 708, 711, 755, 1025
Cigarette industry, 438, 880
Cinchona production, 420
Cinnamon production, 118, 447
Circumcision, female, 1042, 1048
Ciskei (South Africa), 476, 477, 486, 489, 494, 503
Citicorp, 176, 861, 863
Cities, 982
Citrus fruit production, 8, 360, 522, 557, 588
Civil rights: Angola, 17; Egypt, 146
Civil service employment, 1023
Civil war: civilian casualties, 1009; and famine, 926, 927, 930; and health services, 1009-10; religion and, 1056-58; Soviet Union and, 712; by country: Algeria, 6-7; Angola, 17-18, 20; Burundi, 62; Chad, 102-7, 108, 295, 697-99, 1085; Eritrea, 173; Ethiopia, 172; Gambia, 195; Nigeria, 407-8, 1085; Rhodesia, 612-14; Rwanda, 418; Somalia, 468; Sudan, 507, 509, 510, 511, 513, 514, 694, 699-701, 880, 955; Zaire, 585-86, 693
Clark amendment, U.S., 748

Clarke, John I., vi; "Africa's Population," 969-87

Class relationships, 884-86, 1106-9, 1057-58

Claustre, Françoise, 111

Climate change, 931

Clock manufacture, 351

Closed-city programs, 986

Clothing industry, 496

Clove production, 118, 308, 529, 535

Club du Sahel, 930

CMLN (Comité Militaire pour la Libération Nationale), Mali, 330

CMNS (Military Committee for National Salvation), Mauritania, 339

CMRN (Central African Republic), 92-93

CMRN (Comité Militaire de Redressement National), Guinea, 219, 222-24

CMRN (Military Committee for National Recovery), Mauritania, 341

CMRPN (Comité Militaire de Redressment pour le Progrès National), Burkina Faso, 49

CMS (Conseil Militaire Suprême), Niger, 394

CNETU (Council of Non-European Trade Unions), 1028

CND (Conseil National de Développement), Niger, 394

CNR (Conseil National de la Révolution), Burkina Faso, 47

Coal: deposits, 371-72; 475, 537, 589, 597; production, 397, 495-96, 522, 534, 589, 616

Coalizão Democrática de Oposição (São Tomé and Príncipe), 426

Cobalt: deposits, 94, 597; production, 589, 593, 603; underground economy, 876, 877

Cockroft, Lawrence, 924

Coco yam production, 209

Cocoa, 929; smuggling, 873. See also Agriculture

Coconuts, Guinea-Bissau, 232

COD (Congress of Democrats), South Africa, 485, 1030

Coffee, 878, 879-80; underground economy, 876, 877; production, by country: Angola, 20, 21; Burundi, 59, 62, 63; Cameroon, 76; Cape Verde, 85; Central African Republic, 94, 95; Congo, 127; Equatorial Guinea, 166; Ethiopia, 176; Guinea, 217, 225; Ivory Coast, 235, 241; Kenya, 248, 260-61; Liberia, 284; Madagascar, 308; Malawi, 322; Mozambique, 371; Rwanda, 419; São Tomé and Príncipe, 423, 426; Sierra Leone, 458; Tanzania, 535-38; Togo, 543, 547; Uganda, 561, 565, 572-74; Zaire, 588, 593; Zimbabwe, 617

Cold war, 706, 712; Middle East, 709

Collective bargaining, 1019-20, 1025, 1027

Collective farming, 221, 369, 371, 531, 535

Colonial boundaries, 953, 1080; and defense, 726-27

Colonial towns, 674

Colonialism, 671-72, 678, 882, 970, 992; banking, 858-60; Belgian, 61, 417-18, 583; EC countries and, 782; and economic performance, 803, 805; and education, 1049; end of, 706-7; Eritrea, 701; and Eurafrica concept, 771-72; forced labor, 675; German, 375, 380-81, 417, 529-30, 544, 547; and health services, 1002-3, 1005; and international finance, 825-26; and Islam, 1072, 1075-79; Italian, 172, 292, 682; nationalism and, 1102-12; North Africa, 1073; regional associations, 890; and religion, 1064; South Africa, 482-83; Spanish, 162-63, 341, 683; trade unions, 1015-16; and wars, 693-95; Western Sahara, 695; British: 680, 682; Botswana, 38;

Cameroon, 70-71; Gambia, 193; Ghana, 205; Kenya, 250-53; Libya, 292; Malawi, 316-18, 321; Mauritius, 348, 349; Namibia, 375, 380; Nigeria, 406; Rhodesia, 600; Seychelles, 446; Somalia, 466; Southern Rhodesia, 610-11; Sudan, 509, 699; Swaziland, 520; Tanzania, 530; Uganda, 565; *French*: Algeria, 5-6; Benin, 28; Burkina Faso, 48; Cameroon, 70; Central African Republic, 91; Chad, 102-3, 694, 697; Comoros, 115-16, 117; Djibouti, 135-36; Gabon, 183; Guinea, 219-20; Ivory Coast, 238-39; Madagascar, 305-6; Morocco, 357; Niger, 394-95; Senegal, 434; Tunisia, 554; *Portuguese*: 681; Angola, 17, 19-20; Cape Verde, 84; Guinea-Bissau, 227, 230; Mozambique, 367-69, 370-71; São Tomé and Príncipe, 426, 427-28

Coloured people: Namibia, 378, 382; politics, 736-37; South Africa, 476, 477, 481, 485, 499-501

Coloured People's Organization, South Africa, 485

COMINOR, 340

Commission of Mediation, Conciliation and Arbitration, OAU, 690

Committees for the Defence of the Revolution, Ghana, 1019

Common Man's Charter, Uganda, 566

Commonwealth Arts Festival, Edinburgh, 766

Commonwealth countries, African involvement, 762-69

Commonwealth Development Corporation, and Uganda, 576

Commonwealth Games, 766

Communciations, 953; Congo, 121; Gambia, 197; Ghana, 211; Ivory Coast, 240; OAU and, 691;

SADCC and, 750; Sierra Leone, 457; Somalia, 470

Comoros, 113-20, *114*, 802; health figures, 658; Muslims, 1068, 1069; population, 626, 975; tourism, 1121; *economy*: 118-19, 628, 644, 656, 804; currency, 643; employment figures, 630; foreign debt, 844; foreign trade, 638, 640; manufacturing, 913, 916; mineral exports, 919

Compaoré, Blaise, 47, 50-52, 56

Compensatory fund facilities, IMF, 832

Competition for education, 1095

Compradorism, 884-85

Computers in Africa, 1131

Conakry (Guinea), 217, 219, 225, 874, 875

Concessional lending, 848-49

Conditionality, 813-17, 829-30, 848-52, 856

Condoms, 1061

Confédération Nationale des Travailleurs Guinéens, 1017

Confédération Nationale des Travailleurs Sénégalais, 440

Confederation of Senegambia, 436-37, 439-40, 442, 894

Congo, 121-32, *122*, 183, 802; agricultural production, 646, 650; Burkina Faso and, 52; education, 1092; food imports, 928; food production, 648, 652; health figures, 658, 662; Muslims, 1068; population, 626, 660, 976; refugees, 988, 991; *economy*, 127-29, 628, 644, 654, 656, 804; currency, 643; employment figures, 630; foreign debt, 844; foreign trade, 632, 634, 636, 638, 640; imports, 923; manufacturing, 913; mineral exports, 919; underground economy, 876; wages, 1021

Congo Affair, 708

Congo River, 121. *See also* Zaire River

Congress Alliance, South Africa, 485

Congress for the Second Republic (Malawi), 316, 320

Conombo, Joseph, 49

Consas (Constellation of Southern African States), 749

Conscience, African, 1053

Conservation measures, 948

Consessional loans, 846

Constantine (Algeria), 4, 5, 8

Constitutional monarchy, 519

Construction industry, 371, 498, 616, 618, 1023; material imports, 470; material production, 538; underground economy, 875, 876

Consumer goods: imports, 922-23; production, 360, 590, 921

Consumption, 792; military spending and, 719

Conté, Lasana, 222-24

Continental unity, 686, 690

Contraception, 977, 1011

Convergencia Social Democrática, 162

Conversions, religious, 1054

Coombs, Philip, 1087

Coordinating Board of Opposition Forces, Equatorial Guinea, 162

Copper: deposits, 128, 176, 344, 377, 475, 597; price decline, 853; production, 10, 41, 388, 495, 568, 573, 589, 593, 603

Copperbelt (Zambia), 597, 598; riots, 601

Copra production, 118, 368, 371, 447

Coptic Christian Church, 1057, 1069

Corn, Sierra Leone, 456

Corporatism, 1015

Correia, Paulo, 231

Correspondence education, Commonwealth plan, 768-69

Corruption in government, 677, 839, 843; refugee aid, 992; *by country*: Angola, 21; Burkina Faso, 48; Central African Republic, 92, 94-95; Comoros, 116, 117; Egypt, 147, 151; Equatorial Guinea, 166; Gambia, 195; Ghana, 206-7, 208, 873; Guinea, 874-75; Ivory Coast, 239; Kenya, 255, 256, 257; Liberia, 281, 283; Mali, 333; Mauritius, 350; Niger, 395; Nigeria, 408, 409, 410; Senegal, 435, 875; Sierra Leone, 455, 458; Tanzania, 532, 958; Uganda, 574

Corsairing, 1073

COSATU (Congress of South African Trade Unions), 489-90, 492, 739, 743-44, 1032-33, 1035-38

Costs of education, 1094

Cotonou (Benin), 25, 28, 398, 399

Cotton: ginning, 398, 470; *production*: 939-40; Angola, 20; Benin, 30; Burkina Faso, 53; Burundi, 63; Cameroon, 76; Central African Republic, 94, 95; Chad, 108; Egypt, 152; Ivory Coast, 235, 241; Kenya, 260, 262; Madagascar, 309; Mali, 332, 333; Mozambique, 368, 371; Niger, 397; Rwanda, 420; Senegal, 437; Sudan, 505, 512-13; Tanzania, 535, 537, 538; Togo, 543, 548; Uganda, 561, 568, 572, 573, 574; Zaire, 588; Zimbabwe, 617

Council for Mutual Economic Assistance, 177

Council of Malagasy Churches, 307

Countries, diversities, 982-84

Coups, political, and tourism, 1114

CP (Conservative Party), South Africa, 481, 731-34

CPP (Convention People's Party), Ghana, 205-6

CPSA (Communist Party of South Africa), 479

Creative writing, suppression of, 1109-11

Creole people, 115, 161, 348, 349, 445, 452

Crisis management programs, 829-31

Crocker, Chester A., 694, 704
Crops. *See* Agriculture; Cash crop economy
Crystal Mountains, 181
CSR (Conseil Suprême de la Révolution), Madagascar, 304-5
Cuango River, 13
Cuanza River, 13, 15
Cuba: aid recipients, 164, 173, 174, 369, 682; diplomatic relations, 52, 127, 206, 208, 272, 427; *and Angola*, 694, 704; troops, 17, 18, 386-87, 487, 711, 748
Cubango (Okavango) River, 13
Cultural issues: EC and, 782; Lomé Convention, 776
Cultural revolution, Libya, 293
Cunene River, 13
Curepipe (Mauritius), 347
Currencies, 642-43; black market, West Africa, 873; colonial, 859-60; cooperative groups, 904-5; depreciation, 1022; devaluation, 808, 814, 828, 850; overvaluation, 807, 941-42; precolonial, 858. *See also* Economy
Currency and Banking Act, South Africa, 859-60
Curtis, William, 283
CUSA (Council of Unions of South Africa), 1031
CUSA (Customs Union of South Africa), 39, 42
Cushite people, 465
Customs unions, 890; CEAO, 898; CUSA, 39, 42; ECOWAS, 902; MRU, 900; SACU, 906-7
Cyclones, Mauritius, 347
Cyrenaica (Libya), 289, 292, 1075; Arab conquest, 1070
Czechoslovakia, 240

da Costa, Manuel Pinto, 425, 426-27, 430
de Graça, Carlos, 426-27
Dacko, David, 91, 92, 95, 97

Daddah, Moktar Ould, 339, 340-41, 345
Dahhab, Abdul Rahman Siwar al-, 511
Dahomey, 28. *See also* Benin
Daka River, 201
Dakar (Senegal), 431, 434, 436, 438, 439; Islamic Institute, 1089; trade unions, 1016
Daloa (Ivory Coast), 237
Damara people, 377, 378, 379, 380
Danakil Depression, 169
Danjuma (Gen., Nigeria), 408
Danquan, J. B., 205. *See also* Nkrumah, Kwame
Dar es Salaam (Tanzania), 420, 486, 525, 527, 528, 537, 538, 750, 1120; Commonwealth education programs, 765; PAC headquarters, 480
Darbo, Bakary B., 199
Darfur (Sudan), 1008, 1076
Darod people, 465
Dasuki, Ibraham, 410
Date production, 8, 337, 342
Davidson, Basil, vi, 1103-5; *The Liberation of Guiné*, 1101; "Two Decades of Decline: A Burden for the Future," 669-85
Davies, Wendy, vi; "Women in Africa," 1041-52
De Beers Group, 41, 387
de Klerk, Wiempie, 735
De Vos, Antoon, 935
de Wilde, John C., *Agriculture, Marketing and Pricing in Sub-Saharan Africa*, 941, 942
Death rates, 788
Debbech oil field, 557
Debt crisis, 839, 841-57
Debt figures, 644-45
Debt payment suspension, 679
Debt service costs, 669, 679, 842-43, 848
Decentralization policies, 986
Decolonialization, 672-73, 680
Defense capability, 726-27, 728

Defense contracts, South Africa, 723
Defense spending. *See* Military
  spending
Deforestation, 10, 173, 419, 935-36,
  944
De Gaulle, Charles, 6, 219-20
Deger, Saadet, 720-21
Degodia people, 259
Demand elasticities for agricultural
  exports, 939-40
Demand-control policies, 816
Dembélé, Mamadou, 331
Democratic Coalition of Opposition,
  São Tomé and Príncipe, 427
Democratic Party (DP), Uganda, 565,
  570
Democratic Republic of the Sahrawi,
  683
Demographic data, 970-72
Denard, Bob, 116, 117, 120
Deng, William, 700
Denkyira kingdom, 205
Denmark, 204, 770, 771
Density of population, 969-70
Dependence, economic; of SADCC
  states, 757; on single crop, 196,
  210, 410
Dependency ratios, 789, 1006
Deregulation, South Africa, 1035
Dergue (Ethiopia), 170, 172-73,
  178-79, 702
DESCON (Consultative Group for
  Desertification Control), 950
Dese (Ethiopia), 169
Desert areas, 3, 35, 36, 133, 141-42,
  247, 248, 289, 337, 375, 393, 551
Desertification, 936-37, 944, 945-51,
  1008
Desertification Control Program
  Activity Center, 950
Desktop publishing, 1127
Desta, Fisseha, 178
Destabilization policy, South Africa,
  487, 489, 492-94, 681, 694, 703-5,
  748-61, 1010; costs of, 759-61;

Seychelles, 446; Mozambique, 369;
  Zambia, 602; Zimbabwe, 614
Destour Party, Tunisia, 554, 1079
Detained (Ngugi wa Thiong'o), 1111
Developing countries, 787-801;
  desertification, 947; economic
  forecast, 809
Dhlakama, Afonso, 374
Dia, Mamadou, 434, 435
Diakité, Yoro, 330
Diama Dam (Senegal), 438
Diamonds: deposits, 128, 185, 475,
  483, 859; underground economy,
  873, 875-76, 877, 878, 880;
  production: by country: Angola,
  20-21; Botswana, 41; Central
  African Republic, 94-95; Guinea,
  225; Lesotho, 273; Liberia, 285;
  Namibia, 375, 382, 387; Sierra
  Leone, 451, 455, 457, 458; South
  Africa, 495-96; Swaziland, 522;
  Tanzania, 534, 537; Zaire, 589, 593
Diani Beach (Kenya), 1119-20
Diarra, Amadou Baba, 335
Diarrheal diseases, 1012
Diawara, Ange, 125
Dibba, Sherif, 194, 196
Dictatorships, 163-164, 508, 564-71,
  670; colonial, 672-73; postcolonial,
  673
Diego Garcia, 350
Deit, comparative, 662-63
Digil people, 465
Dikeledi, Paul, 745
Dingaan (Zulu leader), 482
Dini, Ahmed, 139
Dinka people, 507, 700
Diola people, 435
Diop, Cheikh Anta, 435
Diop, David, 688
Diori, Alhaji Hamani, 400
Diori, Hamani, 394-95
Diouf, Abdou, 74, 195, 433, 434, 442,
  1054
Dioula people, 433
Diplomacy, African, 693

Dir people, 465

Dire Dawa (Ethiopia), 169

Disease, 110, 214, 299; preventable, 1012; religion and, 1058-60; Western introductions, 1002

Disinvestment in South Africa, 497; Inkatha and, 738

Distribution of income, 790, 815; and market economy, 803-5; state-controlled economies, 808

Distribution of population, 981-82

Djerma-Songhai people, 393

Djibouti, 133-39, *134*, 802, 1081; Arab League, 1079; drug abuse, 1063; health figures, 658; Muslims, 1068, 1069; population, 626, 975; refugees, 985, 988, 991, 998; *economy*: 136-37, 628, 644, 656, 804; currency, 642; employment figures, 630; foreign debt, 844; foreign trade, 638, 640; manufacturing, 913, 916; mineral exports, 919

Djogo, Negue, 106

Dlamini, Bhekimpi Alpheus, Prince of Swaziland, 521, 524

Dlamini, Sotsha Ernest, 524

Doctors, 1003-4

Dodge, Cole P., vii; "African Health and Medical Services," 1002-13

Doe, Jackson F., 280, 283

Doe, Samuel Kanyon, 280, 282-84, 288

Dogon people, 327

Doiuf, Abdou, 435-37

Dolbahante people, 467

Domestic military production, 719, 722-23

Dominican Republic, 780-81

Dongola, 1070

Dorobo people, 248

dos Santos, José Eduardo, 16, 18, 21, 23

dos Santos Franca, Antonio, 16

Douala (Cameroon), 67, 77

Dourado, Wolfgang, 532

Draft animals, 949

Drakensberg Mountains, 267, 473, 475

Drought, 669, 682, 718, 725, 792, 803, 937, 945; and famine, 927-28, 930-31; and health services, 1008; refugees, 985; *by country*: Algeria, 3, 10; Angola, 20; Benin, 29, 30; Botswana, 41, 42; Burkina Faso, 48, 52; Cape Verde Islands, 81, 84, 85; Chad, 99, 107-8, 109, 683; Ethiopia, 169, 173; Gambia, 196; Ghana, 209, 211; Guinea-Bissau, 227, 231; Ivory Coast, 242; Kenya, 248, 260, 262; Lesotho, 267, 273; Libya, 289; Madagascar, 307; Malawi, 322; Mali, 327, 331, 332, 333; Mauritania, 337, 339, 340-41, 341, 342, 344; Mauritius, 347; Morocco, 360; Mozambique, 365, 369, 371, 372; Namibia, 377, 378, 387, 389; Niger, 395, 396-97, 398; Senegal, 437; Sierra Leone, 456; Somalia, 467, 469, 471; South Africa, 475, 495; Sudan 505, 511, 512, 514; Tanzania, 531, 867; Tunisia, 557; Zimbabwe, 616, 617

Drug abuse, 1062-64

Drum, 1109

Drum East Africa, 1130

DTA (Democratic Turnhalle Alliance), 379, 385-86

du Toit, Wynand Petrus, 755

Dube, J. L., 687

DuBois, W. E. B., 687

Dukakis, Michael, 779

Duleb oil field, Tunisia, 557

DUP (Democratic Unionist Party), Sudan, 508, 1078

Durban (South Africa), 476, 477, 497; labor unrest, 1030

Dutch East India Company, 482

Dutch Reformed Church, 379, 477

Duval, Charles Gaetan, 349, 353

Dyola (Jola) people, 192

EAC (East African Community), 259, 527, 534, 568, 893, 895-96

EADB (East African Development Bank), 893, 896

Earthquakes, Algeria, 3

East Africa, 1070-71; AIDS, 978; imports, 922; military spending, 717; population, 975, 986; tourism, 1119-21

East African Currency Board, 866

East Germany, 19, 240, 370, 470

East London (South Africa), 476, 477

Eastern bloc countries, 21, 230, 558, 787-801

Eastern Catholics, Egypt, 143

Ebrahim, Gora, 747

Ebrahim, Ismail, 745

ECA (Economic Commission for Africa), 833-35, 947

EC/ACP trade arrangement, 8

ECCAS (Economic Community of Central African States), 74, 894, 904

Economic diplomacy, religion and, 1064-66

Economic growth, 719-28; transportation and, 953-54

Economic imperialism, 671-72

Economic reform, 727-28, 807-22, 829-39, 849, 911

Economic refugees, 985

Economy, 787-810; banking, 858-70; colonial, Kenya, 251; continental variations, 811-12; decline, 669; and education, 1095; future prospects, 820-21; global, and tourism, 1114-15; and health services, 1005-6; and media, 1123; and military spending, 716-28; OAU and, 691; and population distribution, 981-82; refugees and, 992; regional integration, 890-911; superpower relations, 714; underground, 871-81; worldwide, postwar, 708-9; by country: Angola, 880; Benin, 29-30; Burkina Faso, 49, 51, 52-54; Burundi, 62-64;

Cameroon, 73, 74-78; Cape Verde, 85-86; Central African Republic, 94-95; Chad, 107-9; Comoros, 118-19; Congo, 127-29; Djibouti, 136-37; Egypt, 148, 150, 151, 152-55; Equatorial Guinea, 164-67; Ethiopia, 175-77; Gabon, 185; Gambia, 196-98; Ghana, 206-7, 209-14, 873-74; Guinea, 221-22, 223-26, 874-75; Guinea-Bissau, 231-33; Ivory Coast, 239-42; Kenya, 257, 260-63; Lesotho, 273-75; Liberia, 282, 283, 284-87; Libya, 292, 295-98; Madagascar, 306-10; Malawi, 318, 321-23; Mali, 330, 331-33; Mauritania, 342-44; Mauritius, 349-52; Morocco, 358-62; Mozambique, 370-73; Namibia, 382, 387-89; Niger, 395, 396-99; Nigeria, 408-12, 864-66; Rwanda, 418-21; São Tomé and Príncipe, 427-29; Senegal, 435-40; Seychelles, 447-48; Sierra Leone, 455-59; Somalia, 467, 469-71; South Africa, 483, 494-99, 733; Sudan, 512-14, 880; Swaziland, 521-23; Tanzania, 531, 532, 534-38, 866-69, 958; Togo, 547-49; Tunisia, 556-59, 568, 570, 572-777, 879-80; Zaire, 587-93, 876-79; Zambia, 602-4; Zimbabwe, 615-18, 860-63

ECOWAS (Economic Community of West African States), 193, 222, 546, 834, 894, 901-3; Liberia and, 281

Eden, Anthony, 147

EDF (European Development Fund), 773-74, 775, 777-80

Edo people, 403

EDU (Ethiopian Democratic Union), 171

Education, 670-71, 1087-1100; and birth rates, 977; Commonwealth and, 765, 766, 768-69; comparative figures, 664-65, 796-97; and economic performance, 803; ecological, 951; health care, 1012; medical, 1003; of women, 1046, 1049-50; and working age, 789; *by country*: Algeria, 11; Angola, 22; Benin, 30, 31; Botswana, 43; Burkina Faso, 55-56; Burundi, 64-65; Cameroon, 78-79; Cape Verde, 86-87; Central African Republic, 96; Chad, 110; Comoros, 120; Congo, 130; Djibouti, 138; Egypt, 156-57; Equatorial Guinea, 167; Ethiopia, 177; Gabon, 187; Gambia, 193, 198-99; Ghana, 206, 214-15; Guinea, 223, 226; Guinea-Bissau, 233-34; Ivory Coast, 243-44; Kenya, 264; Lesotho, 275-76; Liberia, 287-88; Libya, 299; Madagascar, 310-11; Malawi, 324; Mali, 334-35; Mauritania, 344; Mauritius, 352-53; Morocco, 362; Mozambique, 373; Namibia, 381-82, 390; Niger, 400; Nigeria, 412-13; Rwanda, 421; São Tomé and Príncipe, 429; Senegal, 441; Seychelles, 447, 448; Sierra Leone, 460; Somalia, 471; South Africa, 498, 499-501, 737; Sudan, 515; Tanzania, 539; Togo, 549-50; Tunisia, 559; Uganda, 577; Zaire, 594; Zambia, 605; Zimbabwe, 618-19

Eglin, Colin, 481

Egypt, *140*, 141-58, 678, 688, 709, 1073-74, 1080; agriculture, 646, 650; Arab conquest, 1070-71; and Arab League, 1079; birth rate, 972; contraception, 977; diplomatic relations, 104, 294, 470, 509, 510, 512, 555, 707-8; education, 664, 1090, 1091, 1092; female circumcision, 1048; food production, 648, 652; health figures, 658, 662; Islam, 1081-83; life expectancy, 987; Muslims, 1068, 1069; population, 626, 660, 974, 986; refugees, 988, 991; Suez crisis, 706-7; tourism, 1116; *economy*: 152-55, 628, 644, 654, 656, 917; currency, 642; employment figures, 630; foreign debt, 842, 843, 846, 853; foreign trade, 632, 634, 636, 638, 640; imports, 923; manufacturing, 913, 915; migrant workers, 298; military production, 721; mineral exports, 919

Eisenhower Doctrine, 707

Ejalu, Ateker, 569

Ekpu, Ray, 1129

Ekwensi, Cyprian, *Beautiful Feathers*, 1106

El Bayadh (Algeria), 4

El Hajdar (Algeria), 4

El Hor (Mauritanian political group), 341

El Molo people, 248

El Obeid (Sudan), 507

El-Borma oil field, 557

Electrical appliances, 351; underground economy, 876

Electronics manufacture, 360

Elmenteita Lake, 247

Elephants, Zaire, 877

ELF (Eritrean Liberation Front), 701-2

ELF-PLF (Eritrean People's Liberation Front), 171, 173-74, 175, 702

Elgeyo people, 249

Ellis, William S., 936-37

Embezzlement, Guinea, 875

Embu people, 248

Employment, 630-31; and education, 1093-95; and military forces, 724-25; public-sector, 1023; of women, 1045, 1046. *See also* Economy

Enahoro, Peter, 1128

Energy usage, comparative, 793

English language: Botswana, 36; Egypt, 143; Ethiopia, 170; Gambia, 192; Ghana, 202; Kenya, 249;

Lesotho, 269; Liberia, 280; Libya, 291; Malawi, 314; Mauritius, 348; Namibia, 378; Nigeria, 403-4; Seychelles, 445, 448; Sierra Leone, 452; Somalia, 465; South Africa, 476, 477; Sudan, 507, 515; Swaziland, 519; Tanzania, 528; Togo, 544; Uganda, 563; Zambia, 598; Zimbabwe, 609

Entebbe (Uganda), 561, 563, 568

Entrepreneurship, 814

Environmental concerns, 401-3, 815, 944-52; agricultural, 934-37; and health services, 1008

EPG (Eminent Persons Group), 762-64

EPRP (Ethiopian People's Revolutionary Party), 171, 172

Equatorial Airlines, 428

Equatorial Guinea, 159-67, *160*, 802; health figures, 658; Muslims, 1068; OAU and, 690; population, 626, 976; refugees, 991; *economy*, 166-67, 628, 644, 656, 804; currency, 643; employment figures, 630; foreign debt, 844; foreign trade, 638, 640; manufacturing, 913, 916

Eritrea, 172-73, 682; Arab conquest, 1071; colonialism, 1076; Ethiopia and, 694, 701-3; Islam and, 1081; literacy campaign, 1049; Qadhafi and, 293; refugees, 996-97; religion, 1057; Somalia and, 466; superpower relations, 709-10, 712-13

Eritrean people, 170

ERPs (Economic Recovery Programs), 197, 198, 210-14

Eshira people, 181

Esparto grass, 296

Espoir oil field, 241

Estate farming, 260-61, 321, 423, 574

Ethanol production, Libya, 297

Ethiopia, *168*, 169-79, 469, 679, 682-83, 688, 725, 802; agriculture, 646, 650; and EC, 770; diplomatic relations, 136, 259, 466, 467, 468, 708; drought, 930-31, 1008; education, 664; emergency aid, 1011-12; famine, 926, 927, 930, 978; female circumcision, 1048; food production, 648, 652; health figures, 658, 662; Islam and, 1081; military spending, 717, 722; Muslims, 1068; Oromo people, 996; population, 626, 660, 975; refugees, 985, 988, 991, 998; religions, 1057; road system, 956; superpower relations, 709-10, 712-13; tourism, 1121; urban primacy, 982; women's work, 1043; *economy*, 175-77, 628, 644, 654, 656, 804; currency, 642; employment figures, 630; foreign debt, 845; foreign trade, 632, 634, 636, 638, 640; industry, 915; manufacturing, 913, 916; mineral exports, 919; *warfare*, 694, 701-3; armed forces, 713; civil war, 996-97; Sudan, 700, 701

Ethiopian Airlines, 176, 1115-16

Ethiopian Orthodox Church, 170

Ethnic groups, 970; education, 1088; religion and, 1056-58. See also Tribalism

Ethylene production, 297

Eurafrica concept, 771-72, 781

Europe, infant mortality, 978

European Community (EC), and Africa, 767-68, 770-83; export tables, 638-39; *relations by country*: Botswana, 41; Chad, 110; Equatorial Guinea, 164, 166; Ethiopia, 177; Guinea, 222; Guinea-Bissau, 232, 233; Lesotho, 274; Liberia, 285, 286; Mauritania, 343; Mauritius, 351; Morocco, 358, 360; Niger, 397, 398; Rwanda, 420; São Tomé and Príncipe, 427, 428; Senegal, 438; Swaziland, 522; Uganda, 574, 576; Zaire, 593

European countries: sanctions against South Africa, 757; trade relations, 42, 359

European Monetary System, 780

Europeans, by country of residence: Djibouti, 133; Equatorial Guinea, 161; Guinea-Bissau, 229; Lesotho, 269; Liberia, 280; Malawi, 314; Morocco, 356; Mozambique, 366; Namibia, 377, 378, 380; São Tomé and Príncipe, 425; Seychelles, 445; Sierra Leone, 452; South Africa, 483; Tanzania, 528; Tunisia, 553, 554; Uganda, 563; Zambia, 598

Evangelical sects, Malawi, 314

Ewe people, 202, 204-5, 544, 545, 1042

Exchange media, precolonial, 858

Exchange rates, 642-43, 722, 806, 814, 843; and agricultural economy, 941-42; IMF and, 828; reforms, 808; state control, 807

Expenditures, comparative figures, 792-93

Export-led growth strategies, 921-24, 939

Exports, 774, 820, 919-20; agricultural, 929, 1007; cash crops, 675; colonial, 825; colonialism and, 671; comparative figures, 634-35, 640-41, 792-94, 799-800; forecasts, 809; and foreign debt, 842, 843; minerals, 918-24; price decline, 669, 812; primary-products, 815; smuggling, 877; stabilization of earnings, 773; timber, 935; world market share, 938. *See also* Economy

Expulsion of refugees, 999

Eyadéma, Etienne Gnassingbe, 544, 545-48, 550

Eyasi Lake, 525

FACP (Front d'Action Commune Provisoire), 698

Factional politics, 677

Fadil, Fawzi Ahmed al-, 515

Faith healing, 1060

Falasha, 993

Falémé (Senegal), 438

Family planning, 977, 1011, 1048

Famine, 682, 714, 718, 792, 926-28, 930-34, 944, 978; and drought, 945; and health services, 1008; and military spending, 725; South African destabilization and, 760; *by country*: Angola, 20; Eritrea, 172; Ethiopia, 173-74, 175; Madagascar, 307; Somalia, 469; Sudan, 514

FAN (Forces Armées du Nord), 103, 698

Fang people, 161, 162-64, 181, 183-84, 188

Fanon, Frantz, 1057, 1102; "The Pitfalls of National Consciousness," 1101-2

Fante people, 202, 204

Farafenni (Gambia), 192

Farah, Nuruddin, 1110

Farim (Guinea-Bissau), 229

Farouk, King of Egypt, 143

Fassi, Allal al-, 1079

FAT (Forces Armées Tchadiennes), 103, 698

Faya-Largeau, Chad, 295

FCRD (Front Congolais pour la Restauration de la Démocratie), 582, 586

FDA (Algerian Democratic Front), 5

Federation of Welfare Societies, 600

Federations, 896-97

Female circumcision, 1042, 1048; and AIDS, 1062, 1061

Female literacy, Malawi, 324

Female-headed households, 1045, 1047. *See also* Women

Fernandino people, 161, 162

Fernando Póo (Bioko Island), 159

Fertility of population, 972-77, 1006-7

Fertilizer production, 153, 262-63, 371

Fertilizer use, 944; and women's work, 1044

Fes (Morocco), 356

Fezzan (Libya), 289

Fianarantsoa (Madagascar), 304

Field, Winston, 611

Financial sector, 351, 352, 495, 498, 858-70

Finland, 53, 63

Firearms, underground economy, 876

Firestone Tire & Rubber Company, 281, 284

Fishing industry, 794; Cameroon, 76; Cape Verde, 85, 86; Chad, 107, 109; Congo, 127; Djibouti, 137; Equatorial Guinea, 166; Gambia, 197; Ghana, 210; Guinea-Bissau, 232, 233; Kenya, 248, 262; Liberia, 284, 287; Malawi, 313, 321-22; Mali, 332, 333; Mauritania, 342, 343; Mauritius, 352; Morocco, 359, 361; Namibia, 375, 382, 387, 388; São Tomé and Príncipe, 428, 429; Senegal, 438, 440; Seychelles, 443, 447; Togo, 547; Western Sahara, 695

FLAM (Forces de Libération de Mauritanie), 339-40

FLEC (Frente de Liberatação do Enclave de Cabinda), 16

FLN (Front de Libération Nationale), Algeria, 4-7

Floods, 369, 512

Flour: mills, 343, 398; underground economy, 876

Fluorspar mining, Tunisia, 558

FNETU (Federation of Non European Trade Unions), 1028

FNLA (Frente Nacional de Libertação de Angola), 16, 17, 384, 487, 585, 703, 748, 754

Folio, Dan, 1074

Fomboni (Comoros), 113

Fon people, Benin, 25, 29

Foncha, John, 71

Fonka, Lawrence Shang, 73-74

Food and Canning Workers Union, South Africa, 1031, 1034

Food imports, 669, 927, 944; comparative figures, 636-37, 791-92, 794; increase of, 675-77; and military imports, 725; by country: Angola, 22; Botswana, 41; Central African Republic, 94; Comoros, 119; Congo, 127; Djibouti, 137; Egypt, 152, 155; Ethiopia, 175; Gambia, 197-98; Ghana, 209, 212, 214; Guinea-Bissau, 233; Kenya, 262; Lesotho, 273; Liberia, 284; Libya, 296; Madagascar, 306; Mauritius, 352; Mauritania, 343; Morocco, 360; Mozambique, 371, 372; Nigeria, 410, 412, 920; São Tomé and Príncipe, 428; Seychelles, 447; Sierra Leone, 456, 458; Swaziland, 522; Tanzania, 532, 536; Zaire, 588, 593; Zambia, 604

Food processing, 654-55, 912; Angola, 21; Burkina Faso, 53; Chad, 109; Egypt, 153; Gambia, 197; Kenya, 262; Liberia, 285; Madagascar, 309; Malawi, 322; Mauritania, 343; Somalia, 470; South Africa, 496; Uganda, 572-73; Zaire, 590

Food production, 332, 456, 669, 921, 926-43, 944; comparative tables, 648-49, 652-53; decline of, 675-77; and famine, 927; OAU and, 691; SADCC and, 906; underground economy, 878-79; women's role, 1043-45

Food shortages, 10, 20, 108. See also Famine; Food imports

Foodstuffs, underground economy, 876, 880

Foot travel, 959

Forced labor, 316, 368, 675

Forces Armées Occidentales, Chad, 102

Foreign aid, 795; Commonwealth countries, 767; development assistance, 948-49; economic,

817-21; food, 792, 1008; Lomé
Convention, 773-74; refugee
assistance, 992-95, 998-99;
recipients: Burkina Faso, 51; Cape
Verde, 86; Chad, 108, 927;
Comoros, 116, 117, 119; Djibouti,
137; Egypt, 152, 153; Equatorial
Guinea, 164, 166, 167; Ethiopia,
177; Gambia, 193; Guinea, 224,
226; Guinea-Bissau, 231, 233;
Liberia, 282, 286; Libya, 292;
Madagascar, 306; Malawi, 324;
Mali, 332; Mauritania, 342-44;
Mozambique, 371; Namibia, 389;
Niger, 397, 399; Rwanda, 420; São
Tomé and Príncipe, 428; Somalia,
470, 471; Sudan, 510-13; Tanzania,
534, 537; Togo, 549
Foreign debt, 669, 679, 718, 803,
829-30, 841-57; comparative
figures, 644-45, 794-95; and
export-led growth, 924; and health
services, 1005-6; Lomé
Conventions and, 778-79; military
spending and, 719; service costs,
812. *See also* Economy
Foreign fishing fleets, 447
Foreign investment, 806, 808, 814,
853, 917; ECOWAS and, 901-2;
and industrialization, 924; Lomé
Conventions and, 779. *See also*
Economy Zaire, 590-91
Foreign relations: labor issues,
1024-25; superpowers and, 706-15;
refugees and, 995-98
Foreign trade, 632-33, 638-39,
793-94. *See also* Economy
Forests, 935-36; exports, 794
Forna, Mohammed, 454, 455
FOSATU (Federation of South
African Trade Unions), 1031, 1034
Foster, Philip, 1097
Fostering, 977
Fouladou, 431
Fouta Djallon (state), 1074
Fouta Djallon highlands, 191, 217, 431

Fouta Djallon mountains, 327
Fouta Ferlo, 431
Fouta Toro, 1074
FPLM (Popular Forces for the
Liberation of Mozambique), 366
FPV (Front Progressiste Voltaïque), 47
Fragments (Ayi Kwei Armah), 1106
Franca, Arnaldo Vasconcellos, 83
France, 770, 772; Algerians in, 4; and
EC, 777; exports, 638-39; imports,
640-41; and trade unions, 1016; *aid
recipients*, 821; Central African
Republic, 92-93; Chad, 108, 295,
698-99; Comoros, 119; Djibouti,
137, 138; Guinea, 226; Mali, 332;
Mauritania, 341, 343; Niger, 397,
400; Rwanda, 420; Zaire, 585;
colonialism, 682, 707, 771,
1077-78; Algeria, 5-6; Benin, 39;
Burkina Faso, 48; Cameroon, 70;
Central African Republic, 91-93;
Chad, 102-3, 694, 697; Comoros,
115-16, 117; Djibouti, 135-36;
Gabon, 183; Guinea, 219-20; Islam
and, 1076-77; Ivory Coast, 238-39;
Mauritania, 340; Mauritius, 349;
Morocco, 357; Niger, 394-95;
Senegal, 434; Togo, 545; Tunisia,
554; *diplomatic relations*: Algeria,
7; Benin, 29; Burkina Faso, 50, 51;
Cameroon, 72, 73, 74; Chad, 104-7,
698; Egypt, 147; Equatorial Guinea,
164-65; Gabon, 184; Guinea, 221,
222; Ivory Coast, 240; Libya 292;
Madagascar, 305-6; Mali, 330, 331;
Mauritania, 340; Morocco, 357-58;
Mozambique, 370; Namibia, 386;
Niger, 395, 396; Senegal, 434, 437;
Tunisia, 554-55; Zaire, 587; *trade
relations*: Algeria, 9, 10, 11;
Angola, 20, 21; Benin, 30; Burkina
Faso, 53; Burundi, 63; Cameroon,
77-78; Central African Republic,
95; Chad, 109; Comoros, 119;
Congo, 129; Egypt, 154; Gambia,
198; Ghana, 204; Ivory Coast, 242;

Liberia, 286-87; Libya, 296, 298; Madagascar, 309; Mali, 333; Mozambique and, 371, 372; Niger, 397-98, 399; Nigeria, 411; Senegal, 440; Seychelles, 447; Sierra Leone, 459; South Africa, 496; Sudan, 514; Togo, 546; Tunisia, 558

Franceville (Gabon), 181

Francistown (Botswana), 36, 41

Franco-Mauritians, 348

Fraser, Malcolm, 762, 767

Free marketeering, 736

Free port, Djibouti, 136-37

Freedom Charter (ANC), 485, 490, 743

Freedom of press, 1123. *See also* Censorship of press

Freedoms, medical personnel and, 1004

Freetown (Sierra Leone), 451, 452, 454, 455, 457, 460, 461

Free-trade areas: CEAO, 898; UDEAC, 900; West Africa, 900

Frelimo (Frente de Libertação de Moçambique), 366-71, 374, 534, 681, 694, 704, 749, 755, 1104

French Equatorial Africa, 102, 124; Chad and, 697; Gabon, 183. *See also* Congo

French language: Algeria, 4, 11; Benin, 25, 31; Burkina Faso, 47; Burundi, 59, 65; Central African Republic, 90; Chad, 101; Comoros, 115; Congo, 123, 130; Djibouti, 133; Egypt, 143; Gabon, 181; Guinea, 219; Ivory Coast, 237, 243; Libya, 291; Madagascar, 304, 310; Mali, 328, 334; Mauritania, 339; Morocco, 356; Niger, 394; Rwanda, 415; Senegal, 433; Seychelles, 445, 448; Togo, 544; Tunisia, 553, 559; Zaire, 581

French people, 304, 356

French West Africa, 434

Fria (Guinea), 225

Fringe benefits, 1021-22

FRNSTP (São Tomé and Príncipe National Resistance Front), 427

Frolinat (Front de Libération Nationale du Tchad), 102, 103, 111, 295, 697-98, 1085

Front de Libération de la Côte des Somalis, 135, 136

Front Patriotique Oubanguien-Parti du Travail, 90

Frontline states, 39, 749

Fruit production, 127, 152, 260-61, 447, 475, 495, 522, 557, 588

Fuels, 959; charcoal, 936; exports, 634-35, 794; imports, 447, 457, 593, 636-37, 793, 794; underground economy, 876; wood, 949

Fula people, 192, 229

Fulani people, 47, 219, 327, 339, 401, 433, 452, 1085; jihads, 1074-75

Fulani-Peulh people, 393

Fundamentalism, Islamic, 143, 150, 357, 508, 511, 1079, 1081-85

Future outlook, 669-85; economic, 809-811; organized labor, 1025-26; regional cooperation, 909-11

Ga-Adangbe people, 202

Gabbia people, 249

Gabes (Tunisia), 551

Gabon, *180*, 181-89, 788, 802; agriculture, 646, 650; birth rate, 972; diplomatic relations, 72, 427; education, 664; food production, 648, 652; health figures, 658, 662; Muslims, 1068; OPEC membership, 1064; population, 626, 976; refugees, 991; tourism, 1117; *economy*: 185-86, 628, 644, 656, 804; currency, 643; employment figures, 630; foreign debt, 844; foreign trade, 632, 634, 636, 638, 640; manufacturing, 913; mineral exports, 919; oil exports, 774; wages, 1020-21

Gaborone (Botswana), 36, 39, 750, 752

Gadama, Aaron, 319-20
Galana River, 247
Galla people, 249, 1071
Gambia, *190*, 191-99, 802;
  agriculture, 646, 650;
  Commonwealth aid, 768;
  ECOWAS membership, 901; food
  production, 648, 652; free press,
  1123; health figures, 658; Muslims,
  1068, 1069; population, 626, 975;
  refugees, 991; road system, 956;
  and Senegal, 436; Senegambia,
  903-4; tourism, 1117; *economy*:
  196-98, 628, 644, 656, 804;
  currency, 642; employment figures,
  630; foreign debt, 842, 844; foreign
  trade, 638, 640; manufacturing,
  913; mineral exports, 919
Gambia river, 191, 193, 431
Game, illegal trade, 877
Game reserves, 1119
Ganja, 1063
Gara Djebelit (Algeria), 10
Garang, John, 510, 515, 700
Garoua (Cameroon), 67, 77
Gas: production, 8, 9, 76-77, 128, 153,
  298, 388, 438; reserves, 176, 371,
  420, 421, 537, 558
Gasoline, underground economy, 875
Gastil, Raymond G., 1123
Gastrow, Peter, 735
GATT (General Agreement on Tariff
  and Trade), 824n
Gazankulu (South Africa), 477
La Gazette (Cameroon), 1124
Gbalazeh, Emmanuel, 281
Gbaya people, 89
GDP, 798-99, 801, 1006; forecasts,
  809; and foreign debt, 842; least
  developed countries, 916;
  manufacturing, 913-14;
  underground economy, 879. *See
  also* Economy
Geba/Corubal River, 227
GECAMINES, 589, 590, 592, 593
Geldenhuys, Deon, 756

Gemstones, Tanzania, 537
General Workers Union, South Africa,
  1031, 1034
Genital mutilation, female, 1042,
  1048, 1061, 1062
Georgetown (Gambia), 191
German East Africa, 417
German East Africa Company, 529
German language, Togo, 544
Germanium deposits, 377
Germany, 250, 772; colonialism, 70,
  380-81, 417, 529-30, 544, 771; and
  EC, 781; exports, 638-39; financial
  aid, 821; imports, 640-41; and
  sanctions against South Africa, 779
Gezira region, Sudan, 512
Ghana, *200*, 201-16; 678, 688, 802,
  1074; agriculture, 646, 650; Akan
  society, 1042, 1051; Asante market
  women, 1046-47; censorship of
  press, 1109; Commonwealth aid,
  768; diplomatic relations, 51, 52,
  546, 765; ECOWAS membership,
  901, 902; education, 664, 1088-89,
  1091-96; food imports, 928; food
  production, 648, 652; health
  figures, 658, 662; labor relations,
  1016, 1022, 1024; marriage laws,
  1050; maternity leave, 1045;
  military budget, 721n; Muslims,
  1068; population, 626, 660, 975,
  986; refugees, 991; road system,
  956; tourism, 1117; trade unions,
  1018, 1019, 1021, 1026;
  unemployment, 1023; *economy*:
  209-14, 628, 644, 654, 656, 804,
  819, 852, 917; currency, 642, 828;
  employment figures, 630; farm
  credits, 1044; foreign debt, 844;
  foreign trade, 632, 634, 636, 638,
  640; imports, 922; industry, 913,
  915, 916; mineral exports, 919;
  reform of, 808; underground
  economy, 873-74
Ghana Democratic Movement, 204
Ghannounchi, Rached, 553, 1083

Ghazala, Abdel Halim Abu, 157
Ghys, Roger "Commandant Charles,"
    120
Gio people, 279
Girl Guides, 1012
Giscard d'Estaing, Valéry, 95, 222
Gisenye (Rwanda), 415
Gitega (Burundi), 59
Giwa, Dele, 1129
Giza (Egypt), 143
Glass manufacture, 371
Gleneagles Agreement, 766
Glycol production, Libya, 297
GNP, 798; comparative tables,
    628-29; and health services, 1006;
    See also Economy
GNPP (Greater Nigeria People's
    Party), 409
Gold: deposits, 30, 109, 128, 167,
    185, 451, 475, 483, 514, 589;
    discovery, South Africa, 859;
    smuggling, 873, 876-80;
    production: Burkina Faso, 53;
    Burundi, 64; Central African
    Republic, 94-95; Ethiopia, 176;
    Ghana, 204, 211, 212; Guinea, 225;
    Liberia, 285; Mali, 332-33; South
    Africa, 495-97; Tanzania, 534, 537;
    Zimbabwe, 617
Gold Coast, 205, 1015; See also Ghana
Goldberg, Dennis, 486
Golden City Post (South Africa),
    1125-26
Goma, Louis Sylvain, 131
Gomina, Fousseni, 29
Gonder (Ethiopia), 169
Gongola River, Nigeria, 401
Gorbachev, Mikhail, 174, 712
Gouled, Hassan, 136
Goumba, Abel, 90, 92
Gourad, Barkat, 139
Gourmantche people, 47
Gourounsi people, 47
Government administration, Niger,
    399

Government budgets, 795-96;
    reductions, 814
Government control: of economy,
    805-8, 815-16, 851, 866-69,
    882-89, 921; banking, 870;
    agricultural policies, 941-42; labor
    issues, 1019-24; trade unions,
    1016-18, 1033-39; and
    underground economy, 881; of
    media, 1124-27
Government structure: Algeria, 4-5;
    Angola, 15-17; Benin, 27;
    Botswana, 36-37; Burkina Faso, 47;
    Burundi, 59-61; Cameroon, 69-70;
    Cape Verde Islands, 83; Central
    African Republic, 90-91; Chad,
    101-2; Comoros, 115; Congo,
    123-24; Djibouti, 133-35; Egypt,
    143-46; Equatorial Guinea, 162;
    Ethiopia, 170-72; Gabon, 182-83;
    Gambia, 192-93; Ghana, 203-4;
    Guinea, 219; Guinea-Bissau,
    229-30; Ivory Coast, 237-38;
    Kenya, 249-50; Lesotho, 269-71;
    Liberia, 280-81; Libya, 291-92;
    Madagascar, 304-5; Malawi,
    314-16; Mali, 328-29; Mauritania,
    339-40; Mauritius, 348-49;
    Morocco, 356-57; Mozambique,
    366-67; Namibia, 379; Niger, 394;
    Nigeria, 404; Rwanda, 417; São
    Tomé and Príncipe, 425-26;
    Senegal, 433-34; Seychelles, 445;
    Sierra Leone, 452-54; Somalia,
    465-66; South Africa, 479-82;
    Sudan, 507-8; Swaziland, 519-21;
    Tanzania, 528-29; Togo, 544;
    Tunisia, 553-54; Uganda, 563-64;
    Zaire, 581-83; Zambia, 598-600;
    Zimbabwe, 609-10
Governments, oppressive, 669-70
Gowon, Yakubu, 407, 408, 1056
GPC (General People's Congress),
    Libya, 291
GPP (Gambia People's Party), 193,
    196

Graham, Efua, vii; "Women in Africa," 1041-52

Grain production, 927-29

Gran Caldera, 159

Grande Comore (Comoros), 113, 117, 119, 120

Grape production, 309

Grazing land, Botswana, 40

Great Britain, 855; aid recipients, 273, 576, 614, 767; and Asante empire, 205; and EC, 770, 772, 781; and EDF, 773; exports, 638; financial aid, 821; imports, 640-41; nationalization, 888; road system, 957, 961; and SADCC, 905; and sanctions against South Africa, 757, 762, 763, 764, 779; and trade unions, 1015-16; *colonialism*: 682, 694, 707, 771, 1077-78; Botswana, 38; Cameroon, 70; Egypt, 1074; Ethiopia, 701; Gambia, 193; Kenya, 250-51, 253; Libya, 292-93; Malawi, 316; Mauritius, 348, 349, 350; Namibia, 380; Nigeria, 406; Seychelles, 446; Somalia, 466; South Africa, 482-84, 859-60; Sudan, 509, 699; Swaziland, 520; Tanzania, 530; Uganda, 565; *diplomatic relations*: Egypt, 146-47; Kenya, 255, 258; Libya, 294, 296; Mauritius, 350; Mozambique, 370; Namibia, 386; Nigeria, 408, 693; Rhodesia, 764; Uganda, 567; Zimbabwe, 612, 615; *trade relations*: Angola, 21; Botswana, 42; Cape Verde, 86; Egypt, 154; Gambia, 198; Ghana, 204, 213; Kenya, 261; Lesotho, 274; Liberia, 287; Libya, 298; Malawi, 323; Nigeria, 417; Seychelles, 447; Sierra Leone, 459; Somalia, 470; South Africa, 496, 497; Sudan, 514; Swaziland, 523; Tunisia, 558; Zambia, 604; Zimbabwe, 617

Great Karroo plain, 473

Great Rift Valley, 247, 313, 579

Great Scarcie River, 451

Great Zimbabwe ruins, 1118

Greater Morocco policy, 358

Greece, 771, 781

Grek Orthodox Church, 581

Green, Reginald, 759

Green Book, Qadhafi, 293, 301, 1082

Green March, 358

Greenville (Liberia), 285

Grey Zulu, A., 606

Grindlays Bank, 866, 961

Grootfontein (Namibia), 377

Groundnut oil, 398, 930

Groundnut production, 929-30; Burkina Faso, 45, 53; Cape Verde, 85; Gambia, 193, 196-97; Guinea-Bissau, 232, 233; Mali, 332, 333; Niger, 395, 397, 399; Senegal, 437; Sudan, 512; Togo, 543, 547; Uganda, 573, 575; Zaire, 588

Group Areas Act, South Arica, 485, 491, 733, 737

Growth, economic, 798-801

Growth of population, 626-27, 970-77

Grunitsky, Nicholas, 545- 550

Grusi people, 202

GSRP (Gambia Socialist Revolutionary Party), 195

GTUC (Ghana Trades Union Congress), 1016, 1019

Guan people, 202

Guano works, Namibia, 375

Guban (burned) lands, 463

Guerrilla activity, 1009; Horn area, 682-83; puppet armies, 754; Western Sahara, 696; *by country:* Chad, 697; Mozambique, 369, 372; Namibia, 384; Rhodesia, 612-14; South Africa, 487, 744-47; Sudan, 699; Uganda, 570-72; Zimbabwe, 613-14

Guerrilla groups, 369, 372, 467, 468, 479, 556, 582

Guinea, 217-26, *218*, 670, 802; agriculture, 646, 650; diplomatic relations, 231, 282-84, 331, 437, 454, 456; education, 664, 1092; food production, 648, 652; health figures, 658, 662; Muslims, 1068, 1069, 1077-79; population, 626, 660, 975; refugees 991, 994-95; road system, 956; trade unions, 1017; *economy:* 224-26, 628, 644, 656, 804; currency, 642; employment figures, 630; foreign debt, 844; foreign trade, 632, 636, 638, 640; manufacturing, 913, 916; mineral exports, 919; underground economy, 874-75

Guinea corn, Burkina Faso, 45

Guinea-Bissau, 227-34, *228*, 681, 802, 1104-5; agriculture, 646, 650; diplomatic relations, 83, 84, 437; ECOWAS membership, 901; food production, 648, 652; health figures, 658; Muslims, 1068; population, 626, 970, 975; refugees, 991; tourism, 1118; trade unions, 1017; *economy:* 231-33, 628, 644, 656, 804; currency, 642; employment figures, 630; foreign debt, 842, 844; foreign trade, 198, 632, 638, 640; manufacturing, 913, 916; mineral exports, 919

Guinea-Bussau Bafatá Resistance Movement, 229

Gulf of Guinea, 401

Gulf of Suez, oil, 153

Gulu (Uganda), 561, 563

Gum arabic, 512, 513

Gumede, Archie, 480, 490

GUNT (Gouvernement d'Union Nationale de Transition), Chad, 101-7, 111-12

Gurma people, 202

Guthrie, Peter, vii; "Road Transportation in Africa," 953-66

Guyana, and South Africa, 763

Gweru (Zimbabwe), 609

Gypsum deposits, 322, 344, 397

Gypsum production, 537

Habré, Hissène, 101, 103-7, 111, 295, 587, 698-99, 1085

Habyarimana, Juvénal, 418-20, 422

Hachim, Said Hassan Said, 117

Hadj, Messali, 6

Haidalla, Khouna, 341-42

Haidalla, Mohammed Khouna, 345

Haile Selassie, 172, 466, 467, 682, 688

Haiti, 780-81

Hall, Richard, 1130

Hamalliyya, 1077, 1079

Hamid, Seif Sharif, 533

Hamitic people, 170, 248, 249

Hamiz River, 3

Hammamet (Tunisia), 551, 558

Hanlon, Joseph, vii, 704; "South Africa's War on its Neighbors," 748-61

Harare (Zimbabwe), 607, 609, 611, 619, 752; banking, 862; press, 1130; tourism, 1118

Haratin people, 341

Harbors. *See* Port cities

Hardwood production, 94, 185. *See also* Forests

Harer (Ethiopia), 169

Hargeysa (Somalia), 463, 468, 470

Harmattan winds, 201, 279, 403

Harper (Liberia), 285

Harrell-Bond, Barbara E., vii; "Refugees in Africa," 988-1001

Hashish, 1063-64

Hassan II, King of Morocco, 8, 293, 357-59, 361, 362-63, 683, 688, 694, 696

Hassan, Muhammad Abdille, 1077

Hassan, Yusuf, 258

Hassan Gouled Aptidon, 135, 139

Hassaniya-speaking Arabs, 339

Hausa people, 393, 403, 1074, 1085; education, 1089

Hausa-Fulani people, 403, 406, 407

Hauts Plateaux (Madagascar), 303

Hawiya people, 465
Hazlewood, Arthur, vii-viii; "African Regionalism," 890-911
Healers, Muslim, 1060
Health services, 662-63, 797, 1002-13; Christianity and, 1058; South African attacks on, 760-61; for women, 1047-48, 1050; *by country*: Benin, 31; Botswana, 43; Burkina Faso, 54-55; Burundi, 64; Cameroon, 78; Cape Verde, 86; Central African Republic, 96; Chad, 109-10; Comoros, 119; Congo, 129; Egypt, 156; Gabon, 187; Gambia, 193, 198; Ghana, 206, 214; Guinea, 226; Guinea-Bissau, 233; Ivory Coast, 242-43; Kenya, 263-64; Lesotho, 275; Liberia, 287; Libya, 299; Madagascar, 310; Malawi, 324; Mali, 333-34; Morocco, 362; Namibia, 382, 389; Niger, 399; Nigeria, 412; São Tomé and Príncipe, 429; Senegal, 440-41; Seychelles, 447, 448; Sierra Leone, 459-60; Somalia, 471; South Africa, 499; Sudan, 514-15; Swaziland, 523; Tanzania, 538-39; Togo, 549; Tunisia, 559; Zaire, 593; Zambia, 604; Zimbabwe, 618
Heavy industry, 912
Hehe people, 528
Heikum people, 378
Helwan steel complex, 153
Hendrickse, Helenard Joe (Allan), 481, 488, 503, 737
Herero Chiefs Council, 382
Herero people, 377-80
Het Volk Party, 484
Heunis, Chris, 732
Hewitt, Adrian, viii; "The European Community and Africa," 770-83
Hide processing, 53, 333
High-income oil countries, 787-801

Higher education, 664-65, 797, 1091-92, 1097-98. *See also* Education; Universities
Highways. *See* Road systems
Himba people, 378
Hindus, 348, 349, 477, 609
Hlengwe people, 609
HNP (Herstigte Nasionale Party), 481, 487, 492
Hoarau, Gabriel, 446
Hoare, "Mad" Mike, 446
Hodd, Michael, viii; "A Survey of the African Economies," 787-810
Hoggar mountains, 3
Holy Spirit movement, 571-72
Homelands. *See* Bantustans
Homosexuality, 1061
Hong Kong, 924
Honwana, Luis Bernardo, 1109
Horn of Africa, 682-83, 709; drought, 930; drug abuse, 1063; Islam, 1071; refugees, 990; superpower relations, 710, 712-13; warfare, 694
Hospitals, 1003-4, 1012. *See also* Health services
Hottentots, 378, 472, 476
Houni, Abdul Moneim al-, 292
Houphouët-Boigny, Félix, 52, 237, 238-40, 245, 394-95, 688, 697, 853
Housing: Algeria, 11; Benin, 31; Botswana, 42-43; Burkina Faso, 54; Congo, 129; Djibouti, 138; Egypt, 156; Gambia, 198; Ivory Coast, 243; Kenya, 263; Lesotho, 275; Namibia, 389-90; Nigeria, 412, 866; São Tomé and Príncipe, 429; Senegal, 440; Sierra Leone, 460; South Africa, 499, 737, 1033; Zambia, 604; Zimbabwe, 618, 862
Houtondji, Jean, 29
Huambo (Angola), 15
Human rights, medical personnel and, 1004
Humbe people, 15
Hungary, Ivory Coast and, 240
Hunger. *See* Famine

Hussein, Karim, "Refugees in Africa," 988-1001
Hutchful, Eboe, viii; "Militarization and Economic Development in Africa," 716-29
Hutu people, 59, 61-62, 66, 415, 417-18
Hwange (Zimbabwe), 609
Hydroelectric power, 949; Burkina Faso, 53; Cameroon, 77; Congo, 121; Ethiopia, 176; Guinea-Bissau, 233; Liberia, 285; Mozambique, 371; Nigeria, 401; Rwanda, 420; Senegal, 439; South Africa, 475; Uganda, 561, 573, 576; Zaire, 590; Zambia, 597; Zimbabwe, 616

Ibadan (Nigeria), 403
Ibibio people, 403
Ibn Badis, 1079
Ibo people, 403, 404, 407, 693, 1056, 1085
Ibrahim, Waziri, 409
IBRD (International Bank for Reconstruction and Development), 849
Ibru, Alex, 1129
ICARA (International Conferences on Assistance to Refugees in Africa), 994
Iceland, Cape Verde and, 85
ICFTU (International Confederation of Free Trade Unions), 708, 1024
ICU (Industrial and Commercial Workers Union), South Africa, 1028
IDASA (Institute for a Democratic Alternative in South Africa), 736
Ideology, religious, 1053
Idiagbon, Tunde, 409
Idris, Muhammad al-, King of Libya, 292, 293
IFAA (Institute for African Alternatives), 832, 837
Ife (Nigeria), 406
Igbo people, 1042
Igue, O. J., 872-73

Ijaw people, 403
Ikejiani, O., 1087
Ikhwan (Muslim Brotherhood), 1083
Illegal aliens, expelled from Nigeria, 409
Illegal trade. See Underground economy
Illiteracy, 1091-93, 1096; See also Education; Literacy
Ilmenite deposits, 309
ILO (International Labor Office), 1017
Imatong Mountains, 505
IMF (International Monetary Fund), 644-45; 779, 795, 811-39, 846-47; adjustment programs, 718, 727; conditionality, 850-51; and debt crisis, 848-49; and economic reform, 808; and labor issues, 1021; and social services, 1006; and unemployment, 1023; and state control of economy, 887-88; structural adjustment facility, 820-21, 848-49, 854-55. See also Economy
Immigrants, Liberia, 280
Immorality Act, South Africa, 485, 491
Immunization programs, 310, 1012
Imperialism, economic, 671-72
Imports, 636-39, 792-94, 774, 800, 820, 922-23; and economic reform, 818; food, 669, 675-77; forecasts, 809; and foreign debt, 846; military, 719, 721, 722, 724; mineral producing countries, 917; oil, Zimbabwe, 616; power, Niger, 397. See also Economy
Import-substitution industries, 398, 470, 807, 912, 918, 921
Incomes, 790, 863; and foreign debt, 846; intra-family distribution, 1007. See also Economy
Indaba, 738-39
Independence, 672, 706-7, 748, 1102-12; Islam and, 1078-79;

refugees, 996-97; South Africa and, 681; trade unions and, 1015

Independent African States, Accra conference, 688

Independent Party, South Africa, 732, 735

India, 765, 788; agriculture, 940; aid to Africa, 767; and South Africa, 763

Indian Ocean: tourism, 1121-22; U.S. Navy, 709

Indian people, 445, 452; Islamic, 1078; South Africa, 476, 481, 736-37

Indigenization, 882

Indigenous religion, 1053-55. *See also* Traditional religion

Indirect rule, colonial, Islam and, 1075, 1077-78

Indo-Mauritian people, 347-48

Indonesia, 118, 308, 1064

Industrial Conciliation Act, South Africa, 1027, 1029, 1031, 1034

Industrial countries, economy, 787-801, 809

Industrial development, 912-25

Industrial relations, 1016-18. *See also* Trade unions

Industrial revolution, slave trade and, 858-59

Industrial Workers of Africa, 1028

Industrialization, 10, 127, 371, 815, 1014; cooperative plans, 910; Lagos Plan of Action, 909; Lomé Convention and, 774; state control, 806; South Africa, 1028-29; women and, 1045

Industry, 791; development of, 671-72, 887; employment figures, 630-31; employment of women, 1045; government policies, 882-83; military, 721-22; minimum wage, 1020; SADCC and, 906. *See also* Economy

Inequalities in education, 1094-96

Infant mortality, 658-59, 797-98, 972, 974-76, 978, 1002-3, 1004, 1011-12; civil war and, 1010; reduction of, 931; South African destabilization and, 760-61. *See also* Health services

Infectious diseases, 1003, 1012

Infitah policy, Egypt, 153

Inflation, 718, 798-801, 807, 1021; and foreign aid, 774; forecasts, 809; military spending and, 719, 722. *See also* Economy

Informal economy, 871n; of women, 1046. *See also* Underground economy

Infrastructure, 953-66; Central African Republic, 95; Chad, 108; Congo, 128; Egypt, 152; Equatorial Guinea, 165; Gambia, 197; Ghana, 211; Mali, 332; Morocco, 359; Mozambique, 372; Namibia, 389; Sierra Leone, 457; South Africa, 483

Inga Dam, Zaire, 590

Ingram, Derek, viii; "Africa and the Commonwealth," 762-69

Inhambane (Mozambique), 366

Inkatha, 481, 489-90, 492, 737-40, 1032, 1036

INM (Imbokodvo National Movement), Swaziland, 519-20

Insurance business, 448

Integration, economic, 890-911

Intellectualism, 1106-9

Interest rates, 803, 812, 855; Tanzania, 867, 868; Zimbabwe, 863

Intermediary role of states, 884-85

Internal security, 727, 728

International Court of Justice (ICJ), 358, 695; and Namibia, 379, 381, 383, 703

International Development Association (IDA), 820, 824n, 834; and Chad, 108; and Uganda, 574

International Finance Corporation, 824n

International financial center,
Mauritius, 352
International Monetary Fund. *See* IMF
International monetary system, 838;
reforms, 836
International organizations, and
refugees, 1000
The Interpreters (Wole Soyinka),
1106-7
Interstate relations, refugees and,
995-98
Investment, 792-93, 799; external
support, 817-21; manufacturing,
914; military spending and, 719.
See also Economy; Foreign
investment
Iran, 117, 469, 556, 709, 751, 1064-65
Iraq, 151, 155
Ireland, 770, 771
Iron: industry, 21; 285, 496, 616;
mining, 10, 128, 225, 235, 340-44,
438, 455, 458, 558; *deposits*: Benin,
30; Cameroon, 77; Central African
Republic, 94; Chad, 109; Congo,
1281; Gabon, 185; Libya, 297;
Mali, 333; Mauritania, 337;
Namibia, 377; Niger, 397; Sierra
Leone, 451, 457; South Africa, 475
Ironsi (Ibo General), 407
Irrigation, 792; Algeria, 3; Burkina
Faso, 45; Mali, 332; Mauritania,
343; Morocco, 360; Nigeria, 411;
Somalia, 470; Sudan, 505, 512;
Swaziland, 517; Tunisia, 557;
Zimbabwe, 607
Isaka Seme, P. K., 687
Isaq people, 465, 467, 468
Isis oil field, Tunisia, 557
Islam, African, 1058, 1067-86; and
Christianity, 1053-54, 1056-58;
drug use, 1063; education, 1089;
fundamentalist, 143, 150, 357, 508,
511, 1079, 1081-85; and OPEC,
1064-65. *See also* Religion
Islambouli, Khalid, 150
Islamic Call society, 1083

Islamic Jihad, 556
Islamic law, 340, 405, 700
Islamic Liberation Party (Tunisia),
1084
Islamic militants, Senegal, 435
Islamic National Front, Sudan, 508,
516
Islamization, 1070-75, 1082
Ismailia (Egypt), 142
Israel, 294, 691, 725, 1079;
diplomatic relations: Cameroon,
73; Egypt, 147, 148-51; Equatorial
Guinea, 165; Ivory Coast, 240;
Lesotho, 273; Liberia, 282; Libya,
293; Malawi, 321; Morocco, 357;
Togo, 546; Tunisia, 555; Uganda,
567, 568; Zaire, 587
Issa people, 133, 135-36, 139
Istiqlal, 357, 1079
Italian East Africa, 466
Italian language, 170, 465
Italy, 576, 781, 821; colonialism, 172,
292, 466, 682, 701, 771; *trade
relations*: Algeria, 10; Angola, 20;
Chad, 109; Sudan, 514; Tanzania,
538; Congo, 129; Egypt, 154;
Liberia, 286-87; Libya, 296, 298;
Nigeria, 411; Seychelles, 447;
Somalia, 470
Iteso people, 563
Itumbi (Tanzania), 612
Ivory, smuggling, 876, 877
Ivory Coast, 52, 235-45, 236, 546,
679, 802; agriculture, 646, 650,
917; CEAO membership, 898;
deforestation, 935-36, 944;
diplomatic relations, 52, 209,
394-95, 1079; ECOWAS
membership, 900; education, 664,
1092; food imports, 928; food
production, 648, 652; health
figures, 658, 662; marriage laws,
1050; Muslims, 1068; population,
626, 660, 975, 986; refugees, 988,
991, 995; tourism, 1115, 1117;
trade relations, 53, 333, 440; urban

primacy, 982; *economy*: 240-42, 628, 644, 654, 656, 804, 812; currency, 643; employment figures, 630; foreign debt, 842-44, 847, 850, 853; foreign trade, 632, 634, 636, 638, 640; imports, 922; industry, 915, 924; manufacturing, 913; mineral exports, 919; smuggling, 873; unemployment, 1023; wages, 1020-21

Jabavu, D. D. T., 687
Jagersfontein (South Africa), 475
Jalloud, Abdel Salem Ahmed, 299-300
Jamahiriya, 1092
Jaona, Monja, 305, 311
Japan, 771; exports, 638; financial aid, 397, 821; imports, 640-41; and South Africa, 757; *trade relations*: Algeria, 10; Egypt, 154; Ghana, 213; Liberia, 287; Libya, 298; Malawi, 323; Mozambique, 372; Niger, 395; Sierra Leone, 459; South Africa, 496, 497; Sudan, 514; Zambia, 604
Jawara, Dawda Kairaba, 194-96, 199, 436, 930, 1054
Jebel Akhdar (Libya), 289
Jebel Marra (Sudan), 505-7
Jebel Nefousa (Libya), 289
Jeffy, Paul, 283
Jehovah's Witnesses, 314
Jerba Island (Tunisia), 558
Jeune Afrique, 1128
Jewish people, 143, 356, 477, 553, 609
Jewish religion, Zaire, 581
Jihads, 1074-75, 1077
Jinja (Uganda), 563, 1059
Joffe, George, viii; "Islam in Africa," 1067-86
Johannesburg (South Africa), 476, 477, 1030, 1036
John Paul II, Pope, 307, 1060
Johnson-Sirleaf, Ellen, 283
Joint banks, Nigeria, 864-65
Joint financing funds, 849

Jonathan, Leabua, 269, 271-72, 276, 752-53
Jong River, 451
Jonglei Canal, 510, 700
Jordan, Egypt and, 151
Jos plateau, 403
Journalism, 1123-27
JRDA (Jeunesse de la Révolution Démocratique Africaine), Guinea, 220
Juba (Sudan), 507
Jubba River, 463, 469, 470
Jugnauth, Anerood, 348, 350, 353
Jumbe, Aboud, 531, 532
Jusu-Sheriff, Salia, 455, 461
Juxon-Smith, Andrew, 454
Jwaning (Botswana), 41

Kabila, Laurent, 582
Kabale (Uganda), 561
Kabre people, 544
Kabwe (Zambia), 598
Kabylia (Algeria), riots, 1084
Kadile, Clements, 1028
KADU (Kenya African Democratic Union), 249, 253
Kaduna (Nigeria), 865
Kaduna River, 401
Kadzamira, Cecilia, 319, 325
Kaédi (Mauritania), 337
Kafue River, 597
Kagera Basin Organization, 420
Kaggia, Bilad, 253
Kainji Dam, 401
Kakwa people, 568
Kalabule (black market), 873
Kalahari Desert, 35, 36, 41, 375, 475
Kalana (Mali), 332-33
Kalanga people, 621
Kalenjin people, 249, 254, 255
Kamara, Abubakar, 461
Kamau, John, 258
Kamba, Dr., 1097-98
Kamba people, 248, 249, 250
Kambia (Sierra Leone), 452
Kambona, Oscar, 529

Kamil, Abdallah, 139
Kamina (Zaire), 587
Kamiriithu Educational, Cultural and
   Community Centre, 1108
Kamougoué, Abdelkader, 104, 106
Kamougoué, Wadal Abdelkader, 111
Kampala (Uganda), 563, 1059; travel
   facilities, 1121
Kamuyambeni, Grey, 316
Kananga (Zaire), 581
KaNgwane (South Africa), 477
Kanifing (Gambia), 192
Kankan (Guinea), 219
Kano, Alhai Aminu, 409
Kano (Nigeria), 403, 406
Kanu, Hassan Gbassay, 456
KANU (Kenya African National
   Union), 249, 252, 253-58, 265
Kanuri people, 403
Kaolack (Senegal), 431
Kaolin production, 537
Kaonde people, 598
Kapwepwe, Simon, 601
Karakul sheep, Namibia, 377, 382,
   387, 388
Karamojong people, 563
Karanja, Josephat, 258, 265
Karefa-Smart (Sierra Leone
   politician), 454
Kariba Dam, 607, 1118
Karim, Muhammad bin Abd al-, 1077
Karimou, Abodel, 1124
Kariuki, J. M., 255
Karoo plains, 473, 475
Karume, Abeid, 531
Kasai River, 13, 590
Kasai/Kwango/Lulua River, 579
Kasavubu, Joseph, 583, 584, 594-95
Kathrada, Ahmed, 486
Katsina (Nigeria), 406
Katumba, Ahmed, 575
KAU (Kenyan African Union), 251
Kaunda, Kenneth David, 39, 599,
   600-602, 603, 605-6, 883, 1055-56
Kavango people, 378
Kawawa, Rashidi, 530, 531

Kayès (Mali), 327, 439
Kayibanda, Grégoire, 418
Kayiira, Andrew, 569, 570-72
Kayira, Legson, 1110
Keiriku people, 378
Kéita, Mobido, 329-31, 688
Kemal, Ali, Prince of Comoros, 116
Kenema (Sierra Leone), 452
Kengo wa Dondo, 586
Kenya, *246*, 247-66, 534, 673, 677,
   709, 750n, 802, 945; age of
   population, 981; agriculture, 646,
   650, 917; AIDS, 1062;
   antidesertification projects, 950;
   birth rate, 972, 1006-7; currency,
   642; desktop publishing, 1127;
   diplomatic relations, 418, 466, 569,
   571; drug abuse, 1063; EAC treaty,
   895-96; education, 664, 1092,
   1095-96; family planning, 1048;
   female circumcision, 1048; food
   production, 648, 652; health
   figures, 658, 662; literary
   suppression, 1111; military
   spending, 717; Muslims, 1068;
   population, 626, 660, 970, 975,
   986; press, 1124, 1131; refugees,
   988, 991, 996; road system, 956;
   tourism, 1113, 1115, 1116,
   1119-20; trade relations, 119, 420,
   574; trade unions, 1017, 1018;
   women's status, 1045; 1046;
   economy, 260-63, 628, 644, 654,
   656, 804, 819, 916-17; banking
   headquarters, 866; employment
   figures, 630; foreign debt, 842, 845;
   foreign trade, 632, 634, 636, 638,
   640; imports, 922; industry, 913,
   915, 924; mineral exports, 919;
   underground economy, 876
Kenyatta, Jomo, 252, 253-55, 687
Kerekou, Mathieu, 27-29, 32-33
Kesselly, Edward, 280, 283
Kgosana, Philip, 747
Khalil, Abdallah, 509
Khama, Seretse, 37-40

Khama, Tshekedi, 38
Khama I, ruler of Botswana, 37-38
Khanga, Melvin, 320, 321
Khartoum (Sudan), 505, 507, 514
Khashoggi, Adnan, 510
Khatmiyya *Tariqa*, 1071, 1078, 1082
Khoi people, 378
Khoi-San people, 15, 35-37, 476, 482
Khung people, 378
Khutse Wildlife Park, 35
Kibaki, Mwai, 255-58, 265
Kigali (Rwanda), 415, 421
Kigeri V, Mwami of Rwanda, 418
Kikongo language, 15, 123
Kikuyu people, 248-56, 258
Killick, Tony, viii-ix; "Africa, the
    International Monetary Fund and
    the World Bank: Adjustment and
    Finance," 811-22
Kilwa, 1071, 1072
Kimathi, Dedan, 252, 257-58
Kimbanguist Church, 581, 594
Kimberley (South Africa), 475, 477,
    483
Kimbundu language, 15
Kinshasa (Zaire), 581, 583, 585, 590,
    593, 876-77, 982
Kinyarwanda language, 415
Kipsigis people, 249
Kirunda, John Luwuliza, 570
Kirundi language, 59, 64
Kirya, Balaki, 570
Kisangani (Zaire), 581
Kisekka, Samson, 571, 578
Kismaayo (Somalia), 463, 470
Kissi people, 248, 452, 460
Kissinger, Henry, 711
Kisumu (Kenya), 248, 254
Kiswahili language, 415
Kivu (Zaire), 876, 878-79
Kiwanuka, Benedicto, 565
KNDP (Cameroon), 71
Koffiefontein (South Africa), 475
Kohl, Helmut, 74
Koinange Mbiyu, 255, 687
Koka Dam Conference, 511

Kola nut, 1063
Kolingba, André, 90, 92-93, 95-97
Kolwezi (Zaire), 581, 585
Koma, Kenneth, 36, 38, 40, 44
Komati River, 517
Komoé River, 235
Kompienga Dam, 53
Kone, Ibrahima, 50
Kongo people, 15, 581
Konkouré River Dam, 225
Kono people, 452
Korambo people, 452
Koranic schools, 334, 1089
Korea, Libya and, 298
Koroma, Alhaji Abdul Karim, 461-62
Kotiga, André, 105
Kouandété (Benin Major), 28
Koudougou (Burkina Faso), 45, 53
Kougaberge range, 473
Kouilou River, 121
Koulamallah, Abderaman, 102
Koumba Mbadinga, Max Anicet, 188
Kountché, Seyni, 395-96
Kouyou people, 125
Kpelle people, 279
Kpolleh, William Gabriel, 280, 281,
    283
KPU (Kenya People's Union), 250,
    254
Krio language, 452
Kru people, 237, 279
Kudu gas field, Namibia, 388
Kuhangua, Jacob, 382
Kumasi (Ghana), 202
Kunene River, 375, 377
Kuntaur (Gambia), 191
Kuria people, 248
Kutako (Herero Chief), 382
Kuwait, and Sudan, 510
Kwa people, 202
KwaLuthi people, 378
KwaMbi people, 378
Kwame Nkrumah Revolutionary
    Guards, 204
KwaNatal Indaba, 738-39
KwaNdebele (South Africa), 477, 490

KwaNgali people, 378
Kwangu-Kwilu people, 581
KwaNjama people, 378
Kwanyama language, 15
KwaZulu (South Africa), 477, 489, 738-39
KwaZulu-Natal Indaba, 489

La Digue Island (Seychelles), 443
La Skhirra (Tunisia), 558
La'youn (Morocco), 359
Labor costs, Morocco, 361
Labor issues, South Africa, 1032-33
Labor legislation, South Africa, 733
Labor unions. See Trade unions
Labor Party, South Africa, 481
Labor unrest, 1016, 1019-24
Labor-based road-building, 961-66
Labour Party: Mauritius, 348, 349; Namibia, 379; South Africa, 736, 737
Labour Relations Act, South Africa, 1035
Lacaze, Jeannou, 587
Lagos (Nigeria), 403, 865, 982, 1116-17, 1118
Lagos Plan of Action, 691, 851, 892, 895, 908-9, 947
Lagu, Joseph, 699
Lake Albert, 561, 579
Lake Bisina, 561
Lake Chad, 89, 99, 109, 401
Lake Edward, 561, 579, 1120
Lake George, 561, 1120
Lake Kariba, 597, 607, 1118
Lake Kivu, 415, 420, 421, 579
Lake Kossou, 235
Lake Kwania, 561
Lake Kyoga, 561
Lake Malawi. See Lake Nyasa
Lake Mweru, 597
Lake Nasser, 141
Lake Nyasa (Malawi), 313, 316, 322, 365, 525
Lake Nyos disaster, 73
Lake Tana, 169

Lake Tanganyika, 59, 64, 525, 579
Lake Turkana, 247, 248, 1120
Lake Victoria, 247, 248, 250, 262, 525, 561, 563, 1120
Lake Volta, 201
Lakwena, Alice, 572, 1054, 1055
Lala, Idi, 90, 92
Lalibela (Ethiopia), 1121
Lall, Sanjaya, 882, 887
Lama Depression, Benin, 25
Lambarené (Gabon), 181, 1117
Lamizana, Aboubakar Sangoulé, 48-49, 56
Lamrani, Mohammed Karim, 356, 363
Land Act, South Africa, 483-84
Land Apportionment Act, Southern Rhodesia, 610-11
Land areas, 788-89
Land colonization, 986
Land distribution, 389, 476
Land reform, 61, 85, 147, 152, 175, 252, 253, 1044-45
Land use plans, 768
Langeberg range, 473
Lango people, 563, 567, 571, 1058
Languages, 970, 1093
LAP (Liberia Action Party), 280
Laraki, Moulay Ahmed, 356, 363
Larich oil field, Tunisia, 557
The Last of the Empire (Ousmane Sembene), 1110
Lateritic soil, 935, 936
Latin America, 781, 928, 977
Lawson, Nigel, 854-55
Laye, Camara, 1110
Lazarus, Neil, ix; "Literature and Politics in Africa," 1101-12
LD-MPT (Ligue Démocratique-Mouvement pour le Parti du Travail), Senegal, 434
Lead: deposits, 128, 185, 377, 597; mining, 10, 388, 558
League of Human Rights, Algeria, 5
League of Nations, and Namibia, 381, 703

Least-developed countries, 549, 774, 776, 947

Leballo, Potlako, 480

Lebanese people, 280, 452

Lebowa (South Africa), 477

Legal Age of Majority Act, Zimbabwe, 1050

Legal status of women, 1050-51

Legum, Colin, ix; "The Organization of African Unity," 686-92

Lekhanya, Justin, 269, 272-73, 276

Lenshina, Alice, 1055-56

Leon, Tony, 735

Leonard, Richard, 723

Leopard skins, 877

Léopoldville, 585. *See also* Kinshasa (Zaire)

Leribe (Lesotho), 269

Léro, Etienne, 688

Lesoma (Socialist League of Malawi), 315, 320

Lesotho, 267-77, *268*, 473, 680, 748, 802, 945; agriculture, 646, 650; education, 664, 1088, 1090; food imports, 928; food production, 648, 652; health figures, 658, 662; Muslims, 1068; population, 626, 660, 976; PTA membership, 908; refugees, 985, 988, 991; road system, 956; SACU membership, 906-7; and SADCC, 749, 905; South Africa and, 486, 489, 705, 752-53, 755, 757; travel facilities, 1119; *economy*: 273-75, 628, 644, 656, 804; currency, 642; employment figures, 630; foreign debt, 845; foreign trade, 638, 640; manufacturing, 913, 916

Less-developed countries, birth rates, 977

Letsie David, Prince of Lesotho, 276

Levantine people, 229

Leys, Colin, 916

Liberation movements, 369, 534, 602, 708, 748; Islam and, 1075

The Liberation of Guiné (Basil Davidson), 1101

Liberation wars, 601, 612-14

Liberia, *278*, 279-88, 546, 688, 802; agriculture, 646, 650; diplomatic relations, 455, 708, 1079; education, 664, 1092; food production, 648, 652; health figures, 658, 662; MRU membership, 900; Muslims, 1068; population, 626, 660, 975; refugees, 991; road system, 956; tourism, 117; *economy*: 284-87, 628, 644, 654, 656, 804, 843, 918; currency, 642; employment figures, 630; foreign debt, 844, 847; foreign trade, 632, 634, 636, 638, 640; imports, 922; manufacturing, 913, 917; mineral exports, 919; wages, 1021

Liberia Grand Coalition, 280-81, 283

Libreville (Gabon), 181, 183, 187

Libya, 289-301, *290*, 678, 688, 725; agriculture, 646, 650; Arab League, 1079; cities, 986; education, 664, 1092; and Egyptian workers, 155; food production, 648, 652; health figures, 658, 662; military spending, 717, 724; Muslims, 1068, 1069, 1076, 1080, 1082-83; population, 626, 660, 974; and Sudan, trade, 513; and Uganda, aid, 567; warfare, 693-94, 696, 697-99, 701; *diplomatic relations*: Algeria, 7; Burkina Faso, 52; Central African Republic, 90, 92, 93; Chad, 102-7, 683, 1085; Egypt, 149-50; Gabon, 184; Gambia, 195; Ghana, 107; Liberia, 282; Mauritania, 341, 343; Morocco, 357; Niger, 395; Senegal, 435, 437; Sudan, 509-10, 512; Tunisia, 555; *economy*: 296-98, 628, 644, 654, 656; currency, 642; employment figures, 630; foreign debt, 846; foreign trade, 632, 634, 636, 638, 640;

industry, 918; manufacturing, 913; mineral exports, 919

Life expectancy, 549, 658-59, 797-98, 931, 974-76, 978, 1002-6. *See also* Health Services

Light industry, 77, 241, 360, 912

Lilongwe (Malawi), 313, 314, 322

Lim, D., 720, 722

Limann, Hilla, 207, 216

Limba people, 452, 456, 461

Limestone: deposits, 30, 128; production, 77, 332

Limpopo River, 35, 473, 475, 607

Lingala language, 123

Lingani, Jean-Baptiste, 50, 51

LIPAD (Ligue Patriotique pour Développement), Burkina Faso, 50

Lissouba, Pascal, 125

Lister, Gwen, 1127

Literacy, 796-97, 1091-92; and birth rates, 977; female, 1049. *See also* Education

Literacy campaigns, 1049-50

Lithium deposits, Namibia, 377

Little Karroo plain, 473

Little Scarcie River, 451

Livestock production, 1008. *See also* Agriculture

Living standards, 790, 801, 811-12; conditionality and, 850-51; and economic reform, 818, 819; forecasts, 810; and foreign debt, 846; Uganda, 879

Livingstone, David, 316

Livingstone (Zambia), 598, 599

Livingstone Mountains, 525

LLA (Lesotho Liberation Army), 269, 271-72, 489

Lloyds Bank of Britain, 861

Lobamba (Swaziland), 520

Lobatse (Botswana), 41

Lobi-Dagari people, 47

Lobito (Angola), 15, 750

Local self-government, 684

Locust plagues, 10, 41, 231, 397, 438

Lodge, Tom, ix: "South African Politics," 730-47

Lofchie, Michael F., ix; "Africa's Agrarian Malaise," 926-43

Logone River, 99

Loko people, 452

Lokoja (Nigeria), 401

Loma Mountains, 451

Lomami River, 579

Lomé (Togo), 398, 543, 544, 547

Lomé Convention, 177, 222, 274, 470, 522, 679, 767-68, 770-82

Lomponda wa Bontende, 587

London Club, 847

Long-distance trade, precolonial, 858

Loubomo (Congo), 121

Low-income countries, 788

Loxley, John, ix; "The African Debt Crisis," 841-57

Lozi people, 598

LPAI (Ligue Populaire Africaine pour l'Indépendance), Djibouti, 135-36

LPP (Liberian People's Party), 281

LSP (Liberal Socialist Party), Egypt, 145

Lualaba River, 579

Luanda (Angola), 15, 17, 22, 752, 1119

Luanda people, Islam, 1072

Luangwa River, 597

Luanshya (Zambia), 598

Luapula River, 597

Luba/Lulua/Songe people, 581

Lubango (Angola), 15

Lubumbashi (Zaire), 581

Luckham, Robin, 717

Lüderitz (Namibia), 388

Luganda language, 563

Lugard, Frederick, 565

Lugbara people, 568

Luhya people, 248

Lule, Yusufu K., 569, 1054

Lumago, Isaac, 571

Lumpa Church, 1055-56

Lumumba, François, 582

Lumumba, Patrice, 583-84, 594, 708

Lunda people, 598
Lunda-Chokwe people, 15
Luo people, 248, 249, 250, 252-54, 256, 258
LUP (Liberia Unification party), 280, 283
Lusaka (Zambia), 479, 486, 598, 602, 764, 908
Lutchmeenaraidoo, Vishnu, 353
Lufti, Ali, 151
Lutheran Church, 378, 404, 477
Luvale people, 598
Luvuvhu River, 475
Luwero Triangle, 570-71
Luwum, Janani, 568, 1057-58
Luxembourg, 771
Luz, Silvino Manuel da, 83
Ly, Sékou, 335-36
Lycett, Andrew, ix; "Africa's War Zones," 693-705

Mabole River, 451
MacGaffey, Janet, x; "The African Underground Economy," 871-81
Machel, Samora, 39, 84, 321, 368, 369, 370, 371, 704, 752
Machinery: exports, 634-35; imports, 119, 263, 447, 458, 470, 593, 636-37, 794; manufacturing, 654-55
Machungo, Mario de Graça, 367
Macías Nguema, Francisco, 161, 163-64
MacMichael, Harold, 699
McNamara, Robert, 827
Madagascar, 302, 303-11, 350, 680, 802; agriculture, 646, 650; deforestation, 936; education, 664, 1090, 1091, 1092; food imports, 928; food production, 648, 652; health figures, 658, 662; Muslims, 1068; population, 626, 660, 975; refugees, 991; tourism, 1121; economy: 308-10, 628, 644, 654, 656, 804, 819; currency, 642; employment figures, 630; foreign debt, 844; foreign trade, 632, 634,

636, 638, 640; imports, 922; manufacturing, 913; mineral exports, 919; trade with Comoros, 119
Madar, Abdi Ali, 468
Madrid Agreement, 341, 358
Mafremo (Malawi Freedom Movement), 316, 320
Mafue people, 378
Maga, Hubert Coutoucou, 28, 29, 33
Magadi Lake, 247
Magendo (black market), 879-80
Maghreb, Islam, 1073, 1083-84
Maghribi, Mahmud Sulaiman, 300
Mahajanga (Madagascar), 304
Mahdi, Muhammad Ahmad al-, 509
Mahdi, Sadiq al-, 151, 508, 509, 511-12, 515-16, 701
Mahdist movement, 1075-77
Mahdiyya, 1076
Mahé Island, 443, 445
Maherero, Samuel, 380
Mahuilili, Nathaniel, 383
Maigari, Bello Bouba, 72
Maintenance of roads, 954-57
Maitatsine, Muhammad Marwa, 1085
Maitatsine movement, 1058
Maize, 876; production by country: Angola, 20; Benin, 30; Burkina Faso, 45; Cameroon, 76; Cape Verde, 85; Congo, 127; Egypt, 152; Ghana, 209; Guinea-Bissau, 232; Kenya, 262; Lesotho, 273; Madagascar, 309; Malawi, 322, 1007; Mali, 332; Mozambique, 371; Sierra Leone, 456; Somalia, 470; South Africa, 495; Swaziland, 522; Tanzania, 537-38; Togo, 543-47; Uganda, 575; Zaire, 588; Zimbabwe, 616
Majeerteen people, 467
Maji Maji war, Tanzania, 1055
Majuba (South Africa), 483
Makanne people, 465
Makatini, Johnny, 746
Make, Cassius, 745

Makeni (Sierra Leone), 452
Makgadikgadi Salt Pan Reserve (Botswana), 35
Makhrouga oil field, 557
Makonde people, 366, 528
Malabo (Equatorial Guinea), 159, 161, 162
Malagasy people, 115, 304
Malan, D. F., 484
Malan, Magnus Andre de Merindol, 117, 503-4
Malan, Wynand, 732
Malaria, 120, 310, 1012
Malawi, *312*, 313-25, 521, 612, 680, 680, 748, 802, 897; agriculture, 646, 650, 917, 1007; diplomatic relations, 370, 486, 527, 704, 749, 755, 905; education, 664; food production, 648, 652; food shortages, 927, 928; health figures, 658, 662; military spending, 717; Muslims, 1068, 1072; population, 626, 660, 975; refugees, 366, 988, 991; repressive laws, 1109-10; road system, 956; travel facilities, 1119; *economy*: 321-23, 628, 644, 654, 656, 804; currency, 642; employment figures, 630; foreign debt, 844, 847; foreign trade, 617, 632, 634, 636, 638, 640; imports, 922; industry, 913, 915, 916; mineral exports, 919; reform of, 808
Malekite rite, Islam, 339
Mali, *326*, 327-36, 802, 1074; agriculture, 646, 650; CEAO membership, 898; education, 664; female circumcision, 1048; food production, 648, 652; health figures, 658, 662; Mauritania and, 340; Muslims, 1068, 1069, 1077, 1078; population, 626, 660, 975, 986; refugees, 991; road system, 957; war with Burkina Faso, 48-49, 51; *economy*: 331-33, 628, 645, 654, 657, 804; currency, 643; employment figures, 631; foreign debt, 844; foreign trade, 632, 634, 636, 638, 640; manufacturing, 913, 916; mineral exports, 919
Mali Federation, 434
Maliba, Kibassa, 582
Malinke people, 219, 223, 327
Malinke/Mandingo people, 229
Malley, Simon, 1128
Malloch-Brown, Mark, 1000
Malloum, Félix, 101, 103, 698
Malnutrition, 119, 214, 306, 310, 333, 944
Maloti Mountains, 267
Malta, Qadhafi and, 294
Mamane, Oumarou, 395-96
Man Mountains, 235
A Man of the People (Chinua Achebe), 1105, 1107
Manantali Dam, 332, 438, 439
Mancham, James, 445, 446, 449
Mandé people, 47, 237
Mandela, Nelson Rolihlahia, 480, 485-86, 504, 763
Mandela, Winnie, 488
Manding language, 237
Mandingo people, 327
Mandinka people, 192, 194, 196
Mandyako people, 229
Manganese: deposits, 94, 167, 333, 589; mining, 10, 53, 185
Mangoky River, 303
Maniom, Irwin, 1125, 1126
Manjia people, 89
Mano River Union, 281, 282, 283, 894, 900-901
Mansôa River, 227
Mansour, Kamel Hassan, 300
Manufactured goods, 794; imports, 263, 636-37; underground economy, 876
Manufacturing, 654-57, 791, 882-83, 912; exports, 634-35; state control, 806-7. *See also* Economy
Manyara Lake, 525
Manzini (Swaziland), 517, 520
Mapanje, Jack, 1110

Maputo (Mozambique), 365, 366, 371, 372, 373, 750, 752, 753, 758, 1119

Maputso (Lesotho), 274

Mara River, 247

Maradi (Niger), 393, 394

Marais, Jaap, 481

Marakwet people, 249

Marble production, Mali, 332

Marehan people, 465, 467

Margai, Albert, 454

Margai, Milton, 454

Marijuana, 1063

Market planning, 805-8

Markets and States in Tropical Africa (Robert Bates), 941, 942

Maroua (Cameroon), 67

Marrakech (Morocco), 356

Marriage age of girls, 972, 1047

Masai people, 249, 250, 528

Masai Steppe, 527

Masaka (Uganda), 563

Maseko Ngoni people, 316

Maseru (Lesotho), 269, 272, 274, 751, 752

Masire, Quett Ketumile Joni, 36, 40, 44

Masmouda Berbers, 1073

Mass media, 951-52, 1123-31; Angola, 22-23; Benin, 32; Botswana, 43; Burkina Faso, 56; Burundi, 65; Cameroon, 79; Cape Verde, 87; Central African Republic, 97; Chad, 110-11; Comoros, 120; Congo, 130-31; Djibouti, 138-39; Egypt, 157; Equatorial Guinea, 167; Ethiopia, 178; Gabon, 187-88; Gambia, 199; Ghana, 215; Guinea, 226; Guinea-Bissau, 234; Ivory Coast, 244; Kenya, 264-65; Lesotho, 276; Liberia, 288; Libya, 299; Madagascar, 311; Malawi, 324-25; Mali, 335; Mauritania, 345; Morocco, 362; Mozambique, 374; Namibia, 390; Niger, 400; Nigeria, 413-14; Rwanda, 421; São Tomé and Príncipe, 429; Senegal, 441; Seychelles, 448; Sierra Leone, 460-61; Somalia, 471; South Africa, 501-3, 731; Sudan, 515; Swaziland, 523; Tanzania, 539; Togo, 550; Tunisia, 559; Uganda, 577-78; Zaire, 594; Zambia, 605; Zimbabwe, 619

Massamba-Débat, Alphonse, 124-25, 126

Massif des Bongos, 89

Masubia people, 378

Masuku, Lookout, 613

Masuku (Gabon), 181

Matabeleland, warfare, 613-14

Matadi (Zaire), 590

Matana people, 66

Matari III, Mwami of Rwanda, 418

Matenje, Dick, 315, 320

Maternal mortality rates, 1047

Maternity leave, 1045

Mathu, Eliud, 251

Matlou, Patrick, x; "Refugees in Africa," 988-1001

Matrilineal societies, 1042, 1051

Matthews, Gabriel Baccus, 281, 282

Mau Mau movement, Kenya, 252

Maun (Botswana), 36

Mauritania, 337-45, *338*, 683, 802; agriculture, 647, 651; Arab League, 1079; CEAO membership, 878; education, 665, 1089; food production, 649, 653; health figures, 659, 663; Morocco and, 358; Muslims, 1068, 1069, 1077; and OAU, 686; population, 627, 660, 975; refugees, 991; road system, 957; Saharan warfare, 695-96, 996; *economy*: 342-44, 629, 645, 655, 657, 804, 819, 843, 918; currency, 642; employment figures, 631; foreign debt, 842, 844; foreign trade, 633, 635, 637, 639, 641; manufacturing, 914; mineral exports, 919

Mauritius, *346*, 347-53, 774, 802;
   agriculture, 647, 651;
   contraception, 977; education, 665,
   1090, 1091; food production, 649,
   653; free press, 1123; health
   figures, 659, 663; life expectancy,
   978; Muslims, 1068; population,
   627, 661, 970, 975, 978; refugees,
   991; tourism, 1115, 1121; *economy*:
   351-52; 629, 645, 655, 657, 804;
   currency, 642; employment figures,
   631; exports, 815; foreign debt,
   845; foreign trade, 309, 633, 635,
   637, 639, 641; manufacturing, 914;
   mineral exports, 919; reform of, 808
Mawema, Michael, 611
Mayekiso, Moses, 1035
Mayombé Mountains, 121
Mayotte (Comoros), 113, 115, 117
Mazrui, Ali A., x; "Religion and
   Social Forces in Africa," 1053-66
M'Ba, Léon, 183, 188
M'Ba-Adessole, Paul, 188
Mbabane (Swaziland), 517, 520
Mbalantu people, 378
Mbale (Uganda), 563
Mbanzeni (Swazi ruler), 520
M'bao oil refinery, 438
Mbarakwengo people, 378
Mbarara (Uganda), 563
Mbeda people, 181
Mbéi River, 181
Mbeki, Govan, 486
Mbere people, 248
Mbeya (Tanzania), 538
Mbida, André-Marie, 71, 79
Mbini River, 159
MBLD (Mouvement Béninois pour la
   Liberté et la Démocratie), 29
M'Bochi people, 123
Mboro, Clement, 700
Mboya, Tom, 252-54, 1017
Mbugua, Beden, 1127
Mbuji-Mayi (Zaire), 581, 878
Mbukushu people, 378
Mbum people, 89

Mbunza people, 378
MCP (Malawi Congress Party), 315,
   318-19, 325
MDA (Mouvement pour la
   Démocratie en Algérie), 5
M'Dilla (Tunisia), 558
MDS (Mouvement des Démocrates
   Socialistes), Tunisia, 553
Meany, George, 708
Meat-processing industry, 41
Mébiame, Léon, 184, 188-89
Mechanized farming, 1008, 1044
Media. *See* Mass media
Medical and Research Foundation,
   1012
Medical schools, 1003, 1004
Medicines, underground economy, 876
Medjerda River, 551
Medjo, Pierre Minlo, 74
Megharief, Mohammed, 291
Meguid, Ahmad Esmat Abdel, 157-58
Mekambo (Gabon), 185
Meknes (Morocco), 356
Melilla (Morocco), 355
Melka Wakena hydroelectric power
   station, 176
Mende people, 452
Menelik II, Emperor of Ethiopia, 682,
   701
Mengistu Haile Mariam, 170, 172,
   173-74, 177, 179, 682-83; Soviet
   support, 712
Mensa-Wood, W. M., 204
Mercenary forces, 116, 117, 120, 494
Merchant fleet, 285-86
Mercury, 10, 94, 880
Merina people, 304
Mersa Brega (Libya), 297, 299
Meru people, 248
MESAN (Mouvement pour
   l'Evolution Démocratique de
   l'Afrique Noire), 91-92
Mestiços (mixed race), 15
Mestiri, Mahmoud, 553
Metal goods industry, 398
Metal-based engineering, 912-13

Metals exports, 634-35, 794, 919-20
Methane gas, Rwanda, 420, 421
Methanol production, 297
Methodists, 202, 379, 404
Mexico, foreign debt, 794
Mfansabili, Prince of Swaziland, 521
MFJA (Movement for Freedom and Justice in Africa), 281
MFM (Madagascar), 305, 307
MFP (Marematlou Freedom Party), Lesotho, 269, 271
Mhlaba, Raymond, 486
Mica production, 309
Micombero, Michel, 61
Middle East politics, 708-9
MIFERMA, 340
Migrant workers, 776, 977, 984-85, 1045
Migration patterns, 981-82, 1045-46
Mijikenda people, 248
Milingo, Emmanuel, 1060
Military aid recipients: Angola, 17; Chad, 104-6, 107; Egypt, 149, 707; Ethiopia, 172-74, 682; Guinea-Bissau, 230; Lesotho, 273; Liberia, 284; Libya, 296; Mozambique, 704; Somalia, 469; Sudan, 510, 511; Tanzania, 534; Togo, 546; Uganda, 567-68; Zaire, 585
Military governments, 669-70, 677-78; Benin, 28; Burkina Faso, 48-50; Central African Repubic, 92-94; Egypt, 146; Equatorial Guinea, 164-65; Ethiopia, 170-71, 682, 702; Ghana, 203, 206-7; Guinea, 219; Lesotho, 269; Liberia, 282; Madagascar, 304, 306; Mali, 328, 330; Mauritania, 339, 341; Namibia, 379; Niger, 394-96; Nigeria, 404-5, 408-10; Rwanda, 418; Sudan, 511; Togo, 545; Uganda, 566, 569, 571-72; Zaire, 584
Military production, domestic, 719, 722-23
Military spending, 716-28. *See also* Armed forces
Military training, 719
Millet production: Burkina Faso, 45, 53; Cameroon, 76; Central African Republic, 94; Chad, 927; Guinea-Bissau, 232; Mali, 332; Mauritania, 337, 342; Niger, 397; Senegal, 438; Somalia, 470; Togo, 547; Uganda, 561, 575
Minah, Francis Mishek, 456, 461
Mindelo (Cape Verde), 81
Mineral exports, 634-35, 794, 919-20
Mineral producing countries, 918-24
Miners revolt, South Africa, 484
Minimum wage, 1020
Mining equipment imports, 399
Mining industry, 982; and AIDS, 1061; colonial economy, 859; EC loans, 775; smuggling, 875, 880. *See also* Economy
Ministerial Conference on the Environment, 947-48
Minorco, 861n
Miraa (qat), 1063
Misratah (Libya), 291
Mission schools, 577, 1049
Missionaries, 316, 317, 1058
Mitterrand, François, 9, 106, 117, 295
Mitumba Mountains, 579
Mkhatshwa, Smangaliso, 488
Mlambo, Johnson, 480
Mlangeni, Andrew, 486
MLPC (Mouvement pour la Libération du Peuple Centrafrican), 90, 92
MLSPT (Movimento de Libertação de São Tomé e Príncipe), 425-26
MMM (Mouvement Militant Mauricien), 348, 349-50
Mmusi, Peter, 36, 40, 44
MNC (Mouvement National Congolais), 582, 583
MNR (Mouvement National pour le Renouveau), 49

MNR (Movement National Pour Le Renouveau), Congo, 125
MNR (Mozambique). *See* Renamo
MNRCS (Mouvement National pour la Révolution Culturelle et Sociale), Chad, 103
Mnthali, Felix, 1110
Mntonga, Eric, 736
Moa River, 451
Moabi Uplands, 181
Mobutu Sese Seko, 105, 581-83, 585-87, 592, 594-95
Mobutu, Joseph-Désiré, 583-85. *See also* Mobutu Sese Seko
Mocumbi, Pascoal Manuel, 367
Modder River, 475
Mogadishu (Somalia), 463
Mohammed V, King of Morocco, 357, 362-63
Moheli (Comoros), 113, 117, 119
Moi, Daniel T. arap, 249, 253-58, 265-66, 571
MOJA-G (Movement for Justice in Africa-Gambia), 195
Mokhehle, Ntsu, 271-72
Mokoena, Aubrey, 488
Molala, Knosi, 480
Mole-Dagbani people, 202
Molefi, Solomon, 745
Molopo River, 35
Mombasa (Kenya), 248, 263, 418, 1120, 1072
Momoh, Joseph Saidu, 453, 454, 456, 458, 460, 461
MONALIGE (Movimiento Nacional de Liberación de Guinea Ecuatorial), 163
Monarchies, 356, 519, 520-21
Monastir (Tunisia), 551, 558
Mondlane, Eduardo, 368
Monekaso, Lobe, 1011
Monetary cooperation, 904-5; Lomé Conventions and, 780
Mongo people, 581
MONIMA (Madagascar), 305, 307
Monogamy, 1061

Monokutuba language, 123
Monrovia (Liberia), 279, 285; diamond smuggling, 876
Monrovia group, 688
Monteiro, José Oscar, 367
Moore language, 47
Moorish people, 328, 339, 340, 342
Mopti (Mali), 327
Moratoria on foreign debt, 852, 853-54
Moremi Wildlife Reserve, 35
MORENA (Mouvement de Redressement National), 184, 188
Morne Seychellois, 443
Moro River, 451
Moro River Convention, 455
Morocco, *354*, 355-63, 678, 683, 688, 709, 1073; agriculture, 647, 651; and Arab League, 1079; diplomatic relations, 7, 8, 165, 166, 293, 294, 340, 341, 437, 585, 587; education, 665, 1090, 1091, 1092; food production, 649, 653; health figures, 659, 663; liberation movement, 1079; military spending, 717; Muslims, 1068, 1069, 1076-77, 1081, 1084; and OAU, 686; population, 627, 661, 974, 986; refugees, 988, 991; Saharan warfare, 695-96; *economy*: 360-62, 629, 645, 655, 657; currency, 642; employment figures, 631; foreign debt, 842, 843, 846, 847, 850, 853; foreign trade, 633, 635, 637, 639, 641; imports, 923; manufacturing, 917; mineral exports, 919
Moroney, Sean, x; "The Media in Africa," 1123-31
Moroni (Comoros), 113
Mortality rates, 972, 977-78
Moshoeshoe I, 270, 276
Moshoeshoe II, King of Lesotho, 269, 271, 276
Mossi people, 45, 47
Motherless children, 1047
Mothers, status of, 1042

Motlana, Nthato, 488
Motsoaledi, Elias, 486
Mou, Lepatou, 272
Mouazoir, Abdallah, 116, 117, 120
Moundou (Chad), 99, 102
Mount Afadjato, 201
Mount Binga, 365
Mount Cameroon, 67
Mount Chambi, 551
Mount Elgon, 561
Mount Inyangani, 607
Mount Karisimbi, 415
Mount Karthala, 113
Mount Kenya, 247, 1120
Mount Kilimanjaro, 525, 527, 1120
Mount Meru, 525
Mount Moco, 13
Mount Mtambama, 517
Mount Mulanje, 313
Mount Namuli, 365
Mount Nimba, 217
Mount Tahat, 3
Mount Vavele, 13
Mourou, Sheikh, 1083
Mouvement Politique Congolais, 124
Mouvement Togolais pour la
    Démocratie, 544
Movement for the Liberation of the
    Sahara, 695
Movimento Nacional da Resistência
    de Moçambique (MNR). *See*
    Renamo
Mozambique, *364*, 365-74, 487,
    680-81, 703, 725, 802; agriculture,
    647, 651; and EC, 770; civil war,
    1009, 1010; diplomatic relations,
    117, 319, 320-21, 521, 534, 614,
    615, 749, 750, 905; education, 665,
    1090; famine, 926-28, 930; food
    production, 649, 653; health
    figures, 659, 663; life expectancy,
    978; military spending, 717, 722,
    726; Muslims, 1068, 1072;
    population, 627, 661, 975, 986;
    refugees, 988, 991; and South
    Africa, 489, 493, 694, 748, 749,
    753-58; tourism, 1119; trade
    unions, 1017; warfare, 704, 752,
    760-61; *economy*: 370-73, 629,
    645, 657, 804; Commonwealth aid,
    768; currency, 642; employment
    figures, 631; foreign debt, 842, 845,
    847; foreign trade, 633, 639, 641;
    manufacturing, 914; mineral
    exports, 919; trade relations, 322,
    617
MP (Mouvement Populaire),
    Morocco, 356
Mpakati, Attati, 320
MPC (Multi-Party Conference),
    Namibia, 386
MPLA (Movimento Popular de
    Libertação de Angola), 17-18, 23,
    384, 534, 585, 587, 681, 694,
    703-4, 711, 748, 1104
MPLA-PT (Movimento Popular de
    Libertação de Angola-Partido de
    Trabalho), 15-16, 18
MPR (Mouvement Populaire de la
    Révolution), Zaire, 581, 582, 584-85
MRDN (Mouvement Révolutionnaire
    pour la Démocratie Nouvelle),
    Senegal, 434
MRND (Mouvement Révolutionnaire
    National pour le Développement),
    417, 418
Mroudjae, Ali, 117
MSM (Mouvement Socialiste
    Mauricien), 348, 350, 353
Msonthi, John, 319
Msuya, Cleopa, 532, 533, 536
Mswati III, King of Swaziland, 519,
    521, 524
MTI (Mouvement de la Tendance
    Islamique), Tunisia, 553, 556,
    1083-84
Mtwara (Tanzania), 537
Mubarak, Muhammad Hosni, 144,
    151, 158, 511
Muchinga mountains, 597
Mudge, Dirk, 385-86, 390
Mueshihange, Peter, 382

Mufulira (Zambia), 598
Mugabe, Robert, 39, 609, 611,
    612-14, 620, 621, 681, 749; South
    African attack, 752
Muhammad, Murtala, 408
Mulaisho, Dominic, 1130
Mulamba Léonard, 584
Multinational corporations, 884-85,
    1014
Mulumba, Mabi, 586
Muluzi, Bakili, 319-20
Muna, Solomon T., 71, 73
Mundia, Nalumino, 606
Mungai, Njoroge, 254
MUNGE (Movimiento de Unión
    Nacional de Guinea Ecuatorial), 163
Muntasir, Omar al-, 291, 295, 300-301
MUP (Mouvement de l'Unité
    Populaire), Tunisia, 553
Muqdisho (Somalia), 463, 468, 470
Muradiyya movement, 1077, 1079
Murchison Falls, 1120
Museveni, Yoweri Kaguta, 259, 563,
    568-72, 574-76, 587, 993, 1009,
    1054
Muslim Brotherhood, 1083; Egypt,
    145; Sudan, 511, 516
Muslims, 1067-86; and AIDS, 1060,
    1061; birth rate, 972; OPEC,
    1064-65. See also Religion
Musokotwane, Kebby Sililo, 606
Mutai, Abdeslam, 1084
Mutare (Zimbabwe), 609
Mutebi, Ronnie, 572
Mutesa, Kabaka of Buganda, 565, 566
Mutsamudu (Comoros), 113, 116
Muwanga (Uganda), 569-70
Muzenda, Simon Vengai, 614, 620,
    621
Muzorewa, Abel, 612, 613, 749
MVA, growth figures, 914-15
Mwadju, Mustafu. See Bob Denard
Mwakenya, 250, 257-58
Mwambutsa IV, Mwami (King) of
    Burundi, 61
Mwanza (Tanzania), 528

Mwinyi, Ali Hassan, 532-33, 536,
    539-40, 958
Myerscough, Dunstan, 1057
Mzali, Mohammed, 556
Mzuzu (Malawi), 314

Naamani, Muhammad, 1084
Nababsingh, Prem, 350
Nabudere, Dan, 569
Nacala (Mozambique), 750
NACTU (National Council of Trade
    Unions), South Africa, 1032, 1036
Nafashi, Ali, 1025
Naguib, Muhammed, 146
Naidoo, Jay, 1032
Nairobi (Kenya), 248, 263, 264, 945,
    1116, 1119-20
Nairobi University, 258
Naivasha Lake, 247
Nakuru Lake, 247
Nama language, 375
Nama people, 377-80
Namib Desert, 375, 378
Namibia, 375-91, *376*, 703, 787;
    agriculture, 647, 651; alternative
    press, 1127; Commonwealth and,
    766-67; diplomatic relations, 18,
    19, 534, 602, 681, 694, 710-11; and
    EC, 770; education, 1096; food
    production, 649, 653; Lomé
    Conventions and, 780; population,
    627, 976; trade unions, 1038-39;
    economy: 387-89, 629, 657;
    currency, 642; employment figures,
    631; foreign trade, 639, 641
Nampula (Mozambique), 366
Nandi people, 249
Naron people, 378
Nasser, Gamal Abdel, 146-49, 673,
    688, 707, 1080, 1083
Natal, 475, 477, 737-40
Natali, Lorenzo, 776
National Alliance Party, Sierra Leone,
    454
National Geographic, 936
National identity, Islam and, 1080

National liberation movements, Islam and, 1078-79

National Parties (NP): Namibia, 379; Nigeria, 408; South Africa, 481-82, 484-93, 731-34, 736, 737

National Resistance Council, Uganda, 563, 564, 571

National sovereignty, and refugee aid, 994-95

National Statutory Council, South Africa, 733

National Union of Mineworkers, South Africa, 1035

National Union Party, Sudan, 509

Nationlism, 673, 678; Afrikaner, 734; literature of, 1101-11; and pan-Africanism, 688; rural people and, 676; Southern African 600-601, 611-12, 736; and trade unions, 1016; and urbanization, 675; and World Bank programs, 826

Nationalization, 806, 882, 883-89; Algeria, 7, 9-10; Egypt, 147; Ethiopia, 172, 175, 177; Guinea, 221; Libya, 293, 296-97, 300; Madagascar, 306; Mali, 329, 331; Mauritania, 340; Mozambique, 369; Nigeria, 408; São Tomé and Príncipe, 426; Seychelles, 448; Sudan, 509; Suez Canal, 707; Tanzania, 866-69; Togo, 546, 547; Uganda, 566, 567; Zaire, 590; Zambia, 601

Natron Lake, 525

Naval base, U.S., Somalia, 467

Naxi Pan National Park, 35

Nazrey (Ethiopia), 169

Nbagui, Sambwa Pida, 581, 586

NCNC (National Council for Nigeria and the Cameroons), 406-7

NCP (National Convention Party), Gambia, 193, 194, 196

Ndau people, 366, 609

Ndebele people, 476, 477, 609, 610, 613, 619, 620

Ndembu people, 598

Ndjamena (Chad), 99, 102-4; warfare, 697-98

Ndlovukazi (Queen mother of Swaziland), 521, 524

Ndola (Zambia), 598

Ndonga people, 378

NDP (National Democratic Party): Egypt, 144-45, 150; Zimbabwe, 611, 620, 621

NDPL (National Democratic Party of Liberia), 280, 282

Negritude concept, 688

Nel, Louis, 758

Neocolonialism, 671, 839, 1103

Neo-Destour Party, Tunisia, 554, 560

Nepotism, Somalia, 468

Netherlands, 771; trading partners, 10, 21, 30, 77, 86, 198, 204, 242, 287, 429, 459

Neto, Agostinho, 16, 17, 18, 23, 39

Neto, Albertino, 427

New African, 1128

New Democratic Movement, Ghana, 204

New Nation (South Africa), 1126

New Republican Party, South Africa, 732

New Wafd Party, Egypt, 151

New Zealand, aid from, 767

Newsletters, 1130

Newspapers, 1123-27. *See also* Mass media

Newswatch (Nigeria), 1129

NFSL (National Front for the Salvation of Libya), 291-92, 294

Ngami Lake, 35

Ngandjera people, 378

Nganguela people, 15

Ngara, Emmanuel, 1104

Ngimbi, Nimy Mayidika, 586

Ngoni people, 314, 316, 519, 520, 610

Ngorongoro conservation area, 527

Ngorongoro Crater, 525, 1120

Ngouabi, Marien, 125-26

Ngugi wa Thiong'o, 1106, 1107-11; "Wole Soyinka, T. M. Aluko and the Satiric Voice," 1106-7

Nguni people, 482

Nguza Karl I Bond, 586, 595

Niamey (Niger), 393, 394, 398, 400

Niari valley, Congo, 121

Nickel deposits, 64, 94, 475

Nickel mining, 235

Nidal, Abu, 294

Niger, *392*, 393-400, 802; agriculture, 647, 651; CEAO membership, 898; education, 665; food production, 649, 653; health figures, 659, 663; Muslims, 1068, 1069, 1077; population, 627, 661, 975; refugees, 991; road system, 957; *economy*: 396-99, 629, 645, 655, 657, 804, 819, 843; currency, 643; employment figures, 631; foreign debt, 845, 847; foreign trade, 633, 635, 637, 639, 641; imports, 923; manufacturing, 914, 916; mineral exports, 919

Niger plains, 217

Niger River, 45, 327, 393, 397, 398, 401

Niger-Benue River basin, 401

Nigeria, 296, 401-14, *402*, 669-70, 676, 678, 762, 802; Abjua conference, 833-35; agriculture, 647, 651; AIDS, 1062; banking system, 864-66, 869; cities, 987; civil war, 693, 1056; colonialism, 1076; and Commonwealth Games, 766; desertification, 945; drug trade, 1064; ECOWAS membership, 901, 902; education, 665, 1088-89, 1090, 1091, 1092, 1093, 1094; food imports, 928; food production, 649, 653; health figures, 659, 663; imports, 923; labor issues, 1020, 1022, 1024, 1025, 1026; military production, 723; military spending, 717, 718, 724; Muslims, 1068, 1069, 1077, 1078, 1080, 1084-85; OPEC membership, 1064; pan-African publishing, 1128; population, 627, 661, 975, 986; press, 1128-29, 1131; protest movement, 1083; refugees, 988, 991; religious conflict, 1058; repatriation of Ghanians, 213, 214; tourism, 1117-18; trade unions, 1014-15, 1015, 1017, 1018; urban primacy, 982; *diplomatic relations*: Angola, 18; Benin, 29; Cameroon, 71, 72, 74; Chad, 104; Equatorial Guinea, 164, 165, 166; Ghana, 209; Israel, 1079; Niger, 395, 396; OAU, 690; South Africa, 763; Togo, 546; *economy*: 410-12, 629, 645, 655, 657, 804, 812, 882, 883, 918-20; currency, 642, 828; employment figures, 631; foreign debt, 842, 843, 844, 850, 852-53; foreign trade, foreign trade, 633, 635, 637, 639, 641; IMF and, 826, 830, 932; manufacturing, 914; mineral exports, 919; oil exports, 774; trade relations, 30, 213, 399, 440; unemployment, 1023; wages, 1021

Nigerian Enterprises Promotion Act, 864

Nile Divide, 415

Nile River, 141-42, 505, 969

Nilo-Hamitic people, 248, 249, 507, 563

Nilotic people, 248, 507, 563

Nimeiry, Jaafar Muhammad al-, 507, 509-11, 516, 700, 1056, 1059, 1082

Nixon, Richard M., 708, 711

Njonjo, Charles, 254, 256-57, 265

Nkala, Enos, 620

Nkayi (Congo), 121

Nkolonkati people, 378

Nkomati Accord, 370, 492, 758

Nkomo, Joshua, 39, 487, 611-14, 620-21

Nkongsamba (Cameroon), 67

Nkosi, Lewis, 1107

Nkrumah, Kwame, 205-6, 672, 673, 687, 688, 765, 915, 1053, 1102
Nkuete, Jean, 73
Nkumbula, Harry, 600
NLC (National Liberation Council), Ghana, 206
NLC (National Labour Congress), 1026
NNC (South African Native National Congress), 484
NNLC (Ngwane National Liberatory Congress), 519, 520, 524
No Easy Walk to Freedom (Nelson Mandela), 504
Nobel Peace Prize, 504
Nomadic people, 339, 340, 344, 401, 465
Nonalignment, 148, 615, 679, 707, 1080
Nonmineral producing countries, industry, 915-18
North Africa: contraception, 977; foreign debt, 842, 846; imports, 923; liberation movement, 1079; military spending, 717; Muslims, 1073-74, 1081; population figures, 974
North Korea, 127, 240, 311, 370, 614, 615, 696
Northern Frontier District Liberation Front, Somalia, 258
Northern Rhodesia, 317-18, 598, 600, 611, 897. *See also* Zambia
Northern Rhodesia African National Congress, 600
North-south divide, 671, 679
Norwegian Church Aid, 958
Nouadhibou (Mauritania), 337, 343
Nouakchott (Mauritania), 337, 339, 341, 343
Noumazaly, Ambroise, 125
NP. *See* National parties
NPC (Northern People's Congress), Nigeria, 406-7
NPP (National People's Party): Nigeria, 409; South Africa, 481, 737

NPUP (National Progressive Unionist Party), Egypt, 145
Nqumayo, Albert, 319
NRA (National Resistance Army), Uganda, 1009
NRC (National Redemption Council), Ghana, 206
NRM (National Resistance Movement), Uganda, 570, 571-72, 577
NSC (National Salvation Committee), Libya, 292
Ntare V, Mwami (King) of Burundi, 61
Ntumazah, Ndeh, 70, 73
Nubia, 1070
Nubian people, 143, 1070; Uganda, 566-67, 568
Nujoma, Sam, 382, 390-91
NUNW (National Union of Namibian Workers), 1038
Nupe people, 403
Nur, Ramadan Mohammed, 171
NUTA (Tanzania), 1019
Nutrition, 797; for women, 1047
Nuweveldberge range, 473
Nyakusa people, 528
Nyamwezi people, 528
Nyaneka people, 15
Nyanja people, 598
Nyasaland, 317, 611, 896-97. *See also* Malawi
Nyasaland African Congress, 317-18
Nyerere, Julius, 39, 529, 530, 531-33, 540, 568, 658, 688, 856, 883, 958, 1054; *Education for Self-Reliance*, 1087; and Uganda, 569
Nyika Plateau, 313
Nzambimana (Lt. Col., Burundi), 66

OADP (Organisation de l'Action Démocratique et Populaire), Morocco, 357
OAS (Secret Army Organization), Algeria, 6
Oases, Tunisia, 551

Oasib (Nama chief), 380

OATUU (Organization of African Trade Union Unity), 832, 837, 1024-25

OAU (Organization of African Unity), 17, 104, 281, 383, 437, 455, 683, 686-92, 698, 995, 996, 1080; Angola, 17; APPER, 832-35; Burkina Faso/Mali conflict, 48-49; Cameroon, 72; Chad, 104; and colonial borders, 693; Comoros, 116; conditionality and, 851; Convention Governing the Specific Aspects of the Refugee Problems in Africa, 989-90, 995; debt conference, 855; Djibouti, 136; environmental concerns, 947; health care, 1012; international finance, 831, 832; Kenya, 255, 258-59; Morocco, 358; religion, 1065; and Saharan war, 683; Seychelles, 446; Somalia, 469; and Soviet Union, 712; and SWAPO, 383; Tanzania, 534; Zaire, 587

Obasanjo, Olasegan, 408, 762

Obbo, Christine, 1046

Obeng, P. V., 204, 216

Obiang Nguema Mbasogo, Teodoro, 164-65

Obote, Milton, 419, 564, 565-67, 569-71, 574-75, 578, 993

Ocaya, Charles, 569

October War, 150

Oculi, Okello, 1059

Odendaal Plan, 381-82

Odinga, Oginga, 249-50, 252-56

Oduho, Joseph, 700

OECD (Organization for Economic Cooperation and Development), 821

Official development assistance (ODA), 834

Offset printing, Mauritius, 351

Ogaden, 171, 172, 682, 683; conflict, 467, 702

Ogaden people, 249, 467

Ogo Highlands, Somalia, 463

Ogooué River, 181

Oil: employment, 412; exploration, 176, 447; exports, 774; imports, 399, 420; nationalization, 296-97, 300; politics, 709, 751; refining, 9, 153, 263, 285, 297, 343, 438, 514, 548, 557; transport from Middle East, 708; *deposits*: Benin, 30; Burundi, 64; Central African Republic, 94; Chad, 109; Equatorial Guinea, 166-67; Guinea-Bissau, 232-33; Liberia, 285; Madagascar, 309; Mozambique, 372; Niger, 397; Nigeria, 407-8; Senegal, 438; Sierra Leone, 451; Sudan, 510, 514, 700; Tunisia, 557; *prices*: 9-10, 75, 128, 185-86, 242, 282, 411, 708-9, 807; and banking, 866; and economic performance, 803; and foreign debt, 843; and health services, 1005; IMF and, 827; Libya and, 293, 294, 297-98; and Lomé Convention, 772-73; and military spending, 717-18, 724; and pan-African publishing, 1127-28; *production*: 8, 153; Algeria, 8, 9; Angola, 20; Benin, 29, 30; Cameroon, 74-75, 76; Chad, 109; Congo, 127-29; Egypt, 153; Gabon, 185; Ghana, 211; Ivory Coast, 241; Kenya, 260; Libya, 289, 292-93, 296-98; Mozambique, 371; Nigeria, 410, 411, 920; Senegal, 438; Tunisia, 556-58; Zaire, 589-90, 593

Ojukwu (Ibo Lt. Col.), 407-8

Okara, Gabriel, *The Voice*, 1106

Okavango Delta, 35, 1118-19

Okavango River, 13, 375

Okello, Basilio, 570, 571

Okello, John, 531

Okello, Tito, 567

Okoya, Pierino, 566

Ol Doinyo Lengai, 525

Old Mutual, 496, 861

Older women, status of, 1042

Olduvai Gorge, 525

OLF (Oromo Liberation Front), 171, 175, 702

Olifants River, 475

Olive oil exports, 557

Olympio, Sylvanus, 545

Omani traders, 1072

Omdurman (Sudan), 507, 515; battle of, 1075

Omgulumbashe (Namibia), 383

Omo-Fadaka, Jimoh, x; "Africa's Environmental Crisis," 944-52

OMVS (Organisation pour la Mise en Valeur du Fleuve Sénégal), 438

Omyene people, 181

One-party states, 807, 1015, 1017-18. See also Government structure

Onimode, Bade, xi; "Africa's Response to the International Monetary Fund-World Bank Programs," 823-40

Onions, Burkina Faso, 45

OPC (Ovamboland People's Congress), Namibia, 382

OPEC (Organization of Petroleum Exporting Countries), 9, 1064-65; Libya and, 293, 297-98; military spending, 724; and Niger, 397, 398; Nigeria and, 411, 920; Tunisia and, 558

OPO (Ovamboland People's Organization), Namibia, 382

Opposition parties, trade unions as, 1018, 1022. See also Political parties

"Oppressed Black African Manifesto," Mauritania, 342

Optical goods, Mauritius, 351

Oran (Algeria), 4, 5

Orange Free State, 270, 473, 475, 477, 483

Orange River, 267, 375, 473, 475

Oranje Unie Party, South Africa, 484

Orapa (Botswana), 41

Organisation des Nationalistes Mauritaniens, 339

Organisation du Peuple Rodriguais, 349

Organization of African Unity. See OAU

Organizations, regional, 892-95

Organized crime, Ghana, 873

Organized labor. See Trade unions

Orlam people, 377, 380

Oromo people, 465, 683, 996

ORP (Organization of Popular Resistance), Algeria, 7

Osman, Abdul Magid, 367

Oti River, 201

Otto, John Ya, 383

Ottoman Empire, 701, 1073

Ouagadougou (Burkina Faso), 45

Oubangi-Chari. See also Central African Republic

Oubangui River, 121

Oueddei, Goukouni, 101-7, 111-12, 295, 698, 1085

Ouedraogo, Gérard, 48

Ouedraogo, Jean-Baptiste, 50

Ouémé River, 25

Ouenza iron mine (Algeria), 10

Oujda (Morocco), 356

Ouko, Robert John, 266

Oumar, Acheikh Ibn, 102, 106

Ousmane, Sembene, 1109

Out of Africa, 1113

Output levels, 789-90

Ovambo people, 15, 377, 378, 379, 380, 381

Overgrazing, 40, 936, 1008

Overseas Press Club, 1129

Overseas students, 353, 421, 448

Overvaluation of currency, 941-42

Ovimbundu people, 15

Owen Falls (Uganda), 561, 573

Owen Falls Dam, 259, 576

Oxford Refugee Studies Programme, Symposium, 1000

Oyite-Ojok, David, 567-70

Oyo (Nigeria), 406

PAAERD (Program of Action for
African Economic Recovery and
Development), 832-35
PAC (Pan-African Congress), 271,
479-80, 485-86, 614, 746-47, 1032,
1036
PACD (Plan of Action to Combat
Desertification), 945-46, 949-50
Package tours, 1116
Pagalu, 159, 161
PAICV (Partido Africano da
Independencia de Cabo Verde), 83,
84
PAIGC (Partido Africano da
Independencia da Guiné e Cabo
Verde), 83, 84, 221, 229, 230-31,
681, 1104-5
Paihama, Kundi, 16, 24
Pakistan, Seychelles and, 447
Palm kernel production, 127, 284, 588
Palm oil production, 930; Benin, 30;
Cameroon, 75, 76; Gambia, 191;
Ghana, 210; Guinea-Bissau, 232,
233; Ivory Coast, 241; Liberia, 284;
Nigeria, 411; Sierra Leone, 458;
Togo, 543, 547; Zaire, 588, 593
Pan-African Congress. See PAC
Pan-African publishing, 1127-28
Pan-Africanism, 207, 686-90, 691,
995; Kenyatta and, 251
Paper manufacture, 371
Paraguay, Cape Verde and, 85
Parallel economy, Zaire, 591. See also
Underground economy
Parasitic infections, 1047
Parastatal organizations, 883n; goals
of, 886-87
Paris Club of Western donors, 167,
323, 344, 456, 459, 469, 549, 591,
582, 847, 854
Parkes, Russell J., xi
Parliamentary government, 673, 678
Parmehutu (Parti pour l'Emancipation
du Peuple Hutu), Rwanda, 418
Parti de la Révolution Populaire,
Zaire, 582

Parti de la Révolution Populaire du
Bénin, 27
Parti de l'Unité Togolaise, 545
Parti Démocratique Congolais, 124
Parti Islamique (Mauritania), 341
Parti Ouvrier et Paysan du Congo, 582
PAS (Parti de l'Avant-garde
Socialiste), 5
Pastureland, 451; loss of, 944
Patasse, Ange, 92-93, 98
Patchouli production, 118
Patrilineal societies, 1042, 1050
Payments reforms, 911
p'Bitek, Okot, 1059, 1106
PCT (Parti Communiste Tunisien),
554, 556
PCT (Parti Congolais du Travail),
123-27
PDCI (Parti Démocratique de la Côte
d'Ivoire), 238-39
PDG (Parti Démocratique de Guinée),
219-23
PDG (Parti Démocratique Gabonais),
182, 183-84
PDNC (Provisional National Defence
Council), Ghana, 203-4, 207-9, 216
PDOIS (People's Democratic
Organization for Independence and
Socialism), Gambia, 193
PDS (Parti Démocratique
Sénégalaise), 434, 435-36
Peacekeeping role of OAU, 690
Peanut smuggling, 875
Peitermaritzburg (South Africa), 476,
477
Pemba Island, 525, 1120
Penrose, Edith, 885
Pension funds, 861n, 1033
People's Caretaker Council, 612
Pepel people, 229
Pereira, Aristides Maria, 83, 84, 87
Perfume essence, 118
Peters, Lenrie, The Second Round,
1106
Petersen, Hector, 488
Petroleum. See OIL

PF (Popular Front), Burkina Faso, 51
PFP (Progressive Federal Party), South Africa, 481, 731-32, 734-35, 737
Pharmaceuticals, 309
Philippines, Qadhafi and, 293
Phosphates: deposits, 30, 185, 232, 344, 695; production, 10, 332, 359, 360-62, 397, 438, 547, 556, 558, 573, 696
Phosphoric acide, 360, 558
Pickett Hill (Sierra Leone), 451
Pico de Moka, 159
Pico de Santa Isabel, 159
Pidgin English, 161
Pienaar, Louis, 379
Pietermaritzburg (South Africa), 476, 482, 739
Pineapples, 225, 241, 522
Pinto (Guinea-Bissau), 229
Piracy, state-controlled, 1073
Pires, Pedro Verona Rodrigues, 83, 84, 87
PIT (Parti de l'Indépendence et du Travail), Senegal, 434
Pityana, Barney, 488
Plaatje, Sol T., 687
PLAN (People's Liberation Army of Namibia), 385
Plantain production, 127, 209, 419, 588
Plantation agriculture, 308-9, 316, 321, 368, 370, 426, 470, 588
Plastics industry, 309, 371, 398
Platinum production, 495
PLO (Palestine Liberation Organization): Amin and, 567; Egypt and, 151; Libya and, 293, 294, 295; Morocco and, 357
PLP (Parti pour la Libération du Peuple), Senegal, 434
Plywood factory, 284-85
PMSD (Parti Mauricien Social Démocrate), 348, 349-50
PND (Parti National Démocratique), Morocco, 356

PNDC (Provisional National Defense Council), Ghana, 207-9, 216, 1019
Podier, Nicholas, 283
Pointe-Noire (Congo), 121
Pokomo people, 248
Pokot people, 249
Police violence, Kenya, 258
Policy-related lending, 830-31
Polisario Front (Frente Popular para la Liberación de Saquia al-Hamra y Río de Oro), 8, 341, 343, 355, 358-59, 683, 695-97
Political elite, 1106
Political instability, 714; and famine, 926-28; and tourism, 1114
Political literature, 1101-12
Political parties: Algeria, 4-5; Angola, 16, 703-4; Benin, 27; Botswana, 37, 38; Burkina Faso, 47, 49; Burundi, 60; Cameroon, 69-70, 73; Cape Verde, 83, 84; Central African Republic, 90; Chad, 101, 103, 697-98; Comoros, 115, 116; Congo, 123-24; Djibouti, 135; Egypt, 144-45, 151; Equatorial Guinea, 162, 163, 164; Ethiopia, 170-71, 701-2; Gabon, 182-83; Gambia, 193-96; Ghana, 204, 207; Guinea, 219-220; Guinea-Bissau, 229; Ivory Coast, 238; Kenya, 249-50, 252; Lesotho, 269, 271, 272; Liberia, 280-81; Libya, 291-92; Madagascar, 305; Malawi, 315; Mali, 328-29; Mauritania, 339-40, 341; Mauritius, 348-49, 350; Morocco, 356-57; Mozambique, 366-67; Namibia, 379, 382-83, 703-4; Niger, 394-95; Nigeria, 405-9; Rwanda, 417; São Tomé and Príncipe, 426; Senegal, 434-36; Seychelles, 445, 446; Sierra Leone, 453, 454; Somalia, 465; South Africa, 479-82, 484-89, 731-47; Sudan, 508, 509, 700; Swaziland, 519-20; Tanzania, 528-29, 530; Togo, 544; Tunisia, 553, 555-56,

1084; Uganda, 565-66, 569; Zaire, 582; Zambia, 599-600; Zimbabwe, 609-10. *See also* Trade unions

Political power, 673

Political stability, 801, 809

Political support of refugees, 996-97

Politics, factional, 677

Polygamy, 977, 1050, 1061

Pondo people, 476

Population, 626-27, 660-61, 787-89, 969-87; refugees, 988-1001. *See also* Urbanization; *growth*: 669, 714, 788-89, 944, 970-77, 1048; and agricultural production, 931-34; and drought, 945; and education, 1087, 1094; and foreign aid, 774; and health services, 1006-7

Population Registration Act, South Africa, 485, 491

Port cities: Angola, 20; Benin, 25; Gambia, 197; Liberia, 285; Mauritania, 343; Morocco, 355, 359; Mozambique, 365, 372; Namibia, 375; SADCC, 750-751; Senegal, 439; Seychelles, 443; Somalia, 470; South Africa, 496, 497; Tanzania, 537; Zaire, 590

Port Elizabeth (South Africa), 476, 477, 497

Port Gentil (Gabon), 181

Port Harcourt (Nigeria), 398, 403, 866

Port Louis (Mauritius), 347

Port Said (Egypt), 142

Port Sudan (Sudan), 507, 514

Porto Novo (Benin), 25

Portugal: diplomatic relations, 221, 319, 370, 427; EC membership, 771, 781; revolution, 383-84, 487, 748; trade relations, 21, 86, 109, 204, 233, 371, 372, 428, 429; and Western Sahara, 695; *colonialism*: 681, 771; Angola, 13, 17, 19-20; Cape Verde, 84; Guinea-Bissau, 230; Mozambique, 367-69; Nigeria, 406; São Tomé and Príncipe, 426

Portuguese colonies, 227, 1017, 1072

Portuguese Guinea, 681. *See also* Guinea-Bissau

Portuguese language, 15, 83, 229, 366, 373, 425, 476

Portuguese people, 380

Postal service, 910

Potash deposits, 128, 176

Potash mining, 558

Potassium-based minerals, 128

Potatoes, 309, 352, 557

Poultry, 41, 76, 397, 438

Power needs, Zaire, 590

Power output, 397-98, 420, 439

PPA (Algerian People's Party), 6

PPM (Parti du Peuple Maurtanien), 339, 340-41

PPN (Parti Progressiste Nigérien), 394-95

PPP (People's Progressive Party), Gambia, 193, 194, 196, 199

PPP (Progressive People's Party), Liberia, 282

PPT (Parti Progressiste Tchadien), 102-3, 697

Praia (Cape Verde), 81, 84

Praslin Island (Seychelles), 443

Prawns, Mozambique, 372

PRC (Parti Révolutionnaire Centrafricain), 90, 93

PRC (People's Redemption Council), Liberia, 280, 282

Precious metals, Rwanda, 420

Precolonial trade, 406, 858

Preferential Trade Area (PTA), 602, 907-8

Presbyterians, 202, 314, 404

Press, 1123-27. *See also* Mass media

Pretoria (South Africa), 475, 477, 482

Price incentives, 814, 816

Prices, 939; cash crops, 1007; controls, 807; and nationalization, 886; regulation, 806; suppression, 942; worldwide decline, 812

Primary education, universal, 1087-88. *See also* Education

Primary products, 679, 815; exports, 410, 774, 794, 939; imports, 794

Príncipe Island, 423. *See also* São Tomé and Príncipe

Private consumption, 792

Private enterprise, 814, 816

Private sector industry, 153

Privatization, 371, 439, 548, 814, 816, 887-88

PRM (Parti du Régroupement Mauritanien), 340

Production, comparative figures, 791-92, 799

Productivity, 1024; of women, 1044

Progressive Reform Party, South Africa, 737

Prostitution, 1046, 1061; and AIDS, 1059

Protectionism, 815, 921

Protest movements, Islam and, 1083-86

PRP (People's Redemption Party), Nigeria, 409

PS (Parti Socialiste), Senegal, 434, 435-36

PSD (Parti Socialiste Destourien), 553, 555

PTA (Preferential Trade Area), 895, 907-8

Public employees, 1022, 1023

Public spending, 796, 807

Publishing, pan-African, 1127-28

Pulse production, 342, 397, 573, 588

PUN (Partido Unico Nacional), Equatorial Guinea, 163

PUNT (Partido Unico Nacional de los Trabajadores), Equatorial Guinea, 163

Puppet armies, South Africa supported, 753-54

Purified Nationalist Party, South Africa, 484

Pygmies, 67, 123, 415

Pyrethrum production, 260-61, 420, 535

Qadhafi, Muammar al-, 52, 103, 149, 291, 293-96, 300, 301, 683, 694, 697-99, 1082-83

Qadiriyya Muslims, 1071, 1072, 1075

Qadr, Abd al-, 1076

Qat, 880, 1063

Qaud, Abdul Majid Mabruk, 301

Qibla, 747

Qoboza, Percy, 1125

Quainoo, Arnold, 204

Quatre Bornes (Mauritius), 347

Que Que (Zimbabwe), 609

Queen Elizabeth National Park, 1120

Quelimane (Mozambique), 366

Quiwonkpa, Thomas, 282

QwaQwa (South Africa), 477

Rabat (Morocco), 355-56

Rabemananjara (Madagascari), 688

Rabih Fadl Allah, 1077

Race relations, 342, 349, 418, 610-11, 1057; South Africa, 476, 484-93, 757-59, 1027, 1029-30

Radio. *See* Mass media

Radioactive minerals, 371

Rahanwein people, 465

Rail embargo, Zimbabwe, 753

Railways, 755; Cameroon, 77; Djibouti, 135; Ivory Coast, 240; Liberia, 285; Libya, 297; Malawi, 316, 322; Senegal, 439; South Africa, 497; Tanzania, 535, 537; Uganda, 565; Zaire, 590; Zambia, 597

Rajbansi, Amichand, 481, 490

Rake, Alan, xi, 1128

Rakotonirainy, Lucien, 307

Rakotonirina, Manadafy, 305

Ramanantsoa (General, Madagascar), 306

Ramboolam, Seewoosagur, 349, 353

Raoul, Alfred, 125

Rapid Deployment Force, 709

Ras al-Unuf (Libya), 297

Ras Dashen, 169

Rastafari movement, 1063

Ratsimandrava (Colonel, Madagascar), 306

Ratsiraka, Didier, 304-7, 311

Rawlings, Jerry John, 51, 203, 204, 207-8, 216, 1019

Razanabahiny, Marajolam, 311

RDA (Rassemblement Démocratique Africaine), 48, 238, 291, 697

RDC (Rassemblement Démocratique Centrafricaine), 90

RDPC (Rassemblement Démocratique de Peuple Camerounais), 69-70, 72, 73

Reagan, Ronald, 298, 681, 698, 710-11, 751, 779

Recession, economic, 803, 843

Red Cross, 1009-10, 1012

Redistribution of population, 986-87

Reforestaton, 128, 241, 262, 285, 397, 948

Reform, economic, 807-22, 911; World Bank and, 849

Reformist policies, 1102-12

Refoulement (extradition) of refugees, 997-98

Refugees, 985, 988-1001; education, 765, 766, 1096; and famine, 930

Regional cooperation, 684-85, 890-911, 925; environmental, 947-48; OAU and, 690, 691

Rehoboth Free Democratic Party, Namibia, 379

Rehoboth people, 377, 378, 703

Religion, 1053-66; conflicts, 508-9, 683, 702, 1070-71, 1081, 1082; freedom, Egypt, 146; fundamentalist, 143, 150, 357, 508, 511, 736, 1079, 1081-85; oppression, 62; persecution, 161, 164, 258; schools, 287, 334. See also Christianity; Islam

Rembrandt Group, 497

Remittance of profits, 863, 865

Remote Areas Development Programme, Botswana, 41

Renamo (Resistência Nacional Moçambicana), 117, 320-21, 369-70, 372-74, 489, 681, 694, 704, 717, 753-55, 926; South Africa and, 492-93, 758; terrorism, 756

Rendille people, 249

René, France-Albert, 445, 446, 449

Repatriated earnings, 11, 52, 86, 154, 274, 298, 323, 360, 559

Repatriation: of migrant workers, 425; of refugees, 997-98

Repressive laws, 379, 381-82, 733, 1109-10

Republican Brothers, Sudan, 510

Rescheduling of debts, 846-48

Research: AIDS, 1062; military, 721

Respiratory infections, 1012

Responsibility of states, 1001

Return to the Shadows (Robert Serumaga), 1106

Réunion, 787; agriculture, 647, 651; food production, 649, 653; infant mortality, 978; life expectancy, 978; mineral exports, 919; population, 970, 975, 978; trade relations, 309, 447

Revolutionary Command Council of Socialist Guinean Patriots and Cadres, 162

Revolutionary rhetoric, 1101

Rhodes, Cecil, 600, 610

Rhodesia, 487, 681, 896-97; Botswana and, 39; Commonwealth countries and, 764-65; Malawi and, 319; Mozambique and, 368, 369, 374; Nigeria and, 408; South Africa and, 748, 749, 753; Zambia and, 602. See also Northern Rhodesia; Southern Rhodesia

Rhodesian Front, 612

Rice: import, 119, 197, 412, 428, 437-38, 458; processing, 333, 398; smuggling, 873, 875; production: Burkina Faso, 45, 53, Cameroon, 76; Egypt, 152; Gambia, 191; Guinea, 224; Guinea-Bissau, 232;

Liberia, 284; Madagascar, 303, 309, 310; Mali, 332; Mauritania, 342; Niger, 397; Nigeria, 411; Rwanda, 415, 419; Sierra Leone, 451, 456; Zaire, 588

Richard's Bay (South Africa), 496, 497, 499

Rif Mountains, 356

Rif war, 1076-77

Rift Valley, 169, 247, 313, 525-27, 579

Rimal al-Abiod, 551

Rinderpest outbreak, 469

Río de Oro, 683, 695

Rio Grande River, 227

Río Muni (Equatorial Guinea), 159, 161, 162-63, 166-67

River blindness, 54

RND (Rassemblement National Démocratique), Senegal, 435

RNI (Rassemblement National des Indépendents), Morocco, 356

Road systems, 953-66; Cameroon, 77; Liberia, 285; Malawi, 322; Morocco, 355; Mozambique, 372; Niger, 398; OAU and, 691; Rwanda, 420; Senegal, 439; Seychelles, 443; Sierra Leone, 457; Somalia, 470; South Africa, 497; Tanzania, 535; Zaire, 588, 590; Zambia, 597

Roberto, Holden, 23, 703

Robson, Peter, xi; "African Regionalism," 890-911

Rodrigues, Manuel Alexandre Duarte "Kito," 16

Rodgues Island, 347, 349

Rokel River, 451

Rôlas Island, 423

Roman Catholic Church: and AIDS, 1060, 1061; and contraception, 1011; schools, 64; See also Religion

Romania, 128, 154

Rossing Mountain, Namibia, 377

Rotary Club International, 1012

Rouge River, 45

RPP (Rassemblement Populaire pour le Progrès), Djibouti, 135, 136

RPT (Rassemblement du Peuple Togolais), 544, 545-46

Ruaha River, 525

Ruanda-Urundi, 61. See also Burundi

Rubber production, 75, 76, 241, 284, 287, 588

Rufiji River, 525

Ruhengeri (Rwanda), 415, 421

Rukwa Lake, 525

Ruling class, African, 885-86

Rural areas, 675-77; civil war, 1009; populations, 20, 366, 389, 505, 676; women in society, 1042

Rustication policies, 986

Rutile deposits, 451, 458

Ruvu River, 525

Ruwenzori Range, 1120-21

Ruzizi River, 59, 420

Rwagasore, Ganwa (Prince) of Burundi, 61

Rwanda, 61, 415-22, *416*, 802; agriculture, 647, 651; AIDS incidence, 1062; Burundi and, 62; education, 665; food production, 649, 653; health figures, 659, 663; Muslims, 1068; population, 627, 661, 975; refugees, 985, 988, 991; road system, 957; tourism, 1120; *economy*: 419-21, 629, 645, 655, 657, 804; currency, 642; employment figures, 631; foreign debt, 844; foreign trade, 633, 635, 637, 639, 641; imports, 923; manufacturing, 914, 916; mineral exports, 919; underground economy, 876

Saamstaan (South Africa), 1126

SAAWU (South African Allied Workers Union), 1031, 1034

Sab people, 465

Sabbe, Osman Saleh, 702

Sabry, Ali, 149

Sachs, Albie, 745

SACP (South African Communist Party), 479, 502
SACPO (South African Coloured Peoples Organisation), 1030
SACTU (South African Congress of Trade Unions), 502, 1029-30
SACU (South African Customs Union), 274, 521, 895, 906-7
Sadat, Anwar, 143, 149-50
SADCC (Southern African Development Coordination Conference), 18, 21, 39, 42, 320, 521, 522, 527, 749-51, 834, 894-95, 905-6; Lesotho and, 272, 273, 274; and PTA, 908; publication, 1130; and sanctions against South Africa, 757-59; South Africa and, 755; Zambia and, 601-4; Zimbabwe and, 615
SADR (Sahrawi Arab Democratic Republic), 341, 358, 683, 686, 695, 996
SAFTU (South African Federation of Trade Unions), 1029
Sahara Desert, 3, 99, 337, 551, 683, 936, 1008
Saharan plateau, 289
Sahel region, 693; desertification, 936, 945; drought, 930-31, 945, 1008; Islam, 1074-75; life expectancy, 978
Sahrawi people, 683, 694, 695, 996
SAIC (South African Indian Congress), 485, 1030
Saint Helena, 970
St. Louis (Senegal), 431
St. Paul River, 279
Sakuye people, 249
Salafiyya movement, 1075, 1077
Salek, Ould, 341, 345
SALF (Somali Abo Liberation Front), 171
Salim, Salim Ahmed, 532, 540-41
Salisbury (Southern Rhodesia), 611
Salt lakes, 551
Salt production, 10, 109, 375, 397, 558, 576

Samaale people, 465
Samatar, Mohammed Ali, 472
Sambju people, 378
Samburu people, 249
San people, 377, 378, 379
Sanaga River, Cameroon, 67
Sanctions against South Africa, 497, 745, 751, 752-53, 757-59, 907
Sandougou River, 191
Sandveld. See Kalahari Desert
Sanga people, 123
Sangala, John, 320
Sango language, 90
Sanhadja Berbers, 1073
Sanhaja people, 683
Sankara, Thomas, 47, 49-52, 54, 56, 107
Sanlam, 496
Santo Antonio (Príncipe Island), 425
Sanusiyya movement, 1075
Sanyang, Kukoi Samba, 195
São Tiago Island (Cape Verde), 81
São Tomé (city), 425
São Tomé and Príncipe, 423-30, 424, 681, 802; economy, 427-29, 629, 645, 657, 804; currency, 642; employment figures, 631; foreign debt, 844; foreign trade, 639, 641; health figures, 659; manufacturing, 914, 916; mineral exports, 919; Muslims, 1068; population, 627, 976; refugees, 991
Saquia al-Hamra, 683, 695
Sara people, 89, 99, 102, 111, 697, 1085
Sarh (Chad), 99, 102
Sassandra River, 235
Sassou-Nguesso, Denis, 123, 126, 131
SATCC (Southern African Transport and Communications Commission), 905
SATLC (South African Trades and Labour Council), 1029
Saudi Arabia, 709, 1064-65; diplomatic relations, 143, 151, 357, 469, 510-11, 696; Islamic law,

1059; trade relations, 343, 470, 514; and war in Eritrea, 702

Savimbi, Jonas, 16, 23, 587, 694, 703

Savings, domestic, 817

Sawyer, Amos, 281

Scandinavia, 855, 978

Schweitzer, Albert, 1058, 1117

SDP (Seychelles Democratic Party), 445, 446

SDSF (Somali Democratic Salvation Front), 465, 467, 468

The Second Round (Lenrie Peters), 1106

Secondary education, 664-65, 797, 1087-88, 1091

Secret societies, female, 1042

Sector adjustment loans, 830

Sedki, Atef, 144, 151, 158

Seeiso, Mathealira, 276

Ségou (Mali), 327

Seibou, Ali, 396, 400

Seidman, Ann Willcox, xi; "Banking Institutions in Africa," 858-70

Sekhonyana, Evaristus Retselisitsoe, 272, 277

Sekondi (Ghana), 202

Selebi-Phikwe (Botswana), 36, 41

Self-employment of women, 1046

Self-government, local, 684

Self-management by workers, 1018-19

Self-reliant agricultural development, 775-76

Self-rule, experience of, 673

Self-sufficiency in food production, 815

Selim, Ali Bazi, 117

Sélingue dam, Mali, 332

Sembene, Ousmane, 1110

Semi-Bantu people, 69

Semiprecious stones, 377

Semitic people, 170

Sena people, 609

Senegal, 431-42, *432*, 802, 945, 1054; agriculture, 647, 651; CEAO membership, 898; diplomatic relations, 74, 192-95, 329, 340; ECOWAS membership, 900; education, 665, 1089, 1092; food imports, 928; food production, 649, 653; health figures, 659, 663; literary suppression, 1110; Muslims, 1068, 1069, 1074-75, 1077, 1079; population, 627, 661, 975; press, 1124; refugees, 991, 994; road system, 957; Senegambia, 903-4; tourism, 1117; trade unions, 1018; *economy*: 437-40, 629, 645, 655, 657, 804, 819; currency, 643; employment figures, 631; foreign debt, 844, 847; foreign trade, 233, 633, 635, 637, 639, 641; imports, 922; industry, 914, 915; mineral exports, 919; underground economy, 875

Senegal River, 337, 339, 342, 343, 431, 439

Senegambia Confederation, 193, 195-96, 199, 436-37, 442, 894, 903-4; budget, 439-40

Senghor, Léopold Sédar, 434-35, 441-42, 688, 1054

Senoufo people, 47, 327-28

Serengeti National Park, 527

Serengeti Plain, 1120

Serer people, 433, 441, 442

Serra Zuira Mountains, 365

Serrekunda/Bakau (Gambia), 192

Serumaga, Robert, *Reutrn to the Shadows*, 1106

Service sector, 630-31, 791

Sesame production, 512, 513, 573, 575

SeSotho language, 269

Setswana language, 36

Seventh-Day Adventists, 314

Sewa River, 451

Sexual politics, 1044

Sexuality, and religion, 1060-62

Seychelles, 443-49, *444*, 788, 801, 802; Commonwealth aid, 768; currency, 642; economy, 447-48, 629, 645, 657, 804; employment figures, 631; foreign debt, 844;

foreign trade, 639, 641; health figures, 659; life expectancy, 978; manufacturing, 914; mineral exports, 919; population, 627, 970, 975; refugees, 991; South African attack, 752; tourism, 1115, 1116, 1121

Seychelles National Movement, 446

Sfax (Tunisia), 551

Shaba (Zaire), 876

Shabani, Nyembo, 586

Shadiliyya, 1071

Shafi Islam, Comoros, 115

Shagari, Shehu, 408, 409

Shah of Iran, fall of, 751

Shaka (Zulu leader), 482

Sharia (Islamic law): and AIDS, 1059; Egypt, 143, 1082; Nigeria, 405; Somalia, 466; Sudan, 507, 508, 510-12, 516, 700, 1056, 1070-71, 1082

Sharpeville (South Africa), massacre, 485

Shemarke (Somali president), 466

Sherbo people, 452

Shia Islam, 1078

Shidle people, 465

Shifta bandits, 258-59

Shikuku, Martin, 255, 257, 258

Shipanga, Andreas, 382

Ships, Liberian-registered, 285-86

Shirazi people, 530

Shire Highlands, 365

Shire River, 313

Shoan people, 701

Shoe manufacture, 309

Shona people, 366, 609, 610, 620

Shrimp production, 309

Shuwa Arabs, 1074

Sibon, Guy, 307

Siddick, Abba, 697

Sidi Bel Abbès (Algeria), 4

Sidi, Ahmed Ould, 339

Sierra Leone, *450*, 451-62, 802; agriculture, 647, 651; education, 665, 1094; food production, 649,

653; health figures, 659, 663; infant mortality, 978; Liberia and, 281-84; marriage age of girls, 972; MRU membership, 900; Muslims, 1068; population, 627, 661, 975; refugees, 991, 995, 997; tourism, 1117; trade unions, 1015, 1017; urban primacy, 982; women's status, 1042, 1044; *economy*: 456-59, 629, 645, 655, 657, 805, 819, 918; currency, 642; employment figures, 631; foreign debt, 845, 847; foreign trade, 633, 635, 637, 639, 641; manufacturing, 914, 916; mineral exports, 920; underground economy, 875-76; wages, 1021

Sijeyo, Wasonga, 1111

Sikasso (Mali), 327

Silver deposits, 377, 475

Simbananiye, Artemon, 66

Simien Mountains, 169

Sinai, 142, 150

SiNdebele language, 609

Singapore, 924

Singh, Shamsher, 940

Single-crop dependency, 210, 410, 1007

Sirte Basin (Libya), 289

Sisal production, 260, 261-62, 368, 371, 535, 538

Sissoko, Filifing, 335

Sisulu, Albertina, 480, 486, 490

Sisulu, Zwelakhe, 1126

Siswati language, 477, 519

Sithole, Ndabaning, 611-13

Six Day War, 148, 293

Sixishe, Desmond, 272

Skeleton Coast, 375

Slabbert, Frederick Van Zyl, 481, 735, 736

SLAM (Sierra Leone Alliance Movement), 454

Slash-and-burn agriculture, 936

Slave trade, 858-59, 931, 970; Ghana, 204, 205; Malawi, 316; Nigeria,

406; São Tomé and Príncipe, 426; Sudan, 509; Zanzibar, 529

Slavery: abolished in South Africa, 482; Mauritania, 339, 341; Mauritius, 349

Slaves, former, Liberia, 281

SLDP (Sierra Leone Democratic Party), 454

Sleeping sickness, 54

Slovo, Joe, 479

SLP (Socialist Labor Party), Egypt, 145

SLPP (Sierra Leone People's Party), 454

Slums, urban, 674

Smelting industry, Rwanda, 421

Smith, Ian, 611, 612-13, 764; South Africa and, 749

Smuggling, 676, 807, 872-73, 876; Angola, 20; Central African Republic, 94-95; Chad, 109; Equatorial Guinea, 166; Gambia, 196; Ghana, 210; Guinea, 224, 225; Mali, 333; Niger, 397; Senegal, 875; Sierra Leone, 455, 457, 458; Togo, 547; Uganda, 879; Zaire, 589, 591, 877. *See also* Underground economy

Smuts, Jan, 484, 1027

SNM (Somali National Movement), 465, 467, 468

Soap production, 285, 398, 428

Soba, 1070

Sobhuza, King of Swaziland, 519, 520-21

Subhuza II, King of Swaziland, 524

Sobukwe, Robert, 480

Social change, and state control of economy, 888-89

Social class, religion and, 1057-58; South Africa, 730, 731

Social conditions, urban, 674-75

Social influences of military forces, 724-25

Social reform, Egypt, 147

Social security programs, 64, 299, 1033

Social service employment, 412

Social wage, 1022

Social welfare, military spending and, 719

Socialism, 805-7, 884; and debt crisis, 837-39; and international finances, 831-32; Pan-Africanism, 687. *See also* Government structure

Socialist bloc countries, Ethiopia and, 176-77

Socialization of women, 1048

Society: and education, 1093-94; postcolonial, 684

Soda ash plants, Kenya, 262

Sofaniama River, 191

Soglo (Dahomey General), 28

Soil conditions, 935-37; conservation, 397, 768; depletion, 40, 52, 251, 273, 332; erosion, 10, 267, 419

Soilih, Ali, 115-16

Sokodé (Togo), 544

Sokoine, Edward, 531-33

Sokoto (state), 1074; Sultan of, 410

Sokoto River, Nigeria, 401

Somali jihad, 1075

Somali language, Djibouti, 133

Somali people, 170

Somalia, 463-72, *464*, 709, 801, 803; agriculture, 647, 651; Arab League, 1079; diplomatic relations, 135-36, 171-74, 258-59, 702-3, 996; drug abuse, 1063; education, 665; female circumcision, 1048; female warrior, 1055; food production, 649, 653; health figures, 659, 663; liberation movement, 1079; literary suppression, 1110; military spending, 717; Muslims, 1068, 1069, 1077, 1080-81; population, 627, 661, 975; refugees, 985, 988, 991; road system, 957; *economy:* 469-71, 629, 645, 655, 657, 805; currency, 643; employment figures, 631; foreign debt, 842, 845; foreign

trade, 633, 635, 637, 639, 641;
industry, 914-17; mineral exports,
920

Sombe people, Benin, 25

Somerville, Keith, xi-xii

Songhai people, 327

Soninke (Serahuli) people, 192

Sorghum production: Benin, 30;
Burkina Faso, 53; Cameroon, 76;
Central African Republic, 94; Chad,
927; Egypt, 152; Guinea-Bissau,
232; Lesotho, 273; Mali, 332;
Niger, 397; Rwanda, 419; Senegal,
438; Sierra Leone, 456; Somalia,
470; South Africa, 495; Sudan, 505,
512; Tanzania, 538; Togo, 547;
Uganda, 575

Soroccos, Tunisia, 551

Sotho people, 36, 270, 476, 519, 520,
609

Soudan inutile, 699

Soudanic Negroid people, 99

Sousse, Eric, 1124

Sousse (Tunisia), 558

South Africa, 473-504, *474*, 670, 679,
725, 803; agriculture, 647, 651;
Basuto people and, 270-71; birth
rate, 972; contraception, 977;
drought, 931; education 1096,
1098; food production, 649, 653;
government structure, 477-82;
health figures, 659, 663; history,
482-94; incomes, 788; internal
politics, 730-47; life expectancy,
978; migrant populations, 986;
military production, 721, 723;
military spending, 717, 724;
Muslims, 1069; population, 627,
661, 976; press, 1124, 1125-26,
1131; refugees, 366, 997; religion,
1057; tourism, 1113; trade unions,
1026-38; *diplomatic relations*: 694,
703-5, 728, 748-61, 1010; Angola,
17, 18-19, 693; Botswana, 38-39,
40; Commonwealth, 762-66;
Comoros, 117; Equatorial Guinea,

165; Ivory Coast, 240; Lesotho,
271-73; Libya, 293; Malawi, 319,
320, 321; Mauritius, 350;
Mozambique, 369-70; Namibia,
379, 381-88; Nigeria, 408; OAU,
686, 690-91; Seychelles, 446;
superpowers, 710-11; Swaziland,
520, 521; Tanzania, 534; Zambia,
601, 602; Zimbabwe, 614-15, 955;
economy: 494-99, 629, 655,
680-82, 787, 805; currency, 643;
employment figures, 631; foreign
debt, 843-45, 847, 853-54; foreign
trade, 633, 635, 637, 639, 641;
underground economy, 876; *trade
relations*: Comoros, 119; EC, 770,
779; Malawi, 322, 323;
Mozambique, 368, 371, 372;
SACU, 906-7; SADCC, 905;
Seychelles, 447; Swaziland, 522,
523; Zambia, 604; Zimbabwe, 616,
617

South Africa Party, 484

South African Reconnaissance
Commandos, 754

South African settlers, Namibia, 377,
378

South America, economic reform, 808

South Korea, 298, 548, 924

South West Africa. *See* Namibia

South West African Territorial Force,
Namibia, 387

Southern Africa: colonialism, 859;
imports, 922; military spending,
717; population, 976; refugees, 990,
993; tourism, 1118-19; warfare,
694-95, 703-5

Southern African Economist, 1129-30

Southern Rhodesia, 39, 317, 369, 600,
610-13, 897; religious murders,
1057-58. *See also* Rhodesia;
Zimbabwe

Southern Sudan Liberation Front, 509

Soviet Union, 706-15, 771; economy,
629, 655, 805; education, 665;
health figures, 659, 663;

population, 627, 661; *aid recipients*: Angola, 19; Congo, 128; Equatorial Guinea, 164; Ethiopia, 682; Libya, 296; Madagascar, 309; Mozambique, 369; Somalia, 470; Uganda, 567-68; *diplomatic relations*: Algeria, 7; Angola, 18, 487; Burkina Faso, 52; Congo, 127; Egypt, 147, 149-51; Equatorial Guinea, 166; Ethiopia, 172-77, 679, 702; Ghana, 206; Guinea, 221-22; Guinea-Bissau, 230; Ivory Coast, 240; Liberia, 282; Libya, 293; Madagascar, 306; Mali, 329, 330, 331; Morocco, 359; Mozambique, 370; São Tomé and Príncipe, 427; Somalia, 467; Tanzania, 534; Zambia, 602; Zimbabwe, 615; *trade relations*: 633, 639, 641; Angola, 21; Egypt, 154; Guinea-Bissau, 233; Mali, 333; Mozambique, 372; Namibia, 388; São Tomé and Príncipe, 428; Sudan, 513; Zimbabwe, 614

The Sowetan, 1125

Soweto uprising, 487-88, 499-500

Soweto Youth Congress, 741

Soybean production, 573, 575

Soyinka, Wole, 1106, 1107-8; *The Interpreters*, 1106

Spain, 358, 395, 771; colonialism, 162-65, 341, 683, 695, 771, 996; EC membership, 781; expulsion of Moors, 1073; Islam and, 1076-77; trade relations, 21, 30, 109, 129, 154, 296, 372

Spanish language, 161, 356

Spanish Morocco, 787

Spanish Sahara, 695

Spare parts, underground economy, 876, 880

Special interest magazines, 1131

Speculation in rice, 309

Spice production, Comoros, 118

SPLA (Sudan People's Liberation Army), 294, 510, 700-701

SPLM (Sudan People's Liberation Movement), 700-701

Sports, 684, 765-66

SPP (Swaziland Progressive Party), 520

SPFF (Seychelles People's Progressive Front), 445, 446

SPUP (Seychelles People's United Party), 445, 446

Sra Ouertane (Tunisia), 558

Ssemogerere, Paul, 569, 571

SSRP (Somali Socialist Revolutionary Party), 465

SSU (Sudan Socialist Union), 509

Stabex, 108, 166, 437, 773, 775, 776

Stability, political 801, 809

State terrorism, South Africa, 756

Steel industry, 10, 21, 153, 371, 496, 548, 616

Stevens, Siaka, 454-56, 461, 1017

Storage facilities, 262, 537

Straits of Gibraltar, 355

Strikes, 383, 435, 1020, 1030, 1031, 1035, 1038

Structural adjustment facility (SAF), IMF, 813, 820-21, 848-49, 854-55

Structural adjustment programs, 727-28, 830-31, 835, 837-38. *See also* IMF; World Bank

Students overseas, 43, 86, 177, 198, 768

Subregional magazines, 1129-30

Subsidies, 1022

Subsistence economy, 676, 1007

Subukwe, Robert, 485

Sudan, 505-16, *506*, 688, 803; agriculture, 647, 651, 1007; Arab League, 1079; armed forces, 713; civil war, 694, 699-701, 1009, 1056; colonialism, 1077, 1078; diplomatic relations, 151, 259, 293, 294, 566-67, 571, 703, 996-97; drought, 930-31, 1008; education, 665, 1092, 1094; famine, 927; female circumcision, 1048; food production, 649, 653; health figures, 659, 663; health services, 1012; IMF riots, 851; liberation movement, 1079; military spending, 717; Muslims, 1069-71, 1076, 1080, 1082; population, 627, 661, 974, 986; refugee aid, 992-94; refugees, 985, 988, 989, 991, 996, 1096; road system, 954, 955-58; *economy*: 512-14, 629, 645, 655, 657, 805; cotton exports, 939-40; currency, 643; employment figures, 631; foreign debt, 842, 845, 847; foreign trade, 633, 635, 637, 639, 641; imports, 923; manufacturing, 914, 916, 917; mineral exports, 920; reform of, 808; underground economy, 876, 880

Sudan African National Union, 699-700

Sudanic Lugbara people, 563

Sudd (marsh), 505

Suez Canal, 141, 154, 701, 706-7; nationalization, 147

Sufi Muslims, 1069, 1071, 1072, 1075

Sugar beet production, 557

Sugar cane production, 475, 495

Sugar, 780; exports, 522; processing, 333, 438, 470; *production*: Benin, 30; Burkina Faso, 53; Cameroon, 76; Cape Verde, 85; Congo, 127; Egypt, 152; Guinea-Bissau, 232; Kenya, 262; Madagascar, 309; Malawi, 322; Mauritania, 343; Mauritius, 347, 351-52; Mozambique, 368, 371; São Tomé and Príncipe, 426; Sudan, 512; Swaziland, 522; Uganda, 574-75; Zaire, 588; Zimbabwe, 617

Sukuma people, 528

Sukuta (Gambia), 192

Sulphur deposits, Namibia, 377

Sultan of Sokoto, 410

Sunmonu, Hassan, 1025

Sunni Muslims, 4, 143, 291, 465

Superphosphates, Morocco, 360

Superpowers, 706-15; and colonialism, 771; European Community as, 771, 781-82; and South Africa, 747

Supplementary fund facility, IMF, 830

Suppression of Communism Act, South Africa, 485, 1029

Susu people, 219, 223

Swahili culture, 1072

Swamps, Gambia, 191

SWANU (South-West Africa National Union), 379, 382-83, 386

SWAPO (South-West Africa People's Organization), 18-19, 377, 379, 382-87, 391, 681, 694, 703-4, 717, 1038; and Commonwealth, 766; refugee assistance, 992-93; Zambia and, 602; Zimbabwe and, 614

Swartberge range, 473

Swazi Nation Land (SNL), 521

Swazi peole, 476, 519

Swaziland, 517-24, *518*, 680, 748, 803; agriculture, 647, 651; and ANC, 745; food production, 649, 653; health figures, 659; Muslims, 1069; population, 627, 976, 986; PTA membership, 908; refugees, 988, 991; road system, 957; SACU membership, 906-7; South Africa and, 486, 705, 752, 753, 757, 758; travel facilities, 1119; *economy*: 521-23, 629, 645, 657, 805; Commonwealth aid, 768; currency, 643; employment figures, 631; foreign debt, 845; foreign trade, 639, 641; manufacturing, 914; and SADCC, 749, 750, 905

Swaziland National Front, 520

Sweden, 85, 233

Sweet potato production, 63, 85, 419, 543, 575

Switzerland, trade relations, 198, 274, 496, 497

SYL (Somali Youth League), 466

Somali Youth League (SYL), 466

Syncretist churches, 452

Sunthetic substitutes, 940
Syria, diplomatic relations, 148, 293, 357, 555
Sysmin, 775

TAA (Tanganyika Africa Association), 530
Taha, Mahmoud Muhammad, 510, 1082
Tahoua (Niger), 393, 398
Taita people, 248
Taiwan, 924
Takawira, Leopold, 611
Tako, Hawo Osman, 1055
Takoradi (Ghana), 202
Tamale (Ghana), 202
Tambo, Oliver, 486, 504, 766
Tamesmida oil field, 557
Tana River, 247
Tandon, Yash, 569
Tanga (Tanzania), 528, 537, 538
Tanganyika, 417, 529-30, 675. See also Tanzania
Tanger (Morocco), 361
Tanning industry, 94, 398
Tano, 201
Tantalum production, 64
TANU (Tanganyika African National Union), 528-31
Tanzam railway, 958
Tanzania, 250, 263, 525-41, 526, 677, 748, 751, 803, 1054; agriculture, 647, 651; AIDS incidence, 1062; diplomatic relations, 259, 320, 370, 446, 568-69, 587, 615, 704, 763, 996; EAC treaty, 895-96; education, 665, 1090, 1096; food production, 649, 653; health figures, 659, 663; health services, 1012; Maji Maji war, 1055; military spending, 717; Muslims, 1069, 1072; population, 627, 661, 975, 986; refugees, 985, 988, 991; road system, 957, 958-59; tourism, 1116, 1120; trade unions, 1016-19; women's wages, 1045; economy:

534-38, 629, 645, 655, 657, 805, 819, 872n, 917; banking system, 866-69; Commonwealth aid, 768; currency, 643; employment figures, 631; foreign aid, 767; foreign debt, 842, 845; foreign trade, 633, 635, 637, 639, 641; and IMF, 832; imports, 922; industry, 914, 915, 916; mineral exports, 920; nationalization, 883; reform of, 808; and SADCC, 749, 750, 905, 906; wages, 1021
Tanzania-Zambia Railway (Tazara), 534, 537, 1120
Tariqas, 1069, 1071, 1075; colonialism and, 1077-78, 1078
Taveta people, 248
Taxes, 796; British, in Kenya, 150-51; military spending and, 719; Southern Rhodesia, 611; Sudan, 513
Taya, Sid'Ahmed Ould, 342, 345
Tazara railway, 534, 537, 1120
Tazarka oil field, 557
Tchad utile and inutile, 697
Tchibouela oil field, 128
Tchicaya-Thystère, Jean-Pierre, 131-32
Tea: production, 63, 248, 260-61, 322, 368, 371, 419, 447, 535-38, 561, 565, 568, 572-74, 617; underground economy, 876, 880
Teachers. See Education
Technical aid, 768
Technical training, 951. See also Education
Technology, 918; agricultural, and women's work, 1044; military, 720, 721; and military contracts, 723
Tedla, Addis, 179
Teff, price in Ethiopia, 175
Teixeira (Guinea-Bissau), 227-29
Telecommunications, 137, 910; OAU and, 691
Televised education, 243
Television. See Mass media
Telli, Diallo, 221

Tema (Ghana), 202

Tembo, John, 319-20, 325

Tembu people, 476

Temne people, 452

Terms of trade, 799-80, 812, 843; and agricultural economy, 937-39; and economic reform, 820; Tanzania, 867; Zambia, 917

Terreblanche, Eugene, 481, 492

Terreblanche, Sampie, 735

Terrorism, 293-94, 756

Tete (Mozambique), 366

Textbooks, 1093

Textile industry, 634-35, 654-55, 912; Angola, 21; Benin, 30; Burkina Faso, 53; Egypt, 153; Guinea, 225; Madagascar, 309; Malawi, 322; Mauritania, 343; Mauritius, 351; Morocco, 361, 362; Niger, 398; São Tomé and Príncipe, 428; Senegal, 438-39; Somalia, 470; Togo, 548; Uganda, 573, 576

Teyateyaneng (Lesotho), 269

TFL (Tanganyika Federation of Labour), 1017

Thailand, Gambia trade, 198

Thangata (forced labor), 316

Tharaka people, 248

Thatcher, Margaret, 763-65

Theater, experimental, 1108

Thermal power, 397-98, 439

Thiam, Habib, 435

Thiès (Senegal), 431, 438

Third World countries: EC and, 771; economic demands, 773; debt, 842; military spending, 719

This Earth, My Brother (Kofi Awoonor), 1106

Thompson, Carol, 759

Thonga people, 366

Tibesti Mountains, 99, 289

Tibesti people, 698

Tibu people, 1085

Tigre, literacy campaign, 1049

Tigre people, 170, 682, 996

Tigrigna language, 170

Tijaniyya movement, 1075

Timber: resources, Congo, 121, 127-28; processing, 322, 576, 590; production, 76, 94, 95, 166, 185, 210, 233, 235, 241, 284-85, 287, 589, 935; smuggling, 873

Tin: deposits, 94, 377, 475; production, 397, 419-20, 537

Tindouf (Algeria), 358

Tipis, Justus ole, 258

Tire manufacture, 371

Tiris el Gharbia, 341

Titanium deposits, 167, 451

Tiv people, 403, 407

Tloome, Dan, 479

Toamasina (Madagascar), 303, 304

Tobacco production, 921; Algeria, 8; Burkina Faso, 45; Egypt, 153; Ivory Coast, 235; Madagascar, 309; Malawi, 322; Rwanda, 420; Swaziland, 522; Tanzania, 535, 536, 538, 868-69; Uganda, 574; Zambia, 603; Zimbabwe, 616, 617

Todd, Garfield, 611

Togo, *542*, 543-50, 803; agriculture, 647, 651; education, 665, 1090, 1092; food production, 649, 653; health figures, 659, 663; Muslims, 1069; population, 627, 661, 975; refugees, 991; road system, 957; smuggling, 873; tourism, 1115, 1117; *economy*: 547-49, 629, 645, 655, 657, 805; currency, 643; ECOWAS membership, 901; employment figures, 631; foreign debt, 845, 847; foreign trade, 633, 635, 637, 639, 641; manufacturing, 914, 916; mineral exports, 920; trade relations, 52, 209

Togo people, 202

Toto-Atacora Mountains, 543

Toivo ja Toivo, Andimba (Hermann), 382, 383, 391

Toko, Wilson, 571

Tolba, Mostafa, 946

Tolbert, William, 281-82, 284, 288

Toliara (Madagascar), 303, 304
Tomato production, 557
Tombalbaye, François, 102-3, 697
Tombouctou (Mali), 327
Tongo people, 314, 316, 598, 609
Torit mutiny, 699
Torture allegations, Kenya, 257-58
Tourareg-Berber people, 99
Toubou people, 99, 103, 111
Toucouleur people, 433
Touré, Ahmed Sékou, 219-22, 454,
   670, 673, 688, 1017, 1024; and
   UNHCR, 994
Touré, Soumane, 49, 51, 56
Tourism, 1113-22; Comoros, 119;
   Egypt, 154; Gambia, 197, 198;
   Kenya, 248, 262; Lesotho, 274;
   Malawi, 322; Mauritius, 350, 351,
   352; Morocco, 360, 361; São Tomé
   and Príncipe, 428; Senegal, 439;
   Seychelles, 443, 447; Swaziland,
   522; Tunisia, 558; Uganda, 576
Towns, 674-76
TPLF (Tigre People's Liberation
   Front), 171, 174, 175, 702;
   women's rights, 1050
Trade: nineteenth century, 316;
   precolonial, 250, 406
Trade deficit. See Economy
Trade preferences, EC, 773
Trade relations: Lomé Conventions
   and, 779; SADCC and, 750n
Trade routes, ancient, 871-72
Trade unions, 600, 708, 1014-40;
   economic proposals, 837-38; and
   nationalization, 886
Trading sectors, illegal, West Africa,
   872-73
Traditional education, 1088. See also
   Education
Traditional religion, 1053-54; and
   AIDS, 1059-60; and alcohol, 1062.
   See also Religion
Trans-Med pipeline, 558
Transgabonais Railway, 185, 186

Transkei (South Africa), 476, 477,
   478, 486, 489, 494, 501, 503
Transnational banks, 863, 864, 867
Transnational companies, and
   women's work, 1045
Transportation, 910; equipment
   imports, 447, 470; road systems,
   953-66; SADCC and, 750-51, 905,
   906
Transvaal (South Africa), 473,
   475-76, 477, 483, 859
Traoré, Diarra, 222-3
Traoré, Moussa, 328, 330-32, 335
Traoré, Youssouf, 336
Travel, 1113-22. See also Tourism
Treaty of Abidjan, 898
Treaty of Lagos, 901
Treaty of Mersa, 554
Treaty of Oujdah, 294
Treaty of Paris, 446
Treaty of Rome, 770
Treaty of Versailles, 381
Treurnicht, Andries, 481, 492
Triangular slave trade, 858-59
Tribal land tenure, Botswana, 43
Tribal Trust Lands, Rhodesia, 611, 615
Tribalism, 677
Triple burden of women, 1043
Triple phosphate production, 558
Tripoli (Libya), 289, 291, 299; U.S.
   attack, 295
Tripolitania (Libya), 289, 291, 299;
   oil fields, 298
Trovoada, Miguel, 430
True Whig Party, Liberia, 282
Tsetse fly infestations, 127, 371
Tsévié (Togo), 544
Tshisekidi wa Mulumba, 586
Tshombe, Moise, 584, 595
Tsiba, Florent, 132
Tsikata, Kojo, 204, 209, 216
Tsimihety people, 304
Tsiranana, Philibert, 305-6
Tsodilo Hills (Botswana), 35
Tsumeb Corporation, 388
Tswana people, 37, 378, 476

Tuareg people, 328, 393, 395-96
Tubers production, 232
Tubman, William, 281, 688
Tucker, Bob, 736
TUCSA (Trade Union Council of South Africa), 1029
Tugela River, 475
Tugen people, 249
Tumbuka people, 314, 316
Tungsten deposits, Zaire, 589
Tungsten production, 64, 420
Tunis (Tunisia), 551, 553
Tunisia, 551-60, 552, 688; agriculture, 647, 651; Arab League, 1079; birth rate, 972; contraception, 977; education, 665, 1090, 1092; food production, 649, 653; health figures, 659, 663; IMF riots, 851; liberation movement, 1079; Libya and, 294, 295; life expectancy, 978; migrant workers, 298; military spending, 717; Muslims, 1069, 1081-84; population, 627, 661, 974, 986; refugees, 991; trade unions, 1016; *economy*: 556-59, 629, 645, 655, 657; currency, 643; employment figures, 631; foreign trade, 633, 635, 637, 639, 641; imports, 923; industry, 914, 915; mineral exports, 920
Tunisian Armed Resistance, 556
Turabi, Hassan al-, 516
Turkana people, 249
Turkey, EC membership, 781; migrant workers, 298; trade with Libya, 296, 298
Turok, Ben, xii; "State-Sector Policies in Africa," 882-89
Tutsi people, 59, 61-62, 66, 415, 417-18
Tutu, Desmond, 492, 504, 1057
Twa people, 59, 415
Two Thousand Seasons (Ayi Kwei Armah), 1109

UAR (United Arab Republic), 148, 149. *See also* Egypt

Uaso Nyiro River, 247
Ubangi people, 89, 123
Ubangi River, 89, 90, 579
UCP (Union Comorienne Pour le Progrès), 114
UDAO (Union Douanière et l'Afrique Occidentale), 897-98
UDEAC (Union Douanière et Economique de l'Afrique Centrale), 78, 164, 894, 899-900
UDEAO (Union Douanière Economique de l'Afrique Occidentale), 897-98
UDF (South Africa), 480, 490-92, 733, 737, 739-43, 763
UDPM (Union Démocratique de Peuple Malien), 328, 330-31
UDPS (Union pour la Démocratie et le Progrès Social), Zaire, 582, 586
UDSG (Union Démocratique et Sociale Gabonaise), 183
UDV (Union Démocratique Voltaïque), 47, 48, 49
UFM (Uganda Freedom Movement), 570
Uganda, 250, 561-78, 562, 670, 678, 725, 803; agriculture, 647, 651; AIDS, 978, 1062; and EC, 770; civil war, 1009-10; diplomatic relations, 259, 418-19, 534, 1083; EAC treaty, 895-96; education, 665, 1095; food production, 649, 653; health figures, 659, 663; health services, 1004; life expectancy, 978; marijuana, 1063; military spending, 717; Muslims, 1069, 1080, 1081; OAU and, 690; population, 627, 661, 975; religions, 1054-55; religious murders, 1057-58; soldiers, 1061; tourism, 1120-21; trade with Rwanda, 420; war with Tanzania, 536, 867; women's status, 1046; *economy*: 572-77, 629, 645, 655, 657, 805; currency, 643; employment figures, 631; foreign

debt, 845, 847; foreign trade, 633, 635, 637, 639, 641; manufacturing, 914, 916; mineral exports, 920; underground economy, 876, 879-80; *refugees*: 985, 991, 996; aid to, 993; attacks on, 997

UGGC (United Gold Coast Convention), 205

UGTAN (Union Générale des Travailleurs de l'Afrique Noire), 1024

UGTT (Union Générale des Travailleurs Tunisiens), 555-56

Uitenhage (South Africa), 476; massacre, 491

Ujamaa villages, Tanzania, 868, 867n, 917

Ukenya, 257-58

Ulama movement, Tunisia, 1079

UMAO (Union Monétaire de l'Afrique de Ouest), 904-5

Umbundu language, 15

Umfolozi River, 475

Umkhonto we Sizwe (ANC guerrillas), 479, 485-86, 494, 504, 740, 744-45

Umma party, Sudan, 508, 1078

UMOA (Union Monétaire Ouest Africaine), 331, 332, 333, 399, 440

UNC (Cameroon), 71-72

UND (Union Nigérienne Démocratique), 394

UNDD (Union Nationale pour la Défense de la Démocratie), Burkina Faso, 49

Underdeveloped countries, military spending, 716, 719-20

Underground economy, 591, 871-81. *See also* Smuggling

Unemployment, 1023; and military spending, 728. *See also* Employment

UNEP (U.N. Environment Program), 945-50

UNESCO: and Ethiopia, 177; and, Niger, 400

UNICEF programs, 441, 470

Union Démocratique Centrafricaine, 92

Union des Travailleurs Libres Sénégalais, 440

Union Nationale des Travailleurs Congolais, 584

Union Nationale des Travailleurs du Zaire, 593

Union Nationale Tchadienne, 102

Union of South Africa. *See* South Africa

Union Socialiste Tchadienne, 102

Union Soudanaise, 329

Unions. *See* Trade unions

UNIP (United National Independence Party), Zambia, 598-601, 606

UNIR (National Union for Independence and Revolution), Chad, 101, 105

UNITA (Angola), 16-21, 23, 384, 487, 489, 587, 681, 694, 703-4, 717, 748, 753, 754, 760; South Africa and, 755; United States and, 711

United Democratic Party, South Africa, 736-37

United Nations: environmental concerns, 948; and Eritrea, 701; and Liberia, 281; and Namibia, 377, 381-83, 385-87, 767; OAU and, 691; refugee villages, Central African Republic, 96; and Rwanda, 418; and São Tomé and Príncipe, 427; and South Africa, 703, 861n, 862; and Togo, 545; trust territory, Cameroon, 70-71; and Western Sahara, 358, 359; and Zaire, 583-84; and Zimbabwe, 612; *agencies and committees*: Advisory Group on Resource Flows to Africa, 856; Children's Fund, 110, 120; Commission for Trade and Development, 679; Conference on Desertification, 945; Council for Namibia, 379; Decade for Women, 1041, 1050, 1051; Development

Program, Zaire, 593; Economic Commission for Africa (ECA), 892, 893; Environment Program (UNEP), 945-50; High Commission for Refugees (UNHCR), 137, 985, 994, 988-89, 998-99, 1000; PAAERD, 832-35

United States of America, 706-15, 771, 781; Agency for International Development, 813; agriculture, 647, 651; Caribbean Basin Initiative (CBI), 772; CIA, 1025; citizens in Liberia, 280, 283; economy, 629, 655; education, 665; export tables, 638-39; financial aid, 821; food production, 649, 653; foreign trade, 633, 635, 637, 639, 641; health figures, 659, 663; import tables, 640-41; income figures, 790; Islam in, 1065; military bases, Zaire, 587; population, 627, 661; road system, 953, 955; sanctions against South Africa, 757; satellite tracking station, Seychelles, 447; and world economy, 824; *diplomatic relations*: Algeria, 7-8; Angola, 17, 18, 19, 748, 755; Burundi, 62; Chad, 104-7, 698-99; Egypt, 146-47, 150-51; Ethiopia, 172, 177; Ghana, 209; Guinea, 222, 224; Kenya, 255, 258; Liberia, 281-83, 286-87, 292-95, 298, 558; Madagascar, 306; Morocco, 357, 358; Namibia, 386-87; Niger, 396; Nigeria, 408; SADCC states, 758, 905; São Tomé and Príncipe, 427; Somalia, 172, 467, 469; and South Africa, 487, 679, 680, 681; Sudan, 510, 511, 512, 514; Zaire, 587; Zimbabwe, 615; *trade relations*: Algeria, 10; Angola, 20, 21, 704; Benin, 30; Botswana, 42; Cameroon, 77; Cape Verde, 86; Chad, 109; Comoros, 118; Congo, 129; Egypt, 154; Ghana, 213; Ivory Coast, 242; Lesotho, 274;

Madagascar, 309; Malawi, 323; Mozambique, 372; Nigeria, 411; Sierra Leone, 459; Somalia and, 470; South Africa, 496, 497; Sudan, 514; Swaziland, 523; Togo, 548; Zaire, 593; Zambia, 604; Zimbabwe, 617

United Party of Nigeria, 409

Universities, 1097-98; and health care, 1012. *See also* Education

University of the Commonwealth, 768-69

UNLA (Uganda), 571, 572, 1009

UNLF (Uganda National Liberation Front), 534, 564, 568-69

UNRF (Uganda National Rescue Front), 570-71

UNTA (União Nacional de Trabalharodres), 22

UNTM (Union Nationale des Travailleurs Maliens), 333

UP (United Party), Liberia, 280

UPC (Comoros), 114

UPC (Uganda People's Congress), 565-66, 570

UPC (Union des Populations Camerounaises), 70-71

UPDA (Uganda People's Democratic Army), 572

UPDM (Uganda People's Democratic Movement), 571-72

UPDS (Zaire), 586

Upington (South Africa), 476, 477

UPM (Uganda), 570

UPP (United People's Party), Liberia, 281

Upper Volta, 1077. *See also* Burkina Faso

UPRONA (Union pour le Progrès National), Burundi, 60, 61

UPS (Union Progressiste Sénégalaise), 434-35

UPV (Union Progressiste Voltaïque), Burkina Faso, 49

Uranium: *deposits*: Burundi, 64; Cameroon, 77; Central African

Republic, 94; Chad, 109; Congo, 128; Equatorial Guinea, 167; Liberia, 285; Namibia, 377; South Africa, 475; *production*: Central African Republic, 94; Gabon, 185; Mali, 332; Namibia, 382, 387-88; Niger, 395, 397, 399; South Africa, 495; Tunisia, 558
Urban areas: Egypt, 141, 142, 143; South Africa, 475-76
Urban economy, women in, 1045-47
Urban populations, 660-61, 789, 974-76; and agricultural economy, 941-42; and economic reform, 815; growth of, 674-75; Libya, 291; political power, 807; unemployment, 42, 372, 440. *See also* Population; Urbanization
Urbanization, 40, 42, 78, 129, 155-56, 674-75, 982, 986, 1045-46
URDC (Union Pour une République Démocratique aux Comores), 116
USDG (Gabon), 183
USFP (Union Socialiste des Forces Populaires), Morocco, 357
USSR. *See* Soviet Union
Usutu River, 517
Uwechwe, Ralph, 1128
UWUSA (United Workers Union of South Africa), 489-90, 1032, 1036-37

Vaal Triangle uprising, 491
Vaccination programs, 110, 120, 441
Vai people, 279
Van Buren, Linda, xii; "African Tourism and Business Travel," 1113-22
Van Eck, Jan, 735
Van Hear, Nicholas, xii; "Labor Issues and Trade Unionism in Africa," 1014-40
Vanadium deposits, 64, 377, 475
Vanadium production, 495
Vance, Cyrus, 711

Van-Dunem Mbinda, Afonso, 16, 23-24
Van-Dunem, Pedro de Castro dos Santos "Loy," 16, 24
Vanilla, Comoros, 118, 308
Vatican, 62, 74
Vegetable production, 152, 260-61, 352, 557
Vehicles, underground economy, 876
Venda (South Africa), 476, 477, 486, 489, 494, 501, 503
Venda people, 609
Venereal disease, 977
Venice Summit, 854
Vereeniging (South Africa), 477
Versailles Treaty, 381
Verwoerd (South African PM), 487
Victoria (Seychelles), 443
Victoria Falls, 1118, 1119
Victoria Nile River, 561
Vieira, João Bernardo, 229, 230, 234
Vieria, José Luandino, 1109
Villagization programs, 173, 531
Virunga Mountains, 415
Vocational training, 1096-97. *See also* Education
Vogel Peak, 403
The Voice (Gabriel Okara), 1106
Voice of America, 708
Voice of Ethiopian Unity, 171, 178
Voice of Namibia, 390
Voice of the Arabs, 157
Voice of the Broad Masses of Eritrea, 171, 178
Voice of the Western Somali and Somali Abo Liberation Fronts, 178
Volcanos, 113, 159, 525
Volta Blanche River, Bagré Dam, 53
Volta Noire River, 45
Volta River, 201
Voltaic people, 237
von Trotha (German General, Namibia), 380
Vonjy (Madagascar party), 305, 307, 311
Vorster, B. J., 487, 488, 749

Vridi Canal (Ivory Coast), 235, 240
VS-MONIMA (Madagascar), 305

Wad Medani (Sudan), 507, 1012
Wadai plateau, 99
Wadaian people, 99
Wade, Abdoulaye, 434, 435, 436
Wage earners, 1014
Wages, 1020-22; and nationalization, 886; of women, 1045. *See also* Economy
Wakil, Abdul, 533
Waldheim, Kurt, 383
Wall, Saharan, Morocco-built, 358, 696
Walvis Bay (Namibia), 375-77, 385, 388
War zones, 693-705; military spending, 717
Warfare, and AIDS, 1061; Arab conquest, 1070-71; Chad, 295; and economy, 724; Egypt-Israel, 148, 150; Ethiopia, 172-73; and famine, 930; Horn region, 682-83; Mauritania, 341; Namibia, 384-85; Nigeria, 407-8; refugees, 989, 990, 996; regional, South Africa and, 748-61; and religion, 1054-57; Saharan area, 683; Somalia-Ethiopia, 467; South Africa, 483; Tanzania-Uganda, 534; tribal, 970; Western Sahara, 358-59
Warioba (Tanzania PM), 533
Watches, Mauritius, 351
Water supplies, 949; accessibility, 959; superpowers and, 714-15; women and, 1043
Waterways, Zaire, 590
WDCs (Ghana), 1019
Weber, Max, 1056
Webi Shabeelle River, 463, 470
Weekly Mail (South Africa), 1126, 1127
Welfare programs, 129, 214, 263-64, 389, 412, 440, 447, 593, 618
West Africa, 1129

West Africa, 693, 974-75; colonialism, 1076; drought, 930-31; imports, 922-23; Islam, 1074-75; military spending, 717; regionalism, 897-98; tourism, 1117-18; underground economy, 872-76
West African Highway, 285
West Germany: diplomatic relations, 73, 386, 397, 470; road system, 957; *trade relations*: Algeria, 10; Angola, 21; Benin, 30; Burundi, 63; Cameroon, 77; Chad, 109; Egypt, 154; Ghana, 213; Ivory Coast, 242; Liberia, 286-87; Libya, 296, 298; Malawi, 323; Mozambique, 371, 372; Nigeria, 411; São Tomé and Príncipe, 429; Sierra Leone, 459; South Africa, 496, 497; Sudan, 514; Tunisia, 558; Zambia, 604; Zimbabwe, 617
Western Contact Group, Namibia, 386
Western Sahara, 8, 355, 686; Morocco and, 358, 361; warfare, 694, 695-97
WFTU (World Federation of Trade Unions), 1024
Wheat, 676-77; imports, 428; production, 8, 152, 262, 273, 411, 495, 512, 557
White majority, South Africa, 478
White Nile River, 505
White people, Namibia, 378; South Africa, 476, 477, 483, 495, 499-501; Zimbabwe, 609
White politics, South Africa, 730-36, 747
White trade unions, South Africa, 1027-28
Whitehead, Edgar, 611
Wiehan, Nic, 1039
Wildebeest, 35
Wildlife: Gambia, 191; Kenya, 248; reserves, 35; safaris, 1116, 1119, 1120; Tanzania, 527
Williams, H. Sylvester, 687
Wilson, Harold, 765

Wilson Airport, Nairobi, 1119
Windhoek (Namibia), 377, 378, 389
Wine production, Algeria, 8
Witbooi, Hendrik, 380, 382
Witwatersrand (South Africa), 473, 475, 483
Wogderes, Fikre Selassie, 179
Wolfram deposits, 109, 377
Wollo, famine, 172
Wolof people, 192, 339, 433
Wologisi Mountains, 279
Women, 1041-52; AIDS, 1061; economic concerns, 1007-8; education, 362, 1095-96; employment, Somalia, 471; literacy, 86, 156, 299, 429; status of, Burkina Faso, 54; and war, 1054-56
Women's League, Malawi, 315
Wood-based industry, 128, 322, 522, 912-13. See also Forests
Wool processing, Mali, 333
Woolen goods, Mauritius, 351
Work force, 630-31, 789, 791, 1014; Algeria, 10-11; forced labor, 675; military, 724; productivity, 1024; self-management movement, 1018-19; urban, women, 1046; women, 1043-44; 1095-96. See also Employment
Worker's Defence Committees (WDCs), Ghana, 1019
Working conditions, south Africa, 1033
Workplace discipline, 1023-24
Workshop theater, 1108
The World (South Africa), 1125
World Bank, 811-22, 824, 848; adjustment programs, 727; African responses, 823-39; conditionality, 850; and debt crisis, 849; and economic reform, 808; and education, 1088, 1097-98, 1099; income groups, 788; International Comparison Project (ICP), 790; Social Dimensions of Adjustment project, 779; special action program, 854-55; and state control of economy, 887-88; and unemployment, 1023; wages, 1021. See also Economy
World Food Program, 512
World War I, 381, 417, 484
World War II, 251, 484
Worrall, Dennis, 732, 735
Worsley, Peter, 1101
WPE (Worker's Party of Ethiopia), 170-71, 178-79
WSLF (Western Somali Liberation Front), 171, 175, 467, 702

Xai-Xai (Mozambique), 366
Xala (Ousmane Sembene), 1110
Xhosa language, 269, 477
Xhosa people, 476, 483
Xitole (Guinea-Bissau), 229
Xuma, A. B., 687

Yacé, Philipe Grégoire, 240, 245
Yacine, Abdeslam, 1084
Yam production, 30, 127, 209, 543, 547
Yameogo, Maurice, 48, 56
Yan Tatsine riots, 1083-85
Yao people, 314, 316, 366, 528
Yaoundé (Cameroon), 67, 70, 78, 79
Yaoundé Convention, 767, 770-71, 772
Yhombi-Opango, Joachim, 124, 126, 132
Ylang-ylang, 118
Yoruba people, 25, 403, 407, 1062; political party, 409
Youlou, Abbé Fulbert, 124
Young Pioneers, Malawi, 315, 319, 320, 321
Young Tunisian movement, 554
Youth Brigade, South Africa, 739
Youth for South Africa, 735
Youth League, Zimbabwe, 611

Yugoslavia, 20, 297, 696

Zaire, 61, 420, 579-95, *580*, 679, 803; agriculture, 647, 651; AIDS, 1060, 1062; and Angola, 17; Cape Verde and, 86; and Chad, 105; civil war, 693; Congo and, 127; education, 665, 1090, 1091; food imports, 928; food production, 649, 653; health figures, 659, 663; hydroelectric power, 420; Muslims, 1069, 1072; population, 627, 661, 976; refugees, 985, 988, 991; road system, 957; and Togo, 546-47; urban primacy, 982; *economy*: 587-93, 629, 645, 655, 657, 805, 819, 832, 918; currency, 643, 828; employment figures, 631; foreign debt, 842, 843, 845, 847; foreign trade, 633, 635, 637, 639, 641; imports, 923; manufacturing, 914, 917; mineral exports, 920; underground economy, 876-79

Zaire River, 579, 589, 590

Zakat, Sudan, 513

Zambezi River, 13, 35, 365, 371, 375, 597, 607, 1118

Zambia, *596*, 597-606, 612, 677, 679, 680, 748, 803, 897; agriculture, 647, 651; diplomatic relations, 320, 587, 703; education, 665, 1088, 1090, 1092, 1093, 1095-96; food imports, 617; food production, 649, 653; health figures, 659, 663; IMF riots, 851; labor issues, 1022; military spending, 717; Muslims, 1069; population, 627, 661, 975, 986; refugees, 366, 985, 988, 991; religious warfare, 1055-56; road system, 957; and South Africa, 705, 752, 753, 755, 763; tourism, 1119; trade unions, 1014, 1018, 1025-26; urban primacy, 982; *economy*: 602-4, 629, 645, 655, 657, 805, 819, 843, 883-84, 918; currency, 643, 828; employment figures, 631; foreign debt, 842, 845, 847, 853; foreign trade, 633, 635, 637, 639,

641; and IMF, 826, 832; manufacturing, 914; mineral exports, 920; reform of, 808; and SADCC, 749, 905; trade relations, 323, 617; underground economy, 876; unemployment 1023; wages, 1021

Zande people, 581

ZANLA (Zimbabwe African National Liberation Army), 612

ZANU (Zimbabwe African National Union), 369, 611-12, 614, 615, 620-21, 681, 749, 755

ZANU-FPF (Zimbabwe African National Union-Patriotic Front), 609, 613, 620-21, 752

Zanzibar, 525, 528, 529-30, 532, 533; economy, 535; Muslims 1072, 1078; tourism, 1120. *See also* Tanzania

ZAPU (Zimbabwe African People's Union), 18, 39, 487, 609-15, 620-21, 755

Zar cults, 1069

Zaria (Nigeria), 406

Zebra skin trade, illegal, 877

Zelten (Libya), 292

Zerbo, Sayé, 49, 56-57

Zezuru people, 620

Zimba people, 620

Zimbabwe, 607-21, *608*, 681, 705, 725, 801, 803; agriculture, 647, 651; contraception, 977; diplomatic relations, 39, 293, 368, 369, 370, 534, 764-67; education, 665, 1089-93; food imports, 928; food production, 649, 653; foreign aid, 767; health figures, 659, 663; military spending, 717; Muslims, 1069, 1072; population, 627, 661, 975, 986; press, 1124, 1131; refugees, 366, 985, 988, 991; road system, 955, 957; and South Africa, 480, 749, 752, 753, 755, 763; tourism, 1115, 1118; trade unions, 1017; urban primacy, 982;

women's status, 1050; *economy*: 615-18, 629, 645, 655, 657, 805; banking system, 860-63, 869; currency, 643; employment figures, 631; foreign debt, 845; foreign trade, 633, 635, 637, 639, 641; and IMF, 832; industry, 914, 918; mineral exports, 920; PTA membership, 908; and SADCC, 749, 750, 905; trade with Malawi, 323; unemployment, 1023; wages, 1021
Zimbabwe Congress of Trade Unions, 618, 1017
Zinc deposits, 128, 176, 185, 377, 589, 597

Zinc production, 10, 558
Zinder (Niger), 393, 394, 398
Zinsou (Benin president), 28
ZIPRA (Zimbabwe People's Revolutionary Army), 612
Zirconium deposits, 167
Zobeir, Robah, 697
Zomba (Malawi), 314
Zongo, Henri, 50, 51
Zouerate (Mauritania), 343
Zulu kingdom, 316, 482, 483
Zulu language, 269, 477
Zulu people, 476; Inkatha, 481, 738-40
Zwane, Ambrose, 524